D1538791

Macropolitics

Consulting Editor,
Inis L. Claude, Jr.
University of Virginia

Also by Richard W. Sterling,
Ethics in a World of Power: The Political Ideas of Friedrich Meinecke

Macropolitics

INTERNATIONAL RELATIONS
IN A GLOBAL SOCIETY

Richard W. Sterling

Dartmouth College

Alfred A. Knopf New York

THIS IS A BORZOI BOOK
PUBLISHED BY ALFRED A. KNOPF, INC.

First Edition
987654321
Copyright © 1974 by Alfred A. Knopf, Inc.

Book design: Karin Batten

Library of Congress Cataloging in Publication Data

Sterling, Richard W
  Macropolitics.

  Bibliography: p.
  1. International relations. I. Title.
JX1395.S76   1974   327   73-21769
ISBN 0-394-48521-1
ISBN 0-394-31102-7 (textbook)

The book's cover shows a portion of a stained glass panel located at United Nations Headquarters, in New York. Designed by Marc Chagall, the window is a memorial to Dag Hammarskjöld and those who died with him in the service of world peace. United Nations/NAGATA

Quotations in this book from the *New York Times* for the years 1967, 1968, 1969, 1970 are reprinted by permission of the New York Times Company.

Manufactured in the United States of America

This book is dedicated
with love and hope to my children,
Mary, John, Whit, and Jim

We hold these truths to be self-evident,
That all men are created equal,
That they are endowed by their Creator
With certain unalienable rights,
That among these are life, liberty
And the pursuit of Happiness

I have never had a feeling, politically, that did not spring from the sentiments embodied in the Declaration of Independence. I have often pondered over the dangers which were incurred by the men who assembled here and framed and adopted that Declaration. I have pondered over the toils that were endured by the officers and soldiers of the army who achieved that independence. I have often inquired of myself what great principle or idea it was that kept this Confederacy so long together. It was not the mere matter of separation of the colonies from the motherland, but that sentiment in the Declaration of Independence which gave liberty not alone to the people of this country, but hope to all the world, for all future time. It was that which gave promise that in due time the weights would be lifted from the shoulders of all men, and that all should have an equal chance.

ABRAHAM LINCOLN
Independence Hall, Philadelphia
February 22, 1861

Preface

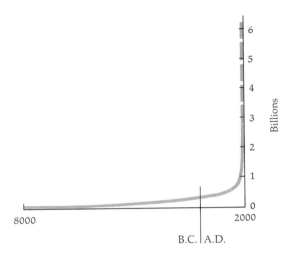

This 10,000-year curve is familiar to every student of world population growth. The long segment rising slowly from the horizontal base line registers the nearly imperceptible increase in numbers of people living on earth during the first ninety-six of the hundred centuries recorded by the curve. The marked upward swing, beginning in the seventeenth century A.D., signals the onset of an unprecedented quickening of the population growth rate. In the twentieth century the curve becomes nearly vertical, graphically representing what has come to be known as the population explosion.

The curve demonstrates that never in history has the earth had to sustain so many human beings as in our own time. It also records the evidence that never before has the earth had to accommodate increasing numbers of human beings so rapidly. Finally, it points toward a future in which, unless arrested by countertrends, the population growth rate will continue to accelerate, generating human beings in such numbers as to overwhelm and exhaust the resources of a finite world.

The upward thrust of the population curve compels the conclusion that the human race has arrived at a predicament without historical parallel. Man is threatened by a danger so novel and so massive that the difference between present and past has become qualitative as well as quantitative. Man's augmented ability to populate the planet has literally transformed the conditions governing his survival.

If human numbers alone have sufficed to produce so fundamental a transformation, they have not been the only transforming agents at work. On the contrary, the population explosion accounts for only one of a number of revolutionary transformations; it is only one of many dimensions of human experience in which incremental change has been superseded by quantum leaps. A graphic portrayal of the histories of nearly all major factors affecting individual and society would result in a series of curves nearly symmetrical to the recorded trend of world population increase. The growth of human economic productivity and consumption, of science and technology, of the diffusion of education—and of man's capacity for destruction—all exhibit the same linear characteristics as the 10,000-year population curve: an almost horizontal segment persisting for millennia and then a rising curve, approaching verticality in the twentieth century.

A realistic analysis of the contemporary world must therefore place the population explosion in the context of a multiplicity of erupting forces, each of which is adding its own energies to an accelerating process of global transformation. The projected sixty-five-year tripling of world population (1935–2000), for example, must be connected conceptually to the tripling of the world's economic product in a mere twenty years (1950–1970). The development of military air power from zero effectiveness in 1900 to the mid-century nuclear missile is terrifying testimony to the verticality of the contemporary science-technology curve. But it is only one of the most obvious aspects of the unprecedented scientific explosion that has revolutionized the entire range of warfare. In turn, the armaments revolution is only part of the still larger process in which science and technology have converted human societies and economies into forms hitherto unknown and evolving rapidly into still newer forms.

On any time scale steeply rising curves signal acceleration. They record that production, consumption, learning, reproduction—or change in general—is occurring more and more rapidly. But the consequences of acceleration extend beyond their significance for time; they also contribute to a compression of space. Rapid population growth has resulted in increased physical crowding of human beings. Expanding consumption requirements crowd the local and global resource bases that must sustain the population. Science and technology have made possible the construction of an ever more dense and comprehensive network of rapid transport and instantaneous communication. It is a network that speeds the circulation of people, goods, information, and ideas, bringing all parts of the globe into unprecedented proximity. It has also transformed the once spacious earth into a unified target for nuclear destruction.

Time and space, then, have been altered in both function and effect by new realities whose form is measured by the vertical curve. The measurement reveals a world that has become a small, crowded planet undergoing multiple and accelerating transformations.

These vast changes in the human condition signal danger, but they also signal opportunity. The greatest danger lies in failure to understand the new realities and their implications. Conversely, the achievement of understanding is the key to opportunity, which rational policies must then shape, nurture, and mature.

The obstacles to developing such creative policies were never more formidable, but man's resources—science, education, and productivity—have never been more abundant. And the new global proximity, which for the first time gives the human community tangible form, makes possible the rational organization of these resources to the benefit of all mankind. If man has now reached the point where he faces the question of survival or extinction in its ultimate dimensions, he is also at least as well equipped as he ever was to solve the survival problem.

In the traditional world most men attempted to cope with survival problems according to the formulas of micropolitics: they linked their safety and their chances for happiness to the life and power of their tribe, city, class, or state. The environment surrounding these parochial political entities was composed of essentially identical structures. Yet this environment has traditionally been perceived as alien. Parts of it might be perceived as hostile or as friendly, but almost never as "belonging." The idea of an organic link between a particular society and societies external to it, of the existence of a common set of problems requiring common solutions and obligations, and of the individual as belonging to both the society and its environment has been a historical rarity. It has been rarest of all at that level where the environment is the globe itself. Traditional international politics has never given tangible expression to the idea of common destiny and common responsibility for the world at large.

In any context micropolitics can be understood as assigning greater value to the parts than to the whole within which the parts function. In the international context these micropolitical valuations find their most significant expression in the still-dominant assumptions concerning the supremacy of the sovereign state. The powerful presence of these assumptions, in turn, defines the central political problem of our time: Can an international system of political thought and political action based on micropolitical values cope successfully with a world in radical transformation, a transformation whose chief effect is to compress time and space and thus to fuse whole and part, sector and environment?

Micropolitical doctrines reflect and were designed to manage events and behavior during the long history when the human process could be measured, at least in gross terms, by a horizontal curve. The world of vertical curves, suddenly come upon us, necessarily challenges the adequacy of those doctrines at almost every point of contact—and nowhere more decisively than in the matter of precedence between the whole and the parts.

The main purpose of this book is to present, analyze, and where the evidence permits, reinforce these challenges to the adequacy of inherited micropolitical doctrines. In essence, then, the book stages a confrontation between micropolitics and macropolitics. The argument will be that men have survived during the long ascendancy of micropolitics only because the conditions of human life have hitherto been characterized by the horizontal curve. Survival in a world of vertical curves, however, requires conformity to the new rules of macropolitics. They are rules whose purpose is the protection and nurture of the whole society of man, and their adoption is the indispensable condition for the survival of all its parts.

October 1, 1973   R. W. S.

Acknowledgments

My chief debt of gratitude in connection with this book is to Inis Claude, Professor of Government and Foreign Affairs at the University of Virginia. A leading authority in international organization and international politics and consulting editor to Random House, his enthusiasm for the manuscript at an early stage in its evolution was a great encouragement. Each chapter benefited from his thoughtful comments and criticisms. Whenever there were substantive disagreements between us, he gave cogent expression to his own point of view and at the same time respected the right to differ. In short, he has been the best of editors.

I am also grateful to Professor John Herz of the City College of New York, who read all but the last few chapters of the manuscript. His observations, whether approving or critical, were always thoughtful and to the point.

The three teachers who have had most impact on me were Arnold Wolfers, Hajo Holborn, and Friedrich Meinecke. Their intellectual and moral excellence set an enduring standard for their students. In their memory, I record here my abiding and affectionate gratitude and admiration.

A number of Dartmouth colleagues, particularly Denis Sullivan and Meredith Clement, have been kind enough to read and comment upon individual chapters or have helped to answer various technical questions. I thank them for their interest and assistance. I am also grateful to several officials in the United Nations Secretariat who checked over the statistics in some of the appendices.

Over the years I was fortunate to have the help of some exceptionally talented undergraduate research assistants, particularly in connection with the preparation of the appendices. I am indebted to all of them: Donald Pogue, Dennis Young, Lynn Breedlove, James Sligar, and Joost van Nispen.

I am also grateful to many people at Knopf for their thoughtful and imaginative participation in the making of this book. My thanks go especially to Jane Cullen and to Barry Rossinoff, whose initiative is responsible for the book's cover.

Ruth Morrison typed almost the whole of the first draft, and Caroline Parr most of the revisions. Their skill, patience, and conscientiousness are much appreciated.

Dartmouth College and the Rockefeller Foundation, in the person of Kenneth W. Thompson, were generous with timely financial support in connection with my first book and again with the present work. I am thus doubly grateful to both.

My final word of thanks, appropriately, goes to the indexer. I am most appreciative of Dorothy Beck's fine work and willingness to cope with the time pressures that unavoidably accompany the compiling of an index.

Contents

PART TWO **The Macropolitical World**   325

Macroanalysis: Objectives and Implications

Macroanalysis: Objectives and Implications

This inquiry into the meaning of international politics bears the title of *Macropolitics* for a very specific reason. It seeks to be cosmopolitan rather than parochial in its analysis of the actors, institutions, and transactions that contribute to the world's political life. It aspires to achieve a stance that views the international system as a whole rather than from the perspective of the actors within the system.

The fundamental question underlying the entire inquiry is: What are the needs and resources of the world as a whole? Consequently, questions regarding the needs and resources of the nation-state, the regional organization, or the United Nations itself are necessarily secondary. They are important and require careful examination, but they are subordinate to the main purpose of achieving an understanding of global reality. Thus, they will be investigated as a means of obtaining a surer grasp of that reality.

The term macropolitics is borrowed explicitly from the field of economics. Macroanalysis and microanalysis have been employed in many different disciplines, notably in the natural sciences. But the development of macroanalysis in economics has the most obvious relevance for the present undertaking. Robert Heilbroner, for example, has observed that:

> When economics focuses its study on the individual agents of the process, the individual owner of labor, capital or land, or when it highlights the manner in which a typical entrepreneur organizes land, labor and capital in his firm, we call the resulting study *microeconomics*. When, however, economics opens its lens to the widest possible extent, to study not so much the individual participant in the production process but the total activity of all participants, we call the study *macroeconomics*.[1]

[1] Robert L. Heilbroner, *Understanding Macroeconomics* (Englewood Cliffs, N.J.: Prentice-Hall, 1965), p. 13.

Heilbroner's explanation of the two major sectors of economic analysis is easily translated into politics. Micropolitics gives primary attention to individual agents in the political process; macropolitics is concerned with the sum of political interactions to which all the individual agents, or actors, contribute.

One could identify macropolitics as equivalent to the political system of the state itself, specifying as micropolitics those activities of voters, parties, pressure groups, legislatures, and the like, that take place within the macropolitical structure of the nation. This is, in fact, the model most economists have used, equating macroeconomics with the national economy and microeconomics with the various sectors of economic activity within the national economy. As Barbara Ward once remarked, however, this nomenclature is indicative of the provincialism sometimes found in economic as well as political concepts. However imposing the gross national product of any given state, authentic economic macroanalysis would properly focus on the economy of the globe in its entirety.

So too in politics. If it is a truism that this is an interdependent world and that the nation-state cannot exist unto itself, political science must draw the conclusions the truism dictates. In order to understand better the parts as well as the whole, we must examine the system as a whole. Macroanalysis in politics requires the student to focus on the global political system.

In international politics, then, the foreign policies of individual states and the decisions within those states that contribute to foreign policy positions essentially fall under the rubric of micropolitics. Macropolitics, on the other hand, extends the analytical base to encompass the external forces bearing in upon the state. These forces emanate not only from other states but also from the world environment in its entirety. Surely it is an environment to which all the individual states or actors have contributed. Yet it is also a world they never made. Instead, it is the result of their combined actions that time and space, accident, and the intricacies of aggregation transmute into something apart and often unanticipated.

A cosmopolitan outlook is difficult to attain. Every individual is caught in a web of subjectivity whose strands are spun by personality, class, color, nation, culture, civilization, and faith. Every person is born and raised within the confines of parochialism, and he can emerge from those confines only by a sustained effort to transcend them. Parochialism is stamped on the birth certificate. To be cosmopolitan one must first grow up.

In essence, parochial attitudes are those which assert, explicitly or implicitly, that only familiar values and behavior have any real worth. Parochialism is the posture of the ingroup, the conviction that divides the world into us and them. What we do is natural, reasonable, and good; what they do is at best quaint or bizarre and at worst, abominable. What the parochial person is really trying to do is to impose his subjective views of reality upon mankind. The cosmopolitan person, in contrast, attempts to discipline and expand the scope of his understanding by actively and seriously considering unfamiliar values and ways of life. The parochial man stays close to routine. The cosmopolitan man, in the process of expanding his base of information and experience, necessarily becomes accustomed to novelty.

Cosmopolitanism is not a prescription for the suppression of individual or cultural subjectivity. Any such exercise in the alienation of selfhood is as futile as it is undesirable—and it is therefore dangerous. What the transition from narrower to broader perspectives does require of the individual, however, is a growing capacity to empathize with the subjective preferences of other individuals and other cultures. The culmination of this process is the maturing of a will that identifies the common concerns of humanity as the proper measure of the more restricted interests of the several societies into which humanity is divided. It is at this point that cosmopolitanism and macropolitics meet.

The cosmopolitan standards of macropolitics are obviously no novelty. They are rooted in the longing for peace, which is as old as history. They take their cue from all those who have sought to discover common interests compelling enough to overcome enmity and war among particular interests. They draw strength from all the ancient and modern doctrines that have avowed the oneness of mankind, and from individuals and groups who sought to act on the premise of human unity.

Above all, macropolitics is the product of a twentieth-century understanding that has spread ever more widely and rapidly since World War II. It is the understanding that the world is becoming too small and vulnerable to survive unless global needs are recognized and acted upon with the same commitment and energy that have traditionally characterized responses to national needs. Macropolitics reflects the work of those ecologists, demographers, agronomists, politicians, jurists, businessmen, and social, biological, and physical scientists who have contributed to that understanding. It is they who have demonstrated the presence of a rapidly growing aggregation of dangers and opportunities that can be dealt with effectively only if men are willing to move beyond their national compartments.

The data collected and the conclusions reached by this growing corps of scientists and policy makers can be summarized in one basic message: the survival and prosperity of the globe is the necessary condition for the survival and prosperity of its parts. The negative corollary is easily deduced: unconcern for the whole will jeopardize its continuing existence, with the parts suffering the necessary consequences.

MACROPOLITICS AND NATIONAL INTEREST

Macropolitical analysis must therefore begin with the questions central to its global concerns: What is the *international* interest? What policies and institutions appear to benefit all men, and what appear to benefit some but not others? What is likely to disadvantage them all? It must ask what any given nation-state contributes to the international interest and judge the value of any particular national interest in terms of the answer to that question.

These questions are the necessary products of a shift in the focus of concern from the nation to the globe. They also clearly imply a relativization of the national interest. The macropolitical concern for the survival and welfare of the global whole logically requires an equal concern for the component national parts. But this allocation of attention is nonetheless a radical departure from the traditional and still dominant micropolitical concepts of international life. This is true because macropolitics erects a standard for international behavior alongside and sometimes in conflict with the traditional standard of the national interest. In the world of academic analysis as well as in the world of policy makers, this inherited standard of national interest has long been regarded as the ultimate justification of foreign policy. The political macroanalyst is forced to insist that the justification is insufficient.

Macropolitics weighs the particular advantages and disadvantages of the parts against the functioning of the whole. Many of its propositions, therefore, derive from analogies between the relationships of globe and nations, on the one hand, and the relationships of central and state, provincial, or local governments, on the other. A closer analogy, because the center has less power than the parts, is the European Economic Community (EEC). However tight or loose, the political nub of the analogy is the proposition that the purposes of the parts cannot be pursued at the expense of the whole.

So formulated, macropolitics implies restrictions on state behavior in international relations. The implication provokes an obvious question: By what agency will these restrictions be declared and enforced? The answer at this stage can only be that the sovereign states themselves—in their individual policies and in multilateral arrangements, in the United Nations, and in other international organizations—must be the originators and guardians of such restrictions. This raises, in turn, a further issue: What could motivate states to define and serve interests larger than their own and to accept restrictions upon themselves? The only possible answer—at any time—is that states will do these things if they perceive them to be in their own interests.

There is a long record of cooperative undertakings in international politics, economics, and law which reveals that states are quite capable of disciplining themselves to serve a common interest and a common purpose. But there is a much longer record demonstrating that states have been highly selective in their approach to international cooperation and in their willingness to submit to restraints. When one considers still another international record—that of outright conflict—it is evident that past precedent offers only a tenuous expectation that macropolitical concepts will recommend themselves without qualification to those in charge of foreign policies.

Past behavior should not be discounted. But humanity's present predicament is a more relevant measure of the value and prospects of the analytical and policy concepts of macropolitics. An inquiry into this predicament is a major purpose of the following chapters. But it is appropriate at the outset to state the governing question accompanying this inquiry: What are the overriding interests of the individual states (and their citizens) given the realities of the contemporary world and its likely future? The data and arguments that make up this book offer a detailed answer, but its main outlines are already evident: men and states, if they seek to be rational in the pursuit of their interests, must cease to restrict their concerns and loyalties to the confines of their own societies. They must learn to accept responsibility and to care for the fate of the global system upon which their own fates depend.

While this conception of interest requires restrictions on the self-will of states, it also offers unprecedented opportunities. A world in which states effectively reconcile their policies to global needs will benefit from a less menacing environment. Such a reconciliation could make possible the conquest of poverty. Those already affluent would collect their usual benefits from such a transformation: hundreds of millions of paupers would become customers—and contributors to world productivity in their own right. A cooperative world could more easily master the growing ecological crisis and, indeed, make human life more rewarding in all its aspects. Interest calculates in terms of gains and losses. Macropolitics promises more gains and fewer losses. Traditional micropolitics promises the reverse.

COOPERATION, CONFLICT, AND REALISM

The global concerns of macropolitics add up to a radical break with much of past international thought and behavior. There is no doubt that the history of international relations has customarily exhibited an ascendancy of the parts over the whole. The search for competitive advantage—and even the cooperative undertakings among states—have characteristically been micropolitical in nature. That is, the objectives of both struggle and cooperation have been designed to advantage some states and not others. The most conspicuous, though not exclusive, model for international behavior has been the zero sum game in which gain for one player must result in loss for another. The assumptions of such a model obviously provide little incentive to consider the needs of the environs in which the game is played.

If international relations has been typically micropolitical in practice and parochial in outlook, a macropolitical analysis runs the danger of losing touch with reality. If men's preference for the parts over the whole is so amply documented in international history, an approach that focuses on the needs of the whole may miss some of the basic dynamics of international behavior. This danger can be avoided only if careful attention is also paid to the characteristics and objectives of the parts.

It is wise to be aware of the pitfalls that await any given analytical approach. If macroanalysis, in departing from the conventional wisdom in international politics, runs risks of error, it will have no monopoly in the risk market. We have lived in a parochial world since time began, and microanalysis in international politics has faithfully reflected that reality. Hence the practitioners of microanalysis, who have stressed the persistent ascendancy of the parts over the whole, have with some reason been pleased to call themselves "realists." But whenever the claim of "realism" is made, one is obligated to try to define reality in order to ascertain whether the avowed realism is in fact realistic.[2]

The persisting parochialism of the nation-state is an indisputable and long-standing reality. But it is an equally indisputable reality that the contemporary world is bound together by unprecedentedly comprehensive communications networks, by a ferocious intimacy of ecological, economic, political, and ideological relationships unknown in all previous history, and by a nuclear community of common life or death. Moreover, many aspects of international behavior, most notably the reciprocal caution of the nuclear superpowers, demonstrate that states are beginning to leaven their traditional parochialism with a new awareness of their common perils. States have also given considerable attention to the promise of common opportunities. Thus a macropolitical approach, addressing itself to both the perils and opportunities of a fundamentally transformed world, may be able to discover realities about the global society that microanalysis cannot see.

The relentless multiplication of mankind's numbers, for example, is quite tangential to the policies and disputes of self-regarding nation-states. Yet the prospect of some 3 billion additional human beings on earth by the year 2000 threatens to become a tidal wave rising in the southern hemisphere and smashing to pieces the entire international

---

[2] William Lee Miller gave to a review article discussing the bitter disagreements between former Secretary of State Dean Acheson and former Ambassador George Kennan the wry title "Two Really Realistic Realists." *Piety Along the Potomac* (Boston: Houghton Mifflin, 1964).

system of which the self-regarding nation-states are a part. Transistor radios and television communication are inherently apolitical, but they are efficient mobilizers of tastes and demands to the point that they may provoke a worldwide confrontation between the affluent and the miserable, regardless of national allegiance.

The color of human skin continues to be an issue that both divides and transcends the nation-state. To say the least, the concept of the national interest is liable to look very different to white Americans and black Americans—or to black men and brown men in, for example, East Africa. Finally, the self-regarding nation-states have gotten themselves into a nuclear bag from which there is no exit except by seeking solutions on a global basis. These are the kinds of problems that cry out for a macroanalytic approach in international relations in which the concerns of the parts cease to obscure the reality of the whole.

The parochial liturgy of political "realism" has adopted as its leading theme the phenomenon of conflict. Cooperation and the resolving of differences are generally relegated to a subordinate status—useful, but only if they do not interfere with the main aim of combat efficiency. This approach permeates the conventional analysis of both domestic and international politics. Just as self-regarding nation-states conflict and compete with one another in a struggle for power, so, within the state, self-regarding parties, classes, and pressure groups also carry on a comparable struggle for advantage. Most analysts assert that an overarching allegiance to the state usually prevents the combat within the state from attaining the ferocity of the international struggle. But even these analysts nonetheless share the basic persuasion that the essence of politics is conflict.

The preoccupation with conflict in contemporary political science is somewhat surprising in light of the fact that most political scientists tend to praise the practicing politician who succeeds in resolving conflict situations and to condemn politicians who exacerbate them. Here, it may be argued, they speak as citizens and not as scientists. Yet, in the end, scientific observation must also record that the arts of cooperation are more sophisticated and productive than those of strife. The success of a political organization, whether party, trade union, or nation-state, is finally measured by the amount of cooperation it can achieve within its ranks and in its relationships with its relevant environment.

Cooperation, then, stakes out its own title as the essence of political activity as well as the proper goal of political effort. The validity of this claim and the functional relationship between cooperation and conflict will be examined throughout this book. But let it be said at the outset: no one could deny that political action and conflict are forever inseparable. Let it also be said that the concern for security—particularly in the international arena where states have typically had to depend upon themselves for survival—was and is a real and legitimate concern. Failure to pay close attention to the phenomenon of enmity and to the pervasive role of conflict in politics can only produce illusions. Illusions at least as grievous, however, obscure the landscape whenever it is forgotten that the true vocation of the politician is to create conditions of consent. Conflict often cannot be avoided, but both morality and economy in the exercise of power always point to voluntary cooperation as the preferred and ultimate solution.

Coinciding interests and cooperative undertakings are just as familiar to both domestic and international politics as are conflicting interests and competitive behavior. Each kind of interest and behavior must be given its full due if analysis is to be realistic. An approach that limits the definition of politics to a struggle for power among conflicting interests offers a dramatic but bogus realism.

The nature of contemporary international life lends urgency to the quest for an authentic realism offering a careful appraisal of actual and potential modes of cooperative behavior as well as of the phenomenon of conflict. As Raymond Aron has noted, for the first time in human experience we have a truly universal history.[3] Men and civilizations are no longer compartmentalized in various sectors of the globe. Instead, they are increasingly participating in, and reacting to, events with worldwide impact. More and more they are investing, willingly or not, in a common fate.

The decompartmentalization of the world opens up exhilarating possibilities. No longer remote from one another, men and cultures have an opportunity to strengthen their common ties. A significant number of the earth's inhabitants who have historically regarded each other as strangers and aliens have discovered and cultivated a new sense of kinship. And the multiplying networks of global relationships have provided the necessary substance with which to transform the visions of earlier prophets of cosmopolitanism into at least the beginnings of a human community.

But at the very moment that technology is collapsing distances between nations and cultures the earth is becoming ominously crowded. Unprecedented increases in population raise the specter of famine not only in nutriments but along the whole spectrum of the natural resources that keep men and civilizations alive. Indeed, the pressures of population, production, and consumption—and the resulting pollution of the earth's environment—menace the ecological balance of the biosphere itself. If, as Thomas Hobbes insisted, realistic political analysis must give due regard to man's desire to survive, a realistic assessment of today's shrunken world must conclude that the goal of survival can be reached only if cooperation outdistances conflict.

---

[3] Raymond Aron, *The Dawn of Universal History* (New York: Praeger, 1961), p. 3.

Yet survival is increasingly endangered. The obvious reason is that in a world in which mankind is converging upon itself conflict in international politics continues to engage more energies than cooperation. Antagonisms within the developed world have generated powers of destruction capable of ending life on earth. But the profusion of volatile and desperate circumstances in the underdeveloped world are more likely to serve as the catalysts which could finally unleash these forces. Korea, Cuba, the Middle East, and Vietnam make the point. They are, in turn, only parts of the danger zone that now spreads over most of the globe and finds its most massive form in the confrontation between the world's rich minority and its poor majority.

The revolution of rising expectations that once described attitudes in the world of the poor has been overtaken by the revolution of disappointed hopes. The virtual demise of formal colonialism, profoundly desirable in itself, has done nothing to change the global process in which the rich have been growing richer and the poor poorer. Moreover, liberation from empire has enabled former colonial peoples to observe this process with greater clarity and hence greater resentment than ever before. As they look out upon the world, they see that every relevant economic, and noneconomic, yardstick shows a massive and growing gap between the developed countries and the underdeveloped countries. Polite usage, to be sure, currently decrees that the latter be called developing countries, but in this case courtesy obscures too many brutal facts.

It is true that in many underdeveloped countries there have been noteworthy achievements in building more productive economies. It is also true that in many of the same countries these achievements have been cancelled out by population increase. If one adds to net population increase the multiplication of urban and rural slum populations, political strife, governmental repression, civil war, corruption, loss of traditional values, inflation, rising indebtedness, and declining foreign exchange earnings, a summation of gains and losses yields a negative balance. Many of the "developing" countries are growing poorer, not only relative to the dynamic growth of the rich countries but in an absolute sense. Under these conditions one may well ask: What price development?

It would be well to leave behind terminological disputes about underdeveloped and developing and simply start from the fact that about two-thirds of mankind, including the massive majority of states, is desperately poor. If present population and economic trends are not radically altered, by the year 2000 the world will be divided into a minority group of 20 to 30 percent of moderately to very rich people and a majority group of 70 to 80 percent for whom hunger, disease, ignorance, and personal frustration are the iron laws of daily life. In such a world the dominant emotion among the poor is bound to be envy; among the rich it is bound to be fear.

WORLD OLIGARCHY AND WORLD MASS

Such a world will reproduce on a macrocosmic scale the classic confrontation of mass and oligarchy that plagued the ancient city-state (and more modern types of political organization as well). The typical outcomes resulting from this confrontation are five. The first is a more or less successful defense of the status quo. The oligarchy maintains its ascendancy and its privileges against the mass challenge. It exploits the divisions among the poor majority and manages to prevent tensions within the oligarchy from degenerating into apocalyptic warfare. In a word, it manages to perpetuate the inherited system of big power politics in which the fate of all mankind is decided by the powerful few. The improbability of such an outcome—and the price it must exact—will be another of the major themes in the subsequent analysis.

The other four outcomes depart from the status quo: either the oligarchy shares its perquisites with the mass to the point where it ceases to be an oligarchy; the oligarchy destroys itself by fragmenting into quarreling factions; the oligarchy is swept away by the mass; or the whole society collapses and falls prey to some stronger neighbor.[4] In each case, these outcomes are revolutionary in the strictest meaning of the term.

Of the four typical outcomes in a revolutionary situation one is not a possible option in the present global crisis. There is no stronger trans-atmospheric neighbor that might seek to impose its order on a disintegrating earthly society. The other outcomes are more relevant. Certainly the oligarchy of the developed nations is beset by quarrels and factions. The United States and the Soviet Union, as the most powerful of the oligarchs, set the pace for the rest of the developed world, sometimes clashing and sometimes moderating their conflicts of interest. Indeed, they are occasionally able to find areas of common interest, as, for example, in the limitation of nuclear testing and arsenals, in delineating spheres of influence, in traditional balance of power operations, and in matters of trade.

Some, in fact, have argued that the United States and Russia are moving toward a duopoly in which each would tacitly agree to a mutual guarantee perpetuating their joint predominance as against the rest of the world. But few would regard such a duopoly as anything more than a precarious marriage of convenience. The causes of faction within the international oligarchy are deep-rooted. There will be stringent limits to collaboration among the oligarchs as long as the nemesis of a nuclear showdown haunts both their fears and their rational calculations. And

---

[4] Concrete examples of these outcomes, of course, usually exhibit features of two or more of these types in various combinations.

only transient solidarities can be attained by ad hoc attempts to keep the lid on an increasingly tumultuous world of the poor.

Besides, the oligarch cannot let the mass alone. Each faction seeks to recruit allies from the world of the poor in its struggle with opposing factions in the oligarchy. The recruiting process explains at least in part the massive economic and military aid programs carried on by the United States, the Soviet Union, and other developed (and some under-developed) countries. Commercial, ideological, and moral motivations all play their important and often autonomous roles in foreign aid policy, but they can never be wholly divorced from considerations of factional advantage. Even if they could it would still remain true that all these motives, singly or in concert, reinforce each other to propel the developed world ever deeper into the affairs of the underdeveloped socie-ties. By the same token, the underdeveloped countries are so desperate for customers, capital, technical assistance, and sometimes military aid that they accept the intrusion of the international oligarchy. In an ideal world, no doubt, they would prefer isolation, or, at least, effective insulation.

Wittingly and unwittingly, the world's rich are exciting the hopes, demands, resentments, and capacities of the world's poor. It is clear so far that the capacities of the poor societies—economic productivity, edu-cational base, military power—have lagged behind hopes, demands, and resentments. But these capacities in some parts of the underdeveloped world have nonetheless grown significantly; the United States made that uncomfortable discovery in Vietnam and the Soviet Union in China. The overall pattern in the world of the poor, however, is that hopes are outpacing achievements. Unless a tolerable balance is restored between hope and achievement the poor are likely to prefer the risks of violence to the prospect of mounting frustration over the costs and vexations of long-range development. It is this only quasi-irrational temptation to violence to which Communist China has long made its key ideological appeal. By the early 1970s the Chinese Communists were indicating some preference for a less dangerous approach. But even if Peking holds to less provocative policies in the name of its own self-preservation, the mood of violence in the world of poverty will be upon us for a long time to come, and will grow in intensity if present trends are not reversed.

Just as the oligarchic factions have always sought and found allies among the mass, so the mass has always found allies among the oli-garchy. It too can recruit. In international society as in domestic politics the small and the weak have often known how to use the powerful for their own ends. Frequently it is difficult to judge whether the strong or the weak exercise more influence in their mutual relations; the United States and South Vietnam, Russia and China, Britain and Rhodesia are cases in point. It is obvious that ruling groups in underdeveloped countries find clienteles within the hierarchies of the developed countries. It is equally obvious that revolutionary sentiments in the Third World have a powerful attraction for disadvantaged minorities in the industrial states.

International reality is becoming an ever more intricate network of both unifying and divisive relationships. In this network, mass and oligarchy, revolutionary and reformer, city dweller and peasant, compatriot and foreigner, developed and underdeveloped, rich and poor are bound together to a common fate overriding all traditional notions of separate national destinies. If the divisive forces in the network gain predominance to the point where massive revolutionary violence occurs, it will be the product of both oligarchy and mass, both caught up in the contradictions of a global tragedy.

One of the four revolutionary outcomes of the politics of confrontation remains to be discussed: the oligarchy shares its perquisites with the mass to the point where it is no longer an oligarchy. To effect such an outcome in the global confrontation between mass and oligarchy would require the application on a global scale of democratic principles that have hitherto been reserved in practice to the domestic politics of some of the developed countries. A global democratization would require the dismantling of the international hierarchy at whose apex one finds, in traditional language, the Great Powers and, in contemporary language, the superpowers. It is neither feasible, necessary, nor desirable that the dismantling operations be precipitate. It is feasible, necessary, and desirable that as large a sector as possible of the global oligarchy recognize and resolve to satisfy the urgent need for an equitable distribution of power and wealth among the peoples of the world.

The central imperative in contemporary world politics can be stated in a still more demanding way. One cannot solve the problems of the world's poor except by abolishing the world's poverty. One cannot solve the problems caused by massive ignorance except by education. But education and wealth generate power, both for the individual and for the society. Ultimately, then, the spread of wealth and education among the two-thirds of mankind now lacking both is a process which will create power where none existed before. The imperative of development thus requires the oligarchs to dilute their virtual monopoly of power to the point where the monopoly is broken. Once this occurs the oligarchy disappears, and one enters the arena of more or less democratic politics in which the rich and the not-so-rich, the educated and the less educated, the powerful and the not-quite-so-powerful, the white and the nonwhite enjoy reasonably equal footing from which to engage in bargaining, debate, conflict, and cooperation. In a word, world development requires the demise of world oligarchy.

If this seems a harsh prospect for the oligarchs, historical perspective can soften it a bit. After all, the dismantling of the oligarchy was central to the democratization process in the domestic politics of the Western countries. The individual human beings who made up the oligarchy were not always driven out of their positions of privilege by fire and sword. Frequently the process was a gradual one in which the oligarchs remained rich and powerful—only their wealth and power were no longer inordinate in relation to the rest of society. Sometimes the oligarchs were struck down by violence, but this outcome was usually associated with a blind determination to hang on to absolute power. Wherever democracy developed with a minimum of violence it was because the rulers were persuaded of the necessity of sharing power.

CLASS INTEREST AND NATIONAL INTEREST

Karl Marx insisted that the oligarchs would never share power with the mass because they were caught up in a historical determinism that decreed the defense of class interest and class privilege to the bitter end. Hence, Marx reasoned, only violent revolution could effect a redistribution of power and wealth. Fortunately for the lives and happiness of hundreds of millions of people in the last four or five generations, this crudely deterministic view of history and politics was refuted by the democratization process in the West, whose revolutionary dynamic owes far more to reform than to violence.

If, however, we now move from the arena of domestic politics back to the global society, Marxian perspectives and prophecies have an uncomfortable relevance. Marx predicted that within every bourgeois state the rich would grow richer and fewer and the poor would become poorer and more numerous. In fact, to the lasting embarrassment of Marxists, the opposite occurred. But at the global level we have already seen that poverty is expanding every day while the rich minority becomes a steadily smaller and less representative segment of mankind. One is forced to ask the question whether the national interest (or race interest) will demonstrate the disastrous qualities that Marx attributed to the phenomenon of class interest. In other words, are the nations of the developed world entangled in a deterministic doctrine of national interest that dictates the defense of their privileged position down to the moment when only violence can take it from them?

The modern theory and practice of international relations has lived off the fundamental proposition that there is no higher value than the national interest. Before the rise of the nation-state, divine right kingdoms, medieval monarchies, ancient empires, city-states, and tribes all preached and practiced an analogous "sacred egotism" which political theorists generally endorsed. If there were dissident voices among the theoreticians, it is nonetheless true that the mainstream of thought about international relations from Thucydides in Greece and Kautilya in India down to our own day has been Machiavellian in content. The world was assumed to be (with considerable accuracy) a congeries of states, each pursuing its own parochial interests. In such a world the formula for survival was that each state should pursue its interests as vigorously as possible. It should do nothing to promote the fortunes of a possible rival. The first duty of the state—to borrow from the classical parlance of international relations—is to itself. The other duties, if any, are feeble admonitions when compared with the dynamic imperative of the state, or national, interest.

The empirical history of international relations and the long tradition of thought about them suggest the formidable difficulties besetting any endeavor to relativize the national interest in the way that the democratization process in domestic politics relativized the class interest. Anyone in contemporary domestic politics, even in nondemocratic societies, who would advocate (overtly, at least) a single-minded pursuit of class interest would properly be regarded as a museum piece. But the single-minded pursuit of whatever is conceived to be the national interest remains an eminently respectable point of view. Transnational structures like the European Economic Community have accomplished much, but they have yet to demonstrate that the member nations are willing to fuse their primary interests with the needs of a larger unity. The claim to national sovereignty, however tenuous in many instances, continues to define the rules of the international game.

A careful examination of the facts of contemporary international life will show just how tenuous the concept of sovereignty has become. A global perspective will reveal the extent to which the traditional rules of the game have become antiquated. Yet the paramountcy of the national interest continues to serve as the major premise of foreign policy making, and sovereignty still functions as the fundamental legal basis for international relationships.

Realism therefore demands recognition of the persistence of the national interest concept and the durability of the nation-state. Realism must acknowledge that the national interest is a more formidable barrier to political and social change on a global scale than the obstacle of class interest that had to be overcome in the process of political and social change in domestic society. But realism is also obligated to examine the forces that are eroding the traditional world of sovereign states and to ascertain the relative pulling power of old habits and new challenges. Above all, realism must avoid the trap of a determinism which assumes that nationalism and sovereignty are the only conceivable principles upon which to organize international life.

If analysis is to be realistic, it must expose the growing contradictions in the nationalist credo. But it must also identify the transnational forces already in movement that promise all men a better and more abundant life than the old system of national exclusiveness was ever able to attain. A new realism need not be at war with the old national societies, insisting that they sacrifice their security, wealth, and uniqueness on a global altar. The relativization of the national interest need not mean the devaluation of the nation. Instead, it offers liberation from a parochialism that cannot in any case live safely among the world's new realities. And it prescribes to nations and states not so much sacrifice as life-enhancing investments in the growth of all societies and in the environment they share in common.

It is realistic, then, to attempt to look at the behavior and needs of more or less sovereign states in terms of the behavior and needs of the environment in which they exist. The significance and destiny of class interest could not be understood without an appreciation of the larger society in which it operated. The significance and destiny of national interest can be grasped only by assessing its interaction with the global society. It is this interaction between the parts and the whole that constitutes the central concern of international relations and which, in this book, is referred to as macropolitics.

MACROPOLITICAL PERSPECTIVES

As a minimum macroanalysis can offer fresh insight into the realities and needs of our time. Its maximum contribution would be a major overhaul of international theory comparable to the transformation of economic theory that took place when macroeconomics achieved ascendancy over microeconomics. Microeconomics, focusing on the behavior of the individual units of production and consumption, was unable to explain or cope effectively with the massive cumulative forces shaping the environment in which individual buyers and sellers operate. During the worldwide economic crisis of the 1930s, macroeconomics emerged as a new theoretical framework to explain and manipulate economic phenomena of great magnitudes. By encompassing the total economic process within the nation-state, macroeconomics clarified and facilitated management of the dynamics of national economic life. Similarly, macropolitics, by probing the cumulative forces constituting the global environment in which all of today's states must pursue their destinies, offers the prospect of a more rational understanding and management of the dynamics of international life.

Crisis was the midwife of macroeconomic theory, and it is also the midwife of macropolitical theory. The fundamental forces in world politics—manpower, resources, technology, and human values—have joined to produce a situation that threatens to defy all rational control. A quantum leap in world population coincides with quantum leaps in technological development and in threats to man's natural environment. At the same time, there is an ominous and increasingly radical inequality of human access to the resources for livelihood and to the creative technology capable of expanding those resources. The rapidity of change reflected in technological acceleration, in the population explosion, and in resource exhaustion is, in turn, shaking the foundations of inherited values. Technology's cruelest gift—the threat of nuclear oblivion—completes the crisis setting. Those living during the remaining years of the twentieth century must deal with the crisis of our time realistically and successfully on pain of extinction.

Realism in contemporary international politics demands that the world be dealt with more as a community and less as a hunting ground for the pursuit of parochial national or ideological interests. It requires less concern for the competitive advantages of the parts and more concern for the common advantages of the whole. It needs to build on the cosmopolitan understanding Lord Keynes achieved at the peace conference at Versailles when he saw (and vainly argued) that the impoverishment of vanquished Germany could only contribute to the impoverishment of the victorious Allies. Keynes left London an Englishman; the Versailles experience transformed him into a "European in his cares and outlook."[5] Nations, Keynes insisted, are not isolated political-economic units; they are caught up in an international network of supply and demand. The national welfare is dependent on other parts of the network and on the welfare of the network as a whole.

It took a second world war before Keynesian doctrines in both national and international economics finally flourished. After 1945 the United States helped to rebuild the economies—and consequently the political power—of victors and vanquished in both Europe and Asia. Economic internationalism gained ascendancy over economic nationalism, and the economic and political power of all concerned has flourished accordingly. But a massive qualification must be appended to this otherwise admirable if still incomplete record of learning from past error. It was an economic internationalism which embraced only a minority of mankind. The Soviet world was excluded, largely by its own choice. Above all, the new world of Asia, Africa, and Latin America, beginning to emerge from the status of colony or satellite, was excluded because of problems of habit, prejudice, and poverty whose magnitude even a Keynes could not possibly foresee. Yet his formula, which he applied fifty years ago to what he called the European family, is as valid as ever for the crisis that today confronts the family of nations as a whole: the impoverishment of some of the parts can only contribute to the eventual impoverishment of the others. And we know today, perhaps more poignantly than Keynes did, that poverty and mutual impoverishment are political and spiritual as well as economic phenomena.

---

[5] John Maynard Keynes, *The Economic Consequences of the Peace* (New York: Harcourt, Brace, 1920), p. 5.

Clear understanding and effective action in the international economy of the late twentieth century requires a kind of fusion of Keynesian concepts in both international and domestic economics. First, it is necessary to see the world economy as a unity. Second, it is necessary to project the Keynesian formula for domestic economic prosperity onto a global screen: the building up and maintenance of a high level of consumption among all segments of the global society is as essential to the highly productive sectors of that society as it is to the sectors of relatively low productivity. Mass consumption is the key to the wealth, power, and stability of the internal economies of the Western nations. It is also the key to affluence in the world economy. The achievement of rising levels of global affluence is, in turn, the indispensable condition of global peace—in the same way that increasing well-being of the mass kept the peace within most of the presently developed states. Only a steady contraction of poverty's world domain can save world society from disaster. It is no mere rhetoric to assert, as President Lyndon Johnson did, that "the rich nations can never live as an island of plenty in a sea of poverty."

A high level of mass consumption is not simply an economic objective; it is also a political objective. It has already been noted, and all of political history confirms it, that economic power is a crucial element in political power. A commitment to a diffusion of wealth among the total population is a commitment to mass economic power and hence to political democratization. Confirming evidence in the history of the industrial West has already been noted. The totalitarian industrial societies offer additional confirmation with a different kind of evidence. Avowing the goal of the mass state, they simultaneously rejected political democracy. The necessary result of this contradiction negated the promise of economic equality as well, for political systems committed to the concentration of power cannot afford the deconcentration of wealth.

The lesson should be clear: the interdependence of wealth and power manifests itself in all societies. Wherever there are great inequalities in wealth there are bound to be great inequalities of power, and vice versa. Reinforcing one another, these inequalities produce and perpetuate elite rule. By the same token, equitable distributions of power and wealth are the preconditions and guardians of democratic government.

But if it is important to underline the inseparability of politics and economics, it must also be stressed that they are not identical. Their intimate relationship does not contradict an ultimate judgment that political will decides the impact of economic processes on society at large. The experience of modern totalitarian societies has already served as a case in point. The case is strengthened by the history of the modern West, where, in almost every instance, political democracy developed ahead of economic democracy.

The fact is that the political idea of human equality has been the restless and indispensable critic of economic inequality. Political egalitarianism, culminating in the principle of one man, one vote, has been the moving force in narrowing the gap between rich and poor in the internal history of the nations of the West. There is no reason to suppose that the economic gap between the rich and poor nations of the globe will be narrowed without a reaffirmation of that same political commitment to human equality—but this time on a transnational basis.

Transnational concerns are the hallmarks of macropolitics. Hence its terms of reference are still more comprehensive than those of macroeconomics. While macroeconomics shifted the focus of attention from the individual transactions of the marketplace to the national economy, macropolitics shifts the focus of attention from the nation to the world. The resulting perspective reveals a shrunken, crowded, and interdependent world radically unfamiliar to previous history. It is a world and an environment whose impact on the international system, though by no means wholly new, is generating an array of challenges unknown and unimagined by the politicians and analysts of the past. Accordingly, macropolitics is a reflection of the uniqueness of the contemporary world. At the same time it registers the continuing presence of those classic features and issues of the international system that bind the present to the past.

The cumulative result of these shifts in perspective is a new way of looking at the relationship between international and domestic politics. What is external and foreign to a particular nation-state in micropolitical analysis becomes in macroanalysis an internal and domestic component of the global system. Concern for the global system, in turn, translates into concern that the interactions of its internal components should enhance rather than endanger the survival chances of the system. Thus the international society, under the novel constraints of a new age, becomes subject for the first time to the rule that has perennially governed all domestic societies: survival requires a quantitative and qualitative ascendancy of cooperation over conflict.

With due regard to differentiating specifics, then, macropolitics asserts the essential identity of international and domestic politics. A shrunken globe is viewed as an expanded domestic society, and the particular characteristics of that society bear the stamp of oligarchy. Traditional great power politics, now curbed by the nuclear menace, strongly resemble the in-fighting and the accommodations typical of oligarchial regimes. By the same token, relationships between the developed and underdeveloped worlds come more and more to exhibit the traditional malaise of oligarchy. The vast majority of the world's population is excluded from the world's government, and significant international decision making is reserved to the minority of the rich and powerful. The outcomes of the resulting tensions may vary, but they all threaten the viability of the system.

Only if the system itself evolves away from oligarchy can the tensions and their dangers be eased. This is a truth about the phenomenon of oligarchy that most of the developed societies have learned, resisted, and relearned in terms of their own domestic politics. In order to survive, they must now learn and apply the lesson in and to the world at large. Otherwise, they must run the risks, now on a global scale, that Plato diagnosed in the ancient oligarchies of the city-states: "A city of that sort is by necessity not one but two—a city of the rich and a city of the poor, living together and always plotting against one other."[6]

The macropolitical approach to international relations claims to be realistic, but it is already obvious that it is no more value free than other approaches. The national interest and power politics schools of thought praised their own capacity to see the world realistically and forcefully criticized the misguided idealism of utopian prescriptions for international life. But they themselves inevitably mingled in with critique and analysis a whole set of normative as well as expediential propositions which they commended to students and practitioners of international politics. These schools have taught that an analysis of the world as it really is will lead the student to assign supreme value to the national interest or power, as the case may be, along the somewhat Hegelian line that what is assumed to be real must also be assumed to be right. It will be argued in this book that such assumptions, when tested against contemporary international reality, will be found wanting. In any case, they demonstrate once again that the self-styled realist is no more able than the professed idealist to break the indestructable link between what is and what ought to be. Meaningful analysis must not deny that link; it must seek to illuminate it.

Thus it is proper to make explicit at the outset that the present endeavor to subject international relations to macroanalysis is animated by a central thesis that is both expediential and normative. The thesis is that there must occur a far-reaching global redistribution of power, wealth, education, and status and of the psychological satisfactions that go with the enjoyment of these values. Without such a redistribution there can be no hope for a viable (a reasonably peaceful) world society.

Such a thesis raises issues of the first importance for the understanding of both international and domestic politics. The following chapters seek to probe these issues in depth.

---

[6] *The Republic*, Book VIII (551 D).

Take but degree away, untune that string,
and, hark what discord follows! each thing
    meets
In mere oppugnancy: the bounded waters
Should lift their bosoms higher than the
    shores
And make a sop of all this solid globe:
Strength should be lord of imbecility,
And the rude son should strike his father dead:
Force should be right; or rather, right and wrong . . .
Should lose their names, and so should justice
    too.
Then every thing includes itself in power,
Power into will, will into appetite;
And appetite, an universal wolf,
So doubly seconded with will and power,
Must make perforce an universal prey,
And last eat up himself.

SHAKESPEARE
Troilus and Cressida, I, iii

PART ONE

The Micropolitical World

Chapter 1

Power

Politics is inseparable from power. Because the partnership between them is both obvious and irrevocable politicians and political thinkers alike have often enough concluded that politics and power are identical. Or, in what amounts to a variation on the main theme, they have assumed that power considerations are the only ones that really count in politics. These conclusions have been particularly apparent in the theory and practice of international politics. It is therefore appropriate to begin this study with an inquiry into the phenomenon of power—and into the contending interpretations of its nature.

Power is influence. Power over nature is the ability to influence the behavior of atoms, molecules, metals, plants, or any of a long list of organic or inorganic phenomena. Power in politics is the ability to influence phenomena of a different order: the attitudes and behavior of human beings relevant to such matters as voting, legislation, forms of government, ideological values, alliances, treaties, peace, and war. Any study of international relations will obviously deal with the concept of power in the political sense.

In the context of politics, power is a loaded word—even a menacing one—and it must be handled with care. One need only think of the emotions aroused by such terms as black power, student power, corporate power, power structure, and, the classic epithet, power politics. If at the outset power is recognized simply as being identical with influence it may lose some of the overtones of menace. Such a recognition should make possible a more objective and emotionally neutral analysis of the nature of power.

We shall see later in this chapter, however, that the simple equation of power with influence is itself a highly controversial and unorthodox proposition. The majority of contemporary political analysts view the exercise of power as an activity that unavoidably involves or threatens the use of coercion. In this view political power is not just any kind of influence; it is coercive influence. Constraint, duress, and force are imputed to power as inherent attributes. Social action in which these attributes are lacking, it is argued, may involve the exercise of influence but not of power: "It is the threat of sanctions which differentiates power from influence in general."[1]

The mistaken identification of power with coercion is the fundamental reason why power is so generally regarded as a menacing and dangerous phenomenon. It also compounds the problem of understanding the nature of politics. If it is assumed, first, that politics equals power and, second, that power equals coercion, it follows that politics itself must deserve the unpleasant reputation of its stereotype. The need to disentangle realities from stereotypes is always an urgent one; the arguments in this chapter and in the ones to follow will frequently be engaged in this task.

The intellectual and emotional controversies that swirl around the concept of power are primarily concerned with the manner in which it is exercised and with the purposes it serves and only secondarily with the sources from which power is derived. Since it is the intention of this book to confront these controversies at the outset, more systematic examination of the sources of power will be deferred until later chapters. But it is appropriate at the beginning of the analysis to offer at least a preliminary catalog of the components of power, of the assets whose presence contributes strength and whose absence contributes to weakness. It is a catalog corresponding to the general agreement among analysts of international relations concerning a list of ingredients, elements, or components of power that need to be factored into any assessment of capabilities in the exercise of power. A power profile, so to speak, can be drawn up for any state by calculating its resources in the following categories: geography, population, economics, political organization, and general value structure.

This list can be expanded almost at will depending on how many subcategories (military organization, ideological dynamism, diplomatic skill, technological sophistication) one wishes to raise to the level of a full-fledged category. They are treated as subcategories here because they can be conveniently located under one of the five more abstract headings above. Their importance in assessing the power of a state is in any case obvious.

One could also compress the list into the two fundamentals of land and people and develop a power estimate of any given state by asking what kind of human superstructure has been erected on the natural base. Whether the initial list is short or long, abstract or more concrete, all the components of power in their greater or lesser complexity must be included in any accounting of strength and weakness. In such an accounting, of course, it is crucial to recognize that power is a relative

---

[1] Harold Lasswell and Abraham Kaplan, *Power and Society: A Framework for Political Inquiry* (New Haven, Conn.: Yale University Press, 1950), p. 76.

concept and that the power estimate is not complete for any state unless its assets and liabilities are measured against the assets and liabilities of all other states relevant to its interests.

THE SCHOOL OF POWER POLITICS

International relations or international politics (despite some opinion to the contrary, the two terms are often used interchangeably without serious conceptual confusion) are frequently declared to be equivalent to "power politics." Those who advocate this equivalency maintain that behavior in the international system can be explained exclusively or at least essentially in terms of a struggle for power. It is not too much to say that in the last thirty years "power politics" has become the orthodox approach in the academic study of international relations in the United States. Abroad, international relations has not received nearly the scholarly attention lavished upon it in America. But to the extent that it has been a subject of professorial investigation in other countries one can speak of a near consensus among academics with respect to the nature and meaning of world politics. Communist scholars exhibit only superficial deviations from the mainstream. The proposition that power is and ought to be the central concern of international relations provokes few dissenting voices.

It is noteworthy that the power politics concept has spilled over into domestic politics as well. It is standard practice for texts and monographs on American government and on domestic politics in general to define *all* politics in some such phraseology as "the pursuit and exercise of power."[2] On the basis of the available evidence one can fairly conclude that the patron saint of American political science—in both its international and domestic aspects—is that most eminent exponent of power politics, Niccolò Machiavelli.

A brief account of the rise of the power concept in contemporary political thought will help to explain not only the reasons for its present ascendancy but also something about the nature of power itself. The academic study of international relations is very new; it was only just before World War I that a growing number of universities began to offer courses labeled "International Relations." Diplomatic history and international law were the long-established disciplines that provided the underpinnings for most of these new courses. But teachers were mainly concerned with the present and with a whole range of phenomena beyond the rather narrow competence of international law. Above all, they were concerned with the problem of war. The dominant interest in inter-

---

[2] Marian Irish and James Prothro, *The Politics of American Democracy*, 4th ed. (Englewood Cliffs, N.J.: Prentice Hall, 1968), p. 5.

national relations teaching and research was the discovery of causes and cures for armed conflicts among states.

This search found both an academic and a political leader in Woodrow Wilson. As a professor, Wilson was an eminent political scientist renowned primarily for his published works in American domestic politics. As President, Wilson was the commanding political figure in the final act of World War I. His interpretation of the Allies' struggle as "a war to end wars" and his vision of a new world system of cooperation and peace offered both intellectual and moral guidance to his erstwhile academic colleagues. Most of them regarded Wilson's League of Nations as the best hope for the prevention of future wars, and they shared his bitter disappointment when the United States Senate (and, when all the evidence was in, the American people) rejected membership in the international organization that was so largely the handiwork of an American president.

The academic result of these painful events was the emergence of international organization as a key issue in the field of international relations. Many teachers were advocates of American entry into the League on the reasonable grounds that the League could not keep the peace if so powerful a country as the United States continued to reject membership. There was also a general assumption that the United States would be a more benevolent influence than any of the so-called Great Powers then members of the League. Most important, there was widespread agreement that the only cure for war resided in a world organization that would bind the member states to forswear the ancient practices of power politics. In the language of these teacher-reformers the term power politics can be translated as the politics of selfishness, of self-centeredness, or of national self-interest. Such a translation is clearly related to the double equation noted earlier: politics = power = coercion.

Adopting the rhetoric of Woodrow Wilson, his academic followers called for an end to power politics and its familiar companion, the balance of power. Instead of each state relying on its own power (or that of its allies) to ensure its security, all states should join a "community of power"—that is, the League of Nations, or an improved version thereof. International organization would provide collective security. The collective membership of the organization (presumably minus the aggressor) would come to the aid of any member whose security was threatened by aggression. The aggressor would likely be awed by the might of the community power ranged against him and abandon his warlike intentions. If not, then community sanctions—economic pressure or even full-scale military operations—would bring about his rapid defeat. The Wilsonians argued that this was the path the world must take in order to redeem Wilson's pledge that World War I was a war to end wars. It was also the path which the academic study of international relations must both explore and advocate.

Collective security operating within the framework of an international organization has belied the hopes and reasoning of the Wilsonians. This is as true, essentially, for the United Nations as it was for the League of Nations. The multiple causes for the failures of collective security will be examined later in some detail. But here the chief reason for the miscalculations in the Wilsonian approach must be noted: it posited an international community of interests that did not exist. This was the fatal weakness in the Wilsonian orthodoxy on American campuses in the 1920s and early 1930s. It was unrealistic.

The mounting attack on the Wilsonian vision and against the dominating place of international organization in the study of international relations was thus carried forward in the name of realism. In the mid-1930s Yale led other American universities in laying the foundations for what would eventually become the new intellectual orthodoxy in the realm of international politics. The new orthodoxy dubbed itself "realistic"—in contrast to the "idealism" of the Wilsonian approach. The fundamental reality for the new school of thought was a world which continued to be divided into competing states each seeking to serve its own interests by amassing or hanging onto as much power as possible. Given the facts of such a world, the dream of an international community of security was a hopeless illusion. There was no security beyond what national power and a shrewd calculation of national self-interest could provide. The shorthand name for the new orthodoxy was power politics. As noted earlier, it continues dominant today.

The new school was, of course, the Old School. As a sequel to the brief interlude of Wilsonianism, it resurrected the traditional European modes of thought about international politics and diplomacy. Bismarck, Cavour, Talleyrand, Castlereagh and Canning, Metternich, Frederick the Great, Richelieu—these were the men who understood best the realities of international politics. They proved it by achieving high marks (at least most of the time) in that most rigorous test that history offers, the test of success. Their common intellectual ancestor was Machiavelli, and their common skill was the ability to exert power in the interest of the states they served (and in their own interests as well). These were the schoolmasters of the Old School of Europe, and they became the schoolmasters of the new school, too. In American universities, in fact, the new orthodoxy of power politics was largely the creation of refugee or otherwise transplanted European scholars of the 1930s who brought the old, deeply rooted traditions to the New World.

These European scholars also brought with them an understanding and a terror of Nazi Germany. The newcomers joined those already in the United States who insisted that peaceful attitudes and high internationalist ideals would not stop Hitler; only armaments, alliances, and all the traditional instrumentalities of diplomacy and war could do the job. In short, the only effective answer to Nazi power, they argued, was counterpower. They were right; World War II was a massive and bloody ratification of their diagnosis and prescription.

While men do not always learn from experience, teachers of international relations learned well the lessons of World War II and the era of appeasement that preceded it: in international politics the thing that counts is power. The Cold War, coming hard on the heels of the hottest war man had ever experienced, reinforced the lesson. Few were prepared to dispute the key formula advanced by one of the most eminent of the European refugee scholars: "International politics, like all politics, is a struggle for power."[3]

Hans Morgenthau's formula, equating international politics with politics in general, dovetailed with then current academic formulations of domestic politics. When American political science began to emerge in the latter part of the nineteenth century as an autonomous intellectual discipline, the major share of its attention was devoted to the institutions of the state. Over the years, however, the analysis of constitutions, legislatures, courts, and laws came to be perceived as an incomplete and therefore rather arid exercise. Parties, pressure groups, political machines, reform movements, and ideological confrontations offered exciting areas for political research, and they all existed outside the formal institutions of government. Political science responded to these new perceptions by moving away from its preoccupation with legal structures and toward the investigation of politics as a social process.

In so doing the study of political science began to lose its sense of unity, cohesiveness, and purpose. Some political scientists recovered a sense of purpose by adopting the position that the end result of political research should be political reform. In this they paralleled the scholars in the international field who sought by means of reason and empirical investigation to reform the world of traditional power politics. But other political scientists eschewed, at least explicitly, the role of reformer. Instead, they tried to restructure political science as a descriptive and value-free discipline incorporating both the governmental and nongovernmental aspects of politics. The unifying theme that came to dominate their understanding of politics in all its ramifications was the concept of power.

Still another European scholar, though not a transplanted one in this case, was the major inspiration for the new approach: Max Weber. Weber deeply influenced sociologists and political scientists alike, but his message to political scientists proved to be particularly penetrating and persuasive. For Weber (as for Marx) law was simply the rules of the game as defined by the powerful. Power was the ability to impose one's own will even in the face of resistance by other wills. He defined the

---

[3] Hans J. Morgenthau, *Politics Among Nations*, 1st ed. (New York: Knopf, 1948), p. 13.

state as "a human community that (successfully) claims the *monopoly of the legitimate use of physical force* within a given territory."[4]

Despite some modifying elaborations, these interpretations of the state and its laws as essentially and predominantly the manifestations of a power process resting ultimately on force constitute the heart of Weberian political doctrine. It was this doctrine, which coincided notably with the political ideas of Machiavelli and Marx, that began to pervade teaching and research in American political science. The mention of Machiavelli alone documents that the doctrines were nothing new—one could, after all, trace their lineage at least as far back as Thrasymachus. But they were new in their massive impact on an American political science whose intellectual heritage and—let it be said with equal force—ideological presuppositions derived from the rather different concepts animating the Declaration of Independence, the Constitution, and the Gettysburg Address.

This shift in focus from the study of the state to the study of power relationships carried with it a multitude of implications. Political science now had vast new frontiers to explore. The whole range of non-governmental political activities became a legitimate area for research. International politics, though still bereft of any solid overarching governmental institutions, could logically fit under the rubric of the new political science (despite which the relation of international politics to political science remains a subject of vigorous dispute). Political activity could be studied wherever it occurred without reference to the time-bound and culture-bound assumptions that politics could not take place in the absence of a fully developed state. Indeed, the state itself came to be looked upon simply as a particular kind of power relationship among a whole series of power relationships observable in human life.

POWER AND REALISM

The new proponents of the power approach in political science, like the critics of Wilsonianism in the study of international relations, claimed for themselves the mantle of "realism" in contrast to the "legalism" and sometimes "moralism" of those who had focused their attention on the state as an institution of laws. The attitude toward law and the state was the same: both were to be understood as sets of power relationships. In this interpretation the normative and ethical connotations of law were bound to fade into the background; so, too, the ancient questions concerning the purpose of the state. At most, one could assert that the pur-

---

[4] Max Weber, "Politics as a Vocation" and "Class, Structure, Party," in Hans H. Gerth and C. Wright Mills, *From Max Weber: Essays in Sociology* (New York: Oxford University Press, 1946), pp. 78, 180, and *passim*. Italics in original.

pose of the state was to effect a distribution of power best calculated to ensure its survival and, ideally, its increasing power. To be "realistic" meant to recognize with Weber, Marx, and Machiavelli that politics, the state, and the law all boiled down to power.

Plato had defined the purpose of politics as the pursuit of justice. Aristotle prescribed that politics should be in the service of the good society. But all such normative approaches to political analysis and activity were repugnant to a generation of thinkers rebelling against the reformers of the previous generation. Many of the norms of the reformers, particularly in the international field, were demonstrably unrealistic and untenable. Many of the rebels drew the conclusion that norms per se are the blinders that prevent men from seeing reality. Hence their desire to build a value-free science of politics that would set aside what "ought to be" and devote itself exclusively to fact, to what "is."

The most obvious fact in the real world of politics, both domestic and international, is the concern for power. It would perhaps be unkind to say of the new realists that they made haste to celebrate the obvious. Indisputably, however, they equated what is most obvious with what is most important and proceeded to build their version of political reality on the proposition that politics is "the pursuit and exercise of power." Suspicious of norms and proud of their commitment to empiricism as they understood the term, many of the new realists refused to take a stand concerning such matters as the proper and improper uses of power. It was often argued that these judgments are beyond the competence of the empirical scientist, who, by self-definition, concerns himself only with "the facts."

Of course, no man's perception of reality is ever devoid of normative appraisal; in Stanley Hoffmann's words, "we evaluate as we breathe." Despite all their efforts, the new political realists in America were no exception to this rule. Explicitly, sometimes straddling their dual roles of scientist and citizen, they often took occasion to affirm established traditions by endorsing democratic norms governing the uses of power and by condemning undemocratic procedures. Implicitly, in strictly scholarly analysis, the democratic values were also usually apparent.[5] But this value position was consistently overshadowed by preoccupation with the processes of power. It is this preoccupation that exposes the realists to the charge that they have made power an end in itself.

Part of the realist rebuttal is that power should be seen not as an end but simply as a means to realize whatever ends political man may aspire to. But it is the standard temptation, in politics as in all of life, to prize the means so highly that the ends they are supposed to serve get lost in

---

[5] Even those who have contributed to elitist theories of contemporary political life generally profess adherence to basic democratic ideas.

the shuffle. Moreover, power is not merely one of a number of means available to realize any given set of political objectives. Power—influencing people—is the indispensable instrument of political activity.

Here, indeed, is the nub of the problem. It is the indispensability of power that has given it the dominant role in the history and literature of politics. Indispensability accounts for the relative ease with which power considerations can deflect political man from the goals (stability, reform, revolution, justice) in whose service he might originally have enlisted. Because it is indispensable power functions both as a means and as an end. Because it is indispensable the politician is constantly tempted to value power above every other consideration. Thus it is that an implicit or explicit worship of power becomes the occupational disease of political life.

Nowhere is that propensity of power to become an end in itself more evident than in international politics. In the world of empires, nation-states, transnational ideologies, armaments, and wars, the preoccupation with power is manifest. It is built into the very nomenclature of international relations. We speak of superpowers, Great Powers, middle and small powers, regional powers, spheres of influence (that is, power). The nineteenth-century European Concert of Powers has given way to the Nuclear Club, but the idea is the same: they are both groupings of the most powerful states in their respective historical periods. In international politics, moreover, legal and cultural restraints on the exercise of power are at their weakest. Small wonder, then, that it is at the global level where power commands the highest premiums. Small wonder also that the practitioners of international politics can often be led to believe that power is the measure of all things.

The obvious centrality of power in the realities of international life helps explain the propensity to label international relations power politics per se. Whether such a label is valid can only be judged after a closer look at the nature of power. This chapter began with the statement that power is influence. The equation was offered in part to dilute the negative and sometimes hostile or fearful emotions that the term power frequently evokes. But even the word "influence" is not without its unsavory connotations; witness the usage of such phrases as influence peddler and influence seeker and the stock political character who exercises influence behind the scenes. In the ordinary uses of language, then, both power and influence are tainted concepts. The taint is essentially moral: the seeker of influence (power) tends to be regarded as unusually selfish, unusually ruthless in his methods, unusually manipulative in his relations with other human beings, unusually ready to subvert social ends to his own purposes. (Of course, the ordinary citizen, unmindful of the self-centeredness common to all men, will ignore his own resemblance to the influence seeker.)

The concept of power raises the emotional ante. Not only does power connote selfish and illicit behavior, it conjures up the image of coercion and violence. It conveys ideas of domination and control. This countenance of power is no mere figment of the imagination. When the power of a state is measured in terms of the size of its nuclear arsenal (or, earlier, by the number of its catapults or its cross-bowmen) the coercive aspects of power are evident enough. Moreover, the imperiousness of power is manifest throughout history. Again and again men and societies have not been content merely to affect or influence to some degree other men and other societies but have sought instead a degree of power that would permit them to dominate, often to the point of tyranny and slavery. Man's power over other men has been a perennial and prime source of violence and human degradation.

Those who defined international politics as power politics wished to underline the prevalence of war, conquest, and empire in interstate relations. Insofar as this is simply an empirical observation there can be no objection. But most of these new-old realists have also insisted that violence and the struggle for dominion have always been and will continue to be the governing realities in international relations. It is not too much to say that for the realist school (despite denials by some of its members) the master concept in the analysis and appraisal of world politics is not peace but war. These points of view obviously raise the most serious kinds of intellectual and moral issues and will be dealt with continuously throughout this book. Here, however, the focus is on the concept of power to which the realists have given paramount importance.

COERCION, CONTROL, AND CONSENT

The difficulty with the realist position is that it has failed the test of authentic realism. The realists have built the intellectual foundations of power politics on an inadequate conceptualization of power itself. They have given overwhelming stress to power as the ability to coerce. And they have given equally overwhelming stress to power as the capacity to control. This double emphasis requires careful examination, for it is a key issue in the matter of conceptions and misconceptions of power.

The proposition of Lasswell and Kaplan that power is equivalent to the capacity to impose sanctions has already been noted. They develop this definition with the assertion that power, as a special case in the exercise of influence, "is the process of affecting policies of others with the help of (actual or threatened) severe deprivations for nonconformity with the policies intended." The definition leaves no doubt that the authors equate the deployment of power with coercive action despite their subsequent and somewhat paradoxical observations that power may also be used in noncoercive ways.[6] These qualifying observations are not, in any event, reflected in the definition itself, which thus conforms to the orthodox penchant to identify power with constraint. Indeed, Lasswell and Kaplan's influential work did much to solidify that orthodoxy.

Conventional doctrines that label power as inherently coercive are characteristically reinforced by a companion proposition: one exercises power in order to achieve domination or control over others. Hans Morgenthau puts the matter succinctly: "When we speak of power, we mean man's control over the minds and actions of other men." Morgenthau's concept of politics as a struggle for power, then, rests on a prior and still more basic concept. The quest for power is a product of the drive to dominate—one of "those elemental biophysical drives by which . . . society is created."[7]

The Lasswell-Kaplan stress on power as coercion and Morgenthau's identification of power with domination are united in Max Weber's proposition, cited earlier, concerning the nature of the state. This coincidence of views should suffice to indicate the formidable intellectual authority sanctioning the judgment that power is inherently a matter of coercion and domination.

Any critique of this judgment must start with two simple facts. First, there is such a thing as power without coercion. Second, there is such a thing as power without control. These two facts are not likely to be disputed whenever they are explicitly raised. But they tend to be lost from sight in a view of the world that highlights the pain and drama of violence and the clash of imperial wills. The practical result of such a view is the equation of power politics with the politics of coercion and control.

A fully realistic view must recognize that there are many ways of exercising power. From this perspective power ceases to be wedded to constraint and domination. Instead, power relationships can be plotted along a spectrum ranging between the extremes of coercion and consent. It is probably impossible to isolate instances of pure consent or pure coercion. But one can analyze power relationships in terms of a lesser or greater degree of consent or coercion. The most obviously coercive relationship in international politics is total war. Physical force of all kinds—and the threat of it—dominates the coercive end of the power spectrum. At the same time, one should not forget that economic and

---

[6] Lasswell and Kaplan, *Power and Society.* See pp. 76 and 77 for the definition of power together with the qualifying observations. The authors cite violence, the use of police or military force, public disgrace and excommunication as examples of the imposition of sanctions or "severe deprivations."

[7] Morgenthau, *Politics Among Nations*, 5th ed. (New York: Knopf, 1973), pp. 28 and 34.

ideological weapons can sometimes be more effective instruments of coercion than raw violence. The uses of force will be examined in some depth in a later chapter, and extended attention to ideology and economics will come in due turn. At this point attention will be focused on the consent end of the power spectrum.

AUTHORITY, LEGITIMACY, AND CHARISMA

Robert Dahl has observed that:

> *Leaders in a political system try to insure that whenever governmental means are used to deal with conflict, the decisions arrived at are widely accepted not solely from fear of violence, punishment, or coercion but also from a belief that it is morally right and proper to do so.* Belief that the structure, procedures, acts, decisions, policies, officials, or leaders of government possess the quality of "rightness," propriety, or moral goodness and should be accepted because of this quality—irrespective of the specific content of the particular act in question—is what we mean by "legitimacy."
>
> [Therefore,] *Leaders in a political system try to endow their actions with legitimacy.* When the influence of a leader is clothed with legitimacy, it is usually referred to as authority. . . . Hence, our . . . proposition is also equivalent to:
>
> Leaders in a political system try to convert their *influence into authority.*[8]

Dahl goes on to make the key observation that authority, as the exercise of legitimate power, "is a highly efficient form of influence. It is not only more reliable and durable than naked coercion but also enables a ruler to govern with a minimum of political resources."[9]

It should be evident from these observations that consent is the defining element in legitimacy and authority. The lifeblood of authority as Dahl defines it is the ability to elicit willing compliance from those subject to its influence. It may exact obedience by means of coercion, but only at the price of diluting its claim to legitimacy. Hence, the degree of authority in any political system is measured by the level of consent prevailing among its membership. The greater the authority of its institutions and processes, the less coercion will be involved in governing and in responding to government.

Members of a political system, therefore, have a profound stake in authority—that is, in a consensual governmental structure—because au-

---

[8] Robert A. Dahl, *Modern Political Analysis* (Englewood Cliffs, N.J: Prentice-Hall, 1963), p. 19. Italics in original.
[9] *Ibid.*

thority promises a minimum of coercion for all members of society. For the active politician or leader it offers an additional bonus: a very great degree of reliability and efficiency in the exercise of power made possible by a situation in which consent is maximal and resistance minimal. It follows that rational politicians should seek to avoid coercive relationships and strive to create consent relationships, "to convert their influence into authority."

It must be noted, however, that Dahl's definitions of legitimacy and authority leave room for both coercion and consent. Coercion is involved in that a person or a group may be willing to submit to punishment or other forms of duress meted out by an authority deemed legitimate. After all, the entire judicial and electoral systems of modern states rest on the willingness of individuals to accept at least some judgments adverse to their interests or desires. Judicial decisions may involve execution, imprisonment, or fines for the convicted. Electoral decisions may require the minority to abide by majority policies. Similarly, in heresy trials in religious or ideological matters the accused has often been willing to abide by the decision of a tribunal he considers legitimate. Readiness to support compulsory military service and acceptance of the police powers of the state are other examples of consent to the coercive exercise of power by legitimate authority.

Yet it is still possible to equate legitimacy with the politics of consent. Legitimacy stands or falls not by virtue of the coercive power to which it may at times resort but by reason of its capacity to elicit continuing consent that it is the "right," "proper," and "morally good" repository of power. Machiavelli himself asserted that it is the illegitimate prince who must most often resort to force while the legitimate prince need not rely so heavily on coercion. The moral to be drawn here is that if one desires to get away from the politics of force one must cultivate the politics of legitimacy.

An additional point needs underlining. In the long run, and usually even in the short run, the policies of legitimate authority must seem more beneficial than punitive in order to elicit continued consent. It has been assumed, with some justification, that modern democratic governments have met this test of legitimacy better than any previous forms of the state. Yet the racial crisis in the United States, the rebellion against the warfare of the modern state, the revolt of ethnic or economically deprived minorities, and the general disenchantment of youth in both affluent and not-so-affluent societies all symbolize a withdrawal of consent and hence a crisis of legitimacy. Legitimacy is difficult to establish and not easy to perpetuate. At an optimum, its overtly coercive acts must be minimal, the punishments it inflicts must seem judicious and fair, and the benefits it confers upon those who are politically effective must seem adequate and likely to increase. This is a formidable political prescription, but the durability of governments and states in their particular historical contexts is a function of how well this prescription is met.

One must ask whether there is any room for the politics of legitimacy in the world at large. The word itself has been used (and misused) often enough in the annals of diplomacy. Metternich's resort to the concept of legitimacy to justify suppression of various national and liberal movements across Europe is hardly exemplary of the consensual basis for legitimate power. In the modern history of international politics, in fact, Metternich bears chief responsibility for the ominous connotations attached to the term—connotations of international reaction, interference in the internal affairs of states (chiefly weak states), and oppression and political stagnation in general. The fact that a concept is deceptively used, however, need not detract from its value. The real question, then, is whether there has been or could be a legitimate power whose relative restraint in the use of coercion and whose distribution of benefits could elicit the consent of the world society or a very large portion of it.

As far as the past is concerned, the answer is clearly yes. Both the Roman and the Chinese empires came to be accepted as "legitimate authority" by widely diverse groups of people remote from the center of imperial power and from one another. For a thousand years after the fall of Rome the history of the West was dominated by the contest to inherit what was deemed the universal mandate of Rome. Pope and emperor struggled with one another for centuries to establish who ought to obey whom. Both claimed the Roman heritage and a jurisdiction that was, in theory at least, coextensive with Christendom.

Legitimacy always suffers when it is the subject of a major contest and tends to vanish when the contest is prolonged. Medieval Europe was no exception to this rule, but the idea of a supreme legitimate authority for the peoples of the Western world persisted long after the fact. It still haunted the national monarchies and the republican movements of modern Europe. They were followed by transnational ideologies of democracy and Marxism that, each according to its own lights, once again tried to define legitimacy and illegitimacy in both domestic and world politics.

Today, the United Nations represents the most comprehensive embodiment of international authority. Its Charter elaborates at length what is legitimate and what is illegitimate in international behavior. Above all, the charter rules out violence among nations without previous or retroactive approval by the United Nations. On paper, the Security Council has a monopoly of the legitimate use of force in international affairs. But in practice the old struggle between pope and emperor in effect repeats itself. The power to act, insofar as it rests on force, is negated by the conflicting Charter interpretations and policy goals of the two superpowers.

The element of consent in UN power is almost as tenuous. The degree of loyalty enjoyed by most national governments far exceeds the amount of loyalty and consent accorded the United Nations. Even for dissident groups in the domestic politics of most states, the individual state is their own thing in a way that a remote United Nations cannot be. The limited, but nonetheless valuable, material and cultural benefits provided by the UN combine with psychological remoteness and the subordinate role of international organization in the great issues of war and peace to reduce United Nations authority from a fact to little more than a notion.

The Holy Roman Empire of medieval Europe was also more of a notion than a fact, and for many of the same reasons. But the presence of parallels need not indicate similar destinies. The revolutionary context of contemporary world politics opens up radically new perspectives in the ordering of international life, and the UN itself, as we shall see later on, has helped to create these perspectives.

The key challenge remains: Is there any room for the politics of legitimacy in the world at large? We know that ancient Rome and China established such a legitimacy over enormous geographic expanses (not forgetting that it was a legitimacy based on imperial deference rather than egalitarian association). We know that throughout history men have sought to establish or reestablish a legitimate world authority. We know that despite—and also because of—the weaknesses of the United Nations legitimate authority is the most effective restraint on the politics of force. Most importantly, we need to know (and the second part of this book will elaborate on this theme) that the developing international system must provide the basics of legitimate government: adequate benefits for the peoples of the world, particularly of the underdeveloped world. It must create conditions conducive to the growth of individual and cultural self-respect, to meaningful participation in the processes of international decision making, and to protection from arbitrary uses of violence. Failure to approximate this measure of legitimacy will, insofar as we can see ahead, doom the international system to self-destruction.

All these considerations argue that the precepts of legitimacy have a rightful and intellectually tenable place in international politics just as they do in domestic politics. It is true that legitimate government has often been realized in domestic societies and only seldom in the larger world. But this is no reason to abandon the norm of legitimacy and the values it represents in the conduct of international affairs. The alternative is to abandon the quest for consensual policies and to accept coercion as the governing principle in world politics—until that principle finally succeeds in destroying the global political system.

There is no need to assume that a legitimate international system must resemble the structure of any one of the numerous legitimate governments, past or present, in domestic political societies. Legitimacy has taken root in unitary, federal, imperial, and feudal forms of government. In a highly diverse world, legitimacy would have to rest on a pluralistic basis. Whatever its structure, if the system is relatively benign it will command a degree of consent sufficient to generate the values that legitimacy represents. What is obvious here is that the functions of legitimacy are more important than the forms. Legitimate power is ultimately a psychological relationship; it rests on the belief that those who exercise power constitute proper authority. Legitimacy presupposes allegiance.

Dahl's assertion that "leaders in a political system try to endow their actions with legitimacy" is just as applicable to international as to domestic politics. Many political leaders have been able to exert great power beyond the boundaries of their own states by virtue of the appeal of their policies, personalities, or both, at home and abroad. Napoleon, Hitler, Lenin, Stalin, Lincoln, Wilson, Franklin Roosevelt, John Kennedy, Mao Tse-tung, Nasser, and Castro are cases in point. While some of these leaders have been men of coercion and violence, their power in international affairs was or is in significant degree a function of the allegiance more or less freely accorded them by significant numbers of people in other countries. Since all these men are past or present leaders of states, the power of their transnational appeal goes beyond simply a personal relationship to affect the fortunes and influence of the states they have represented.

Charismatic leadership is a term often used to describe this phenomenon—by which is meant, roughly, political sex appeal. People are attracted to and fascinated by the charismatic leader; they identify with his personality and style and see at least a linkage if not a complete congruity between his interests and objectives and their own. Charisma is a manifestation of hope. People will voluntarily support and follow the charismatic leader because they hope that he will bring them peace, justice, a better life, adventure, power, or any assortment of desired goods. It is evident, then, that policies as well as personality are involved in the charismatic phenomenon.

Public response to the assassination of John Kennedy and then his brother Robert demonstrated once again that people will revere the personal incorporations of their hopes even after the leaders themselves have been struck down and there can no longer be any realistic expectations of concrete benefits from their leadership. On every continent the Kennedy name has been memorialized in monuments, schools, cultural centers, and "Ciudad Kennedys." Of Brazil it is reported that "almost every Brazilian town has a Kennedy school." On the west coast of Africa "the word 'Kennedy' in both Pidgin English and French is a superlative. It is used to describe anything from a great event to a pretty girl. . . . At Christian churches in Africa a whole new generation of young Africans is emerging with the given names of John Fitzgerald-Kennedy."

After the death of Robert Kennedy a resident of Ciudad Kennedy in Colombia was interviewed in her home. The living room wall bore two adornments: a colored picture of Jesus and a photograph of John F. Kennedy. " 'Now I will have to get one of Robert for the other side,' Mrs. Patiño said. . . . 'We all had such hopes for him. . . . He was one of the family. . . . He was the darling of everyone here. Even if he had been a Protestant, we would have loved him for his consolation of the poor.' "[10]

Some have responded to these outpourings of sentiment with the wry and regrettably apt observation that people are liable to love dead heroes better than live ones. Yet when all allowances are made for this quality in the human character, the power of heroes, both living and dead, remains manifest. The candidate for succession to power who can claim the mantle of the dead hero has an advantage denied to his rivals, a fact that helps to explain the long persistence of the hereditary principle in politics. But the charismatic hero dramatizes a still more important fact of political life: he derives a major source of his strength and sometimes the crucial increments of power from consent freely given rather than from his command of the instruments of coercion. Attractive personal style and attractive policies attract consent, all of which adds up to power.

Legitimacy is customarily associated with orthodox institutions and leadership while charisma evokes the image of a revolutionary leader. But history has often reversed these connotations: the charismatic leader has promised a return to the old order, and radical change has been preached in the name of a new or revised concept of legitimacy. Whatever the connotations, the linkage between legitimacy and charisma should be evident. Both are products of the followers rather than of the leaders; neither kind of leadership can be detected except in the allegiance proffered by the led. The legitimate or charismatic leader, therefore, is by definition one whose power depends on retaining or winning the voluntary support of others and not on coercing them into obedience. This does not mean that he will not coerce, but only that coercion is not the key instrument of his power.

---

[10] The material in these paragraphs is taken from reports in the *New York Times*, November 24, 1967, and April 2 and June 10, 1968. The June 10 report continues: "The speaker at the memorial service in Ciudad Kennedy said, 'The disappearance of Senator Robert Kennedy has injured the hopes of all the towns and all the people and all the hearts of Colombia. Like the people of America, we feel frustration. We loved him so much, we hoped for him so much. Our hearts cry with those around the grave at the cemetery of Arlington.' "

The report adds: "In Ciudad Kennedy, as in most places in Latin America, 'Kennedy' is the only name known in American politics. It is almost universally associated among ordinary people with the good the United States has done. Yesterday, *El Tiempo*, one of Bogota's leading newspapers, made this observation on its editorial page: 'Latin America has lost a great friend in Senator Kennedy. We have absolutely no interest in the other candidates. Nixon took with him painful impressions. We do not know McCarthy or Humphrey.' "

Voluntary support is the indispensable ingredient in the maintenance or creation of community. Community, in turn, is the strongest possible basis for power. A single man without followers is obviously powerless; he has no one to influence. A small elite can monopolize power and rule a state by command and repression. Indeed, this kind of power may bear some of the marks of legitimacy insofar as the mass looks on its own subordinate status as customary and unalterable. But such a society cannot begin to match the power of a society whose inhabitants, or at least the overwhelming majority of them, regard themselves as willing members of a community and as partisans with a common cause. These observations apply to domestic and international politics alike. It is axiomatic that party leaders who have the broadest appeal both within and outside their own parties always achieve greater power than those who operate from a narrower base of support. States whose policies are most acceptable to the world are also in the best position to influence the world—if they are also powerful in terms of other indices. For the party leader and the foreign policy maker the master formula for power is the same: seek to cultivate a sense of community.

POWER AND COERCION

Communities can be broadly or narrowly based, however, and it must not be overlooked that even the most encompassing community has typically managed to locate an external enemy. Thus political man can be said to fluctuate between cooperation and conflict. He seeks to generate a community of volunteers not simply for the purpose of achieving mutual benefits among themselves but also to enhance the community's combat efficiency in the outside world. The pattern is repeated over and over again by the corporation, the pressure group, and the party in domestic politics, and by the state in the world at large. Democrats call for more ardent dedication within their ranks in order to inflict a more resounding defeat on the Republicans, and vice versa. Nations call for greater solidarity and self-sacrifice from their populations in the battle with the common foe. Thus one is confronted with the ironic spectacle in which a community based on consent is seen not as an end in itself but as the most serviceable instrument for coercing those outside the community. Consent is demoted back to the level of means, and coercion reemerges as the final purpose of the game.

It is at this point that the power theoreticians make their claim that politics is essentially a game of coercion. Indeed, many argue that coercion is the prerequisite of consent, that no community is ever built except in response to danger from an external foe, and that foreign danger is the most effective stimulus to domestic solidarity. History offers too much counterevidence to let these generalizations stand (the

Napoleonic danger united Spain but not Germany, the Kaiser's ambitions united France but not Russia, Hitler's assault united England but not France). Nonetheless, the interaction between internal goals and external threats is so pervasive and intricate at every level of social organization that it is possible to make a highly persuasive case that coercion is both foundation and apex, both beginning and end of political life.

It is undeniable that coercion is to be found at the beginning of politics and will be present at the end, but the same thing can be said of consent. The key question concerns the proportions between the two: Which predominates? This question cannot be answered by the simple assertion that an external threat is necessary to the cohesion of internal organization. It requires instead an examination of the purposes of the internal organization of a society and the nature of the external threat to which it believes itself to be exposed.

Such an examination will show that the internal dynamics of a society must be considered before one can assess the impact of the external threat. If the society exhibits an already high level of consent, then an outside threat is likely to solidify it still further. Conversely, if the level of consent is low, it follows that an external threat is not much of a menace to those whose stake in the society under pressure is already minimal. In such circumstances, outside pressure will sooner shatter the society than unite it. Hence the level of internal consent defines the effectiveness of external pressure and is consequently the key element in deciding unity or disunity in any given society or state.

At the same time, it is no denial of the reality of external threats to point out that organizations with parochial and self-serving purposes are marvelously efficient multipliers of external hostility. The parochial nationalism of Hitler and the parochial communism of Stalin or Mao head an endless list of examples demonstrating that enmity toward the outside world begets enmity from the outside world. Conversely, a policy that seeks to avoid or mitigate hostility abroad can achieve its objectives without necessarily undermining consensus at home.

The weight of the evidence does not support the Hobbesian notion that men cooperate only because they fear coercion by, or desire to coerce, others. What the evidence does reveal is that the fear of coercion and the desire to coerce can never be eliminated from the ensemble of motives involved in human cooperation. But coercion cannot automatically be assigned first place (or last) among these motives. Exactly the same can be said about consent. The quest for unity and consent in human life is as ineradicable as the taste for conflict and coercion. Which dominates in a given space or time is a matter of human choice.

Wise choice, in turn, is guided by both experience and purpose. Experience shows that coercion begets coercion and consent, consent. The wise politician will therefore resort to coercion only if it appears to be an unavoidable means for the maintenance or the restoration of consent.

This applies as well to the police riot squad as to the declaration of war. As for purpose, each must decide whether coercion or consent is the legitimate standard for the conduct of politics and be prepared to live with the consequences of his decision.

Power based on consent is the most solid and stable basis possible for a domestic political regime. The same formula holds true in the world political structure: other things held constant, the foreign policy of any country is most effective where it commands the greatest consent. It follows that for both the domestic politician and the foreign policy maker the governing objective must rationally be to create conditions of consent. Apart from other considerations, as Dahl has noted, the presence of consent permits power to be exercised with a maximum of economy. It takes less effort to influence and move people in desired directions when they are already well disposed to the leadership being exercised. Otherwise one has to resort to bargaining, bribery, or force in order to persuade them.

Bargaining, bribery, and force will never disappear from politics—at least, not until conflicting interests, crime, policemen, and jails disappear from the life of domestic societies nor until both national armies and international "peace-keeping forces" vanish from world society. But recognizing that coercion and other unpleasant methods of influencing people will persist indefinitely does not mean that they should be regarded as the most important or even the most interesting weapons in the political arsenal.

The realist school has given undue emphasis to political activity nearer the coercive end of the power spectrum for at least three reasons. First, there is so much of this kind of activity throughout history that one is tempted to overvalue its significance for the social process. The rise and fall of individual states and the human and material destructiveness of war are more convenient and at first glance more portentous landmarks of history than the subtler and more continuous developments of the arts and sciences, economics, political forms, ideologies, and religions. Second, the realists have not paid enough attention to the fact that men and states have historically spent more time and effort in peaceful pursuits than in war with one another. Third, they assume that force is the final arbiter in relations among states, that victory on the battlefield is the supreme payoff, and that the test by arms determines winners and losers in international politics. Yet the resurgence of Germany and Japan in the post–World War II period made the "victories" of Britain and China, for example, look somewhat ambiguous. And it would be difficult to determine the extent to which the force at their disposal or the relative vigor of their political, social, and economic institutions accounts for the respective world impact of the United States and the Soviet Union since 1945.

In any event, it should be clear that while force can be an effective way of exercising power, the achievement of consent without coercion is a still more effective—and far less costly—path to power. It is true that it is not always possible to achieve political objectives by the methods of consent. But it is equally true that it is not always possible to achieve political objectives by the methods of coercion—witness the years of nuclear stalemate in which the two superpowers have been too terrified to use force against one another. The threat and capability of force are obviously significant in the mutual relations of the superpowers. But the actual use of force would destroy them both. In such a predicament, only evolving consensual relations can meet their needs as living and changing societies.

Power politics, interpreted as the politics of coercion, cannot be a guide for rational behavior in international relations. It not only obscures the nature of power; it also posits a framework for the analysis of international politics in which peace and the striving for consent are seen as necessarily secondary to conflict and war. One need be neither pacifist nor utopian to insist that such an approach distorts both intellectual comprehension and policy priorities. Above all, it offers a self-defeating recipe for survival in a nuclear world.

POWER AND CONTROL

A similar indictment must be leveled against power politics when it is interpreted as the politics of control. The objectives of a seeker of power may vary from a modest amount of influence in a decision concerning a single issue all the way to the goal of omnipotence. The citizen who promotes the one man—one vote principle and the aspirant to world conquest are both power seekers. The difference between them lies in the degree and scope of power sought and the purpose it is designed to serve. In international politics governments (and individuals and nongovernmental organizations) seek to exercise influence at many different levels of intensity in matters that vary enormously in narrowness or breadth of scope.

Most of the time, power politics in international life consists of exercises in influence aimed at achieving very limited goals. The bulk of economic negotiations and the lining up of votes on most of the issues that come before the United Nations fall into this category. Power politics takes on a sharper edge when nations are in serious dispute with one another. The cross-purposes of policy characterizing relations between the United States and Gaullist France and the Soviet-Chinese dispute are cases in point. Even here, however, one cannot say that it is the objective of the one antagonist to dominate the other. (Among other considerations, the effort to dominate would be prohibitively expensive.) Instead, the disputants attempt to persuade one another to desist from or adopt certain policies. While the methods of persuasion can often be unpleasant, it is not their purpose in these kinds of disputes to bring about the surrender or total subjugation of one party to the will of the other.

It is a rare occasion when the power seeker in international relations aspires to total control. These occasions, however, are among the most dramatic and significant that world history records. It is largely because of them that international relations is so often interpreted as the politics of control. In the history of the West, Charlemagne and his successors, Charles V, Louis XIV, and Napoleon, stand as monuments to the will to dominate. Our own century has outdone all the others in the production of would-be world conquerors; the legacies of Wilhelm II, Hitler, and Stalin are still at work among us. Small wonder that world politics is so often seen as a struggle for dominance.

Today, moreover, the United States, Russia, and China each charge the other with harboring ambitions for world supremacy. Western Europe fears it will lose its independence in the face of massive American economic power. Eastern Europe longs to restore its independence in the face of massive Soviet military power. In Asia, Africa, and Latin America, where imperial subjugation is a recent memory and where political, economic, and military weakness is still the order of the day, the fear of continued or renewed domination by the world of industrial states is the leading political concern. Thus the politics of control is very much at issue in the contemporary world. The weak fear control by the strong, and the strong fear control by those who are or may become still stronger. It is even true that there are some among the strong who seriously aspire to world dominion.

Yet the undoubted presence of ambitions to control and fears of being controlled cannot justify the generalization that world politics is inherently and necessarily a politics of domination. Such a conclusion would have to rest on evidence revealing aspirations for control in all, or at least the overwhelming majority of, international transactions. No such evidence has ever been assembled. The politics of control is a recurrent and dangerous threat to both domestic and international society. But it is no more the name of the political game than is coercion.

By the same token, the politics of control is no more rational than the politics of coercion. Nothing is more productive of conflict than the attempt by one society to control another, and this kind of conflict was never more costly than it is now. Even in the past, most empires were ultimately self-defeating. Today, dominion and empire are wholly unnecessary to the political, economic, and even ideological fortunes of the world's societies. Whether a country is developed or underdeveloped, internal growth—not external conquest—is the key to political influence and economic gain.

Of the past it can be said that the control relationship accounted for only a fraction of the totality of international relations. In the present, any desire to exercise control over foreign societies is destructively unrealistic. This does not mean that a rational government ought never to pressure another government to do what it does not want to do. It does mean that it is unnecessary and futile to try to make puppets out of the weak or to plan for the downfall and powerlessness of one's rivals among the strong. It is true that men have often been enlisted in unnecessary and futile undertakings. It follows that there is no guarantee that the politics of control will not once again plunge the world into war and, this time, irretrievable disaster. But this would be the climax of the ancient irrationality that drives men to make other men slaves and not the outcome of a rational understanding of the uses of power in international politics.

There is an obvious causal relation between the politics of control and the politics of coercion. Persons or states influencing one another in varying degree and manner have the option of running the gamut from consent to coercion in the methods they use. Control of one human being or one society by another, however, is by definition a coercive relationship. Being subject to some degree of external influence is the human condition and is more or less tolerable according to the nature and intensity of the influence. But the question of control raises issues of a different order of magnitude. Control implies omnipotence for one party and powerlessness for the other. It is the relationship between master and slave, the evident negation of freedom. Without at this point drawing any moral conclusions from these observations, it is clear that the only recourse for those who seek control—and for those who resist it—is the politics of coercion.

Coercion always has played and always will play a role in every political system, domestic or international. Its scope and intensity varies over time and with the efforts of men to foster, regulate, or diminish its use. But the politics of control places coercion at center-stage. It is there not occasionally or incidentally but continuously and necessarily. Thus even those in the school of power politics who explicitly observe that power may be exercised in nonviolent and noncoercive ways nonetheless weight both their abstract definitions and their concrete discussions of power on the side of coercion. They are unerringly driven into this position by the explicit or implicit premise that politics, and especially international politics, is the politics of control. Freighted with these assumptions, then, it is hardly surprising that the terms "power" and "power politics" have acquired an aura of violence and injustice.

POWER REDEFINED

If there is ever to be a normatively neutral and nonemotive understanding of the nature of power, the concept of power will have to be purged of its coercive bias. In order for this to come about the assumption must be abandoned that the power seeker is *necessarily* one who seeks control. Instead, an authentic realism must see the politics of control as a more or less frequent aberration from the norm of rational politics. With every appearance the intention to control adds its own inherent coercive dynamics to the existing potential for coercion, with the result that the prospects for consent must wither. The politics of control is not the standard for political activity; it is the corruption of politics.

If it is argued that many domestic and international politicians have proved themselves corrupt one can only observe that the contrary is also true. Political man has a wide choice of techniques in the exercise of power. He can use them effectively only if he is liberated from the assumption that posits a causal connection between power and control and, hence, between power and coercion. Free of the intent to dominate and control, the politician (or the state in international politics) can give priority to the politics of consent and mutual gain and use coercive power not to promote the politics of control but to combat it.

The simple proposition that power equals influence brings back into focus the full range of possible power relationships, benevolent as well as malevolent. It removes any justification for those immature and self-satisfied attitudes that automatically condemn all politics as evil because they involve "power seeking." At the same time, it provides a set of rational criteria for judging a politician or a state in the exercise of power: What techniques of influence are being used along the spectrum between consent and coercion? Are they appropriate to the specific situation in which they are being used? What measure of influence is sought along the spectrum between freedom and control? All these questions are wholly appropriate to the calculus of power. But the answers in each specific case will lead beyond the orthodox understanding of power politics. Not only will they distinguish between the rational and the irrational. They will also offer a basis for moral judgment providing distinctions between good and evil in the usage of power.

Once again the issue of values comes to the fore. The conventional wisdom in power politics almost ostentatiously refuses to subject politics to normative judgments. This position is, in fact, quite understandable. The orthodox assumption is that politics equals the pursuit of power and that the pursuit of power equals the quest for control; control, in turn, is by definition a coercive relationship. Such a model of politics is cheerless enough to make anyone who adopts it diffident about passing moral judgments on political behavior. On the other hand, to define power simply as influence permits the analyst to recognize the ranges of power existing outside the realm of coercion or control. It restores to the politician the consciousness of choice in the exercise and objectives of power. So doing, it reunites politics with the realm of moral values.

Chapter 2

Power and Purpose

The adherents of orthodox power politics usually agree that a monopoly of power is undesirable. They are generally forthright in their opposition to despotism in domestic society or to any would-be world conqueror. But their assumption that politics is by nature a struggle for control makes it difficult on either rational or moral grounds to condemn the presumptive Caesar. After all, if the purpose of the game is domination, one can hardly blame a politician (or a state in international politics) for playing the game with zest and the will to win.

THE BALANCE OF POWER

In the absence of viable criteria for judging the purposes and proper and improper uses of power, however, one can still hope to avoid power monopolies in domestic and international politics by counting on the presence of a plurality of conflicting interests. The point may be made abstractly: if it is the interest of every politician or state to achieve as much control as possible over the others, it is equally the interest of the other politicians or states to be as free as possible from external control.

Still abstractly, if State A accumulates and employs power in order to establish control over State X, X will accumulate and employ power to frustrate A's designs. In this example it is clear that A is on the offensive and X on the defensive. But the basic assumption that the purpose of the game is control means that the roles could just as well be reversed. Offense and defense are here simply functions of the distribution of power. If X were convinced that its power resources were superior to those of A, X would go on the offensive and A would be the defender. This is the simplest possible illustration of the classic concept in international politics known as the balance of power.

The balance of power, however, is a reasonably complex concept. Recognition that the power resources available to one politician or state may be superior to the resources of another requires that one must reckon on the possibility—and, indeed, probability—that the stronger will in fact achieve domination. If this outcome is to be avoided, the struggle for control must cease to be a simple two-way contest (which it never is in real life anyway). Balance of power doctrine prescribes that the weaker side must enhance its inferior power by drawing on the power of others; that is, it must recruit allies. If we designate X once again as the weaker side, it is clear that if X is successful in building an alliance whose combined strength matches or surpasses the power of A, A's aspirations to control X will be blocked.

Both the simpler and more complex games of balance of power can be played with either threats or force or both. In international politics, World War I and World War II exemplify the massive use of force to beat back attempts at world hegemony by Germany and its associates. Individually, the Allied Powers in both wars were weaker than Germany. Together, however, they were finally able to put together an unbeatable combination. In the years leading up to 1914 and 1939 the balancing game was played (very poorly by the West in the latter period) primarily with threats of force rather than with force itself. Armaments build-ups, military demonstrations, *faits accomplis*, vigorous and sometimes devious recruiting of allies, economic pressures, and, finally, ultimatums were the techniques used in the quest for preponderance. In the pre-1914 period, it should be noted, it was somewhat difficult to tell who was more enthusiastically aspiring to control whom.

The Cold War, in its turn, has been an exercise in the balance of power employing both the threat and use of force. Alongside the familiar pattern of alliance and counteralliance, arms races, and eyeball-to-eyeball duels in Berlin and Cuba, there have been large-scale resorts to force in Korea and Vietnam and numerous other outbreaks of violence more or less linked to the Cold War balance.

The standard interpretation of these major conflicts in twentieth-century history stresses that A (the stronger) is ultimately blocked by the coalition organized by an initially weaker X. If A can excel X in the recruiting of allies, however, it is obvious that A's original superiority will be enhanced and that its aim of controlling X will be realized. But here a crucial mitigating factor enters the calculations. As the weaker side, X has a built-in advantage in the search for allies. State A, the stronger power and actively seeking to extend its control, is more likely to inspire fear and hostility among all the participants in the game than is the relatively weaker X. Should A conquer X, A's increased strength would magnify its capacities to extend its control over other players in the system. The sum of the capacities of the whole system to resist A is then reduced by the loss of X. It follows that the other players in the system would have reason to ally with X and to oppose A.

Of course, the defensive alliance with X might prove so successful that A is overwhelmed and conquered; then X may attempt to control A.

Even so, as the originally weaker side, X will be a more comfortable ally than would A. In a victorious alliance X could not enjoy so dominant a position as a victorious A would have achieved. In no case, therefore, can the purposes of the other players be served by alliance with A. Such alliances would ensure A's triumph and the subordination of A's allies as well as of the defeated X. After all, the name of the game is the struggle for power, and the only restraint on the quest for power is the fear of superior counterpower. Remove the main bastion of counterpower (the coalition led by X) and A will proceed to subjugate friend and foe alike, all in accordance with the logic that the need for power equals the desire for control. Thus one of the immutable rules of balance of power doctrine is: always ally with the weaker side.

Another rule is: alliances must always be looked on as temporary. This is the answer to the dangers that would emerge from a victory of the defensive coalition led by X. The more extensive the victory, the more reason for the allies to desert the winning coalition and create a new front opposing the newly enhanced power (and therefore ambitions) of X. Since there are relatively few instances of total defeat and total loss of power by the vanquished, a prime candidate for membership in the new front opposing X is the erstwhile enemy, A. Humbled and weakened, A has become an acceptable alliance partner—until that day, at any rate, when A might again recover its previous strength. At that moment balance of power doctrine requires A's new friends to switch sides once more and rejoin X, who, victories faded and long bereft of allies, is again the weaker side.

The logic of these fluid dynamics is translated into two empirical generalizations in balance of power analysis. The first is that after a successful war the victorious coalition tends to disintegrate. The second is that today's friends may be tomorrow's enemies—and today's enemies, tomorrow's friends.

If the generalizations sound cold-blooded, they are no more so than the totality of the game from which they derive. Any critique must await an evaluation of the game as a whole. But at this point it is well to note the magnitude of the critic's task by observing that the concrete events of history abundantly illustrate the presence of these abstractly described processes and the rules and generalizations emerging from them. A recent major historical illustration was the diplomatic revolution after World War II, when the former enemies Germany, Japan, and Italy joined the West against the West's erstwhile Russian and Chinese allies.

A contemporary illustration, and one still in the making, is the current world position of the United States, whose enormous power may itself be the leading cause of its difficulties in holding old alliances together and in building new partnerships. If we accept the proposition that the Cold War waned in the 1960s because the American-led coalition stymied the Soviet challenge by mobilizing superior power resources, it follows that there has been something of a reversal in the American and Soviet roles. The military might and political and ideological aggressiveness of Stalinist Russia neatly coincided with the characteristics traditionally associated with A. The United States, on the other hand, performed the standard functions of X. The performance was brilliantly successful—so successful that a clearly out-classed Soviet Union no longer looks very persuasive in the role of A. Instead, correctly or incorrectly, most of the world now tends to classify the American colossus as A, and Washington is feeling the consequences of this new classification.

Pertinent, though not conclusive, evidence of this switch in perception of the American and Russian roles in the international system can be found in multination Gallup polls conducted in 1959 and 1969. Respondents from countries in the non-communist world were asked to estimate which nation would in ten years' time be the world leader militarily and scientifically. In the 1959 survey it was the Soviets who were ahead on both counts; 36 percent anticipated Soviet superiority in military prowess and 42 percent in the sciences. The corresponding figures for the United States were 24 percent and 23 percent. By 1969 opinion had changed dramatically. Of those polled, 36 percent believed the United States would be the leading military power in 1979, and 54 percent assumed that the Americans would be foremost in science. The corresponding figures for the Soviet Union had shrunk to 22 percent and 10 percent.[1]

It should be stressed that the analysis to this point has been governed by the central assumption of balance of power theory. That is, states are presumed to be concerned first of all with the coercive power of other states; the substantive policy goals of foreign states, benevolent or malevolent, are subordinate considerations. As we shall see, this assumption manifests itself again and again in the actual conduct of foreign policies.

The 1971 crisis between India and Pakistan that led to war and the emergence of Bangladesh provides an already classic example. In the international jockeying for position the United States decided to "tilt" against democratic (and stronger) India in favor of the weaker Pakistani military dictatorship. The official American rationale was moral and legal: India, by marching troops into Bengal (then East Pakistan), was

---

[1] It should be noted that in 1959 "other countries" and "no opinion" options were chosen by 40 percent (military prospects) and 35 percent (scientific prospects). Corresponding percentages for 1969 were 41 and 47.

The 1959 survey was conducted in the following countries: France, Great Britain, Greece, India, The Netherlands, Norway, Switzerland, Uruguay, and West Germany. In 1969 polling was carried out in Brazil, Canada, Colombia, Finland, Great Britain, Greece, India, Israel, Japan, Spain, Uruguay, and West Germany. *New York Times*, January 22, 1970.

the aggressor. At the same time, however, Washington attached little weight to Pakistan's cruelly oppressive acts against its own citizens in Bengal—the future Bangladesh—and the resulting flow of millions of Bengali refugees into India.

The operative rationale of American policy was more coherent. It centered on China and on a "tilt" taking place at several levels. China backed Pakistan against India in the hope that its chief Asian rival would be humbled. The United States, for its part, was newly embarked on a policy of wooing China (its weaker antagonist) as a means to pressure the more powerful Soviet Union. Thus the United States had its own ulterior reasons for aligning itself with the China-Pakistan position, independent of the merits of the India-Pakistan dispute. To complete the picture, the power of China was the paramount concern of the Soviet Union; it therefore supported India as the major counterweight to that power.

Such churlish calculations were but another manifestation of a perennial and universal phenomenon in international politics—and, indeed, in all politics. But this does not mean that policy is always made exclusively or even primarily in conformity with its postulates. Who appears weaker or stronger in a particular contest depends very much on the perspectives and purposes of all those affected by it. In the Bangladesh crisis what mattered for China was that India was the stronger; for the United States, that Russia was the stronger; for Russia, that China was the stronger. Hence differences in perspective break up the simplicity of the dictum that one should aid the weaker against the stronger.

Such differences were also evident in the postwar alliance of the United States with Western Europe and Japan. It could be (and has been) argued that the Soviet Union was X, the weaker power, all along. According to balance of power premises, Western Europe and Japan should therefore have aligned themselves with Moscow, and not with Washington. Yet the coercive power of the Soviet Union loomed much larger and more immediate, particularly in Europe, than did that of the United States. Geographically, in Asia as well as in Europe, the Soviet power base was near and the American far away. Thus the Russians, even if they could not and did not match the power potential of the Americans, were perceived from Europe and Japan as the greater danger.

Yet these perceptions were not solely the product of balance of power considerations based on fear of coercive power—even as modified by place, time, and circumstance. They were also the product of hope, the opposite of fear. The hope was that a partnership with the United States would offer security for the pursuit of individual and social values that the expansion of Soviet power threatened to extinguish. The alignment of Western Europe, Japan, and America, then, resulted from ideological affinity as well as balance of power calculations. Even if the United States appeared actually or potentially the stronger of the superpowers, it could still bring allies to its side so long as the attractiveness of its substantive policies compensated for the risk that it might abuse its superior power.

The presence of these kinds of considerations in the making of policy clearly refutes any claim for the balance of power as a comprehensive model for political behavior. It also suggests the quality of remedy for the vexations that beset A when its friends and allies begin to waver. The power to coerce can often compel submission, but it also repels. Those subject to its influence must constantly be lured by the possibility of alternative connections. State A can combat these centrifugal forces by warning against the menacing intent of X, but the most effective antidote is to restore confidence in the benevolent substance of its own policies.

The power to attract finally outweighs the power to compel. This is the ultimate critique of balance of power theory. Yet the arrogance—born of insecurity—that afflicts the wielders of great power repeatedly blinds them to this fundamental truth of politics. The result is that the balance of power calculus with its stress on coercion and fear of coercion often enough passes as an adequate explanation of political reality and an adequate model for political action. Thus it will be useful to examine further characteristics of the balance of power and of orthodox balance of power analysis before proceeding to a more detailed and extensive critique.

THE HOLDER OF THE BALANCE

The abstract process sketched above describes an unspecified number of states moving back and forth between A and X, allying with one and then the other according to the relative strengths and weaknesses of both. This function of augmenting the weaker side to restrain or defeat the stronger can be performed either by several players or by only one. Hitherto, the relative power of the players other than A and X has not been specified, but there was an implication that they were all weaker than A or X. Let us now set aside that implication and identify among the players State B. B's power matches or surpasses the power of X and perhaps even comes close to rivaling the power of A. B's weight alone is therefore sufficient to determine the outcome of a showdown between A and X. In this situation B is designated the "balancer" or "holder of the balance."

B occupies the most fortunate position in the balance of power constellation. Both A and X will bid for B's favor. While B's interest dictates support of the weaker side, there is no need for an outright alliance with X except in the direst circumstances. Failing these, B can afford to entertain overtures from A and in return for cooperation with A in minor matters can extract concessions to buttress its already favorable power position. Nor will B neglect to remind X that desperately needed assistance always comes at a high price. Great Britain in the four hundred years between the Reformation and the nuclear age is generally regarded as the classic personification of B in international politics. In domestic politics, if we look closely at presidential nominating processes in the United States for an example, B might easily be the Mayor of Chicago.

Like the bevy of states oscillating between A and X in the earlier example, B as the balancer is theoretically indifferent to ideological or moral issues that might be involved in the contest between A and X. State A may be a creative and humane society with as much justice in its political life as an imperfect world affords. X may be a despotic state led by fanatics whose subversive efforts to weaken A have provoked A into retaliation. Whatever B's ideological preferences, it must invariably support X in a showdown on the single consideration that X is weaker than A. It must assume that the apparent benevolence of A's political institutions and attitudes does not suspend the rules of the game and that A will control what it can. Should A drastically weaken X, B would lose its role as balancer, since A's power would then be greater than B's even if B could still effect a combination with the residual power of X. Indeed, B would face the direct pressure of a victorious A; consequently, its own independence would be threatened.

Adherents of balance of power doctrine, as noted at the outset of the chapter, praise the system as a method for perpetuating a multiplicity of power centers. This is clearly a value judgment, despite the professed dedication of the power politics school to theorize about what is rather than what ought to be. In the case of B, the balancer or holder of the balance, the venture into the realm of values goes one step further. B is generally pictured as benevolent in its own right, and for two reasons. First, abstractly, B is the obvious guardian of the system of balance. It can tip the scales this way or that more effectively than can any combination of otherwise disunited smaller states. State B is clearly an asset if one desires to maintain a pluralistic system of power. Second, concretely, is the fact that Great Britain has been so prominently associated with the functions of B in modern international history. Admirers of traditional British foreign policy and admirers of the balance of power are virtually interchangeable (in the United States and Britain, at any rate). Their admiration leads to a subtle and sometimes not so subtle interweaving of the concrete characteristics of British policy with the abstract functions of B.

Thus it is noted that Britain resisted the overweening ambitions of, say, Louis XIV, Napoleon, the Kaiser, and Hitler, and a vote of thanks is duly recorded. It is no denigration of Britain's sometimes heroic achievements to observe that only the last of these great confrontations could fairly be labeled a generally clear-cut contest of good and evil. Yet

Britain—and B—tends to be accorded a whole string of honorific titles such as defender of democracy, protector of the weak, vindicator of the liberties of Europe, scourge of aggression, champion of international justice, and staunch foe of tyrants. Winston Churchill, unsurprisingly, claimed all these virtues for Britain insofar as Britain played the role of balancer. But he did not forget the abstract functions of B, either:

> Observe that the policy of England takes no account of which nation it is that seeks the overlordship of Europe. The question is not whether it is Spain, or the French Monarchy, or the French Empire, or the German Empire, or the Hitler regime. It has nothing to do with rulers or nations; it is concerned solely with whoever is the strongest or the potentially dominating tyrant. Therefore, we should not be afraid of being accused of being pro-French or anti-German. If the circumstances were reversed, we could equally be pro-German and anti-French. It is a law of public policy we are following and not a mere expedient dictated by accidental circumstances, or likes and dislikes, or any other sentiment.[2]

If the words "tyrant" and "overlordship" are eliminated from this otherwise candid and nonemotive statement, it suggests why those who are not British partisans have traditionally denounced the foreign policy of England as cold, calculating, and perfidious. In this connection, Lord Palmerston's celebrated observation that "England has no eternal friends and no eternal enemies but only eternal interests" was a choice bone for the critics to pick on. They could also note that while Britain characteristically opposed any overlordship in Europe, it was not averse to establishing its own overlordship in the form of a global empire outside of Europe—with the usual negative consequences for the liberties of the peoples subject to imperial rule.

The point here is not to rekindle old controversies but to document the fact that controversy exists concerning both the utility and benevolence of the role of balancer. Those who prefer the diffusion of power in a plurality of power centers (or "sovereignties") will judge B to be useful and convenient to have around. Those who prefer a concentration of power and a diminution of the roles of the multiple sovereignties will deem B an enemy and a spoiler of aspirations for unity. This latter image was indeed the visage of Britain in the eyes of continental unifiers, whether they were revolutionaries under Napoleon or antirevolutionaries under Metternich and the Tsar. On one point only was there agree-

---

[2] Winston S. Churchill, *The Gathering Storm*, Vol. I: *The Second World War* (Boston: Houghton Mifflin, 1948), pp. 207–211. The quotation is from a March 1936 speech. After reproducing the speech Churchill goes on to observe that, with some modification, "the argument is not necessarily without its application" in the post-1945 world.

ment between the perspectives of the British and those of the continental unifiers: Britain, faithfully playing the role of B, made the continuing division of the Continent the cardinal principle of its policy. To complete the story, while Britain was acting as balancer, there were many individuals and states on the European continent that had no desire to be unified. To them "unification" signified conquest by whichever continental power was strongest. For these, of course, Britain in the role of B was a providential support and refuge.

DIVIDE AND RULE

Whatever the perspective, it is clear that B thrives on division. Conflict between A and X enhances B's influence over both; each must try to woo B in its own way. Should there be agreement or reconciliation between A and X, B must necessarily play a more modest role in their reckonings. Hence B's maximum opportunities for power are found in a political system, domestic or international, that is characterized by fragmentation. In this situation the most obvious temptation for B is to play upon and magnify the dissensions within the system, a technique classically defined (and denounced) as "divide and rule." This was the standard reproach leveled against Britain by the continental unifiers. It was also the reproach made against the British Empire by colonial peoples, whose internal religious, ethnic, linguistic, or tribal quarrels offered ideal conditions for the application of divide and rule techniques by a sophisticated but numerically weak imperial bureaucracy.

If B's role and Britain's interpretation of it begin to sound morally somewhat sleazy, it is time to recall that Britain is only the best-known of innumerable B's and only one of the many practitioners of divide and rule tactics in the history of domestic and international politics. Furthermore, the more benign aspect of B's—and Britain's—function must not be forgotten: to restrain the strong and protect the weak. In Imperial India, Muslims were grateful for the protection of the British Raj against the numerically stronger Hindus, just as the American Indians were grateful for London's restraining hand on the expanding ambitions of the colonists. Thus the vocation of the balancer is an ambiguous one in terms of humane and moral values. Indeed, it could be argued that if there are going to be divisions anyway, B's function is indispensable as a means of moderating their ferocity and preventing the more powerful from gobbling up the lesser players in the system. These considerations join the others previously listed in accounting for the esteem in which B is held by balance of power theoreticians.

One other attribute of B's position requires mention. To attain the status of holder of the balance is to come as close to achieving actual domination as a diverse, multipower system permits. Balance of power analysts point out, as we have noted, that never in history has one state achieved a monopoly of power in the international system. (One should add that no one faction in a domestic political system has ever monopolized power either, though there have been some close approximations.) Their sensible premise is that it would be both bloody and futile to embark on a policy of world domination. But since international politics is by their definition a game whose purpose is to control as much as possible and to be controlled as little as possible, one can achieve the purpose of the game by becoming the balancer.

Of course, only those with an adequate basis of power can aspire to become B, but this is also true for any state aspiring to world conquest. The aspirant B does not try to destroy the power of those who stand in the way so much as to exploit the divisions among them. B deflects the animosity of the others from itself and back into the ambit of their own intramural disputes. Such a policy involves a minimum expenditure of resources, a minimum of opposition, and hence a minimum of danger. This contrasts with a maximum of resources, opposition, and danger involved in a policy of world conquest—a policy whose ultimate goal is anyway beyond reach. If A and X are otherwise the strongest powers in the international system, and if B can decide the outcome of any contest between them, it is obvious that B has reached the summit of the international hierarchy of influence. By the same token, if A and X are the strongest powers in a given geographical region, a regional B is stronger still. The calculus of power politics offers no greater rewards than these.

BALANCE OF POWER IN DOMESTIC POLITICS

The examples used to illustrate balance of power politics have so far been drawn almost exclusively from the domain of international relations. But examples in domestic politics are by no means confined to the Mayor of Chicago. Indeed, David Hume, in his oft-cited essay on the balance of power, traced its origins to the practices of domestic politics in the Hellenic world. Hume pointed to the institutions of ostracism in Athens and petalism in Syracuse, which provided for the expulsion of any individual citizen whose power within the civil society threatened to become overweening.[3] The Athenians were notably cold-blooded in these matters: they invoked the ostracism procedure to exile Themistocles, who had been the chief architect of Athens' historic victory over the invading Persians. Modern political ostracism still resorts to exile (Trotsky, Tshombe, Perón, Juan Bosch, perhaps even Ché Guevara), though appointment to choice or not so choice ambassadorial posts far from the

---

[3] David Hume, "Of the Balance of Power," *Essays, Moral, Political and Literary* (London: Henry Frowde, 1904), pp. 339–348.

home front is a more frequent device. The parallels are evident: in domestic politics as in international politics A is a prime target for the hostility of an X-led coalition.

The American Constitution is a milestone in the domestic political history of balance of power doctrine. It deliberately provided for a government of checks and balances by establishing a plurality of power centers, each of which was accorded constitutional protection against control by the others. These legal guarantees were substantially strengthened by the very existence of a plurality of autonomous political forces. Any one of these forces—executive, legislature, judiciary, big states, small states, federal government, or state governments—could find allies against whichever one of them sought domination. When one adds to this ensemble the multiplicity of economic, sectional, ethnic, ideological, and other interest groups it is evident that the American power balance is one of the most complex in the world. Most countries do not exhibit the constitutional pluralism of the United States, but all display varying degrees of the diversity that is the foundation of all balance of power politics.

There are, of course, differences in the way the balance of power operates in a relatively integrated society like the United States or Britain and in the relatively unintegrated international society. The reasons for these differences will be discussed at a later point. But it should be noted here that a major reason is the presence in an integrated society of a unity of purpose and allegiance to the community that surmounts, restrains, and sometimes transforms the behavior of those playing the balance of power game in internal politics. At the same time, it must not be forgotten that unity of purpose and allegiance is a matter of common will, something that is often absent in so-called domestic politics. Unity of purpose in the United States broke apart over the issue of slavery. As a result, every restraint on the struggle for control collapsed. The massive use of force and the desperate diplomatic search for allies in the Civil War made the great domestic collision essentially indistinguishable from the classic balance of power contests associated with international politics.

None of the major nations of the world has escaped a similar fate at one point or another in its history. This is true of most of the smaller states as well. In the contemporary world the prevalence of "internal wars," revolutions, coups and coutercoups in dozens of so-called domestic societies testifies to the absence of any authentic unity of purpose in their political life. Accordingly, it is no surprise to find individuals and groups within these societies playing the balancing game in conformity with the rules familiar to international life. Vietnam is a particularly mournful example.

It should be clear that a sense of common purpose is a highly useful and valuable restraint on the process of matching power with counterpower in a struggle for control. One measure of the political health of any state is the degree of unity and allegiance among its citizens. This means the degree to which the citizens will subordinate their own strivings for power and advantage to the welfare of the state or community as a whole. But subordination of self does not come easily to human beings, and therefore allegiance to a community is a tender plant requiring constant cultivation. In many countries it is trampled upon again and again with the result that the struggle for internal control is carried out with the most radical and violent devices. We have noted similar, if less frequent, problems in more integrated societies. But the massive problem in international politics, in the eyes of balance of power theoreticians, is that the tender plant simply doesn't exist. Beyond the sovereign state there is no allegiance, there is no sense of common purpose.

THE BALANCE OF FEAR

It follows that in international politics the only possible restraint on the ferocity of the struggle for power is fear. Each state must make the others afraid. State A must be so strong that X will be afraid to attack; X must be so strong that A will be afraid to attack. If, as we have seen, this equality of fear cannot be achieved in a two-way confrontation because of an inequality of power resources, X and/or A can recruit allies to establish a balance. The balance of power is thus generically a balance of fear. The nuclear balance of terror is therefore nothing essentially new, but simply the ancient pattern of the balance of power implemented with the most modern devices.

But if the balance of terror is nothing new, the Soviet-American conflict since 1945 has nevertheless been characterized by a novel configuration of the balance of power. The presence of a balancer and/or a number of states able to move back and forth from A to X according to the power ratio between them indicates that the other players at least approach the level of power represented by A and X. This configuration is known as a multipolar balance of power, and it typifies most of the history of international relations. But since 1945 A and X have been superpowers; even the so-called major powers are incomparably weaker than the top two. This configuration has been dubbed a bipolar system to signify that only A and X really count. By definition bipolarity excludes a balancer (at the global level) because there is no state to play the role of B. That is, there is none with enough strength decisively to alter the balance between A and X. Even a combination of states moving to one side or the other would have mainly a psychological impact; the military and economic might of the superpowers and the ratio between them would persist relatively undisturbed.

In this situation the value of allies for A and X declines. Allies may be useful (geographically, tactically, ideologically) but not crucial, because they cannot alter the strategic balance. If alliances nonetheless abound, it is because A and X are less the recruiters of allies and more the recruited as the smaller powers seek protection from one superpower by attaching themselves to the other. Just as Western Europe embraced an American alliance after World War II, so the communist governments, if not peoples, of Eastern Europe sought refuge with Moscow. These alliances between strong leaders and weak followers have been called blocs as a means of indicating their unusual cohesiveness and solidarity in contrast to the fickle attitudes that commonly prevail among allies in a multipolar system. It has even been contended that the bloc system is not a balance of power at all because allies are not free to join or abandon A or X at will but are tied to their bloc by ideological as well as power considerations.

While it is true that bloc politics lacks the flexibility of a multipolar system in respect to alliance formation, the presence of the balancing process is still unmistakable. It expresses itself in the armaments efforts of A-bloc and X-bloc and in the competition between them in terms of economic growth and ideological appeal. The lack of significant allies to add or detract weights from one side or the other is thus compensated for by the dynamic development of internal power resources. The frequency of technological surprises and breakthroughs even restores some of the flexibility characteristic of the multipolar system, for each breakthrough is just as surely a new source of power as the acquisition of an alliance was in the so-called classic days of diplomacy.

The pattern of bloc politics began to break down in the 1960s. The defections of China and France from their respective alignments were only the most spectacular events in a continued loosening of bloc ties. But the facts of bipolarity are more resistant to change. If nuclear war does not upset all calculations, the year 2000 will still find the United States and the Soviet Union alone at the summit and only China (and perhaps a unified Europe) as a serious candidate to join them. One must estimate, then, that the full reemergence of a multipolar system will be a matter of at least two generations—beyond that it is useless to speculate. This means that international relations in our time must continue to be played out largely within the relatively unique configuration of bipolarity. It also means that every major undertaking by one superpower must be calculated in terms of its effect on the other.

Are these calculations going to be made primarily in the context of mutual terror, that is, according to the rules of the balance of power? We have seen that fear is the basic principle of the balance of power in both multipolar and bipolar versions. We have also seen that balance of power theoreticians have argued that there is no available substitute as the foundation of international politics. But all the evidence demonstrates that fear is a highly precarious restraint on the game of power politics. If the game threatens to get out of hand, the only possible way to prevent an explosion (other than capitulation) is to raise the level of fear.

If A threatens to injure X, X can counter with a threat to injure A. But A is still more likely to be restrained if X's counterthreat is not merely to injure but to destroy. The premium on escalation in this dismal game is obvious. Long before the term escalation entered the political vocabulary, balance of power theoreticians described the same phenomenon in different terminology. They recognized that the dynamics of the system require states to strive not for equality of power with rival states but for a margin of superiority.

Restraint could still obtain so long as A's attempts to gain the lead are countered by the efforts of X to wrest the lead from A. Thus the system of balance of power is less a static counterpoise of mutual fear and more a dynamic equilibrium engendered by the competitive search for preponderance. In such an environment, however, it is obvious that the accelerating mobilization of power resources and the rising level of fear must inflate the stakes in the contest. It is also obvious that the interplay of heightened anxieties will increase the likelihood of miscalculations and the probability of crisis. The series of crises that brought on World War I and, to some extent, World War II were, in fact, generated by a flow of concrete historical events that corresponded closely to this abstract description of the dynamic equilibrium of fear inherent in the balance of power system.

The ominous lesson of the world wars (and of every other war, international or civil) is that mutual fear has grave limitations as a restraint on the use of violence in political activity. Many if not all balance of power theoreticians are candid enough to stress the point. Their position is simply that however inadequate and even morally deplorable it may be to rely on fear, it is the only restraint available on the conduct of politics in the international society. If there were a world referee and a common will among men to support his rulings—a unity of purpose to place the welfare of the whole above the interests of the contending parts—then one could subject world politics to the restraints of law and equity. At this point, the argument concludes, the political dynamics of world society would come to resemble those of domestic society.

Even though domestic politics are not immune from even the most extreme forms of violence and often lack a sense of common will, one can agree that the presence of an authoritative referee would be a more effective and desirable restraint on political behavior than would a system of competitive threats. But the balance of power counselors point to the indubitable truth that no such referee exists in contemporary world politics. Moreover, even though ancient Rome and China could serve as prototypes of such a referee, their mandates were clearly limited

geographically and politically. Thus one must see the distinctive characteristic of international politics in the fact that never in history has
there been an authentic global referee, whatever the pretensions of
potentates, emperors, or popes.

Finally, the balance of power theoreticians question the desirability of
such a referee. Their opposition to a monopoly of power is not simply
a paradox in which those who define politics as a struggle for control
refuse to endorse the attainment of control. It also stems from the recognition of the world's diversity and a belief that the establishment of an
effective international referee or government would be at the expense
of diversity. They fear that the most likely and perhaps only path to
world government is world conquest. Once established, such a government or referee could restrain political behavior in so diverse a society
only with the techniques of tyranny. Thus the balance of power and the
politics of fear reemerge as the only "realistic" way to conduct politics
in international society: the world is stuck with the balance of terror.

Ironically, it is the very intensification of terror generated by the
advent of nuclear weapons that has given the balance of power doctrine
a renewed lease on life. Its supporters have usually conceded that the
purpose of the game is not really the prevention of war. Instead, the
purpose is simply to prevent (by war, if necessary) any one of the con-
tenders from achieving a monopoly of power. At the same time, balance
of power advocates have honestly deplored the enormity of war and
have shared the human despair that war creates. War, in this view, is the
historic and tragic price the world has paid for diversity—and for the
values attached to diversity. In the nuclear age, however, the price of
all-out war has skyrocketed, and total war between the superpowers has
become "unthinkable." Hence the nuclear powers, balancing their resources against one another and playing upon each other's fears, would
never dare actually to unleash the full forces of violence. In this situation the balance of power might yet serve both diversity and peace.

In those distant days before 1945 if A and X threatened one another
with "destruction" the term was understood to involve such consequences as complete defeat of military forces, occupation of enemy territory, large-scale indemnities, elimination of the vanquished from the
ranks of Great Powers and, in extreme cases, replacement of the enemy
government by one more to the liking of the victor, or even annexation.
These threats seem pallid in the era of the nuclear fires. Now the term
destruction connotes an abrupt and unquenchable incineration of an
entire society, an entire civilization, or even the globe itself, with only a
few isolated and crazed survivors to recall a world vanished suddenly
and forever. While an actual outbreak of nuclear warfare might not
escalate to these apocalyptic dimensions, the horror it would inflict at
any level of intensity still staggers the imagination. This being so, balance of terror doctrine assumes that neither A nor X, having achieved a

rough parity in nuclear weapons systems, would ever move from threats of destruction to the actual decision to destroy. For parity means that even if A destroys X, X will, during the process of its own destruction, release the salvos that will destroy A.

Without going further into the joyless realms of nuclear strategy at this point, it must be noted that the balance of terror strategists depend on the rationality of the nuclear opponents as the chief barrier to prevent nuclear threat from becoming nuclear force. But fear is notoriously corrosive of reason. The prelude and outbreak of both world wars featured a predominance of irrational over rational behavior, a predominance whose chief cause was fear. It is possible, even likely, that the chilling novelty of nuclear weapons has shocked political leaders and their followers into somewhat more rational behavior today. But as nuclear weapons proliferate despite nonproliferation efforts, the level of rationality is likely to decline and the level of fear to rise.

It is true that the conduct of international relations has always taken place within a network of fear. It is also true that the techniques of threat and counterthreat have not always, nor even most of the time, escalated into violence. But the most important truth is that sooner or later violence occurs. In an atmosphere charged with fear the probabilities of violence at any given time are considerable. In the long run the probability curve rises to the level of virtual certainty. A balance of power—a balance of fear—has never been (nor did its advocates claim it to be) a guarantor of peace. It cannot offer such a guarantee now. If the dangers of nuclear devastation are to be diminished, one must go beyond the inherent instabilities of both the traditional balance of power and the latter-day equilibrium of terror.

BALANCE OF POWER: A REASSESSMENT

Progress toward a more viable foundation for peace requires a thoroughgoing, though not complete, dismantling of balance of power theory. Such a wrecking operation must, first, recognize the frequency with which balance of power politics has been and will be played and at the same time insist that it is not the only rational way to play the game. Second, it must show that even when balance of power provides a rationally advantageous recipe for political action, there are times and places in which it is impossible to follow it. Third, it must demonstrate that the balance of power is more appropriate to relatively static periods of history but ill-suited to periods of massive and rapid change. Finally, it must seek to demonstrate that the supreme purpose of politics is not to excel at the game of balance of power but to transcend it.

The first step in the process of deflating balance of power doctrine is to divest it of the aura of determinism. Many theoreticians and practitioners have elevated the balance of power to the status of a universal law of politics operating regardless of time, circumstance, or the will of men. Hans Morgenthau, for example, asserts that there is

> [a] basic misconception that has impeded the understanding of international politics and has made us the prey of illusions. This misconception asserts that men have a choice between power politics and its necessary outgrowth, the balance of power, on the one hand, and a different, better kind of international relations on the other. . . .
>
> It will be shown . . . that the international balance of power is only a particular manifestation of a general social principle to which all societies composed of a number of autonomous units owe the autonomy of their component parts; that the balance of power and policies aiming at its preservation are not only inevitable but are an essential stabilizing factor in a society of sovereign nations.[4]

The obvious conclusion to be drawn is that this general principle or law of politics cannot be ignored with impunity and that the politician must be governed by its imperatives or court political ruin. Obedience to these imperatives, by the same token, is the only path to success.

The empirical foundations for these deterministic assumptions can be located in the venerability of the balance of power doctrine and in the demonstrated ubiquity of its practice. Twenty-three centuries ago Thucydides wrote his history of the Peloponnesian Wars as a veritable case study in balance of power politics. Demosthenes' oration two generations later urging diplomatic support for Megalopolis was a classic exposition of the intricate virtues of the doctrine. In the same century Kautilya's rule book for kings, known as the *Arthasastra*, advocated balance of power policies in the idiom of ancient India. Subsequent proponents, from Polybius to Machiavelli and David Hume to Winston Churchill, have been legion. As for the persistence of the balance of power in practice, a number of examples have already been considered, and the examples could be multiplied almost indefinitely.

Yet an authentic realism must reject determinism in balance of power doctrines as elsewhere. It must make the empirical observation that the balance of power is a recurrent and very frequent pattern of political behavior, both domestically and internationally. As such, it must always be taken into account in political calculations. But frequency does not mean invariability, and where there is variability the doctrinaire world of necessity and determinism must give way to the real world of probabilities. If we wish to assess the probabilities of balance of power behavior, we need to be able to explain why political man has acted in

---

[4] Morgenthau, *Politics Among Nations*, 5th ed., p. 167.

ways that deviate from the precepts of balance of power doctrine. These explanations can be traced to both rationality and irrationality.

The ineradicable role of irrationality in politics prevents any assumption that men and states are continuously caught up in a balance of power pattern. A simple failure to grasp the rules of the balancing game has again and again broken the pattern of equilibrium. In the name of the balance of power Hume castigated those rulers who failed to support Carthage in its struggle with Rome on the grounds that Carthage was the last significant barrier to Rome's aspirations to dominate Europe, Africa, and the East. He charged that the "private passions" of Massinissa, Attalus, and other princes were the culprits which led them to support rather than oppose an ascendant Rome.[5] Hume has left us to speculate on the nature of these passions. Sloth, cowardice, corruption, avarice, decadence, or sheer stupidity—all may have played a role in causing princes and princelings to line up with the Roman A instead of the Carthaginian X. Only Hiero of Syracuse, Hume observed, seems to have understood the balance of power since he fudged on his alliance with Rome by supplying aid to Carthage. But Hiero's duplicity was not enough to turn the tide.

In any event, Rome did succeed in mastering the Western world, and during the centuries of Roman rule balance of power politics was demoted to a subordinate process within the framework of Roman supremacy. This massive fact is sufficient demonstration that there is nothing inevitable in the operation of the balance of power; whether it operates or not is a matter of human choice. As Hume's examples imply, a choice not to play the balancing game may be irrational. Many analysts have made a persuasive case for American irrationality between the two world wars on the ground that the United States preferred to turn in upon itself rather than accept the painful truth that its security was dependent on the balance of power in Europe. Isolationism is indeed irrational, both then and now, for any state with significant capacity to influence the environment in which it exists. Where such capacity is minimal, however, insulation from the mainstream of regional or global politics may commend itself as a reasonable course of action. Whether rational or irrational, the phenomenon of isolationist policies reinforces the lesson that a theory of world politics that assumes the inevitable operation of the balance of power will err.

Reason and unreason combine to explain why not every state or politician plays the balancing game. State A may seek to monopolize power and rationally order its behavior to that end. The objective itself may be unrealistic, but the behavior of the other players would be even more so if they assumed that A was playing balance of power instead of monop-

---

[5] Hume, "Of the Balance of Power."

oly. State A may be so strong that other states, particularly those in A's immediate vicinity, may simply not be in a position to join an opposing coalition. The rapid rise of Nazi power in the 1930s persuaded many European states that their salvation lay in reaching accommodation with Hitler. Britain and France were accused of both irrationality and cowardice for their parts in appeasing Germany. But Stalin's appeasement of Hitler in 1939, also born of weakness, is generally regarded to be more rational. As for the small states, the willingness of many to accommodate themselves to Berlin may not have been heroic, but they were hard put to find a rational alternative. Balance of power doctrine puts a premium on maneuverability, but there are often circumstances in which room for maneuver is reduced almost to zero. In these circumstances balance of power operations are also virtually paralyzed.

THE INTERNAL BALANCE OF POWER

Maneuverability may be restricted by internal as well as external pressures. If A expounds an ideology that appeals to a sector of the citizens of State Y, the government of Y will find it difficult to oppose A. The same may be true if Y has an ethnic or religious minority with bonds of consanguinity or faith to the people of A. These considerations should help to focus attention on a crucial fact of political life that many balance of power theoreticians are inclined to overlook in their analyses of international relations: management of internal political pressures may match or outweigh the importance of managing external pressures.

It is, ironically, the very universality of the balance of power—its presence in both domestic and international politics—that operates to inhibit its workings in both spheres. External threat may persuade internal factions to put aside their separate ambitions and quarrels and unite under a strong leader to meet the foreign danger. In this case, diffusion of domestic power yields to concentration. Internal threats, on the other hand, may convince one or more factions to solicit aid from a powerful state abroad as a means of subduing its domestic competitors. In this case, the external balance of power is judged less important than the internal.

Those who assert the primary importance of foreign policy will always be unhappy whenever priority is accorded to the internal balance of power. Charles II of England, for example, is frequently pilloried for his failure to assume leadership in an anti-French coalition. In the abstract, Charles should have played X to the A of Louis XIV. In the concrete circumstances, Charles was accepting large subsidies from Louis in return for performing the usual services that subsidies buy. Charles' policy obviously frustrated those who wished to restrain French power in Europe, but Charles was more interested in preserving his throne at home than in asserting himself abroad. Louis might be a danger to Europe and to England itself, but factional opposition, the memory of a beheaded father, and a wobbly throne only recently restored persuaded Charles that civil strife was still more dangerous. He needed the money and political support that Louis provided; in his situation neither rational nor moral criticism is very convincing.

Another Englishman, Stanley Baldwin, is more culpable. It is one thing to fear civil war and the loss of one's head and another to fear the loss of an election. As prime minister of England, Baldwin too refused to play X—this time to Hitler's A. He insisted that the pacifist mood of the British public prevented him from mounting an adequate response to the Nazi challenge. But he was unwilling to risk his personal position and that of his party in an effort to combat a dangerously unrealistic set of popular attitudes. Instead, he played down the Hitler menace, softpedaled the need for rearmament, and presented himself as the peace candidate. Baldwin discussed his motives when he stood before the House of Commons in 1936 and offered a retrospective analysis of the election strategy that brought victory to the Conservatives in the previous year. To use his own words, Baldwin spoke with an "appalling frankness":

> My position as the leader of a great party was not altogether a comfortable one. . . .
>
> Supposing I had gone to the country and said that Germany was rearming and that we must rearm, does anybody think that this pacific democracy would have rallied to that cry at that moment? . . . I cannot think of anything that would have made the loss of the election from my point of view more certain. . . . we won the election by a large majority; but frankly I could conceive that we should at that time, by advocating certain courses, have been a great deal less successful.[6]

This is not the place to strike a balance between Baldwin's personal failings and the general malaise affecting Britain in the years of appeasement. But so much is clear: Baldwin's politics constitutes another variation on the theme that the internal balance of power can take precedence over the external.

The example of Charles II, if not that of Baldwin, suggests the generalization that it is sometimes more rational to give paramount consideration to power in contexts other than international relations. After all, acceptance of an external overlordship in exchange for guaranteed authority within the fiefdom was the political foundation of medieval Europe, as it has been for every other feudal society. A pledge of

---

[6] Speech of November 12, 1936, cited in John F. Kennedy, *Why England Slept*, 2nd ed. (Garden City, N.Y.: Doubleday, 1961), pp. 124–125.

allegiance to the foreign conqueror to redeem autonomy in local affairs has characterized Levantine societies. The same kind of relationship emerged again and again in the West's colonial territories—the colonized chief could continue to reign so long as he performed certain services for the great white chief overseas.

Many of these imperial and feudal arrangements were tawdry in the specific sense that the external guarantee permitted the local ruler or oligarchy to exploit the local population with relative impunity. The great white chief's troops or gunboats were usually available to put down any rebels. Such an arrangement may benefit the restricted interests of a small elite, but it can have no charms for the mass. It is this conflict of interests between colonized elite and mass which has typically produced demands for independence from outside control and for a united front against the foreigner. Translated into the concepts of sovereignty and nationalism, these demands—whether in the sixteenth or the twentieth century—are clearly directed to both the internal and the external distribution of power.

The depressing phenomenon of the colonized society offers the power theoreticians in international politics one of their most compelling arguments in favor of a theory of national interest which seeks to avoid external control at any price. It bolsters the case for a multiplicity of autonomous (that is, sovereign) states each playing the balancing game as an indispensable means for preserving multiplicity and, hence, autonomy. There is, in fact, a certain moral attractiveness in the image of a world of vigorous societies each guarding its independence and dealing with its internal problems without external interference. One difficulty, however, is that there has generally been a poor correspondence between the image and reality. Furthermore, even if the independent nation-state has typically generated greater equality and justice within its borders, the sovereign national ego has multiplied and intensified war and injustice abroad. Finally, even the image itself is being drained of relevance in the contemporary world of ever-growing and ever more irreversible interdependence.

For present purposes, the major conclusion is that throughout history many states and peoples have simply failed to play the international game of balance of power. Some have chosen and some have been forced to opt out of the game abroad in order to play either the game of balance or of control at home. Others have not had the strength to compete. Still others have preferred different values to those of power. The "private passions" of which Hume complained—the love of luxury, ease, or sensuality—are still in evidence. Farouk, the late deposed king of Egypt, and ex-emperor Bao Dai of Vietnam are symbols of a sybaritic addiction among elites that afflicts a not inconsiderable number of contemporary societies. On the other hand, a preference for the tranquil arts of life over the pulling and hauling of the power struggle can hardly be termed an automatic vice. For all these reasons only a part of international society ever plays the balancing game at any one time. It follows that balance of power doctrine can account for only part of the world's political behavior. One must conclude, therefore, that the balance of power is neither actually nor potentially omnipresent and that assumptions to the contrary are necessarily erroneous.

THE CONFLICT BETWEEN BALANCE OF POWER AND CHANGE

Political change means many things. It can mean the transfer of power from one set of rulers to another. It can mean that power is being more widely diffused or more narrowly concentrated. It can mean a change in the purposes for which power is used. All of these changes in various combinations are occurring with extraordinary and unprecedented rapidity in our own time. In this situation the old balance of power recipes are becoming obsolete. The reason for this is that balance of power doctrine recommends essentially static techniques, most of which are out of tune with an increasingly dynamic world.

In international relations, balance of power politics is designed to perpetuate the existence of a multiplicity of sovereign units. But nuclear weapons make a mockery of the military defense of sovereignty even, and especially, at the superpower level. The danger they represent has persuaded most of the nonnuclear states in the world to forego their "sovereign" right to manufacture or use them, even though the five nuclear powers continue to assert that right for themselves. The superpowers themselves have instituted a number of international controls governing aspects of the nuclear problem, culminating in the 1972 Strategic Arms Limitations Talks (SALT agreements). It is true that the net effect of all the nuclear treaties so far signed falls far short of a system of adequate safeguards. Yet each has advanced and strengthened the proposition that what is needed in nuclear weaponry is not more sovereignty but less.

Economic sovereignty is just as dubious. The dynamics of the world economy overshadow the economies of the individual states as never before. The presence of the American super-economy and a few lesser giants among the multitudes of economic pygmies belies the egalitarian claims of sovereignty. Every state is not—and cannot be—as sovereign as every other. What is needed in the economic sphere is not dogmatic insistence upon a bogus autonomy but a rational and equitable adjustment to the facts of interdependence. In every sphere of life sovereignty means separateness. But science, technology, economics, and rational politics in today's world require expansion and intensification of human interrelationships across sovereign borders.

The balance of power concept is obsolescent because it conflicts with the world's need to stress unity. The existence of a need does not mean that it will necessarily be satisfied. But it is clear that satisfaction will more likely result from political behavior whose norm is unity rather than division. These arguments bear close resemblance to the perennial debates about domestic political organization: To what extent should power be concentrated, to what extent dispersed? The similarity cannot be doubted since we have already seen examples of the domestic balance of power, and balance of power politics presupposes a tension between unity and dispersion of power.

The resemblance is increasingly striking with the development of the industrial revolution. As the economies of the West became more productive, expansive, and complex, as new techniques of transport and communication transformed distance into proximity, as people in different economic strata and different geographical regions became more dependent on one another, the need for stronger central government and comprehensive central services could not be ignored. In every case, the countries of the West responded to the industrial revolution by moving away from the separation of powers and toward a synthesis of power.

This process has not been free of abuses. Some of the industrializing countries—past and present—have succumbed to arbitrary government and the pall of uniformity. But if the values of diversity have suffered, they have retained enough vigor to be both boon and challenge to the inhabitants of most of the contemporary industrial societies. Above all, the policies that gave priority to unity over division produced in the industrial West more wealth, more power, more internal peace, and more widely shared freedom than in any societies previously known to history.

It is obvious that one can neither anticipate nor recommend for the world at large exact replicas of the centralizing processes that have characterized Western domestic politics. Within the West itself, after all, these processes found expression in highly diverse forms. Movements toward a greater synthesis of power on a transnational basis will either reflect the still greater diversity of the world beyond the West or they will fail of their objective. All this being said, it remains true that the realist in today's world must identify unity and not division as the touchstone of policy.

As we saw earlier, the lack of a sense of unity is the final argument that balance of power theorists use to justify the politics of division. This is fair enough, for where there is no unity, there must be division, and balance of power policies are a rational response to the facts of division. They do not, however, represent a rational response to the challenge of unity. In every society that has achieved successful unification, balance of power politics has been subordinated to (though not eradicated by) the unifying processes. This has been true whether one cites the Chinese or Roman empires or the internal consolidation of the Western nation-states since the eighteenth century. Any progress toward greater unity on a transnational or global level must reproduce this same subordination of the balance of power to the politics of unity. Since deep divisions in the world persist, however, the principle of the balance of power is bound to exhibit continued vigor. If it is destined to retain its vigor and to become nonetheless subordinate, the politics of unity must necessarily be more vigorous still.

The lessons to be drawn at this point are several. Balance of power will be around as long as there are divisions and conflicts among men; its longevity is thus assured. It offers rational techniques for dealing with divisions and conflicts whenever they will not yield to the techniques of unity, and it can function as a desirable restraint should power threaten to become overcentralized (or should A threaten to become overbearing). But the balance of power is not the only principle of politics. Other techniques are essential if unity is to be strengthened. No coherent society could ever have emerged if the techniques of unity had not been successfully applied. In today's world there is a desperate need for greater unity. In these circumstances a rational foreign policy formula might read: hold in defensive reserve the techniques of balance of power; assume the offensive with the techniques of unity.

FROM DIVISIVENESS TOWARD UNITY

What, then, are the techniques of unity? They are obviously those at the consent end of the spectrum of power. As soon as there is greater reliance on consent and less on coercion the politics of balance of power begins to yield to the politics of unity. In other words, the mutual fears of A and X diminish and mutual confidence grows. But the key question is: What will diminish the role of fear? The answer can only be that A and X must cease trying to control the other. They must also cease trying to control the fate of the remainder of the world.

If the solution to the problem of fear is obvious, the efforts to achieve it are obviously complex. Yet the solution is not beyond reach for a very simple reason: there is no need for A and X to try to control the other or the rest of the world. This is particularly true for the A and X of America and Russia. The politics of control has always rested on illusion, but at no time in history has there been a greater opportunity to banish the illusion than now. This is because the two nuclear giants today stand unchallenged and unchallengeable. Avoidance of nuclear war and wise internal policies will guarantee their impregnability into the indefinite future. No one can endanger them if they will give up endangering each other.

But balance of power doctrine prescribes that each state must try to avoid being at the mercy of the others. The prescription is a response to the assumption that the concern for power observable in all states is indistinguishable from the desire to dominate other states. The will to power, as previously noted, is equated to the will to control. This being so, every state must distrust every other state. Each must jealously husband its own power and limit the power of others since weakness invites domination. Each is by definition a danger to the other. All must fear the advent of a powerful A, and prudence dictates alignment (formal or tacit) of the rest with a not so powerful X as the only feasible counterweight to A. Finally, the doctrine asserts, the others can hope to avoid domination as long as the strongest two are restrained by their dread of one another. The others therefore have a stake in the persistence of mutual fear and mistrust between A and X. Their stake is virtually guaranteed: since A and X do not differ from other states except in the massiveness of their power resources, each would seek to control the other if it could. Therefore, the persistence of their mutual fear is practically assured.

This set of assumptions is vitiated, however, by three crucial observations already elaborated. First, the concern for power and the will to dominate are not identical. Second, empirical political behavior deviates so often from balance of power doctrine that its assumptions can account for only part of political reality. Third, there is no objective need for either of the present A and X titleholders to attempt or fear control of the other.

On the other hand, the superpowers have more rational grounds for a different kind of fear, namely, that other players in the game will try to exacerbate the tensions that persist between them. Self-nominated candidates for the position of balancer are clearly in evidence, though none with the historic advantages that Great Britain once enjoyed. The prospects that a bona fide B will once again emerge are still cloudy, but so much is clear: B is a symbol of division and will always be an obstacle to the politics of unity.

Once again the temptation to make B the villain in the piece must be resisted. As befits a symbol, B is a reflection and not a first cause of the politics of divisiveness. Whether in domestic politics or in international politics at the regional or global level, B has emerged again and again only because there was an already existing context of divisiveness. As of now, the chief agents of division or unity can only be the policies of the superpowers—toward each other and toward the world at large.

In their policies toward the rest of the world, stronger powers throughout history have sought to dominate weaker powers for any or all of three reasons. State A or X sought to dominate Y for the intrinsic benefits anticipated: access to additional land, manpower, raw materials or markets, geographical advantages, ideological satisfactions, or the pleasures of being the master. Or, A sought to control Y in order to enhance its capacity for eventually controlling X. Or, conversely, A sought to control Y in order to prevent X from controlling and exploiting Y as a means of overtaking the power of A. In terms of objectives sought, then, policies of control can be labeled intrinsic, offensive, and defensive.

None of these motives for control has any relevance for American or Soviet policy today. Neither superpower can attempt to control the other without committing suicide. This revolutionary change in the traditional relationships between A and X also carries with it revolutionary implications for their relationships with the rest of the world. In essence, it destroys the time-honored rationale for policies of offensive or defensive control of smaller powers. Russia and America are already impregnable: so long as they maintain their superpower status in a (militarily) bipolar world, their security does not depend on third parties. Their defense is located first and last in the nuclear, political, and economic power generated within their own borders and not in client states or conquered territories.

In regard to intrinsic benefits from policies of control, it can only be said that control of smaller powers for the sake of material gain is a ludicrous ambition for economic giants. It is also an evil ambition in a world desperate to be freed from both internal and external exploitation. As for ideological zeal, it should at last be manifest that the diversity of the world is an insuperable barrier to any universal way of life. Time, space, culture, and personality inevitably limit the numbers of people any ideology can expect to convert. By the same token, the persistence of diversity warrants confidence that different and even inimical ideological positions can coexist with reasonable self-confidence.

It must be stressed that all these arguments are prescriptions for rational and relevant politics and not descriptions of actual international behavior. Policies of control for strategic, economic, and ideological reasons are still in evidence despite their growing illogic. Their stubborn persistence is intimately connected with a perennial motivation unaffected by time or change and with which we are already familiar: the ancient lust to dominate, to enjoy the role of master. Cravings for power, glory, and deference are characteristically present in those who yearn for top dog status. But the ambition to play Caesar is still more generally a product of a deeper emotion—once again the emotion of fear. The victim suspects that the world is composed only of masters and slaves and that if he would not be one he must be the other. The itch to command is as resistant to rational criticism as it ever was. Strategic, economic, or ideological counterarguments can make little impression because the victim is not really interested in listening to them; he hears a different drummer.

And so the ancient and tragic drama continually repeats itself. The recognition of the impulse to dominate (in oneself and in others) produces the fear of being dominated. Fear, in turn, reinforces the original impulse; it argues that winning the game of domination oneself is the only way to frustrate the other players' aspirations for mastery. The vernacular version of this prescription is dog eat dog; in a more traditional idiom, every man must either be hammer or anvil. This is the classic vicious circle of arrogance and fear in mutual hot pursuit. To negotiate an exit from this depressing maze only the contrary qualities can help: modesty and courage.

Vicious circles are by definition difficult to break. The effort takes time, imagination, and staying power, and success is uncertain. But the initial step remains the lead line all the way to liberation: the understanding that irrationality is both start and finish in the game of control, that rationality in politics requires not control but consent. Since the Cuban confrontation of 1962, the United States and the Soviet Union have given some evidence of such an understanding, but the burden of mutual fear constantly tugs them backward, as Vietnam, Czechoslovakia, and the Middle East have demonstrated.

It is hard, of course, to be confident about one's own invulnerability when one is constantly probing for vulnerabilities in others. Hence recognition that the game of domination is irrational needs to be reinforced by the development of an active distaste for the game. In this connection it is just possible that the experiences of white America in its own cities and of Communist Russia with the results of its own ideology at home and abroad will eventually help to convince both that the role of the master is an expensive and demoralizing luxury as well as a dangerous and self-destructive objective.

In any case, the lesson for both the superpowers is clear: they can both be powerful and secure without pursuing an illusory omnipotence. Each has an indestructible nuclear retaliatory capacity, and since neither can dominate the other, both have a guarantee against being dominated. The presence of such a guarantee negates the case for superpower domination anywhere in the world. Their nuclear stalemate has forced the superpowers to stress the politics of consent toward one another. It has also freed them, if they can only see it, to move toward consensual relationships with every lesser power in international politics.

The old hankering after supremacy and the burdens of suspicion and fear cannot be sloughed off quickly; indeed, their legacies will persist for the foreseeable future. But this does not detract from the revolutionary reality that the superpowers can *safely* move away from the politics of coercion and control and establish the politics of consent as the norm and objective of their international conduct. Even realistic norms are often violated, of course, and conflicts will never be eliminated. But their number and intensity are more easily reduced where the purpose of policy is cooperation than where the assumption prevails that there is no alternative to conflict.

It is, then, realistic to advocate the subordination of balance of power politics to the goal of cooperation. Both superpowers can afford it without endangering their own security. But how rapidly and how far they can move away from coercion and toward consent depends on two basic factors: the degree of realism with which each understands its own invulnerability and the recognition that each has a stake in the invulnerability of the other. That is, mutual and symmetrical vulnerability is the equivalent of mutual invulnerability. These rules and conditions add up to the precise opposite of balance of power politics. Balance of power is a game geared to vulnerability and not invulnerability, to conflict and not to cooperation; its basic assumption is that each would control if it could and that the threat of control can be modified only by a continuing and escalating confrontation of coercive power with coercive counterpower.

TRANSCENDING THE POWER CALCULUS

To transcend the balance of power is to move toward the consent end of the power spectrum. It follows that all that has been said so far still fits within the calculus of power politics. We have seen that consensual relationships are also power relationships and that renouncing the ambition to control does not mean renunciation of power as such. All this suggests that power remains the central concern of political action and the proper organizing concept for the understanding of politics.

One might infer that all that matters is the awareness of the consensual as well as the coercive aspects of power and the rational selection of techniques from the full range of the power spectrum according to the requirements of the concrete situation. One might draw the further implication that the rational management of power presently excludes the politics of control but that as yet unforeseeable changes might make it possible to resume the game of domination in earnest without the fear of mutual suicide. These inferences and implications would clearly reinforce the central thesis of power politics that political behavior is motivated exclusively by concerns for power.

It is here that the question of purpose emerges once more. We have seen that the politics of control is necessarily coercive. Both the aspirant to domination and his often similarly motivated prospective victims are caught up in the process of threat and counterthreat, injury and reprisal. Only when the will to dominate abates among all the players do consensual relationships have a chance to prosper. But even should such an abatement occur, what are the prospects for the politics of consent when the will to dominate again waxes strong? In the calculus of power politics the intensity of the will to power among the relevant players is the exclusive determinant of the range of choice between coercion and consent. The question then arises whether there is any way of constraining the will to power within the bounds of moderation so that the politics of consent could enjoy better prospects for durability. In other words, how can the relationship that makes the politics of consent dependent on the politics of control be reversed?

The answer can only come from outside the power calculus. When power is properly understood as involving both consensual and coercive relationships the power calculus offers the politician a choice between them. But its single imperative of enhancing power devalues choice to the level of automatic selection: in each situation one chooses the methods of consent or coercion according to whether they promise net gains in power. The power calculus is theoretically as indifferent to freedom and control as it is to consent and coercion. In some circumstances the rational management of power prescribes the politics of freedom and consent, but in others it may not. However, if just one player, rationally or not, insists on playing the game of force and domination, the others have no choice but to follow his lead. It is at this point that power politics loses its theoretical neutrality. Preoccupied with the will to dominate and the fear of domination, it weights the game, after all, on the side of coercion and control.

The only effective counterweight to the calculus of power is the normative proposition that the purpose of politics is not to control men but to liberate them. Once subjected to an external norm, power can no longer be an end in itself. Political behavior can no longer be deemed rational simply because it enhances power but only if it serves the purposes of freedom. The most critical function of the autonomous norm of liberty is that it devalues power itself: devaluation is inherent in the demotion of power from the realm of ends to that of means. But its effect is more dramatically evident whenever the imperative of freedom requires that power be curtailed rather than enhanced. The power calculus is wholly resistant to such a requirement. But only a readiness to comply can build a lasting framework for the politics of consent.

As noted in the introductory chapter, the secret of success in the development of the Western democracies was the ongoing redistribution of power, wealth, education, and status. Violence was avoided to the extent that class interest was subordinated to the welfare of the nation. Consent was strengthened to the extent that class power was diluted and shared rather than reinforced and hoarded. It was also suggested at the outset that the process of democratization in the West has a profound significance for the understanding of contemporary international politics and offers peculiarly relevant guidelines for the formulation of international policy in the late twentieth century. The material and psychological obstacles to their application are formidable, but one obstacle is overcome as soon as one recognizes that for both domestic and international politics power should be subordinate to freedom and not the other way around.

This restatement of priorities does not rule out the concern for power, but it does conflict with those who label international relations power politics per se. It does not deny that many of those active in international politics continue to behave in accordance with a model that identifies power as both the indispensable means and the supreme objective of policy. But the alternative model subordinating power to freedom derives credibility from two major sources. First is the evidence that a great deal of international behavior cannot be explained by the conventions of power politics. Second, the massive inflow of data reaching us from every area and aspect of our contemporary world demonstrates that objective conditions have now emerged in which a continuation of the game of power politics must end in global catastrophe. Safety can be won only by playing politics with a number of different rules in a fundamentally revised model for international behavior.

In this book the new model is called macropolitics. Its fullest elaboration appears in Part Two, but it is already apparent that the conflict between macropolitics and power politics is basic. Macropolitics asserts that the power politics label is empirically misleading as a generalization about all international relations. It also asserts that the label is normatively misleading because it implies that there is no reality in international political life other than power and that one must, after all, play the game as it "really" is. As for the balance of power, the macropolitical model makes no denial of its rationality, but only as a defensive technique and only in tandem with an offensive strategy that seeks to move away from division and toward unity.

The argument between power politics and macropolitics will continue throughout this book, and the bulk of the evidence still remains to be considered. But at the close of the initial formal analysis of power and purpose in politics, it is in order to make reference once again to the two major actors in the contemporary international system. It was contended earlier that the two superpowers, barring nuclear war or internal upheaval, will continue to be superpowers thirty years hence. But their international policies can be deemed successful only if by that time their disproportionate share of the world's power has been significantly diminished.

The norm of freedom does not demand the destruction of power, but it does require its more equitable distribution. Freedom's demand for greater equality is also identical to the requirements of rational international policy—an identity that becomes increasingly evident as one moves from micropolitical to macropolitical concepts of the global society. The nub of the matter is that if the present drastic imbalance in the global division of power and wealth persists, the global majority of the weak and the poor will have no stake in keeping the peace and no alternative but to incite the strong against one another. As for the superpowers, the search for still more power is equivalent to the pursuit of war. Peace is possible only if they learn the lesson that power politics doesn't teach: power is something not only to covet but also to share.

Chapter 3

Force

Force has often been called the *ultima ratio* in political life. Correct usage employs the Latin phrase to signify that in political dispute violence is the ultimate arbiter or court of last resort. The message is that when all other forms of power have failed to persuade, one can then reach for the weapons of coercion.

There is, however, an understandable ambiguity surrounding the idea of *ultima ratio*. The concept of force as the court of last resort suggests that all other means for the solution of disputes should be employed before recourse is taken to coercion. At the same time, it suggests that force is, after all, the supreme argument beside which other techniques of power seem puny. The words that Thucydides put into the mouths of the Athenians in their ultimatum to Melos echo throughout history: the strong do what they can and the weak suffer what they must. Updated versions of this ancient proposition include Napoleon's dictum that God is on the side of the biggest battalions and Stalin's rhetorical question asking how many divisions has the Pope. These archetypal sentiments identify superior force as the trump card in politics. Placing a premium on force, they loosen the restraints implied in that sense of the *ultima ratio* concept which admonishes against resort to force before other methods have been exhausted.

The presumption that force is decisive in the outcome of political struggle can therefore initiate a transformation in which men see the role of force not as an *ultima ratio* but as a kind of *prima ratio*. The court of last resort becomes the court of first resort whenever significant numbers of people believe that no methods other than those of force will bring meaningful political results. Here politics, both domestic and international, becomes identical with war. Mao's doctrine that "political power grows out of the barrel of a gun" is the best known contemporary formulation of the reasoning that interprets the ultimacy of force as the primacy of force. Ché Guevara, Régis Debray, and Frantz Fanon go still further with their intimations that it is violence which gives birth to ideology and not the other way around. Their explicit or implicit revolutionary advice is first to build an army and shed some blood and then find an idea. It fits well with a markedly counterrevolutionary tradition of thought that celebrates war as the mother of all things.

The Guevara-Debray-Fanon appreciation of violence is also, however, only a far-out version of Marxian orthodoxy. Despite occasional concessions to the observed reality of social reform, Marx clung tenaciously to his central proposition that only violence could bring about significant social change. Those who benefit by an unjust status quo, he contended, cannot be persuaded to change it by reasoned argument, economic pressure, or even the fear of revolution. Instead, they can be driven from their positions of privilege only by the actual application of revolutionary force. The fundamental intransigence of the ruling class derives not from the circumstance that many of its members may be men of greed and ill will but from the ideology, necessarily shared by all its members, that declares the class interest to be absolute and sacrosanct. In this analysis violence inexorably becomes the only significant instrument for social change and the only meaningful relationship between classes and ideologies.

Against this analytical background it is understandable why Khrushchev came to be denounced as a revisionist both within and outside the Soviet Union. Khrushchev advanced the possibility of a peaceful transition from capitalism to socialism and of peaceful coexistence between capitalism and communism on a global basis. His concept of peace might differ from that of Western leaders, but it was patently heretical in the world of Marxian communism. Khrushchev could cite some quotations from Lenin to support his stand, but the main thrust of Leninist analysis accentuated and dramatized the imperative of violence in the thought of Marx. Thus Mao—and to a lesser extent Guevara, Fanon, and others of their persuasion—can credibly claim to represent the true orthodoxy of Marxism-Leninism. In their eyes the whole argument between *prima ratio* and *ultima ratio* is persiflage: whether violence should be the court of first or last resort is a false issue. The resort to force establishes the only court whose judgments count.

FORCE IN THE NUCLEAR CONTEXT

Among other things, Khrushchev's heresy was an attempt to deal with a world in which new instruments of force have revolutionized the entire meaning of international politics and, inevitably, of domestic politics as well. The advent of nuclear weapons radically altered every calculation known to history concerning the role of force in the pursuit of political objectives. But it did not change everything. While many societies, both domestic and international, have often succeeded in relegating force to subordinate and infrequent use, none has ever been able wholly to disprove the claim that force is indeed the *ultima ratio*. Despite the terrifying growth of nuclear arsenals, the claim still stands.

As one instrument of power, force may be uneconomic and morally undesirable, and the results obtained by its use may be of ambiguous value. As the sole instrument of power, force is clearly an abomination. But it is undeniable that force has achieved objectives that seemed otherwise unattainable. It is equally undeniable that the option of force is always open to all who are justly or unjustly discontent. And it is undeniable that the use of force may sometimes be legitimate. All these history-tested considerations according force an ineradicable and even legitimate role in political life now rend man's consciousness and conscience as he contemplates the nuclear giant.

Since 1945 the debate over the role of force has been tortuous and tortured. The absurdities and paradoxes into which many of the debaters have been driven testify to the agonizing nature of the issue. Many of those who declared that there was no alternative to peace or who asserted that nuclear war was unthinkable have themselves been responsible for building up the world's ever more sophisticated nuclear military forces. There is general agreement that the actual use of nuclear weapons would be a wholly irrational act. But within this same consensus most accept, more or less reluctantly, the rationality of nuclear threats.

After all, nuclear threat is the alpha and omega of the official policies of deterrence and balance of terror, and these policies of the superpowers are the keystone in the entire structure of contemporary international politics. But those who deny the rationality of use and affirm the rationality of threat are almost turned back upon themselves when the issue of credible and effective policy is raised. No threat is credible if it is obvious that under no circumstances will it be implemented. Hence the game of deterrence literally demands that one must act as if there are, in fact, circumstances in which it would be rational to light the nuclear fires. Thus the irrational is made rational, the incredible credible, and once again force, even in its nuclear incarnation, stakes out its claim to be the *ultima ratio*.

It is probably true to say that since 1945 the nuclear apparition has so far prevented a resort to all-out violence. Without the fear it has instilled the frequency and intensity of crises afflicting international politics would, almost without doubt, already have produced a third world war. But we have noted in Chapter 2 that fear is a notoriously unstable foundation for peace. It would be folly to assume that nuclear fear can function as a kind of indefinite salvation. The truth is that nuclear war is not at all unthinkable. The terrible gift of the atomic physicists has not narrowed the range of man's political choices in the sense of creating a situation in which there is no alternative to peace. The nuclear alternative will haunt international politics and the life of man into the unforeseeable future.

During the remainder of the twentieth century, then, the nemesis of nuclear power must condition all realistic debate about the role of force in the world's politics. The debate cannot assume that nuclear weapons will not be used. Nor can it be assumed that an initial resort to conventional weaponry can always be contained at the conventional level. Neither governments in international politics nor those who would settle domestic political issues in the streets can ignore the nuclear dimension of violence except at awful peril to themselves and to all men. It is ironic that the nuclear age has so far produced more terrorists than pacifists. Perhaps the proportions could be reversed if it were understood that the doors of the nuclear arsenals are not necessarily closed for all time. Whoever promotes violence at whatever level of politics must share responsibility for that day, if it comes, when the doors open.

It will require enormous exertion to keep those doors closed. The requirements are all the more exacting because the pacifist solution is not a live option in a world of turbulence, anger, and injustice. Ideological passions, racial hatreds, and human inequities are too massive to suppose that men will not resort to force even with serious and effective efforts being made to deal with the causes of human degradation and conflict. There will continue to be clashes between force and counterforce. Their frequency and intensity will diminish only when human misery across the globe begins to diminish—and even then only after a time lag—and the short-run prospect is for more misery rather than less. It is therefore imperative that the problem of force be brought into focus.

Rational understanding cannot accept the claims that force is either a *prima* or an *ultima ratio*. Force must be seen instead as something in between the first and final instruments of politics. Rational policy must seek to prevent violence, but it cannot condemn its use out of hand and in every circumstance. Nor can rational policy renounce the resort to force on its own behalf in situations where its own existence is at stake. There will continue to be those, in both international and domestic politics, who argue that violence is the only way to get things done, and it is necessary to be prepared to deal with them should they move from words to deeds. The terrible and historic dilemma is still operative: the rational man can neither desire nor reject violence, and the nuclear dimension has only intensified the anguish of his situation.

If the banishment of violence is an illusory hope, it is equally illusory to suppose that the world can survive without unremitting effort to eliminate the causes of violence. Since even the wisest and most vigorous efforts cannot be wholly successful, however, one must be prepared to restrict the intensity of violence wherever preventive measures have failed. This unavoidable acceptance of the possibilities and probabilities of violence, in turn, demands a set of guidelines for thinking about the phenomenon of force. Every political society, of course, has a policy toward the use of violence, but the rush of events has often thrown these policies into disarray. Since Hiroshima, moreover, the manifest irrationality of nuclear war has made rational thinking about the use of force infinitely more difficult. A viable policy toward force at every level from bricks and paving-stones to nuclear warheads seems almost impossible to achieve. Yet there must be at least an approximation of such a policy if catastrophic mistakes are to be avoided.

A viable policy to deal with the problem of force should be able to identify its wellsprings and anticipate the likelihood of its use. It should be able to judge the utility of violence. It should also be able to judge the justice of a resort to force, with the understanding that utility and morality are not obviously identical. Finally, such a policy can be viable only if it seeks simultaneously to root out the causes of violence and limit its use. In short, it must be animated by a resolute will to move away from the coercive end of the power spectrum and toward consent. Neither pacifists nor terrorists could endorse such guidelines. A more detailed examination is now in order to see whether these guidelines will commend themselves to others.

It has already been argued in this chapter and in the preceding ones that any policy which does not anticipate continuing outbreaks of violence is wholly out of touch with reality. World history since 1945 is sufficient testimony concerning things still to come. In addition to the direct and indirect collisions of the major powers, civil and international violence has broken out again and again in the underdeveloped world. To make the lesson complete, it is necessary to record the ominous increase in violent acts and violent attitudes within the societies of the developed world. Whether one looks at ideologies of the Right or the Left, at international society or domestic society, it is evident that there are many who accept and some who prefer violence as an instrument of politics.

VIOLENCE AND POVERTY

The causes that produce violent events and violent attitudes are many and will not soon disappear. Most evident, of course, is the marked correlation between poverty and violence. Equally evident is the fact that most of the world is poor and will be for some time to come. When he was secretary of defense, Robert McNamara used the years 1958 to 1966 to illustrate some lessons about the role of violence across the world. Of the 164 "internationally significant outbreaks of violence" in these eight years, only fifteen were military conflicts between two or more states; the rest were internal upheavals. Of the internal conflicts, more than two-thirds occurred in the eighty poorest countries and nearly one-third in the thirty-seven middle-income countries. Among the twenty-seven rich countries there was only one such outbreak.[1]

The lesson to be drawn, from this period at least, is that the poorer the society, the more likely it is to experience violence, whereas the rich societies are virtually immune. The subsequent rise in violence in the industrial nations, whatever its own intrinsic dangers, is not likely to alter significantly these correlations between poverty and appeals to arms. Indeed, as the United States in particular demonstrates, the presence of poverty within the developed society is the most evident source both of violence and of justifications for its use.

It has been pointed out often enough—and correctly—that the poor are not necessarily more prone to violence than other people. As long as poverty is accepted by the poor as an immutable fact of life there is little inclination to attempt to better their lot by force. It is only when a persuasive hope for betterment is injected into the culture of poverty that a significant potential for violence emerges. From this point on the elements making for an explosion multiply, and the longer poverty persists, the greater the prospects for the use of force. This infiltration of hope into the culture of poverty has now occurred across the globe and constitutes the greatest single breeding ground for violence in the last third of the twentieth century.

The Machiavellian lament, still heard, that the poor should not have been offered hope in the first place is now as unrealistic as it is unjust. The rich minority of mankind cannot help but continue to give daily demonstrations of the possibilities for massive change in every corner of the globe; its very existence is a daily stimulus to prodigious hopes. The minority literally brandishes the fruits of its own development before the eyes of the poor and both consciously and unconsciously prescribes emulation. The rich themselves initiated the dynamic of world development, and it cannot be interrupted or slowed down without the most tragic consequences for both rich and poor.

It is for some of these reasons that Secretary McNamara rejected the notion that military hardware is the best security against violence. In-

---

[1] Secretary McNamara used World Bank categories in classifying the countries involved: rich nations are those with more than $750 annual per capita income (in 1966 the United States per capita income was more than $2700); middle-income nations are those with $250 to $749 annual per capita income; poor nations: $100 to $249; very poor nations: under $100.

McNamara used another statistical probe to make the same point: in the period under consideration "87 percent of the very poor nations, 69 percent of the poor nations, and 48 percent of the middle-income nations have suffered serious violence." Robert S. McNamara, Address to the American Society of Newspaper Editors, Montreal, May 18, 1966.

stead he advanced what for a defense secretary is a rather dramatic formulation: "security is development. Without development there can be no security." While McNamara used this definition of security within the specific context of the developing state, he also made it clear that the security of the United States and other economically advanced countries is directly related to the degree of success attained by the developing world itself in achieving the security that only development can bring.[2] Without development the incidence of violence will increase. The spread of violence among the global poor affects the security of the global rich just as surely as civil violence in the ghetto affects the security of the suburb. The challenge is clear: whoever would diminish violence in international or domestic society must commit himself to a sustained attack on poverty at home and abroad.

FORCE, LAW, AND ORDER

There is more than one parallel between domestic and international politics to be found in this issue. McNamara's discussion of world security reflects the familiar debate on the home front between the idea of law and order and the idea of social justice. "Law and order" advocates generally promote the use of enhanced police power (military hardware) as the preferred instrument to drive down the crime rate and reduce the frequency of other forms of violent and illegal behavior in civil society. "Social justice" partisans, on the other hand, rely primarily on recipes for social change (development) designed to reform the environment from which violence and illegality emanates.

McNamara, both as defense secretary and, subsequently, as head of the World Bank, has clearly represented the social justice school of thought. It is obvious, of course, that one who for seven years presided over the world's mightiest armed forces would also have a sober appreciation of the importance of military hardware. For just this reason McNamara's consignment of the military to an auxiliary role in the search for security has unique cogency—even if one finds irony in the fact that during McNamara's own period in office the American military budget was on occasion almost thirty times the amount of money devoted to foreign economic aid.[3]

There are plenty of ironies in the debate between justice and law and order precisely because each needs the other to be durable and because,

---

[2] Ibid. The McNamara formulation is essentially identical with the pronouncement of Pope Paul VI that "development is the new name for peace." "Populorum Progressio" (On the Development of Peoples), the fifth encyclical of Paul VI, March 26, 1967.

[3] It should be noted that McNamara, more than any other secretary of defense, allocated major sums of defense monies to quasi-military and military-support activities that could double as investments in development.

ideally, they should form a unity. But the basic issue must not be obscured: force of arms can offer that kind of law and order, or "peace," associated with the garrison. On the other hand, only the satisfaction of legitimate demands and the social changes this satisfaction necessarily entails can offer the kind of peace, law, and order that do not rest on fear and repression and that can therefore promise durability, trust, and a life worth living.

We have seen that there is a distinct correlation between poverty and violence only where there has been an injection of hope for justice into the daily lives of the poor. The concept of social justice moves us still further beyond the simplistic assumption that economic deprivation, by itself, is the sole or even chief source of violence. It is true, once the global masses of poor are aroused from their traditional passivity, that only a successful attack on world-wide poverty can reduce the level of world-wide violence. But the attack on poverty is only part of the task. Social justice has many other meanings besides the righting of economic wrongs. Racism, chauvinism, class arrogance, intellectual or ideological exclusivism—in short, egotism and elitism of every kind—are all enemies of social justice and agents of violence. The presence of these dismal phenomena in all their abundance will be examined in some detail later in this book. Here it should be noted that all the elements of elitism are operative in international and domestic politics alike and produce similar results in both contexts.

It is obvious that human egotism, whether of the individual or group variety, is a far more complex problem than human poverty. Given the technical resources available in our own time, it is possible to speak realistically about such a goal as the effective elimination of poverty. But it would be wholly unrealistic to suppose that one could ever eliminate the self-centeredness of either mass man or man as individual. At the same time, anyone concerned with the problem of violence cannot avoid the truth that human pride far outclasses human poverty as a fomentor of conflict. Imperial ambitions, ideological and religious crusades, racial obsessions, and Caesarian complexes have killed many more millions of people than the desire to escape from poverty. Indeed, most of those who made war for material gains were already rich and merely wanted to become richer. Not their poverty but their greed made them violent. The relief of human destitution must therefore be regarded only as a necessary but not sufficient answer to the problem of violence. Violence can be controlled, regulated, and diminished only where benevolence countervails selfishness, and this can occur only where mutual trust and respect outweigh mutual fear and contempt.

The inescapable conclusion has already been drawn in the previous chapters: the central task of the politician is to create conditions of trust and consent. But it is evident that the task is one of extraordinary difficulty. The ineradicable persistence of human conceit creates and recreates conditions of violence. It is therefore an illusion to suppose that the goal of pacification can ever be fully achieved. Vanity can never be conquered; it can only be contained. For this reason alone violence will challenge man's existence as long as history endures. Ever new expressions of individual and group egotisms will tax the imaginations of ever new seekers of community in a dialectic that points to no foreseeable end or resolution. Those who desire to inhibit violence in our own time must therefore regard every success—and every failure—as temporary. They must accept violence as a permanent nemesis that can be contained in each era of history only by an expanding sense of community responding to the manifest needs of the time.

One can assert that pride is more violent than poverty and still identify poverty as the prime breeding ground of violence. This is because the masses of poor have always been, and are now more than ever, recruitment reservoirs for men who preach an end to poverty but whose real objectives are often only tenuously related to economic uplift. The strength of numbers, even in the nuclear age, is not to be denied, and throughout history, with the exception of the modern industrial West, this strength has resided with the poor.

At the global level the poor today constitute the vast majority. Living in misery and obsessed with the desire for change, the impoverished majority is the demagogue's fortune and the ideal instrument with which to gratify ulterior motives. The demagogue teaches violence to the poor not as a means to free them from poverty but in order to enlist them in the service of nation, race, class, or ideology and, above all, for the gratification of the demagogue's own distended ego. If the demagogue's happiest hunting ground is denied him by virtue of the conquest of poverty, he always has other contexts in which to operate. But the elimination of human penury would reduce the scope and impact of the demagogue's violence more than any other single achievement.

THE UTILITY OF FORCE

The presence of human poverty and the permanence of human selfishness make it both possible and necessary to speak of the utility of force. Force is an expensive technique for the exercise of power, it is often counterproductive, and it is morally perilous. But none of these strictures can deny that there are circumstances in which force is useful. Its primary utility is defensive. In an environment where many are willing to use force wherever they detect weakness, the presence of counterforce is a useful restraint. It becomes indispensable once an attack is actually launched. The only qualification comes when resistance to armed attack is clearly hopeless. If the ratio of forces is such that submission to enemy demands is inevitable, it is usually wiser to submit before rather than after the ordeal of death and destruction and seek to live on in hope of a better day. Denmark in 1940 and Czechoslovakia in 1938 and 1968 are tragic but telling instances of the choice for capitulation.

The defensive utility of force is ancient doctrine, but it needs to be tested against two objections, one of long standing and one that is new. In their abhorrence of violence, pacifists have traditionally argued the case for nonviolent resistance. In the ideal world of pacifism, of course, there would be nothing to resist since all men would be living together according to the precepts of human brotherhood. But as soon as it is conceded that in the real world there are men of violence, the problem of resistance becomes manifest. The pacifist does not wish merely to avoid violence; he must condemn it. He must therefore oppose all who wield or condone resort to the instruments of force. He cannot run from violence but must fight against it—with nonviolent means. His weapons are verbal and symbolic. When their arguments have failed, many pacifists have literally laid their bodies on the line and suffered the pain of martyrdom.

Despite the heroism of many in their ranks, pacifists have not been able to demonstrate the efficacy of their principles. If one were merely intent upon avoiding physical combat, a commitment to passive non-violence might offer a fairly good probability of physical survival. But the pacifist is not interested so much in survival as in the vindication of his values. Thus, just like the nonpacifist, he will resist threats to the values he cherishes. He must be actively nonviolent. It is at this juncture that the issue is joined: Are nonviolent techniques of resistance adequate to the purposes they are designed to serve?

The answer can only be negative. The movements led by Gandhi and by Martin Luther King demonstrated that the ideology and practice of nonviolence could generate a formidable political power. But it was not sufficient to achieve the objectives sought. Neither movement was en-tirely free of violent acts. The successes of both, moreover, were due in considerable part to the fear that the injustices they dramatized would provoke greater violence if no concessions were made while the rebel-lion was still pacifist in commitment. Further, both the independence of India and the gains in racial equality in the United States have been products of a complex history only one of whose elements was the per-suasive energy of nonviolence. Finally, neither Gandhi nor King could have achieved their unique moral and political eminence if their aims had not been shared to a significant degree by their antagonists. In a totalitarian society they would have been shot by the government rather than, as it happened in fact, by outlaws.

Pacifism has no chance whenever contestants believe that their aims are diametrically opposed. One can attribute the phenomena of both non-violent dispute and cooperation to the happy fact that such beliefs do not always obtain. But they recur with enough regularity in both domestic and international politics to deny the possibility of any final farewell to arms. History admonishes men to anticipate violence even as they seek peace, and to be prepared for both. Pacifism can be a useful and even admirable tactic to deal with specific challenges. But it can never serve as a strategy to deal with all contingencies.

NUCLEAR PACIFISM

The new argument against the defensive utility of force was born with the atomic age. The nuclear presence has enveloped the ancient debate concerning the role of violence in an even more somber atmosphere. Proponents of nuclear pacifism argue that no human value (such as national independence, political freedom) is so important that it could justify lighting the nuclear fires in its defense. The argument is pressed home by the assertion that the value to be defended would in any case be automatically destroyed by the very act of resorting to nuclear defense. It is true that most competent analysts envision a variety of possible outcomes in a nuclear war and reject the automaticity of oblivion. But they cannot deny the presently existing possibilities for approaching total destruction of life and environment, nor the fact that the possibilities grow more numerous as technology continues to refine the instruments of annihilation. The challenge of nuclear pacifism is one with which it is agonizingly difficult to deal because nuclear weaponry has eroded all the familiar rationales for the use of all-out force.

The nuclear years have, in fact, marked the supreme triumph of relativism. They have injected an unprecedented uncertainty into human existence: uncertainty about the future, uncertainty about whether the old rules of domestic and international politics still make any sense, uncertainty about human survival and human purpose. How many would risk igniting the holocaust to defend liberty and equality or, for that matter, authority and hierarchy? The answer certainly is: a sufficient number. But most of these are among the reckless rebels and reactionaries who willfully refuse to consider the consequences of their acts.

Those who understand nuclear consequences, on the other hand, cannot help but wonder about their values and about their own loyalty to these values. Thus the relatively rational and moderate center of the political spectrum is tempted to agree that no human purpose can justify a nuclear test of strength. The results are a tendency to discourage any search for verities that might be worth dying or killing for and a desire to keep the nuclear lid on at all costs. Another result is that the moderate center runs the danger of being drained of energy and conviction and, consequently, weakened in its confrontations with the extremes. The final and ironic product of this exercise in relativism is the emergence of survival itself as an absolute value to which all others must be sacrificed.

Thus the nuclear giant puts human integrity on the spot more poignantly than ever before. It is, however, the same old spot—mightily magnified—that numberless heroes and martyrs, servants of peace and defenders of justice, including pacifists like Gandhi and King, have known so well in the past. They took the classic position: survival is not everything. It is, still today, the only position that can prevent the erosion of all values—and the ultimate delivery of the nuclear choice into the sole possession of the reckless. Once this juncture is reached, the game is up anyway. If one must fear escalation to the nuclear peak, one must also fear that deescalation in which every norm is tossed aside in the struggle to stay alive. The courage to endure risks continues to be relevant even in the new dimensions of the nuclear age.

It is certainly man's interest and duty to reduce the risks of nuclear confrontation, but it is an illusion to suppose that all risks can be banished. The knowledge of the nuclear secret has become an irrevocable part of human history and cannot be unlearned. It has often been argued that armaments are only symptoms and not causes of conflict. The thesis is oversimple, but it nonetheless expresses a truth whose significance is mightily enhanced in the nuclear age. Since the nuclear symptom can never be permanently exorcised, the premium on success in dealing with the causes of conflict has never been greater. The continuing resolve to remove the sources of belligerence and the continuing pursuit of the politics of consent are the only available insurance against the holocaust. They also offer the only hope that nuclear armaments may in time be reduced to less dangerous levels.

In the meantime, the policies of both the United States and the Soviet Union, as their arsenals attest, are committed to the use of nuclear weapons as the ultimate instruments of their wills. One may disagree with the policies, but one cannot ignore the fact that they exist. The nuclear commitment is the heart and soul of deterrence strategy, and even if the gulf of suspicion between the superpowers narrows, there are no rational grounds for supposing that the deterrence relationship will soon be drastically transformed. Indeed, mankind lives in a world in which the governments of all the nuclear powers—and the available evidence indicates that they have the active or tacit support of the vast majority of their citizenry in this matter—would prefer to pull the atomic trigger rather than permit their opponents to dictate their fate.

If only a long-range enterprise to remove the causes of hostility can prevent an ultimate resort to nuclear weapons, only the will to use them in the interim can make the enterprise possible. A peaceful world in which enmity is replaced by a creative mixture of cooperation and disagreement can be achieved only by mutual accommodation and never by a process in which one state or ideology dictates to the rest. Here the balance of power, now in its nuclear guise as the balance of terror, plays its essential role. Those who hold power with no fear of counterpower will serve only the interests of the powerful—that is, their own. Those who possess and have the will to use nuclear power will dictate to those who lack nuclear weapons or nuclear will, or both.[4]

Some friends of peace via unilateral disarmament have fostered the illusion (borrowed, ironically enough, from Hobbes) that the surrender of all nuclear capacities to a single nuclear power might result in an evolution from an admittedly repellent short-term slavery to an eventually benevolent society of undivided humanity. The illusion is intrinsic because the presence of counterpower is essential, if not sufficient, to transform relationships of command into relationships of consent. Moreover, the illusory nature of the proposal can easily be put to empirical test as soon as one asks which of today's nuclear powers would be ready to nominate one of their number—or even the United Nations—to be sole custodian of nuclear weapons. One must admit, however regretfully, that the world is going to have to continue to live with a multiplicity of atomic arsenals. The idea of a nuclear monopoly provides no real exit from a dilemma destined to persist for an indeterminate period of time.

In such a world no one can escape the terrible question: Are there any circumstances in which I would endorse the use of nuclear weapons? Each person must find his own answer. Those who answer yes, as does the writer, assume an appalling responsibility and may be tragically wrong. But the same may be said of those who answer no. Those who prefer, for themselves or mankind, survival over all other values frequently get what they are looking for—a valueless existence. Frequently, too, the sacrifice of all other values does not achieve the survival so ardently desired. In the final analysis, no one can say with certainty whether nuclear pacifism or acceptance of the nuclear contingency represents the more dangerous stance. The only certain result of nuclear pacifism is that the nuclear option will eventually be vested in men and nations less pacifically inclined.

OFFENSIVE AND DEFENSIVE FORCE

So far the whole discussion of the utility of force, both nuclear and conventional, has assumed a defensive rather than offensive motivation. But it must be said that the offensive use of force has also demonstrated its

---

[4] It is for this reason that nonnuclear states such as India seek nuclear "umbrellas" —guarantees from friendly nuclear states that will commit the guarantor to threaten and, if need be, use nuclear force to protect the nonnuclear state from having to capitulate to a hostile nuclear state. It is also, of course, the American nuclear capacity that provides the crucial protection for a militarily weak Western Europe just as the Soviet atomic arsenal is the final support of the militarily and politically weak governments of Eastern Europe.

utility, up to and including the nuclear level. After all, the first and so far only military resort to atomic weaponry was offensive in nature. The bombs that fell on Hiroshima and Nagasaki did not constitute a last-ditch response to an intolerable threat; they functioned instead as a means to hasten the end of a war with an enemy doomed in any case to certain defeat. It is clear that they cruelly fulfilled that function. This is not the place to join in the unending argument of whether the achievement of an important but obviously secondary goal justified the American decision either in terms of expediency or morality. Here it must suffice to record as dispassionately as possible that the offensive use of nuclear weapons attained the objective sought.

Imperial Japan, of course, was not an atomic power; in 1945 the United States was the nuclear monopolist and did not need to fear retaliation in kind. The moment the nuclear monopoly was broken, however, the value of offensive nuclear use plummeted. The lesson to be drawn is that the threat or actual use of offensive nuclear power can be extremely effective against a nonnuclear state devoid of reliable nuclear allies but that the margin of utility virtually vanishes when the foe has comparable nuclear strength.

No one can read the massive literature of nuclear strategy without conceding the possibility that in some circumstances a nuclear offensive against a nuclear enemy could confer the benefits of "victory." It is this possibility that is at the heart of the nuclear arms race. It generates the fear that one's opponent will discover a technique of self-protection which so reduces his vulnerability that he will consider an offensive nuclear strike "worth" the terrible wounds he would inevitably sustain himself.

In the language of the nuclear strategists, each side is tempted to build a first strike capability on the grounds that the one who strikes second—in retaliation—must necessarily be less effective since his nuclear system will have already been damaged. It is true that during the 1960s both the United States and the Soviet Union developed retaliatory systems assumed to be invulnerable—that is, each could strike back and destroy the other no matter how much initial damage was inflicted by the one who struck first. But it is also true that the validity of the invulnerability assumption must be constantly tested in the light of unfolding military technology. Should, for example, one side alone deploy an even partially effective antiballistic missile (ABM) system against incoming nuclear warheads, both the offensive and the retaliatory capability of the opponent would be drastically reduced. In this situation the relative equality of vulnerability (or invulnerability) would vanish.

These are some of the considerations that finally produced the 1972 Treaty on Limitation of Anti-Ballistic Missile Systems, the first concrete achievement of Soviet and American negotiators in the Strategic Arms Limitation Talks (SALT) begun in 1969. The Treaty, in effect, arrested the installation and evolution of ABM technology at an early stage. Rather than risk precipitating a costly and destabilizing new phase of the arms race, Moscow and Washington agreed to confine their ABM systems to the two deployment areas each had already begun to develop. The Treaty restrictions confirmed in the most dramatic way possible the enormous pressures on the strategic nuclear balance that the ABM has generated. As we shall see subsequently, the Treaty was linked to an interim agreement providing for a five-year freeze on the number of offensive missiles each side could deploy.

The major effect of SALT 1972, therefore, was to prolong the situation reached in the 1960s: a rough parity in the terrifying offensive capabilities of the two superpowers and in the terrifying weakness of their defensive capabilities. Vulnerability to hostile attack and invulnerability of retaliatory forces—this is the combination that treaty and agreement together sought to perpetuate as the formula for nuclear balance and security. Their rationale is evident. If neither superpower can defend its own population from catastrophic nuclear attack (by means of a comprehensive ABM or other defensive system), and if both can visit the other with catastrophe no matter which one attacks first, the inhibitions against launching an attack are virtually absolute. Unless, that is, new technologies and new fears and suspicions once again upset the balance—and the agreements.

Thus the stability of nuclear deterrence must always be the product of ad hoc agreements not to let technological capabilities, or political ambitions, destroy superpower parity. But ad hoc agreements are not always easy to reach (or to abide by), and the SALT agreements have certainly not brought the evolution of nuclear technology to a halt.

If one then factors into the deterrence problem the growing capacities for chemical and electronic warfare and the rise of nuclear powers other than the United States and Soviet Russia, stability begins to look more like instability, subject to only the most precarious restraints. In such a context of dynamic change one can never reject out of hand the offensive utility of nuclear or any other kind of nonconventional force. The entire history of techniques of warfare has been marked by a dialectic of offense and defense in which first one and then the other gained the advantage in an unending seesaw race. While the nuclear age is profoundly revolutionary in many respects, it has not succeeded in bringing this ancient dialectic to a halt.

If one must concede that the offensive use of nuclear force may have "utility," the offensive utility of conventional violence is illustrated almost daily. In international relations the attacker (provoked or unprovoked) often achieves his objectives: China in Tibet and India, North Vietnam in Indochina, India in Goa, Israel in the Middle East, Russia in Hungary and Czechoslovakia are some of the obvious examples since

World War II. In many areas of Africa and Asia it was the decision of those who suffered under colonialism to take the offensive, to resort to revolutionary force, that finally convinced the defenders of the colonial status quo that their brand of imperialism was bankrupt. If we think of Indonesia, Indochina, Kenya, and Algeria as outstanding examples of successful armed revolutions against twentieth-century colonialism, it is also useful to recall their eighteenth-century prototype, the American Revolution.

The offensive utility of force is demonstrated in domestic revolutions as well as in international wars and colonial revolts. Soviet Russia, Franco's Spain, Communist China, and Castro's Cuba stand as monuments, however tarnished, to the efficacy of violence in internal politics. In an age of coups and countercoups, ethnic and class rebellions, and struggles between elites and urban and rural guerillas on nearly every continent it is manifest that violence, or the threat of its use, calls the political tune for far more of mankind than does the peaceful and equitable implementation of the majority or public will.

The evidence is clear: almost everyone at one time or another and in one circumstance or another deems violence useful. Victory in war or revolution is the supreme, if often tragic, reward that political violence can offer, but there are many other forms of the utility of force. They begin with the primitive sense of self-assertion and gratification the schoolboy feels when he discovers the power of his fists. The discovery leads some into the sado-masochistic world of the Marquis de Sade, although most learn to accept various combinations of physical, social, psychic, and moral limitations on the uses of violence. No one, however, is immune to the arguments that both emotion and reason can summon up in favor of force. In times of great international or domestic upheaval only the few can maintain their stance in opposition to violence, and still fewer exhibit inner confidence in their nonviolent convictions.

Whether the times are quiet or not, it is a generally accepted rule of social existence that the police power must include the option of force in upholding the civil authority. No government in history has functioned in the absence of this rule, but many have collapsed because they have failed, for whatever reason, to apply it. On the other side of the coin, the revolutionary must ultimately challenge the police power of the state, matching threats and actual use of rebel force against the existing and potential instruments of violence at the disposal of the state.

Even ineffectual displays of rebel violence against the state are valued by dissidents as a means of "radicalizing" public opinion—at least that portion of it most likely to resent the use of force by civil authority. This is an ancient technique in the use of violence; yet it is treated as a novelty each time a new generation of rebels rediscovers it. The recurring surprise is due, certainly in part, to the fact that both the fear of violence and the taste for it slumber in every individual. Most people, for good and sufficient reasons, would just as soon not think about the problem too deeply or too often.

More than ever in the nuclear age, however, violence needs to be thought about. Both in the social context in which he lives and in the individuality of his psychic structure, man's problem with violence is an insoluble one. That is, it is not a problem which can be mastered and finally disposed of. It will haunt mankind as long as there are boys with fists. The real challenge is not one of eliminating violence but of putting it under restraints and limiting its domain. It is one of creating conditions domestically and internationally that offer the prospect of peaceful and equitable resolutions for disputes and grievances.

Such a prospect can emerge only from a climate of hope based on previous visible achievement. Since the disputes and grievances within and between nations across the globe are numerous and all too often immense, the short-run prospects for limiting and restraining violence are not encouraging. A measure of success in dealing with some of the causes of violence would promise, at best, somewhat better odds against outbreaks of violence over the longer run.

Rational analysis cannot escape the conclusion that violence has its uses and gratifications from the level of individual self-assertion all the way up to the level of major wars and revolutions. Only the gullible will believe that violence never achieves anything or that the achievements of violence are always outweighed by the evil they involve. Lovers of peace must proceed from the fact that political violence can be a highly effective means of achieving political goals. They may decry the resort to force, but their real task is to demonstrate the superiority of alternative methods in the political process. Only convincing and continuing demonstrations of this kind can keep violence at bay and prevent it from dominating man's political life.

FLAWS IN THE UTILITY CONCEPT

Effective restraints on the use of violence cannot be derived from any analysis which restricts itself simply to a consideration of the utility of resorts to force. If it is conceded that force has sometimes proved itself useful, one must necessarily ask not whether force should ever be used but under what circumstances. The concept of utility can offer only one underlying and fundamental answer: force should be used when one is strong but not when one is weak. The utility of force assumes the immediate or eventual triumph of physical strength over physical weakness. It does not require the strong always to use force; it merely provides a criterion to decide, when occasion demands, whether the resort to force is rational.

But the criterion of physical superiority is beset by multiple difficulties, the first of which is the uncertainty involved in the measurement of superiority and inferiority. It is easy to conclude that the Soviet Union is stronger than Czechoslovakia. It is more difficult to determine the relative strengths of the Soviet Union and the United States. Moreover, as we have seen from the discussion of the balance of power, the weaker state in any given dispute may compensate for its weakness by recruiting allies. As in the case of Germany in two world wars, recourse to violence by the initially stronger state can lead to its own ruin at the hands of a hostile coalition. The belated entry of the United States into both wars illustrates a characteristic phenomenon in international politics (and in domestic politics as well): the unleashing of violence by the "stronger" is the chief stimulus in mobilizing an opposing coalition that eventually may be stronger still.

Finally, the element of "surprise" can never be eliminated from the calculations. Not only "secret weapons" but general mobilization potential in technology and economics fall into this category. A test of strength between a heavily armed government and a ragged band of guerillas may reveal unsuspected social and political weaknesses where strength was assumed—and vice versa. At the international level, the military confrontation between the United States and North Vietnam is a painful and portentous example of this kind of "surprise."

Balance of power dynamics join the inherent difficulties in accurately measuring military strengths and weaknesses to make the criterion of physical superiority a highly ambiguous guide to the application of force. Ambiguity, in turn, vitiates the restraints on violence that the calculus of force is supposed to provide. The utilitarian assumption that violence will be restrained by the fear of counterviolence is undermined by the long history of miscalculations concerning the relative strengths of the parties in contention. In case after case they have gone to war in violation of the utilitarian standard of physical superiority because they did not or could not measure "superiority" accurately.

Still more frequently, of course, the utilitarian standard was abandoned because of a combination of faulty assessments of military might and a commitment to values other than those included in the concept of utility. There have always been both individuals and societies that preferred, wisely or not, to go down fighting a superior enemy rather than capitulate at the outset. In such situations, of course, there was usually an eminently utilitarian hope that a powerful friend, a "surprise," or a "miracle" would save the weaker from otherwise inevitable defeat. These hopes have in fact been fulfilled often enough so that they will continue to play their parts in the drama of war and peace for the foreseeable future.

The rule of thumb that one should not use violence if one is inferior in strength is certainly not without its relevant message. It tells India or Mexico that it would be folly to attack China or the United States (though the message becomes garbled if the issue is not attack but resistance to attack). But it is too crude a rule of thumb: the probabilities are high that a policy guided exclusively or even primarily by its precepts will in the long run fail of its objectives.

Any crude and ambiguous standard of conduct is bound to be more often violated than honored. Indeed, reliance on the concept of the utility of force fosters more violence than it hinders because it places a premium on the competitive acquisition of physical strength by all parties concerned. It assigns coercion the leading role in political life. As noted in the discussion of power, the greater the emphasis on coercion, the more intense the emotion of fear. While fear is not necessarily an irrational emotion (it is obviously rational to fear nuclear war) it is a more fertile source of irrationality in politics than any other. The conclusion is evident: utility and irrationality must inevitably conflict, and any concept of utility that incites rather than diminishes irrationality is clearly self-defeating.

It is a commonplace though frequently neglected understanding of political science that no society can endure in peace whose internal structure is held together chiefly because the physically weaker faction fears to attack the stronger. Such a society is bound to be ungovernable except by violence. This is the prime meaning of the time-honored observation that one can do everything with bayonets except sit on them. It is true that fear has been a way of life for many societies over long periods of time, but it is also true that their histories have been punctuated by every kind of violence from palace coups and purges to mass imprisonments, mass executions, and civil war. If the thrall of fear makes domestic societies ungovernable except by violence, the same applies to international society. Indeed, mutually enhancing premiums on force and fear have characterized the international way of life since its inception with all the predictable violent results.

Force can serve useful functions but not unless it is governed by considerations other than relative capacities for violence. In those cases where one can accurately distinguish between strength and weakness, reckoning in terms of the utility of force can certainly be useful—at least in the short run—to the strong. It can serve the weak, also in the short run, only in confirming their weakness. In the long run, however, the weak have often absorbed the lessons taught by the utility of force and have set about developing the capacities for violence which finally overmatched their erstwhile masters. This is the core history of every successful armed revolution. Not every revolutionary movement is successful, but even aborted rebellions force the strong to make sacrifices they would otherwise prefer to avoid. A society governed by the utility of force is thus a high-risk society—and for every element in the society. Superior force may protect the rulers for a long time, in some cases even for generations. But the risks are high, and regimes of force inevitably build up a terrible legacy.

FORCE AND JUSTICE

The crux of the issue is reached when one asks: What is the utility of force for all men? Politics governed by the standard of superior strength can only result in advantaging one part of mankind and disadvantaging the other part: it benefits those who are currently strong and harms those who are currently weak. Far more often than not, whether in domestic politics or in the world at large, the strong constitute a minority and the weak a majority. This is abundantly true today in the confrontation between the developed and underdeveloped worlds. There is thus a high correlation between minority rule and the kind of politics that reckons in terms of the utility of force. If force is to perform a useful function for more than a minority—ideally for all men—the concept of utility must be supplemented by, and subordinated to, the concept of justice.

This proposition, of course, is an extension of themes introduced by the opening chapters on power. It was argued there that the power calculus is an inadequate frame of reference if one wishes to maximize consent and minimize coercion and control in either domestic or international politics. It was further argued that a realistic pursuit of such an objective requires the introduction of a value judgment rooted in considerations other than power, namely, that the purpose of politics is not to control men but to liberate them. Similar considerations apply to the calculus of force. The utility of force cannot be gainsaid, but whoever wishes to minimize its frequency and intensity and maximize its service to all men must condone a resort to force only in the cause of justice.

Such a proposition opens up a Pandora's box of issues. Who is to decide what is "just"? What of the Machiavellian dictum that the only real choice is between the greater evil and the lesser; how can evil, even if a lesser one, be just? How can one deal with concepts of justice that produce bloody crusades and inquisitions instead of peace and liberty? What of the concept of relative justice that springs from the knowledge that no dispute in human affairs ever reveals one side to have a monopoly of right and the other of wrong? How can one posit a universal standard of justice in the face of a bewildering diversity of cultures and of individual and social norms? Is not the idea of justice always fated to be only a smoke screen masking less benevolent concerns? Is there not a natural repugnance between justice and force? What *is* justice?

An analysis of world politics can examine such a formidable array of questions only as it gains in depth and comprehensiveness; the subsequent chapters will seek to further this process. Even then, what answers do emerge must of necessity be controversial and not final. But the issue of justice must be raised now. Violence is the tragedy of politics and justice its promise. Those who seek from politics the good society must come to grips with the phenomenon of violence. Those who define politics simply as the pursuit of power—by violence, if necessary—must not be permitted to duck the issue of justice. Without a moral evaluation of the role of violence any analysis of international politics (or domestic politics) must be rootless, timid, and, in the end, unconvincing.

Any discussion of justice must begin with a definition: justice is that behavior, individual and social, which treats human beings as ends in themselves and not as means to the ends of others. This paraphrase of Kant also paraphrases the central ethical norms of the Christian and Judaic doctrines of which Kant's categorical imperative is the best-known secular expression. If one were seeking a more comprehensive pedigree, one could easily link Islam to this ethical heritage and then proceed, perhaps with gradually diminishing returns, to research all the other great and obscure religions and philosophies of the world. In political analysis, however, it will be more profitable simply to treat the definition of justice just given in the approved scientific manner, that is, as a working hypothesis whose validity must be tested against factual knowledge and by rational examination.

On this hypothesis, force may be justly used only when it furthers the objective of treating all men as ends in themselves. This assumption provides, at first glance, a reasonably watertight rationale for criminal justice. The criminal is one who, by definition, flagrantly violates the proscription against using other men to serve one's own purposes. Murder, rape, abduction, arson, and theft are among the obvious and standard crimes against the rights of other human beings. The whole idea of rights, in turn, stems from political, social, philosophical, or religious attempts to give expression to the concept that men should be treated as ends in themselves.

But the situation of the criminal is not unambiguous. Even a cursory survey of the diversity of culture and custom among states, and within states, makes it evident that what is criminal in one jurisdiction may not be criminal in another. Variation in space is matched by variation in time. Noncriminal behavior (prostitution or slaveholding, for example) may become criminal, and criminal behavior (such as peddling pornography or lynching) may become noncriminal as social attitudes change. Fluctuating standards for judging criminal acts and for subjecting the criminal to forcible punishment constantly undermine a universal and essentially moral definition of crime as a violation of human rights.

Several other objections suggest themselves. Many sociologists and psychiatrists argue that the criminal is a victim of his social or psychological circumstance and question how he can be held responsible for a situation over which he has minimal control or none at all. Here they come close to Marx and others who generally tend to deal with crime as the inevitable product of a faulty socioeconomic system. In this school of thought punishment is fundamentally out of place. The reform-minded would substitute "rehabilitation" for punishment and prefer "houses of correction" to prisons, thus coupling their ideals with a reluctant acceptance of forcible confinement. For their part, the revolutionaries make their practical compromise with the idea of criminal incarceration with the argument that it is unavoidable until that day when social revolution finally banishes criminality. Even the less extreme position that holds criminal and society jointly responsible poses the question which asks why the criminal alone should suffer punishment in cases where society should be regarded as a codefendant. The fact that society ordinarily pays the costs of adjudication and custody is hardly a satisfactory response.

In the abstract, the criminal arbitrarily deprives his fellow man of life, liberty, happiness, or property and is therefore unjust. The conclusion is that crime must be punished by forcing the guilty to endure similar kinds of deprivations, on the understanding that these deprivations are not arbitrary but legitimate penalties to chastise the transgressor and to warn any would-be imitators. But those who regard the criminal as more sinned against than sinning or arraign society at least as codefendant cannot be satisfied with a system that simply matches criminal with judicial ferocity.

When civil law and political crime enter into consideration the relativity of human justice requires a still more searching scrutiny. To cite only two examples, sanctity of contract and sanctity of property have served as classic façades to camouflage the realities of human exploitation. This does not mean that such concepts have no intrinsic moral worth as guardians of human integrity, but the global record shows a long and still unfinished history of legal toleration, and even approval, of abuses for which they have often provided a rationale. Legislatures and courts have, of course, punished abuses and reinterpreted concepts in order to prevent their being suborned. But all this is still further testimony to the uncertainty and variableness of human standards of right and wrong.

The ambiguities of moral obligation in human society are in evidence at every level from the practice of violence by the individual criminal to the uses of violence in revolution and war. In the Western theory of sovereignty the state alone has the legal right to use violence in its role as protector of the community. But those who believe a given state exploits rather than protects the community and who deny the possibility of peaceful reform of civil society will reject the legitimacy of state-sanctioned violence and assert their revolutionary right to resort either to nonviolent civil disobedience or force.

History offers an abundance of examples in which friends of justice could endorse either the triumph of revolution or the successful assertion of state authority. For Americans, the contrasting roles of Washington and Lincoln should be enduring symbols of the relativity of the claims advanced by both governments and revolutions. Thus if one advocates recourse to violence only in the cause of justice it is clear that one must be guided more by the concrete situation under consideration than by legal or ideological formulas.

What is true for revolution is also true for war. The state's claim to the right of self-defense in international politics may serve merely to rationalize the forcible perpetuation of an intolerable status quo, particularly when the state's "self" is sprawled out over a spacious and ill-gotten empire. By the same token, the state that resorts to violence first, usually labeled the aggressor, is not automatically convicted of moral ignominy. It is worthy of note, in this connection, that neither the League of Nations nor the United Nations has been able to come up with an agreed definition of aggression. The complexities of the problem can be illustrated by the observation that in retrospect few would condemn Britain and France had they been more aggressive in trying to bring down the Hitler regime—even by forcible intervention—while they were still relatively stronger than Germany.

Whether in war or revolution, the coupling of the just use of force with self-defense is useful insofar as it places the main burden of moral proof on the attacker and so acts as a restraint on those seeking occasions for violence. But the defender is never absolved from his share of the burden, namely, to demonstrate that what he would protect is in fact morally defensible. Just as it was impossible to argue that force has only defensive utility, so it is impossible to contend that only the defensive use of force is just.

After exploring the relativity of some of the standards designed to reconcile force and justice, one is tempted to question the viability of any absolute criterion for just behavior. Indeed, the prevailing intellectual orthodoxy of relativism generally dismisses justice as a nonoperational concept. This position is quite consistent, of course, with its definition of politics as simply the pursuit and exercise of power. Yet the presence of human degradation in civil society and across the world constantly injects new urgency into the Founding Fathers' declaration that the purpose of government is justice.[5] It does the same for the more ancient words of St. Augustine: "What is the state without justice but a great band of robbers?"[6] The Augustinian formulation also facilitates the linking, once again, of domestic and international politics within a macropolitical framework by identifying justice as the final measure of both domestic and foreign policy.

---

[5] *The Federalist*, Number 51.
[6] *The City of God*, Book IV, Chap. 4.

THE RELEVANCE OF JUSTICE

Macropolitics inevitably provokes a debate on the ancient issues involved in a universal standard of justice. Without, at this point, pressing the debate to a conclusion, let it be noted that the tradition that Kant summed up in his proposition that all men be treated as ends in themselves has no serious rival as a substantive definition of justice. Indeed, Marx, as the chief critic of that tradition, merely substituted a negative formulation of the same principle when he envisioned a society in which man would no longer be exploited by man. In Western and Western-influenced society, at least, one finds not diversity but a rare unanimity concerning the substance of justice, and the relativists must retreat from substance to method to make their case credible.

Here, as we have seen, relativism is firmly entrenched because history constantly reveals the persistent deficiencies of variable human institutions and concepts in realizing—making operational—substantive justice. Since it is extraordinarily difficult to meet the requirements of justice—of treating all men as ends in themselves—men are constantly inclined to desert these requirements in favor of less rigorous standards. Those who desert, however, contribute to making justice nonoperational not only as an intellectual concept but also in the daily reality of political life.

To treat men as ends in themselves is perfectly tenable as an absolute definition of justice so long as one accepts that men will suffer to the degree that the norm it embodies is violated. Such a definition is also wholly compatible with the conventional wisdom of relativism that lives from the unassailable premise that there is nothing perfect in man or his works. One need not argue that the absence of justice is the sole cause of human misery in order to affirm that injustice invariably damages human relationships by transgressing against human dignity. Those who would better the human condition cannot evade the Kantian definition of justice. It is a definition that can be dismissed only by those who also dismiss the notion of human dignity as an attribute inhering in all men.

This much must be conceded to relativism: the standard that permits force to be used only in the cause of justice can, in an imperfect world, be applied only in relative terms. Since the just and the unjust cannot be neatly separated, the use of force even in the name of justice (judicial penalties, revolution and counterrevolution, war) must inevitably cause injustice. The resort to force is only the most dramatic demonstration that men cannot help using other men for their own purposes and that there is some injustice in the course and outcome of every conflict. The issue then becomes one requiring a judgment in each instance of conflict: Which user of force (criminal or society, government or revolution, State A or State B?) is more likely to further or subvert the aim of treating men as ends in themselves?

Here Machiavelli's choice between greater and lesser evil reemerges.

It is at this point that relativity of viewpoint and interest and fallibility of perception corrode the standards for decision. A completely accurate and disinterested appraisal of the relative justice on each side of a dispute is no more possible than a completely accurate estimate of the power of the contestants. But meaningful decisions are not possible without criteria, vulnerable or invulnerable. The vulnerable criterion of justice is at least an authentic restraint on the use of violence; in contrast, the vulnerable standard of utility necessarily increases the reliance on force. Far more important, a decision between two claims to justice is qualitatively different from a judgment of the relative capacity for violence possessed by each of the contestants.

A Kantian concept of justice cannot produce those reckless moral crusades that understandably terrify the power politics school of thought. Its spokesmen are quite right to recognize the cry for justice as the most passionate of all political emotions. They are also right to fear the impact passion can have on reason, reasonableness, and moderation. These are the considerations that move the most humane among them to counsel abandonment of the idea of justice in politics in favor of a presumptively detached and utilitarian calculus of power.

But their fears are misplaced. They ought properly to be directed to the counterfeits of justice that turn judicial process into persecution, social energy into imperialism, and religion into inquisition. After all, in the absence of an authentic understanding of justice, bogus concepts are bound to proliferate and so magnify the very dangers of violence the power calculators seek to avoid. A multiplicity of falsehoods about the nature of justice does not demonstrate that nothing true can be said about it. Nor does it demonstrate that passions aroused in the name of justice must necessarily divide men rather than provide formulas for their reconciliation.

In an unjust world it is true that the idea of justice is inevitably disruptive, and the more intensely men perceive themselves the victims of injustice, the more profound the disruption. But their fear and anger will not be calmed and their disposition to violence will not be diminished by the message that there is no justice—or injustice—but only power and the utility of superior force. Yet this is the only answer the pedagogy of power politics has to offer. In domestic politics the answer is covert insofar as there is a grudging recognition that men cannot bear to live in a state that denies even the obligation to be just.

In international politics, however, the answer becomes overt. Since the power politics model assumes that states have no obligations beyond their own self-interest, the idea of international justice is openly identified as myth. The degree to which states treat other states and peoples as ends in themselves is deemed a matter of convenience and not duty. The unavoidable conclusion concerning force is that its use in defense or pursuit of power is rational (with the frequently attached humanitarian proviso that its application must be "discriminating"), but that recourse to force on behalf of a necessarily mythical justice is not.

Power politics to the contrary, the most relevant message for those who fear violence—in domestic or international politics—is that justice is the chief guardian of peace and injustice its chief enemy. Even this proposition, however, cannot dispose of the problem of violence because it does not exclude violence in defense of justice. Further, one must recognize that force, whether motivated by concern for power or for justice, inevitably violates the Kantian norm. At the same time, there may be considerable agreement that the norm ought not to be left defenseless. In this context the championing of justice by forcible means must be regarded as a tragedy whose participants can find vindication to the extent that they seek to remove the causes of conflict and repair the ravages of the violence they both suffer and inflict.

The resort to force in the name of the power calculus, on the other hand, is not a tragic act and can have no other result than to debauch the norm of justice. The debauchery is magnified by the fact that the practitioner of power politics (sometimes in contrast to his theoretical mentors) is never satisfied to rationalize his concrete acts of violence solely in terms of power and the utility of force. Instead, he invariably must embellish them with whatever spurious concepts of justice are conveniently at hand. Hypocrisy here joins physical injury to compound injustice—and to perpetuate the vicious circle of violence and counterviolence.

Those who agree that violence will never be permanently excluded from international or domestic politics may also be able to agree on some other propositions: that injustice is the chief instigator of violence; that justice is its chief remedy; and that the Kantian norm is the standard by which to measure all concepts of just behavior. There may also be some agreement on a further set of propositions: that the norm of justice will constantly be violated; that it must nevertheless stand as a model and be defended against violation; that its forcible defense is in itself a violation of justice; but that this category of violation (and only this category) can be regarded as morally tolerable.

Those who cannot accept these propositions are obviously free to reject the ethic of justice as a more hopeful and effective guideline than the ethic of power for dealing with the problem of violence. But the proposition that men should be treated as ends in themselves epitomizes the idea of consent and hence is undeniably averse to coercion. The power calculus, on the other hand, is essentially indifferent to violence; ungoverned by a concept of justice it is more attracted to coercion than consent. For those wishing to inhibit the resort to violence the choice of standards should be clear.

Every policy must establish a set of objectives and identify means, or instruments, designed to achieve them. For those who value violence for its own sake—and there are some, notably among those who oscillate between the *prima ratio* and *ultima ratio* approaches to political violence—force is a purpose as well as an instrument of policy. For all others, force is always a means to an end and never consciously an end in itself. It must not be overlooked, of course, that even the most earnest efforts to preserve the means-ends distinction can disintegrate in the heat of conflict. The means one selects have a well-known way of affecting the ends one has set, even to the extent of contradicting or superseding the original objectives. Yet the effort to maintain the distinction between goals and methods must be continued, most particularly when the method is force. Of all methods, violence is the most dangerous; of all purposes, it is the most pernicious.

If force ought properly to be treated as a means, then its use should be commensurate with the value of the objective sought. It follows that the rationale or justification for the resort to violence lies solely in the purpose served. Since force is inherently cruel and dangerous, its use cannot be defended by reference to some paltry end but only in the cause of a goal or value of major consequence. In civil society, political thought based on natural law traditions has generally designated justice as the prime rationale for resort to violence. Relativist thought, on the other hand, using labels such as security and prudence, has given primacy to the rationale of social self-interest in its manifold guises.

In the world at large even those who defend resort to force in civil society only in the name of justice are generally content not to press their theoretical case much beyond the national boundary. Thus the relativist school is understandably dominant in international politics, where the standard approach, buttressed by the concept of sovereignty, sees the supreme justification for force in the self-interest and security of the state. This view, however, has not gone unchallenged; the most massive if unsystematic critique in recent times was developed at the Nuremberg trials.

No one will deny that the self-interest of states whose citizens number hundreds of thousands to hundreds of millions is a matter of major consequence. It is therefore not surprising that the theory of power politics should be content to rest its case for the use of force by invoking the sovereign will of the state acting in its own interest. But in the real world, no war has ever been fought without both sides justifying the violence and the suffering in terms that go beyond self-interest. Each always asserts the superior worth of its cause within a framework of moral values alleged to be binding on both antagonists and, indeed, on mankind at large. Legal rights, equitable division of territory, self-determination of peoples, democracy versus autocracy, or liberation from bourgeois exploitation are familiar samples of the moral banners that appear on the battlefield wherever men are struggling for power.

One can interpret all this as pious sound and fury; indeed, much of it is. Yet the persistent unwillingness of men to shed blood simply in the name of calculated self-interest and their persistent tendency to move into the realm of moral norms for self-justification are phenomena that cannot easily be dismissed. If Thucydides saw the Peloponnesian Wars exemplifying the proposition that the strong do what they can and the weak suffer what they must, it should be recalled that his history was not intended as a eulogy but as a critique and requiem. Machiavelli himself was not content to let the well enough of power politics alone but insisted that his ideal prince be "inspired by a just cause," namely, the liberation of Italy from the "barbarians."[7]

The just war is a concept that has been elaborated and defended most notably by Roman Catholic thinkers. But the idea it embodies hovers over every social conflict throughout history and cannot be confined by any boundary lines between civil and international society. It is an idea which asserts that the only conceivable legitimation for violence derives from the same source that condemns its use—from the province of ethics. It requires that one never resort to force except in a cause that morally deserves the support of its enemies as well as its defenders. This proposition is the foundation of every aspiration for justice in civil society. The concept of the just war, in turn, seeks to give specific expression to that aspiration in international society. If both the domestic and international manifestations of this proposition are always and inevitably imperfect, they are always and inevitably present. Anyone who sees these manifestations simply as more or less effective exercises in camouflage can never reach the heart of the problem of violence—or of justice.

No policy toward force has avoided reference to some concept of justice, and no policy toward force ever can. Those who wish to come to terms with the phenomenon of violence must also come to terms with competing concepts of justice and the distortions thereof. Only such an effort in political theory and practice can lead to that firm ground where the causes of violence can be realistically identified and treated and the outbreaks of violence diminished. Such an effort is also a prerequisite to reasonable individual judgments about the kinds of circumstances in which one would oneself resort to force. Finally, it would yield some tenable criteria for the choice of weapons, whether they be bricks, machine guns, or nuclear warheads.

---

[7] *The Prince*, Chap. XXVI.

Chapter 4

Force and War: Stimuli and Restraints

As is true of all complex problems, every aspect of the problem of force affects and is affected by every other. Restraints on force, for example, derive in part from the desire to prevent violence from reaching a level which threatens irreparable injury to the values whose protection the use of force is supposed to serve. Devices to restrict violence must therefore be seen not merely as limitations on armed conflict but also as exercises in the commensurability of ends and means.

Limitations on arms and curbs on their use also relate to the efficacy of a resort to force. While limited violence may provoke only limited response, all-out violence may not only stimulate all-out response but also maximize mobilization efforts on both sides and draw other parties into the conflict. As we have seen, in such an intensification of the struggle, the calculation of relative strengths becomes a precarious and extremely high-risk undertaking. A policy designed to maximize the efficacy of force must therefore not only develop capacities for destruction but also seek means to limit it. It should go without saying that the nuclear era has given a new and terrible urgency to this ancient but often neglected truth.

Judgments about the efficacy of force, its appropriateness to the goals it is supposed to advance, and the restraints to which it should be subject can be linked into a single prescription: force should be used in such a way as to cause the least possible damage in the achievement of a realistic approximation of the objectives sought. But all policy aims are subjective in content and elastic in practice, and what constitutes a realistic approximation is always a matter of debate. Furthermore, assessment of the adequacy of the means for attaining the desired goals is always inexact.[1] If, therefore, one wants to prevent violence from becom-

---

[1] The Cuban missile crisis of 1962 offers an apt illustration of these problems. There was profound disagreement among those who influenced the American policy decisions concerning the adequacy of the naval "quarantine" (or blockade) as a means of reversing the Soviet decision to deploy missiles on Cuban soil. Preemptive air strikes, invasion, or both were strongly urged, particularly by the military, as the most

ing counterproductive, the prescription of minimum force for optimum gain is insufficient as a rational guide to the use of force. It must be fortified once again by value judgment: the judgment that the use of physical coercion is an intrinsically undesirable form of political behavior because of the human suffering it entails and because the proper vocation of politics is not coercion but consent.

THE NORMALCY OF VIOLENCE

The supreme skill of the politician is not the management of violence but the ability to create situations in which the likelihood of violence is minimal. This is a proposition which harmonizes with the sentiment that deplores violence in civil societies, a sentiment widely held by people generally and by political scientists in particular. Even the Marxist tradition does not regard force as desirable; it is regarded simply as a necessary means of reaching the promised land of a classless society in which violence would no longer have a function.

Jefferson's ruminations about the usefulness of a little bloodshed every generation to refresh the tree of liberty are not without significance. But they did not vitiate Jefferson's own preference for civil peace over civil war, nor do they contradict the general preference in political thought for maximizing nonviolence and minimizing violence. This preference both affects and is affected by the commonly made empirical observation that a high level of violence indicates a badly functioning society and a low level of violence indicates that a society is functioning well or, at least, that it is in "equilibrium." In this context equilibrium is often

---

effective methods to achieve the desired objective. Moreover, there was conflict about the objective: Was it enough simply to compel the Soviets to back down in the current confrontation or should the Castro regime be destroyed so as to prevent similar contingencies in the future?

Finally, did the policy chosen achieve a realistic approximation of the objectives sought? The Soviet-American agreement called for UN inspection teams to supervise the dismantling of the missile emplacements and to verify the elimination of all such installations on the island. Castro successfully refused to permit such teams on Cuban soil, and the Kennedy administration's unwillingness to press the issue and its subsequent decision to rely instead on aerial surveillance caused some of its more hawkish critics to express doubts that the Soviets had fully implemented the agreement reached. From the Soviet point of view, it should be noted, the United States never officially fulfilled its part of the bargain to issue a formal anti-invasion pledge as an integral part of its policy toward Cuba.

In retrospect, it can be said that both the United States and the Soviet Union, given the relative intensity of their interests and the relative strengths of their bargaining positions, achieved reasonable approximations of their goals: there are no missiles on Cuban soil and Cuba has not been invaded. One could then deduce that the goals were realistic, or realistically altered, and that the methods used to achieve them were adequate. But at the time of crisis, decision, and agreement there remained grave uncertainties about all these matters.

interpreted as a situation in which relatively few members of the society are so dissatisfied that they are willing to resort to force rather than continue to tolerate the existing political and social structure.

The judgment that peace is the preferable state of domestic politics does not extend to international politics. Since the military usually offers a more spacious opportunity for prestigious careers than does the internal police function, it is understandable that there is an imposing array of soldier-statesmen who stand as historic and persuasive advocates of the virtues of military activity. They are joined by a smaller and generally less illustrious group of civilian admirers, among whom the most notable modern representatives are Mussolini and Hitler.

But worship of the war god is only a secondary contributor to concepts of international relations that place violence at the center of the action. The main contribution has come from the dominant tradition in political thought which deplores war but nonetheless regards it as "normal." It would be too pat to assert that this view holds violence to be an aberration in domestic politics and peace to be an aberration in international life. But such an inference is not far off the mark; even in our own time so distinguished an analyst as Raymond Aron identifies peace as the norm of the domestic polity and "either peace or war" as the norm of international society.[2]

Aron then draws the conclusion that in the absence of an overreaching system of government and laws all sovereign parties in international relations have the right to resort to violence—in contrast to domestic politics where the sovereign government monopolizes the instruments of force and is their sole legitimate internal user. As we have already observed and will observe again, so categorical a distinction between domestic and international politics is deceptive. Yet there are enough elements of truth to lend the distinction plausibility and then to infer from it the legitimacy of war as a means of settling international disputes.

Tolerance toward war as a normal phenomenon of international politics has many explanations, most of which are connected with the essentially micropolitical history of international life noted in the introductory chapter. The diversity of peoples and states and the practical impossibility of creating satisfactory and durable institutions for the nonviolent settlement of disputes among them made self-protection and self-assertion the unavoidable rules of the international game. In this context it is understandable that over the centuries even the most humane thinkers, if they grappled seriously with the given realities, should have doubts about the possibilities for extending the realm of peace beyond the sovereign border.

---

[2] *Peace and War: A Theory of International Relations* (New York: Doubleday, 1966), pp. 6, 7, and *passim*.

Within the state one could strive to build an island of internal peace, but to calm the surrounding sea of violence characteristically seemed to be beyond man's best capacities. This view was neither unrealistic nor immoral, and it would be presumptuous to try to apportion praise or blame. It is cited rather as a necessary part of the explanation for the consistent record of failure over time to regulate and reduce international violence to a tolerable level. The historic probabilities of success in such an enterprise have so far been virtually nil, and it should cause little wonder that men have generally been prone to accept war as a painful fact of life not much subject to their wills.

An act of will is the crucial component in any program of action. When men believe that no amount of willing can alter any given set of conditions, an effective policy to deal with these conditions is necessarily a contradiction in terms. At best, one can prepare contingency plans to deal with a variety of typical accidents that occur with the force and inevitability of nature. In the standard phraseology, one deals with symptoms but not with causes. This has been the characteristic approach to the problem of violence in international relations.

The historic inability to control international violence has resulted in uncounted hundreds of millions of violent deaths. If the record is a monstrous one, it is nonetheless true that mankind itself has so far survived and multiplied. Currently, indeed, the rapid rate of human proliferation threatens to burden mankind more heavily than most of the conventional wars of the past. But since 1945 the problems of conventional war have been overshadowed by the problems of nuclear war. The lessons that history teaches about the human capacity for survival are no longer so convincing. Before Hiroshima the acceptance of world politics as the realm of unavoidable and essentially uncontrollable violence did not necessarily imply despair over man's fate or cynicism about his nature. But the destructive power conjured up by the atomic physicists, as many of them recognized, for the first time laid the question of mankind's future on the line.

The nuclear revelation restates the ancient challenge of war and peace in the most dramatic terms possible. Is it feasible for men to treat the causes of international violence instead of merely coping with its effects? The question is not addressed to any specific dispute; instead it raises a generic issue: Can men master the art of international relationships to the point where violence need no longer be considered "normal" but rather—analogous to its role in the well-functioning civil society—as an aberration? And then can men go on to devise techniques and institutions that can effectively prevent the "aberrations," whenever they occur, from attaining catastrophic proportions? Unless affirmative answers can be developed in a dangerously limited span of time the sea of violence traditionally associated with international politics will engulf all the islands of peace that civil society has so far managed to sustain.

The thermonuclear menace has demonstrably roused many from the lethargy of traditional international theory. But it has not dissipated the doubts that man's will can alter the micropolitical dynamics that have hitherto characterized international relations. These doubts may begin to yield to hope if a macropolitical approach can demonstrate a viable logic and practicality. That is, a macroanalysis of world politics ought to be able accurately to identify the causes of international violence and to prescribe effective means to deal with them. Effective means, in turn, should be understood as those that offer a realistic prospect of holding violence to a minimum and transforming it from a rule of international life into an exception.

If this seems a formidable task, one might note that it is not so very much out of proportion to the long-standing aspirations of balance of power theory, which also offers guidelines for the regulation of international violence. Balance of power theory, of course, has been chiefly concerned with the perpetuation of the micropolitical system of a multiplicity of sovereignties. But it has not been unmindful of the tragedy of violence and has sought ways to mitigate it while continuing to assume its "normalcy." Indeed, the assumption is correct; violence is in fact the normal product of micropolitics. The micropolitical system, as defined in the introductory chapter, is one in which each participant absolutizes its own interests and relegates the interests of every other participant and of the system as a whole to subordinate status. To the degree that states approximate the micropolitical model, war is the normal relationship, just as "class war" is the normal relationship between classes when they play (necessarily, as Marx would have it) the game of micropolitics within the class structure.

The argument is obvious: the problem of violence in international relations can be dealt with effectively only to the degree that micropolitical values give way to macropolitical values, that is, to the degree that the good of the whole gains ascendancy over the good of the parts. The argument still needs a great deal of exploration, but perhaps enough has been said so far to foster a reasonable anticipation that macroanalysis offers better prospects than the micropolitical assumptions of balance of power theory for the control of international violence.

THE INTENSIFICATION OF VIOLENCE

If the emergence of nuclear weaponry has stimulated efforts to rethink the role of violence in politics, the event has ample precedent. Every significant innovation in the history of military technology has been the signal for stocktaking and reflection. The crossbow in the hands of yeoman infantry not only conquered the mounted knight but also contributed to the collapse of medieval social and political organization.

Gunpowder drastically reduced the defensibility of the walled city and joined the ensemble of forces pushing in the direction of the more spacious territorial monarchy. The Industrial Revolution began to produce sufficient goods and services to make possible the provisioning of mass armies equipped to fight on a year-round basis. Hence there was no longer any need for that historic annual respite from battle when troops withdrew to winter quarters.

Every one of these technological achievements challenged the viability of inherited institutions and released new energies; each time the dominant sociopolitical structures either adapted to them or disintegrated. Those that failed to adapt demonstrated in the most convincing way possible their deficiencies in the management and control of violence. The losers, at least, had cause to wonder whether there was not some better way than force to settle political disputes.

It is common knowledge that the twentieth century has enormously accelerated the rate of innovation in military technology. The submarine and tank have drastically altered sea and land power. The airplane created a totally new military dimension whose boundaries have been steadily and spectacularly extended by jet engine, rocket, space capsule, moon landings, and planetary probes. If we add biological, chemical, electronic, and nuclear weaponry the list is still not complete. But it is sufficient to make the point that this assembly-line productivity of technology has made and broken empires, nations, and ideologies with unprecedented rapidity. Once again, the vanquished and those who cannot hope to compete have cause to wonder about the efficacy of violence. Moreover, if they reflect at all, they also have cause to rebel against the proposition that in international politics the resort to force is "normal."

What is truly new, however, is that the forces of destruction which daily accumulate in the nuclear arsenals threaten to extinguish the difference between winners and losers. The management and control of nuclear violence, once the violence is actually unleashed, bids fair to become a contradiction in terms for all belligerents. In all previous history, the victor in warfare generally suffered light wounds in comparison with the defeated foe. It is true that among the vanquished states there were few that experienced the fate of Carthage and many that lived to prosper and even to conquer another day. But with infrequent exceptions the consequences of victory in major wars were profoundly different from the consequences of defeat for the societies concerned. Victory was held to be "worth it." In a nuclear war, however, the hideous injury that both sides must inevitably suffer would be tantamount to a shared calamity of unimaginable magnitude, if not to mutual suicide.

The various battle scenarios projected by Herman Kahn and other nuclear strategists seek to demonstrate the possibility of controlling nuclear exchanges so that the warring states could opt for any one of a large number of intensities of violence below the level of reciprocal annihilation.[3] The assumptions governing these exercises in limited nuclear warfare would necessarily leave each contestant at the end of hostilities with part of its nuclear arsenal intact. Then neither side could dictate to the other, and both would have "survived." But the mutilation suffered by all the main contestants in a "limited" nuclear exchange would be both terrible and comparable in severity. To pay such a fearful price for a "compromise" peace is, in its own terms, as much a mockery of rational policy as nuclear Armageddon itself.

But the assumption that a nuclear exchange could be limited once it was actually under way must itself be questioned. The proposition that restraint will prevail in the panic atmosphere of nuclear detonations does not carry much conviction. Moreover, an additional factor of uncertainty must enter into the calculations, compounding the instability of strategies designed to prevent the ultimate act of destruction. Every one of the lower rungs on the nuclear escalation ladder offers footing only to the extent that there remains a prospect for a negotiated peace. Everything depends on confidence on both sides in the opponent's will to restraint—in a context singularly subversive of confidence. Once that confidence fades on either side in the course of nuclear battle the pressure to abandon all remaining inhibitions would be enormous.

Thus limited nuclear war approaches total nuclear war in catastrophic effect and under combat conditions tends to become identical with it. Whatever the outcome, victory and defeat lose their meaning. This follows by definition in the limited war outcome of a "compromise" peace. In a war to the death, the concepts of victory and defeat can have functional significance only as a means of distinguishing a virtually destroyed society from one that is completely obliterated. This would, in fact, be the only possible description of a victor's peace between the United States and the Soviet Union.

In the nuclear context, then, and for the first time in history, the application of unlimited force in pursuit of unlimited victory is a flat negation of rational policy. If the conclusion seems too obvious, it is not at all obvious that it has been built into the war strategies of the nuclear powers as a governing principle. After all, total violence and total conquest were the bloody *leitmotifs* of both world wars and thus the dominant military legacy of the first half of the twentieth century. Further, all-out force has realized, or could have realized, tangible and sometimes enormous payoffs for the stronger side in every period of history except where balance of power configurations have limited the feasibility of their attainment.

Finally, total violence permeates the theory of sovereignty itself inso-

---

[3] Herman Kahn, *On Escalation* (New York: Praeger, 1965), and *On Thermonuclear War* (Princeton, N.J.: Princeton University Press, 1960). *On Escalation* describes forty-four rungs on the escalation ladder, thirty-five of which involve either credible threats or actual use of nuclear weapons.

far as it demands (as, for example, in the case of Nazi Germany) the sacrifice of every human value in preference to submission to the external foe. It is evident that both the history and logic of the micro-political system of international relations have resisted the notion of limited violence. The idea that all-out force is no longer a rational option is so essentially novel that only the most rigorous intellectual—and moral—discipline can succeed in removing it from the list of policy options.

Under Defense Secretary McNamara, the American military establishment sought to establish a new set of options by developing a whole spectrum of capabilities, both nuclear and nonnuclear, that would permit it to be effective at all levels of violence from guerilla warfare to operations just this side of holocaust. Above all, United States policy became committed to the proposition that limited war is the only conceivable framework for rational military strategy and that total war must be relegated to the category of desperation.

The category of desperation, however, was not banned from military doctrine. It has remained as a freak component of official policy in both the United States and the Soviet Union. Produced and then consecrated to nonuse, the ultimate American and Russian megatonnages nonetheless function as wild cards in the game of deterrence and constantly influence the players' moves. Nuclear strategy, therefore, is one that gives overwhelming preference to limited violence but does not rule out the possibility of total violence. As we have seen, this possibility is built into the entire structure of the deterrence system of threats.

RECIPROCITIES BETWEEN FORCE AND THREAT

These considerations should serve to underscore the inherited knowledge that threats are by definition dangerous. But they do not and cannot negate the inherited experience that threats have their uses. This experience applies to the nuclear era as well as to any other. The nuclear saber rattling of Khrushchev and Bulganin in the Suez crisis of 1956 was not without its effect. The far more spectacular evocation of the nuclear menace (combined with more limited threats) by President Kennedy in the Cuban missile crisis not only led to the resolution of the crisis but also marked the beginning of the years of Soviet-American détente. Whatever the insufficiencies of the détente period, its easing of the superheated atmosphere of the late 1940s and 1950s brought about a general decline in the intensity of mutual fear and permitted at least some promising steps to be taken in improving Soviet-American relationships. One cannot gainsay the truth that in international politics, as in domestic law enforcement systems, threats can serve creative as well as destructive purposes.

One can speak of limited and unlimited threats. In international politics, for example, there is obviously a profound difference between threatening to bombard or occupy a port city (Haiphong, Guantanamo, Gibraltar) and threatening to transform an entire society into a radioactive wasteland. But for analytical purposes it is convenient to assign the concept of threat to the lower rungs of the ladder of escalating violence. The qualitative differences between types of concrete threats become manifest anyway in the course of examining the differences between the kinds of violence actually unleashed. The distinction between word and deed is not the only analytical guideline in considering the problem of force, but it remains a fundamental one. The situation before the killing starts is fundamentally transformed once the killing has begun. Hence we shall deal with threat as typifying a desire to limit the use of force in the sense that threat tries to make the point with words and symbols instead of acts.

The scale of violence thus runs from threat through various intensities of actual force in which the framework of restraints on its use is progressively dismantled. At the end of the process stands violence without limit, a situation in which the user of violence employs it to the maximum of his capabilities. At the individual level, this process can be illustrated by an escalation pattern that starts with truculence, proceeds to a fight with fists or knives, and ends with murder. In the context of the political use of force, however, the absolute and final violence represented by murder has hitherto been unattained. The collective equivalent of murder is genocide, and though from time to time there has been intent to commit genocide and approximations thereof, there is no instance in which all the intended victims have been murdered. Even some Carthaginians survived.

Since 1945, however, the scale of violence for collective action has become complete. Absolute violence is now a feasible technique of political action, and continuing advances in technology are in process of making it not only feasible but easy. This fact constitutes a revolution in many senses, but most particularly in the sense that for the first time in man's history the maximum utilization of force could result not only in the obliteration of enemy peoples but also of all human life. Thus absolute novelty combines with sheer horror to state the case for urgency in developing reliable limitations on violence.

Threat, as we have noted, represents the most restrained kind of violence, in the sense that it does not involve physically forcible acts. Words, of course, may provoke violence; indeed, they may be so designed. But threatening words may also prevent violence by persuading an individual or state on the brink of using force that the plunge into action will prove too costly. Since the one making threats has not yet moved into action and since his words can either precipitate or hinder violence, it remains legitimate to begin a consideration of rising levels of violence with the concept of threat.

Threat is not confined to words; its message can be conveyed by other than verbal symbols, including nonviolent acts. Increased military spending, expansion of armed forces, massing of armies at sensitive borders (or deployment of sea power at strategic locations or air power alerts), partial or total mobilization, well-publicized reports about secret diplomatic consultations, economic sanctions of all kinds, subversive propaganda and agitation—all these activities constitute only a sampling of the techniques of menace. None subject the target of the threat to physical constraint, but all place him under pressure or damage his interests.

Threat continues to play a role even after the process of physical compulsion has begun. The actual resort to force always stimulates expectations that the initial level of violence will be raised to maximum intensity unless the dispute is settled. The only exception to this rule, as we have noted, emerged for the first time when the nuclear age opened up the possibility of murdering the enemy society at one stroke so that there would be no target left to threaten (and the possibility that there would be no one left to engage in further threats). Aside from the nuclear Armageddon, then, force and the threat of more force are inextricably linked together. This fact defines the context—and the dangers—of limited war.

LIMITED WAR

In the nuclear era, the idea of limited war received its initial doctrinal elaboration in the pioneering effort of Henry Kissinger.[4] The Korean War, of course, provided the first large-scale, postwar contrast between a major international war fought with limited means for limited ends and the all-out war philosophy that characterized World War II.

But Kissinger's *Nuclear Weapons and Foreign Policy* spotlighted for the first time the central dilemma of nuclear power, namely, that its unlimited use is equivalent to the collapse of rationality—and of society. A trenchant critic of John Foster Dulles' policy of massive retaliation, Kissinger warned that a predominant or, worse yet, exclusive reliance on strategic nuclear power to defend vital American interests would confront the United States with an impossible choice every time a major international crisis erupted. The choice would be either to back down in the face of Soviet threats or push the Armageddon button. If the United States was to extricate itself from this unbearable dilemma, Kissinger argued, it must enhance its ability to fight limited war by augmenting its conventional military capabilities and by developing a sophisticated

---

[4] *Nuclear Weapons and Foreign Policy* (New York: Harper Bros., 1957). See also *The Necessity for Choice* (New York: Harper Bros., 1961).

capacity for deploying tactical atomic weapons.[5] The latter were deemed necessary to counter Russian and Chinese superiority in manpower. They were deemed desirable since they exploited the advantage of an assumed American technological superiority.

Uneasiness among some European allies who envisioned themselves as the likely locale of tactical nuclear explosions, uncertainty whether there could be any way to prevent tactical nuclear use from escalating to strategic use, and the subsequent maturation of missile technology were among the reasons why Kissinger later deemphasized the nuclear aspects of limited war. His original advocacy, however, was influential in stimulating expansion of the evolving arsenal of tactical nuclear arms and foreshadowed the shift in official American policy from massive retaliation to graduated deterrence.

So far as techniques of limitation are concerned, it is a standard proposition that war may be limited in terms of geographical scope, of military and other social resources invested, and of objectives sought. The Korean War, in global perspective the post-1945 archetype of limited war, is customarily cited as a model of almost classic simplicity. Fighting was rigidly confined to a narrow peninsula and to a single, though artificially divided, society. The possible use of nuclear weapons was considered and rejected. None of the intervening participants ventured to maximize their conventional military capabilities. All the intervening parties pursued limited goals: they sought to effect political solutions in Korea, though not without recognizing the impact of such solutions on issues outside of Korea.

But this classic example of limited warfare was about as total as the Koreans themselves are likely to have desired. As the armies surged back and forth and air and naval power rained destruction from the skies and along the coasts, every part of the peninsula suffered devastation. The total number of Korean soldiers killed on both sides was 436,000. The civilian death toll in South Korea alone stood at 373,000. If one esti-

---

[5] The distinction between tactical and strategic in nuclear weaponry has presented some difficult problems, beginning with the essentially qualitative difference between nuclear and nonnuclear explosives. Roughly, however, nuclear parlance measures strategic weapons in megatonnages (multiples of 1,000,000 tons of the explosive force of TNT) and tactical weapons in kilotonnages (multiples of 1,000 tons of TNT equivalent). This distinction is closely related to the greater and lesser explosive potential, respectively, of fusion and fission weapons. Only nuclear fusion explosions are properly called "thermonuclear"; devices that generate their explosive force from the process of nuclear fission are fabricated on the same principles as the original atomic bombs that fell on Hiroshima and Nagasaki.

Tactical nuclear weapons have been developed for battlefield use whose explosive force is much less than that which incinerated Hiroshima. On the other hand, other "tactical" weapons are in existence that are capable of surpassing the destruction inflicted on Hiroshima by an unknown order of magnitude. The result is that the distinction between tactical and strategic nuclear warfare becomes ominously obscure.

mates the number of North Korean civilian deaths (for which there are no accurate figures available) as correspondingly great, it is probable that close to 1 million North and South Korean soldiers and civilians lost their lives by the time the fighting ceased. Military and civilian wounded in South Korea totaled 423,000. If one continues the assumption that North Korea, with a 1953 population of approximately 10 million compared with South Korea's 20 million, suffered proportional losses, the combined death and wounded figure for the peninsula as a whole is an appalling 1,650,000, or 5.5 percent of the total Korean population.[6] These figures begin to approach the percentage level of casualties suffered by the most heavily engaged countries in both world wars.

Such terrible losses should occasion no surprise because the two Korean governments, unlike the intervening powers, were pursuing unlimited goals. That is, each wanted to eliminate the other, each used force to the maximum of its capabilities, and each had to rely on outside assistance to stave off collapse. For the governments in Seoul and Pyongyang it was a war to the death and hence total; only the balance of military force and power established by the intervening states prevented the death of the southern regime in the first part of the war and of the northern regime in the latter part. Indeed, the continuing presence of outside powers and their persistent concern with the fate of the Korean peninsula have contributed significantly in preventing the outbreak of another round between North and South. These circumstances continued to obtain even after the two governments in Korea began to negotiate in 1972 in quest of eased relations.

Vietnam does not offer an exact parallel, but there are enough similarities to warrant attention. Once again, the aims of Hanoi and Saigon can be characterized as total. Ho Chi Minh's policy was clearly one of eliminating the southern regime and uniting Vietnam on his own terms. His successors have faithfully adhered to that policy, and neither the January 1973 cease-fire agreement nor the ensuing military activities and peace negotiations offer evidence that they have conclusively renounced it. For its part, and from the very beginning, Saigon desired an end to the communist government in the North but lacked the strength to translate that desire into a concrete policy. Hence it was forced to content itself with trying to preserve its own viability. Thus in Vietnam, too, it has been a war to the death with the inevitable fearsome toll of human lives and goods and, in contrast with Korea, a tragic rending of South Vietnam's social fabric.

In South Vietnam's case, the Saigon government was on the verge

---

[6] Figures are based on those supplied by the Embassy of the Republic of Korea in a letter of July 2, 1969. They do not, of course, include casualties suffered by the United States, of other countries under United Nations command, or of Red China.

of collapse more than once until 1965 when the United States began to inject massive numbers of troops and arms. Hanoi, on the other hand, was never in such desperate straits, but it is certain that it could not subsequently have kept up the fight without the enormous increase in military and economic aid from Russia and China. In Vietnam as in Korea, then, outside powers fought, financed, or supplied what for them was a limited war but which was terrible in its totality for those whose homeland became the field of battle.

Hence one man's limited war is often another man's total war. Those who concentrate on great power relationships and the need to prevent direct all-out violence at the superpower level often fail to pay adequate attention to the suffering of people whose home territory is the locale of a limited (in the sense of localized) war. Indeed, some analysts of pre-1945 international politics have pointed to the colonial frontier as a convenient outlet for great power aggressiveness and violence. In Asia and Africa, it was assumed, great powers could attack one another directly or through proxies without provoking the all-out war likely to result from similar behavior in the supersensitive Western and Central European arena. Military technicians, by the same token, tended to regard the localized war as a useful testing ground for the newest weapons, tactics, and strategies and as a dress rehearsal of things to come in the next big-scale war.

This highly expediential approach to the phenomenon of geographically limited wars is still in evidence. If such an approach seems morally offensive, it nonetheless has a certain realism to it. It is the counterpart of the classic remedy for domestic strife which Shakespeare ascribes to the dying Henry IV:

> I cut them off; and had a purpose now
> To lead out many to the Holy Land,
> Lest rest and lying still might make them look
> Too near unto my state. Therefore, my Harry,
> Be it thy course to busy giddy minds
> With foreign quarrels[7]

The deflection of violence from the central zone of conflict to peripheral areas has on occasion undoubtedly served to lower tensions between a set of powerful antagonists. By permitting an actual test of military (or political) strength in an area some distance from the concentration of paramount security interests, a limited engagement of military forces has sometimes persuaded the opponents not to press the issue nearer home. In such instances, then, the limited use of military resources at the disposal of major powers in a geographically remote region is certain

---

[7] *Henry IV, Part II.*

to be less destructive of human values in the aggregate than an all-out war effort resulting from a head-on collision between them in their respective strategic front yards.

But geographical displacement of the theater of conflict has often provided only temporary respite from major wars between major powers. Skirmishes in the Near East, Africa, and the Balkans turned out to be preludes to World War I. Two of the three classic "rehearsals" of the 1930s—China, Ethiopia, and Spain—were still in progress when World War II preempted the stage. Thus localized military struggles, more or less removed from the center of political gravity, can often serve to raise levels of tension rather than lower them. The staging of side shows is not a reliable recipe for avoiding the main event; if one seeks greater reliability it can be found only in the degree to which the major powers are willing to compromise their central interests among themselves.

The process by which local wars have escalated into central wars between great powers has taken many forms over time, but one of the most notable and repetitive of the phenomena in this process has been the pressure on the intervening major powers to become wholly identified with the ambitions of their respective local allies. The American experiences in Vietnam and Korea, both of which threatened global war, are obvious cases in point. But the Soviet Union has also known painful moments of overinvolvement with its Cuban and Arab friends. The constant tendency of the local belligerent is to extract a total commitment from its great ally, while the latter, if it is rationally committed to keep the war from spreading, must continually guard against overplaying its hand and must seek to maintain at least a minimum of flexibility in its policies toward the major powers intervening on the opposing side.

This conflict of purposes is characteristic of every alliance between stronger and weaker powers, and it has been dealt with in many different ways and often satisfactorily for both parties. But the emotional pull is usually in the direction of heeding the call for total involvement of the great ally in the fate of its small partner. Once the alliance has been transformed from paper pledges into common military action, the bonds forged on the battlefield are not easily broken. Both the military and civilian personnel of the metropolitan power must develop a sense of combat solidarity with the local ally if the morale of both partners is to withstand the shocks and miseries of war. The drama and suffering of the war zone lend urgency to the views of those on the scene, while the calculations of the policy makers in the distant capital of the metropolitan ally seem pallid by comparison.

A sense of guilt intensifies the emotional involvement. After all, it is the local ally whose population is being decimated and whose land is being ravaged; the metropolitan power only suffers limited military and economic losses. Moreover, should all the sorrow and sacrifice end in defeat, the metropolitan power simply withdraws to its homeland, but the local ally must remain to face the unpleasant aftermath. Thus the soldiers, diplomats, and citizens of the great ally who are on the scene of battle almost invariably tend to become partisans of and spokesmen for their small and beleaguered partner and host.

These are some of the dynamics which typically pressure a major power into raising the ante—originally perhaps very modest—in political and military struggles occurring far from its home base. It is indisputably good advice to admonish the great powers that they are the big dogs and that tails should not wag dogs. But good advice and high emotion are notoriously incompatible. Further, it is not, in any case, an easy matter to determine either in advance or in the midst of events what constitutes the expedient upper limits of involvement in peripheral wars. The premium on success increases as the casualties multiply, and the prestige of victory (or the avoidance of defeat) becomes more desirable as the price being paid to achieve it manifestly rises.

In the longer run, it is not always readily apparent to powers with global interests which areas or regions are expendable. Which continent on earth could the Soviet Union or the United States afford to view with studied detachment? Even Antarctica has required regulation by treaty between them. One must add that the flow of events is usually more important than geographic locale in deciding the degree of involvement in a local dispute which a major power might deem expedient. The outbreak of war in Korea in 1950 might not have seemed so important to the United States had it not been preceded by a rush of extraordinary and ominous events: the fall of Czechoslovakia and the Berlin blockade in 1948 and the first Soviet atomic explosion and the victory of Mao in China in 1949. Similarly, the twin humiliations of the Bay of Pigs and the Berlin wall in 1961, the ongoing struggle in Laos, and the Cuban missile crisis in 1962 clearly contributed to the determination of the Kennedy administration to hold the line in Vietnam and defy the challenge emanating from Hanoi and the Vietcong.

APPEASEMENT AND THE DOMINO THEORY

Here we come face to face with the true meaning of the "domino theory." The image of a row of standing dominoes inevitably falling one after another once the first domino has toppled backward has been a popular debating device for those who have a penchant for standing pat. The image is most often linked to a geographic area: if one domino in Southeast Asia falls (Vietnam), all the other dominoes will fall too (Laos, Malaysia, Thailand). Some of the image makers in this particular region have gone on to include Indonesia and the Philippines and/or the entire Indian subcontinent in the chain reaction. Indeed, the most ardent adherents of the domino theory in the United States have argued that the fall of any Asian domino (Korea, Taiwan, Vietnam) would initiate a chain of events irresistibly forcing American power all the way back to San Francisco.

The absurdity of these alarmist generalizations derives from the primitive nature of the political and strategic suppositions in which they are entangled. But faulty or overblown conclusions ought not to discredit the premises on which they are based; the premises must be evaluated in their own right. Such an evaluation can only yield the judgment that the domino concept has both enhanced and distorted realistic analysis of concrete situations. After all, in response to a series of aggressive thrusts by one great power, or its local allies, the opposing great power must either draw a line beyond which it will not retreat or lose its credibility as an ally or potential ally, or even as a power in its own right. Continual retreat brings with it the reputation of being a paper tiger. This became the fate of Britain and France in the 1930s as they steadily yielded ground before the forward surges of the Axis powers. The dominoes did indeed fall, one by one, until the situation was beyond repair.

The lesson was not lost on Washington policy makers after 1945, and determination not to repeat the story of appeasement became a key characteristic of American foreign policy in the postwar period. This determination expressed itself formally in the concept of containment and produced a long series of confrontations with the Soviet Union beginning with Iran, Turkey, and Greece and extending through Berlin and Korea to Cuba and Vietnam.

It is possible to argue that the United States may have been too rigid and unyielding at one point or another, that it overvalued a specific alliance or piece of territory, or that it exaggerated a particular threat and overreacted to it (Guatemala, the Dominican Republic). But even the harshest critics of American behavior have not denied the necessity of frequent confrontations with Soviet and other brands of communist power in various parts of the world if the major objectives of American policy were to be realized. The most alienated critics, of course, take issue with the objectives themselves, but the detached observer of the Cold War years must affirm the generally benevolent and creative intent embedded in American purposes. The United States may have erred by seeing the danger of falling dominoes in too many places, but its willingness to take stands in lands far removed from American shores has been the chief support for whatever freedom and order the postwar world has been able to achieve.

The domino image is thus only an element in the larger problem of appeasement. Appeasement in general means making concessions to the wishes of an antagonistic power. Such a procedure, as Winston Churchill observed, need not be unwise or ignoble if it is designed to produce a more equitable distribution of power or other worldly values among states. It is only when the antagonist's appetite for concessions becomes voracious and insatiable that appeasement becomes futile and dangerous, and it has been the attempts to satiate the insatiable which have helped to give appeasement its bad name in the twentieth century. Still more specifically, appeasement has been associated with concessions by a major power sacrificing the interests of a small ally or friend. It is here that appeasement comes to be regarded not only as unwise but craven and dishonorable. Hence opponents of appeasement cite the obligation to honor commitments as well as the expedience of preventing dominoes from falling.

Both appeasement and its component domino imagery, however, must be analyzed in terms of time, space, and the intent of the parties in conflict. If an expanding power lays claim to more and bigger concessions at an accelerating rate, it is reasonable to fear the domino effect. If an isolated concession is demanded, or if the claim comes after the claimant has been successfully rebuffed in a number of other disputes and is in an otherwise sober frame of mind, domino theories and anti-appeasement rhetoric are less plausible. As we have noted, the time sequence in these matters is usually more decisive than geographical considerations. Nonetheless, spatial relationships must also be given their due. Every power has a set of strategic geographical priorities, and it will regard antagonistic ambitions in one area of the globe as intrinsically more dangerous than in another.

Objectively, one must seek to discriminate between the various rows of dominoes alleged to be in danger of falling. Mere proximity to the home base, however, is not an adequate criterion: the United States can more easily accept communist control in Cuba than in Western Germany or Japan. Nor is the indiscriminate evocation of the domino image in every geographic region a satisfactory substitute for rational political appraisal. Almost all the smaller powers surrounding Nazi Germany were uniformly weak, and in Eastern Europe in particular they were highly ambivalent in their attitudes toward German expansion. It was therefore not surprising that when one fell the others also eventually collapsed. But a whole different set of circumstances, including American power, has prevented a chain reaction to the fall of the Cuban domino.

The same can be said of the massive collapse of the Chinese domino in the Far East in 1949. In the case of Southeast Asia, communist control in Saigon would not necessarily lead to communist control in Bangkok or Jakarta; the weaknesses of Thailand or Indonesia are many, but they are not identical to the weaknesses manifested in Vietnam. In sum, the loss of one position does not necessarily lead to the loss of others; the domino effect occurs only when the defending metropolitan power is itself weak or lacking in resourcefulness or when the region in which it has involved itself is comprised of uniformly unstable and irresolute governments.

These considerations lead directly into the problem of intent. What set of purposes animates the opposing forces in any given area? What objectives does the small ally seek to realize? A hostile metropolitan power may indeed desire to create an exclusive sphere of interest in an entire geographic region. If its capacities match its ambitions—and if the region is a vital element in the global balance of power—resistance by the other metropolitan power, including major military confrontations, is both rational and necessary. But the hostile objectives may be more modest or the muscle needed to achieve them may be lacking, in which case the defending metropolitan power may err on the side of over-reaction rather than underreaction. Further, the opposing forces may be divided in their goals: the hostile major power may seek regional hegemony, but its local ally may prefer a regional power balance to safeguard its own independence and, therefore, may turn against its metropolitan sponsor after (and sometimes even before) a victory of arms has been gained. Of the many tragic and costly American errors committed in Vietnam, not a few resulted from mistaken assumptions of an unbreakable solidarity between Hanoi and its allies in Peking and Moscow.

It hardly needs to be stressed that the enemy camp has no monopoly on divisiveness. The local ally of the defending metropolitan power is also more interested in its own objectives than in those of its distant partner. Divergent aims, of course, have characterized every alliance ever consummated, but the only successful alliances have been those in which the signatories have seriously gone about the business of resolving their differences. Thus both the metropolitan power and the local ally must show the capacity for harmonizing their interests and efforts. If the local ally is unwilling to do what is necessary to maintain its own integrity, the metropolitan power will do better to let that particular domino fall and concentrate its efforts on shoring up more promising dominoes in the rest of the row. On the other hand, the metropolitan power cannot treat the small partner as a mere pawn in its sphere of influence strategy and expect to have a reliable regional ally.

In the final analysis, then, whether the domino effect occurs depends upon will and concrete circumstance; it has nothing to do with mechanical inevitability. But once the unreal simplicity of the inevitable is replaced by the complexity of the real and highly contingent world the difficulty of assessing the stakes in limited confrontations and limited wars is evident.

A FORMULA FOR LIMITING VIOLENCE

Limited or not, war is generally the most serious commitment a politician can make. Once the decision for war is made, it will not be easily revoked except when military operations lead one side to rapid victory and the other to a precipitate and crushing defeat. Fighting that stretches out over months or years generates its own pressures for continuing the struggle. If not victory, then a draw; if not a draw, then defeat with honor (that is, let's hang on to something); if not an honorable defeat, then at least a glorious fight to the finish—these are the typical, though fortunately not inevitable, psychological dynamics of a faltering war effort.

These dynamics become more complex when more than one government is involved on either side of the struggle. If a metropolitan power is making a limited commitment to a joint war effort with a local ally, it is reasonable to consider cutting its losses and getting out if the contest begins to look unpromising. Such a consideration is in fact central to the whole concept of limited war. But it is frequently, if not always, in direct conflict with the policies of the local ally, whose very existence may be dependent on the contributions of the metropolitan power. In this situation, the local ally will use every expedient available to pressure its metropolitan partner to identify completely with its own local goals. Since it bears the brunt of death and destruction, the local ally persuasively claims the right to be somewhat fanatical about these matters.

All these observations point to the fact that once a war has started, the belligerents are as a rule more strongly pulled in the direction of escalation than of deescalation. It follows that if the war is to remain a limited confrontation instead of a struggle to the death, the key to limitation obviously resides in the aims of the belligerents. What degree of defeat do they wish to inflict on the enemy? Did the belligerents originally set limits on the resources they were willing to invest in this particular struggle? Is the side for whom the fighting is going badly able to discipline itself to abide by its original projections concerning the upper limits of its commitment? If intervening events have made the struggle more momentous than anticipated, does a reassessment of the economy of warfare produce a new set of upper limits or does the effort now become all-out? As for the side currently enjoying military advantage, does its appetite increase with the eating so that it begins to shift its sights from limited to total victory?

All these questions concerning belligerent aims have been answered differently in different conflicts, and the answers have determined the boundary line between limited and total war. Hence if limited war is by definition preferable to total war—and such a preference has come to be virtually universal since the advent of the nuclear age—an ability to discipline belligerents, or potential belligerents, to keep their aims limited is imperative. Both the Soviet Union and the United States, in their relations with one another, can rely on nothing else than self-discipline born of mutual fear. Ideally, every other state would also understand the need for self-discipline in a highly inflammable world. But here ideal and actual behavior are radically at odds, so that what self-discipline lacks must be supplied by externally imposed discipline. The most effective discipline, of course, would be that exercised jointly by the two superpowers.

The unwillingness or inability of one or both superpowers to apply restraints on local belligerents necessarily enhances the probabilities of total war at both regional and global levels. If one fears total nuclear war in a shrunken and terribly vulnerable world, one must also fear total conventional war at any given point on the globe. In the first place, no region on earth is now really remote from the zones of prime international sensitivity. Moreover, the excess of commitments and passions that total war characteristically generates constantly threatens to breach the original geographical limits of the conflict as the local belligerents desperately seek to augment their sources of external support. The Vietnamese and Korean wars are only two of the latest examples of this process. It is a process observable throughout history and includes such notable instances as the confrontation of Austria-Hungary and Serbia in 1914, the efforts of the Confederacy to involve both England and France in the American Civil War, and the success of the internal factions in the French Revolution in involving all of Europe in the fate of France. Experience admonishes those seeking to avoid total war among metropolitan powers to pursue policies designed to prevent total war among nonmetropolitan powers.

Those who insist on perpetuating the sovereign game of micropolitics will deplore the implication that the major powers have any right or obligation to regulate the policies of small powers, still less of warring factions within small powers. Yet the constitutional structure of the United Nations itself explicitly designates the great-power-dominated Security Council as the executive arm and enforcer of the international community will. One may add that Article 2, Paragraph 3 of the United Nations Charter requires that "All Members shall settle their international disputes by peaceful means in such a manner that international peace and security, and justice, are not endangered."[8] Thus the United Nations posits a community interest in preventing violence wherever it might occur.[9] It also prescribes that the aims of the parties to any dis-

---

[8] Articles 33 and 34, among others, contain language that makes it possible to translate almost any kind of a domestic political conflict into a matter of international concern.

[9] Article 51 recognizes the legitimacy of self-defense in response to armed attack.

pute, whether there has been a resort to force or not, must not endanger the security of the remainder of the community nor transgress (undefined) norms of justice.

Whatever the deficiencies of the United Nations in practice, the framers of the charter were eminently realistic in recognizing that restraints must be placed upon the policy aims of the membership as well as on the means employed to achieve them. The largely negative record of the United Nations in preventing violence and indifferent success in limiting its intensity has only underscored the realism of its macropolitical premise: the peace of the world is essentially indivisible. Its failing authority to implement the charter has in fact devolved upon the two superpowers acting singly or in concert. If they do not exercise this authority, no one else will or can. Insofar as they accept any responsibilities, then, the superpowers have the twin responsibility of placing limits on their own aims and the means used to achieve them and on the ends and means that other powers pursue. If this is not to be a mandate simply for repression, it must be linked to a positive obligation to assume leadership in a macropolitical effort to build a world society that rescues all states from the desperation which produces total conflict.

It will serve no purpose, at this point, to speculate on the prospects for concerted and systematic efforts in this direction by the superpowers. But the rather frequent ad hoc and pragmatic actions of both, singly or jointly, in curbing conflict in various parts of the world—including the Middle East and even, on occasion, Vietnam—offer precedents for policies of a longer range and more deliberate nature. In any event, if the threat of total war among the nuclear powers is to be diminished, the probabilities of total war among nonnuclear powers must also be reduced. This means that obliteration of the opposition in any given international (or internal) dispute must become as unacceptable a policy objective as it is in any domestic society that calls itself free. In turn, the political, economic, social, and cultural contexts in which the disputants operate must be altered at least to the point where the satisfactions they offer inhibit rather than provoke the impulse to all-out hostilities.

Thus the preference for limits on violence at the nuclear level cannot be realized with any sense of security unless effective limits on conventional violence are also established. Total violence in one region of the globe is a standing invitation to total violence in all regions. Moderation in the setting of policy goals and moderation in methods of attaining them across the entire board of global politics—and not just at the superpower level—are the inescapable requirements of any program of violence limitation. This is merely a restatement of the provisions of the United Nations Charter, but the persistent inadequacies of the United Nations in translating charter language into reality indicate the formidable international tasks that remain before these provisions can be given meaningful effect.

Life for the peoples of the world must be made tolerable enough so that they are ready to consent to live it or change it peaceably. These are the only conditions under which violence can be progressively diminished. It follows that the achievement of such conditions must be the central purpose of any rational international policy to limit violence, whether under the aegis of the United Nations or under other forms of authority. One can definitively move away from total war toward limited war only in the process of striving for the kind of global society in which there need be no war at all.

In any war, the aims of the stronger side will be decisive in determining the intensity, duration, and outcome of the struggle. Hence the admonition to moderation must be addressed particularly to the potential winners of any conflict, once it has broken out, if the dangers of total war are to be avoided. Similarly, it is the stronger powers, and especially the strongest, that bear the chief responsibility for creating conditions of consent and peace around the globe that can rob violence of its political appeal. Limits on force can emerge only from limits on selfish ambition—on the part of great and small powers alike—in the name of justice and peace in the world community.

Since the great powers are by definition strong and rich and the small powers weak and mostly in desperate poverty, both justice and surcease from violence make identical demands: that the great powers aid the small to achieve a rapidly growing share of the world's wealth and power. The policy formula offered at the close of the introductory chapter—a global redistribution of power, wealth, education, and status —is also the formula that will yield the most effective limitations on violence. Failure to implement it will mean that the more or less limited wars of our time will constitute only another dismal and perhaps final interval between the intensifying military spasms leading to total war.

Chapter 5

Force and War: The Weapons Dynamic

Efforts to diminish the frequency and intensity of threatened and actual violence have often taken the form of proposals for disarmament or arms control. These efforts have occupied a very significant place in twentieth-century diplomacy, but their practical results have in sum been minimal. The basic reason for this discouraging outcome is the extraordinary number and intensity of conflicts that have characterized most of this period and the consequent premium on building instead of curtailing armed might.

It would be oversimple to infer from this that weapons function only as symptoms and not as causes of conflict. Yet it remains true that any reduction in the level of armaments by adversaries or potential adversaries is bound to be temporary unless their political purposes toward one another change. The chief lesson learned from attempts to limit wars applies equally to ventures in limiting arms: the substantive goals of policy are all-important. Mutually hostile intent will produce armaments just as surely as mutually peaceful intent will produce plowshares.

A world which has reduced its stock of weapons to a minimum can only be a world whose peoples are maximizing their satisfactions to the point where force is no longer an attractive option. Hence the shipwreck of innumerable schemes for the elimination or reduction of military establishments in an international society far removed from such idyllic circumstances. It is, therefore, hardly surprising that since World War II a deeply divided humanity has used a revolutionary technology to fabricate armaments of indescribably destructive force. The ingenuity of weapons manufacture has at least matched the inventiveness of civilian technology and has far outstripped the efforts to achieve some measure of control over the burgeoning arms race. The test-ban treaty, the nuclear nonproliferation treaty, the hot-line agreement, the establishment of nuclear-free zones in Antarctica, Latin America, and outer space, and the first SALT agreements in 1972 are all important achievements. But they are also only palliative measures; they do not and cannot touch the fundamental sources of the danger that threatens all human beings with oblivion.

In a single decade, from 1962 through 1971, the world spent approximately two trillion dollars on armaments. (The digital equivalent of $2,000,000,000,000, or two thousand billion, may be a more graphic way of conveying the message.) This vast sum expended on war and preparation for war in a ten year period is roughly equal to the value of all the goods and services produced by the United States in the two years 1971 and 1972. To put it as succinctly as possible, it is double the 1971 GNP of the world's richest country. The global armaments bill in 1971 alone, the last year of the period for which figures are available, was $216 billion—a new record.[1] During the longer period from 1945 to 1971, the United States alone spent $1.3 trillion on its military establishment and the Soviet Union an estimated $1 trillion.[2]

The most significant development in the postwar history of armaments was the breakdown of efforts to reach an international agreement giving the United Nations a monopoly of ownership and production of nuclear energy. It gave notice that national armaments would continue to be, as before, a matter for national discretion. Those who could afford it, economically and politically, were free to build conventional or nuclear arms as they saw fit.

These are the conditions that produced the fantastic expenditures (and dangers) of the postwar arms race. Successive revolutions in weapons technology occurring at an accelerating rate combined with the Cold War and endemic instability in the underdeveloped world to create and perpetuate a boom in the arms market.

In many ways the impact of new weaponry has been the most spectacular of these causal factors. The replacement of piston engines by jet propulsion increased the costs of air forces by about as much as it increased flying speeds. Mastery of the nuclear fusion process and manufacture of hydrogen weapons by the mid-1950s multiplied the dangers and expense of military competition by several orders of magnitude. The

---

[1] These figures are based on data from 120 countries, and money values are calculated in 1971 dollars. Thus they reflect inflation as well as more arms and more military manpower.

The share of rising prices in the growth of world military expenditure is measured by the difference in expenditure increase over the decade if it is calculated in 1971 prices (82 percent) and in 1961 prices (33⅓ percent). Even after allowing for inflation, however, the annual arms bill was $40 billion greater in 1971 than in 1962.

The contribution of manpower costs to rising military budgets is evidenced by the increase in the number of men under arms around the world: from 19 million in 1961 to an average of more than 23 million during the years from 1968 to 1970. See United States Arms Control and Disarmament Agency, *World Military Expenditures 1971* (Washington, D.C.), 1971.

[2] Department of State, Bureau of Public Affairs, News Release, Washington, D.C., August 1, 1972.

subsequent shifts from bomber to missile delivery systems and then from liquid- to solid-fueled rockets led to new strategic deployments on air, land, and sea and to another massive expansion of military budgets.

In the latter part of the 1960s still another weapons revolution took place. It was a compound revolution in the sense that it vastly augmented offensive nuclear power and, for the first time since the beginning of the atomic age, produced a strategically significant defensive weapon. The new offensive device was labeled the Multiple Independently Targeted Re-entry Vehicle (MIRV). The new defense is best known under the generic term of antiballistic missile, or ABM.

ABM AND MIRV

The development and virtually simultaneous emergence of MIRV and ABM gave still another push to what Secretary of Defense McNamara called the mad momentum of the arms race. But the new weapons also threatened to drive costs and risks up to levels from which even the superpowers recoiled. Consequently, the United States and the Soviet Union decided to enter into negotiations which, for the first time in twenty-five years, resulted in a marked deceleration in the production and deployment of some key weapons in their nuclear arsenals.

The threat posed by ABM contributed most to the new effort at slowing the arms race. Deterrence, or the balance of terror between the superpowers, has been a function of their roughly equal ability to absorb a nuclear attack and still retain sufficient undamaged nuclear weapons to cause the attacker to suffer as terribly as the defender. ABM, however, threatened to upset this balance by making it possible for the attacker to ward off or blunt a counteroffensive (second strike) with defensive missiles capable of intercepting and destroying retaliatory strikes. The chief threat of ABM, then, was to move the "unthinkable" strategy of nuclear attack (a first strike decision) back into the realm of the "thinkable."

The Russians were the first to deploy an ABM system; its existence was verified in early 1967. Concentrated around Moscow, the system was judged by most American military experts to be only marginally effective in terms of both quantity (number of missiles) and quality (ability to intercept incoming missiles). The United States officially described the Soviet installation as a "thin" system. But its presence generated enormous internal political pressure on the American government to match the Russian move with an ABM system of its own.

During most of the 1960s American policy makers rejected an ABM system because of cost, doubts about its possible effectiveness, and disinclination to sharpen antagonisms between the nuclear opponents. Thus two prototype ABM systems of the early 1960s, Nike-Zeus and Nike-X, never became operational. But when the Soviet's "thin" system became public knowledge, the United States responded, in September 1967, by announcing the decision to build a thin system of its own.[3]

The new ABM system was called Sentinel until 1969 when the incoming Nixon administration renamed it Safeguard. It is actually an aggregate of weapons including two types of missiles (Spartan and Sprint) armed with different kinds of nuclear warheads and integrated with sophisticated radar and computer complexes.[4] The prime function of the system is to protect missile installations, but it also has some potential for intercepting attacks directed at cities and urban populations. This dual defense capability of Safeguard (and of its Soviet counterpart) intensified ABM's pressure on the strategic weapons balance that had hitherto rested almost exclusively on the offensive capabilities of each side.

Awareness of the dangers involved in destabilizing the balance of terror played a significant role in limiting initial commitments on both sides to thin ABM systems. Indeed, the United States announced that Sentinel was directed primarily against whatever missile capacity China might have developed by the mid-1970s. Moreover, even its most ardent proponents did not claim that Sentinel-Safeguard could be more than a "partial defense" against a full-scale Soviet attack on U.S. missile bases.

---

[3] See Secretary of Defense McNamara's speech in San Francisco, September 18, 1967, printed in the *New York Times*, September 19, 1967. The text clearly indicates McNamara's reluctance concerning the ABM decision. Public reaction to the speech made it evident that the decision had been precipitated by fears of political vulnerability to domestic hawks as well as by military threats from abroad.

[4] The system is designed to operate as follows: after detection of an enemy missile by the system's radar, Spartan ABM would be launched on a trajectory that would bring it into the vicinity of the incoming missile while still deep in space (anywhere from 400 to 800 miles above the earth's surface). At this point the Spectrum (2 megaton) thermonuclear warhead carried by Spartan would detonate and destroy the enemy missile with massive bursts of X-rays. Sprint is a secondary interceptor with a very much smaller (kiloton) warhead and limited range. It is designed to intercept and destroy offensive ICBMs in the earth's atmosphere up to an altitude of 20 miles.

A megaton nuclear burst is equivalent to the explosion of 1 million tons of ordinary TNT. A kiloton nuclear bomb is equivalent to 1,000 tons of TNT. The bomb dropped on Hiroshima was a 20 kiloton device. The explosive force released by Spartan is therefore 100 times greater than that released at Hiroshima. Sprint's kilotonnage is substantially less than the Hiroshima bomb.

The kilotonnage and megatonnage of nuclear arithmetic explain the otherwise inexplicable: that a single nuclear submarine carries weapons capable of unleashing more explosive force than all the bombs dropped on Germany and Japan during nearly six years of World War II.

The admittedly limited effectiveness of ABM systems therefore lent additional weight to the argument that a heavy investment in defensive nuclear weaponry would be wasteful as well as provocative.

In any case, provocation was a bigger problem than waste. Sentinel-Safeguard was a thin response to the thin Soviet ABM challenge. But massive investment could convert both into "thick" systems in terms of quantity of operational units and quality as measured by improved accuracy and effectiveness of antimissile defense. Such investment by one side would necessarily trigger a like investment on the other. Disequilibrium in the balance of terror would follow, increasing fears on each side that the other would gain a strategic advantage during this new and unfamiliar phase of the arms race and that the advantaged side would then exploit its favorable position to confront the opponent with a choice between surrender and annihilation.

These dangerous instabilities in disequilibrium, it should be added, would be generated not only by crash ABM programs but also by intensified efforts to counter their effectiveness with new offensive devices. Ironically, then, and consonant with the entire prenuclear history of arms races, a major commitment to nuclear defense must also be the greatest stimulus to the quest for a more sophisticated, costly, and devastating nuclear offense.

Fear of such a sequence of developments was equally evident in the United States and the Soviet Union. This is the fundamental reason that each unilaterally kept its ABM system thin from the first. It is also the reason that finally led them to formalize their prudential policies in the bilateral ABM treaty signed as part of the SALT agreements of 1972 (SALT I).

Another consideration also played a major part in American and Soviet decisions concerning ABM. It was obviously a possibility that the dangers inherent in the anticipated period of disequilibrium could be successfully avoided and that the two superpowers could eventually reach a new level of equilibrium based on both offensive and defensive capabilities. But the cost estimates for achieving the new equilibrium began at upward of $40 billion for each side.

The disadvantages of attempting to develop a full-scale nuclear defense system were abundantly and fearsomely apparent. In the continuing race in offensive weaponry, however, the associated dangers and disadvantages weighed less heavily with decision makers in Washington and Moscow. Although the advent of MIRV was recognized as having revolutionary implications for attack strategy, MIRV was also only the latest among a growing array of offensive weapons. Several years earlier the Soviets had begun installation of the SS-9, an enormous missile, larger than any in the American arsenal and equipped with multiple warheads capable of delivering an explosive force up to 25 megatons (equal to the explosive power of 25 million tons of TNT, see note 4). In

1967 the Soviets also began developing and testing FOBS, a system the United States had earlier tested and shelved.[5]

The massiveness of SS-9 and the sophistication of the FOBS delivery system, however, were wholly overshadowed by the attack capabilities of MIRV. First, MIRV makes possible a quantum jump in the destructive power of nuclear offense. It does this by converting ICBMs (Intercontinental Ballistic Missiles) and SLBMs (Submarine-launched Ballistic Missiles) carrying single nuclear warheads into vehicles equipped with five, ten, or an even greater number of warheads. Thus the United States, with approximately 1,700 strategic missiles in 1972, could multiply the number of its deliverable warheads to 17,000 or more.[6]

Second, MIRV greatly expands the operational range of every missile so equipped. Each warhead can be detached during flight so that the vehicle can visit nuclear destruction upon five, ten, or more areas instead of only one. Finally, as the acronym MIRV signifies, each one of the multiple warheads is independently targeted. Upon separating from its

---

[5] FOBS is the abbreviation for Fractional Orbital Bombardment System. As its name indicates, FOBS actually goes into orbit and is therefore, strictly speaking, a space rather than a ballistic weapon. Technically, however, it does not violate the provisions of the Outer Space Treaty (1967) which forbid orbiting military vehicles. FOBS is designed to make only a partial (fractional) orbit before its nuclear warhead is guided to its terrestrial target. Still, the FOBS vehicle itself continues in full orbit after its warhead is ejected with the result that its legality under the space treaty is ambiguous, to say the least. The trajectories of all long-range ballistic missiles also traverse outer space, but they do so only briefly between launch and target and are not designed to orbit or otherwise remain in space for extended periods.

[6] The SALT I agreements of 1972 froze the number of operational strategic missiles on each side for five years at the level of the then current inventories. Hence, if the agreements are not superseded or violated, the United States will continue to deploy about 1,700 strategic missiles and the Soviet Union approximately 2,300 through mid-1977.

The smaller number of missiles permitted the United States is compensated for principally by the American lead in converting to MIRV. At the time of signing the SALT agreements, the Soviets had not as yet tested their version of MIRV. Thus the United States, with fewer missiles, was estimated already to have a launch capacity of more than 7,200 deliverable warheads. See Morton Halperin, "Light Through the Cloud of Doom," News of the Week, New York Times, May 28, 1972.

It should be noted that some estimates put the number of deliverable American warheads in the 5,000 to 6,000 range. Also, on June 8, 1972, Defense Secretary Melvin Laird announced that the Soviet Union had begun testing its version of MIRV and predicted a Russian MIRV capability by late 1973 (New York Times, June 9, 1972). Subsequently, however, there has been uncertainty concerning the kind and status of Soviet testing. What has remained certain is that at the beginning of 1973 the Soviet Union was two or more years behind the United States in MIRV technology.

Other American advantages offsetting the greater number of Soviet missiles include a three-to-one lead in strategic heavy bombers, a comparable lead in nuclear warhead inventories, qualitative superiority in submarines and submarine logistical support, and a generally higher level of weapons sophistication and demonstrated reliability. See Department of State, News Release, August 1, 1972.

vehicle, the individual warhead is controlled by an independent guidance system that permits several changes of trajectory before it zeros in on its preselected target. These are the properties that led the chief of the Defense Department's research operations to confer on MIRV the macabre name of "space bus." Describing the capacity to release nuclear bombs one by one as it passes over enemy territory, he pointed out that MIRV operates rather like a bus discharging passengers at various points along its route.

Thus MIRV has accomplished a triple revolution in nuclear offense: in terms of quantity, range, and accuracy. The strategic significance of the revolution, in turn, goes far beyond the increased capacity to devastate enemy territory. The heart of the matter is the enormously enhanced ability to cripple the opponent's retaliatory system. Assuming 80 percent to 90 percent accuracy, as few as ten MIRV vehicles, each carrying ten warheads, could destroy in their silos 80 to 90 of the opponent's missiles. If the latter were also "MIRVed," this would be equivalent to the demolition of 800 to 900 warheads on the ground. To destroy the same number of warheads once the opponent had launched them, on the other hand, would require at least 800 to 900 ABMs to intercept them.

It should be evident, then, that MIRV not only reaffirms the primacy of nuclear offense over defense but that it poses a still more immediate threat than any foreseeable ABM system to the security upon which both superpowers have depended during the era of deterrence. As shown earlier, this security has derived from the knowledge that each superpower disposes of a second strike capability—the ability to absorb damage from a first strike and still deliver a death blow to the attacker's society. MIRV places a retaliatory second strike capacity in doubt. It magnifies the anxieties of each side that it will be helpless if the other side strikes first, and therefore raises the premium on striking first oneself. As Robert Kleiman put it, "The logic of this arithmetic—by increasing the fear that the other side may pre-empt—could turn the relative stability of mutual deterrence into a nightmare of nuclear nervousness."[7]

What MIRV did, then, was to cancel out much of the potential defensive effectiveness of ABM, at least at the stage of development it had reached by 1972. It undoubtedly discouraged the Soviets from investing rapidly and heavily in a comprehensive ABM system likely to become obsolescent even before it became fully operational. MIRV also lessened pressure on, and from, the Defense Department to buy a thick ABM program by bolstering the orthodox doctrine of the nuclear age that the best defense is a good offense.

Indeed, the continuing primacy of the offense was dramatically registered in the SALT I agreements themselves. While ABM development was drastically limited by a formal treaty of indefinite duration, the five-

---

[7] *New York Times*, October 9, 1967.

year numerical freeze on nuclear offense weapons was incorporated into an "interim agreement." Far more important, the interim agreement imposed no qualitative restrictions of consequence on missile "modernization." In effect, this was a green light for both sides to expand their MIRV capabilities, and other offense technologies, as rapidly as their resources permit.

Thus despite the welcome results of SALT I in terms of numerical limitations on ABM systems and on offensive missiles, the instabilities that began to endanger the deterrence pattern in the late 1960s have by no means been eliminated. After SALT I, as before, the superpowers continue in a situation in which each side must fear that the other may achieve a first strike capacity—that one side may become capable of destroying so much of the enemy missile strength in a surprise attack that it need not fear catastrophic reprisal. The remedy, of course, lies in still further hardening the missile systems of both superpowers by means of mobile ICBMs, more undersea deployment, sea bed emplacements, and the like.[8] After more colossal expenditures and psychological strains generated by and during the quest for new defensive systems, still further military innovations in both offense and defense will almost inevitably raise armaments budgets—and the level of danger—several notches more.

Only if the superpowers agree to qualitative as well as quantitative restrictions on nuclear arms will there be some prospect for really significant relief from the terror and profligate expenditures of the arms race. Qualitative problems were a leading item on the agenda of the second phase of the SALT talks (SALT II) as they got under way in November 1972. But both sides publicly anticipated lengthy and still more difficult negotiations before any further agreements could be reached.

"GENERAL AND COMPLETE DISARMAMENT"

Thus the dynamics of the mad momentum deplored by Secretary McNamara continue to gather new energy. All attempts since 1945 to stop or even slow down the arms race, including SALT I, are demonstrably puny by comparison. Any prospect for the actual elimination of nuclear weapons disappeared by the mid-1950s when it became evident that even the most intricate inspection system offered no way of discovering all the nuclear warheads already manufactured. Khrushchev

---

[8] The 1971 treaty forbidding nuclear weapons emplacements on the ocean floor and sea bed excepts sea bed within a twelve-mile zone coextensive with the coastal waters of maritime states. This treaty was signed February 11, 1971, and entered into force May 18, 1972.

put the matter succinctly when he observed that a nuclear bomb could be hidden "in your aunt's closet." In the late 1950s, the development of the ICBM made the entire globe into a unified field for nuclear operations; no part of the earth's surface was any longer immune to sudden catastrophic attack. (Agreements to create nuclear free zones may prohibit the installation of nuclear weapons within their perimeters, but they cannot prevent nuclear powers from covertly targeting them from afar.)

These developments made certain what was already highly probable since the beginning of the nuclear age: nuclear weapons and the means to deliver them within minutes anywhere in the world have become ineradicable features of international politics. It follows that disarmament, in the sense of actually eliminating armed forces around the world, is not a live option. The new circumstances make a mockery of all proposals, chiefly Soviet-inspired, for "general and complete disarmament" (dubbed GCD in the jargon of disarmament diplomacy). Such proposals, calling for complete elimination of all nuclear weapons, can never signify anything more than propaganda exercises in a world where their elimination cannot be verified.

As GCD implies, these proposals also call for the elimination of all conventional weapons down to the level needed for the maintenance of "internal order." It hardly need be noted that the demand for armaments to preserve internal order in the one-hundred-fifty-odd states around the globe will vary widely and will be subject to unpredictable fluctuations over time.[9] Hence the conventional weapons aspects of GCD proposals are as paradoxical, and hypocritical, as the nuclear clauses.

It may or may not be historical accident that Soviet Premier Khrushchev chose to introduce GCD into the disarmament debate in 1959. It was then that the superpowers' essentially uninspectable thermonuclear stockpiles had grown from few to many, and it was then that the successful operation of nuclear-tipped ICBMs had been assured. In any case, the GCD concept, which the Soviets had used to embarrass various futile disarmament conferences prior to World War II, could hardly be rejected without stigmatizing the nay sayers as enemies of peace. Hence Britain and, more tardily and reluctantly, the United States supported GCD in principle and submitted relatively detailed proposals for its realization. The United Nations membership unanimously endorsed the GCD principle (which cost no one anything), and negotiations under UN sponsorship duly began. It should cause no surprise that after protracted and fruitless discussions the talks petered out in the early 1960s. Since then, GCD has been reinjected into disarmament debates from time to time with no concrete consequences.

---

[9] The number of armaments the Soviet Union would require to preserve internal order would obviously differ from the number of armaments required by Denmark or, more pointedly, Czechoslovakia. A similar comparison could be made between the needs of the United States and, say, the Dominican Republic.

In addition to the impossible problem of inspection, the question of who would keep the peace in a relatively but still unequally disarmed world proved insoluble. The United States proposed a veto-free UN security force whose numbers and armaments would be superior to any single nation-state, including America and Russia. The proposal was feasible only within the still more unlikely framework of a limited world government. The Soviets, on the other hand, insisted on subordinating any such force to the double yoke of control by the contributing states and by the veto-ridden Security Council and therewith once again championed the principle of undiluted national sovereignty. There the matter rested.

ARMS CONTROL

If the probabilities of GCD are demonstrably nil, more circumscribed approaches to the arms race have achieved some significant but necessarily tangential successes. The decade of the 1960s, responding to the faits accomplis of military technology and registering a greater degree of realism, saw arms control rather than disarmament become the top item on the negotiating agenda. As disarmament, in the sense of eliminating or drastically reducing existing arsenals, languished, arms control, in the form of efforts to restrict the deployment of weapons, to reduce the likelihood of their use, and to slow the development of new weapons, made sufficient gains to justify hope that nuclear catastrophe is not inevitable. These achievements have functioned as both cause and effect during the lengthening American-Soviet quasi-détente that began after the Cuban missile crisis in the fall of 1962.

The first major breakthrough in arms control was, of course, the nuclear test-ban treaty signed by the United States, Britain, and the Soviet Union on August 5, 1963.[10] The treaty was initialed nearly six years after the 1957 UN General Assembly had called upon the nuclear powers to cease all testing immediately and to establish effective means to verify and police the ban. In 1958 the three powers pledged themselves to a voluntary moratorium on testing which was broken by the Soviet Union in the fall of 1961 and by the United States, in response to the Soviet test resumption, shortly afterward. All during the test-ban nego-

---

[10] Of the arms control treaties and conventions to be discussed here, almost all are multilateral instruments signed by at least a majority of the states of the world.

An exception is the Antarctic Treaty, whose original signatories were maritime states with special geographical or explorational interests in the Antarctic region. Other states are free to accede to the treaty but by 1971 there were only seventeen states that had either signed or acceded. Another exception is the regional treaty banning nuclear weapons in Latin America.

Finally, there are the Soviet-American hot line agreements and the SALT I agreements, which were bilateral undertakings.

tiations, which began in October 1958, inspection (in this case verification of test-ban violations) was a key issue. The Soviets, as usual, virtually equated inspection with espionage and were determined to keep inspectors of whatever nationality (other than Soviet) few in number, infrequent as visitors, and as far away as possible from installations on Soviet soil. The United States stressed its consistently held position that agreements are worthless unless they include binding provisions enabling the signatories to detect and verify transgressions.

When the treaty was finally completed, the nub of the perennial argument over inspection remained unresolved. Hence the treaty did not ban underground nuclear tests, which would be impossible to detect without elaborate on-site inspections. Instead, the ban extended only to explosions in the earth's atmosphere, outer space, and under water, all of which existing scientific instrumentation could monitor from afar with a high degree of accuracy. Pledges by the United States and the Soviet Union to seek a supplementary agreement banning underground tests are as yet unredeemed, and, predictably, both powers have greatly expanded their nuclear testing activities beneath the earth's surface.

France and China, determined to obtain full membership in the nuclear club and unwilling to agree to anything that would slow down their growth as nuclear powers, refused to join the other nuclear powers and the majority of nonnuclear states in signing the test-ban treaty. From their point of view, one not without a certain cogency, the treaty would function as a confirmation of the virtual monopoly of fully tested nuclear weapons enjoyed by the three original nuclear powers. The same consideration, of course, was basic to the French and Chinese rejections of the subsequent nuclear nonproliferation treaty.

The resistance of Paris and Peking points to the fundamental long-range problematics of partial measures in dealing with the nuclear menace: any arms control expedients that serve to perpetuate a Soviet-American duopoly of nuclear arms will provoke recurrent criticism, resentment, and demands for reappraisal. In the absence of profound improvements in the political, economic, and social status of the vast majority of mankind during the years from 1970 to 2000, treaty arrangements that divide the world into nuclear haves and have-nots will become intolerable. The result can only be that such treaties, whether banning the deployment or the testing of nuclear weapons, will inevitably be denounced. Both treaties, after all, permit the signatory unilaterally to revoke its agreement, in the name of its own "supreme interests," on three months' notice.

The shortcomings of the test-ban treaty should not, however, obscure its achievements. The agreement by nearly all the nations of the world to drive nuclear testing underground was a signal event in mankind's effort to deal with the new and massive complex of problems set in motion with the advent of the nuclear age. The dangerous contamination of the earth's atmosphere caused by radioactive fallout from test explosions came to a halt—with the exception of that generated by the relatively infrequent and limited testing activities of France and China. Underground confinement complicated, and made more costly, the American and Soviet testing programs and thus, to some extent, slowed down the process of weapons development. Above all, the test ban was, as President Kennedy described it in one of his favorite Chinese proverbs, the "first step in a journey of a thousand miles." A beginning had been made along the path to nuclear safety, and it encouraged the taking of further small but important steps forward.

The first such step predated the actual signing of the test-ban treaty by a little more than six weeks, but it was taken in clear anticipation of the new atmosphere that the imminent test ban would generate. On June 20, 1963, the Soviet Union and the United States agreed to establish a "hot line" between the White House and the Kremlin. This is an instantaneous communication system that enables the two governments to be in immediate and direct contact at the highest level whenever a crisis situation should arise. The intention is that both governments should have a way to make clear their purposes in any international situation in which events are moving rapidly and dangerously. Thus the hot line can serve to diminish the risk that one or both sides will heighten the tension by acting out of ignorance or misunderstanding of the other's position.

The hot line would obviously be useful in the event of an inadvertent nuclear explosion or missile launching as well as in the explanation of more deliberate diplomatic or military activities. It was put into actual use for the first time during the crisis caused by the Arab-Israeli war of 1967 and was presumably helpful in efforts to keep the violence from spreading beyond the confines of the Middle East. It hardly needs saying that the utility of the hot line, now that it is installed, depends wholly on the capacity and will of the two governments to use it in a rational manner. A much more important, and much more hopeful, consideration is that the policy decision that originally led to the installation of the hot line assumed that the two governments will use it cooperatively.[11]

The next small step in the thousand-mile journey was the simultaneous declaration by the United States and the Soviet Union in April 1964

---

[11] The hot line predictably became something of a status symbol. De Gaulle persuaded the Kremlin of the desirability of a hot line between Paris and Moscow, and Britain asked for and received the same arrangement between London and Washington.

The American-Russian hot-line agreement was "modernized" in a supplementary agreement signed September 30, 1971, and effective as of that date. The modernization undertaking was signed simultaneously with a second agreement designed to reduce the risks of an accidental outbreak of nuclear war.

of voluntary cutbacks in the production of fissionable materials. Britain, in turn, announced the imminent cessation of the production of plutonium for military purposes. As these actions were entirely voluntary and unilateral, however, there is no way of knowing the actual volume of current production of nuclear materials for the military establishments of the superpowers. At the same time, the Soviet Union refused to accept more far-reaching American proposals for procedures to verify cutbacks; it also declined to agree to a complete halt in the production of fissionable materials for war. Moscow further refused to consider a proposal for the supervised transfer of 100,000 kilograms of already fabricated enriched uranium from military to peaceful uses and the destruction of some of the existing weapons stockpiles on both sides. Hence the cessation of military nuclear production and the dismantling of nuclear arsenals, in part or *in toto*, remain as unresolved issues on the disarmament agenda of the 1970s.

The nuclear off-limits agreements (Antarctica, Latin America, and outer space)[12] represent further steps, each with its own significance. The 1959 Antarctica Treaty was especially significant in the evolution of arms control policies since it preceded the test-ban treaty by four years and became the prototype for the subsequent outer space and Latin American negotiations. But its intrinsic importance obviously falls far short of the test-ban agreement; its historic role is best characterized as a precursor of the series of arms control achievements beginning with the test ban.

The previous discussion of FOBS and MIRV has already pointed out some of the ambiguities tending to undermine the effectiveness of the treaty barring nuclear weapons from outer space. Yet the principled agreement by virtually all the nations of the world that outer space shall be used only for peaceful purposes is a precious warranty for the security of mankind as more and more of the universe beyond the earth's atmosphere is opened up to human activity. The fact that FOBS begins to blur the suborbital edges of space ought not to be cause for jettisoning a crucial undertaking that there must not be full-fledged space weapons.

Another approach to arms control focuses on the vehicles that deliver nuclear warheads rather than the warheads themselves. This was indeed

---

[12] The Antarctic Treaty was signed December 1, 1959, and entered into force June 23, 1961. It banned not only nuclear weapons from Antarctica but all military activities of any kind.

The Treaty for the Prohibition of Nuclear Weapons in Latin America was signed on February 14, 1967, and entered into force on April 22, 1968.

The Treaty on Principles Governing the Activities of States in the Exploration and Use of Outer Space, Including the Moon and other Celestial Bodies was signed January 27, 1967, and entered into force October 10, 1967.

the center of concern in the SALT I agreements. France was an early proponent of this approach, being the first to propose a complete ban on military ballistic missiles. That the French should take the lead in this area was hardly surprising since France was far behind in the race to develop missile systems. Any agreement to limit military activity to conventional aircraft would have significantly enhanced the relative standing of France as a nuclear power, for in contrast to the absence of missiles, France had some nuclear bombs and an abundance of jets. This was only a reenactment of what has become one of the classic ploys of disarmament diplomacy: each party to the negotiation is eager to limit or outlaw those categories of weapons in which others enjoy a particular advantage while exhibiting uncompromising opposition to like proposals affecting weapons categories in which one's own advantages are evident.

This repetitive masquerade in disarmament strategy is accurately caricatured in the fable of the animals' disarmament conference. The eagle is in favor of outlawing teeth. The tiger suggests the banning of beaks and tusks. The elephant opposes the tiger but supports the eagle's anti-teeth proposal, provided it is extended to cover claws. The eagle responds by raising the question whether a distinction is to be made between claws and talons. At this point the bear interrupts with a classic GCD formula: every kind of armament should be outlawed and all should embrace one another in a fervent fraternal hug.

This dismal comedy has particular relevance for vehicular arms control. Since the superpowers have already produced more nuclear explosives than they could conceivably detonate even in an Armageddon madness, the sophistication of delivery systems in offense and defense is now the crucial issue. We have already seen how FOBS, MIRV, and thin and thick ABM systems complicate the problem of vehicular arms control. In addition, one should note a special difficulty that MIRV introduced: the value of aerial or orbital surveillance of emplaced missiles has been drastically reduced because only on-the-spot inspection could determine whether any given missile is equipped with one or many nuclear warheads. The long history of Soviet intransigence with regard to inspection bodes ill for any hopes for meaningful progress in this and other aspects of vehicular arms control. The American commitment to MIRV technology constitutes an equally formidable obstacle.

The nuclear nonproliferation treaty, after more than four years of negotiation in the Eighteen Nations Disarmament Committee (ENDC) established by the United Nations, was approved on June 12, 1968, by the UN General Assembly in a 95–4 vote.[13] Ratification by individual

---

[13] Albania, Cuba, Tanzania, and Zambia voted nay. There were twenty-one abstentions: France, Argentina, Brazil, India, Spain, Portugal, Algeria, and Saudi Arabia were the most notable among the group of abstainers.

governments followed, and the treaty went into effect March 5, 1970, upon completion of the ratification process by the United States, Britain, and the Soviet Union and by the first forty of the other signatories.

The nonproliferation treaty is in many ways the outstanding achievement of the global arms control efforts of the 1960s. It marked an unusual degree of Soviet-American cooperation even to the point of joint submission of a draft treaty to the ENDC. The treaty outlaws the further spread of nuclear weapons by forbidding nuclear powers to transfer them to nonnuclear powers or to assist nonnuclear powers in their manufacture. The nonnuclear signatories, in turn, are forbidden to manufacture nuclear weapons on their own or to receive assistance in building or otherwise obtaining them. In return for full and cooperative access to atomic energy for peaceful purposes, the nonnuclear signatories agreed to accept the authority of the International Atomic Energy Agency to inspect their nuclear activities.[14] Finally, the treaty pledged the signatories to intensify their efforts to slow the nuclear arms race and to go on from there to the problem of nuclear disarmament and, once again, GCD.

The willingness of the vast majority of the nonnuclear states legally to divest themselves of the right to possess the most powerful weapons the world has ever known (and to sanction the continuing possession of such weapons by those that already have them) is a remarkable event in international politics. This remains true even though, as we have already noted, any signatory may unilaterally terminate its agreement with three months' notice. Moreover, while most of these nations are not in a position to create nuclear arsenals, a significant minority, perhaps as many as twenty, are or soon will be perfectly capable of using nuclear technology for military purposes. For them, in particular, the treaty represents an historic sacrifice in terms of their ability to make their voices heard at the highest and most fateful levels of decision in international politics. The unwillingness to make such a sacrifice was at the heart of French and Chinese opposition to both the test-ban and the nonproliferation treaties. De Gaulle and Mao were in complete agreement that in today's tough world political power requires a nuclear gun.

The attitudes expressed by Paris and Peking lie just below the surface in many of the nonnuclear countries that signed the treaty. They will inevitably gain in strength if the nuclear signatories do not make good on their pledges to bring about agreed reductions in their own over-

---

[14] Primarily at the insistence of the Soviet Union, the treaty does not subject the nuclear powers to inspection. The irony of requiring states still innocent of nuclear arms to submit to inspection, but not those already amply equipped, offers possibilities for further embellishments upon the fable of the animals' disarmament conference.

whelming military power. On the face of it, the treaty perpetuates the monopoly of the five nuclear powers and condemns the rest of the world to second-class citizenship in the realm of armaments. That the non-nuclear signatories should accept this consequence is a tribute to their wisdom as well as witness to their fear of indiscriminate proliferation of nuclear arsenals. But unless the restraint of nonnuclear powers is matched by restraint on the part of the nuclear powers in terms of a serious effort to reduce inequities between nuclear haves and have-nots, the durability of the nonproliferation agreement will be imperiled.

In the series of efforts to curb the arms race during the thirteen years from 1959 to 1972, the convention banning biological weapons is a unique achievement in several respects.[15] First, it was preceded by a unilateral action of the United States to renounce germ warfare and to destroy its existing inventories of biological weapons.[16] Second, the United States and the Soviet Union presented a joint draft of the convention to the UN Conference of the Committee on Disarmament (CCD), thus repeating their collaboration in the nuclear nonproliferation treaty.

Third, the peculiar horror that attaches to the deliberate spread of debilitating or killing diseases generated a rare consensus in favor of prohibition within and among states. Finally, and the most unusual feature, is the provision in the convention that all biological weapons must be destroyed within nine months of the date the convention enters into force. The agreement was therefore the first that could be categorized as an authentic act of international disarmament rather than simply another in the series of arms control efforts. In consonance with its unilateral renunciation of germ warfare, the United States began the destruction of its existing stocks of biological weapons even before the convention was signed.

There is a less encouraging aspect of the successful agreement to ban biological warfare. Among experts there was widespread doubt as to the military utility of biological and toxic weapons and a corresponding belief that their renunciation would not constitute any real sacrifice of military advantage. For one thing, the very nature of the weapons prevented their being tested with anything like the precision that has characterized the testing of nuclear weapons; hence their efficacy in combat conditions was open to question. Further, the possibility was all too obvious that the users of germ warfare could infect their own populations as well as those of the enemy. Thus the danger of backlash makes biological weap-

---

[15] Convention on the Prohibition of the Development, Production, and Stockpiling of Bacteriological (Biological) and Toxic Weapons and on Their Destruction, signed April 10, 1972. By early 1973 the ratification requirements had not yet been met.
[16] Statement by President Nixon, November 25, 1969.

ons cumbersome and ambiguous in effect as well as morally and psychologically repugnant.[17]

In the light of these observations one might be inclined to downgrade the importance of the biological weapons convention, but it would be a mistake to do so. If germ warfare capability is an unproven and therefore dubious military asset, its outright prohibition, extending to the destruction of all existing biological weapons stocks, is nonetheless testimony to the willingness of most sovereign states to set at least some limits to the cruelties and terrors of the arms race. Recognition of the need for international restraints and, above all, success in negotiating such restraints strengthens the credibility of efforts to achieve further cooperative undertakings. Actual disarmament in one category of weapons and operative international restraints and controls in others provide the most persuasive evidence that there can be mutually beneficial resolutions of issues generated by a world in arms—and of the deeper lying issues and conflicts that are the prime source of the world-wide demand for arms.

SUPERPOWER RESPONSIBILITY

Yet the mad momentum of the arms race continues. It has been slowed only slightly by the array of agreements, treaties, and conventions negotiated from the late 1950s through the early 1970s. Because of them, the rising curve of world arms expenditures is somewhat less steep. But because none of them have lessened in any fundamental way the fear of force or the faith in counterforce, the curve continues to rise nonetheless. Research and development of new, more efficient, and more apocalyptic weapons continues unabated. As long as the quest for combat advantage goes on, the agreements on arms control and prohibition reached so far will remain frail reeds against the threatening storm.

The storm center has been and will continue to be located in the relationships of the American and Russian superpowers. While other military structures around the world are formidable and dangerous, they are dwarfed by the masses of men and machines commanded by Washington and Moscow. Together the two giants account for nearly 70 percent of the annual global expenditure on military force, and they command more than one quarter of all men under arms around the globe. As Figure 4.1 shows, 1970 military expenditures of the superpowers together were

---

[17] It is noteworthy that the convention also pledged the signatories to continue negotiations for an agreement to ban chemical and gas warfare as well. But compared with biological agents, the military value of chemical weapons is much more clearly established. Hence a convention prohibiting the military use of chemicals and gases will be correspondingly more difficult to attain.

Figure 5.1

Ten Major Military Powers, 1970

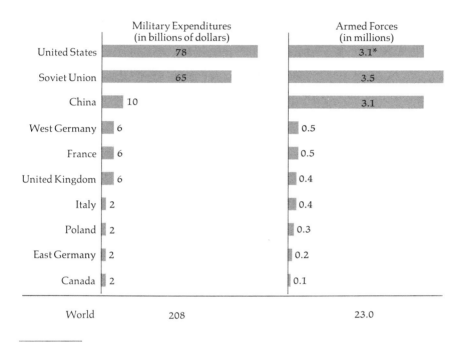

	Military Expenditures (in billions of dollars)	Armed Forces (in millions)
United States	78	3.1*
Soviet Union	65	3.5
China	10	3.1
West Germany	6	0.5
France	6	0.5
United Kingdom	6	0.4
Italy	2	0.4
Poland	2	0.3
East Germany	2	0.2
Canada	2	0.1
World	208	23.0

Source: United States Arms Control and Disarmament Agency, *World Military Expenditures 1971.* Washington, D.C., 1972.

*This figure was scheduled to be reduced by mid-1973 to 2.4 million, plus approximately 1 million reservists. (*New York Times,* January 27, 1973.)

more than fourteen times greater than those of China, the next ranking military power.

This colossal imbalance of armed might affects every particular configuration of the general and world-wide problem of armaments. Only the two superpowers are in a position to introduce—or obstruct—new generations of ever more costly and dangerous weapons. Only their decisions can ease some of the regional military impasses around the world. The preparatory talks on reducing military force levels between member states of NATO and the Warsaw Treaty offer a case in point. There was an evident irony as the negotiations got under way in Vienna in early 1973. For the junior European partners in these alliances, the major objective was to diminish the American and Soviet military and political presences in the heart of Europe. But for the United States and the Soviet Union, a measure of disengagement in Europe was only one of a number of regional and functional aspects of their shifting military strategies. They would judge the issues primarily in terms of their global deployments of force and only secondarily in terms of intrinsically European objectives. And because of their European allies' dependence on them, the superpowers would also have the last word.

The regional influence of Russia and America is equally evident in the Middle East. As the chief political supporters, respectively, of the Arabs and Israelis, they are also the chief purveyors of armaments to the contending sides in an area that has not known real peace at any time since 1920. If the leading causes of the hostilities are now to be found in the Middle East itself, their lethal effects have been terrifyingly amplified by the flood of imported Soviet and American armaments. This profusion of weapons in the arsenals of the Middle East has transformed small states into significant military powers; in consequence, the Arab-Israeli struggle has become an endemic threat not only to the peoples of the Middle East but to the peace of the entire global system.

The two major wars since 1945 have been fought in East and Southeast Asia, chiefly with American and Soviet arms. The direct and massive military involvement of the United States in Korea and Vietnam ought not to obscure the major role that Soviet weapons of all kinds also played in the outcome of the fighting. Here more than anywhere else the armed might and the clashing wills of the superpowers turned strife among small and poor societies into fearful conflagrations. And here, once again, the intensity of conflict not only brought untold misery to the peoples of these areas but also almost destroyed the shaky foundations of global peace. Although China also played a conspicuous role (which in Korea, of course, resulted in a direct military intervention), it was the state of American-Soviet rather than American-Chinese relations that weighed most heavily in deciding the issues of war and peace in the Korean peninsula and in Indochina.

Only a global measurement, however, can convey the full import of the superpowers' role as arms manufacturers and suppliers to the rest of the world. Between 1950 and 1971 the third world (*excluding* North and South Vietnam) imported from the developed world more than $18.5 billion worth of major arms. Of this huge sum (colossal in terms of the fragile economies of the recipient countries) the United States provided $6.76 billion and the Soviet Union $5.16 billion. Together, then, American and Soviet shipments constituted nearly two-thirds of the total arms flow to the underdeveloped world over a twenty-year period. (Their combined contribution to the arms flow into Vietnam was, of course, proportionally much higher.) The two other major arms exporters, Britain and France, together accounted for approximately another 23 percent of the total flow.

This distribution among the suppliers of arms has held fairly constant over the 1950–1971 period, but the total volume has increased nearly 500 percent: from under $400 million annually at the beginning of the twenty-year span to $1.8 billion in 1971.[18] The long-term acceleration of arms imports into the underdeveloped world grimly reflects the long-term increase in total armaments production to which reference was made earlier. Both dramatize the fact that this is a far more heavily armed and far more dangerous planet than when the first serious efforts at arms control began in the late 1950s.

One need not condemn all arms manufacture or export in order to contend that the swollen flow of arms into the underdeveloped countries threatens the peace of the rich as well as the poor. It drains away funds and saps the will necessary to realize the goals of development. Complicity in the competitive arming of the poor is as dangerous and irresponsible as the recklessness which, despite efforts at control, characterizes the nuclear arms race among the rich. If controls are going to be effective at any level of the world military structure, they will have to be applied effectively at every level. Restraint in weapons competition between the superpowers can only be temporary unless they also exercise restraint in their arms traffic with the volatile third world where, as we observed in Chapter 3, most of the violence since 1945 has occurred.

In every era of international history the strongest have asserted rights of regional or global leadership. They have been less willing, however, to accept responsibility for the results of the influence they wield. The global influence and responsibility of the strong have never been more visible than in the age of the nuclear superpowers. If the numbers, cost, and destructiveness of weapons around the world continue to increase, the major cause will be found in the decisions of the superpowers. By the same token, only they can provide the leadership to halt and reverse the global arms race.

SALT I and the arms control achievements that preceded it were only initial tests of such a leadership. The progress of the SALT II negotiations will be a far more decisive test. Unless the superpowers reach understandings far more comprehensive than those of SALT I, their armaments budgets will dwarf the $2 trillion aggregate expended from 1945 through 1971. Official American projections based on current (post-SALT I) defense spending indicate that the two countries together could spend another $5 trillion or more during the remaining years of the century.[19] The many-sided threats to peace and the ruinous misuse of resources represented by expenditures of this magnitude defy rational calculation. Indeed, if in future years the superpowers actually spend in

---

[18] These statistics and those in the preceding paragraph are taken from *World Armaments and Disarmament, SIPRI Yearbook, 1972* (Stockholm: International Peace Research Institute, 1972), pp. 100–110.

[19] Department of State, News Release, August 1, 1972.

accordance with these steeply rising projections it will signify the collapse of rationality altogether.

Yet the difficulties of ending the arms race are enormous. The superpowers are jointly responsible for setting its pace, but the responsibility is created not by their common will but by the antagonisms that divide them. Each would be ready to invest less in armed might if it did not fear the other would gain advantage, and these fears will play a much greater role in SALT II than in SALT I. This is true, first, because the SALT II agenda goes beyond freezes and ceilings on numbers of weapons to address the problem of actual disarmament measures—that is, the reduction of stockpiles of existing weapons. Second, the negotiators are committed to discussing across-the-board reductions in all offensive strategic weapons and not just ICBMs and SLBMs. Both objectives are much to be desired, but they raise issues whose resolution is formidably difficult.

While both sides are agreed, for example, that strategic bombers (of which the United States has a vastly greater number) should be included in the offensive weapons category, they disagree whether other weapons systems are offensive or defensive. In the opening rounds of SALT II, the Soviets contended that the approximately 700 American tactical aircraft in Europe capable of reaching Soviet territory with nuclear warheads are strategically offensive. The Americans asserted that "tactical" weapons cannot be regarded as "strategic" and that the mission of the aircraft is not offensive but rather one of defending Western Europe against attack. Conversely, when the Americans suggested that any reductions in tactical aircraft should be matched by decreasing the number of Soviet intermediate range missiles (IRBMs) aimed at Western Europe, the Soviets argued that they could not be considered "strategic" since the IRBMs are incapable of reaching the United States.

Arguments about what constitutes offensive and defensive weaponry have perplexed and stymied disarmament conferences both before and since the advent of the nuclear age. But as we have already seen, inspection and verification of compliance with agreed reductions of weapons stocks constitute a still thornier problem. It is true that satellite reconnaissance now functions as a substitute for ground inspection and verification in locating both numbers and kinds of missile emplacements. But satellites cannot detect the number of warheads clustered in each missile. And it is precisely the multiple warhead launcher, MIRV, that is now the crucial element in the offensive arms race.[20]

Once the Soviets have successfully flight-tested their version of MIRV,

---

[20] The Soviets and the Americans have had MRV launchers for some time. MRV denotes a multiple warhead missile but without the capability of targeting each warhead independently. This is the capability that converts MRV to MIRV and that constitutes a revolution in nuclear launcher technology.

they can "MIRV" their missiles undetected, just as the United States has been able to do since 1970. Then the MIRV race will be on in earnest, the Russians attempting to catch up and the Americans attempting to maintain their lead. Neither side can be certain how many MIRVs the other has. The result for both sides can only be intensified insecurity and intensified pressures for still greater expenditures and still more sophisticated and terrible weapons.

As of June 1973, there remained some hope of an agreement to ban MIRV before the staging of Soviet test flights gave the signal that the Russians were fully in the MIRV race. It was a slim hope, based on two dubious possibilities. One was that the United States would be willing to dismantle, with Soviet observers on hand, its already installed MIRVs. The other was that the Soviets would agree to cancel the scheduled test flights. Since the flights would be observable by satellite, the United States would be able to monitor a Soviet pledge to forego a MIRV capability, one which it could not perfect without testing. Thus the need for on-site inspection of Soviet missiles would be obviated.

If this hope fails,[21] SALT II negotiators must then confront directly the issue of mutual on-site inspection, and the Soviet aversion to inspection would come into play once again. If the Soviet position remains unchanged, there is little likelihood that SALT II will be able to halt or even slow down the mad momentum of MIRV. Whatever else SALT II may be able to achieve, it will not have been able to defuse the greatest of the dangers threatening Russia, America, and the world at large.

PREREQUISITES OF DISARMAMENT

Whatever the outcome of the SALT II talks, it is inescapable that the bigger and richer states, and particularly the superpowers, will remain more heavily armed than the smaller and poorer countries. We have seen that this would be true even in the wholly unlikely event of an actual GCD agreement because of the varying levels of armament needed (that is, demanded) by the several states to maintain "internal order." Moreover, it should be pointed out that mankind at large has some stake in the continuation of mutual nuclear deterrence between the superpowers and, thus, in an inequality of arms between superpowers and other states. If it is true, as suggested earlier, that the fear of nuclear weapons has been the chief deterrent to World War III, one can hardly wish the nuclear fear out of existence without providing some substitute restraint.

---

[21] The hope failed two months later when Defense Secretary Schlesinger announced that the Soviets had successfully flight-tested MIRVS (*New York Times*, August 18, 1973).

The fact is that arms control and deterrence (nuclear and nonnuclear) are unavoidably locked up in the same box. Reductions of, or restrictions upon, military arsenals will be acceptable only if those agreeing to them are convinced that the efficacy of their deterrent strategy is unimpaired. This was as true for all other ages as it is for the nuclear age. As for disarmament proper (in the sense of a large-scale dismantling of military establishments), such an objective can be realistically pursued only in an atmosphere where the felt need for deterrence policies is no longer so intense. In other words, one can move from the initial and limited measures of arms control toward major efforts to reduce the staggering dangers and costs of massive armaments systems only when the world is less possessed by fear than it has been so far in the twentieth century. Indeed, the most hopeful thing about the arms control measures that have actually been implemented is their contribution to a process that could slowly lead away from the fear of violence that has so long dominated international politics.

The function of diminishing fear and enhancing hope (provided hope is not confused with illusion) is not only creative in itself but also gives the lie to the argument that arms must be seen only as symptoms and not as causes. While it is true that hostile attitudes in international politics will almost invariably produce armaments races, it is also true that the accumulation of arms by opposing sides will reinforce reciprocal hostility and fear. It is in this familiar circular process that arms acquire causal as well as symptomatic characteristics and join the ensemble of factors that can make for war.

The causal function of armaments is equally evident in the reverse process when hostile powers begin to diminish the intensity of their antagonism. An authentic détente requires that the erstwhile opponents alter their policies toward one another in significant, substantive ways. Abstinence from at least the more obvious efforts to subvert one another, a measure of collaboration in political and economic matters, and a freer exchange of ideas and persons are among the typical indicators of détente. But willingness on both sides to deemphasize, restrict, or partially dismantle their military establishments is a signally important warrant of more peaceful intent. As such, it plays a causal role in the movement away from war just as surely as rising military outlays stimulate movements toward war.

If a competitive build-up of armaments increases international tensions and cooperative curtailment of military capacities diminishes them, it is obvious that continuing efforts in the area of arms control and of disarmament itself are eminently desirable. Contrary to the contentions of a number of analysts of international politics, such efforts need not wait upon the solution of more basic substantive questions (for example, reunification of currently divided countries, pacification of specific geographical areas, or overt alteration of policy goals by contesting powers).

One of the major difficulties with those doctrines which prescribe the settlement of substantive conflicts prior to attempts to reduce the level of arms is that new substantive conflicts constantly emerge. Hence the real world will defer both arms control and disarmament until the millenium to the degree that political settlement first and arms reductions later are believed to constitute an irreversible sequence.

Efforts at cooperation in terms of substantive matters and in terms of levels of armament need to be made in tandem. The ancient lesson that means have a profound impact on ends needs to be applied specifically to the relationship between the objectives of foreign policy and the military instrumentalities designed to promote or protect them. It is clear that the successful arms control agreements and the nonproliferation negotiations then in progress helped create an atmosphere conducive to containing the Middle East crisis of 1967. It is equally clear that failure to end the MIRV race will diminish future possibilities for the containment or resolution of any of the substantive issues (long-standing or upcoming) making for conflict between the superpowers.

Political agreements and arms limitations are mutually reinforcing in the same way that political conflicts and arms build-ups are mutually reinforcing. The hopes for continuing advances in the realm of arms limitation must wither without ongoing gains in political reconciliation. By the same token, efforts to resolve substantive controversies cannot get very far without lightening the burden of fear inspired by the presence of massive armaments. Diplomacy thus has substantive tasks to perform in South and Southeast Asia, in Western and Eastern Europe, in the Middle East, and in a host of other geographic and policy areas; it also has the urgent and continuing task of attempting to restrain and eventually undo the dynamics that both generate and are generated by arms races.

If there is still a diplomatic agenda by the year 2000, the problem of armaments will be one of the items on it. The dream of a weaponless world can only be fantasy in an international society that has not purged itself of injustice, and rational men must sorrowfully concede that a global society securely governed by justice lies beyond any future that can be projected with any degree of plausibility. For these reasons alone, nostrums such as unilateral disarmament or moral principles such as nonviolent resistance are incapable of solving the problems of war or other kinds of violence. We have seen in previous chapters that there are circumstances in which force has an undeniable utility and can even be the servant of justice. Any supposition that the international task is simply one of eliminating force is therefore misleading; the great task is rather one of building social structures on both regional and global bases in which utilities—and justice—can be realized by methods other than violence.

Moreover, the key political, social, and economic roles that military organizations often play in domestic affairs of the state—particularly in underdeveloped societies, in totalitarian regimes, or, indeed, in any heavily armed state—suggest once again the many ramifications of force. For many nations, the threat or reality of violence is much more a domestic than an international problem. In these countries, military forces are designed primarily to deal with civil strife rather than for foreign conquest or defense against invading armies. Indeed, for better or worse, in most underdeveloped countries today the military is the most important power organization in domestic politics and often the only mainstay of order. It should be obvious that until the social conditions in which the preponderant majority of mankind now lives are changed to the point where *domestic* disarmament becomes a realistic objective, the prospects for major achievements in international disarmament must be unpromising.

All these considerations point to the inescapable conclusion that the goal of a disarmed world can be pursued only within the framework of a global policy that steadily lightens the burden of human injustice. Such a policy must by definition address itself to the kinds of political, social, and economic conditions that produce violence and the corollary demand for weapons. At the same time, it must recognize the causal as well as the symptomatic aspects of armaments and pursue the essentially compatible objectives of social justice and the reduction of military arsenals. Such a policy cannot be expected to eliminate violence in any foreseeable future, but it can diminish the frequency of resorts to force by enhancing the opportunities for peaceful change.

Above all, a viable policy to strengthen the hope for justice and decrease the fear of force cannot accept the orthodox view of the normalcy of violence in international politics. It is undeniable that international relations and violence have had an historic affinity for one another, but it is an affinity that can be readily explained in terms of the highly erratic and arbitrary distribution of power, wealth, and status over the centuries both among and within states. To the extent that global commitments to global development mean anything at all, they signify that these kinds of unjust maldistributions can no longer be tolerated as "normal"; it follows that the violence they produce ought not to be considered normal, either. A rational global policy will adopt a different model in which violence, poverty, and other kinds of deprivations are designated as abnormalities which must be corrected if humanity is to survive. Such a policy can do no better than to proceed on the understanding that violence and justice are mutually repugnant.

In the specific matter of armaments, rational policy must seek first to bring the mad momentum of the arms race to a halt and then to reverse its direction. The arms control measures so far realized could serve, if the superpowers so choose, as the beginnings of a movement for sanity in the direction of disarmament. To the degree that social justice begins to be realized in the underdeveloped world, the military needs of the superpowers will eventually decline. Their major armaments burdens, however, derive from their mutual opposition—and their joint opposition to China. Here the threat of violence arises not so much from problems of social justice as from fundamental individual and social emotions such as fear and pride. These kinds of emotions are tenacious and intransigent and underscore the difficulties that will plague any serious disarmament efforts at the superpower level. But if there are difficulties, they need not be deemed insuperable; the superpowers may feel compelled to overcome them in the name of their own safety. The pressure from the nonnuclear world to scuttle the nonproliferation treaty will grow insistent if the nuclear powers do not reach agreement to scale down their monopoly.

A still more effective pressure would emanate from the recognition of the simple truth referred to in Chapter 2: neither the United States nor the Soviet Union, and one may now add China, has any objective need of conquest. The key to wealth and power, actual or potential, lies in internal development and policy and not in foreign domination. Neither the survival, the security, nor the greatness of these three giants requires the enormous efforts that each of them now expends on arms. In view of the terrible and evident dangers that beset all men in the nuclear age, it is not unreasonable to hope, or even to anticipate, that the three giants will gradually come to realize that the competition in arms is not only dangerous, futile, and self-defeating but also unnecessary. When this lesson is learned (and there is no reason it should not be learned in the 1970s), one can then look to cooperative efforts to achieve major reductions in the world's most formidable arsenals. In other words, disarmament as well as arms control can then be translated into a meaningful program of action.

Once this stage is realized, men can realistically reject the ancient proposition of the normalcy of war in international relations. But there can be no halfway house in which "either peace or war" is accepted as the standard for international behavior. As in reasonably free and satisfied domestic societies, the international norm must be equated to peace —and to justice as the only guarantee of a peace that can endure.

Chapter 6

Ideology

Since the beginning of human history, force has shared the stage with ideology as an instrument for the governing of men. While force and ideology have often been in partnership with one another, their essential characteristics are antagonistic. Force governs by coercion and fear; ideology governs by consent and hope.

This set of contrasts may understandably offend those who are aware of the destructive role played by ideological passions over the centuries in both domestic and international politics. There is no intention here to gloss over the havoc created again and again by ideologies that have deified particular religions, races, nations, classes, or political systems. All history has demonstrated that fanaticism is the occupational disease of ideologists. Yet the world lives at least as much by ideology as by force, and it is vital that the nature and function of ideology be understood as clearly and dispassionately as possible. From such an understanding should come a more realistic assessment of the contribution ideology can make to peaceful cooperation as well as to conflict among men in both domestic and international society.

Ideology is a set of ideas that purports to give meaning to the past, to explain the present, and to prognosticate the future. It necessarily couples these explanatory and predictive functions with a series of value judgments: ideology distinguishes between what has been good and what has been evil in the past; it decrees what kind of behavior is or is not virtuous in the present; and it prescribes desirable objectives for the future and the means to achieve them.

It should be added that the value judgments inherent in every ideology need not involve ethical principles. Often they are expressed in terms of such nonethical criteria as rational or irrational, advantageous or harmful, and true or false. Finally, in order to qualify as an ideology, this set of explanatory and judgmental ideas cannot simply be the speculations of an individual thinker (or thinkers) isolated from the surrounding world, but it must move into the world and affect the lives of significant numbers of men. In other words, ideology is by nature a social phenomenon.

It is apparent from the foregoing definition that ideology is also an extraordinarily powerful social phenomenon. While each case differs in the degree of specificity with which the basic ideological functions are carried out, every ideology is a variation on the theme of Goethe's famous questions: Where did we come from? Why are we here? Where are we going? However often fashion decrees the death of God—or, indeed, the end of ideology—men are not going to cease asking such questions. It follows that there will always be a market for ideologies because ideologies profess to probe these questions and offer answers to them. Whatever the factual or moral validity of any particular ideology, it is clear that ideology as a generic phenomenon performs a crucial social function. It offers a sense of meaning and purpose to individual and corporate existence. Ideology is therefore a vital and indispensable ingredient in the building and maintenance of human communities.

Communities take many forms: religious, political, economic, racial, geographic, professional, and fraternal. Each form displays more or less visibly its ideological countenance in its efforts to explain reality (or that part of reality deemed relevant) and to proffer criteria for judging the reality discerned. Whatever the nature of the community, its ideology is designed to reconcile its members to the communal life, to prevent members from becoming alienated, and often to attract new recruits to the community.

It should be evident, then, that ideology's role in political or any other kind of social organization is characteristically one of persuasion. In professing to offer a plausible interpretation of social existence, a set of attractive values, and a guide to a hopeful future, ideology must rely on consent rather than force in order to prosper. While it may threaten the heretic with coercion, its continuing power and vitality can come from no other source than the continuing and willing loyalty of the bulk of its followers. Ideology's chief function is the legitimation of the social organization it represents, and, as was seen in the chapter on power, legitimacy is fundamentally a matter of consent. Hence the distinction made at the beginning of this chapter between ideology and force.

Before we subject ideology to more detailed scrutiny, the cardinal features of ideology in the abstract bear recapitulation. First, ideology is an essential component of social organization and, as such, cannot be eliminated from human existence. Second, in the absence of the explanatory and evaluative functions performed by ideology, men and societies suffer a sense of alienation and meaninglessness. Third, the alternative to government based on the loyalties that ideology cultivates is government by raw force in either of its two classic forms—tyranny or anarchy. Finally, to give additional stress to its role in social organization, it should be noted that ideology can be variously translated as doctrine, creed, belief system, and social myth. Neither rulers, churchmen, citizens, nor revolutionaries could avoid agreement that in these matters one is dealing with fundamentals.

THE CONCEPT OF IDEOLOGY IN HISTORY

Of course, the definition of ideology offered here is by no means universally accepted. The term "ideology" has been in use for nearly two hundred years and has gone through a number of metamorphoses of meaning. It was coined by Antoine Destutt de Tracy, a French Enlightenment philosopher, who desired to use the word in its precise logical meaning, that is, to denote a science or theory of ideas. But despite the politically and socially neutral ring of this definition, de Tracy endowed his verbal invention with the polemical tone with which it has since been associated. He and like-minded philosophers believed the science of ideas would serve not only as a path to objective truth but also as a means to discredit religious, metaphysical, and other traditional explanations of reality. From the beginning, then, ideology was, among other things, a partisan battle cry, a declaration of war against another belief system (or doctrine, creed, or social myth). Only its newly minted and verbally neutral name created the illusion of a categorical distinction between ideology and all the other belief systems that had preceded it.

Ideology's claims to realism and objectivity were rudely denounced by Napoleon when the teachings of the "ideologues" ran counter to his imperial ambitions. He accused the ideologues of being unable to grasp the realities of the practical world and so relegated them to the same intellectual limbo to which they themselves had previously consigned churchmen and metaphysicians. However self-serving Napoleon's motives, his accusation was historic in the sense that ideology has ever since had to contend with the implication that it embodies an unrealistic and, therefore, false set of ideas. Napoleon also set the precedent for making ideology a dirty word: he pinned it on the adversary while denying any ideological contamination of his own policies and doctrines.

It was left to Marx to place ideology at the center of political and intellectual debate. Marx' attack on ideology was no longer directed at the specific school of thinkers against which Napoleon had vented his ire. Ideology had become a class phenomenon: Marx equated ideology to any network of ideas whose function is to serve class interests. Therefore, ideology could take many forms: bourgeois economic theory, religion, the chivalric ideal, natural rights doctrines, philosophic idealism, nationalism.

The Marxian view attributes to all these ideologies the property of deceit, and in two senses. First, ideology's representatives deliberately lie to protect and further the interests that ideology camouflages and for which it provides moral justification. Second, and more important, class interests *necessarily* distort the perceptions of those who are caught up in them, so that the ideological superstructure generated by class (or other) interests is intrinsically fraudulent—quite independently of any conscious intention to lie. For Marx, then, the central political task becomes only incidentally one of exposing and punishing liars; the primary task is to destroy the false ideas themselves by means of a radical overthrow of the existing social conditions from which they spring.

Thus de Tracy's ideology took on connotations opposite from those he had claimed for it. Instead of being the instrument of truth to destroy error, ideology had itself become a prime source of error which must be expunged by new truth. If Marx, like Napoleon, brands ideology less as deceit and more as illusion, its malign influence becomes still more deep-seated because it incorporates a whole substructure of unwitting falsehood far more difficult to combat than conscious lies. In this light, ideology becomes a melange of deceit, irrationality, superstition, and want of comprehension. And since ideology always serves particular interests at the expense of general interests, it is always both consciously and unconsciously hypocritical.

In the face of a long history of polemical usage of the term ideology, Karl Mannheim conducted a rescue operation—of sorts—in his famous study *Ideology and Utopia*. While Mannheim was generally critical of ideology, defining it at one point as a set of ideas circulated by and among a ruling group and functioning to perpetuate its rule,[1] he was interested in a matter of more fundamental importance. This was the proposition that *all* social groupings are caught up in subjective points of view and that their conceptions of reality are always socially conditioned. Accordingly, he concluded that "the thought of all parties in all epochs is of an ideological character."[2] Mannheim's conclusion cut the ground from under any contention that only the adversary is caught up in the toils of ideology. Instead, all "parties" operate within the confines of given ideologies.

Mannheim distinguished ideologies from utopias, describing the latter as sets of ideas generated by oppressed groups and committed to radical change of the status quo. Without getting into the sometimes tortuous argumentation by which Mannheim arrives at his preference for utopian over ideological thought, it suffices for the purpose here to note that Mannheim saw both as being imperfectly in touch with reality. To this extent, then, ideology and utopia are identical. Moreover, conscious and

---

[1] Karl Mannheim, *Ideology and Utopia* (New York: Harcourt, Brace, 1936), p. 36. The foregoing discussion of the usage of the term ideology is drawn in part from Mannheim's book.

[2] Ibid., p. 69.

unconscious preoccupation with self-serving interests and desires constitutes the chief source and measure of their common blindness to reality. Thus both ideology and utopia symbolize the subjectivity and par-
tiality that afflict all men and all social groupings in which they
participate.

Mannheim's effort to make a qualitative distinction between ideology
and utopia did not succeed insofar as general usage of these terms is
concerned. Utopia retains its traditional meaning as a radical and sometimes visionary critique of and alternative to existing society, but it is
generally treated as a variant of ideological thought. Ideology has prevailed as the generic term for belief systems located along the whole
spectrum between reactionary and radical, and utopian thought is thus
necessarily subsumed under it. There is still no consensus in so viewing
ideology. But there has been enough agreement in theory and practice
to further the process of dislodging the polemical implications of the
word and employing it instead as a descriptive-analytical term. Such
usage makes it possible to discuss the role of ideology on its merits rather
than as an inherently noxious phenomenon.

If ideology performs a crucial social function, it does so in both domestic and international society. In domestic politics, it can protect the community by combating factionalism and the threat of anarchy. In international politics, it can protect the several communities by infusing each
with a sense of identity resistant to external pressures. Internally, it
defines and justifies the rules of social organization. Externally, it ration-
alizes the community's behavior in the international arena. It functions
as the interpreter of both internal and external reality; as such, it offers
a purpose and perspective without which events within and beyond the
community would dissolve into unintelligible chaos.

The interpreting, ordering, and unifying functions of ideology so far
stressed constitute, in essence, social cement. But since ideologies are
almost invariably tied to local interests, or at least to local origins, their
solidarity function almost invariably ceases at one or another physical
or cultural boundary. As soon as ideology is examined as an international problem, then, it is more often seen as a divisive force than as a
force for cohesion. In particular, the presence of conflicting ideologies
has been one of the chief characteristics of twentieth-century world
politics—to the point where one is tempted to forget that there are differing ideologies that coexist in relative compatibility and that there are
other eras of international politics in which hostile ideological confrontation was of little or no importance. But whatever the modifying observations, contemporary international experience has been a tragic witness
to the degree of enmity that clashing ideologies can produce.

The contemporary world also provides a reminder, if one is needed,
that ideology does not always play the role of a unifying force within
the civil society. If the world scene has always displayed a multiplicity

of ideologies, the domestic society has frequently exhibited the same characteristic. The ideology of the nation or state, which claims to incorporate the standards of the whole community, is often confronted with subnational or transnational ideologies based on class, religion, race, or other values. Unless a mutually acceptable coexistence can be agreed upon (and sometimes agreement is very difficult to achieve) the society runs the danger of civil war—just as mutually intolerant ideologies in the international arena heighten the risks of international war.

It should therefore be evident that ideology confronts us with a profound dilemma in that it both unites men and divides them from one another. It has been argued that ideology's unifying functions are socially indispensable. It is now time to examine its divisive aspects in some detail. They arise from three broad characteristics that all ideologies tend to display: deceptiveness, emotionalism, and exclusivity.

IDEOLOGY AND DECEIT

In the brief history of the term ideology we have already seen it used to signify something hovering between a lie and an illusion. The reasons for this negative assessment (characteristically made by the political Left) were two. First was the view of ideology as a set of presumably attractive symbols (religion, patriotism, imperial glory) deliberately manipulated by the ruling class for the purpose of hoodwinking the masses into supporting the particular interests (profit, power, prestige) of the manipulators. Since the masses would respond to the symbols unaware of the selfish interests they concealed and since the furtherance of the interests of the rulers would benefit only themselves and not the masses, the critics charged that the whole operation was a lie from start to finish. The deception was compounded by the fact that such a manipulation of ideological symbols fostered a bogus sense of unity between rulers and ruled, while in truth it was hardening and confirming the barriers separating the rich and powerful from the poor and powerless.

The concept of ideology as illusion softened or removed altogether the role of deliberate falsehood; its place was taken by the lie which is both involuntary and preordained. In this version, the ruling class cannot help equating its own interests with those of society at large. The values and aspirations of the ruling group are the products of its own group experience; it cannot imagine that anyone outside its circle could speak for society or that there might be opposing interests worthy of consideration in the making of policy. In essence, the ruling class grants itself a monopoly of command and the masses a monopoly of obedience. Religion or patriotism or other overarching symbols are invoked—not cynically, but as a matter of course—to legitimize these arrangements.

Marx and Mannheim called these attitudes "false consciousness," which might be translated as extreme subjectivity of viewpoint caused by an unreflective and therefore relentless preoccupation with self-interest.

No one who has studied historical or contemporary elites will dismiss these sketches as mere caricature. If they do not faithfully reflect all aspects of the reality of politics, they fit the case in enough instances to define one of the great and perennial problems of political life. The tendency toward "false consciousness"—and toward the use of the deliberate falsehood—is built into every society. Nor is it restricted to the "ruling class" in the classic sense of a group controlling society as a whole. It appears in bureaucracies or segments of bureaucracies, in powerful economic, religious, professional, or intellectual groups, in the figure of the man who lives in the white house on the hill. And, as Mannheim pointed out, it appears in oppositional and revolutionary groups. Utopians, too, pursue their interests to the exclusion of others and in more or less blind defiance of the real world.

Subjectivity and self-interest are obviously at the root of these spectacles, but it is the claim to objectivity and common interest that raises the issue of deception. The individual who candidly proclaims his single-minded intention to gratify his personal desires may, with luck, achieve his purpose, but he will be functioning outside the sphere of social action. Society and politics presuppose the group, and the group presupposes a number of individuals linked by common interests and values. Hence group purposes stress those things which unite the members and play down divergent interests among the membership.

Thus tensions arise between unity and diversity, between common and individual interests, which are fundamental to group life at every level from a neighborhood gang through trade unions or ethnic associations to nation-states and transnational ideological movements. The inevitable bias in group values in favor of group unity distorts reality to the extent that it ignores, misrepresents, or suppresses the deviant aspirations of the individual members. This is the point of generation for both false consciousness and the deliberate lie; here group purpose is represented as being something other than it is.

Ideally, group purposes would be limited to those areas where there is an authentic community of interest among the membership and would not presume upon those areas where individual interests diverge. But the premium on unity, the necessity for individual service to the group, the varying intensity of individual loyalty to group enterprises, and the need for both exhortation and punishment to ensure the durability of group norms constitute continuing pressures to transgress those limits. Even if the transgressions are nil or minimal, these necessary aspects of group life create a group mystique that is already at one remove from the reality of man's life in society.

The group is larger and more powerful than the individual, its behavior is institutionalized, and, in the case of such major groups as state and church, it is more durable than the individual. Hence, out of fear, respect, convenience, ambition, and a host of other motivations, the individual is constrained to conform to group values and to subordinate or conceal those values of his own which stand outside the group consensus. Thus the group stakes its claim to decide issues in areas outside the authentic common interests that bind its membership together.

If group values assert a greater measure of common interest than in fact exists, this is not the only source of illusion and deception. Fostering the appearance of group harmony, which, within limits, may be real enough, inevitably obscures the undercurrents of tension generated by the individual's attempts to adjust to the claims of group life. To the extent that the group is one of free men, there is opportunity for ongoing negotiation and adjustment of the relations between individual and group values on the principle that the major purpose of group life is to benefit the members, and not the other way around. Such negotiation and adjustment constitute the only means by which the group mystique can be kept in touch with reality. All groups, of course, claim to benefit their memberships, but to the extent that the claim cannot be debated and demonstrated on a continuing basis the group mystique moves more and more into the realm of deception. It is in these circumstances that group values—ideology—are converted into an orthodoxy that tolerates no criticism.

The primary sources of the frauds and fallacies that subject ideology to the reproach of its critics are the insistence that unity is always the primary value, that loyalty must transcend the actual ensemble of shared interests, and that criticism cannot be tolerated. The reproach is legitimate, but the remedy is often elusive. This is because overweening ideological demands are invariably rooted in authentic social values: the need for social unity in a great many crucial matters, the need for a social loyalty that will persist even when individuals are asked to make sacrifices for the common interest, the need for a set of symbols and institutions that command the respect of all sectors of society and are thus ordinarily insulated from partisan criticism. These needs are fundamental in the life of social groups, and ideology will be the fundamental response to them as long as men seek to formulate common interests and common social purposes.

Explaining, interpreting, and affirming these interests and purposes, ideology will inevitably reflect the quality of the motivations to which they are linked. Thus arguments for banishing ideology (ideology would presumably disappear in Marx' classless society) miss the point. Ideologies are permanent denizens of the political and social world, and their role as a force for reason or unreason and for good or evil will always depend first of all on the way in which men deal with the issues emerging from the unity-diversity problem present in every social group.

So far in this discussion of ideology and deception the emphasis has been on the individual and the group. But groups, particularly those with more elaborate ideological systems, are not simply congregations of individuals. They are characteristically made up of a more or less numerous set of subgroups. The simplest model, and sufficient to the purpose here, is a group comprised of a leadership subgroup and a number of other subgroups outside the leadership. By virtue of its official position and power, the leadership claims to be the legitimate interpreter of the group ideology. But since it is interested in protecting its leadership position, there is a proneness to manipulate ideological symbols in a way that will benefit the leaders. In this way the idea of the common interest of the group is suborned to serve the special interests of the subgroup. This is the process that provoked Marx' attack on the ruling class in bourgeois society.

The conflict between group and subgroup offers even greater opportunities for ideological obfuscation and sleight of hand than the conflict between group and individual. But the phenomenon of the subgroup can also furnish a remedy. Its effectiveness, of course, varies with the power of the one or more subgroups outside the leadership to call the leadership group to account or to replace it. The nonleadership subgroups have a vital stake in preventing the leadership from misappropriating the ideological symbols of the community to consolidate or increase its own power. They, too, assert rights of ideological interpretation for the community as a whole, rights that may be expressed in a full-fledged counterideology.

Whatever their stance, of course, the subgroups out of power are not necessarily any freer of subgroup bias in their exposition of community ideological values than is the leadership group. Thus competition among subgroups in ideological interpretation will never eliminate error— indeed, its sources are multiplied. But insofar as mutual criticism disciplines the contending parties and forces each to search for links to the group as a whole, error is not likely to be so gross as when a single subgroup monopolizes the ideological function.

EMOTIONALISM AND EXCLUSIVITY

Ideological commitment characteristically involves emotional commitment. Nationalism, religious faith, class consciousness, or racial pride are obviously not matters of pure reason; love, hatred, anger, fear, and a host of other emotions are built into these affinities. Ideology lives by loyalty, and loyalty is not authentic if it is merely the product of a set of rational calculations whereby the individual decides that it is in his interest to adhere to a certain group or set of ideas—with the proviso that if his interests change his affiliations will also. Although it is true that the group cannot be justified if it does not benefit the individual interest, it is also true that the individual must make sacrifices if group purposes are to be achieved. It follows that the willingness to make such sacrifices in the absence of immediate personal benefits, or at times when group purposes are in conflict with the individual's desires, is the first test of loyalty.

The ultimate test of loyalty, of course, bluntly asks whether the individual loves his ideological community to the point where he is willing consistently to place its welfare before his own and to derive his most cherished personal rewards from an ethic of service to it. The priest in the church, the patriot in the nation, the soldier in the army, or the militant in the revolutionary cause are expected to answer in the affirmative. In each concrete case the affirmation may be true or false, but the general norm of loyalty based on love is an indispensable element of any viable ideology.

Ideology thus articulates a community of reason and emotion; the balance between them varies from case to case—and in every case eludes precise measurement. Now it is a fundamental assumption of the case against ideology that reason and emotion are inherently inimical. It argues that the emotional component inevitably tends to obscure or overwhelm the rational; in so doing, it effects a divorce between the true believers and reality. Irrationality, in turn, reinforces subjective preferences instead of disciplining them. Hence the ideological community is given to quixotic behavior: it launches crusades, it makes claims of universal validity for its own culture-bound values, it becomes blind to its own shortcomings and unable to appreciate or even understand alternative sets of values. Its sense of self-importance is inflated to the point where it becomes, as Hobbes said of the state, "a mortall god." And the servants of mortal gods necessarily become idolaters and fanatics.

These arguments describe accurately enough the pathology of ideology, and there is an abundance of cases on which they can draw for illustrative material. The Inquisition, the Terror, Hitlerism, Stalinism, the communal fanaticism that tore apart India and Pakistan and Nigeria and Biafra, and the racial conflict that today poses the gravest threat to the United States since the Civil War—all these are examples of emotionalism rampant. Each represents the triumph of fear, hatred, pride, anger, and greed over reason. But they also represent a triumph over the contrary emotions: courage, love, humility, sympathy, and generosity. Hence the issue is drawn not simply between reason and emotion but also between the warlike and pacific emotions. Reason is necessary to prevent courage from becoming foolhardy or love from becoming idolatrous. But its still more important task of curbing the belligerent passions would become impossible without reinforcement from the passions that make for harmony. Thus a call for the suppression of passion in political and social life is as undesirable as it is unrealistic.

In society as in the individual, reason has always lived together with an ensemble of emotions. The presence of rational-emotional ideological structures is a reflection of that fact, and every attempt to purge ideology from political life on the charge of irrationalism will fail before this elementary truth about man in society. The need for a unifying myth, for group as well as individual self-esteem, for social expression of the emotional as well as rational elements of man's life all guarantee ideology's future. The pathology of ideology with its delusions of grandeur that transform the self into Saint George and all the world into a dragon is a perennial threat in a dangerous world. But the danger can be forestalled only when reason is united with the pacific emotions to curb the warlike ones. It is a matter of refining and disciplining emotions and not of suppressing them. The same holds true for ideology itself.

Exclusivity is the third major ideological vice. It emerges from many interrelated sources; the most fundamental is that human subjectivity which forever precludes any final objectivity in knowing and evaluating the meaning of man's life. Ideas of social organization and values necessarily rest on incomplete and incompletely understood data and must therefore inevitably lack universal validity. The situational variant of subjectivity is parochialism in which the thing observed is distorted because of the viewer's point of observation.

Subjectivity guarantees that there will always be a multiplicity of ideas attempting to explain human society and purposes. Parochialism guarantees that there will always be conflicts in interpreting the meaning of these ideas. Thus the stage is set for ideological combat in which one complex of ideas is declared superior to another and, at the same time (paradoxically, perhaps), is endangered by the inferior complex. All of which has led many observers to accept what might be called a corollary to the phenomenon of ideology: there is no ideology without a counterideology. Each claims an exclusive patent on the truth; each excludes the adherents of the other. The in-group of one is the out-group of the other. Thus the world is divided into any number of mutually exclusive and intolerant blocs.

The case for accepting the corollary that ideology presupposes a counterideology is very strong. It has already been noted that the word itself, whatever the stated intent of its coiner, was born to do doctrinal battle. And it is generally true that throughout history the religious, political, and social belief systems that later came to be called ideologies emerged in the face of opposition and, in turn, opposed the emergence of new belief systems.

The pagan-Christian confrontation in Rome and the subsequent clash of Christianized Rome with the "barbarians," the rise of Islam in the

Arab East, the struggle between Muslim and Hindu in India, between Catholic and Protestant in Europe, *ancien régime* versus revolutionary democracy in France, liberty versus slavery in the United States, communism versus tsarism in Russia—all these exemplify belief systems in conflict. In each case one party to the confrontation defeated the other. Yet in no case was the defeat total—the belief systems of the victors were always infiltrated by the ideologies of the defeated. To take Rome as a single example, the victorious Christians retained the imperial ways of the pagan Romans who had once been their persecutors. In turn, the barbarian conquerors of the late Empire converted to Christianity, thus imitating the Romans who centuries earlier had borrowed the gods and intellectual values of conquered Greece.

What these brief historical references can only hint at is that there are areas of compatibility among ideologies. Even in the massive and historically critical conflicts just cited there was a degree of mutual conversion between victors and vanquished. To some extent this was because they had to live together after the battles were done. To some extent it was because the opposing ideologies were not wholly repugnant to one another; each contained elements more or less acceptable to many on the other side. To some extent it was because ideologies, after all, reflect human experience and thus, despite their parochialisms, cannot be wholly alien to men operating within the framework of other parochial ideologies.

If each major ideology addresses itself to the portentous questions concerning the origin, significance, governance, and destiny of man, the form is the same even if the content differs markedly. Moreover, there is overlap in content both because ideology addresses itself to the human condition and because of mutual borrowing among disparate ideologies. Christianity and Islam, Catholicism and Protestantism, Marxism and liberalism all demonstrate overlaps of ideological content whose scope varies from case to case.

These observations are not meant to minimize the past terrors or present dangers of ideological conflict. Identity of form and overlap in content have not prevented virulent enmities or massive bloodshed. The ideologies of competing nationalisms, of competing concepts of world order, and of competing racisms constitute the most formidable contemporary threats to peace both among and within states. The point is simply that ideologies have capacities for accommodation as well as conflict. After all, the religious struggle between Christian and Muslim in most parts of the world has long since been laid to rest. The centuries of bitterness between Catholicism and Protestantism have given way to a growing ecumenism. Communism and democracy respond to the imperatives of nuclear reality by seeking, often painfully, ways to coexist. The conclusion to be drawn is that the presence of contending ideologies does not necessarily foretell inevitable bloody battle. If one accepts the corollary that ideology presupposes an opposing ideology, the question remains as to the intensity of their opposition. Only an answer to this question can provide an estimate concerning the likelihood of major conflict.

THE PROBLEM OF PAROCHIALISM

It should be evident that intensity of ideological opposition is closely related to the problems of parochialism and subjectivity. Parochialism, it will be recalled, occurs when the thing observed is distorted because the vantage point of the viewer conditions and biases his observation. When the myopic provincial views, judges, and condemns the city and the world in terms of the values of his own rural bailiwick, his vantage point, in the classical usage of the term parochial, is spatial. Spatial parochialism is equally, and more dangerously, apparent in the nation or creed that sets itself up as a universal standard from which the rest of the world is seen as regrettably or maliciously deviant. Parochialism in both individuals and societies has its roots in the sheer geographical distance and relative infrequency of contact between cultures. The vantage point can also be temporally remote in that men tend to impose their judgments on past events without understanding that values are time bound as well as space bound. Finally, the vantage point can be social in that the objects observed are seen through the filter of class, ethnic, occupational, or religious allegiances.

Since all these parochialisms have to do with human relationships, they distort both the observer and the thing observed. Because the observer draws conclusions from his inaccurate observations, his behavior will be unrealistic. Because the thing observed is man in another culture, the observer's tendencies to parochialism will be reinforced to the extent that he knows *himself* to be the subject of biased observation. This is the contribution of parochialism to the state of affairs in which human cultures, though occupying the same planet, seem to exist in different worlds. Parochialism certainly does not account for the far-reaching objective differences among human cultures. What it does do is to obscure the similarities and to transform what is merely different into something bizarre, evil, or dangerous.

Parochialism clearly intensifies the divisions among men; it follows that ideology, to the extent that it is parochial in outlook, will play a divisive rather than a unifying role. It is therefore an exercise in windmill tilting to try to solve the problem of divisions in domestic or global society by declaring that ideology is the enemy that must be driven from the field. The real contest is with parochialism, and the relative values of ideologies need to be measured in terms of the balance between their parochial and cosmopolitan elements.

A cosmopolitan perspective, as noted at the outset of the introductory chapter, is one that seeks (always imperfectly) to understand the whole as well as the parts by moving from the parochial starting point toward the vantage point from which the whole can be viewed with minimal distortion. Thus the emigrant village dweller becomes mobile, experiences and learns from the city, becomes acquainted with other countrysides, and sees his former way of life as part of a larger social system. The narrow sectarian leaves his parish and discovers the wealth of unities and diversities that gives his religion its overall significance. The nationalist goes abroad and discovers other ways of life; his own becomes one among many, each of which has its unique values. These sketches do not pretend to capture the profundities of the transition to cosmopolitanism, but they do pinpoint the kind of experience that can lead to the broadening of perspective. This broadening, in turn, is the essence of the cosmopolitanization process.

The conquest of parochialism depends on an ongoing process of learning and growth. There is nothing inherently static in the relationship between the observer and the thing observed. On the contrary, observation is an inherently dynamic activity that invites further observation. It can provoke the observer to reflect on the adequacy of the presuppositions and values that characterize his initial vantage point and instill the desire to remold them in the light of what he has observed.

The process is not without pain and loss as old certainties become new relativities. It is at these points of pain (alienation from one's surroundings, hostility from one's more sedentary fellows, uncertainty concerning the directions further observation should take) where inhibitions against further learning emerge. The pull of parochialism makes itself felt, and the observer is tempted to shun and even fear new experience instead of engaging in further pursuit. If he moves too far away from the ambit of his original environment he becomes rootless unless he can put down roots in another community or social group, small or large. But new roots mean new involvement in parochial perspectives if there is to be solidarity instead of hostility in his relations with his fellow members of the new community. Thus the pressure to accept parochial values is unavoidable and unrelenting.

Ideology experiences the same pressures that accompany the pilgrimage of our harassed individual observer. As a religious, political, or social creed seeking to explain and judge reality, ideology by definition is something that reaches out beyond the realm of routine existence. It claims to see what most men have not seen: revelations, intellectual explanations, new purposes or norms for society. Ideology is, therefore, by nature a generalizing and universalizing phenomenon, admonishing men that there are purposes and significances in life larger than themselves. It presents itself as the answer to all the necessary questions and urges (or pressures) the individual to abandon his isolated and fragmentary perspectives for the more spacious and encompassing ideological vantage point.

But since the attractive power of ideology depends on persuasion and conviction and only incidentally on force, it cannot stray too far from what its partisans want to hear. It must present itself as protecting and advancing their interests. If it demands sacrifices of individual desires in the name of the ideological community, it must promise rewards greater than the sacrifices—on the unassailable principle that the ultimate justification of the group is benefit to the individuals comprising it. Thus the generalizing bent of ideology is countered by the particularizing pressures of its constituency (and, of course, by the particularistic viewpoints of the ideologists themselves).

Ideology's self-portrayal is always and necessarily benevolent, but benevolence can be stretched only so far beyond the immediate circle of the faithful. Assertions of universal benevolence are likely to make the home precincts restless. Ideologies that have gone the furthest in cosmopolitan aspirations, such as Christianity, democratic liberalism, and communism, have claimed to represent the hopes of all mankind. But quite apart from the unbelievers, authoritarians, or class enemies who must disappear before the claim is validated, their representative function is severely limited by the demands of their various home constituencies and by internal struggles within these constituencies. Quarreling factions, objective differences in human cultures, and the role that propinquity and remoteness play in the setting of priorities all converge to put in question whatever authenticity there might be in claims to universal representativeness and benevolence.

The claim of universality for values that are in fact projections of parochial interests may be hypocritical or naïve or both. In any case, the Marxist term "false consciousness" is apt. But frankly parochial ideologies are no remedy for the problem of hypocrisy or of naïveté. Worship of an explicitly local or tribal god in the form of nation, race, class, or church can be as deceptive and dangerous as the proselytizing creed that seeks to embrace all mankind. Fascism, initially based on what was deemed to be the unique genius and mission of the Italian people, was declared to be, in one of Mussolini's most quoted phrases, "not for export." Those given to irony might draw the inference from the no-export doctrine that only the Italians deserved to live under fascism. But the doctrine soon lost contact with reality in any event as Mussolini began to encourage and support a bevy of local fascisms in Austria, Hungary, the Balkans, Spain, France, and even England.

Hitler, too, long insisted on the specifically German and "Aryan" racial spirit in his National Socialism until his expansionist policies made it expedient to discover racial "cousins" all over Europe who were willing to establish puppet regimes on the Nazi model. In the course of Hitler's sudden conversion to ideological spaciousness, the Italians, the Spanish, and at least some of the French became "Aryanized," while even the Japanese were granted the status of "honorary Aryans." As far as Imperial Japan itself was concerned, it abandoned in due time the explicit concept of an Asian empire for the benefit of the Japanese and instead announced its ambition to create a Greater East Asia Co-prosperity Sphere.

One can draw the lesson that parochial ideologies would be spared these contortions if they would consistently forego all but parochial concerns. Conversely, it is evident that a belief system that aspires to a wider significance in the world must abandon or at least deemphasize provincial symbols. But a still more basic issue is involved. "False consciousness," as we have seen, appears in various guises at every level of social and political organization. A parochial ideology minding its own provincial business may not exhibit the kinds of hypocrisies that characterized the nationalisms of the Axis powers. But it cannot divest itself of its basic nature as a set of generalizing explanations and judgments of social life. If these generalizations do, in fact, stop at the boundaries of the individual tribe, class, or nation, there remains the question concerning their validity within these boundaries.

IDEOLOGY AND COMMUNITY

Here we return to the issues raised earlier concerning the relationship of individuals and groups to the community as a whole. Ideology is a prescription for the life of the community, and even if it restricts itself to the internal life of the community it already operates at a very high level of generalization. In supplying norms, goals, and rules to guide social behavior, ideology must necessarily assert that it represents and generalizes the interests (or at least the "true" interests) of the community and its inhabitants. And the community may vary in size from a small tribe or sect with a few thousand members to a great state or religion with hundreds of millions of adherents. Thus a parochial ideology "not for export" nonetheless exhibits in microcosm (often a massive microcosm) the identical problematic inherent in the cosmopolitan ideology that would evangelize the world. That is, it presents itself as a collective good when, in fact, it may serve the good of only part of the collectivity.

This is the nub of the classic attack of Marx, with which we are already familiar, on the bourgeois ideology of the nineteenth century. It can be directed with still greater force against the communist ideology of the twentieth century. At first frankly class-oriented (dictatorship of the proletariat), then bringing "progressive" intellectuals and peasants into the new establishment, and finally claiming to represent and benefit all those under its rule, the Soviet brand of communism over a period of more than fifty years has at best granted wildly disproportionate benefits to a small elite. At worst it has been an instrument of mass terror and enslavement in the hands of a single man. At the same time, communism's professions of internationalism have been contradicted and discredited by nationalistic behavior.

The betrayal of the collective idea in Stalin's Russia by the ideologue of the collectivity finds an analogue of comparable scope only in Nazi Germany. Hitler's most fundamental appeal was to the god of nationalism and to service in the national interest. Yet he chose to prolong his own rule of terror to the ruinous end instead of seeking a way out of the war that would have spared his nation the agonies and devastation of total defeat. He could have found a rationalization for the choice he made, no doubt, in the manic slogan that was coined during the heyday of Nazi intoxication: "Adolf Hitler is Germany, and Germany is Adolf Hitler." Another judgment of Hitler by General Ludwig Beck, one of the leading conspirators against the Nazi regime, is more apt: "This man has no fatherland."

Whether we find it operating on a world, national, or local scale, ideology is inevitably embroiled in the same set of problems. Professions of objectivity are belied by the facts of subjectivity. Claims of universal validity for ideological values must be discounted because of their parochial origin. Doctrines of collective benevolence are tainted by the particular purposes of the doctrinaires. The common interest is never free of special interests. But these problems are not peculiar to ideology; they are problems inherent in life itself. Subjectivity and parochialism are ineradicable facts of human existence, and the tendency of human beings to prefer self-interest to all other brands is notorious. It is also notorious that subjectivity, parochialism, and the pursuit of self-interest are prime agents in dividing men from one another and in making them enemies instead of friends. If we have observed ideologies that are blatantly or covertly parochial and devoid of community concern, truth, or peaceful intent, they are either exploiting or succumbing to powerful psychological forces at work among those to whom they appeal.

Yet the crucial function of ideology continues to be one of unifying men, of drawing them away from an exclusive concern with self, of infusing life with social and spiritual significance. Whether or not its purposes are morally laudable or intellectually tenable, every ideology is an attempt to get away from the anarchy produced by the unrestrained pursuit of subjectively conceived self-interest. In the language of the social contract theorists, ideology seeks to lead men out of the state of nature and into a state of society.

In fulfilling this function, ideologies have registered both catastrophic failures and prodigious achievements. If the failures have been stressed so far, it is appropriate to mention some of the major successes (all of which, of course, are qualified and time bound): the world religions, democracy, liberalism, nationalism. Its adherents would add communism to this list. Communism's first fifty years or so of practice have certainly demonstrated its ability to mobilize masses of people in the name of an idea. But the persistent reliance on force as a major element in the mobilization process leaves moot the question of communist ideology's long-run viability.

Whether or not an ideology plays a creative or destructive role at any level of social organization will obviously depend on its ideational content. The proposition that one group is superior to all others is inherently more provocative of conflict than the proposition that all men are created equal. This holds true despite the frequency of hypocrisy in the egalitarian camp and despite the fact that in a hierarchical world egalitarianism can be supremely provocative. The long-run contribution to peace and justice made by the human relationship of equality as against the relationship of superior-inferior cannot be in doubt. Ideological propositions concerning such issues as individual liberty and group solidarity, the mutual economic rights and obligations of individual and society, and the role of the society in relation to the larger world are obvious additional instances of the importance of ideational content in an appraisal of the role that any specific ideology is likely to play.

Scope is an additional indicator of ideological promise or threat. To what extent is an ideology culture bound? Does it accept itself as an ideology among ideologies, even when it seeks converts? Or does it insist on being the one true faith that regards all those who do not join up as inferior beings, enemies, or both? The limits of its aspirations must be set by the particularity of its values; otherwise an ideology will inevitably leave the realm of persuasion and consent and turn to fakery and force.

This is not an argument in favor of parochial ideologies. It merely asserts that the common and unifying interests and values that an ideology, local or global, necessarily claims to represent must be restricted to what are in fact common interests and values. Conversely, it must be able to respect the diversity of values that are beyond its compass. Unless ideology strikes a realistic balance between unity and diversity, it becomes an agent of divisiveness rather than of common purpose. In this event it loses the dynamic quality without which no ideology can long persist: the ability to attract converts either from other societies or from the new generation of the society in which it is already the conventional wisdom.

The unavoidable subjectivity and the inevitable degree of parochialism in every ideology constitute an obvious parallel to the plight of every individual. To cope with this plight there is in the individual the capacity (unevenly distributed) for learning, change, and growth. To the extent that an ideology also exhibits this capacity it can continue to perform its unifying functions either intensively or extensively (or both) without departing from a primary reliance on persuasion and consent. To use Karl Deutsch's terminology, ideology can be a system that is self-destroying or self-enhancing. Deutsch defines self-enhancing systems as those "which are able to increase their probability of survival and their ranges of possible action over an increasing variety of environments."[3] Requisite to self-enhancement is receptivity to new information and the ability and will to change goals to the extent that the flow of incoming information reveals previous goals to be self-destructive.[4]

These concepts provide important aids to understanding the dynamism of ideologies in the past and to assessing the prospects of contemporary ideologies. The longevity of the major religious ideologies can be attributed in significant part to their capacities (however intermittently exercised) for self-enhancement. Hopes for peace are closely linked to further demonstrations of communism's ability to absorb new information and willingness to consider changes in objectives. The same can be said for the phenomenon of nationalism. And the challenge is obvious to the American ideological system in many different ways. Among other things, its ability to survive will decrease as will its capacity to operate in a wide variety of environments unless it finally expunges the white supremacy clause that has constantly contradicted its egalitarian professions.

TRANSNATIONAL IDEOLOGY

These observations once again evoke the dangers of exclusivity in ideology in which the in-group is glorified and the out-group degraded. It is this penchant for dividing more men than it unifies that has led the critics of ideology to desire its disappearance from politics. Concerning ideology at the international level in particular, critics are often vehement on the point that ideological strife is bound to turn into crusade and countercrusade in which the infidels must be exterminated. Compromise, the chief art of politics, becomes impossible when each side regards the other as an ideological devil that must be cast out—and whose followers, if they are to survive, must give witness to their repentance. Some of the chief woes of the twentieth century—total war, unconditional surrender, total victory—are thus linked with, if not derived from, the expanded role of ideology in our times.

---

[3] Karl W. Deutsch, *The Nerves of Government* (New York: Free Press, 1963), p. 249. Also see Chaps. 13 and 14 generally of this brilliant study of politics as communication.

[4] Ibid., pp. 239 and 253.

The charges hit uncomfortably close to the mark. Yet the critics' alternative prescriptions are not persuasive. They put them forward as a means of defusing international politics on the assumption that the forsaking of ideology would be tantamount to abandoning the vain pursuit of absolute values in a relative world. A growing capacity for compromise would ensue since the various participants in international politics would entertain an altogether more modest set of ambitions than, for example, saving the world for democracy or communism. The more modest ambitions, to quote Hans Morgenthau, would center on safeguarding national security "defined as integrity of the national territory and its institutions."[5]

But this familiar national interest remedy to which most of the anti-ideology literature in international relations is linked is subject to countercriticism on at least three counts. First, national institutions are themselves infused with ideological content, and most major political systems have at one time or another exported or imposed their "national" institutions abroad. In short, nationalism itself is an ideology. Second, the national institutions of the Soviet Union and the United States, for example, would be drastically altered if the transnational ideological elements in the American tradition and in communist doctrine were expunged—with perhaps greater loss than gain.

Third, the essentially defensive strategy of protecting existing national institutions places a premium on the status quo wholly at odds with a world of massive and accelerating change. The demands being generated in the contemporary rush of events are essentially transnational in character—demands such as those with which the underdeveloped world confronts the industrialized world, demands for security and prosperity that call into question the structure of the nation-states of Western Europe, and demands for protection from nuclear holocaust that call for collaborative instead of unilateral response on the part of the superpowers.

There are, in a word, necessary tasks that go far beyond the protection of the territory and institutions of nations. Indeed, upon the successful performance of these tasks depends whatever long-run security the national units can rationally anticipate. But the nature of the tasks is such that their rationale must be transnational rather than national. Raymond Aron once observed that a Great Power "wants an Idea," an idea that goes beyond its own security and power and that offers "humanity a perspective of stabilization and peace." In the absence of such a concept of international order, Aron warned that "the national interest of the United States, or even the collective interest of the

---

[5] Hans J. Morgenthau, *Politics Among Nations*, 5th ed. (New York: Knopf, 1973), p. 542.

Anglo-Saxon minority, will not win over any country, nor will it inspire any loyalties."[6]

Commitment to the building of communities of consent larger than the community inspired by nationalism is the key to the accomplishment of the world tasks that both dwarf the traditional concerns of the nation-state system and threaten it with a catastrophic finale. Such a commitment, in turn, requires the development of a transnational ideology.

In domestic politics, it is the standard practice of political parties to put forward programs and define objectives that purport to serve not the particular interests of the party but the general interests of society as a whole. We have already observed that such professions are always ambiguous and often, but not necessarily, false. The point to be made here is that party activity is inconceivable in terms other than the norm of service to the community of which it is a part. A party defining its purposes exclusively in terms of its own self-interest is a contradiction in terms. It must either rally recruits under the banner of some larger good or resign itself to impotency. The same conditions for political effectiveness now prevail at the international level. On a shrunken and interdependent planet where poverty, injustice, and the threat of extinction cannot be diminished without the development of transnational communities, commitments that transcend the self-interest of already ambiguous sovereignties are essential.

The objective need for transnationalism is underlined (and often undermined) by the transnational ideologies and quasi-ideologies already on the scene with platforms and policies for reforming or revolutionizing the global system. The various brands of communism—the Soviet, the Chinese, and the Castro third world varieties—are explicitly for export, whatever uneasy compromises they make with nationalism or other local preferences. The ex-colonial world struggles to find transnational solidarity in opposition to the remnants of colonialism and to the forces of neocolonialism. It seeks to build a united front against the white man's racial injustice wherever it may exist. And it calls upon the industrialized world for massive aid in the war against massive poverty, more often than not labeling this aid as a duty and as reparations for past and present sins of exploitation. If the voice of the third world is not as coherent as the various voices of communism, it is nonetheless clear that it conceives of a world society in which there is a set of obligations and rights that go far beyond the traditional concept of each unit tending its own sovereign business.

---

[6] Raymond Aron, "The Quest for a Philosophy of Foreign Affairs," *Revue Française de Science Politique* (January–March, 1953). Reprinted in Stanley Hoffmann, *Contemporary Theory in International Relations* (Englewood Cliffs, N.J.: Prentice-Hall, 1960), pp. 87 and 89.

Quite apart from the objective need for transnationalism, the West, and the United States as the leader of the West, cannot afford to be without transnational propositions of its own. Of course, such propositions have been emanating from the West for a long time: the development of international law, the doctrine of free trade, and the sponsorship of international organization are some key examples in the modern era. All purported to benefit the whole of international society at least as much as the parts, but all were afflicted with the familiar vices of ideology: deceptiveness, parochialism, and a bias in favor of their sponsors' interests. To the non-Western world, Western cosmopolitanism expressed itself as imperialism, a Western monopoly on power and wealth, and the degradation of non-Western peoples.

Thus the non-Western transnational ideologies in the contemporary world must be seen in part—a very significant part—as challenges to the traditional transnational ideas of the West. It hardly needs saying that the record of Western transnationalism falls far short of total benevolence or success. But the demands both to compete and to cooperate in a world that is integrating at an ever more rapid rate rule out the option of retiring from the field of transnational ideology. Transnationalism requires new forms and new content; what these might be will be explored in later parts of this book. But what needs to be said here is that if the West turns its back on the ideology of transnationalism or, what is more likely, plays the game simply to register points against the competition, it is going to have to make most of its points not by persuasion and consent but by force. As was pointed out in the beginning of the chapter in reference to domestic societies: in the absence of a legitimating ideology, political life cannot avoid being dominated by coercion. At the international level, only an ideology that offers the outlines and promise of a community of mankind can swell the ranks of allies, persuade neutrals, and ultimately diminish the role of threats among enemies.

Ideologies can perhaps best be understood as pressure groups in the realm of ideas. The pressure group image reaffirms the typical origins of an ideology in a relatively restricted complex of ideas closely connected with the interests of the originators. But the ideology is immediately less parochial if the ideas and interests it expresses happen to coincide with those of large segments of the society in which it operates. Ideology sloughs off still more of its parochial ballast if it learns from experience that some goals are expendable and that those which are not are best sought after in a relationship of reciprocal services between the ideology and the larger community. Ideology is at its most cosmopolitan when it develops a stake in the survival and well-being of the society in which it functions, even though not all elements of the society are in accord with its premises and goals.

Because of the diversity of mankind, no single ideology will conquer and eliminate the pluralism that defines the pressure group status of each. There is an ultimate limit to the compass of any given ideology. But there is no reason to accept the parochialism, the in-group–out-group syndrome and the hypocrisies that inevitably accompany these phenomena as the governing realities of ideology. They are, rather, the occupational hazards of ideological ventures, and they can be, and have been, combated in the name of an ideology's own life expectancy.

These hazards are formidable but unavoidable because any effort to eject ideology from international life cannot succeed. An invitation to flee from ideology is an invitation to flee from political reality; there will always be other ideologists to replace those who leave the field. Realism demands that the hazards be recognized and resisted; it also demands that they not be permitted to obscure the crucial function that ideology performs in human society. Only ideology generates those unifying myths which can respond to men's yearnings for peace and justice. Only ideology can endeavor to answer the questions which the nuclear age has made more urgent than ever before in history: Why are we here? Where are we going? How do we get there—if we do? Ideology is always threatened by parochialism, but this does not nullify its inherent capacity at any given time to draw men's minds toward larger unities than prevailing custom sanctions.

Ideology may legitimize an existing order, or it may prophesy the legitimacy of a new order. In either case, it functions as an embodiment of social vision. One may realistically quarrel with the quality of any particular ideological outlook, but not with the need for vision itself. Hence any transition from nationalism to transnationalism cannot dispense with the kinds of explanations, projections, and value judgments that ideology characteristically provides. The problematics of such a transition can be more clearly understood if we now examine in some detail the ideology of nationalism itself.

Chapter 7

Nationalism

In the contemporary world the ideology of nationalism is somewhere near the zenith of its influence. Whether its full impact is yet to be felt or whether it has already peaked is a matter of continuing debate. But there can be no doubt that it is now the most powerful and popular of the political ideologies. From its beginnings in eighteenth-century Europe, the nationalist idea has spread to all parts of the globe. Most people in today's world apparently accept the concept of nation in preference to any other as the proper framework in which to organize their political activities and loyalties.

During the course of its development nationalism has challenged and shattered the legitimacy of theocracy, feudalism, dynasticism, and imperialism as systems for governing men. While this development is by no means ended, its success is registered, among other ways, in the fact that all states of the world (however dubiously) are now dubbed nations. Indeed, in both official and common parlance the term "nation" has in effect superseded the term "state." The world organization of states bears the name United Nations; its predecessor was christened the League of Nations. And ordinary usage speaks of international, not interstate, politics or relations.

Nationalism's triumph—in word and deed, so to speak—has given rise to a widespread assumption that the nation is both the "natural" basis upon which to organize the civil society and the "natural" basic unit in international politics. The assumption is invalid on many counts, including the historicity or time-bound characteristics of nationalism. It has just been noted that during its rise to preeminence, nationalism has toppled other forms of political organization which, in their own periods of dominance, seemed to be "natural" patterns for the conduct of internal government and external relations.

Nationalism is a relatively new phenomenon in the history of man, and its "naturalness" was not all that apparent even two hundred years ago. Indeed, for most of the non-European world it has only been during the course of the twentieth century that the nation has come to be

regarded as the "natural" political goal of all peoples. As historical phenomena, the nation and nationalism share history's quality of transience.
For most of the past they did not exist, and it is a safe assumption that
at some point in the future they will cease to exist. Thus the perspective
of history confirms what empirical analysis of the contemporary world
will also make evident: the nation is only one of many ways to organize
the political loyalties of men.

Yet today, nationalism is the reigning political orthodoxy in most of
the world. Where it is not orthodox in doctrine (as in communism) it is
highly orthodox in practice, and where the concept of the nation is only
nascent it is nonetheless the governing aspiration. If the nation is only
one of a number of ways to structure political organization, and if it
has driven rival political ideologies from the field or outclassed their
drawing power, it is evident that nationalism incorporates an extraordinarily potent political appeal. In essence, nationalism's appeal is its
promise of internal freedom and wealth and external power. It is an
appeal that accounts for nationalism's past conquests and present attractiveness and one that will determine its future prospects.

Freedom, affluence, and power have, of course, been much-prized
values throughout history. But they have also tended to be elusive, and
demand has rather consistently exceeded supply. For this as well as other
reasons, they have more often been sought as individual rather than as
social goals. Even the ideal of a society whose inhabitants would all be
"free" or affluent is a relative rarity in the annals of history. Still rarer
are the societies that approximate the ideal in practice. By contrast, there
have been many societies that have exhibited external power; but whatever benefits such power brought with it most often tended to be
restricted to the ruling elites and touched the lot of the mass very little.
Thus the bulk of historical evidence demonstrates that freedom, wealth,
and power, both internal and external, have usually been accessible to
the few and only infrequently to the many. As nationalism developed it
began to manifest a potential for altering that ancient pattern of distribution.

THE APPEALS OF NATIONALISM

Nationalism derives its basic strength from the fact that it involves a
transfer of essential political loyalties from individuals to the group. It
replaces allegiance to the monarch, the feudal lord, the remote emperor—
or to the alien colonial master—with a new and fundamentally communal
allegiance. The object of reverence is the group itself which stands above
all who comprise it: governors and governed, rich and poor, elite and
mass. Ideally, each individual and social component is the servant of the
group—of the nation—as a whole. In the shift from the politics of per-

sonality to the politics of collectivity, government ceases to be a matter of the king's pleasure or of inherited contractual obligation; it becomes instead a joint enterprise to be pursued by and for the benefit of the national community.

This is an obviously abstract and idealized description. But it does not distort the truth that the group concept of political organization opens the door to political participation by far greater numbers of people than does the hierarchical and fundamentally personal principle characterizing monarchical, feudal-aristocratic, or imperial-colonial modes of government. Broader political participation, in turn, is the key to wider access to wealth, freedom, and power. It is because the group principle of nationalism has achieved impressive and demonstrable results in broadening such access that its appeal and prestige have become worldwide. All its failures have not been enough to dim its allure.

A great many of nationalism's failures, of course, can be traced to both the choices and the necessities involved in defining the group in which political loyalty is to be vested. Nationalism, as we noted in the previous chapter, is an explicitly parochial ideology. The national idea proposes the organization of political community not on the model of universal empire or the brotherhood of man, but rather along the lines of the family, the clan, and the tribe. It identifies the national group as uniquely belonging together and, consequently, as distinct and separate from all other groups. Such assumptions create the obvious temptation for each nation to celebrate its uniqueness by avowing its superiority over the rest. If nationalism has often and enthusiastically succumbed to this temptation, it must be said in fairness that it merely follows the precedent set by all the other parochial political societies preexisting or contemporary with it. Yet, as we shall see, nationalism has lent a power and a massiveness to parochial egotism which has made it more destructive than any other kind of political organization. The nation's achievements as a bringer of freedom, wealth, and power are at least matched by its record as a bringer of conflict and death.

What makes a group belong together in the sense of a nation and what distinguishes it from other groups is a matter of longstanding debate. The criteria of common ethnic bonds, common language, a common fund of historical, political, and cultural experience, and a common territorial base are familiar landmarks in analyses of nationalism. Just as familiar is the evidence that weakens those criteria. Four languages are spoken in Switzerland. A Jewish sense of belonging together culminating in the nation of Israel existed and continues to exist despite the continuing world-wide dispersion of the Diaspora. A Soviet nationalism of sorts prevails despite the vast diversity of approximately one hundred ethnic groups living within the Soviet borders. American nationalism has been built from an unprecedented variety of ethnic stocks, linguistic groups, and cultural and political histories.

Just as there are national unities that do not meet one or more of the familiar criteria of nationhood, so there are cases where the criteria are met but the ties do not bind. Thus ethnic, linguistic, cultural, and proximity links have not bound Austria or German Switzerland to the German nation nor Italian and French Switzerland to Italy or France. Centuries of common government have not prevented Scots and Welshmen from periodically attempting to reassert their own sense of nationhood in the United Kingdom any more than they have suppressed similar aspirations among the Bretons in France or the Basques and Catalans in Spain.

It is evident that the presence of the more tangible characteristics commonly associated with nationality is not sufficient to account for the existence of a nation. It is equally evident that the absence of one or another does not prevent a nation from being formed. It follows that the key variable in the building or preservation of a nation is the presence of a political will to unity. This view of the nation as fundamentally a matter of will found what is perhaps its most dramatic expression in the formulation of the nineteenth-century French writer Ernest Renan: "The nation is a daily plebiscite." The message is that if people "will" the nation it will exist; if they do not will to "belong together" they will separate. Thus the tangibles of geography, ethnicity, language, and culture function as stocks of raw materials from which the political will draws in building a national community. If these raw materials are wholly absent, the enterprise will not get off the ground. But if only some are missing or diluted, political will can find substitutes or make do without. Each of the tangibles can help in giving the national community a sense of concreteness, but only political will can generate an awareness of how each fits into the commanding unity of the nation.

Linguistic identity, geographic proximity, and the other variables just discussed obviously preexist nationalism and are encountered throughout history. Nationalism's unique contribution was the proposition that these factors, or at least a selection of them, should constitute the building blocks of political community. The nationalist norm asserts that people ought to form a political unity *because* they are ethnic kin, speak the same language, inhabit a common territory (whose limits are frequently difficult to define), or share a similar cultural heritage. Conversely, people who exhibit these kinds of unities ought not to be kept apart from one another in separate political entities. Since feudal and then monarchical Europe was for the most part made up of political units that either fragmented or subjugated nationalities, the revolutionary quality of the nascent nationalist doctrine is manifest.

From its beginnings, then, nationalism represented a two-pronged attack on the European status quo. It called for a fundamental reconstitution of the territorial basis for political organization. And as the determinants of political loyalty it substituted such impersonal tangibles as geography, ethnicity, and language for the personal symbols of monarchy and aristocracy. Thus nationalism challenged both the right of many a ruler to territories under his dominion and, far more important, the principle of monarchical or aristocratic rule as such. Once reverence for the national group became deeply implanted, reverence for the monarch became functionally superfluous or, at best, secondary.

The building blocks selected by nationalism for constructing political community have proved to be durable. The state with a compact territorial base usually proves superior in political energy to the empire whose strength derives from far-flung and often geographically disconnected possessions. People living in proximity to one another are easier to organize for social action than those whom distance separates. A territorial unit occupied by a loyal populace tends to be internally more peaceful and externally more secure than one where loyalties are split along ethnic, linguistic, or class lines. Where nationalism has brought together many small political entities and fused them into one large political and geographic unit it has collaborated with the forces of economic productivity by removing barriers to trade, creating large internal markets, and making possible economies of scale. Common language obviously makes for easy communication within a society. It also generates an emotional affinity among those who speak it; national literature and national idiom evoke a sense of familiarity indispensable to trust. Shared cultural traditions—religion, folkways, attitudes toward the surrounding world—constitute additional community cement. In sum, the nationalist stress on a homogeneous people residing within clearly demarcated territorial limits has engendered remarkably cohesive political communities peculiarly suited to the conduct of joint enterprises.

These are some of the measures of the nation's success as a form of political community, and they help make understandable the eagerness with which those living in different political forms have desired to copy the nationalist formula. But the crucial links between nationalism, internal freedom, and external power need further exploration if the full magnetism of the nationalist idea is to be understood.

Although the nation as a quasi-geographical, quasi-cultural, and sometimes even quasi-political concept long preceded it, nationalism, as a doctrine preaching the political reification of the nation, was a product of the eighteenth century. We have already noted that nationalism advocated loyalty to the group rather than loyalty to ruling personages as the basis of political legitimacy. This theme was wholly in harmony with the forces in eighteenth-century Europe and America rebelling against arbitrary and unrepresentative government.

Indeed, the histories of nationalism and of liberal-democratic doctrines are inextricably intertwined. The slogan "government by the people" suited nationalism and democracy equally well. "Liberty, equality, and fraternity" were all group values in the sense that they were understood to represent rights and duties of every member of the group. Fraternity explicitly stressed obligation to the group. The principle of equality buttressed group solidarity, by attacking the hierarchies of privilege which divided men into castes, classes, and estates, fostering in the same territory many groups instead of one. Liberty, that most individual of values, can flourish only where loyalty to the group creates an atmosphere of mutual trust and where it is not threatened by a conspicuously unequal distribution of power among members of the group. Reverence for an impersonal and all-encompassing nation was admirably suited to the advancement of these revolutionary values.

"Citizen" became a key word for both nationalism and democracy. Its democratic connotation derives from the proposition that the citizen has a right to participate in the political process, that he is no longer a "subject" of a monarch or a ruling elite. The significance of the concept of citizen for nationalist thought is that it is the nation that defines the citizen. All members of the nation are citizens and can claim the right to political participation; nonnationals have no such right. Practice by no means coincided neatly with theory, but the interaction of these democratic and nationalist ideas of citizenship initiated a progressive extension of the franchise that logically (and actually) culminated in the doctrine of one man, one vote.

Nationalism's stress on collectivity contained obvious potentials for tyranny that manifested themselves soon enough—most particularly in revolutionary France. But the argument that political rights spring from nationality became a battle cry taken up again and again by those who proffered liberation of the many from oppression by the few. In traditional society, power, as well as wealth, education, and status, was restricted to a small elite that regarded these values as its legitimate monopoly. It followed that the prerogative of social decision was an integral part of this monopoly.

Tickets of admission into this charmed circle were few and difficult to come by: criteria for entry were royal or aristocratic birth, sometimes military prowess or skillful churchmanship, and occasionally earned wealth or, more frequently, inherited wealth. Nationalism preached that the charmed circle must be expanded to coincide with the boundaries of the nation itself and that being born within the national territory was the only price for entry. In the nation—in theory—political rights are birthrights. The whole concept of restricted access to political power is swept away in a manifesto dominated by egalitarian, libertarian, and democratic imagery.

This imagery is at the heart of nationalism's continuing revolutionary appeal. During the two centuries of its development, nationalism has expanded its scope to include the norms of mass access to social and economic power as well as political power. Here again, norm and practice have often diverged, but there has been enough correspondence so that nationalism has been able to hold on to its egalitarian credentials.

These credentials have been the chief attraction for nineteenth- and twentieth-century revolutionaries in their struggles to dismantle the hierarchies of traditional society. If the European revolutionaries sought to destroy the authority of emperors, kings, and nobles, the revolutionaries of the non-European world have fought their versions of indigenous autocrats and oligarchs as well as colonial overlords, and all in the name of the egalitarian proposition that power belongs to the people.

If the appeal of nationalism here seems indistinguishable from the appeal of democracy, the unique attraction of nationalism becomes apparent once it is recalled that nationalism defines who "the people" are: not just any people but only the people of the nation, not just some people within the nation but all of them, and no one else. The revolutionary seeking to destroy traditional authority must profess allegiance to an alternative authority. "The people" as authority is too abstract unless it is understood as the national people or, at least, a people living within a defined territory. Thus the nation offered the most tangible authority possible for an egalitarian-democratic doctrine. The retreat of the Russian revolutionaries from communist internationalism to Soviet nationalism and the latter-day spread of national communisms offer eloquent testimony to this point.

Tangibility, familiarity, and empathy are crucial elements in political community. Their disappearance constituted one of the most dangerous deficits of the *anciens régimes* in the face of the rising nationalist tide. The king at Versailles was as distant from the people of France as the king of England was from the American colonists. In the seminal democratic-nationalist revolutions of America and France the enemy was an alien symbolizing an alien world, with no perceivable connection, except one of oppression, to the ordinary cares and concerns of those revolting against him. The revolutions were in a real sense revolts against alienation. They sought a new solidarity in which there would be an identity of rulers and ruled, in which arbitrary prerogative would disappear, and in which internal divisions in the community would be healed. It is not surprising that the quest for solidarity should have produced floods of refugees from both revolutionary America and France whose divisive presence the new communities would not tolerate. In the fraternal community there is no place for the alien, and the difficulties in the doctrine of human brotherhood become once more manifest.

The idea of a national brotherhood presents less difficulty. The relative tangibility of a geographically defined homeland, the familiarity of a national language, and empathy with those sharing one's own culture all reinforce the conviction of community far more powerfully than could the more abstract and universal aspects of the democratic message. It is clear that despite their interaction and overlap of principles democracy and nationalism are not identical. They have often been hostile to one another. But it is also true that nationalism provides a uniquely favorable context for the development of democracy. The nation as home, brotherhood, and body politic offers a basis for community loyalty and trust without which the democratic promise of liberty and equality cannot easily be kept. Those who feel alienated from one another will soon attack one another's liberties, and the old cycle of hierarchy, oppression, and violence will again assert itself. Nationalism represented a new and more attractive form of social obligation; as such it was a necessary complement to the democratic principle of individual freedom.

ANTAGONISMS BETWEEN NATIONALISM
AND DEMOCRACY

If one accepts the argument that both freedom and obligation are indispensable to the good man and the good society, it continues to be evident that the relationship between the two is full of conflict. This conflict has been the most frequent cause of divorce between democracy and nationalism. Both attacked the vested interests of the hierarchical society, and the initial successes of the nationalist-democratic revolutionaries in America and France inspired emulation throughout Europe and later throughout the world. But they also inspired resistance. Thus many of the traditional elites, when the assault turned upon them, did the politically prudent thing and sought to divide the revolutionary enemy. They did this, in essence, by buying nationalism and rejecting democracy.

Despite nationalism's inherent egalitarianism, its connotations of social obligation were far more congenial to traditional ruling groups than the democratic stress on individual rights. Democracy demands the transfer of power from elite to mass. Nationalism demands the transfer of power from elite to nation: here there was room to maneuver. The elite could not become part of the mass and still retain its own identity, but it might become part of the nation and remain reasonably intact in the process. To do this, the elite had to prove its indispensability to the building (or the preservation) of the nation. Judicious and limited concessions to egalitarian demands were in order. Lessons were to be drawn from the course of past revolutions, and from the darker side of the French Revolution in particular. The costs of dismantling the *ancien régime* were rivers of blood and a sea of misery that, except for a brief moment of imperial glory, divided the French nation instead of uniting it. The implication was clear: anyone with a sense of obligation to the nation would wish to spare it such excesses and agonies.

A still more telling argument concerned the defense of the nation from the foreign foe. A divided nation could not resist a foreign conqueror. Napoleon drove home that lesson all over Europe, a lesson from which European elites drew a special inference. If the national brotherhood is to be safe from foreign war and invasion, they argued, it must treasure internal solidarity above the kinds of freedoms that can be had only at the price of anarchy or civil war.

There was a further lesson. Napoleon's military occupations had belied the pretensions to universal truth and brotherhood in the doctrines of the French revolutionaries. Their proposals for restructuring society had no universal validity but were merely foreign—and therefore unsuited to the unique genius of other nations. Slavish imitation of foreign models violated the distinctive character of the nation that should be the model for building a community in harmony with its own historical, social, and cultural context. As a long-dominant part of this context, the traditional elites could find ample room at the top in a new nation so conceived.

These were some of the characteristic arguments used by the rulers of Europe to rally their peoples in an effort to stem the Napoleonic tide. For many of the rulers the choice was simple: either bow to the dictates of Napoleon or gain sufficient mass support to become powerful enough to defeat him. Since virtually the only bonds that united ruler and ruled were attachment to the homeland and fear and resentment of the foreigner, nationalism was the natural battle cry. Xenophobia thus became the taproot of what has been dubbed conservative nationalism. As the name implies, the purpose of conservative nationalism was to preserve inherited institutions of the society and not to revolutionize them. Yet even conservative nationalism was an instrument of fundamental change in that the inherited institutions were no longer self-validating but were forced to justify themselves in terms of service to the nation and to the mass of its inhabitants.

Nationalism's basic egalitarian impulse was not to be denied, and even twentieth-century fascism, as the most extreme reaction against the liberal-democratic forms of nationalism, emitted strong egalitarian signals in practice as well as in theory. Both the Italian and German varieties gutted the power and prestige of the traditional hierarchies in their own countries and in those that they conquered. But fascism's replacement of conservative rule by tyranny led to world-wide disaster. It provided a bloody commentary on the old truth that destruction of elites can be productive of evil as well as good. It showed that propositions about equality need to be assessed in relation to the total content of the creed that proposes them. Above all, although fascism did not deny nationalist egalitarianism, it revealed its cruelest implications. Nationalism holds men equal as nationals rather than as men. In the Nazi apotheosis of nationalism, *only* nationals were men, and those not admitted to the nation were relegated to various levels of subhumanity.

NATIONALISM AS AN INSTRUMENT OF POWER

Liberal or illiberal, nationalist egalitarianism lived by the proposition that the nation served the citizen and that every citizen had a stake in the life of the nation. The expansion of the franchise culminating in universal suffrage was the supreme political expression of this relationship. But far-reaching political implications were also present in the military tenets of nationalism. The mutually benevolent relation between the national and the nation implied for the citizen both a duty and a right to defend the nation.

If the bearing of arms might be a burdensome obligation, it was also a precious right in that the traditional regimes characteristically limited access to arms to the elites and their hired mercenaries. In this way they effectively reserved the powers of physical coercion to themselves. Nationalist (and democratic) doctrine called for an armed citizenry, not merely as a means of toppling the oppressive rule of the moment but as a permanent safeguard against the return of tyrants. Thus nationalism and democracy challenged the military as well as the political monopoly of the ruling minorities and demanded guns as well as votes.

The American revolutionary militia and the citizen armies of the French Revolution epitomized these demands. But they also demonstrated proficiencies in matters beyond the realm of internal rebellion. At different times, both displayed their capacities to transform the nature of international war. In particular, France in the 1790s sought to develop the citizen army into a nation in arms, where every able-bodied male, theoretically at least, was subject to military duty. It was here that the draft and the concept of universal military service, in their modern forms, were born. The capacity to mobilize the entire male population, or a massive portion of it, for military purposes enormously enhanced the power of the revolutionary nation in its struggle with the traditional regimes still depending on the relatively small military organizations made up of elites and mercenaries. By drawing on a larger percentage of its populace, France was able to overwhelm its opponents in sheer numbers of fighting men.

But the quality of the fighting men was also crucial. The overthrow of the French monarchy and the goals of the French Revolution produced among masses of Frenchmen the conviction that they in fact had a vital stake in the new nation. This, in turn, produced a willingness to fight for it. For almost twenty years after 1789, the great military struggles generated by the French Revolution were characterized by a contest between the volunteer spirit of the French armies and the mercenary spirit that pervaded the armies of France's enemies. If the volunteer spirit was decisive in the succession of French victories, its superiority resides not simply in the realm of morale but also in the fact that willingness to fight made possible a new strategy and tactics with which the traditional armies could not cope.

The mercenary army, whose soldiers had little motivation other than their pay, had to rely on severe discipline and close surveillance to ensure against malingering, desertion, and breaking under enemy fire. These requirements necessitated concentration of troops and close-order movements ill-suited to conduct or withstand flanking and envelopment operations. The Revolutionary and Napoleonic armies, on the other hand, could rely on relatively self-disciplined soldiers and thus conduct operations on the basis of extended lines of communication in which the soldier followed orders even in the absence of an overseer. Hence France could overwhelm its enemies by moving masses of men with unprecedented flexibility and speed primarily because these masses were fighting not for money but for their country as a matter of conviction and loyalty. In order finally to destroy the French supremacy, the other powers had to imitate the nationalist political formula, which then began to produce similar military results for them.

The mobilization of masses of people is obviously an economic as well as a military, political, and psychological phenomenon. The prodigious military efforts during the years from 1789 to 1815 could not have reached the level they did without the growing wealth and technology being produced by the Industrial Revolution. The emergence of nationalism and the onset of the Industrial Revolution were roughly contemporaneous events. We have already noted the complementary nature of their needs and purposes: large-scale political units free of internal trade barriers encouraged a rising level of production and exchange. Moreover, the political challenge of the nationalists to the traditional elites reinforced the efforts of the bourgeoisie to rid themselves of the economic controls exercised by the monarchical bureaucracies. In addition, the new bourgeoisie obviously felt more at home with the nationalist ethos than with the old stratified state in which manufacture and commerce were deemed unsuitable and demeaning occupations for the ruling class.

But the most portentous interconnection between nationalism and industrialism was the egalitarian promise of the former and the productive potential of the latter. If every citizen was to have a stake in the nation and if the nation was to be a brotherhood, then the stake must be at least in part material and the brotherhood more tangible than sentimental gesture; otherwise the doctrine would not persuade. Indeed, it did not persuade insofar as the new industrialism failed to distribute material benefits any more equitably—and in some cases the distribution was still more inequitable—than the old aristocratic state. By the mid-nineteenth century the material shortcomings of nationalism, liberalism, and industrialism precipitated the Marxist attack on the bourgeois nation.

Partly in response to this attack, partly as a result of the internal political and social dynamics of the industrializing nations, and partly because
of the sheer volume of wealth and productivity created by the industrial
economy, a significant redistribution of benefits on a nationwide scale
got under way. Once begun, the process of redistribution never ceased.
The bourgeois nation of the nineteenth century was transformed into the
welfare state of the twentieth. The passage was uneven, marked by setbacks, often bloody and sometimes deceptive, but it nonetheless arrived
at a state of mass affluence for which there is no precedent in history.
In short, nationalism, industrialism, and democracy have constituted an
incredibly effective partnership for the mass production and mass distribution of wealth. Despite the continued existence of serious and sometimes scandalous inequities, they have realized the economic aspects of
the egalitarian vision to the point where the vast majorities of the
national populations do in fact perceive their own well-being closely
bound up with the continued well-being of the nation-state.

A concept of human organization that so dramatically expanded the
economic as well as the political franchise could not fail to generate the
most powerful kinds of vested interests in its perpetuation. Nor could
it fail to attract imitators. Marxist internationalism in both the pre- and
post-1914 varieties demonstrated that it was unable to compete with the
political force of nationalism. As a result, communism became either a
nationalist revolution, as in Russia, Cuba, and China, or it was imposed
from without, as in most of Eastern Europe, only to take on the national
coloration of the conquered as time passed. Thus when the era of the
European empires in Asia and Africa began to wane, the West's own
nationalist formula had no serious competitor as ideology and technique
for the new political organization of the non-European world.

If socialism is presently the goal of most of the ideologues of the
developing world, they have linked it with nation rather than with class.
The territorial unit and not the transnational unity is at the center of
their concerns. The achievements of European and American nationalism
in terms of internal affluence and freedom and external power have
simply been too impressive to forego the nation-state as the model for
Asia, Africa, and, in its own special context, Latin America. The appropriateness of the model is something else again, as we shall see later.

NATIONAL SELF-DETERMINATION

Still another facet of nationalist egalitarianism has powerfully attracted
revolutionaries in both the nineteenth and twentieth centuries. This was
the proposition, sometimes explicit and sometimes implicit, sometimes
propagandized and sometimes suppressed, that every nationality, great
or small, had the right to form its own independent nation-state. Here

the equality of nationals was linked to the equality of nations—not, of course, an equality of power, security, or wealth, but nonetheless a fundamental equality of choice whether or not to become an independent nation. Thus the international extension of the nationalist doctrine was the principle of national self-determination which asserted that all peoples are equal in their right to govern themselves as nations.

Ireland in the west, the disunited peoples of Germany and Italy in the center, and the whole of Eastern Europe under the domination of polyglot empires demonstrated the inconveniences that could arise if the idea of national self-determination was taken too seriously by too many. The earliest and most powerful nation-states stood to lose territory they had inherited from the *anciens régimes,* a painful prospect to them no less than to their predecessors. Or they would have to contemplate the loss of buffer areas or political vacuums where the fragmentation of a given geographical region into numerous small states made it possible for the already consolidated nation to influence affairs to its own advantage.

Hence England was not eager to foster Irish nationalism, France did not push the principle of national self-determination as far as Germans were concerned, and both German and Russian nationalism looked with disfavor on the Polish variety. Yet in the long run, for better or worse, the national aspirations of most of the peoples of Europe were realized. The uneven effectiveness of the Soviet attempt since 1945 to weaken the spirit of nationalism in Eastern Europe has shown that here, too, the suppression of the national impulse could register only superficial and temporary successes.

Nationalism's general triumph in Europe was more than a hundred years in the making. Its general triumph in the non-European world is still to come—if it does come. If the more powerful and well-established nations of Europe were not eager to export nationalism to their continental neighbors, they were still less disposed to cultivate the national idea in their overseas empires. Yet they could not hide the principles and achievements of their own nationalism any more than they could hide the facts of imperial oppression. Thus, their colonial subjects appropriated the formulas of national self-determination and the nation-state on their own behalf.

To become an independent nation among independent nations became the standard aspiration throughout the non-European world. After two world wars broke the power of the European empires this aspiration, too, was realized, in form if not in substance. But substantive effectiveness is in the last analysis the only measure of success in political organization as in other matters. In this respect the crucial tests for nationalism in the underdeveloped world are still ahead. Hence the assertion made at the beginning of the chapter: the political form of the nation-state is the global orthodoxy, but in the developing world it is an orthodoxy of purpose and not yet one reflecting established fact.

THE PATHOLOGY OF NATIONALISM

It is now time to turn to the pathology of nationalism. The nation-state has demonstrated its ability to generate more power and wealth and a larger measure of individual freedom and equality than any previous form of social organization. But these fortunate results did not appear in any uniform manner or measure. In many contexts and for long periods of time nationalism has been the destroyer rather than the producer of power, wealth, liberty, and equality.

Of course, like ideologues for other creeds, some nationalists betrayed their principles. The egalitarian promise was revoked again and again as the new rulers built and defended new hierarchies based on property, military organization, or party. As we have seen, national self-determination was regarded with favor for one's own nation but often not for others. Despite the hopes of some of its early and idealistic advocates, the advent of nationalism did not alter the inherited rules of the international system that the strong will try to rule the weak and that it is safer to anticipate hostility than friendship in relations among states.

Nation-states, democratic or not, showed that kings and nobles are not the only ones who can make war and that the higher the proportion of the national population integrated into the political and economic society, the more formidable the war machine. By the same token, the greater the number objectively or subjectively benefiting from membership in the nation, the greater the number ready to fight passionately on its behalf. The result has been the linkage of nationalism with mass armies and mass militancy. Finally, the familiar relationship between power and corruption was enormously magnified by the prodigious growth of material and military power in the nation-state. The non-national, non-European world was too easy and too tempting a target for exploitation by the powerful, and the new nation-states of Europe surpassed all previous imperialisms—in the name of national greatness and national interest.

Yet the chief problem of nationalism is not its failure to eliminate sin. Nationalism was not the beginning nor will it be the end of selfishness, hypocrisy, violence, or injustice in political life. Moreover, it has registered extraordinary and benevolent achievements in both the material and moral realms so that in a summation of its virtues and vices one can hardly avoid the judgment that the record of nationalism has been both glorious and miserable. Nationalism's fundamental problematic and chief source of its pathology is that ideological vice with which we are already familiar: exclusivity.

As noted at the outset of this chapter, the ethos of nationalism is basically tribal. Thus when the nation behaves pathologically in the sense of violating its own professed values of liberty, equality, and fraternity, the behavior may result in response to contingent events. But the pathological behavior of nationalism is more often and more profoundly a reflex of its own tribal presuppositions. The political vision that built the nation from the materials of common language, common ethnic strains, common geographic base, or common culture focused on forces which contribute powerfully to cohesion in a mass society. Since cohesion is crucial to political community, particularly when it is conceived as a joint enterprise of all its members rather than a command-obedience relationship between elite and mass, nationalism built well.

But the political success of nationalism's tenets also reveals their weaknesses. The norm of one country, one language, one culture, one loyalty inevitably places enormous stress on homogeneity, conformity, and uniformity. If these characteristics enable the nation to act more effectively as a unit, they also weaken its ability to deal with diversity. In the established nation-states this weakness has expressed itself, sometimes catastrophically, in the fate of national minorities. In the aspirant nation-states, most of which are multicultural in composition, it raises the question whether nationalism can ever be a viable political solution for the bulk of the underdeveloped world. Finally, in international relations the nationalist aversion to diversity has taken the most terrible toll of all.

Almost all the major European nation-states developing in the nineteenth century were confronted with national minorities. The Catalans and Basques of Spain have already been noted. In addition to Bretons, France also had a small Basque population, but the Germans of Alsace were the main problem and were destined to play a fateful role in three wars between France and Germany. Prussia harbored significant numbers of Poles and Danes, and after uniting under Prussian leadership in 1871 Germany insisted upon a fatal acquisition: some quarter-million Frenchmen along with the German populations in Alsace and Lorraine, which were themselves ambiguous about their national identifications.

Scots and Welsh were relatively quiescent in nineteenth-century Britain, but the Irish problem was terrible in its bloodshed and bitterness. One can hardly speak of a national minority in the case of Ireland; more accurately, it was a matter of imperial exploitation and oppression of a colony. The Russian, Austro-Hungarian, and Turkish empires were conglomerations of minorities conflicting with one another as well as with the dominant national groups. Italy made up for lost time by incorporating reluctant Austrians and Slavs into the Italian nation as part of the spoils of World War I.

The smaller European states mirrored the problems of their larger neighbors. Tensions between Fleming and Walloon have threatened Belgian political unity ever since the international agreements of the 1830s produced Belgian independence. Norwegians broke away from Sweden and formed their own kingdom in 1903. Greeks and Turks persecuted one another on both Greek and Turkish soil and still continue to pursue their communal animosity of a thousand years on the island of Cyprus. After the defeat of Russia and then of the Central Powers in 1918, almost every one of the dozen or so states that emerged from the old empires was burdened with national minorities. The bitterness of minorities that could not find room for a congenial way of life in the new "nations" to which events had assigned them provided high combustion material to fuel the second outbreak of world war in 1939.

The conflict between dominant nationality and national minority reached its climax of horror in Nazi Germany and Soviet Russia. Great Russian nationalism under the tsars was a cruel yoke for the profusion of non-Russian nationalities and cultures within the borders of the empire. Finns, Swedes, the Baltic peoples, Poles, Ruthenians, Ukrainians, Georgians, Armenians, Tatars, Muslims, Mongols, and Jews lived as captives of Great Russian power. After the Revolution, the Bolshevik promise of independence or autonomy was both kept and betrayed. The building of a synthetic, all-inclusive Soviet nationalism based on party loyalty allowed some of the minorities cultural diversity in exchange for political conformity. But the growing terror of the Stalinist regime and the fears and passions unleashed by World War II resulted in mass persecution, imprisonment, slaughter, and physical transplantation of national minority groups deemed dangerous to the security of the regime. Uncounted millions both within and outside the Soviet borders have paid a bitter price for the conversion of Marxist internationalism into Soviet nationalism.

Germany, on the other hand, was stripped of its national minorities by the territorial losses imposed by the Treaty of Versailles. In the pain and fury of defeat it proceeded to manufacture a new minority: the Jews. Anti-Semitism in the prewar German empire had not been much more virulent than in France, less so than in Austria-Hungary, and mild in comparison with the brutal persecutions in Russia. Some 600,000 German Jews, with the partial exception of considerable numbers of post-1918 Jewish immigrants from Eastern Europe, were more thoroughly assimilated into German society than was true of any other country. But in their frustration over the outcome of the war, German nationalists seized upon the Jews as a convenient scapegoat. Powerless against their enemies abroad, the nationalists created enemies at home.

For the extremist-nationalist movements that ultimately gathered under Hitler's banner, communists, socialists, and democrats were also enemies of the nation. But these might still be converted by force or persuasion. The Jews, however, were declared a race apart, inferior and unfit to dwell on German soil. The result of these cruel and fantastic propositions was the concentration camp and the gas chamber from which only a remnant of Germany's Jews escaped. During the few years when Hitler's armies controlled most of Europe the rage to persecute the Jews grew to the colossal proportions of genocide; by the end of World War II 6 million

Jews had died at the hands of their Nazi tormentors. Nationalist obsession with homogeneity and tribal exclusivity can go no further.

The history of the nation-state in the new world both follows the European pattern and at the same time exhibits unique aspects. The most visible uniqueness has been the mass presence of non-European populations—the indigenous Indian population and the Africans imported in slavery. The white men who penetrated the Americas as conquerors and slavemasters set the tone for political society in the Western Hemisphere: the new states were to be built not with the Indian and the black man but on top of them. This arrogant and cold-hearted notion has bloodied the hemisphere for nearly five centuries in defiance of the truth that the strictly white or white-dominated nation is neither morally nor politically viable in most parts of the hemisphere.

The exclusion of Indians and blacks from the nation-building process meant that the embryonic American nations were wholly dependent on immigration if they were to grow and prosper. The new world premium on immigrants collapsed the barriers that had divided peoples into rival nationalities in the old world from which they came. Even though new and different kinds of barriers were erected after their arrival, uncounted millions from every part of Europe (and later smaller numbers of Asians from the Near and Far East) experienced an unprecedented sea change in their passage to the Americas. In all cases alien to one another and in some cases enemies, they took up residence in the new territories and with greater or lesser difficulty developed a common allegiance to their new homelands. Hence those new world nations most attractive to immigrants became far more cosmopolitan than their old world counterparts. This was true even though, with the exception of Canada, the earliest wave of immigrants in each case set the language and the political and cultural tone of the developing societies. The diversity of immigrant ethnicity, language, and religion continued to be divisive, but not to the point where it prevented the emergence of an authentic national sense of belonging together.

Thus the Western Hemisphere witnessed on the one hand the fiercest kind of tribal exclusivity toward nonwhites and, on the other, a historic transcendence of tribal enmities among the white populations. New World experience violated most of the concrete criteria for determining the viability of nationhood and demonstrated again and again that the key variable in the making of a nation is a matter of will. This is the variable at issue now in the still incomplete nations of the Americas. It is at issue in the English-French confrontation in Canada stemming from the unique circumstance that one white population conquered another two hundred years ago, and it is at issue in white Canada's stance concerning its resident Indian and Eskimo populations. It is at issue in Mexico, Central America, and the Andean republics, where discrimination as well as poverty bars Indians from the political community and in so doing frustrates the community's aspirations to nationhood. And it is notoriously at issue in the United States, where ancient and continuing wrongs against Indians and blacks and more recent wrongs against Japanese Americans, Mexican Americans, and Puerto Ricans have shamed the national motto: from many, one.

NATIONALISM IN THE NEW SOVEREIGNTIES

This highly condensed survey of the tribal crimes and follies of nationalism in the West can only underline the dubiousness of the national model as a way of life for the non-West. In all of Asia and Africa, only Japan, Korea, and some of the Arab states are free of significant ethnic, linguistic, religious, or tribal divisions. Heterogeneity and not homogeneity is the fundamental condition of life for all the other aspirant nations from Manila to Dakar, and to a degree that wholly overshadows the problems of diversity faced by European nationalism.[1]

India epitomizes the dilemma on the most gigantic scale. More than half a billion people crowd part of a subcontinent that has spawned hundreds of languages. Fourteen have been accorded status as official languages while one, Hindi, has been designated as the *lingua franca* for all Indians. But unwillingness to accept the paramountcy of Hindi, particularly in southern India, perpetuates the use of English, the tongue of the departed imperial ruler, as the common bond of communication in all parts of India. This common facility, of course, is shared only among the elites and is thus hardly conducive to improving communications between elite and mass.

Linguistic divisions and ethnic animosities have constantly threatened India's federal system; state boundaries have had to be redrawn and whole new states carved out to appease passions aroused by the aversion to living with alien communities. In 1973 India was composed of eighteen federated states, in most of which there is a separate paramount language. Given the multiplicity of lesser languages, the many overlapping patterns of linguistic distribution, and the abundance of regional and ethnic hostilities, the stability of the state system will continue to be a major problem. Add to this the uneasy presence of more than 50 million Muslims and the divisive effects of a lingering caste system, and the barriers to mature nationhood seem almost insurmountable.

If India is the giant reflector of Asian woes, Nigeria performs the same function in Africa. The secession of Biafra and the long ensuing war with its terrible loss of life recall the massacre of millions that accompanied the partition of India and Pakistan in 1947. Christian Ibo and Muslim Haussa could not live with one another. Driven from the Muslim

---

[1] For ethnic divisions within the world's sovereignties, see Appendices D and E.

north back to their eastern homelands, the Ibos retaliated with the weapon of secession. No settlement can heal these wounds for many years; and even if they are healed, the specter of division and secession will haunt Nigeria into the future as it tries to find some basis for unity among nearly 60 million people composed of no less than 248 ethnic groups, each with its own distinct language.

India and Nigeria face the most staggering problems in the search for political unity, but most Asian and African states differ only in scale. At the very moment of its independence in 1960 the Congo was pulled apart by tribalism, sectionalism, and the conflicting ambitions among blacks and among whites who wanted to prolong imperial privileges. Only the extended presence of United Nations forces made it possible to put the pieces together again, but the formula for an enduring voluntary political unity remains to be found. In Sudan the dominant Muslim-Arab community in the north made war for fifteen years on the black Christian and animist minority in the south. In neighboring Chad the situation is the reverse: the black majority in the south wars on the Muslim-Arab minority in the north. In East Africa tens of thousands of the resident Asian populations have been driven into permanent exile, and the remainder live under the threat of future expulsions. In southern Africa, of course, the traditional imperial relationship between majority and minority continues to prevail: the white minority is master and persecutor of the black majority. In Asia there are bitter animosities within and across frontiers between Jews and Arabs, Arabs and Kurds, Pakistanis and Pushtoons, Pakistanis and Bengalis, Hindus and Muslims, Sinhalese and Tamils. Overseas Chinese and their host countries throughout Southeast Asia also defy the nation-state's premise of a will to live together as a community.

Most of these multicultural societies had only one unifying bond: they were administrative units of alien empires. In some cases their one cooperative and unifying experience was the attempt to rid the unit of its imperial occupiers. Once the attempt succeeded, many of the new sovereignties were faced with the question whether they could hold together on a voluntary basis peoples and territories that had been joined only by imperial fiat. Here the political will to build a nation has been tested again and again to the breaking point.

In a majority of the new states only a few factors were at hand to function as forces for national consolidation. The preestablished colonial governmental and administrative overlay that defined the frontiers and the internal political and economic patterns of the state constituted, in most cases, the more or less going concern inherited by the new government. In almost all cases the language of the former colonial rulers served as the medium of communication across ethnic-linguistic lines. In many instances the charisma of the leader of the independence movement and, in some, the common experience of a full-scale revolutionary struggle for liberation contributed to the quest for unity. Finally, the superior power of a particular ethnic, tribal, or religious group has often been employed as a means to persuade or coerce the less powerful groups into accepting the continuance of common government.

Against these unifying factors stands the fundamental fact of diversity in ethnic, linguistic, tribal, or religious affiliations. It is compounded by the physical and psychological remoteness among groups that are supposed to comprise the nation and by the corresponding meagerness of internal lines of communication and of economic ties. Many of the new states share with some of the Latin American countries sharp discontinuities in topography and climate. Not a few face situations in which the boundaries of neighboring states inherited from the respective colonial administrations dissect linguistic, ethnic, or tribal groupings and thus constitute a fertile source for secessionist and irredentist enterprises. Finally, in all of the new states, as in virtually all of Latin America, there is the terrible spectacle of the division between the few who have power, money, and education and the mass which multiplies itself and its resentments, poverty, and ignorance with increasing speed.

Rupert Emerson describes the nation as "the largest community which, when the chips are down, effectively commands men's loyalty, overriding the claims both of the lesser communities within it and those which cut across it or potentially enfold it within a still greater society."[2] With the exception of very few, the new states are far removed from meeting these criteria of nationhood. It follows that most of these division-ridden entities are, in fact, prenations.

The truth is that only a minority of mankind, coinciding closely with the populations of the developed world, lives in what may properly be called nation-states. The emergence of the nation as the object of overriding loyalty on a mass basis depends on the development of an upwardly mobile society in which all members, or at least the vast majority, are regarded as rightful participants in the society's political and economic life. To the extent that the majority or significant minorities are treated as alien and indefinitely consigned to the far side of the gap that divides the good life from misery there can be no common loyalty that unites the total population.

Nationalism cannot build a viable state unless it pursues its egalitarian vocation. As we have seen, the obstacles to political, economic, social, and cultural equality are far greater in the new prenations than they have been in the West where nationalism got its start. Just as it did in the nineteenth-century West, technology offers the presently underdeveloped world the means to realize egalitarian aspirations. But it is evident that these aspirations can be fulfilled in most of the new states

---

[2] Rupert Emerson, *From Empire to Nation: The Rise to Self-assertion of Asian and African Peoples* (Cambridge, Mass.: Harvard University Press, 1960), p. 95.

only if these states accept their heterogeneous inheritance and avoid attempting to duplicate the specifically Western premium on homogeneity. "Liberty, equality, and diversity" is a more suitable motto in the underdeveloped world than the familiar triad that celebrates fraternity as the final virtue. If a sense of fraternity is to emerge, it can only do so to the extent that each group within the state feels that its voice will have due weight in the decisions made by the larger community and that it is master of its own integrity.

These considerations pose difficult but not impossible problems; they are the classic problems to which federalism addresses itself. With greater or less sincerity and success the United States, Switzerland, Germany, and the Soviet Union have served as examples in the developed world of the application of federal principles to deal with regional, ethnic, linguistic, or cultural diversities; India, Malaysia, Mexico, and Nigeria are among the federal states in the underdeveloped world. The frauds and failures that have attended federal experiments in both worlds are hardly conducive to optimism. But success has been frequent enough so that the concept of the division and decentralization of powers to take into account the diversity of groups and regions offers at least part of a model for building prenations into coherent states. The federal concept runs counter to the widespread preference for centralized planning and one-party systems in the underdeveloped world, but experience has shown that it is not incompatible with rapid development and the concomitant upwardly mobile society.

Each of the prenations must obviously find its own path to nationhood —or to a viable multicultural society—and some may find insuperable obstacles in the way. But at least one generalization about the nation-state applies to all. No political community producing internal freedom and welfare and external power can be built in the absence of a voluntary inclination on the part of its peoples to identify their destinies with it. The first premise of nationalism is voluntarism; people who do not wish to be nationals cannot be forced into it. Or, if they are compelled to live in a state in which they do not feel at home, their unwilling presence measures the extent to which the nation-state falls short of the hopes for freedom and power which it has inspired for 200 years.

Whether homogeneous or heterogeneous in composition, the nation-state requires mass loyalty, not just the loyalty of a small elite. In the prenations mass loyalty can only result from steadily expanding political, economic, and educational opportunities. The investment needed to provide increasing opportunity will stretch available resources to the breaking point for a long time to come, and those countries which willfully or otherwise squander resources in ethnic or other forms of discrimination and oppression are candidates for bankruptcy.

Ideally, then, nationalism functions as a unifying force within the state. It seeks to transform the population into a voluntary community.

While homogeneity in ethnicity, language, and culture is favorable to national development, heterogeneity does not necessarily obstruct the path to nationhood. The political will to unity can overcome the qualities of exclusivity in the nationalist psychology and build an authentic nation from diverse materials. If, however, nationalism exacerbates instead of heals the inevitable divisions produced by heterogeneity or perpetuates instead of narrows the gulf between elite and mass, it is malfunctioning and frustrating the achievement of its own goals.

NATIONALISM IN THE GLOBAL SOCIETY

Beyond the state the situation is quite different. In international relations the nation has no unifying mission. Its goal is its own survival or aggrandizement in an irredeemably alien world. Its exclusivistic ethos accepts and solidifies the divisions that characterize global society. For Emerson, "the nation can be called a 'terminal community,' with the implication that it is for present purposes the effective end of the road for man as a social animal, the end point of working solidarity between men."[3] For Morgenthau, "the members of the human race live and act politically, not as members of one world society . . . but as members of their respective national societies, guided by their national standards . . . In politics the nation and not humanity is the ultimate fact."[4] In domestic politics the nation is, ideally, the inclusive society. In international politics it is, ideally, the exclusive society.

In the world, then, nationalism is the agent not of solidarity and egalitarianism but of fragmentation and discrimination. If the nation overcomes barriers within the state it builds new barriers around the state. In traditional society the great division among men was that which divided the ruling elites from the powerless masses. In the world of nation-states the great division is one that divides powerful masses from one another. For the old elites the out-groups were, first, the populations subject to their rule; for the new nations the out-groups became the foreigners. In both cases the absence of community inevitably made for conflict. But nationalism, reconstituting the state on a mass basis and nurturing the rapid growth of technology, provoked conflicts that have dwarfed anything previously known to history. The Napoleonic Wars and World Wars I and II have been the most bitter of the bitter fruits of early and contemporary nationalism. World War III threatens to be its bitterest and final fruit.

On the one hand, nationalism has symbolized and partially realized

---

[3] Emerson, *idem.*

[4] Hans J. Morgenthau, *Politics Among Nations*, 5th ed. (New York: Knopf, 1973), p. 267.

freedom from alien rule, freedom from superior-inferior relationships, freedom from the psychology of master and slave. On the other hand, the nation-state as the embodiment of sovereign independence is the chief breeder of anarchy in the global system. National loyalties inhibit larger loyalties, national rivalries dominate the world's political processes, the interests of each nation assert paramountcy over the interests of all men.

National governments make war and reserve to themselves the fateful choice whether the war shall be conventional or nuclear. Nation-states make the decisions that perpetuate the lopsided allocation of material resources in a world riven by the glaring contrast between the minority rich and the majority poor. Preoccupation with the national self diverts attention from the mounting perils of global incineration and starvation and subverts the will and the reason necessary to combat them. The world is joined together to a degree of intricacy unprecedented in all previous history. Nationalism's continuing tendency to seal off and compartmentalize what is already connected can only be destructive and not creative.

Thus we arrive at the unavoidable conclusion: nationalism, like all ideologies, both unites men and divides them. Explicitly parochial in outlook, the national ideal has nonetheless transcended and transformed the still narrower parochialisms of tribe, province, or class. Insofar as it can perform this function in the new states of the underdeveloped world it must be reckoned as a positive force in the search for freedom, equality, civil order, and economic development. But in many of the new states, nationalism confronts such extremes of heterogeneity that it must demonstrate a capacity for accommodating diversity far greater than its history in the West has hitherto exhibited. In these states the viability of nationalism is uncertain. At the same time, it is possible that the quest for unity in diversity in the underdeveloped world will offer some instructive lessons to those states of the developed world where still persisting cultural and racial discrimination belies their pretensions to consummated nationhood.

Whatever the services of nationalism to internal politics, its external divisiveness constitutes the chief danger to human survival. The conclusion of the chapter on ideology stated the need for transnationalism, for still more spacious concepts of political life than the once spacious principles of nationalism. The second part of this book will attempt to develop a set of transnational concepts in detail. Here, on the basis of the evidence so far presented, it will only be argued that there is no way to avoid what men dread most unless transnationalism begins to displace nationalism in human political loyalties.

This is not a prescription for the early demise of the nation-state. The continuing emotional appeal of nationalism and the extraordinary political and economic benefits it has conferred guarantee its persistence into the foreseeable future. The contention is simply that the nation must begin to slough off its parochialism and become increasingly cosmopolitan. That is, it must recognize that its fate is tied to the fate of the larger world in which it exists and that national decisions which fail to respond to international needs are self-destructive. If the nation-state cannot demonstrate such a capacity for growth and change—for self-enhancement through accommodation to the needs of the global society—it will indeed be the "terminal community" in the most ominous sense of the phrase. Those who live in nation-states have a future only if they begin to see the nation as a transitional community, as one of a still unfinished series of experiments in the history of political creativity.

Chapter 8

Imperialism

Imperialism wears the two-faced mask of Janus. One face reveals imperialism as the embodiment of conquest and domination, the other as the symbol of defeat and bondage. This double image necessarily produces radically different judgments about empire. The conquerors like to look upon empire as a source of power, glory, and profit, and even as an expanded opportunity for moral uplift. Conversely, the conquered see empire as the cause of their powerlessness, their indigence, their humiliation, and their moral debasement.

Churchill and Nehru, the political giants of midcentury England and India, offer dramatic witness to the distance that separates conqueror and conquered, imperialist and victim of imperialism. In the midst of a desperate war whose professed purpose was to vindicate democratic values, Churchill loftily vowed that he had "not become the King's First Minister in order to preside over the liquidation of the British Empire."[1] Nehru's words, though written perhaps two years earlier, provide the essential commentary on Churchill's position: "They talk complacently still of their empire and of their desire to maintain it, forgetting perhaps that the word, which sounds so good to them, is a symbol to us of our own subjection, degradation and poverty."[2] These colliding views of empire illustrate the irreconcilable perspectives of warden and prisoner. Their juxtaposition makes it clear that in addressing the problem of imperialism one has to deal with a form of tyranny.

IMPERIALISM AS A SPECIES OF TYRANNY

The perception of imperialism as a variety of tyranny accords with both its historical and its (Western) etymological origins. The prototypes of

[1] Winston S. Churchill, *The End of the Beginning: War Speeches, 1942* (Boston: Little, Brown, 1943), p. 268.
[2] Jawaharlal Nehru, "The Parting of the Ways," *Toward Freedom* (Boston: Beacon Press, 1958), p. 379.

empire in all parts of the globe resulted typically from political-military actions that broke out of the confines of traditional tribal society. Where these efforts at conquest were successful, the tribal commune was superseded by a more extensive territorial society. The politics of the new imperial society was characterized chiefly by a sharp distinction between conqueror and conquered and by a monopoly, or oligopoly, of power in the hands of the conquerors. The exercise of unlimited power by any faction of a society is, of course, the classic breeding ground of tyranny.

It was from the concept of unlimited power that the Roman word *imperium* gained its original meaning. In early Roman usage the word described a military command whose authority was "not subject to definition or limitation." Here the imperium reflected the presence of the despotic principle in all military organization. By the same token, the measures the Roman Republic took to constrain the military arm reflected deep awareness of its dangerous potentials: "In Republican Rome the imperator or general appointed to command an army was obliged to leave the city directly upon appointment, the mere presence of one holding the imperium or absolute military power being considered repugnant to civil principles and magistracy."[3]

It was, finally, the collapse of distinctions between civil and military power and between Rome and its dependencies that finished the Republic and enabled the imperators to turn the whole of the Roman world into an empire. Now "the holder of the imperium (imperator) absorbed all the powers of the state and became absolute monarch." Thus Roman experience fused government by conquest, usurpation of power, and despotism into the concept of imperium. No accretion of power, glory, or prosperity could henceforth erase the sense of liberties lost through empire, even for the imperialists themselves. The course of imperialism in Rome as elsewhere established beyond doubt that one man's empire must necessarily be another man's tyranny, both at home and abroad.

Imperialism, in the sense in which the word is now generally used, compounds the injury of tyranny in a particular and peculiarly provocative way. By definition, imperialism establishes a government by strangers. Alien rule is the hallmark of empire. The key decisions for the imperial colony are made by persons, processes, and institutions foreign to the colony. Thus the sharp edges of arbitrary power cannot be softened by any collective empathy or intellectual understanding between rulers and ruled. Abuses by private interests in the colony are tied into the politics of the imperial metropole and are, therefore, difficult to check or punish. The outward symbols of authority may be palpable in the person of the local colonial official, but real political and economic

---

[3] The definition and discussion of imperium are taken from *Funk and Wagnalls New Standard® Dictionary of the English Language* (New York: Funk and Wagnalls, 1963).

authority is remote, and redress of major grievances is correspondingly difficult.

To the extent that there is any sense of public responsibility or patriotism animating imperial policy, it attaches first to the country of the colonizer and only secondarily, if at all, to the colony. If the incumbent government was despotic before the arrival of the imperialists, the conquerors rather typically found a use for the despot and by their support made his removal almost impossible. Indeed, imperialism's strongest tendency has been to freeze the status quo and devitalize the politics of the captured colonies so that the inhabitants of the colonies had only the choice of being rebels or being servants in someone else's political house. This tendency corresponds to a favorite assumption of imperialism: those in the imperial dependency are incapable of governing themselves.

The whole imperial argument, of course, contradicts the nationalist and democratic assumptions that home-grown government is preferable to that imported from abroad. In support of their position the empire builders could cite an occasional persuasive case to demonstrate that "benevolent" despotism imposed from the outside can, at a given time, establish a more peaceful civil order and a more productive economy than could the indigenous government. Supporters of imperialism could also draw attention to the classic debates among subjugated peoples in every era questioning whether the imperial strangers or their own countrymen who collaborate with them are the more rapacious and oppressive. Collaboration, of course, is a perennial phenomenon among minority groups in a conquered territory. The foreign masters are usually in need of allies against the hostility or indifference of the local majority, and the collaborators satisfy that need in exchange for grants of local power and privilege. Finally, the imperial argument points to the tangibles: the building of roads, clinics, schools, railways, or airports where none or few existed previous to colonial status. In these and other ways the conquerors can build up a certain clientele among the conquered.

But the clientele is made up of retainers and not partners. Whatever the merits in the imperial arguments—and of those just cited the merits are mostly dubious—they cannot weigh against the central fact that imperialism stands as an insurmountable barrier to the creation of a community between ruler and ruled. The imperialist is always the master and mover; the subject of empire is always the servant and the one who is moved. The colonial servant wears a double yoke: the foreign overlord and the local oligarch; and he cannot confront the one without confronting the other. Hence he is deprived of any role in an autonomous drama of political action, of participating effectively in the clash between the new and the old, between democracy and oligarchy, between the new generation of his own country and its elders.

So long as imperialism persists, these and all matters that shape the destiny of the country are exclusively the province of the colonial governors. In such a context no joint political enterprise such as nationalism offers can possibly take root—except in the nationalist underground movement committed to the overthrow of imperialism. In short, if the native of a colony wishes to become an authentic political being, he must become an outlaw. Gandhi and Nehru, Kenyatta, Nkrumah, Ben Bella, and Ho Chi Minh are at the head of a long list of twentieth-century examples. Washington, Jefferson, Adams, San Martín, Bolívar, and Martí made the same choice for outlawry in earlier periods of decolonization.

Imperialism is arbitrary and alien; it is also predatory. It postulates rule by one group over another group for the benefit of the ruling group. All the rationalizations and justifications for empire cannot disguise the fact that the basic imperial impulse is to conquer and to enjoy the benefits that accrue to conquerors. Empires were not built for the happiness of the conquered colonials but for the convenience of the empire builders. Insofar as the foreign masters could accommodate the needs of the "natives" while pursuing their own purposes they laid the foundations for the morally self-vindicating slogans of sacred trusts and civilizing missions. But underneath everything was the fundamental premise of imperialism: all power to the alien masters and none to the indigenous mass. Whatever the modifications of this premise in particular situations, it was understood on all sides that the imperial will is the sovereign will and that the only effective authority is authority endorsed by the sovereign. Thus, if the essence of imperialism is conquest, the essence of empire is the perpetuation of the distinction between conqueror and conquered.

IMPERIALISM AT HIGH TIDE

It is obvious that many human beings will suffer under an imperial system. It is also obvious that some will profit from it and therefore seek to defend it. But at this juncture of history there are few overt champions of imperialism, and for very particular reasons. The almost universal reticence in expressing imperial ambitions today is a new phenomenon in international politics. At the turn of the century, as in all previous history, it was taken for granted that powerful states would have empires and that weak peoples were obvious and legitimate targets for imperial expansion. To be sure, contemporary critics like J. A. Hobson argued that imperialism was unjust or unprofitable or both. But the key difference between then and now is that those whom Hobson attacked argued back, and their rebuttal was less a defense than a counterattack. Imperialism was a badge to be worn proudly by those who were or who aspired to be masters rather than subjects of empire.

The majesty of imperial self-confidence in the late nineteenth century is best conveyed in the words of the imperialists themselves. Joseph Chamberlain, Lord Lugard, Lord Rosebery, and Lord Baden-Powell epitomize the establishment approach to the British Empire and offer a fair sample of imperial opinion. Chamberlain, as colonial secretary, parliamentarian, publicist, and businessman, was the recognized leader of the imperial prophets. Empire was an obsession with Chamberlain and reached into all aspects of his thinking. Hence the following remarks cannot be labeled representative, only salient:

> I think the duty of this country in regard to all these savage countries over which we are called upon to exercize some sort of dominion is to establish, at the earliest possible date, Pax Britannica, and force these people to keep the peace amongst themselves (cheers), and by so doing, whatever may be the destruction of life in an expedition which brings about this result, it will be nothing if weighed in the balance against the annual loss of life which goes on so long as we keep away.[4]

The note of benevolence sounded more loudly, and that of impatience and force receded, as Chamberlain discovered new aspects of empire in the following year (1897):

> . . . a change has come over the Imperial idea. . . . the sense of possession has given place to a different sentiment—the sense of obligation. We feel now that our rule over these territories can only be justified if we can show that it adds to the happiness and prosperity of the people, and I maintain that our rules does, and has, brought security and peace and comparative prosperity to countries that never knew their blessings before. In carrying out this work of civilization we are fulfilling what I believe to be our national mission.

If Chamberlain praised the benign influence of empire on the native populations and sounded the white man's burden note, he was still more convinced that imperialism meant economic gain for England. Here, however, we shall let Lord Lugard, soldier and distinguished colonial administrator, give expression to one facet of the commercial thinking of the empire builders:

> Let us admit that commercial enterprise in Africa is undertaken for our own benefit, as much as and more than for the benefit of the African. We have spoken already of the vital necessity of new markets for the old world. It is, therefore, to our very obvious advantage to teach the millions of Africa the

---

[4] The quotations from Chamberlain, Lugard, Rosebery, and Baden-Powell are all taken from Richard Koebner and Helmut D. Schmidt, *Imperialism: The Story and Significance of a Political Word, 1840–1960* (Cambridge University Press, 1961). These quotations from speeches and articles, all of which were written during the 1890s, can be found, together with their original sources, in Chapters VII and VIII of Koebner and Schmidt's study. (Reprinted by permission of Cambridge University Press.)

wants of civilization, so that whilst supplying them we may receive in return the products of their country and the labour of their hands.

Lord Rosebery, once Liberal prime minister, twice foreign secretary, and long-time associate of Gladstone, came to imperialism only reluctantly, having spent many years opposing Disraeli's brand of empire. But by 1888 he had declared enthusiastically for Imperial Federation in which the white colonies would join Britain in creating a federal constitution binding them to one another, presumably forever. Five years later, Rosebery provided at least part of a rationale for Imperial Federation in a speech to the Royal Colonial Institute. It was, he said, "part of our responsibility and heritage to take care that the world, as far as it can be moulded by us, shall receive the Anglo-Saxon and not another character." In the election campaign of 1895 Rosebery described himself as a "Liberal Imperialist" and proceeded to define his terms in an eclectic formulation that was not without a certain wry candor and practicality:

Liberal Imperialism implies, first, the maintenance of the Empire; secondly, the opening of new areas for our surplus population; thirdly, suppression of the slave trade; fourthly, the development of missionary enterprise; and fifthly, the development of our commerce, which so often needs it.

While there were voices in opposition to the self-congratulatory themes running through all these professions of faith in empire, they constituted only a small minority. After all, Chamberlain and Rosebery were on opposite sides in the election of 1895 and thus between them virtually monopolized the spectrum of opinion. Both Conservatives and Liberals embraced imperialism; only the pain of the Boer War at the turn of the century began to produce an atmosphere in which dissidence and second thoughts could be effectively heard in England. But the 1890s were the imperial heydays. In the general election of 1892 Robert Baden-Powell, later Lord Baden-Powell and founder of the Boy Scouts, noted with satisfaction that "every candidate promised to uphold the unity of empire." He exuded a classic blend of pride and piety (with Rosebery's help) when he expressed his hopes concerning the work of the newly organized Imperial Institute:

[it should seek] to provide full knowledge in support of the zealous pride in their Empire now so widely instilled into the nation; affording convincing reason to all Imperialists for the faith that is in them. . . . We believe our great Empire to be, in Lord Rosebery's eloquent words, "the greatest secular agency for good the world has ever seen."

The smugness and naïveté of British imperial attitudes found its counterparts and imitators throughout Europe and in America. In both Germany and the United States there were many who were convinced that their countries would soon overtake and supersede Britain as the dominant power on the globe and that as the nineteenth century had brought Britain to the zenith of its power, so the twentieth would be the "German Century" or the American. Similar ideas were stirring in Japan, particularly after the triumph over Russia in 1905. Just as the French imperialists had long been extolling the *mission civilisatrice* as the leading rationale for French expansion overseas, the Germans now wanted to benefit the world by extending the realm of *Kultur.*

Imperialists of every nationality were persuaded that empire was a paying proposition. They also attached political and military advantages to imperial territories. But rewards in the quest for power and wealth were not enough to satisfy the imperial urge; empire was also, and perhaps primarily, a matter of glory and magnificence. The acts of territorial expansion, of conquering and commanding, generated a portion of these less tangible goods, but conquest and command for their own sakes suggested to the imperialists a set of values more appropriate to the barbarism of the non-European world than to the center of civilization. The professed solution was essentially a Platonic one: a good commander could not help but benefit those commanded by him. By bringing civilization to the backward regions and the "lower races of the earth" (even Hobson used these terms and, with some reservations, assented to these ideas), the European powers and the United States could only improve the lot of the rest of mankind. Hence empire had the ongoing task of raising the cultural level of the natives. And since the natives had a long way to go, the morally satisfying cause of advancing civilization appeared to be one of indefinite duration.

All these sentiments for the advancement of civilization and culture found the apogee of their expression in Rudyard Kipling's celebrated poem whose title is perhaps more freighted with significance now than when it was written in 1899. The text of "The White Man's Burden" is properly understood only if it is noted that the poem is specifically addressed to the people of the United States and that its purpose was to persuade them to get on with the business of taking charge in the Philippines. It is worth quoting at length:

> Take up the White Man's burden—
>   Send forth the best ye breed—
> Go bind your sons to exile
>   To serve your captives' need;
> To wait in heavy harness
>   On fluttered folk and wild—
> Your new-caught, sullen peoples,
>   Half devil and half child.
>
> Take up the White Man's burden—
>   In patience to abide,

> To veil the threat of terror
>   And check the show of pride;
> By open speech and simple
>   An hundred times made plain
> To seek another's profit
>   And work another's gain.
>
> Take up the White Man's burden—
>   The savage wars of peace—
> Fill full the mouth of Famine
>   And bid the sickness cease;
> And when your goal is nearest
>   The end for others sought,
> Watch Sloth and heathen Folly
>   Bring all your hope to naught.
>
>   . . .
>
> Take up the White Man's burden—
>   And reap his old reward:
> The blame of those ye better
>   The hate of those ye guard—
> The cry of hosts ye humour
>   (Ah, slowly!) toward the light:—
> "Why brought ye us from bondage,
>   "Our loved Egyptian night?"
>
>   . . .
>
> Take up the White Man's burden—
>   Have done with childish days—
> The lightly proffered laurel,
>   The easy, ungrudged praise.
> Comes now, to search your manhood
>   Through all the thankless years,
> Cold-edged with dear-bought wisdom
>   The judgment of your peers![5]

While the poetic formula imbues empire with an ethic of service, it suggests that in the face of native recalcitrance the service cannot achieve very much. It follows, as the final verse makes rather clear, that the real service is not to the natives but to the novice conquerors. The tough job of building and maintaining empires is an exercise in manliness and a school in the techniques of command. The colony and its people resemble a fief—or a plantation—whose management must be mastered if the novice is to win the esteem of his peers. "Peers," in

---

[5] *The Five Nations.* New York: Doubleday, Page and Co., 1903. By permission of Mr. George Bambridge, Methuen, Macmillan of Canada.

turn, presumably refers to those who are already experienced in the ways of imperialism. The native's chief function is to serve as a foil to test the mettle of the white master. The passive role assigned the native and the paternalistic role urged upon the imperialist make it evident that whatever "improvement" is feasible, the native can rise only to a level that is still far below that of the master. Empire might be "progressive" but never egalitarian.

No one could have responded more enthusiastically to Kipling's concepts of imperial burden or to his specific urgings that the United States take charge of the Philippines than Senator Albert J. Beveridge of Indiana. A close associate of Theodore Roosevelt and the most articulate of the new imperialists, Beveridge's oratorical flights make the British Empire enthusiasts, even Kipling, seem models of restraint. Indeed, no study of imperialism, long or short, is complete without excerpts from Beveridge's speech to the Senate on January 5, 1900, when he announced, in support of his own resolution, that the Philippines "are forever ours." (Two years later, the Speaker of the House of Representatives, Congressman Joseph Cannon, wanted to make it "forever and a day.")

Beveridge's minor theme was that the Filipinos were not capable of self-government: "How could they be? They are not of a self-governing race. They are Orientals, Malays instructed by Spaniards in the latter's worst estate." His major theme was that Americans were not only eminently qualified to govern themselves but were also uniquely suited to govern everyone else:

> Mr. President, this question is deeper than any question of party politics; deeper than any question of the isolated policy of our country even; deeper even than any question of constitutional power. It is elemental. It is racial. God has not been preparing the English-speaking and Teutonic peoples for a thousand years for nothing but vain and idle self-contemplation and self-admiration. No! He has made us the master organizers of the world to establish system where chaos reigns. He has given us the spirit of progress to overwhelm the forces of reaction throughout the earth. He has made us adepts in government that we may administer government among savage and senile peoples. Were it not for such a force as this the world would relapse into barbarism and night. And of all our race He has marked the American people as His chosen nation to finally lead in the regeneration of the world.[6]

One need not take time to ridicule these various examples of imperialist bombast. As comedy they speak grimly for themselves. But their

---

[6] The quotations from Senator Beveridge and Representative Cannon are taken from Albert K. Weinberg's classic study of American expansionism *Manifest Destiny* (Chicago: Quadrangle Books, 1963), pp. 307 and 308. The book was first published by Johns Hopkins Press, Baltimore, 1935.

authors were not comics; they took themselves seriously. What is more important, public opinion took them seriously, too, because they gave expression to the whole melange of ideas that animated the surge of imperialism at the turn of the century: racism, missionary snobbery, avarice, military romanticism, cultural provincialism, and a self-satisfaction that can only be described as brutal. These were the ideas that dominated imperial policy and practice and that the colonial populations had to try to live with at the receiving end. Most important, they persist as nemesis in both the European and non-European worlds long after the formal abandonment of empires.

The superiority-inferiority syndrome continues to poison the relationships between the world of the white rich and the world of the colored poor. Those who have made it in terms of power and wealth are always prone to consider themselves cleverer and more vigorous than those who have not. It is this set of persuasions on a mass basis that reproduces again and again in our own time the characteristics typifying the imperialist attitudes of a Kipling, a Rosebery, or a Beveridge.

By the same token, the urgency with which the non-European world wants to modernize in order to gain power and wealth reinforces the assumption of superiority on the part of the societies that achieved these values first. To the extent that the underdeveloped world is imitating the developed world, it is tempting to conclude, first, that the developed world has a near monopoly of desirable social values and, second, that the societies which fashioned these values have much to teach but little to learn. Such inferences, of course, inhibit reflection on the possibility that there may be a variety of routes to modernization which deviate from those taken in the past by the nations that deem themselves already "modern."

What is at stake at a global level (as it is at the national level in every culturally divided society) is cultural self-respect. The nonwhite world has been able to bear military defeat, political weakness, poverty, and social dislocation better than the white man's condescension. His disdain has been more wounding than all the demonstrations of superior force or superior technology. And the white man's recipe for salvation has been the ultimate expression of that disdain: leave behind native barbarism, the "loved Egyptian night," and imitate the ways of the imperial master. More than any real or imagined political, military, or economic power exercised over nonwhites, it is white arrogance that gives most credence to the charge that neoimperialism, or neocolonialism, is the chief danger now menacing the developing world.

CRITICS OF IMPERIALISM

In the three classic and most influential critiques of imperialism of the early twentieth century, this issue, while not overlooked, was obscured. J. A. Hobson, V. I. Lenin, and Joseph Schumpeter were all more interested in the effects of imperialism on the imperialists than in the fate of colonial populations.[7] Here, ironically, the critics and their targets are at one. This assertion may be too harsh as a commentary on Hobson. In his *Imperialism* he gave frequent evidence of sympathy for the victims of imperial rule and, in the case of Asia, showed a sensitive appreciation of indigenous cultures. Hobson was nonetheless primarily concerned with imperialism as a ruinous misuse of the resources of the metropolitan country, as a danger to its internal political and economic viability, and as an open invitation to devastating wars with other imperial nations. As for Lenin and Schumpeter, they were too preoccupied with making theoretical and ideological points to address themselves seriously to the superiority-inferiority relationship that makes imperialism psychologically as well as economically odious to its victims.

HOBSON ON IMPERIALISM

For Hobson, as for Lenin, imperialism is essentially a matter of economics. The human romance with property and wealth is the force that drives men to use the instruments of government in order to expand the state's territory and to subordinate alien men to their rule. Hobson and Lenin were also in agreement that while imperial expansion and imperial rule did in fact confer economic benefits, these flowed primarily to the smallest and least deserving group in society, the capitalist class. Beyond this point Hobson and Lenin parted company. Faithful to the determinist principle, Lenin saw imperialism as a class interest that would die only with the death of the class itself. Faithful to his reformist creed, Hobson hoped that an informed public and intelligentsia would pressure both government and capital to recognize the danger and folly of imperialism and to embrace more socially beneficent methods for satisfying economic objectives.

Hobson was able to demonstrate with relative ease that imperialism was no boon to the national economy as a whole. Contrary to imperial-

---

[7] J. A. Hobson, *Imperialism*, 3rd ed. (London: Allen and Unwin, 1938). First published in 1902. V. I. Lenin, *Imperialism, the Highest Stage of Capitalism* (Moscow: Foreign Languages Publishing House, 1950). First published in 1916. Joseph Schumpeter, "The Sociology of Imperialisms," *Imperialism and Social Classes* (New York: Augustus M. Kelley, 1951). First published in 1919.

ist propaganda, trade did not follow the flag with any consistency; poverty-stricken millions in the colonial areas made poor customers. At the time when Hobson wrote, the outstanding fact about international trade was the same as it is today: the industrialized nations are each other's best customers, and the overwhelming bulk of world trade is made up of their mutual transactions. Hence the investments that imperialism demands in money, organizational effort, and sometimes blood, Hobson argued, must bring a far smaller return than would a modest increase of commercial effort in the market constituted by the industrial nations.

Hobson did find that the yields from foreign investments averaged out to be significantly higher than the average yield on domestic investment—at least for the years in which he examined the relevant statistics.[8] On the basis of these findings, he concluded that those with money to invest were the chief beneficiaries of empire and therefore constituted the hard kernel of imperialist enthusiasm.

The investing classes, in turn, were the product of a maldistribution of wealth in society at large. Effect a redistribution of wealth within the metropolitan society, Hobson argued, and the excessive concentration of riches and power in the hands of this small segment of the population will disappear. Proceeding from this premise, Hobson concluded that the fate of imperialism would be sealed once the rich ceased to be rich—or at least lacked the wherewithal to invest significant amounts in colonial ventures. At the same time, investment at home in an economy characterized by a more equitably distributed capacity for consumption would enrich the society as a whole in a way that the most glittering empire could never do. Even though Hobson conceded the presence of other than economic motives in the pursuit of empire, he was saying, in essence, that empires would disappear once their profitability to a small group of capitalists in the metropolitan countries disappeared.

But not quite: Hobson raised the question whether the imperial nations could or should remove themselves completely from the colonial areas, and his answer was no. He attempted to wrestle in earnest with the problem of the white man's burden. "The real issue," he wrote, "is whether, and under what circumstances, it is justifiable for Western nations to use compulsory government for the control and education in the arts of industrial and political civilization of the inhabitants of tropical countries and other so-called lower races."[9]

Hobson's response to his own question was two-pronged. First, it is imperative to discover and develop all the world's resources with all due speed, a task that at present only the industrial nations can carry out.

---

[8] The ambiguities in Hobson's observations will be examined shortly in conjunction with similar ambiguities in Lenin's data and conclusions concerning foreign investment.

[9] Hobson, *Imperialism*, p. 228.

Second, Western governments must protect non-Western populations from the unscrupulous attentions of private exploiters from the West. "If these principles be admitted," he concluded, "it follows that civilized Governments *may* undertake the political and economic control of lower races—in a word, that the characteristic form of modern imperialism is not under all conditions illegitimate."[10] Hobson then went on to ask:

> What, then, are the conditions which render it legitimate? They may be provisionally stated thus: Such interference with the government of a lower race must be directed primarily to secure the safety and progress of the civilization of the world, and not the special interest of the interfering nation. Such interference must be attended by an improvement and elevation of the character of the people who are brought under this control. Lastly, the determination of the two preceding conditions must not be left to the arbitrary will or judgment of the interfering nation, but must proceed from some organized representation of civilized humanity.[11]

Contemporary critics of the West must find these reflections of Hobson's unusually satisfying grist for their mills. How better demonstrate the West's incorrigible predilection for empire than to discover imperialist attitudes imbedded in the writings of the chief Western critic of imperialism? Non-Western critics might concede that Hobson abhorred economic exploitation. But they might also observe that paternalistic concerns for the "lower races" would most likely contribute to their cultural exploitation by educating them away from their own cultural heritage and placing before them the alien model of the West —a model at the very least dubious in terms of both desirability and attainability. From this perspective Western partisan and Western critic of imperialism are united in the assumption of Western cultural preeminence. And since the West is largely white, concepts of cultural and racial superiority all too easily blend into a multifaceted but naïve egotism to which Kipling and the other prophets of empire gave classic expression.

But if Hobson was guilty of paternalistic arrogance, he was nevertheless wrestling with a very real practical and moral problem. The last quarter of the nineteenth century marked an already advanced stage in the technological revolution that has made the world ever smaller. New methods of transport and communication were even then making all parts of the globe more and more readily accessible. Distance no longer provided much insulation between the industrial West and the agricultural societies of Asia, Africa, and Latin America. The strong and the weak were now living side by side. The burst of imperial expansion

---

[10] Ibid., p. 232. Hobson's italics.
[11] Ibid.

during this period again demonstrated the age-old penchant of the strong to dominate the weak. But the problem was that now the weak were permanently within easy reach. Should one imperial government set free a colonial territory, it would in all probability be gobbled up by a rival empire. Should all the imperial powers release their overseas dependencies, the former colonies would be defenseless against the financial and technological power of great private entrepreneurs like Cecil Rhodes and all his counterparts. Therefore, Hobson argued, a government cleansed of predatory tendencies had an indispensable overseas role to play in protecting the foreordained victims of exploitation from their foreordained exploiters.

Thus Hobson called for European control of an unspecified amount of non-European territory, exercising authority under the supervision of an agency representing the norms of "civilized humanity." In proposing this internationalization of the imperial function, he anticipated the mandates system of the League of Nations and the trusteeship operations of the United Nations. But international control, though preferable to the arbitrary imperiums of individual nations, is still control by aliens.

If the purpose of control should now be redesigned to benefit rather than exploit the populations controlled—and to forward "the progress of the civilization of the world"—it was likely that the controllers rather than the controlled would take the lead in defining what constitutes benefits, progress, and civilization. In such a context the outlook for participatory democracy, however much Hobson himself might have desired it, was not encouraging. But these considerations only underline the fact that Hobson was dealing with a highly intractable problem. In his day, as in our time, the proximity of strong and weak societies creates a built-in propensity for imperial behavior—to the point where even if the strong are consciously trying to avoid empire building, the weak will still have good reason to fear them.

LENIN ON IMPERIALISM

Lenin and Hobson both treated imperialism like a disease produced by capitalism and curable only with the death or radical transformation of capitalism. Yet both were obviously aware of the long succession of imperialisms before the advent of capitalist society. Lenin referred to Roman imperialism and linked it to Roman slavery. He also spoke of political aspects of empire as though they were separable from an economic analysis of imperialism. But aside from these fleeting references, Lenin treated imperialism exclusively as an economic phenomenon and a product of an overripe capitalism. There is certainly no hint that Lenin's brand of Marxism could produce an imperialism of its own.

Following in Hobson's footsteps, Lenin asserted that the high return on investment in colonial areas was the central driving force behind imperial expansion. "In these backward countries," Lenin wrote, "profits are unusually high, for capital is scarce, the price of land is relatively low, wages are low, raw materials are cheap."[12] These economic characteristics, Lenin argued, must necessarily attract capital investors. To prove his point, he cited figures showing a spectacular rise in the foreign investments of Britain, France, and Germany over the period from 1862 to 1914. In the latter year, the total foreign investment of the three countries, according to Lenin's calculations, amounted to somewhere between 175 and 200 billion francs (35 to 40 billion 1914 dollars).

This is no mean figure, but its significance for understanding the dynamics of imperialism is much diminished once it is pointed out that foreign investment can find its way to many areas other than the backward countries of Lenin's description. Indeed, in his elaboration of another set of statistics, Lenin vouchsafed that, as of 1910, most of French foreign investment was located in Europe (primarily in Russia), that German external investment was "divided almost evenly between Europe and America," and that while British investment in continental Europe was relatively modest, investment in "America" was considerably larger than the total for Asia, Africa, and Australia combined. Lenin's statistics (this time in German marks) show that each of the three investment regions—Europe, America, and Asia-Africa-Australia—attracted approximately one-third of the foreign investment capital of the three leading capital exporters, with the latter region accounting for a slightly smaller share than the other two.

In the scramble for investment markets, the role of Lenin's backward countries shrinks further as soon as the region America is subdivided into the United States and Canada, on the one hand, and Latin America and the Caribbean, on the other. The latter area had, by the time of Lenin's analysis, attracted a considerable amount of foreign capital, but far less than the two economically sophisticated countries of North America.

One must, of course, follow the same procedure of subdivision in the Europe of 1910, distinguishing the industrialized west and north from the primarily agricultural south and east. Hence investments in Europe cannot automatically be identified as the export of capital from one sophisticated economy to another. Eastern and southern Europe were nonetheless far more sophisticated than most areas of Asia, Africa, and Latin America. Thus it is clear that Lenin's own figures, when subject to closer scrutiny, show that on a world scale the more sophisticated economies attracted capital in far greater abundance than Lenin's "back-

---

[12] Lenin, *Imperialism*, p. 100. The discussion of foreign investment that follows draws on material to be found on pp. 98–106 of Lenin's study.

ward" economies. There is an evident parallel here with Hobson's data on foreign trade, the bulk of which was carried on among the already industrialized countries and not between those countries and their respective empires.

LENIN AND HOBSON ON TRADE, INVESTMENT, AND IMPERIALISM

As far as capital exports go, however, Hobson was as careless as Lenin about distinguishing between "foreign" investments as a general category and "colonial" or "imperial" investments as a subcategory. In the only set of statistics in Hobson's study in which even a partial breakdown is undertaken, the total British capital abroad in the year 1893 is calculated to be nearly 1.7 billion pounds. Of that amount, 770 million pounds are accounted for by loans: 525 million "foreign," 225 million "colonial," and 20 million "municipal." Investments in railways account for 388 million, broken down as follows: "U.S.A.," 120 million; "colonial," 140 million; "various," 128 million. As for the balance of 540 million, it is broken down into "banks, lands, mines, etc.," with no indication whatsoever as to the world region in which these enterprises were located.[13] The only certain conclusion to be drawn from these statistics is that of the 1893 total of 1.7 billion pounds of British overseas investment, 365 million was specifically located in colonial areas, 120 million in the United States, and something over 1.2 billion, or about 75 percent of the total, in unspecified areas outside the United Kingdom.

To bring some order out of chaos it will be helpful to cite more complete and reliable statistics, this time for British foreign investments in the peak year 1913.[14] By then the total of British capital abroad had risen to approximately 3.8 billion pounds. Of this amount 47.3 percent was invested in the empire—but it is noteworthy that the most developed "colonies," Canada, Australia, and New Zealand, accounted for more than half (52.3 percent) of all imperial investment. India-Ceylon and South Africa together attracted another 42 percent of the total, leaving a minuscule 5.7 percent scattered around the huge remainder of Britain's colonial possessions. In sum, less than half of Britain's overseas investments were located within the Empire and less than one-fifth in the nonwhite imperial territories.

In the world at large, the United States was the prime area of British investment: 20 percent of the grand total, or 754.6 million pounds. Investment in Europe was the smallest for any continent: 5.8 percent

---

[13] Hobson, *Imperialism*, p. 62.

[14] Royal Institute of International Affairs, *The Problem of International Investment* (London: Oxford University Press, 1937), p. 121.

or 218.6 million pounds. In Latin America, British investment in Argentina stood at better than double the amount invested in next-ranking Brazil. These two countries plus Mexico and Chile accounted for more than 80 percent of the total British capital of 756.6 million pounds invested in Latin America. Finally, in Asia, where investment activity continued to be modest, Japan was the largest recipient of British capital (62.8 million pounds or 1.7 percent of total British overseas investment).

The conclusion is evident: with the exception of Europe (where some governments had made efforts to discourage British capital), the British foreign investment pattern of 1913 consistently favored the more advanced over the less advanced areas. The United States was the largest single recipient of British capital, equalling the total British investment in all of Latin America. South of the Rio Grande, the four most developed countries accounted for more than 80 percent and the seven most developed for 99.3 percent of British investment in Latin America. In the empire and in Asia outside the empire, the picture is the same: the most developed colonies or countries attracted the most investment and the least, least.

This pattern is still more evident in the 1914 geographic distribution of foreign investment of the other two chief sources of international capital, France and Germany.[15] Europe had absorbed 61 percent of French capital exports and 53 percent of German. Only 9 percent of French foreign investment could be found in the French colonies and about half that percentage of German funds in German colonies. The bulk of French and German noncolonial overseas investments was situated in the Western Hemisphere.

In the case of France and Germany, then, investment followed the flag no more conspicuously than did trade. In Britain's case, imperial investment, like trade, followed only where the flag had been flying for a very long time and where the economies were preponderantly white. By contrast, the new imperial territories acquired during the late nineteenth century generally attracted only a meager portion of British investment, similar in magnitude to the very limited sums that found their way to the French and German colonies from their respective metropoles. The British example, both within and outside the empire, states the lesson for the whole of European overseas investment during the peak years from 1880 to 1914. Capital certainly poured out of Europe, but the prime determinant of its destination was not the location of the various European national flags overseas but the prospects for profitability. And, with some exceptions, these prospects were most alluring in the more developed economies.

These points are important for a number of reasons. They argue for a rejection of the Hobson-Lenin thesis that the demands of the investor

---

[15] Ibid., pp. 125, 127.

class—the essence of capitalism—were the sole or dominating causal force behind the enormous acquisitions of colonial territory in the late nineteenth and early twentieth centuries. They leave room instead for a multiplicity of motivations in the building of empires, in this period or in any other. But Hobson's and Lenin's carelessness with distinctions between foreign and colonial investment activities also helps to uncover a more profound point with which both were concerned.

If one removes, like an overlay, the whole network of pre-1914 national and imperial boundaries, an underlying map, or flow chart, would show simply an enormous and otherwise undifferentiated migration of capital from the more industrialized areas to the less industrialized ones. The bulk of this outflow, as we have seen, would not be channeled to the least developed economies but to those beginning to develop a greater productivity and ranging all the way to the highly productive United States. The overall process of international capital movements, in turn, may be compared to the flow of capital in a reasonably sophisticated domestic economy: from the urban financial center, or centers, to the rural areas, small towns, and provincial cities. In both contexts, these capital movements are indispensable to economic development in capital poor areas. But as the symbol of Wall Street signifies (in domestic and international economics alike), the movements are circular: in the absence of countervailing factors, returns on investments tend to profit the metropole more than the provinces. The result is a growing concentration of capital resources and a growing disparity between rich and poor areas. If left unchecked, the whole process must lead to a growing concentration of political power. And this is precisely what Hobson and Lenin were attacking—the power of the rich over the poor in both the domestic and the international society.

In a word, the central thrust (and appeal) of Hobson's and Lenin's critiques is directed at a concept of imperialism identical with the definition offered at the outset of the chapter: imperialism is essentially a matter of conquest and has to do with relationships between conquerors and conquered. Lenin and Hobson saw imperialism as the domination of the many by the few—the many overseas by the few rich countries in Europe, the many poor within the rich countries by the small class of capitalists constituting a domestic imperator. So long as the many within the capitalist societies and the many in the world at large dominated by these same societies could gain no effective redress from exploitation, they were equal in their existential situation: they were both the conquered. If one concedes that these formulations are more Leninist than Hobsonian, it is nonetheless true that the language signifies only a difference in degree and not in kind between the two critics.

This "ecumenical" vision of the meaning and impact of empire is the most durable of the legacies in Hobson's and Lenin's studies of imperialism. Both saw imperialism as in principle a global confrontation between rich and poor, without any precise geographical delimitations. It is a view that brings them into the center of the contemporary debate concerning neocolonialism, or neoimperialism, which has been variously defined as colonialism without colonies and imperialism without an empire. The issues of the metropolitan power's actual physical possession of colonial territory, of military control and formal political authority, which played so major a role in the debate over imperialism in the early part of the century, have almost completely vanished. In their place are issues revolving around what has been labeled economic and cultural imperialism.

Here the matters for debate are intrinsically global; they can be confined to a particular tract of territory only for purposes of illustration. These issues will be considered often during the remainder of this book. At this point, it is important to keep in mind that the terms of reference for understanding the nature of imperialism have drastically altered during the course of the twentieth century. Only then can one comprehend why it is that denunciations of imperialism and colonialism fill the air more loudly at present than when the white man's imperial flags flew over most of Asia and Africa.

Both Hobson and Lenin tended to identify every economic enterprise of the industrialized countries outside their own borders as prima facie evidence of imperialism. Given the lesser and greater degree of economic determinism in their thinking, it should be no cause for surprise that they often went one step further to label as imperialist all external activities of the rich countries, whatever their nature. Their allegations were based on the proposition that the leading capitalist nations were demonstrably imbued with the imperialist ethos and that this ethos necessarily permeated and dominated their entire domestic and international behavior. This wide-angled view of imperialism as all-pervasive and geographically indeterminate generated a concept of global empire in the most complete sense. It was a kind of empire "upon which the sun never sets" more surely and durably than the British prototype.

For Lenin, and only less so for Hobson, imperialism was a global disease. Insisting that imperialism seeks the conquest of industrial as well as agrarian territories ("German appetite for Belgium; French appetite for Lorraine"), Lenin was able to diagnose its presence in the heart of Western Europe as well as in Africa and Asia. Portugal and Argentina were also portrayed as victims of imperialism because of heavy British investment of capital in both countries and on evidence of the special British commercial and investment privileges in Portugal as well as in Portugal's African empire. Lenin's conclusion, of course, was that the presence of such assets enabled Britain to exercise hegemonial, or almost hegemonial, influence in both European Portugal and Latin American Argentina and, by extension, in any other country where a similar economic situation prevailed. Imperialism, then, was not simply a matter of European versus non-European or white versus nonwhite. Instead, it was discernible everywhere on the globe—wherever power confronted weakness.

LENIN AND HOBSON: THEIR RELEVANCE
TO THE PROBLEM OF NEOCOLONIALISM

Those who have a stake in stressing only the racist aspect of empire in current debates over neocolonialism may bridle at the catholicity of Lenin's approach to this facet of the problem. But all serious students of imperialism in the postcolonial world will want to pay attention to the very simple categories Lenin adopts to account for the varieties of imperialism:

> Typical of this epoch is not only the two main groups of countries: those owning colonies, and colonies, but also the diverse forms of dependent countries which, officially, are politically independent but, in fact, are in the net of financial and diplomatic dependence.[16]

This proposition is not original with Lenin, but the simplicity of its formulation and its appearance in the work of the most famous of twentieth-century revolutionaries gives it a peculiar immediacy and authority in the ex-colonial world. It offers a telling counter to any contentions that imperialism had come to an end with the virtually complete dismantling of the European empires after World War II. The response could simply be, and often with good reason, that the number of colonies had declined only to swell the numbers of Lenin's "semicolonies," officially independent but caught, in fact, "in the net of financial and diplomatic dependence."

This is the central issue of neocolonialism: the issue of dependence and independence. For the militant critics of the West, both communist and noncommunist, the post-1945 retreat from empire was a sham; hence the struggle for independence had to go on. In the Americas, of course, all but some of the Caribbean peoples had been formally independent for more than a century. But this only enabled Castro to assert that 1945 had changed nothing and that generations of the peoples of Latin America had been living in semicolonies before the war and continued to live in them thereafter. Thus the struggle must be one of striking at American business and financial power as well as at the American government itself in order to shed the status of semicolony and achieve authentic national sovereignty. Kwame Nkrumah was

---

[16] Lenin, *Imperialism*, p. 137. The foregoing discussion refers primarily to pp. 130–140 and 146–148.

Africa's chief spokesman in warning against the symptoms and dangers of capitalist-produced neocolonialism; in Asia it was Sukarno. In all three continents the theme was the same: behind official Western professions of respect for national sovereignty in the underdeveloped world lies concealed the intent to persevere in a policy of domination indistinguishable in substance from the old imperialism.

Lenin's and Hobson's assertions that the flow of capital, rather than the course of military conquest, is the essence of imperialism are manifestly congenial to the thesis of neocolonialism. There is, however, another aspect of the Lenin-Hobson treatment of capital and colonialism that must disconcert those aspiring to greater wealth and power for the underdeveloped world. For Lenin and Hobson portrayed the export of capital as an unambiguous evil and without any redeeming social value.

Lenin, of course, regarded all forms of private property as exploitative. Hobson assumed that the ownership of property by citizens of rich countries in countries where the poor were in the vast majority and politically helpless could satisfy no other purpose than the greed of the rich. Hence neither was inclined to examine the creative functions of actual or potential investment in the colonial and semicolonial worlds. As a result, their theses offer confusing and unhelpful guidance for those in the underdeveloped world who recognize that one of their indispensable tasks is to persuade the industrialized states to agree to a vastly increased flow of both government and private capital.

The problem is not susceptible of resolution in terms of slogans such as "capital (or aid) without strings." There are always strings between donor and recipient, just as between creditor and debtor. The objective must rather be to fashion ties between capital exporter and importer that will not subvert but will enhance the political independence and developmental progress of the latter. This can be done the more easily to the extent that there is a growth in understanding that political freedom and developmental progress in the third world are in the profound mutual interest of both the capital-exporting and capital-importing countries.

Such an understanding obviously conflicts with the determinism to which Lenin, as a good Marxist, was committed—a determinism that, in this instance, decreed that capitalism and capital export must produce imperialism. What capitalism did do, in fact, was to produce wealth and power in unprecedented amounts and place before the individuals and societies enjoying them a choice as to what to do with the enhanced instruments of political and economic action at their disposal. At the time of Hobson's and Lenin's critiques the overwhelming choice was manifestly for empire, as the arrogant formulations of the imperialists and the slashing attacks of the critics testify. But it is important to keep in mind that imperialism was, and is, a matter of choice and not of necessity, so that in the contemporary world, where charges of covert imperialism and neocolonialism are loud and insistent, the awareness of a continuing freedom to choose will not be lost.

In the case of imperialism, Lenin constructed his deterministic arguments on an underestimation of the profitability of domestic investment within the capitalist countries and an overestimation of the profitability of investment in the colonial and semicolonial countries. Badly out of touch with the realities of most of industrial Europe, Lenin insisted that "uneven development and a semi-starvation level of existence of the masses are fundamental and inevitable conditions and premises" of capitalism. His conclusion was, therefore, that "surplus capital will be utilized not for the purpose of raising the standard of living of the masses in a given country, for this would mean a decline in profits for the capitalists, but for the purpose of increasing profits by exporting capital abroad to the backward countries."[17]

Yet throughout his book Lenin inadvertently revealed the abundance of opportunities for profitable investment in the capitalist homelands through his denunciations of the scandalous profits that capital continued to make within the domestic economy. Indeed, in addition to an individual and corporate profit there was even a kind of social profit which enabled the capitalist class "to bribe certain sections of the workers, . . . for a time a fairly considerable minority of them, and win them to the side of the bourgeoisie of a given industry or given nation against all the others."[18]

Consistency is not immediately apparent in these arguments nor in the confusions that attended Lenin's discussions of "foreign" and "colonial" investments. We saw earlier that the bulk of foreign investment was going to areas hardly deserving the name "colonial." We may now note that the overwhelming proportion of total investment stayed at home in the domestic economies of the European industrial states and did not travel abroad at all. In their belittling of domestic investment prospects both Lenin and Hobson were misled by the relatively short-run high yields of total (and not just colonial) overseas investments. In the long run they were inevitably refuted by the laws of gross national product, which decree that the higher the level of GNP (and per capita GNP), the greater the opportunity for capital.

Lenin and Hobson argued that the capitalist-industrialist countries were producing a supply of both capital and goods far greater than domestic demand could consume. They were therefore forced to search and struggle for commodity and capital markets abroad. Hobson, at least, felt that this pattern could be altered by governmental policies that raised the level of domestic demand through income redistribution, increased production to meet the increased demand, and attracted capital

---

[17] Ibid., pp. 99–100.
[18] Ibid., pp. 89, 134, 202–203.

by virtue of the profitability of investment in plant and production in an expanding economy.

Thus Hobson understood the long-term truth that emerged in twentieth-century economics: the bulk of investment activities will locate in societies characterized by a high level of consumption on a mass basis and not in nonindustrialized societies where GNP and per capita GNP are low. But he did not show himself to be very sanguine about the probabilities of reform; and Lenin, of course, dismissed them out of hand. Hobson saw "investment imperialism" as a mistaken policy that just might still be changed. For Lenin it was, in his own words, "the highest stage of capitalism," that is, the final stage in the irreversible process that dooms capitalism to self-destruction.

SCHUMPETER ON IMPERIALISM

Whatever the differences between Lenin and Hobson, they were in accord that it is the economic system, and specifically capitalism, that produces imperialism. For Schumpeter, the cause was not economic but psychological—the irrational nature of man. He does, however, assign a role to economics in general and a crucial role to capitalism in particular in the dynamics of imperialism. For Schumpeter they function not as cause but as cure. Once again, one man's disease turns out to be another man's remedy.

In any case, Schumpeter selected the irrational nature of man as the prime cause of imperialism; more specifically, man's irrational drive for expansion. Schumpeter's formal definition reads: "imperialism is the objectless disposition on the part of a state to unlimited forcible expansion." Finally, the definition is further refined by an explanation of the word "objectless": it describes "tendencies toward forcible expansion without definite utilitarian limits—that is, non-rational and irrational, purely instinctual inclinations toward war and conquest."[19] One might have thought that Schumpeter, writing at the close of World War I, was warning against tying imperialism to any one economic system in order to stress the perennial presence of irrationality in human affairs. On the contrary, he foresaw the demise of irrationality at the hands of a triumphant capitalist rationalism. (Schumpeter even passed up the opportunity for revision of his thesis during the years of the rise of Nazism and World War II.)

Schumpeter's basic quarrel with Hobson and Lenin derives from his thesis that the propensities for imperialistic behavior stem not from the capitalist but from the precapitalist elements still persisting in modern states. It is the continued presence of autocratic and feudal elements in

---

[19] Schumpeter, *Imperialism and Social Classes*, pp. 7, 83.

contemporary society that accounts for the protracted life of imperialism. In the course of his analysis, Schumpeter traces the social and psychological heritage of autocratic and feudal sectors of society back to the earliest times, when the manifold dangers to individual life and social organization made it necessary, and rational, to develop a warrior class. Once developed, this class naturally discerned a stake in its own survival and thus kept on building or refurbishing warrior states and making wars whether there was any objective need for them or not. This same, essentially mindless, process is then identified as the fundamental cause of imperialism and war in the contemporary world.

At this point it is clear that an element of rationality is reintroduced into Schumpeter's concept of imperialism. By his reasoning, it was at one time (and at different times in different societies) rational to fight and conquer other peoples in the name of security for the individual and society. When security was no longer objectively at stake, however, war and conquest were to be explained in terms of an irrational throwback to the rationality of an earlier period. Therefore, it is the throwback, the atavism, that introduces the element of irrationality. In its pristine form, imperialism is portrayed as a rational response to security problems. The argument that war and imperialism are fundamentally anachronistic linked Schumpeter intellectually, and undoubtedly emotionally, to those who looked on history as "progress" which moved men away from violence and barbarism toward a rational and peaceful social existence.

Yet even without the hindsight supplied by the tragic toll of violence and conquest since 1919, one could have been uneasy about Schumpeter's prognostications. The concept of rationality always raises the question, Rationality in terms of what? Schumpeter, as an economist in a controversy with other economists, generally spoke of rationality in economic terms. Yet he pinpointed imperialism in its original form as rational in terms of security needs, and his analysis of subsequent historical periods frequently revealed the continuing presence of this form of rationality. Schumpeter's assessment of the wars, conquests, and defeats of Louis XIV, for example, makes evident that a whole series of rational considerations—political, military, and social, as well as economic—claimed their due in the making of policy.

Indeed, in the instance of Louis XIV Schumpeter stressed the presence of a phenomenon all too familiar to the history of politics. At the court of Versailles, military and diplomatic decisions were being made not for external gains of state and society but in order to manipulate the internal political and social structure of France to the benefit of those in power. The Sun King's solution to the problems created by the numbers of idle and restive nobles he himself had persuaded to reside at Versailles was to ship them out again to the battlefields. "Foreign campaigns preoccupied and satisfied the nobility," Schumpeter observed, and he concluded that the ancient and sorrowful recipe was once again in use: "If civil war was to be avoided, then foreign wars were required." From there Schumpeter proceeded to the overarching generalization that "the belligerence and war policy of the autocratic state are explained from the necessities of its social structure, from the inherited dispositions of its ruling class, rather than from the immediate advantages to be derived by conquest."[20]

But advantages of some sort, rationally calculated, were accruing to a significant number of persons and groups involved in this process. Drawing appropriate conclusions from "the necessities of the social structure" may not always be either heroic, farsighted, or just, but it often yields highly tangible benefits, including economic ones. Schumpeter's appraisal of Louis XIV and others provides convincing documentation for this point. But if this much is established, then Schumpeter's initial coupling of imperialism with irrationality is called into still more serious question.

If the contention is that the overt imperial program follows a logic imposed by the dynamics of domestic politics, there is no necessary loss but only a displacement of rationality. If internal political aims govern external policies, then imperialism can hardly be an "objectless disposition on the part of a state." Nor can that disposition be one of "unlimited forcible expansion," for those in charge of state policy would presumably set limits according to their anticipated utility in the pursuit of domestic political goals. Certainly neither Schumpeter nor anyone else could label the combined internal-external policies of Louis XIV as "objectless" or as lacking limits. Irrationalities were abundantly evident, but rationalities were, too.

As we have noted, Schumpeter identified capitalism not as the cause of imperialism but as its cure. The cure was to be effected as capitalist rationalism gradually conquered the atavistic irrationalities of less advanced socioeconomic-political systems. This was to occur through a process already under way for more than a century, one that Schumpeter described as democratization, individualization, and rationalization of whole societies. Having defined imperialism as irrational primarily in economic terms, Schumpeter now saw the rational economic objectives and rational life styles of an expanding capitalism bulldozing, as it were, all the remaining anachronisms out of existence:

> In a purely capitalist world, what was once energy for war becomes simply energy for labor of every kind. Wars of conquest and adventurism in foreign policy in general are bound to be regarded as troublesome distractions, destructive of life's meaning, a diversion from the accustomed and therefore "true" task.

---

[20] Ibid., pp. 76, 77.

A purely capitalist world therefore can offer no fertile soil to imperialist impulses.[21]

These dicta are likely to induce a state of acute disbelief not only in Marxists but in all reasonable skeptics. The attribution of so much social and political magic to any economic system whatsoever must be suspect.

Whatever the shortcomings of Schumpeter's theses, he contributed importantly to the understanding of imperialism. Despite his own brand of economic determinism (capitalism as certain cure rather than as necessary cause), he moved the discussion of imperialism and war out of the predominantly economic realm by pointing to the lurking irrationality in human institutions and behavior. If he was oversanguine in his anticipations about the demise of irrationality, the force of his historical illustrations underscores the inextricable, and ineradicable, blend of rationality and irrationality that characterizes human existence.

The result is that his readers are more likely to be fortified against assumptions about the triumph of rationalism than to be persuaded by them. Moreover, if Schumpeter fails to make a convincing case for capitalism as the gravedigger of imperialism, he does succeed in demonstrating that there is no necessary connection between capitalism and imperialism. The lesson that imperialism has flourished under a variety of socioeconomic systems admonishes anti-imperialists to cultivate a greater degree of sophistication in exercising the perpetually necessary vigilance.

IMPERIALISM: THE BASIC REMEDY

After considering the efforts at causation theory on the part of three eminent critics of imperialism, it should be evident that motives, in this as in other areas of life, continue to be elusive. If one replaces the essentially single-factor analyses of these critics with the principle of multiple causation as a technique for the exploration of motive, one will avoid their biases but may become a victim of others. After all, if one takes the position that there are a variety of causes for a given phenomenon, the task of assigning them relative weights remains a formidable challenge. Moreover, the identity of the predominating factor or factors in the causal ensemble will vary with the concrete case. Did the sixteenth-century rulers of Spain see their American empire more as a source of wealth or of power? Since the one translates with some facility into the other, is the answer not bound to be blurred? When the flow

---

[21] Ibid., p. 90.

of gold abated and the political difficulties piled up, to what extent did the sense of Catholic mission, the vision of Spanish glory, and the tradition of adventure and great enterprise replace more prosaic motives as the chief underpinnings of the imperial effort?

The course of empire is obviously and often governed by military objectives. In a typical case, acquisition of territories beyond the borders is called for as a means of protecting the homeland; then still more remote geography is coveted in order that the newly established outlying bastions might themselves not be disadvantaged in defense. Or the accumulation of bases abroad may serve a frankly offensive purpose. Or there may be a mixture of offensive and defensive objectives related to the security of specific geographical entities, to the promotion and protection of commerce, or to both. The string of British bases that once began at Gibraltar and included Malta, Cyprus, Suez, Aden, Capetown, Bombay, Trincomalee, Singapore, and Hong Kong illustrates very well how considerations of military advantage, commerce, adventure, and the desire to dominate mix with "the objectless disposition to expand" to create empire.

In short, the variety of imperial experience defies any attempt to construct a universally or even generally applicable hierarchy of motivations. It is more useful to compare empire to any complex system—to the state itself with its multiple purposes and its variegated history—in which one set of objectives predominates in one context only to recede before another set when times or issues change. The relativity of imperial motivation need not, however, impede one's understanding of the meaning of empire. As distinct from motivations, the essence of empire is universal and unchanging: it is revealed in the phenomena of conquest and subjugation. It is in evidence wherever one group is ruling another group for the benefit of the ruling group. The extent to which imperial exploitation takes place because of the pursuit of military or economic advantage, enhanced prestige or grandeur, or addiction to adventure or "civilizing missions" is of secondary importance. What matters most is the understanding that men are willing to oppress their fellow men in order to gratify any or all of a variety of motivations.

It follows that if one wishes to roll back the forces of imperialism, it cannot help much to designate some particular human motive or social phenomenon as the prime cause and then attempt to eradicate it. Instead, one does better to examine the environment in which the imperial motivations find expression. If the environment is one in which the strong confront the weak, the probabilities of imperialistic behavior will increase. In an environment where power is more equitably distributed the opportunities for imperialism will be reduced. The necessary conclusion is that imperialism can be combated only to the extent that democratic and balance of power principles are applied to international politics. Both are hostile to a monopoly of power in the hands of any group; it follows that both promote a diffusion of power among several groups.

As far as the balance of power is concerned, we have already seen it praised (Chapter 2) as the indispensable barrier to imperial ambition. The actual course that modern imperialism took, however, demonstrated that if balance of power politics is hostile to monopoly, it is well suited to oligarchy. Each of the major industrial powers maintained an empire; each collaborated or conflicted with its fellow empires. But jointly they constituted a closed oligarchy that effectively exercised all the available power and left none for the majority of mankind outside the industrial world.

The balance of power, then, laid some restraint upon imperial and hegemonial ambitions of the industrial nations toward one another but not in their relations with the nonindustrial world. Precisely because of the weakness of the nonindustrial world, no indigenous power balance existed that could save it from the European, American, and Japanese empire builders. As a counter to imperialism, balance of power has had its uses. But it is only a partial remedy; it cannot aid those who have no power.

Hence the ultimate requirement of the democratization of world politics is the most effective answer to imperialism. Such a requirement presupposes deliberate efforts to infuse power wherever powerlessness presently prevails. It assumes the need for a diffusion of power going beyond the minimum necessary to break monopoly and moving toward the maximum goal of effectively enfranchising all peoples and all men. It aims not at the impossible goal of equal shares but at the possible one of equitable shares in which the less powerful will have at least something to contribute to mutually beneficial relations with the more powerful.

An equitable sharing of power among the peoples of the world would not automatically produce community among them, but it would provide the only foundations from which a sense of community could grow. Imperialism, as we have seen, is the negation of community: despots and those they rule can have no interests in common, and community depends on the recognition of common interests. Thus if the reach of empire is to dwindle, the scope of community must grow. Imperialism will not come to an end if capitalism disappears any more than it faded away with the demise of slavery or mercantilism. And there can be no more convincing evidence of imperialism's tenacity than the behavior of twentieth-century communist systems.

Imperialism will not disappear even should the white man vanish. Desires for security, wealth, and glory, the hankering after adventure and crusades, and the readiness to gratify these ambitions at the expense of freedom and dignity for others are human characteristics transcending all distinctions among races or socioeconomic systems. Whence it comes that all social and economic systems and all races require defenses against imperialism. And adequate defenses can be found only in a democratic diffusion of power which offers each individual or group sufficient power to contend effectively for the satisfaction of legitimate needs.

The formal retreat from empire after 1945 has been a historic and indispensable step along the path of democratization. But it has not in itself significantly altered the power ratio between the industrial and the nonindustrial worlds. Consequently, a context favorable to imperial undertakings necessarily persists; hence the virulence of contemporary debate about neoimperialism and neocolonialism. The imperial itch will continue to assert itself as long as the strong live next to the weak without a governing community powerful enough to protect the interests of all. Thus the economic, political, and educational development of the world of the poor serves the double objective of dimming the prospects of imperialism and enhancing the growth of community. But this double objective is necessarily long term, and the problems of imperialism and neoimperialism are immediate. They will be examined at length throughout the second part of this book.

Chapter 9

Diplomacy

The composite that has emerged from the preceding chapters describes a world that is refractory and full of menace. It is a world that characteristically prizes power above all other worldly goods and that repeatedly confuses power with the capacity to coerce. These are among the major reasons why violence and the threat of violence are endemic to international society. Another and inseparably related reason for the recurrent eruptions of violence is the absence of any enduring sense of community and of the mutual trust that community presupposes. In such a context the fear of force and the determination to be skilled in its use necessarily reinforce one another.

As we have seen, the community-building goals of ideology have always stopped short of the globe itself; even those ideologies which have professed the brotherhood of man have almost always exhibited a fatal parochialism in practice. Today, moreover, most of the world is committed to an explicit parochialism that celebrates the nation as the ultimate human community. And despite the partially valid claims of nationalism to be the enemy of imperialism, it has contributed only minimally to the solution of the fundamental condition that gives rise to imperialism: the unregulated coexistence of the weak with the strong.

Such a world is essentially ungovernable. Its stubborn resistance to rules and regulations, whether they are designed to serve justice or only law and order, stems from the central facts of the world's experience. It is a micropolitical world, one in which concern for the parts takes precedence over concern for the whole. If the world is to move away from the tyranny of violence, it must begin to reverse that order of precedence and address itself to the challenge of macropolitics—which is to say that some profound changes must be made.

In assessing the nature of these changes, much can be learned if we first examine the traditional methods adopted to bring some order out of international chaos. These are methods designed to work within the system; they do not assume the need for any fundamental changes. They have evolved over time in the two great and venerable institutions of diplomacy and international law. They have also developed in the more recent institution of international organization, which, despite macropolitical professions, continues to operate within a micropolitical frame of reference.

Diplomacy is the oldest method that men have devised for coping with the problems of war and peace. It involves, essentially, the use of language rather than force—the exchange of ideas rather than blows—in the conduct of relations among societies. This characteristic of diplomacy is obviously most suited to cooperative undertakings such as economic exchanges and military alliances. But adversary diplomacy also features the displacement of violence by talk—in the meetings where enemies are trying to avoid war, in the negotiations that precede the launching of wars, and in the reconvened negotiations that seek to end wars. In adversary diplomacy, however, it is very evident that language and violence are intimately connected. The verbal message is one that threatens force if the diplomatic negotiations fail to attain the objective.

THE DIPLOMAT AS POLITICIAN

Diplomacy has evolved on a continuous basis over the course of history as a method of dealing with a tough world. Its lineage is similar to that of domestic politics, which must operate within the only somewhat less complex structures of individual societies. Diplomacy is, indeed, the politics of international relations; it is international politics in the most precise sense of the term. Apart from the differing contexts, the purposes of politics and diplomacy are identical. Both seek to unite a plurality of interests or at least make them compatible—or both seek to make some interests prevail over others. In pursuit of these objectives, moreover, both resort to three basic modes of behavior: cooperation, accommodation, and opposition. In international as in domestic society, these three options define the spectrum of political activity.

Within this spectrum the classic functions of diplomacy are commonly listed as representation, intelligence (in the sense of gathering and transmitting information), and negotiation. This same classification can be used to describe the main tasks of the domestic politician. Diplomats, except for those employed in global or regional transnational organizations, represent their countries; politicians represent local, regional, or national constituencies. Diplomats must collect information—using both straightforward and devious means—about the countries to which they are assigned. They must screen and assess the importance of the information emanating from their own foreign office as well. The politician, whether legislator or executive, must also ascertain the wishes of his constituencies and at the same time sound out opinion at the capital in order to reach a decision on any given issue. For both diplomats and politicians decisions emerge from negotiation, from the work at the conference table that precedes every legislative action, every executive decision, and every diplomatic agreement.

As representatives, both the politician and the diplomat must reflect the wishes of their respective constituencies and seek to satisfy their demands. If the home district (or powerful individuals and groups within it) wants a dam or an airport, the legislator is well advised to try to get it. If the home government wants a new agreement governing the flow of aid and trade with the country to which the diplomat is posted, he is obliged to try to get it.

Here the rules for politician and diplomat diverge. In the one case, the politician feels pressure to take a certain course of action, and in the other, the diplomat is instructed to do so. This is an important difference in the terms of contract, so to speak, that govern domestic politics and diplomacy. But it by no means destroys the parallels between them. The diplomat's instructions typically, though not always, reflect his own views, and an ambassador has often been able to effect a change in what he regarded as unwise instructions. Thus both politician and diplomat are brokers between two worlds, the home constituency and the domestic or foreign capital. They cannot help reflecting the attitudes and needs evidenced at the site where they carry out their representational activities. Hence they also tend to represent the larger world to the home constituency instead of functioning simply as its agent abroad.

This two-way view of diplomats and politicians is evidenced across the whole range of their classic functions. Their roles as information gatherers prevent them from being mere reflections of their constituencies. They are obligated to collect intelligence about the needs, wishes, and power of other units operating in the larger world in which their constituency is represented. As a result of their intelligence activities outside the constituency, they may try to alter their constituents' preferences. This was the course often taken by such vintage diplomats as François de Callières and Diego de Acuña, Count of Gondomar. Callières, ambassador of Louis XIV and classic figure in the literature of diplomacy, insisted that the ambassador abroad must correct ignorance at home and take decisions on the spot, when necessary, without instructions from superiors.[1] Gondomar, Spanish ambassador to London at the time of James I, went even further in practice. He had so far freed himself from control by Madrid that he not only made Spanish policy in London but, by virtue of his influence over the British monarch, dominated the making of English foreign policy as well.[2]

---

[1] François de Callières, *On the Manner of Negotiating with Princes*, translated and with an introduction by A. F. Whyte (Boston: Houghton Mifflin, 1919), p. 38 and *passim*. Callières's book was first published in Paris in 1716.

[2] For a study of Gondomar see Garrett Mattingly, *Renaissance Diplomacy* (Boston: Houghton Mifflin, 1955).

More recent examples of diplomat-preceptors include those in the 1930s who tried to educate their foreign offices to a clearer understanding of the Nazi menace and argued for a drastic change in course. Robert Coulondre, French ambassador to Moscow and then Berlin, was one of the most eminent of these. The American ambassadors in Moscow and Berlin during this period, William Bullitt and William Dodd, also tried, without much success, to imbue the home front with the urgency felt on the front line.[3] Their counterparts in domestic politics are the presidents, prime ministers, and legislators who try to bring the attitudes of national or local constituencies into line with perspectives that emerge first in the capital.

The same kind of feedback from representatives to those represented can take place in connection with the negotiation functions of diplomat and politician. Each is theoretically an agent obliged to promote and defend the interests of his principal in bargaining with the representatives of other principals. But each is, also theoretically, assumed to be a shrewd judge of what the traffic at the center of negotiations will bear. When the desires of his constituency conflict with those of another and the latter has more power, the diplomat or the politician, as the case may be, will have to retreat. The retreat may be catastrophic, as it was when Chancellor Kurt von Schussnig of Austria was made to understand by Hitler in 1938 that further resistance to a German takeover of Austria was useless. Or a retreat may be less immediately painful but may lead to the gravest long-range consequences, as Woodrow Wilson discovered when he could not cajole the rest of the Big Four at Versailles into renouncing their commitments to a punitive peace. Or the exercise in backing down may occur at a far lower level, as when a legislator discovers he lacks the bargaining power to extract a post office or a harbor installation for his district. (In all these cases the problem, in the idiom of Chicago, is one of insufficient clout.)

If only unsuccessful negotiating positions have been used as illustrations, it is because adversity is the more powerful generator of feedback. Success permits established relationships to continue along routine lines without much examination or reflection, but setbacks cause questions to be raised between representative and constituency. The bringer of bad tidings has to try to persuade constituents to alter their views concerning the attainable and even the desirable, and this may lead to a series of negotiations within his constituency even more unpleasant than those whose outcome he came home to report. In order to survive politically, he must be able to demonstrate convincingly his own negotiating zeal, the pressures that frustrated his aims, the unrealism of constituent expectations, or all three. With greater or less accuracy, he is telling those at

---

[3] For studies of Coulondre, Bullitt, and Dodd see Gordon Craig and Felix Gilbert (eds.), *The Diplomats: 1919–1939* (Princeton, N.J.: Princeton University Press, 1953).

the seat of power (*his* power) what it is like in the outside world. Once again, then, he is an envoy to his constituency as well as from it.

The most dangerous charge that can be made against the politician or the diplomat is that he has defected and sold out to the opposition. The accusation can be and often has been tantamount to the charge of treason. But it can also take the much milder form of calling attention to the recurrent phenomenon of the ambassador so engrossed in the problems of the host country that he becomes its partisan instead of the advocate of his own foreign office.

The instances of "switching sides," ranging in substance from innocuous to treacherous, are legion in politics as in diplomacy. A congressman is accused of selling out to one or many lobbies so that he now sells their points of view to his constituents instead of the other way round. A black politician is denounced as an Uncle Tom because he is said to have become subservient to the white power structure: he gains favors for himself by promising to keep his constituents cool. All these examples violate the representative function. But it would be possible to cite others that have provoked similar charges of betrayal when in fact they simply demonstrated the perfectly desirable and legitimate effort of the representative to let his constituents know that they are not the only ones with hopes, fears, and demands and that they cannot always expect their own wishes to prevail.

Both politics and diplomacy are exercises in two-way communication between a smaller world and a larger one. Both the politician and the diplomat are necessarily mediators between the two worlds. Both must be uneasy because the two worlds are very different, and communication between them is difficult and prone to misunderstanding and distortion. But beyond this line the similarities between politician and diplomat must yield once again to contrast.

THE DIFFERENT CONTEXTS OF DIPLOMACY AND POLITICS

The basic contrast is that the politician operates within a society where, ideally at least, the welfare of the whole is considered to have priority over the welfare of the parts. He is, therefore, assumed to have a proper dedication to serve not only his own constituency but also the larger community of which it is part. In diplomacy there is only a pale and fleeting reflection of this permissible double allegiance, and it is a reflection usually produced by sporadic considerations of convenience and sentiment rather than by a more durable sense of international legal and social obligations. The governing propositions are that the diplomat is the exclusive servant of his state and that the state's interests must outrank every other interest. Their consequence is that international comity and other expressions of the idea of an international community take a back seat in the conduct of international business.

This difference in the context of diplomatic activities is matched by a difference in mandate. We have noted that the politician is free, as the saying goes, to vote his conscience. That is, even if a particular vote represents a craven capitulation to pressures from inside or outside of his district, it is still the politician's own yea or nay. He is not legally bound to do the bidding of his constituency or any portion thereof. He is an uninstructed delegate. This is not true of the diplomat who, in his delegate status, is under instructions.

Representing sovereignty in a world of sovereignties, the diplomat is characteristically on a tighter rein than his domestic political counterpart. He is assumed to be operating in a context where his diplomatic colleagues range from outright enemies to those who, no matter how friendly, are bound to a different allegiance. In a representative and reasonably cohesive domestic political system, despite the realities of class, ethnic, and sectional differences, the formal norms assume that the politician-delegate is operating on friendly territory so long as he is within the boundaries of the state. Hence it is not surprising that there are no formal restrictions on the way in which the politician carries out his mandate.

The diplomat, however, has traditionally found the boundaries between friendly and enemy territory much harder to ascertain. If he recalls the venerable balance of power dictum that today's friends are tomorrow's enemies and vice versa, he must necessarily develop that reserve for which diplomats are customarily noted. Enemy territory is obviously hostile; neutral territory might become so; friendly territory may be deceptive. It follows that the diplomat must be more of a reconnoitering soldier than a tribune of the people. He operates in a hierarchical chain of command and according to binding if not always detailed instructions.

In his official capacity, then, the diplomat characteristically speaks to his counterparts abroad not with his own voice but with that of his foreign minister or his head of government. The caution instilled by holding office in potentially or actually hostile territory is compounded by the caution obligatory for anyone who speaks for someone else. While these patterns of behavior may not be immediately apparent in relations among friendly capitals, they are not far from the surface even there and emerge whenever the atmosphere becomes less cordial.

Over the long span of history international partnerships have been notable for their tenuousness and brevity. Even during periods of intensive cooperation among partners, their diplomats remain under instructions and are more certainly working for their respective foreign offices than for the common purposes embedded in their cooperative undertakings. The recurrent suspicion exhibited by Gaullist France toward the Common Market and the North Atlantic Treaty, even as it continued to affirm its allegiance to both institutions, is a case in point. The tensions that plagued the British-American-Russian alliance of World War II despite the imperative need for wartime unity constitute a dramatic variation on the same theme. One might add the American example of aloofness in World War I, when the United States insisted upon being an "Associated" rather than an "Allied" power as a means of stressing its independence in respect to the war policies and peace aims of the allied coalition.

The problem illustrated in these examples and in others like them is that the will to preserve or enter into an enduring and indivisible community is lacking. Diplomats are typically engaged in effecting ad hoc arrangements among political entities which reserve the right to combine and recombine at their own convenience. As noted in the discussion of the balance of power and elsewhere, the reigning assumption is division rather than unity. Hence diplomacy's reputation for tortuousness and guile. Hence also General de Gaulle's reference to nations as "those cold monsters," eyeing one another as candidates for manipulation rather than as authentic partners dedicated to the building of durable bases for collaboration. Hence, finally, the image of the diplomat as a cynical intriguer whose polish and charm cannot conceal the fact that he plays the game according to the rules of the conflict model of politics.

SECRET DIPLOMACY

In this perspective, diplomacy's affinity for secrecy, its reputation for duplicity, and its linkage with force appear to be all of a piece. Secrecy, in the view of most articulate practitioners of diplomacy, was and is an indispensable aspect of their business. Critics of diplomacy, particularly since 1918, have denounced secrecy as a partner of deception and a cause of uncertainty and misunderstanding among governments and between governments and their own peoples. Above all, they have condemned it as a device for protecting the power of the diplomats and the foreign policy establishment in general by ensuring to them a monopoly of information relevant to effective participation in international politics. Thus the objective of the critics is not only to make diplomacy more honest and pacific but also to make it more democratic.

Secret negotiations and secret treaties—symbols of undemocratic procedures whatever their substantive content—were standard fixtures in traditional diplomacy. Both drew the fire of the reformers' demands for change—demands that were most dramatically expressed by Woodrow Wilson in the famous prescription calling for "open covenants, openly arrived at." Wilson incorporated his striking phrase into the Fourteen Points which he offered at the beginning of 1918 as the basis for peace.

As a result it attained a world-wide currency—something Wilson began to regret a year later at the outset of the long series of executive sessions of the Big Four at Versailles in which the treaties of peace with the Central Powers were hammered out in secret. The clash between practice and precept forced Wilson to recant and affirm the value of confidentiality in diplomatic negotiation (while reiterating his position that upon signature treaties should become public documents). But the critics with less practical experience continued to attack diplomatic secrecy in all its aspects.

Secrecy inevitably carries with it connotations of deception in at least two respects. First, the withholding of information and its restriction to a privileged few denies knowledge of the "whole truth" to the many. Second, the resort to secrecy invites the suspicion that there is something to hide that could not bear public scrutiny. In this context, secrecy easily comes to be regarded as a mere substitute for and interchangeable with deliberate falsehood: its purpose is to permit diplomats to say one thing in private and another in public.

If diplomacy is not engaged in nefarious practices, its critics ask, why do its defenders uphold the doctrine of secrecy in negotiations? If the response is that businesses and baseball teams do not bargain in public either, the typical rebuttal points out that businesses and baseball teams are not involved in matters that can mean life or death for thousands or millions of human beings and whole societies. Nor are businesses and baseball teams political communities in which citizen control is appropriate and legitimate. Finally, the nation that calls itself democratic and simultaneously demands supreme allegiance from its citizens cannot keep secrets from the people without contradicting its own premises of government by consent.

The counterrebuttal will contend that disclosure of secrets to the nation's citizens must also mean disclosure to the nation's enemies. The diplomat must not telegraph his punches; that is, the country will make a less favorable bargain if at the outset the diplomat permits the other side to see everything he has up his sleeve. Further, public negotiation leads to an undesirable rigidity of bargaining positions. In private, the diplomat can raise a demand he does not seriously intend as a means of wringing a concession from his opposite number on a quite different matter. This kind of pressure politics and horse trading would not be possible in public, the argument runs, because to raise a demand, with suitable fanfare, in international negotiations and then retreat from it would inevitably be viewed by the uninstructed citizenry as a betrayal of sacred principle or vital interest.

The same fate would await the procedures known as exploratory non-binding discussions and confidential trial balloons. All these essentially probing techniques, which are useful and sometimes indispensable to the resolution of diplomatic antagonisms would, in public, lose their efficacy because the public could not discriminate between what was to be taken literally and what figuratively in the diplomatic performance. To these procedural aspects of confidentiality one must add its substantive functions: the protection of military, scientific, economic, and even political secrets—for example, the concealment of internal bureaucratic political divisions.

All the counterrebuttal arguments contribute to a powerful case for the continued legitimation of diplomatic secrecy. But they only weaken the case of the critics; they do not demolish it. Under the cloak of secrecy governments have committed their citizens to courses of action that have turned out to be disastrous for individuals and society alike. In such circumstances the meaningfulness of self-government is clearly at issue. Given the indivisibilities of foreign and domestic politics, the penchant for secrecy inevitably makes its appearance on the home front, and credibility gaps open up not only between states but also between governments and their own peoples. Those who operate a policy-making machine that relies extensively on secret information and methods of procedure clearly have in hand an instrument which enhances their power and conceals their mistakes.

In this debate neither pro nor con can triumph. Nor do they cancel each other out. Each side makes points that cannot successfully be refuted, which is to say that secrecy in diplomacy has both uses and abuses. The basic rationale for secrecy is the presence of conflict and antagonism and the resultant fear that if the opponent knows what you are or are not doing he would be in a better position to harm you, or you would be in a less advantageous position to harm him. Secrecy is borne along and sustained, then, by the age-old dialectic of mutual fear and suspicion. It is idle to call for the abolition of secrecy in international affairs so long as this sorry dialectic persists.

It is also idle to make too much of a distinction between negotiations and treaties when discussing the permissability of secrecy. Conventional wisdom generally tends to make this distinction, agreeing with Wilson's revised doctrine of open covenants. That is, the approved solution from both an expediential and moral viewpoint is "open covenants, privately arrived at." Secret negotiation is therefore sanctioned, and secret treaties are condemned. In accordance with these norms, all international treaties entered into by members of the United Nations are required to be registered and published by the United Nations.[4] It is certain that this provision has been adhered to quite strictly, but it is also certain that there have been violations. How many, we cannot know, for the evidence lies buried in the vaults of classified information.

What we do know is that diplomatic negotiations can lead to outcomes other than formal political treaties. They include military pacts,

---

[4] Article 102. A similar procedure was followed in the League of Nations.

or clauses of such pacts, sub rosa agreements to assist or undermine foreign governments or foreign insurrectionaries, informal arrangements tantamount to virtual alliances, and unilateral commitments reached as a result of negotiation but concealed even from the negotiating partner. Such promises or commitments not subject to public scrutiny have abounded both before and since the reformers began to make their voices heard at the turn of the century and during World War I. The complaint against secret treaties is twofold: that their existence increases both uncertainty and fear in international politics, and that they commit the peoples of the governments involved to more or less risky undertakings without their knowledge or consent. The persistent recurrence of these substitutes for formal secret treaties makes it clear that the cause for complaint continues to exist.

Thus the issues raised in the debate over secret treaties have by no means been laid to rest simply because a formal UN treaty registry now exists. They join all the other ongoing issues inherent in secret negotiations and in secret intelligence operations of all kinds. The strongest case against secrecy in all these contexts is that it is itself deceptive, that it creates an atmosphere congenial to deception, or that it is perceived as deception and so causes reactions of suspicion and resentment (and counterdeception). The strongest case for secrecy, on the other hand, is that enemies intending injury to each other do in fact exist. International politics still remains unredeemed, and it is prudent in an enmity relationship to prevent the enemy from gaining too much information about your actions, your assets, and particularly your vulnerabilities.

One can accept the proposition that secrecy is an evil because of its linkage with deception. One must also accept it as a necessary evil so long as the more fundamental evil of enmity persists. These acceptances, however, need not be passive. The norm of realistic policy, most particularly in the nuclear age, is to curb enmity and nurture friendship. Insofar as such a policy is implemented, then, it will diminish the number and intensity of international antagonisms—and with them the chief causes of secrecy. It is only in this context that one can legitimately enjoin those who play a role in the world of official secrecy to strive toward a set of diplomatic standards in which full public information becomes the rule and secrecy the exception.

VIETNAM, SECRECY, AND PUBLIC OPINION

Hovering over all these arguments about secret policy making and secret diplomacy is a much broader question—one so broad that it defies any generalized answer and can be discussed meaningfully only in terms of concrete cases. It is the hoary question whether "the people" or the foreign policy establishment (politicians, diplomats, and generals) are the more reliable guardians of peace. Establishment partisans have often enough been able to point to cases in which public opinion and debate exhibited far more warlike or chauvinistic attitudes concerning a particular international issue than could be found within government itself. These instances of counterpoint between a pugnacious public and a more cautious government suggest that peace is better served by the secrecy and formality of diplomatic procedures, insulated from the pressures of passionate and uninformed opinion.

The point is well taken—but only in some instances. Civilian and military officials in governments, foreign offices, and embassies can be gripped by passions, too. Depending on the circumstances, they can be convinced, justifiably or otherwise, of the necessity for war as well as for peaceful settlement. Either conviction, in turn, may or may not correspond to dominant trends in public opinion. And whatever position is adopted, the foreign policy establishment is obliged by its official status and responsibility to persuade as much of public opinion as possible to share its point of view. In that effort, of course, government exercises a powerful leverage thanks to its monopoly of official and classified information. The governmental prerogative to release or withhold such information is a function of the still more basic political sanction of secrecy.

Hence it is evident that the practice and apparatus of secrecy inhibits democratic control of foreign policy. But it does not follow that secrecy is therefore more conducive to war and conflict than to peace and conciliation. What can be ascertained is that secrecy in foreign affairs frequently compounds substantive antagonisms between government and its own public. Where government and public are divided on substantive matters of policy, governmental exercise of the prerogatives of secrecy will envenom the internal political process, sometimes to the point where trust between government and internal opposition is subverted and each begins to challenge the other's legitimacy.

In American history the Vietnam war provides the most extreme and searing demonstration of the corrosive effect a foreign policy issue can have on domestic political life. Without attempting here to judge substantive matters in contention, one can identify governmental secrecy as a major contributor to the virulence that infected the years of debate over Vietnam policy. Among other accusations, the opposition charged the government with circumventing constitutional procedures by committing American military power behind a veil of confidential diplomacy, with making judgments and setting policies that would not stand the light of public debate, and with public professions of American objectives in Vietnam belied by the private assessments of those in key policy-making positions.

The publication of the *Pentagon Papers* in 1971 brought these charges to a head. The unauthorized public disclosure of more than 7,000 pages of secret government documents powerfully reinforced opposition critics. Yet there was also a reasonable correspondence between many of the secret decisions and public statements of intent by government officials. Moreover, many of the decisions taken were not at variance with the dominant trends in public opinion. Certainly the Pentagon documents could not prove that American policy in Vietnam would have been significantly different if the American public had had unimpeded access to and impact upon the policy-making proceedings during the years of American involvement in Indochina. Which is to say that the well-known reluctance of the policy makers to "lose a war" was widely shared among the electorate at large.

Nevertheless, it is evident that the wall of secrecy surrounding American policy in Vietnam corrupted debate both within official circles and in the public domain. This is particularly apparent in the contradictory formulations of American policy goals in Vietnam. Public discussion was dominated by the official explanation of the war as a defense of free Asian peoples against the spread of communism. The consequence was that critics—unless they were willing to profess themselves as favorable or indifferent to the growth of communist power—were forced to question the sincerity of government statements of purpose. Once the contest took this form, it escalated to the point where rational disagreements and criticisms were virtually eclipsed by unfounded and inflammatory attacks launched by both sides.

Within government, on the other hand, the *Pentagon Papers* made it clear that the standard public articulations of war aims had little relation to what officials felt were the real stakes in Vietnam. The 1965 draft statement of John McNaughton, then Assistant Secretary of Defense for International Security Affairs, can fairly be taken as a representative if not definitive expression of official thinking in this regard. In this memorandum, directed to Secretary Robert McNamara, McNaughton attempted to assign weights to American aims in Vietnam according to their importance. They were:

> 70%—To avoid humiliating US defeat (to our reputation as a guarantor).
> 20%—To keep South Vietnam (and the adjacent) territory from Chinese hands.
> 10%—To permit the people of South Vietnam to enjoy a better, freer way of life.
> ALSO—To emerge from crisis without unacceptable taint from methods used.
> NOT—To "help a friend," although it would be hard to stay in if asked out.[5]

---

[5] *Pentagon Papers, New York Times* edition (New York: Bantam Books, 1971), p. 432. The draft statement is entitled "Plan for Action for South Vietnam," and was appended to a covering memorandum to McNamara. It is dated March 24, 1965.

While there was ample evidence of public concern for American prestige throughout the Vietnam ordeal, it mostly found expression in an unreflective and generalized patriotism and anticommunism. A public policy pronouncement incorporating the specific stress on prestige and credibility set down in the McNaughton statement would, at the very least, have sharpened the focus of debate. It might not have alienated all sectors of opinion, but it could well have forced more rational and honest assessments of the importance of the goals sought and the costs involved in seeking them. Certainly the McNaughton statement of war aims undercuts the anticommunism constantly stressed in the official rationale for the Vietnam war. It also effectively shatters the high moral tone of American solidarity with a small and imperiled ally.

All components of the secret debate on Vietnam were also present in the public debate. Therefore, one cannot say that governmental and public considerations had no relation to one another. But the importance assigned to each of the components varied greatly from one context to the other. Public discussion was dominated by clichés about legal and moral obligations to carry on the war. In consequence, an opposition emerged whose criticisms were dominated by counterclichés. The near absence of clearly and reasonably articulated debate, in turn, resulted in public attitudes variously marked by confusion, apathy, cynicism, frustration, and anger. This set of attitudes produced violent acts often enough to sustain the judgment that the Vietnam issue was seriously damaging the fabric of American society.

In the debate internal to government, on the other hand, the imperative of victory was the prevailing theme. The government's task of public persuasion, therefore, became one of convincing the citizenry of the necessity for victory, or "peace with honor." The companion necessity, of course, was to inspire confidence that the goal sought could be attained at a tolerable cost. The insistence on "winning," then, characterized the debate on both sides of the wall of secrecy, but within the governmental enclosure "winning" was the overriding consideration. In such a perspective the fruits of victory and the likelihood of achieving it were more taken for granted than subjected to rational assessment. The sacrifices required for victory, in this same perspective, necessarily appeared less formidable than they did to a growing body of public opinion which rejected the doctrine that there is "no substitute for victory."[6]

---

[6] General Douglas MacArthur invoked this doctrine during the Korean War in his struggle to free his military strategy from the restraints imposed by the Truman administration's policy of limited war. The subsequent firing of MacArthur, more than anything else, testified to the government's determination to keep the war limited.

The internal political repercussions of Truman's decision, however, included the fury of witch hunting known as the McCarthy era and the massive rejection of the

In sum, the cost-benefit analysis—to use a term given currency by Secretary McNamara—was reckoned differently on one side of the secrecy wall than on the other. As we have already indicated, the Vietnam issue is hardly unique in this respect. On the contrary, variance in public and internal governmental assessments of most foreign policy issues is standard in all societies. Nor is such variance necessarily harmful. But Vietnam joins a long list of examples throughout history and around the world in which the variance exceeded tolerance limits. The result has been grievous damage to the relationships between government and people—to say nothing of the ravages of prolonged and inconclusive military operations visited upon the armed forces and upon allies and enemies alike.

If such disasters are to be avoided in the future, attention must be directed first to the substance rather than the techniques of policy and diplomacy. Policy makers must assess the viability of a proposed course of action in terms of the preferences of domestic public opinion as well as of the perceived exigencies of international politics. If public preferences are at odds with official opinion, government's initiative need not be blocked; it can take its case to the public and attempt to change preferences. In the course of such an exercise, by the same token, government may discover the wisdom of rethinking its own position in the matter at issue.

Give and take between government and public may not always be possible or desirable. Emergency diplomacy and policy making, imperative in such confrontations as the 1962 Cuban missile crisis, set a premium on secrecy. In such circumstances the government must be the actor and the citizen the spectator. Optimally, a responsible leadership will keep the public apprised of the dangers created by the developing crisis and of the efforts by government to deal with them. But policy makers must be highly selective in deciding what information should be released so as not to compromise their strategy in dealing with the opponent. Above all, there is no time to ascertain whether the public approves the leadership's course of action.

It is evident, then, that circumstances may require limits on the principle of candor between government and people. But this is no reason to abandon the principle. Policies designed to bring about reconciliation instead of conflict with an opponent will have an easier time in meeting the requirements of the candor principle. And if reconciliation efforts fail, candor will marshal public support for the ensuing conflict more effectively than if significant sectors of public opinion believe that gov-

Democratic party in the 1952 elections. With hindsight one could draw the lesson that no American government could pursue a "no win" policy and expect to survive politically. It is a lesson that has obviously had its impact on the various managers of the Vietnam war.

ernment has chosen conflict without consulting public preferences. In a word, Immanuel Kant's insistence that nothing should be attempted in diplomacy that cannot be adequately defended in public discussion has profound relevance to Vietnam and to all the major issues of contemporary international politics.[7] There is an affinity between conciliation and openness—and between conflict and concealment.

DIPLOMACY AND DECEPTION

If enmity conduces to secrecy, it is even more directly the parent of deceit. By and large, diplomats and diplomacy have not been highly regarded in terms of the standards of honesty prevailing in the profession. The muckrakers, particularly those of the interwar vintage who were intent on making old-style diplomacy responsible for World War I and most other international disasters, portrayed diplomats as necessarily both victims and perpetuators of a vicious system of subterfuge and cunning. On the other hand, the diplomats themselves and their defenders generally offer a picture of diplomatic rectitude in almost ludicrous contrast to the assertions of the critics.

Sir Harold Nicolson, for example, perhaps the best-known champion of the diplomatic establishment, designates truthfulness as the ideal diplomat's prime virtue: "By this is meant, not merely abstention from a conscious mis-statement, but a scrupulous care to avoid the suggestion of the false or the suppression of the true."[8] These are high standards, indeed, though hardly in accord with the famous instructions that Louis XI issued to his ambassadors before he sent them off to Brittany: "If they lie to you, lie still more to them." Nor can they be easily reconciled to Sir Henry Wotton's punning definition of a diplomat (without which no book on the subject can be complete): "an honest man sent to lie abroad for the good of his country."[9]

One could cite numerous and more contemporary examples to press the point. Throughout history, diplomatic missions have frequently

---

[7] Immanuel Kant, *To Eternal Peace*, Appendix, in *The Philosophy of Kant* (New York: Modern Library, 1949), pp. 469–476.

[8] Sir Harold Nicolson, *Diplomacy* (New York: Harcourt, Brace, 1939), p. 110.

[9] Ibid., pp. 44–45. Nicolson rather defensively remarks that Wotton's "phrase is often quoted against us" (presumably against Britishers and British diplomatic practice). In an attempt to lay Wotton's ghost, Nicolson not only asserts that Sir Henry's effort was a joke (which it was) but also that James I was shocked to the point of banning the miscreant from future ambassadorial service. It is likely, however, that Sir Henry's temerity in expressing his sentiments in public rather than their inherent cynicism roused the king's ire. In any case, Nicolson is willing to concede in further argumentation that Wotton's sentiment was not unique but, rather, representative of the diplomacy of his age.

served as bases from which to carry on the clandestine deceptions of intelligence and counterintelligence operations. During the Cold War the practice became routine, with the result that since 1945 close to fifty mission personnel from the Soviet Embassy in Washington, or the Soviet United Nations mission in New York, and approximately the same number from the American Embassy in Moscow have been accused and/or expelled as spies. The Cold War also witnessed repeated violations of the publicly pledged words of the two governments. Moscow's record of perjury is a formidable one. Any representative sample would have to include Soviet perfidy in Berlin in 1948, Hungary in 1956, Cuba in 1962, and Czechoslovakia in 1968. American denials of the existence of U-2 flights over the Soviet Union in 1960 and of preparations for the invasion of Cuba in 1961 are among the most spectacular derelictions on the Western side.

A different kind of diplomatic turpitude is evidenced in the violation of the Tripartite Declaration of 1950, which obligated the signatories (United States, Britain, and France) to take action against aggression in the Middle East. The operative clause in the declaration provided that "The three Governments, should they find that any of these [Middle Eastern] States was preparing to violate frontiers or armistice lines would, consistently with their obligations as members of the United Nations, immediately take action, both within and outside the United Nations, to prevent such violation." British-French-Israeli aggression against Egypt in 1956 turned the declaration inside out. And while the United States cannot be faulted for inaction in its response to the Suez crisis, the measures it took fell far short of what one might have anticipated under a strict construction of the language of the declaration.

Soviet transgressions quite overshadow those of the West. For example, during most of the eleven-month Berlin blockade the Soviets stubbornly denied that a blockade even existed. In the wake of the Kremlin's bloody suppression of the Hungarian revolution in 1956 the same ostentatious contempt for truth was evidenced in *Pravda's* rebuttal of charges leveled by President Tito: "In his speech Comrade Tito puts forth the slogan of 'independence' of Socialist countries and Communist Parties from the Soviet Union and the Communist Party of the Soviet Union. Everyone knows, however, that the Soviet Union does not require the dependence or subordination of anyone."[10] The Soviets perjured themselves in the same grim manner a dozen years later in conjunction with the 1968 invasion of Czechoslovakia.

One example of early Soviet diplomatic style, by contrast, exhibits a refreshing candor. In recounting the Brest-Litovsk treaty negotiations in 1918, during which Imperial Germany was imposing draconic conditions

---

[10] *Pravda*, November 23, 1956.

in peace negotiations with a newly Bolshevik Russia, Isaac Deutscher cites an incident

> which seemed to transfer the sedate diplomats of the Central Powers into the atmosphere of a Shavian comedy. A preamble to the treaty contained the respectable cliché that the contracting parties desired to live in peace and friendship. The authors of the draft could not expect this to give rise to objections. They were mistaken. "I would take the liberty," Trotsky said, "to propose that the . . . phrase be deleted. Its thoroughly conventional, ornamental style does not correspond to the dry business-like sense of the document. . . . Such declarations . . . copied from one diplomatic document to another, have never yet characterized the real relations between states."[11]

It should be clear from these examples that there is little point in either attacking or defending the diplomat's professional reputation for probity. Personally truthful men (and some untruthful ones as well) in embassies abroad or foreign offices at home are engaged in a process in which the premium on success is enormous and the danger and stigma of failure correspondingly great. Where this process is marked by a high degree of rivalry, or enmity, the pressure to sacrifice every other consideration to the imperative of success mounts to the point where diplomacy moves close to the ethos of war itself. In such circumstances, honesty is hard pressed and often enough, as we have seen, unceremoniously tossed out the window.

If truth frequently suffers in the quest for victory, it is similarly damaged in situations of impasse or defeat. Here the classic concern with saving face has typically produced formulas designed to gloss over any facts that might humiliate the parties involved. This can be a useful and even generous diplomatic technique designed to dissuade the disappointed from desperate and irrational acts. Like the generic concept of tact, face-saving is an indispensable virtue in a sensitive world. Yet it can also obscure public understanding of the real meaning of the diplomatic transactions at issue. In this case, virtue and vice are effectively inseparable—as is also true in personal relations among individuals where the line between tact and untruthfulness is commonly tenuous.

The diplomat, then, works in a world where the premium on success is a massive one and in which strife among those seeking success is endemic. But these are not the only conditions of employment that test the mettle of the diplomat's character. As we have already noted, he is always the agent of a principal: abroad as a representative of the home government, in the home office as a foreign affairs bureaucrat subordinate to the political regime. Even the diplomat who is not content simply

---

[11] Isaac Deutscher, *The Prophet Armed: Trotsky, 1879–1921* (New York: Oxford University Press, 1954), p. 366.

to carry out orders from higher up but also tries to bring before his government points of view other than those it generates, must ultimately speak with the voice of officialdom and not with his own.

Here again is the intermingling of virtue and vice. It is necessary that the diplomat represent his government and not simply himself. At the same time, his position constantly places him in the role of advocate. He is therefore obliged to put his government's case in the most favorable light possible, to suppress or discount facts that might be damaging, and sometimes to discredit the opposing government by subtle distortions or blunt untruths. These pressures are very like those felt by the lawyer who is, after all, the prototype of the advocate. Yet lawyers, at least those in private practice, have far greater latitude in deciding which clients to take on or keep than does the diplomat, whose single legitimate client, so long as he chooses to practice his profession, is his government.

It is the diplomat's highest calling to overcome conflict by effecting compromises—by manufacturing a common interest where previously two or more conflicting interests had been churning up hostility. Even this most important task of reconciliation, however, again presses the diplomat in the direction of embellishing or concealing facts according to whether they promote or hinder the efforts at compromise. The end result is, therefore, apt to be couched in phraseology reflecting only imperfectly the nature of the original problem and how it was resolved. Letting the agreement reached blur the outlines of the disagreements surmounted is sound procedure in personal as well as in diplomatic relations. But, as noted in the earlier discussion of public and secret diplomacy, where initial positions have been ostentatiously taken, subsequent compromises tend to appear hypocritical.

DIPLOMATIC BARGAINING

All these considerations are tied into the process of bargaining. The diplomatic bargainer is like any other in his purpose of selling dear and buying cheap. If he contemplates offering concession X in exchange for concession Y from his opposite number across the negotiating table, the diplomat will typically assert the surpassing value of X and the questionable adequacy of Y as a *quid pro quo*. As in commerce, value in the diplomatic marketplace tends to be defined by the bargaining strengths of the respective participants in the negotiating process, and not as something intrinsic. This economic truth is often harsh for the manufacturers of commodities. It can be far harsher in diplomacy, where the commodities are frequently human beings, slices of territory, social and economic structures, or national self-esteem.

It was Woodrow Wilson again who led the reformers in demanding that diplomacy cease to "barter peoples and provinces." It was also Wilson who found he could not extricate himself from this kind of barter at Versailles. The conversion of China's Shantung Peninsula from German colony to Japanese colony and the transfer of German-speaking South Tyrol from Austria to Italy are usually cited as Wilson's classic derelictions in these matters. But in terms of his own principles of national self-determination there is no reason not to add to the list of deviations the Sudetenland, the Polish Corridor, the forced separation of Germany and Austria, and the German colonial empire that was parceled out in the form of League of Nations mandates to the victor powers. The salient point here is not an indictment of Wilson but an understanding that diplomacy frequently bargains in areas of life that emotionally and morally, as well as materially, are highly sensitive. It follows that the necessary art of bargaining, when it concerns itself with these areas, runs the risk of becoming both callous and devious, thus contributing to the aura of perfidy that plagues the diplomatic reputation.

Bargaining also involves a certain amount of sleight of hand. Side A has duly offered concession X and disparaged side B's offering of concession Y. B then inquires whether A would be disposed to follow an alternate route by conceding Z in exchange for W. A's position is that under no circumstances can Z be a subject for discussion—Z is nonnegotiable. Yet when it appears that B will not raise the ante in the XY deal, A may wish to take another look at the Z problem to see whether there is any flexibility after all. The negotiating struggle over the issue of whether, and how many, North Vietnamese troops would remain in South Vietnam after a ceasefire is at once a neat and deplorable illustration of the impact of the Z factor.

A second scenario portrays A as knowing all along that there is flexibility in his Z position but denying it initially in order to pressure B into making the preferred XY exchange more attractive. A third scenario has B offering Y as a deliberately unsatisfactory concession in order to push A toward serious negotiations about ZW. In still another variation, A may deem it an unpropitious moment to come to any kind of agreement with B. Not wishing to appear hostile to negotiations as such, nor to the peaceful intent they symbolize in the public eye, A puts forward concession X as the ultimate in statesmanship, knowing well that it is Z that really matters to B. A then casts B in the role of making impossible demands, thus bearing the onus for the breaking off of negotiations. (For A and B one can substitute any pair of countries or alliances. For WXYZ one can substitute, for example, missiles, tariffs, agricultural policies in the Common Market, or, once again, Vietnam.)

Thus the initial terms or positions in the bargaining process may vary greatly from or even contradict what emerges at the end. Issues that have no intrinsic meaning for a particular set of negotiations may be spun out only as a means to maneuver one or another of the participants into a discussion of issues that do have a chance of being resolved. Or, more somberly, they may be spun out to avoid a resolution of anything at all. Whatever the motives behind these exercises in the manipulation of symbols, it is evident that they do not create an atmosphere of candor. Still, if the bargaining process has any legitimacy at all—and politics and diplomacy are impossible to imagine in its absence—there needs to be understanding and tolerance for some of its unavoidably opaque characteristics.

The diplomatic bargainer cannot often play with all his cards on the table. Like the domestic politician, he must seek to gain his ends both by promising rewards and threatening punishments in line with the ancient political rule about the indispensability of both carrot and stick. In international relations, however, there is theoretically no upper limit on the punishment to be inflicted. It follows that the use of threats, at least between those powers roughly equal in military strength, becomes a much more delicate and dangerous matter than is usually the case in domestic politics.

Hence the rule of traditional diplomacy that the mailed fist should be insulated inside a velvet glove. Wielding promises and threats in a situation where enmity is a present or potential reality, the diplomat characteristically resorts to the vocabulary of indirection. Insofar as such tactics succeed in their insulating functions and in preventing the migration of conflicts from the conference table to the battlefield, they protect rather than endanger peace. This should be significant compensation for those who are distressed by the diplomat's penchant for calling a spade by some other name.

DIPLOMACY'S CREDIBILITY PROBLEM

The diplomat, then, has a built-in credibility gap. This has fundamentally nothing to do with his personal qualities; it is the product of his working conditions. He operates in a system where the network of official diplomatic relationships is undergirded (and sometimes undermined) by a network of clandestine agents and activities. Insofar as he sometimes establishes links between the two, he can serve as a classic illustration of what is meant by the term double-dealing. The diplomat's connection with and sometimes direction of spies, his dependence on secrecy, his familiarity with the uses of ambiguity, and his status as an agent obligated to obey his principal all combine to conjure up the familiar picture of diplomatic deviousness.

Thus Nicolson's insistence that at least the diplomats he approves of have maintained high standards of personal and official honesty is mostly beside the point. Nicolson cites Callières as a support for his position, and Callières is, if anything, more eloquent than Nicolson:

The good negotiator will never base the success of his negotiations upon false promises or breaches of faith; it is an error to suppose, as public opinion supposes, that it is necessary for an efficient Ambassador to be a past master in the art of deception; dishonesty is in fact little more than a proof of the smallness of mind of him who resorts to it, and shows that he is too meagerly equipped to gain his purposes by just and reasonable methods. Doubtless the art of lying has on occasion been successfully practiced by diplomatists; but unlike that honesty which here, as elsewhere, is the best policy, a lie always leaves in its wake a drop of poison. . . . Even the most dazzling diplomatic triumphs which have been gained by deception are based upon insecure foundations. They leave the defeated party with a sense of indignation, a desire to be revenged and a resentment which will always be a danger.[12]

But the aura of strict candor and virtue begins to fade when one turns to sections of Callières's book from which Nicolson does not quote. The honest ambassador described by Callières must also manage an espionage network:

The ambassador has sometimes been called an honorable spy because one of his principal occupations has been to discover great secrets; and he fails in the discharge of his duty if he does not know how to lay out the necessary sums for this purpose. . . . There is no expense . . . more necessary than that which is laid out upon a secret service.[13]

The ambassador must get his information by purchase and bribery, distributing secret subsidies to impecunious courtiers and even high ranking ministers of state. Callières particularly commends the employment of dancers as agents "who by virtue of their profession have an entrée with the prince less formal and in some degree more intimate than any ambassador can perhaps possess." Flattery and ingratiating oneself by such contrivances as purposely losing at cards to one's "royal opponent" are also well within the bounds of diplomatic propriety.

Callières does set functional limits to the use of bribery: "There is all the difference between the attempt to debauch the subjects of a sovereign prince in order to ensnare them in conspiracy against him and the legitimate endeavor to use every opportunity for acquiring information." Callières was perfectly aware of the existence of envoys who attempted to stir up usurpations, rebellions, or civil wars in the countries to which they were assigned, but he warned that such practices could lead to the breakdown of the entire system by destroying all basis for trust in the ambassador's purposes. But concerning the buying of information,

---

[12] Nicolson, *Diplomacy*, pp. 108–109.

[13] This and the following quotations and paraphases may be found in Callières, *On the Manner of Negotiating with Princes*, pp. 25–27, 86–88, 103, 105–106.

Callières's moral fastidiousness was once again less evident: "no criticism can fall upon a foreign envoy who successfully adopts the practice;
the only culprit in such cases is the citizen of a foreign state who for
corrupt motives sells information abroad." In such transactions, then,
there is a moral stigma upon the suborned but not upon the suborner.

Callières's propositions come close to spelling out a code for honor
among thieves. At the center of the code stands the ambassador who
would not sully his honor by playing the game the way Louis XI advised
—if they lie to you, lie still more to them. He may spy, bribe, flatter, be
a faker at cards and a high-level procurer, but in formal negotiations he
is straightforward, and if he gives his word it may be relied upon. The
prescription is a bit reminiscent of romantic depictions of gangsters or
bandits whose lives are generally a menace to those around them but
who make it a point of honor not to lie their way out of tight spots and
to keep promises, however grudgingly given.

The intention is not to pillory Callières, who was certainly no gang-
ster and whose strictures against deceit in negotiation are to be valued
as wise advice. The issue is that diplomacy's credibility problem cannot
be solved simply by pointing to or insisting upon a high standard of
veracity and reliability in negotiation. It is reassuring to be able to trust
the ambassador's pledged word but less reassuring to know that he is
directing a spy network against you, that he is flattering you and bribing
your associates, and that he would not hesitate to plant a voluptuous
informer in your bed. Behavior of this kind cannot help but give rise to
uneasiness concerning the ambassadorial intentions. It is an uneasiness
that can be only partially mitigated by the knowledge that you have sent
out ambassadors to do the same things abroad.

Callières's rules and regulations for diplomatic behavior are by no
means to be regarded as cynical. Indeed, in the light of the diplomatic record of Europe in the seventeenth and early eighteenth centuries, they can
be looked upon as idealistic exhortations to reform.[14] Although implementation of Callières's code at the time might have improved prospects
for a greater degree of honesty in diplomacy and even reduced the occasions for war, it could hardly have banished mistrust from diplomatic
relations. Nor did Callières aspire to so much. But it is precisely the

---

[14] Abraham de Wicquefort, a Flemish contemporary of Callières who published *The
Ambassador and His Functions* in 1715, offered a perhaps overgloomy characterization of the European diplomacy of his time: "The late King of Sweden did not fear
saying that he did not know what kind of animal a Treaty was. And to speak the
truth . . . it must be confessed that Princes observe Treaties but as far as they
please, and that it is Interest or Whim, and not Honesty of Principle, that guides
their Actions. The Wax and Parchment did not bind faster than a Chain of Straw,
and they seem to glory in out-doing the Florentin Politician, in all he says, concerning the most pernicious Maxims of the worst of Men." Bernard Lintott edition
(London, no date), p. 372.

absence of trust among states that chiefly explains diplomacy's enduring reputation for deceitfulness. Callières himself resorted to the bromide about honesty being the best policy while at the same time demonstrating that he was quite prepared to follow other policies in areas of activity where honesty could not possibly have a place. The phenomenon of selective honesty (or selective dishonesty) in which men resort to truth or untruth as policy dictates is both cause and effect of mistrust and of the stigma of untrustworthiness.

Many contemporary diplomats, perhaps most, will go through their careers without personal involvement in some of the more exotic forms of sub rosa activity. But none will fail to know that their embassy code rooms are subject to special security precautions and that attempts to break codes are often made by allies as well as enemies. The strict regulations concerning the locking of office files in foreign office and embassy is another daily reminder that there are people in the world of diplomacy (or its secret service underground) who will resort to underhanded means to obtain information to which they are not entitled. The omnipresence of secret services is taken for granted, and all know at one time or another what it is like to suspect and be suspected.[15]

Reinforcing the routine reminders of duplicity's role are the great events that shake the diplomatic world: Berlin, Korea, Suez, Hungary, Quemoy-Matsu, the Bay of Pigs, the Cuban missile crisis, Vietnam, the third Arab-Israeli war of 1967, the *Pueblo* affair, the invasion of Czechoslovakia. All these events are deemed crises because they seriously threaten or actually break the peace. But they are also crises of confidence in the sense that those involved in them almost invariably make wildly inflated claims concerning the consistency, steadfastness, and rectitude of their own positions while excoriating in the most unrestrained language the opponent's addiction to falsehood and his contempt for the pledged word. These crises occur frequently enough so that public opinion can without too much difficulty gain an impression of diplomacy as a ruthless and nonstop lying-match (if they lie to you, lie still more to them). Indeed, it is important to note that only crisis diplomacy is likely to attract public attention and that the friendlier arts of cooperative diplomacy play a minor role in the shaping of diplomacy's public image.

If enmity and conflict foster falsehoods, it is obvious that friendship and cooperation are the basic remedies at truth's disposal. In diplomacy as in personal life, one most easily tells the truth to those one can afford to trust. But these fundamental remedies are not always available in a world rent by profound differences in political, economic, military,

---

[15] All these phenomena can be found in domestic as well as international politics, although until the Watergate revelations it was generally held that the internal processes of democratic societies were relatively free of them.

and ideological circumstances. Injustice, hatred, suspicion, and fanaticism are palpable presences around the globe. Because the conditions that breed these presences are deep-rooted and difficult to alter, they will not soon disappear. But it is precisely the alteration of these pathetic and dangerous conditions that is the priority goal of a rational foreign policy and a rational diplomacy. Only a progressive realization of this goal, in turn, will also make possible a progressive emancipation from the legacy of subterfuge that has characterized every era of diplomatic history.

DIPLOMACY AND WAR

Enmity and conflict are also the obvious links between diplomacy and war. Their persistence constantly sabotages diplomacy's claim to be, by definition, a peace-oriented activity. As we have already noted, both politics and diplomacy involve exercises of power, or influence, carried out along a spectrum bounded by force and consent. To the extent that the action in any particular set of diplomatic negotiations moves closer to the force end of the spectrum, threats, vilification, and finally the ultimatum dominate the proceedings and bring them to a climax. In such circumstances, the techniques of diplomacy are being used to prepare for combat and not to effect conciliation. Even if the actual result is not a resort to arms but is instead a capitulation to the ultimatum by the weaker power or the acceptance of a bad bargain, the brandishing of force as the effective agent in reaching "agreement" is manifest. Hence the image of diplomacy as a sinister and sometimes cruel game in which the strong characteristically push around the weak and which frequently becomes so high pressured and reckless as to make war unavoidable.

This image was in high vogue particularly in the wake of World War I. The magnitude and unprecedented horror of a catastrophe that ended a century of more or less peaceful development in Europe spurred the search for scapegoats (as well as authentic causal agents), and the diplomats were fair game. The diplomats and their political chiefs formed, in the public eye, a team. They were the most visible civilians in the prewar and wartime unfolding of tragedy. It is therefore understandable that they were taxed with a large share of responsibility. The oversubtle maneuvers of Sir Edward Grey were subject to unfriendly scrutiny, along with Bethmann-Hollweg's rash characterization of the treaty guaranteeing Belgian neutrality as a scrap of paper. The "blank check" that Germany tacitly offered Austria-Hungary in the dispute with Serbia, the secret British-French military consultations without benefit of an alliance in the years before 1914, the secret treaties signed in 1915 by Britain, France, and Russia carving up southeast Europe and the Ottoman Empire without any intention to consider the wishes of the peoples affected,[16] and the improbable efforts of the German government to lure Mexico into war against the United States with a promise of helping Mexico to recover territories lost in 1848—all these contributed powerfully to the indictment of the inherited diplomatic system. The basic accusation was that instead of promoting peace, diplomacy was promoting war.

Diplomats have been on the defensive ever since. For their activities leading up to 1914 they have been accused of being war-prone. The record during the war has been interpreted as one featuring conspiratorial efforts to undermine the public promises of a just and lasting peace. With the end of the war only the victors counted, and their diplomacy in the making of peace was attacked as vengeful and as a political and economic disaster. There were those, of course (particularly in France), who complained that the peace was not nearly harsh enough. The hard liner–soft liner debate concerning peace enforcement problems was to go on during the 1920s. But the soft liner and generally liberal and left-wing critics who attacked simultaneously the Treaty of Versailles and the whole corpus of traditional diplomacy were by far the more articulate and effective in shaping public attitudes toward diplomacy.

By contrast, the history of diplomacy in the 1930s is preeminently a record of appeasement. As part of that record, its practitioners have been accused of cowardice, of procrastination, of preferring selfish personal or class interests to the larger interests of the nation (or of humanity at large), and of catastrophic miscalculations of international realities. The belligerent diplomacy characteristic of all sides in the pre-1914 period had given way to a different pattern: pre-1939 diplomacy was dominated by the warlike demands of the Axis before which the Western powers executed a series of craven retreats. Different patterns or not, the accusers concluded that the diplomatic system had once again managed to make a world war inevitable.

Like the Germans after World War I, the diplomats have been emphatically unwilling to accept any war-guilt clause. The terrors which the years from 1914 to 1945 brought with them were so overwhelming that it is understandable if those who played prominent roles were reluctant to admit responsibility. Moreover, the arraignment of diplomacy was put in terms going far beyond what the facts would support. Hence, as usual, exaggerated charges provoked exaggerated defensiveness.

Far from sharing any guilt for war, the diplomat defended himself and was defended as a peacemaker by definition. If a persistent critic noted that war nonetheless broke out, the defense could point to the

---

[16] The new Soviet regime took advantage of its control of what had been the tsarist foreign office to publish these documents soon after the Revolution as a means of embarrassing the continuing Allied war effort.

enemy's diplomacy, everybody's generals, or the stupidities of the political leadership, both domestic and foreign, as the real culprits. In sum, in a very large body of literature produced by twentieth-century diplomats and ex-diplomats it is difficult to find any serious explorations of the relation between diplomacy and force. The most candid statement in this regard comes from the distinguished Indian diplomat, K. M. Panikkar:

> An Ambassador's primary, and almost only, duty is to secure the safety and interests of his own country. If that safety and security can be won by peaceful methods he should work for peace. If they cannot be won by peace, it does not follow that he should work for a disturbance of the peace or for war, but he should try by every means to alter the circumstances in his favor.[17]

By contemporary standards, Ambassador Panikkar's observation represents the outer reaches of diplomatic candor. It is not too distant in spirit from Callières's views on the matter:

> A powerful prince who maintains a constant system of diplomacy . . . is in a position to influence the destiny of neighboring states, to maintain peace between all states, or to pursue war where it is favorable to his design.[18]

Both statements avow what has been denied again and again despite the evidence again and again brought forward: diplomacy serves both war and peace.

The diplomat can be directed to provoke a foreign government to the point where, despite dubious prospects, it either declares war or loses its credibility with its own people. Diplomatic talk can be used as a smoke screen for a military attack, as in the case of the Nomura-Kurusu assurances of Japan's peaceful intent during their Washington negotiations with Secretary of State Cordell Hull prior to and on the very day of Pearl Harbor. One can use threats to browbeat the other side across the bargaining table to the point where it surrenders without fighting. An infamous example, alongside the bullying of Austrian Chancellor Schussnigg, is Hitler's summoning, in March 1939, of the ailing President Emil Hacha of rump Czechoslovakia in the dead of night. Hacha was told that unless he signed a no-resistance agreement to a German occupation scheduled to commence in a few hours, Prague would be in smoking ruins by morning. He signed.

Even without detailed documentation one could devise reasonably

---

[17] K. M. Panikkar, *The Principles and Practice of Diplomacy* (Bombay: Asia Publishing House, 1956), pp. 59–60.

[18] Callières, *On the Manner of Negotiating with Princes*, p. 18.

accurate scenarios for comparable exchanges between the Soviets and the representatives of Lithuania, Latvia, and Estonia in 1940 when the Russians announced that the three Baltic republics were about to be admitted into the Soviet Union whether they liked it or not. The United States and the West are not innocent of such dealings. They, too, have used diplomacy by intimidation. After all, Western imperial expansion was accomplished more often by emissaries holding out the prospect of rewards in store for concessions and punishments awaiting those who refused to make them than by actual military operations. These techniques have been used in United States relations with Latin American countries as well as in the more extensive imperial enterprises of the European powers in Asia and Africa.

It should be evident, then, that diplomacy is ambivalent toward force and consent. While there may be a diplomatic bias in favor of genuine agreement and consent, the cardinal consideration must be that for diplomacy war and peace are subordinate categories of concern. Sometimes diplomats are earnestly seeking peace; sometimes—certainly less often—they just as earnestly seek capitulation or war. The diplomat is a servant of the government and part of the foreign policy establishment. If his government desires peace, the diplomat will try to bring it about; if the government is bent on war, the diplomat will seek to foment it. In short, to paraphrase Ambassador Panikkar, the diplomat must be ready to use *every* means to secure the interests of his own country. Once this maxim is accepted as a matter of fact, if not of principle, the sterile polemics characterizing the diplomat either as peace maker or war monger should come to a halt (but they won't).

DIPLOMACY AS MICROPOLITICS

What has really been at stake all along is not the personal affinities of diplomats for peace or war, the antidemocratic attitudes that have been attributed to them, or other deficiencies of intellect or character best explained by the sociology of aristocracy. The real difficulty is that the diplomat has traditionally operated, and still operates, in terms of a micropolitical ethos that he shares with all but a small minority of mankind. The most that one can extract from this ethos, in diplomacy or in any other sector of the individual state and society, is a preference for getting one's way peacefully.

The preference runs roughly as follows: agreement rather than disagreement, disagreement rather than sacrifice or even risk of interests, peace if it avoids such sacrifices or risks, war if deemed necessary to protect the interests at stake. Such an ethos implies a fundamental lack of responsibility to anything other than the self-regarding state, and where there is a multiplicity of such states, the incidence of violence and such other unpleasant things as secretiveness and deception is bound to be high. The rate of incidence can decline only with the growth of a more inclusive sense of responsibility to replace the exclusivity of micropolitics.

The French and German usages of *haute politique* and *grosse Politik* as synonyms for diplomacy translate poorly into English; an accurate rendering would come somewhere between top level politics and high policy. In any case, both the French and German expressions have traditionally been used to convey the sense that on a scale of rising political importance diplomacy—politics among sovereign states—stands at the very top in terms of impact on men and societies. The great diplomatic assemblages in Muenster and Osnabrueck (Peace of Westphalia) in 1648, at Utrecht in 1713, and at Vienna in 1815 epitomize this importance. They brought together many or most of the great and small powers of Europe to make or confirm decisions about war and peace that affected the course of history for a long time thereafter.

Decisions taken at the Congress of Vienna had particularly far-reaching consequences; one of them was the emergence of the Concert of Europe. During its lifetime of nearly one hundred years, the Concert, composed of Europe's great powers, met on an ad hoc basis and dealt with major international issues on the assumption that they could not be resolved unless all of them agreed or at least participated in the decisions taken. The assumption was in accord with the Declaration of February 5, 1814, the genesis of the Concert, in which England, Austria, Prussia, and Russia pledged that they would not act simply on behalf of their own interests "but in the name of Europe which forms but a single whole."

The early restoration of France to diplomatic respectability and the signing of the Holy Alliance and associated treaties in 1815 enhanced the sense of commitment to European solidarity. Even though the Holy Alliance soon fell apart, due primarily to British-Russian hostility, the Concert continued to function and register some significant successes in terms of promoting peaceful settlement and preventing war. Two of the most noteworthy assemblies of the Concert were the negotiations establishing and guaranteeing Belgian independence in the 1830s and the Congress of Berlin in 1878, which succeeded in damping the explosive consequences of the latest round in the centuries-old struggle between Russia and Turkey.

On the other hand, the Concert was certainly not in evidence during the Crimean War in 1854 or the Franco-Prussian War in 1870, and it was tragically moribund in 1914. When it functioned and while it lasted, however, the Concert provided a congressional form of politics in which member states would send instructed but not irrevocably bound delegates to reach political settlements affecting all of Europe. The Berlin Conference of 1884–1885 and the Algeciras Conference of

1906 extended the Concert principle to the resolution of overseas issues and disputes.

Some of the members of the European congresses and conferences saw themselves as engaged in managing the affairs of mankind. This is *haute politique* indeed. In reality, they were not far off the mark as they distributed rewards and punishments, peoples and territories, naval bases and coaling stations, protectorates and commercial spheres of influence. They were engaged at the international level in the undertaking that David Easton defines as the essence of political activity: the authoritative allocation of values for society as a whole.[19]

United in Concert, the great European powers were the rulers of the world. But, of course, the unity was only sporadic. The Concert could be convened only if its members agreed to it (here it bears strong resemblance to the United Nations Security Council, whose effectiveness must always be measured in terms of the veto contingency). Agreement was obviously lacking in 1870 as well as in 1914, and the result was that major political events took place outside the purview of any regulating or controlling body at all. World War I was the terrible culmination of the inadequacies of a hundred years of *haute politique*.

Appalled by the ravages of the Napoleonic wars, the fathers of the Concert system had sought to give practical effect to the ideal of European unity as a way to avoid a recurrence of mass violence. But, as the early demise of the Holy Alliance demonstrated, the vision of a united Europe, and even the less idealistic vision of a united European aristocracy, faded before the often combined forces of the new nationalism and the traditional egotisms of the individual states. Loyalty to the European system as exemplified by the Concert was not absent; it was just that it had to contend with more powerful loyalties focused on the national or territorial state. The powers were willing, sometimes eager, to support the Concert system so long as their interests and those of the system coincided. But when one or more powers felt that the Concert would hinder rather than help them in the realization of their individual aims, the calling of a congress had no point.

Hence the Concert system of diplomacy reflects and is dominated by the balance of power system. As we have seen in Chapter 2, the balance of power concept is a useful policy guide in exploiting or adjusting to the divisions that keep nations apart, but it cannot offer a remedy for those divisions. It is true that a state pursuing balance of power policies frequently has an authentic stake in the functioning of the larger system in which it operates. But whether the system promotes peace or war, security and prosperity for all or only for some, whether it plays a malign or benevolent role in global terms—these concerns are by defini-

---

[19] David Easton, *The Political System* (New York: Knopf, 1953), *passim*.

tion secondary to the primary concern: whether the system promotes the objectives of the particular member.

The key question is always, To what extent does the system serve the interest of the individual state? The question is never, To what extent does the intrinsic value of the system have a claim on the allegiance of the state? Thus in a balance of power system, the state is something like the depersonalized stockholder who invests if the prospects for dividends and growth are good but assumes no responsibility for the viability of the corporation and gets out when he no longer stands to benefit. This was the key problematic in the life and downfall of the Concert of Europe.

Traditional diplomacy can be understood as the politics of indifference. The diplomat's code was to be indifferent to everything that did not affect his own country's interests and to be concerned only with those matters which did. The internal misery or well-being of a society was of diplomatic interest only insofar as its foreign policy was affected. Nothing was valued for its own sake; everything was examined for its possible utility or disutility to the diplomat's state-employer.

Fortunately, not every diplomat (nor every foreign policy) achieved so formidable a degree of intellectual and moral detachment. But the premium on instrumentality made the world of diplomacy generally a place of aloofness inimical to enduring attachments across state boundaries. It promoted an atmosphere caricatured but also characterized by the question attributed to Talleyrand when he was informed of the death of the Russian delegate to the Congress of Vienna: What could have been his motive?

Traditional diplomacy facilitated contact among states on the proposition that each was theoretically impermeable. That is, the diplomat and his secret agent may be straining every resource to penetrate another society and exploit internal political divisions, but the diplomat's formal mission is to have dealings only with the officials authorized to represent that society as an indivisible unit to the outside world. This is, of course, the classic formula for relations among sovereigns and another way of describing the world of micropolitics.

Despite its cosmopolitan pretensions, then, traditional diplomacy has been fundamentally parochial in outlook. The provincialism of its precepts and the recurring disasters resulting from its practice have again and again stimulated men to look elsewhere than to diplomacy for more viable ways of regulating the international system. The chief inventions resulting from this quest have been international law and international organization. But neither has been able to go much beyond diplomacy in transforming micropolitics into macropolitics.

Chapter 10

International Law

For more than three centuries prevailing opinion has regarded Hugo Grotius' *On the Law of War and Peace (De Jure Belli ac Paci Libri Tres)* as the most important of the sources and foundations of Western international law. Insofar as Western concepts of international law predominate around the world, Grotius has played the role of global founder. It is appropriate, then, to take note of the founder's principal legacy. Dedicating his book to Louis XIII of France, Grotius specified the guiding theme and purpose of his work: "For it has been written on behalf of justice."[1]

Grotius also made clear his motives for pleading the cause of law and justice in relations among states:

> I have had many and weighty reasons for undertaking to write upon this subject. Throughout the Christian world I observed a lack of restraint in relation to war such as even barbarous races should be ashamed of; I observed that men rush to arms for slight causes, or no cause at all, and that when arms have once been taken up there is no longer any respect for law, divine or human; it is as if, in accordance with a general decree, frenzy had openly been let loose for the committing of all crimes.[2]

The timelessness of Grotius' lament for the pathologies of international life and his yearning to change them place him at the center of the tradition that has sought to turn men away from violence and make them into lovers of peace. Yet his prescriptions would not please the peace militants of past or present, since Grotius sought only to regulate the use of violence and not to abolish it. Indeed, he explicitly distinguished his own position from that of the pacifists; Grotius set forth his doctrine of war and peace so "that men may not believe either that nothing is allowable, or that everything is."

---

[1] Hugo Grotius, *De Jure Belli ac Pacis Libri Tres* (Oxford: Clarendon Press, 1925), Vol. II, p. 3. Grotius' work was first published in 1625.

[2] Ibid., p. 20. The two immediately following quotations will also be found at the same location.

De Jure Belli, then, is an elaboration of Grotius' conviction that "there is a common law among nations which is valid alike for war, and in war," and, by logical extension, in peace. It is a common law grounded on natural law. Affirming the just war doctrine, Grotius defines the just war and the unjust war in terms of cause, of conduct, and of outcome. He specifies the circumstances in which resort to violence is permissible and those in which it is not. Once a war has broken out, Grotius argues, the law commands restraint in the exercise of violence and prescribes that the general conduct of the war must serve the policy of restoring an enduring peace. This requirement, of course, commends compassion for the vanquished and rules out revenge for injuries sustained by the victors.

Grotius' law of nations recognizes three legitimate occasions for resort to war: in defense of life, in defense of property, and to punish wrongdoing. It is here, of course, that ambiguity enters. Can the victim of an attack claim just cause if his own behavior has been so threatening as to provoke the attacker? Is the property to be defended justly held, or is it loot upon which the passage of time has conferred the respectability of ownership? If the state is committed to the punishment of wrongdoing beyond its boundaries, where is the guarantee for the impartiality of the commitment and of the punitive expedition itself?

Grotius dealt in a comprehensive manner with these and like questions in which "there often comes a moment of doubt, . . . as when day passes into night, or when cold water slowly becomes warm."[3] But, not surprisingly, his answers were not always persuasive. One of the most controversial aspects of Grotius' treatise, for example, is his vigorous defense of absolute monarchy and his condemnation of rebellion. It may be surmised that Louis XIII, as the recipient of Grotius' dedication, was not displeased to note Grotius' admiration for royal rule. At the same time, Grotius set out seven exceptions to the rule against rebellion plus an additional four where usurpation was involved. Several of these exceptions could be construed as ample rationales for the rebellion of Grotius' Dutch compatriots against their Spanish overlords, and one of the qualifying paragraphs could be cited as sanction for just about any kind of rebellion.[4]

THE UNEQUAL CONTEST BETWEEN LAW AND ANARCHY

Grotius emerges, then, as another example of the inevitable presence of particular interests embedded in what are put forward as general prop-

---

[3] Ibid., p. 557.

[4] Ibid., pp. 156–162.

ositions. We have seen this symbiosis of general and particular, of cosmopolitan and parochial, in the precepts of ideology, nationalism, imperialism, and diplomacy. The juxtaposition is particularly poignant in law with its express claim to universality which in its natural law form refers to all mankind and in its positive law form to all who live within an explicitly specified jurisdiction.

The idea of law's universality, in turn, is linked to the concept of justice: if some within its declared jurisdiction are exempt from the law, how will there be confidence in the just behavior of those exempted? In both domestic and international society, the exempt will possess undue privilege and power, and the rest will be at their mercy. Under such circumstances the ideal of equal justice under law must disappear. In domestic society the alternative is tyranny or, at best, oligarchy. In international society the alternative is the anarchy to which we have become accustomed. The fundamental legal problem in internal politics is that some seek to evade the law. The fundamental legal problem in world politics is that all resist establishing law's jurisdiction.

The desirability of justice and the undesirability of anarchy, however, have repeatedly led both scholars and statesmen to assert the possibility, the necessity, or even the self-evident existence of a comprehensive international law. Grotius stood in a long line of "jurisconsults to mankind" which effectively began with his Spanish predecessors, Vitoria and Suárez, and with Gentili in England, and was carried on by Pufendorf, Bynkershoek, Wolff, Vattel, and Austin, to name only the most eminent. Grotius' desire to plead "on behalf of justice" was not absent in the works of his colleagues, but many of their briefs were still more ambiguous than his. With his successors, the ancient natural law basis of justice began to crumble under the pressure of an accelerating secularization of political and intellectual life. Its fate was acidly and accurately described by Jeremy Bentham:

> A great multitude of people are continually talking of the law of nature: and then they go on giving you their sentiments of what is right and what is wrong: and these sentiments, you are to understand, are so many chapters and sections of the law of nature.[5]

Bentham neatly impales the subjectivity of pretensions to objective truth, not only for his own time but as a commentary for the ages. Yet the unmasking of subjective preferences in order to discredit natural law doctrine strikes a heavy blow at any set of propositions that assert the unity of men. Within the state the blow can be countered by massive

---

[5] Quoted in Arthur Nussbaum, *A Concise History of the Law of Nations*, 2nd ed. (New York: Macmillan, 1954), p. 185.

resort to positive law as a means of restructuring community, which is, of course, the remedy Bentham was promoting. But, as Nussbaum notes, Bentham was not addressing himself to the problems of the international society when he took aim at the law of nature. Here the resistance to a comprehensive use of positive law in matters affecting war and peace has been massive and persistent—reflecting, in turn, the massive and persistent resistance to a conception of the world as a community in any authentic sense whatsoever. The state could downgrade natural law and survive, sometimes precariously. But the world had no ready alternative to the punctured assumptions concerning a universal law of nature, except perhaps to follow up the denial of natural law with a denial of international law itself.

Indeed, in the nineteenth century John Austin, the most recent of the classic commentators, stated that international law was not "law properly so-called" because it lacked effective enforcement. Instead, it was better defined as "positive morality" embodied in the "opinions and sentiments current among nations generally." Austin followed Bentham in explicitly rejecting the universal premises of the natural law tradition, but he found no way to dismantle the Babel built by the self-interested interpreters of the law that aroused Bentham's scorn. On the contrary, Austin's "opinions and sentiments" construction offered unprecedented latitude for those who wished to construe international law to their own advantage rather than as an instrument of human justice. It also gave force to the opinion of those who saw the international scene as wholly unsuited to the rule of law and who subscribed to (and/or championed) the proposition that only power counts in relations across sovereign boundaries.

The erosion of a universal normative content in international law has continued and speeded up in our own time despite a revival of interest in natural law concepts. Concomitantly, the paramountcy of parochial self-interest in legal formulas is ever more pronounced. Oliver Lissitzyn identifies one aspect of this process; indeed, he sanctions it as evidence of a desirable correspondence between international law and typical international behavior:

> The very limitations on the sphere of operation of general international law made for its effectiveness. Since to a very large extent it did not purport to regulate the means by which a state could protect its major interests, it was generally not subjected to great strains. Furthermore, the stronger powers, at least insofar as they had common interests, had a preponderant influence on the development of its content and were not restrained from the use of force to repress what they regarded as violations of the law by others. International legal norms underwent constant reinterpretation and development—generally keeping in step with the evolving needs and policies of the

stronger states. International law was thus fairly well adjusted to the realities of power and interest.[6]

The description is realistic, but what is described bears more resemblance to political self-assertion by the powerful than to any concept of law which Grotius once posited as common and applicable to all nations without exception or favor. It is an account of a reality that often makes both idealist and cynic call for an end to a farce which labels as law what is manifestly nothing more than faintly disguised power politics.

The examination of concrete cases does still more to strip international law of the august character which at least the school of Grotius attributed to it. In the case of the endemic Berlin crisis, one analyst observes:

> Neither side is satisfied with the status quo, but any change implies a shift in the power structure on the European continent. This is unacceptable, so the unnatural situation in Berlin is perpetuated. Law has found a useful role in this perpetuation—legal contentions serve as a means to probe the other side's commitment (a substitute for force), and by obscuring the underlying political confrontation in the jargon of the law, they blanket the volatility which characterizes the Berlin situation. This is a modest role, but it is all that reasonably can or should be expected of international law in view of the heterogeneous nature of the contemporary international political system.[7]

Of course, domestic law is also used to probe an opponent's intentions or to muffle conflict in a mass of legalisms. But domestic law in an integrated state has a whole panoply of other functions, including the making of major—and enforceable—decisions in the society under its jurisdiction. It is these functions that endow law with most of its social and political significance.

In comparison with the major decision-making achievements of domestic law, the record of international law is meager indeed. Analysis of another concrete case, the Suez crisis of 1956, offers a forceful illustration:

> The lesson to be drawn . . . is that international law is, in times of crises, still not the controlling factor in the use of force. Britain, France and Israel behaved in ways very similar to those of the Soviet Union and the United States in situations which closely affected their national interest—the main

---

[6] Oliver J. Lissitzyn, "International Law in a Divided World," *International Conciliation* No. 542 (March 1963), p. 7.

[7] Lawrence Scheinman, "The Berlin Blockade," in Lawrence Scheinman and David Wilkinson (eds.), *International Law and Political Crisis* (Boston: Little, Brown, 1968), p. 40.

difference was one not of law but of power. Britain, France and Israel were compelled to withdraw. . . . But the U.S.S.R. and the United States got away with their unilateral actions because their power could not be effectively challenged—at least not in regions within their immediate spheres of influence: Hungary in the case of the Soviet Union, Cuba and the Dominican Republic in the case of the United States.

Nearly half a century after the first attempt made to impose the restraints of international law through a permanent organization on the unilateral use of force, it has to be admitted that international law, at least in situations of vital clashes of national interest, is still used essentially as a point of argument. It has been twisted this way or that to bolster political action, and no state has hitherto found it difficult to contradict its own line of action or reasoning when it believed that national interest required such contradiction.[8]

Yet so eminent an authority as Julius Stone pronounces international law alive and well, though living in limbo:

the international legal order takes the extraordinary course of providing by its own rules for its collision with overwhelming power. It allows the military victor through the imposed treaty of peace to incorporate his dictated terms into the body of international law, thus preserving at any rate the rest of the rules and its own continued existence. By this built-in device, it incorporates into the legal order the net result of what otherwise would be a legal, or even an illegal, revolution. International law, in short, legalizes even that scale of transformation and destruction of legal rights which in national legal systems can come about only from legal revolution.[9]

Despite the elegant and instructive reasoning in this statement, it only embroiders the general proposition already broached: in international relations, law is what the strongest say it is. So construed, law promises vast benefits for the powerful and slim consolation for the weak. Small wonder that the ex-colonial states, in addition to having specific complaints, are prone to look askance at the whole body of law which calls itself international but is in fact Western and whose reality so often contradicts its enveloping rhetoric. They might understandably prefer Soviet candor in this matter:

Those institutions in international law which can facilitate the execution of the stated tasks of the USSR are recognized and applied by the USSR, and

---

[8] Wolfgang Friedmann and Lawrence A. Collins, "The Suez Canal Crisis of 1956," in ibid., pp. 124, 125.

[9] Julius Stone, "Approaches to the Notion of International Justice," in Richard A. Falk and Cyril E. Black (eds.), *The Future of the International Legal Order*, Vol. I: *Trends and Patterns* (Princeton, N.J.: Princeton University Press, 1969), p. 388.

those institutions which conflict in any manner with these purposes are rejected by the USSR.[10]

Grotius wrote *De Jure Belli* because he was appalled by the ruinous competition among states which he saw all around him and by the cruelties—the "frenzy"—that punctuated the competitive process. He was, in fact, responding to one of history's most destructive examples of that process; his massive work was written during the opening years of the Thirty Years' War. Grotius thus resembles the modern student of international relations, troubled by war and injustice and seeking hopeful remedies.

But if, willing justice, the student is contemptuous of the law and order formula in domestic politics, he must be still more contemptuous of a law in international society that provides neither justice nor order in any matters of major importance to men. The copious (and authentic) documentation demonstrating the high degree of law-abidingness among nations in routine diplomatic and commercial intercourse can do little to dispel his contempt; these are not matters he is fundamentally concerned with. Nor can he be satisfied with analyses that depict international law as one of the instrumentalities useful in carrying on the power struggle. Such a thesis does not resolve his problem but only intensifies it. All the insights offered by a power-oriented realism into the pretensions of international law can serve only as a preface to the question whether there is indeed a creative role for international law in the building of peace and justice.

LAW IN DOMESTIC AND INTERNATIONAL SOCIETY

If justice is to be done to international law itself, however, it is necessary to compare the context in which it must operate with the generally more benign conditions under which domestic law has developed. Why has law been so central in the civil state and so marginal beyond the state? Salient comparisons and distinctions may be made in four crucial areas: the sources of law in domestic and international society; the jurisdictional qualities of the law in each type of society; the locus of interpretation in each; and the agencies available to each for the enforcement of the law.

The major source of law in modern domestic societies is legislation, combined with the precedents and procedures established by the execu-

---

[10] F. I. Kozhevnikov in an article written in 1947 and cited by Lissitzyn, "International Law in a Divided World," p. 16. While the bluntness of this language reflects the special truculence of the Cold War, it is quite in line with the classic Marxist position on law as simply an instrument of the ruling class to buttress its own ruling position.

tive implementation of any given statute. In international society treaties constitute the major source of law. Like legislation, they define in reasonably precise terms what the parties binding themselves (or being bound) are supposed to do. Legislation requires those under its jurisdiction to pay certain taxes, to conduct labor-management relations in prescribed ways, to serve in the armed forces, and the like. Treaties require the signatories to aid each other in case of attack, to extradite fugitives from justice, to refrain from the militarization of certain areas, or to abide by a specified set of projections in their trade with one another. Thus treaties and legislation are fundamentally analogous, and often the concrete matters they deal with are similar, as, for example, the regulation of international and domestic commerce.

But here the similarity ends. As sources of law, treaties and legislation readily lend themselves to comparison. But a wide gap opens up as soon as they are examined in the light of their jurisdictional qualities and their relationships to agencies of law interpretation and enforcement. The legislature relies on a well-established executive branch that will enforce legislation not ruled invalid by a well-established court system. The treaty partners, however, must typically rely on themselves for enforcement of the treaty, and they are certainly prone to rely on their own interpretations of its provisions.

As far as jurisdictional qualities are concerned, legislation is the equivalent of a general rule while a treaty embodies a particular rule. That is, the enactment of a law binds all people affected by the law's provisions. The signing of a treaty, however far reaching its impact, almost invariably binds only the signatories. Hence treaties are very much like contract law: two or more parties may make an agreement concerning how they will do their business with one another, but the rules they establish to govern their intercourse are not mandatory for others. The result is, from the global perspective, that treaty law adds up to a very mixed bundle of particularistic and unconnected agreements. Some success has been registered in codifying and universalizing procedures formerly regulated by bilateral or multilateral treaties, but these are characteristically in areas of day-to-day operational convenience (postal traffic, public health operations, regulations dealing with diplomatic representation). While codification is essential to a more comprehensive legal system, it necessarily remains remote from those realms where the issues of war, peace, and justice are generated and settled.

Court decisions are also sources of law in both domestic and international society. *Brown vs. Board of Education* dramatically illustrates what a court can do to precipitate a flow of historic events both in and beyond the law. When the United States Supreme Court in 1954 declared racial segregation inherently unequal, it set into motion mass actions whose impact will be felt well beyond the end of the century. But until now, at least, a court can contribute only modestly to the corpus of international law and the movement of international society. Article 59 of the Statute of the International Court of Justice (ICJ) provides that "the decision of the Court has no binding force except between the parties and in respect of the particular case." Thus the ICJ may be called a "world court," but it is clearly unable to make world decisions. Its judicial competence is, in fact, the mirror image of the legislative competence of treaty makers: the rules bind only the signatories (or, only the parties to the case). With so meager a grant of authority, the ICJ could not hope to pursue the kind of law-building role played by the courts within the United States or even in other domestic societies where the judiciary has a more modest part in the political system.

The weakness of the ICJ can be illustrated in another way. Article 59 makes it clear that the rule of *stare decisis* is not operative in international law; that is, courts are not bound to follow previous precedents. It follows that there is no requirement that court rulings be consistent with previous rulings in similar cases. Article 59 makes it equally clear that there is no hierarchical system in international law. The International Court of Justice is not an international supreme court. National courts, or international courts established by bilateral or multilateral treaties, have no legal connection with the ICJ and are free to ignore its rulings. Without a hierarchy of judicial authority or a binding body of precedent, the court cannot be expected to improve much on a record which identifies it as a useful but not very significant international institution.[11]

If it is asked why the Court has such modest prerogatives, the simple answer is that the nation-states that negotiated the treaty establishing the ICJ statute would not grant more far-reaching powers. The more complex and realistic answer is that the limitations on international judicial power reflect the fact that the Court's statute is the work of many powerful and sovereign policy makers, and not of a single legislature. The policy makers—the nation-states—have been the sole sources of the power to enforce Court decisions, and hitherto they have insisted upon deciding themselves when to employ such power. This is, of course, the cardinal weakness of the ICJ: there is no one sworn to enforce its rulings.

But there are other weaknesses as well. They are also profoundly difficult to deal with because they, too, are neither gratuitous nor ephemeral, but organic and fundamental. Article 59 was not a matter of mere nationalistic caprice on the part of those who wrote the statute; it was also a rational response to all the deficiencies that continued to limit international law to a marginal role in the settlement of disputes.

---

[11] See Hans Morgenthau's incisive discussion of these and other aspects of the problematics of international law in *Politics Among Nations*, Chap. 18.

A judicial system operating on the principle of *stare decisis* would be a much more powerful generator of international legal norms. But the still-sovereign states were not, and are not, willing to see binding precedent arise from particular cases in which states not party to the case have no guaranteed opportunity to make their views heard. Nor could they overlook the fact that there is no way to secure a legislative reversal of any norms the Court might adopt. In a domestic society it is always possible to nullify a court ruling by enacting new legislation, but there is no such recourse in international society. Thus deficiencies in other sectors of the legal structure virtually dictate a severely restricted grant of power to the judicial sector.

Weakness in the legislative and executive aspects of any political system must necessarily mean weakness in its judicial processes. Hence states shy away from law on an international scale not merely because of pride, custom, and an infatuation with sovereignty, but also because that minimum degree of world community is still lacking which alone could give significance to law as an instrument for resolving conflict and regulating the forces of stability and change. In short, there is the familiar vicious circle in which sovereignty fears to bet more on a wider community because the community is too feeble, and the community remains feeble because sovereignty will not make serious bets on its growth and potential strength.

Custom and scholarly commentaries join treaties and court decisions as the remaining noteworthy sources of international law. Just as custom is the original source of law in every domestic society, so it is at the root of international law as well. But as society grows more complex, custom recedes into the background and is overshadowed or replaced by legislation as the working basis for law. During periods of rapid social and technological change this displacement process accelerates, and congresses and parliaments are pressured to produce a large number of statutory solutions to a large number of very thorny problems. In domestic society the displacement of custom by statute has been often painful but generally efficacious. In international society, however, there is no legislative agency, within or outside the United Nations, remotely able to deal comprehensively with the conflict between custom and change—or with the conflict of custom and custom.

It is evident today that profound problems are posed not only by the crumbling and obsolescence of custom but also by the existence side by side of a multitude of highly diverse customary, or mixed customary-statutory, systems. Many of these systems are conscious of one another for the first time in history, and first impressions are bound to be mixed. In any case, custom is diluted by the persistence of diverse practices and is at least shaken by the presence of a variety of custom-built structures. The need to attain an adjustable equilibrium between custom and statute and custom and custom is manifest and urgent, but the international legislative mechanism that could effect such an equilibrium continues to be absent. In the meantime, custom continues to decline in importance as a source of international law.

The same may be said of the scholarly commentary on the law. Time, of course, has eroded the role of the classic commentators, though Grotius, Vattel, Austin, and others continue to be consulted by international lawyers and judges. The works of contemporary scholars are also used in preparing briefs or decisions, but their credibility does not match that once enjoyed by the classic succession. Most important, the contemporaneousness of their work betokens the contemporaneousness of their biases, so that they are less acceptable as authorities than those temporally more distant. Furthermore, scholars and practitioners of international law have generally been overwhelmingly Western, and this alone is enough to make non-Westerners chary of the whole body of scholarly analysis and opinion.

For non-Westerners all the main sources of today's international law—court opinions and treaty law as well as custom and the commentators—bear the stamp of white parochialism. If international law aspires to become truly global law, it must take on the challenge emanating from the underdeveloped world—and from the communist world as well. The challenge is particularly acute in such areas as sovereign prerogatives, human rights, and property rights. International law cannot become an authentically global presence unless it evolves some distance away from traditional Western standards in these matters.

PROBLEMS OF JURISDICTION AND ENFORCEMENT

If we now compare the characteristics of jurisdiction in international and domestic law, the gap between the two grows still wider. Domestic law applies directly to individuals, since individuals are assumed to be the basic movers and creators of events to which the law must address itself. But in international society, law applies to states, with some few exceptions to be noted later. States interpose themselves between international law and their own citizens. The result is that international law is seldom able to reach down into a domestic society to prosecute or defend an individual or a group. With the exception of transnational courts established by the Council of Europe and the European Community, there are no procedures by which individuals or groups can gain direct access to an international court to obtain redress of grievances.[12] Despite the high-minded language of the UN Charter and the

---

[12] The Statute of the International Court of Justice (Article 34) leaves no room for doubt: "Only states may be parties in cases before the Court."

detailed provisions delineating the liberties of man in the Human Rights Declaration and Covenants, international organization is as yet unable to function as a competent global protector of individual rights.[13]

As far as the United Nations is concerned, it is evident that its founders did not wish it to fulfill such a function, for they incorporated into the Charter some blunt wording in Article 2, paragraph 7:

> Nothing in the present Charter shall authorize the United Nations to intervene in matters which are essentially within the domestic jurisdiction of any state or shall require the Members to submit such matters to settlement under the present Charter.

It is true that the word "essentially" has offered some leeway for differing interpretations of Charter duties in this area. It is also true that the final clause in paragraph 7 specifies that the nonintervention principle "shall not prejudice the application of enforcement measures under Chapter VII" of the Charter. These qualifying words and the broad mandates of the General Assembly and the Security Council to consider any purported threats to the peace from whatever source have been used to justify UN concern with the fate of groups and individuals within the borders of sovereign states—most notably Spain in the 1940s and, more recently, South Africa.

In the main, then, states are the subjects of international law. It follows that the subjects of international law are far stronger than the law itself; there are enough powerful subjects, in any case, to make the problem of enforcement first in importance. Domestic law, on the other hand, profits greatly from the fact that individuals living in a reasonably well-organized state are relatively powerless to resist the writ of law. Thus, in terms of the ratio of power between the law s guardians and the law's subjects, international and domestic society are evidently not only different but diametrical opposites. Hence the ability of the states to limit or deny the jurisdiction of international law and to permit international courts to decide only those issues in which judicial procedures would not be likely to inconvenience national policies.

In a situation in which the subject and not the court determines juris-

---

[13] The Universal Declaration of Human Rights was unanimously passed by the General Assembly of the United Nations in 1948 (South Africa and some of the Arab states abstained). As in the case with all General Assembly actions, this resolution was nonbinding. Eighteen years went by before implementing Covenants, one dealing with political and civil rights and one with economic, social, and cultural rights, were completed in 1966. They contain some mild prescriptions for international action in the event that a UN member, signatory to the Covenant, should then violate its provisions. Since a large percentage of the UN membership, including the United States, has not yet ratified or even signed the Covenants, their impact has been slight.

diction, there is logically no room for the principle of compulsory jurisdiction. This principle is one of the indispensable supports of a
functioning system of domestic law: if one individual institutes court
action against another, the defendant must appear in court. In international law, however, one state can hail another before a tribunal only
with the other state's consent. The qualifications to this statement that
accuracy requires are not very impressive. The Statute of the International Court of Justice (Article 36) provides the opportunity for states
that so desire to bind themselves to accept compulsory jurisdiction of the
ICJ in certain categories of "legal" disputes.[14] (They are labeled "legal"
because they concern such matters as treaty interpretation, interpretations of international law, or disagreements as to whether or not a breach
of international obligation has in fact taken place.) These provisions of
Article 36 go under the short name of the Optional Clause.

The restricted set of categories included in Article 36 confines the
principle of compulsory jurisdiction to narrow limits. It is further
circumscribed by the provision that each Optional Clause signatory is
obliged to accept compulsory jurisdiction of the Court only in respect
to other signatories. Thus a state that for some reason had not signed
the Optional Clause could rely only on voluntary will and not on obligation in getting a signatory into court on a matter covered under
Article 36.

Much more serious is the fact that the language of the statute has
permitted the states adhering to the Optional Clause to hedge their
commitments with all sorts of reservations. The most controversial of
these reservations was that demanded by the United States Senate (over
executive branch objections) and which is referred to as the Connally
Amendment. The amendment exempts from the Court's jurisdiction disputes "essentially within the domestic jurisdiction of the United States
of America as determined by the United States of America." In the first
place, the reservation is hardly warranted in view of the very restricted
subject matter the Court is declared competent to consider under the
Optional Clause. Second, the phrase "as determined by the United
States of America" is not only gratuitous but in conflict with the whole
spirit of Article 36 and particularly with Paragraph 6: "In the event of a
dispute as to whether the Court has jurisdiction, the matter shall be
settled by the decision of the Court." Finally, of course, what dispute
might not be defined as lying "essentially" within the domestic jurisdiction of the United States, particularly since the United States does the
defining?

It is this kind of nationalism, at once flamboyant and anxious—and in
this instance American—that has kept the work load of the ICJ far below
its capacity. In its first twenty-five years (1947–1972) the World Court

---

[14] As of mid-1972 forty-six states had so bound themselves. None were from the
Soviet bloc and relatively few from the underdeveloped world.

had been seized of only fifty-six cases. Of these, fourteen involved requests for advisory opinions by the Court. The remainder consisted of
"contentious" cases, so designated because the procedure is one of contest between litigants, requiring a ruling and not merely an opinion from
the Court. As of 1967, only twelve of the contentious cases had been
decided on their merits, and two were still pending. Of the remaining
twenty-four cases submitted before 1967, eight had been removed from
the Court's docket on jurisdictional grounds, six had been discontinued
by the litigants in pursuit of a settlement outside of court, six never got
beyond the preliminary objections stage, and four were unresolved and
withdrawn for a variety of reasons.[15] This meager record makes painfully
clear just how circumscribed the jurisdictional outreach of the World
Court has been.

In domestic society, the chief interpreters of the law are the courts.
The status of the World Court makes it clear that in international society
the powers of interpretation are distributed quite differently. With the
qualified exception of the permanent Court of International Arbitration,
the ICJ stands alone as a judicial body of global competence. It has
already been pointed out that a number of transnational courts have
been established on a regional basis by bilateral or multilateral treaty,
but they have no connection in fact or law to the ICJ.

Given the restrictions placed on the functions of the ICJ and the
regional courts, the foremost interpreters of international law are necessarily the nation-states themselves. The bulk of cases in international
law are tried in national courts, and national courts are most reluctant
to decide a case in any way that would conflict with their governments'
foreign policies. Hence the nation-state's key position as chief legal
interpreter: it interprets the law by modifying or refusing the jurisdiction of an international court and by virtue of its influence on the conduct of its own national courts.

The most obvious contrast between domestic and international law is
found in the realm of enforcement. In the civil state the executive arm of
government provides sanctions, policemen, and jails to punish violators
of the law. At the international level no such executive authority is available. The nations themselves provide the sanctions—if they feel they
have a stake in the issue at hand and if they are of a mind to press the

---

[15] The figures for 1947–1972 are taken from the International Court of Justice,
Yearbook, 1971–1972; (The Hague: 1972), pp. 12–14. The breakdown of cases ac-
cording to their outcome for the years 1947–1967 is taken from Leo Gross, "The
International Court of Justice and the United Nations," in *Recueil de Cours,
Académie du Droit International,* Vol. 120, 1967–I (Leyde: A. W. Sijthoff), pp.
332–333.

During the period from 1967 to 1972, there have been three new contentious cases
and two requests for advisory opinions before the ICJ. The Court rendered judgment
in one case and delivered one advisory opinion (declaring South Africa's presence
in South-West Africa, or Namibia, illegal). Final action on the other three items was
still pending in mid-1972.

matter. To illustrate the starkness of the situation, assume that Nation A wins a case against Nation B (in, say, the Permanent Court of Arbitration) and that B is recalcitrant and refuses to abide by the decision. Until the League of Nations Covenant went into effect, there was no way in which A could make B comply except by using its own coercive powers. No other nation nor any international body was obliged to aid A in enforcing the court's decision.

The League Covenant, however, did not materially alter the situation. Article 13 provided that the League Council would "propose steps" to be taken in case of noncompliance with a decision by the Permanent Court of International Justice (or by any judicial body officially recognized by the Council as competent). But the Council operated on the unanimity principle, a notoriously unpromising basis for vigorous executive action. In any case the Council never had to face a direct test of legal enforcement in its twenty-year history. The closest it came to such a predicament was in the matter of the Corfu incident of 1923.[16]

Article 94 of the United Nations Charter is the analogue to the Covenant's Article 13:

Each member of the United Nations undertakes to comply with the decision of the International Court of Justice in any case to which it is a party. If any party to a case fails to perform the obligations incumbent upon it under a judgment rendered by the Court, the other party may have recourse to the Security Council which may, if it deems necessary, make recommendations or decide upon measures to be taken to give effect to the judgment.

But the League's old unanimity requirement—now modified in the United Nations to apply only to the great power permanent members of the Security Council—remains to vitiate the promise of law enforcement. Moreover, the Charter's language in this area is somewhat less forceful than that of the Covenant. At all events, it continues to be possible for the Security Council to act as an enforcement agency of the World Court in matters of lesser consequence. But any issue affecting important East-West relationships, for example, would be sure to provoke the threat of veto.

Such relationships were very much involved in still another celebrated case involving the island of Corfu. This was the Corfu Channel Case, ironically, the first case (1947–1949) to be argued before the ICJ. The Court awarded Britain a judgment against Albania to compensate for loss of lives and damages suffered by British warships as the result of colliding with illegally placed Albanian mines. But since Albania was at

---

[16] In the Corfu incident Italy had bombarded and occupied the Greek island of Corfu in retaliation for the assassination of Italian nationals on Greek soil. Greece brought the matter before the Council, which then referred the legal aspects of the dispute to a specially selected Committee of Jurists—and not to the Permanent Court of International Justice. The Jurists' Committee responded with an ambiguous set of opinions, and the Council ultimately took no action on the Greek complaint.

the time still a loyal member of the Soviet bloc, it could defy the Court's ruling with impunity. Britain did not even bother to invoke Article 94, since it was sufficiently obvious that in the face of a certain Soviet veto the Security Council's executive power was nil.

Nor were the British prepared to collect from Albania by means of such "self-help" measures as the classic expedient of gunboat diplomacy. Given the formidable presence of the Soviet Union in Southeast Europe as well as in the Security Council, any such action could only be deemed foolhardy. While there have been no further instances of open defiance of Court rulings, the Corfu Channel Case pointed up the lesson that the Court is helpless in making its judgments stick whenever great power, and especially superpower, politics are involved. In this area of international law enforcement the situation remains fundamentally the same as it was before the emergence in 1919 of the League of Nations and the Permanent Court of International Justice and then of their successor institutions after World War II.

SOVEREIGNTY

All the legislative, jurisdictional, adjudicatory, and law enforcement problems that beset international law are inextricably intertwined with the phenomenon of sovereignty. From the time of Grotius, international law grew up, as it were, with the concept of sovereignty. And, as we have noted on several occasions, sovereignty affirms the primacy of the national parts over the international whole. The state aspiring to sovereignty seeks to control its own destiny. It has customarily sought to realize these aspirations by safeguarding the independence of its political and social system from outside influences. Above all, particularly in regard to the policy- and decision-making processes, it adheres to the proposition (much more ancient than the concept of sovereignty itself) that the sovereign will knows no law beyond its own. Such a proposition is in irreconcilable conflict with the building of transnational institutions embodying the legislative, judicial, and executive functions necessary to any authentic rule of law.

If one looks at the history of modern international law, it is evident that for most of the period since Grotius, legal rulings and theorists have simultaneously broadened the claim of sovereignty and narrowed the scope of law's relevance to international relations. Grotius' confident assumption that states have binding legal obligations to one another is replaced by Austin's proposition that international law is not authentic law at all—precisely because it lacks the sanctions to enforce obligations. The just war concept falls away, and in its place stands the nineteenth-century doctrine that any state has the right to make war for any reason it deems sufficient.

It is true that there has been a revival of the just-war concept in the twentieth century. It is embodied in the League Covenant, the UN Charter, and the Nuremberg trials. But it must contend, as always, with the resourceful imaginations of states and leaderships determined to use violence and equally determined to find some legitimating justification for their behavior. And like any other attempt to restrict the sovereign will, it must also contend with the precept as old as Thrasymachus that justice equals the interest of the stronger—and with the variant wisdom of contemporary legal realists like Julius Stone, who assert that law is what the victor says it is.

The uneven contest of sovereign power with international law is obviously not a product of the doctrines of international legal theorists. The chief author of this drama of confrontation in the modern world has been the nation-state. The success story of sovereignty is fundamentally the success story of nationalism which managed to build, on an explicitly parochial basis, the most productive, flexible, and egalitarian societies men had yet known. For more and more people, since the eighteenth century, the nation-state provided a reasonably satisfactory context in which to fulfill human needs for security, economic welfare, and cultural and psychological satisfactions. Despite the recurrence of big and little wars, people in the states of the Western world—and it was the West that called the tune in world politics—flourished well enough. There was no felt need to change the system and, of course, the need was felt least by those whom the system benefited most.

Even the sequential catastrophes of two world wars and their shattering demonstrations of sovereign nationalism's capacities for destruction created no real disposition to alter the traditional framework of international society. The prospect for new departures in the case of both the League and the UN depended from first to last on the way in which the great powers made use of them. The failure of the League and the fact that the United Nations continues to function at the periphery of most of the great issues of world politics testify to the lack of will and imagination on the part of the strongest nations. But they also testify to the obstacles that the system of sovereignty generally places in the way of a community of mankind.

They demonstrate, further, that too few people in places of power have deemed the present and potential dangers of the traditional system so acute as to require a massive alteration of that system. The problems generated by nuclear arsenals, transnational ideologies, shrinking distances between peoples, the poverty that torments and provokes more than two-thirds of mankind—all these dwarf the dimensions of sovereign nationalism and clamor for the elaboration of transcending concepts of law and justice. But the clamor has not yet met with harmonizing responses; nor will they emerge until the nation ceases to be a sovereign end and is seen instead as a means to fashion a larger human community.

REGIONALISM AND LAW

If the prospects for law and justice remain dim at the global level, they are much brighter in the regional context. Here, since World War II, Western Europe has led the way. This leadership was momentous and remarkable in view of the heritage of enmity between France and Germany and the fresh and terrible wounds each had suffered just before the work of reconciliation was begun. But World War II and its aftermath had driven Western Europe into such desperate circumstances that only one meaningful choice remained: either to turn toward reconciliation and unity or give up all hope of having an effective voice in its own destiny. In this context it became evident, in some areas at least, that national sovereignty undermines rather than guarantees the capacity for autonomous social, cultural, and political expression. The legally sovereign and "victor" nations of Western Europe could no more cope on their own with the aftermath of one war and the imminent threat of another than could a defeated, occupied, and divided Germany.

Militarily and politically, the threat came from the Soviet Union. Economically, it came from the decimated and exhausted peoples, the devastated physical plant, and the shortage of capital in Europe itself. The shrunken markets and populations of all the European nations when compared to the newly dominant superpowers made it evident that European preeminence in both power and wealth was irretrievably lost. In these circumstances, national boundaries had become a palpable disadvantage in the struggle to reestablish viable political systems and reconstruct shattered economies. Recovery at an extraordinary rate of progress was possible only as a result of unprecedented intra-European cooperation. It also required an unprecedented flow of extra-European capital—some $17 billion in the form of outright grants over a four-year period (1948-1952) from the United States under the aegis of the Marshall Plan. (The Soviet Union rejected the American invitation to participate in the Marshall Plan and prevented all countries under its control from taking part.)[17]

The experiences and pressures that Europe suffered in the early postwar years generated a whole series of efforts to remove some of the most crippling legacies of the system of sovereignty. The Organization for

---

[17] The Soviets charged that the Marshall proposal was a scheme devised by American imperialists to subordinate Europe to the control of Washington and Wall Street. Moscow's response was not unanticipated, which accounts in part for the rather lukewarm character of the original American bid to the Kremlin. But the major stumbling block in extending the recovery program to all of Europe was the conviction on Stalin's part that Moscow stood to benefit from the prolongation of European weakness and despair that he believed, with the customary cruelty of his brand of logic, would be conducive to further and spectacular gains for the cause of communism.

European Economic Cooperation embraced all the recipient countries participating in the Marshall Plan (and later the United States, Canada, and other countries of Western Europe and, under the new name Organization for Economic Cooperation and Development, Japan). This was the first large-scale intergovernmental enterprise in cooperative economic planning for recovery and development.

The Schuman Plan followed, binding together six Western European countries (France, Germany, Italy, Belgium, the Netherlands, and Luxembourg) in a customs and production union of their coal and steel industries, the European Coal and Steel Community. Known subsequently as the Six, these key countries proceeded to negotiate a more comprehensive framework for collaboration which took form in 1957 in the Treaty of Rome. This treaty marked the birth of the European Economic Community (EEC, or Common Market) whose purpose was not only to integrate all aspects of the members' economies into a single union but also —more cautiously—to lay the groundwork for a measure of political federation. At the same time, EURATOM was established to provide for collaboration among the Six in research and production for peaceful purposes of nuclear energy. The European Free Trade Association (EFTA) was a more limited counterpart to the Common Market, devised in 1959 by the still sovereignty-conscious British. EFTA required gradual elimination of tariffs among its members, but no commitment to genuine economic integration.[18]

Even without examining the details of the structure and history of these transnational institutions, it is evident that they represent the kind of activity conducive to the growth of transnational law. This is especially true of the institutions and policy guidelines of the EEC. In addition to providing for a common external tariff, the Treaty of Rome lays down a common policy for dealing with monopolies, price fixing, restraint of trade, and certain aspects of production. It pledges members to develop common standards to govern working conditions, social security, and bargaining between employers and employees. And it has created institutions to facilitate the development and policing of the

---

[18] In addition to Britain, the founding EFTA members were Norway, Sweden, Denmark, Austria, Switzerland, and Portugal. They were later joined by Iceland and by Finland, as an EFTA associate.

On July 22, 1972, EFTA effected a partial merger with the Common Market in a series of treaties that provided for the gradual establishment of free trade, but not full economic integration, among all members of the two groups. On January 1, 1973, Britain and Denmark, together with Ireland, became full members of the Common Market group.

The future of EFTA, now much diminished geographically and in economic function and power, will depend in large degree on relations with its giant Common Market neighbor.

commonly accepted obligations in the familiar form of executive, legislative, and judicial organs.

If the forms are familiar, however, they are also embryonic and their institutional authority is severely limited. The weakness of the European Parliament and the strength of the Council of Ministers (where each member government has a weighted vote in most issues and a veto in some) underlines the reluctance to dismantle national sovereignty too rapidly. At the same time, and despite its unevenness, the growth in power and stature of the Common Market's executive commission and, under its aegis, the concomitant growth of the "Eurocracy" into a complex European administrative and regulatory institution testify to the attractions of supranational solutions and to the permeability and mortality of national sovereignty.

Above all, the establishment of a Community Court of Justice, acting under very much the same grants of authority (but in a much more restricted framework) as the United States Supreme Court, was an extraordinary step in the subordination of national sovereignty to transnational law. The Court of Justice has the power to decide disputes between member states and to determine violations of the treaties making up the Community. Thus it acts as a high constitutional court whose rulings the member governments are bound to obey (and which so far none has defied). At least as important is the Community Court's breach of one of the major defenses of sovereignty: the barrier that sovereignty places between international law and the individual human being. The Court's charter provides that individuals, and not just member states, have direct access to the Court for the purpose of challenging acts of the commission or of member states. It follows that access is also open to corporations and, indeed, to any legal person in the Community.

These remarkable innovations in legal relationships are products of a will to alter the dimensions of political community. While the progress of the Six toward union has been primarily economic, it has gone forward only because of the assumption that the members of EEC would never again exercise the preeminently political option of making war upon one another. As the degree of economic integration has increased, any realistic prospect that a member state might abandon that assumption and reassert its war-making sovereignty against its fellow members has vanished. In their efforts to become a single economic entity, the EEC members have had to move toward establishing a network of transnational legal regulations and institutions similar to those that govern the internal economic life of still-sovereign nations. While EEC still has a long way to go in this respect, the legal structures and procedures already in operation forecast what the more elaborate institutions will look like if the goal of full integration is attained.

Both the successes and the failures of the Common Market and other

European organizations demonstrate with equal persuasiveness that the rule of law cannot assert itself without a sustaining commitment to political community. In no other area of the world does the will to move away from nationalism and toward transnationalism appear with anything like the intensity it has manifested in Western Europe. Consequently, one does not find in Asia, Africa, the Western Hemisphere, or even within the Soviet–East European bloc any comparable body of transnational law or the complex of regulatory and judicial procedures that gives it force. The Central American Common Market is as close an analogue to the EEC as the rest of the globe offers. But it is comprised of economies that are far less complex, and it continues to be plagued by such virulent manifestations of nationalism as the 1969 war between Honduras and Salvador.

No region on earth matches Western Europe in the degree of confidence that regional neighbors will not use violence against one another. This confidence rests not only on the economic and legal commitments represented by the Common Market and its other primarily economic organizations but also, of course, on the collaborative military arrangements made for the common defense and governed by the provisions of the Western European Union and the North Atlantic Treaty.

The role of the military component in the transnational structure of Western Europe points up the inescapable truth that one must deal holistically with communities; in the final analysis, the whole is crucial and the parts are secondary. Far-reaching economic collaboration among a given group of nations cannot be achieved unless there is a considerable degree of political trust among them. Transnational law can make headway only if its potential subjects calculate that their interests will be benefited, or at least not harmed, by it. Enduring military collaboration on a highly integrated basis requires a conviction that the collaborators are engaged in an association of life and death, that survival is not possible unless the principle is maintained that a threat to one part of the community endangers all parts.[19]

The building of a community must necessarily be a package deal. There must be a degree of readiness to abandon or modify old forms of community in virtually all significant areas of social existence. The embracing of a new community involves developing a whole spectrum of new loyalties and at least leaving moot the question whether these new loyalties may one day supersede the old. When the parties to such transactions in radical political change are nation-states, either long-

---

[19] It should be noted that France resigned from the North Atlantic Treaty *Organization* in 1968 but not from the North Atlantic *Treaty*, of which it remains a member in good standing. The French move was motivated in part by the desire to decrease the role of integrated military cooperation, of which NATO was the institutionalization. But France continues military collaboration with its treaty partners, particularly Western Germany, on a restricted basis.

established or newly formed, it should be clear that transnational unions can be successfully developed only with extreme difficulty.

Western Europe may go considerably further along the path to economic and political integration, but the obstacles are formidable. Prospects within the next decade or two for unions in other areas of the globe to achieve even the present level of Europe's integration are not encouraging. Hence it would be a mistake to hold up Western Europe as a model for other regions.

It would be a still graver mistake to hold up Western Europe as a model for the world as a whole. The network of transnational law that is growing in Europe is the product of a comparatively high degree of community awareness and commitment on a regional basis. The awareness of an inclusive global community, on the other hand, is not shared very widely, tends to be sporadic even among those who share it, and lacks the convenient focus that comes more easily to organizations that are regionally exclusive and functionally specific. It follows that the role of law must be very different in the global context than in either highly or loosely integrated regional organizations.

LAW AND POLITICS

Whether the context is regional or global, the act of submission to law is a matter grave enough to make all candidates hesitate. After all, law implies uniformity, order, universality, permanence, conformity, and strict restraints on coercion. Contemporary international politics, in contrast, is characterized by variety, disorder, parochialism, rapid change, and weak restraints on coercive practices. The antagonism between these two sets of characteristics is a measure of the distance that still separates law from politics in international life.

As we noted earlier, there is an abundance of international law in good working order to deal with the routine problems that beset interstate relations. But it is in terms of its ability to deal effectively with matters of great dispute, to prevent the outbreak of violence, and to build a structure of peaceful settlement that law is essentially absent from the international scene.

Law presupposes generalized compulsion, and we have seen that in the global system there is no general executive endowed with the power to do the compelling. However, neither the degree of variety among nations nor the perversity of sovereign attitudes is enough to explain this deficiency. One cannot understand the full reluctance of states to undertake legal obligations without stressing that law is the most rigid of all sets of rules. Morality is subject to interpretation by the individual conscience, by ecclesiastical laws, or by both, and these are usually devoid of physical sanctions. Political agreements or diplomatic treaties are generally ad hoc, of restricted duration, and limited to specific parties. But law strives to be universal. It requires obedience from all within its jurisdiction and instruments of coercion to impose that obedience. And it assumes its own timelessness; or, to put it in other words, there is a time-honored presumption that the law is not easily changed. Hence states accustomed to independence, including those which recognize that national sovereignty is no longer a viable answer to their problems, remain chary of the obligations and compulsions of law.

It may be useful at this point to push the issue of the compulsory nature of law one step further by making the obvious but nonetheless necessary point that in any sociopolitical context it is desirable to set limits to generalized compulsion. Thus it would be unwise to attempt to arrive at—as well as impossible to achieve—a situation in which law would be substituted for all forms of political relationships. Such a substitution would be the most complete realization yet witnessed of the tyrant's precept that everything not forbidden is compulsory.

The implication should be clear: law can be a dangerous as well as benign technique for social regulation. It can be a weapon of injustice as well as justice. There are areas into which a free society ought not to let law penetrate; hence the Bill of Rights appended to the United States Constitution is largely an exercise in barring the law's entry into certain spheres of American life: "The Congress shall make no law." In a word, law has played and ought to play an important but limited role in every domestic society. It has a long-range chance to do the same, but no more, in international society. If one is going to approach the problems of international relations creatively, exploring avenues of realistic and constructive change, one needs to understand that limitations on the role of law are not only inevitable but desirable.

If it is a mistake to try to banish politics in favor of legal norms, it is more dangerous in the immediate sense to go the opposite route and politicize the law. The idealists who pursue the vision of a world governed in all essential respects by the rule of law are only a minority of a minority. But it is the self-styled realists in international law—as in international politics—that represent the mainstream of contemporary international thought, and they have rendered law and politics almost indistinguishable. This erasure of the boundaries between politics and law is the more ominous in that it takes place largely within the context of a politics understood as the pursuit of power, and of power defined as the capacity to coerce. As noted in the opening chapters, these definitions have the effect of removing justice from the province of politics. It follows that the equation of law and politics under these circumstances necessarily removes justice from the province of law as well.

The legal realists in international relations have striven to carve out a significant niche for law in a context admittedly hostile to juridical order. Persuaded of the desirability of expanding the role of law as a means of diminishing the likelihood of arbitrary and violent acts, they have not been content to let international law remain at the level of housekeeping arrangements. In this attitude the realists themselves display an unmistakable idealism. But in their endeavor to make law relevant to the high politics of the global system, they strip law of essential characteristics and graft onto it characteristics that obscure its identity still further.

Richard Falk, for example, observes that "The range of [legal] norms includes rules of the game and very specific provisions in international agreements." He then adds, "My own preference is to extend the characterization 'law' to any 'norm' that appears to standardize international behavior."[20] This is a noteworthy eclecticism. It derives norms of international law from any kind of international transaction so long as it functions to standardize behavior, but it does not inquire into the quality of the standards set. Such a characterization of law must indifferently legalize cooperative and hostile patterns of interaction to the extent that they exhibit precedent-setting qualities. This is quite in line with the dominant theories in contemporary law, both domestic and international, which assert that law is what people agree to do—with the often explicit commentary appended that what is really meant is: what the most powerful people agree to do.

Insofar as law is seen as a servant of peace—and justice—attempts to neutralize its bias in favor of these values must be resisted. By the same token, the capacity to discriminate among the patterns of behavior that law should or should not incorporate into its normative structure must be protected. This obviously cannot be done if the option is for wholesale eclecticism. Falk's selection of concrete behavior patterns as candidates for the status of legal norms effectively illustrates the problem:

Law provides a convenient way for political rivals to specify limits of permissible behavior. If the consequence of unrestrained conflict is mutually destructive then it is rational to seek common limits that will prevent such unrestrained conflict from taking place. For instance, in the Korean War supply centers behind the Yalu and in Japan were both exempted from military attack. . . .

Cold War rivals are intimidated by the probable fulfillment of collective self-defense commitments and the fear of a retaliation that includes nuclear devastation.[21]

---

[20] Richard A. Falk, "Revolutionary Nations and the Quality of International Legal Order," in Morton A. Kaplan (ed.), *The Revolution in World Politics* (New York: Wiley, 1962), pp. 311–312, footnote 3.

[21] Ibid., pp. 311, 322.

It is, of course, true that law is a convenient way to define permissible behavior, for both allies as well as rivals. The difficulty with these examples is that the political rivals involved have not relied on law to influence each other's behavior but on the threat of unilateral force. The trans-Yalu and Japanese sanctuaries during the Korean War existed by virtue of a military-political, ad hoc, tacit understanding between warring opponents. The enemy sanctuary was not attacked for fear that retaliation in force would cancel out any immediate gains by subsequent losses. Moreover, since the sanctuaries were located on the highly sensitive national territories of China and Japan, those policy makers on both sides who wanted to contain the war had a mutual stake in observing each other's off-limits signs.

But this was an exercise in military deterrence and power politics, not in law. The misnomer is still more apparent in Falk's reference to the global confrontation of alliances and nuclear arsenals. These juxapositions are ordinarily described as balance of power and equilibrium of forces, compounded by the nuclear age into the balance of terror. To turn them into legal concepts because they undoubtedly pattern and restrain behavior is rather like pinning sheriff's badges on rival bands of vigilantes. After all, political-military confrontations at both global and vigilante levels can provoke as well as restrain those involved. Moreover, each side is free to abandon the tacit agreement whenever it seems advantageous to do so—in effect, whenever one side has become so strong that it no longer fears the other.

One can hope that no such eventuality will occur in the realm of nuclear weapons. But this hope ought not to obscure the principal point at issue: whether one can equate a pattern of law with a pattern of mutual fear of mutual force. What nullifies the equation is the by now all too familiar deficiency: a sense of community among the rivals. Enmity has always been the keynote of the kinds of stand-off confrontations Falk cites, and enmity is a notorious scourge of community. The arrangements that the participants make from time to time to try to keep the confrontations from getting out of hand are calculated by each side in terms of maximum gain for one's own interests and maximum loss for the opposition. Each side would like to harm the other more if only it safely could. Military or political stand-offs may, of course, permit contingent conditions to develop that are favorable to the growth of legal norms, but the stand-off phenomenon itself is precommunity and prelegal.

So long as there is no recognition of responsibility to the community but only to the self, there can be nothing properly called law. Instead there is either a condition of tyranny or one of anarchy. While anarchy is the state usually ascribed to international relations, tyranny is equally applicable in the sense that it is here where the weak are most vulnerable to despotic rule by the strong. It is terror and the fear of terror in the anarchic-despotic system that defeats community and, therefore, law. The formula works both ways: law cannot prosper in the absence of community; neither depotism nor anarchy can prosper in its presence.

LAW, COMMUNITY, AND JUSTICE

The formula that identifies community as a condition of law is a measure of the obstacles that stand in the way of an effective international legal order. It spotlights once again the weakness of the community impulse at the global level. So doing, it challenges the advocates of "world peace through world law"—those who argue for the early adoption of comprehensive global legislation in all categories of issues that might result in armed conflict. For without first undertaking the prerequisite exercise in community-building, the slow task of dismantling the barriers of enmity and fear that divide the peoples of the world, one cannot hope to unite them through gestures in law making.

Community cannot be legislated, although legislation can strengthen a community already in process of growth. Desire for community is the seedbed of law, and the greater the commitment to a common destiny, the more solid the legal structure uniting those who are so committed. All these considerations suggest that law should be understood less as the cornerstone and more as the capstone of society. Indeed, the willingness to subordinate oneself to a system governed by legal regulation is the ultimate political commitment because the society (or individual) so committed has confided its very survival to a larger and more powerful institution. A stable rule of law requires that the law's subjects share the conviction that common interests are held widely and profoundly enough to warrant entrusting the largest part of their welfare and safety to the decisions of others. This kind of conviction, in turn, rests on the belief that trust will not be rewarded with oppression or violence.

Community is thus a delicate and intricate phenomenon. Law, as a code that defines what the community members must, may, and must not do, is the most explicit and detailed—and in this sense the most highly developed—statement of the terms of the community contract. Where the sense of community is nonexistent or weak, one can anticipate that legal relationships will be minimal. In the absence of community-building efforts, the obstacles to furthering the development of law will be insuperable. Efforts to build community, in turn, cannot be regarded as casual or goodwill undertakings, since any effective exertions in this direction must necessarily be of a revolutionary nature. This is so because the building of community requires the dismantling of sovereignty. The state of nature–social contract theorists applied this proposition to the relationship between the individual and the civil society; it holds no less true for the state and international society.

We have noted that the system of sovereignty is deeply embedded in the world's values for both good and bad reasons and with both good and bad effects. Its replacement with a system animated by a growing commitment to transnational community requires a series of political decisions by the sovereign partners and a consolidation of political will among them. All this would have to precede the emergence of a community legislature that could persuasively represent a transnational community allegiance.

If the forms that make law obligatory must wait until a relatively late stage in the evolution of community, the spirit that makes men willing voluntarily to bind themselves to law must initiate and power the evolution. This is the same spirit of justice described earlier as one that values all men as ends in themselves. Such a concept is necessarily at war with the concept of sovereignty, because sovereignty rates at full value only those human beings who pledge allegiance to it. Moreover, it values them primarily in terms of their contribution to the power of sovereignty, and not as ends in themselves.

This is the ancient theme of parochialism, which has dominated the political life of men throughout history and of which sovereignty is only a modern expression. Hence the problem posed by sovereignty is nothing fundamentally new. But it cannot be sufficiently stressed that sovereignty has become deeply entwined in the premises of modern international law. The result is that the claims of international law to universality have been eroded by its own parochial assumptions, and the legal ideal of dispensing justice has been negated by the system of sovereign self-worship.

Thus the body of precepts and rulings that make up contemporary international law are generally misleading and unhelpful if one aspires to an authentic rule of law for a transnational society. Despite Grotius' assertion that he wrote "on behalf of justice," the overlap between international law and justice has been minimal. The analysis by Kaplan and Katzenbach of the factors that lend the international legal system at least some effectiveness is strikingly illustrative of this point:

> Such a decentralized system is not utterly chaotic, and state officials do not have unlimited discretion to act arbitrarily. They are deterred from doing so by many considerations: a consciousness of the general need for order and stability in the conduct of foreign relations and the rules regulating transnational problems; the fact that many rules have reciprocal advantages; the existence of widely shared techniques of legal reasoning and argumentation; the desire not to offend other states for a variety of reasons, including the possibility of incurring various sanctions.[22]

---

[22] Morton A. Kaplan and Nicholas de B. Katzenbach, *The Political Foundations of International Law* (New York: Wiley, 1961), pp. 20–21.

The accuracy of the appraisal cannot be doubted. No more can it be doubted that justice has vanished altogether from this list of motivations for legal behavior. Stripped to its essentials, the list specifies the desirability of law and order, in peace and war; reciprocal advantages derived from adhering to many of the rules, especially for those who formulate them; the convenience of perpetuating an established legal ideology; and, finally, the fear of conflict and force. Here is no law which, say, promotes freedom, defends equality, nurtures social obligation, protects the weak, or combats oppression, except perhaps by inadvertence. It is a law designed for the cold world of Machiavelli and Hobbes, in which sovereigns consent to nothing except what they consider convenient to their own interests.

International law has never had any real capability for the effective pursuit of justice precisely because it has been legislated by sovereigns who intended to retain their sovereignty. Sovereigns reserve to themselves the privilege of deciding where legality and morality lie in the great issues of war and peace. This is one of the reasons why more than fifty years of labor by politicians and experts under the aegis of the League and then of the United Nations have failed to produce an agreed definition of aggression that an international body could then apply to specific cases. In principle, the sovereign rejects any restrictions on its external behavior except those to which it has given its consent. And since what it consents to in one set of circumstances may be inconvenient in another, the sovereign power is wary of any act that might suggest the setting of a precedent. Thus, as we have seen, international law is denied that accumulation of precedent and statute without which no legal system can be viable. It is this fundamental infirmity that invited Julius Stone's observation, cited earlier, that the institutions of international law are at the mercy of each successive military victor.

Sovereign power is arbitrary power. This holds true for the internal life of the state as well as for its external behavior. The very real military, political, and economic premiums on national unity have historically supported the state's claim to exclusive control over all that goes on within its own borders and immunity from external interference. (Like almost everything else in the disheartening story of international law, this claim is not the result of idiot choice but is a more or less practical response to a practical situation. Hence the difficulty of altering the response patterns.) The recent scattered and sometimes successful efforts to invoke the UN Charter and the Human Rights Conventions in the domestic courts of the United States and other countries still do not constitute a serious challenge to the internal juridical supremacy of the sovereign state.

The most dramatic rebuff to such a challenge was handed down by the International Court of Justice itself in its 1966 ruling in the South-West Africa (Namibia) case. By an eight to seven vote, the ICJ ruled that the plaintiffs, Ethiopia and Liberia, had no proper legal standing before the Court (in this particular issue) and on these grounds refused to judge the case on its substantive merits. Here, of course, the issue did not even concern the internal jurisdiction of South Africa proper in regard to racial oppression, but only its policies within the South-West African territory that it has administered since receiving it as a mandate from the League of Nations in 1920. By denying legal standing to the plaintiffs on highly debatable grounds, the majority of justices prevented the Court from considering whether or not the practice of apartheid conflicts with the mandate obligation to "promote to the utmost the material and moral well-being and the social progress" of the inhabitants (75,000 white, 451,000 nonwhite). It also avoided a judgment as to whether South Africa is obliged to accept UN supervision of its administration of South-West Africa.

Further, the Court reversed itself (certainly it was a reversal in logic and equity though the matter is arguable in terms of legal technicality). In 1962 it had rejected, also by an eight to seven vote, the South African contention that Ethiopia and Liberia had no proper legal standing before the Court; in 1966 it used the legal standing argument to bring to a close the Court's consideration of the case and effectively to deny all judicial relief in the matter.

The ICJ decision profoundly discouraged hopes that international law would at last begin to address itself to issues of social justice. But the majority could with reason assert that in the absence of relevant international legislation the capability as well as the authority of the Court to adjudicate must necessarily be severely limited. Indeed, the president of the Court resorted to that familiar argument of the judicial conservatives in the American legal system that judges ought only to be judges and not legislators. In international law the states are the prime legislators and the prime executors, and what they will not do judges certainly cannot do for them. To put it bluntly, who was going to enforce a Court ruling against South Africa? Or was the Court to repeat the humiliating experience of the Corfu Channel Case, in which its decision was defied with impunity by Albania because no one was willing to back law with the requisite power?

The issue of Namibia reverted to the United Nations, and in the fall of 1966 the General Assembly voted a resolution terminating the South African mandate and declaring that Namibia was henceforth to be the "direct responsibility" of the UN. The resolution was without practical effect. In 1970 the Security Council also declared South Africa's continuing presence in Namibia illegal, but authorized no sanctions that could give the declaration force. Instead, resort was once again made to the World Court, this time for an advisory opinion on the matter. On June 21, 1971, the ICJ ruled (thirteen to two) that South Africa was indeed illegally occupying Namibia.

As we have seen, however, advisory opinions by the Court do not have the status of Court rulings and thus do not even raise the issue of enforcement action. Hence the Court joined the Security Council and the General Assembly; all went on record as recognizing a breach of international law without taking any measures that could effectively punish the lawbreaker or otherwise vindicate the law as they themselves had defined it. On the initiative of the new UN secretary-general, Kurt Waldheim, the Namibia issue entered another phase in 1972. Dr. Waldheim made a personal visit to South Africa and South-West Africa and obtained an agreement from the South African government to cooperate with a special UN representative in discussions of Namibia's future. The effect was to transfer the issue from the realm of law and formal resolutions to the realm of diplomatic negotiations.

Whatever the outcome of the effort at diplomacy, it is evident that South Africa has successfully defied majority-defined norms of international law and majority votes in both houses of the United Nations. The UN's appointed representative functions neither as prosecutor, judge, nor policeman; he has instead the political task of ascertaining whether any combination of threats and inducements can persuade South Africa to alter its behavior. In a word, he functions as a diplomat, the life of whose mission depends on the continuing willingness of South Africa to tolerate his work and presence. Once again, sovereign prerogative has won its ancient argument with international law. If there is ever a resolution of the Namibia issue, the outcome will be decided not according to the writ of law but by the relative strength of the political pressures mobilized by those sovereign states choosing to involve themselves.

For the most part confined to the world of sovereigns and barred from the relations characteristic of community, traditional international law is simply not equipped to deal with such major global issues as social and racial injustice, inequitable distribution of wealth, or protection against exploitation. Yet these are the kinds of issues on which the fate of the world will turn. They received unprecedented emphasis in the UN Charter and then were raised still more forcefully in the Declaration and the Covenants on Human Rights. But their resolution still awaits implementing legislation.

In order to be effective, such legislation cannot be identified—certainly not in the first instance—with the formalities of the statutory process. What is needed instead is a larger kind of lawmaking which finds expression in partly formal and partly implicit agreements that a given set of major and long-range transnational problems are going to be solved jointly or not at all—and that nonsolution spells catastrophe. However tacit and partial the character of such agreements, the result would be a constitutional commitment to an evolving transnational community. International law "on behalf of justice" will begin to develop on the day such a commitment is made.

Chapter 11

International
Organization

If one locates diplomacy, international law, and international organization along the spectrum of micro-macropolitics, there is a discernible progression, with international organization relatively closer to the macro end of the scale. One can hardly speak of proximity, however, for the contemporary forms and practices of international organization so far represent only the most modest (and sometimes counterfeit) steps in the direction of macropolitics.

Yet it is clear that both of the global international organizations of the twentieth century were founded with more far-reaching purposes in mind. In the League of Nations and in the United Nations the intent was to move away from the unrestricted state sovereignty characteristic of micropolitics and to place certain international restraints upon national behavior. Even though many of the restraints have turned out to be deceptive, only quasi-effective, or simply inoperative, it is still significant that for the first time since the eclipse of the natural law doctrine, the principle of untrammeled sovereignty no longer goes unchallenged.

The twentieth-century critiques of sovereignty drew their force first of all from the mass suffering and horror that convulsed virtually the entire globe in the course of two world wars. During the thirty-one years from 1914 to 1945, ten years of total war cost more than 60 million lives, countless numbers of maimed, diseased, starving, and homeless human beings, cultural and economic losses beyond measure, and the collapse of states, regimes, and whole societies. The nuclear climax at Hiroshima gave warning that still another resort to unrestrained violence on a global scale would magnify the terror to apocalyptic proportions.[1] It is

---

[1] The Charter of the United Nations was drafted in the spring of 1945 and signed in San Francisco on June 26, 1945. It was therefore completed even before the first successful (and secret) atomic explosion test in Alamagordo, New Mexico, in July, and six weeks before Hiroshima. Hence the drafters of the Charter, with the exception of those privy to the secret of the American atomic effort, were not affected by forebodings concerning the potential of nuclear weapons. But once their appalling powers of destruction became manifest, the fear of nuclear war assumed a dominant role in the evolution of the United Nations as well as in the international system as a whole.

292

therefore understandable that those who founded the League and later the United Nations should have been preoccupied with the control of violence.

Such a preoccupation may be justly criticized on the basis that it is concerned with symptoms and not causes of international disorders. But a frontal attack on causes would have required a massive restructuring of the whole of international society. Despite the ravages of world war, those in power among the victors were wholly unready in 1919 or 1945 to consider so drastic a step. Even had the will existed in the places of power, it could not have been expressed with any rationality or justice in documents drafted during the first months of armistice or, in 1945, during the last months of war. In both cases the majority of the world was absent from the proceedings; the losers had no voice, and the colonial world virtually none.

Besides, only subsequent events began to reveal those deeper causes of organized violence in international relations which had long been obscured by the military and economic supremacy of Europe and by the subjection of the world's nonwhite majority to an unyielding white colonialism. In the case of the United Nations, nuclear weapons, the population explosion, consciousness of the disastrously inequitable division of the world's wealth, and the unprecedented intensification on a global scale of racial and ethnic hatreds were all post-Charter phenomena. Such problems could not be meaningfully addressed by papers drafted and signed in 1945, but only as they emerged in subsequent history and darkened the horizon enough to command widespread attention.

Thus the constitution makers of both Covenant and Charter conceived of their tasks primarily as exercises in the inhibition and control of violence. It is true that those who wrote the Charter were much more conscious of the whole spectrum of social and economic issues underlying political violence than were the drafters of the Covenant. But their chief task remained the same: to keep the lid on the use of force in politics without changing the other rules of the game in any essential way. It was within this narrow frame of reference that the attack on sovereignty (such as it was) took place.

THE COLLECTIVE SECURITY EMPHASIS

Collective security was therefore the centerpiece in the efforts of both the League and the UN to organize and regulate the conduct of international relations. The common premise was that the security of the individual state could no longer be adequately safeguarded by the doctrine of self-help that governed the inherited practice of both diplomacy and international law. Consequently, nations were invited to subscribe to a set of rules that, insofar as they reflected collective security doctrines, would transform every dispute that threatened war between individual states into a concern of the entire international community. The appropriate institutions of the community would decide the dispute on its merits and with a view to protecting the legitimate interests of both parties. Then, if one party elected to defy the community decision and attack the other, the aggressor would be punished by the overwhelming power of the remaining members of the community. By the same token, the party abiding by the community decision would enjoy an invincible defense against aggression. As Korea so cruelly demonstrated, however, it may pay a terrible price until the community forces are assembled in sufficient strength to prevail.

The drafters of Covenant and Charter, of course, hoped that the threat of community reprisal would usually be sufficient to deter aggression. But they were not so incautious as to permit the freedom of action of the individual members to be left in doubt—to be suspended between the hope that threats alone could prevent aggression and the fear that collective security might in fact require full-scale military operations against aggressors. They resolved the issue, as we shall see, by watering down the principle of collective security until it was compatible once more with the principle of sovereignty. That is, in both Covenant and Charter, the concept of community response to aggression was transformed, with some qualifications, back into the traditional formula of individual response to aggression by the various states in accordance with the sovereign interests of each.

The connection between the international organizations of the twentieth-century and their nineteenth-century predecessor, the Concert of Europe, is clear. The Concert system also subscribed to the proposition that there must be some common supervision of resorts to force. But the Concert did not aspire to go beyond the micropolitical premises of the balance of power. That is, peace was deemed generally preferable to war, but the great states dominating the Concert had no intention of letting the desirability of peace obstruct their tenacious pursuit of power, empire, and self-glorification. It follows that they sought to guide their policies in terms of the exigencies of power; they were far more concerned with the effects of any given dispute on the European power structure than with the intrinsic merits at issue or with the threat to peace.

The Concert system assumed the desirability of conducting the business of Europe and the world on the basis of unanimous or near-unanimous decisions by a great power board of directors. But the decisions represented an aggregation of their individual interests rather than responsible attempts to serve the common interests of the society as a whole. And whenever such decisions could not be anticipated or proved to be unattainable, each state was free to ignore the Concert principle of consultation. Thus the Concert system was used only when most or all of the powerful deemed it convenient; the convenience of the rest of the world was not taken into much account.

The principle of great power convenience that produced or prevented a resort to Concert procedures and that controlled the guidelines for Concert decisions is clearly fundamental to the nature of oligarchy. As an oligarchy, the Concert was open to the classic radical attack that it was simply an ongoing method of dividing and then redividing the loot among the powerful. The Berlin assemblages of 1878 and 1885 and the Algeciras conference of 1906 are particularly vulnerable targets in this respect. But the longer range significance of the Concert was that it was only the latest in a long line of oligarchical efforts to curb the anarchy of international life for the benefit of the oligarchs.

Indeed, most of world history can be characterized as a contest between oligarchy and anarchy for the lead role in international politics. But it has been an uneven contest. The divisive motives among the oligarchs themselves necessarily result in the periodic breakdown of a precarious order, at which point the anarchy of violence takes over. In the most profound sense, there is never any authentic respite from anarchy because the international oligarchies themselves operate according to presuppositions that are basically anarchic.

The crucial difference between the aspirations of nineteenth- and twentieth-century versions of international organization lies in the intent of the League and then of the United Nations to tame the anarchical principle—in the international system at large and among the great powers in particular. The concept of collective security in effect substituted community obligation for freedom of choice in matters involving the use of violence. It did this by prescribing that the contingency of aggression rather than the sovereign interest must decide the legitimacy of going to war or remaining at peace.

According to this set of rules, if an ally or friend of great power A is judged an aggressor, A would be expected to join the antiaggression coalition loyally upholding Covenant or Charter. Power A would then be required to contribute to the suppression of its own friend or ally; it must suppress any qualms that among the foes of aggression there might be some that are also foes of A. In other words, in following the rules of collective security, A risks undermining its own power position by sacrificing an ally and thus strengthening an enemy. Middle and small powers have similar problems, sometimes in reverse: should A itself be declared the aggressor, what small, vulnerable, and as yet uninvaded neighbor of A could feel comfortable about committing itself forthwith to the anti-A coalition?

These are the kinds of considerations that have caused states to cling tenaciously to the sovereign prerogatives associated with war and peace. The problem of moving away from anarchy and toward community is made still more difficult because one can never be sure who will play the role of A (as aggressor or aggressor's friend) at any given time. Over the last fifty years, and in various contexts, all the great powers have appeared in the guise of A: Great Britain, France, Germany, Italy, Japan, China, the Soviet Union, and the United States. On the other side of the coin, it is difficult to think of a small or middle power that has not at one time or another been cast as A's aggressive friend or vulnerable neighbor. War is a serious business, and states are bound to think the matter through many times before letting someone else declare it for them.

In 1919 and 1945 the majority of sovereign states nonetheless agreed to accept the norm of community authority in matters of war and peace. Subsequent events in both postwar periods showed the norm to be riddled with loopholes and the authority to be feeble. Yet each event has its own significance, and the promises made at Versailles and San Francisco signified that a corner was being turned in history. The ultimacy of sovereignty, virtually undisputed for more than three centuries, was brought into confrontation with a contending doctrine. The stage was set for a debate about something that had never been seriously debated (and certainly not honestly debated) on a global scale before: To what extent should the parochial needs and aspirations of individual states yield to the larger needs and aspirations of mankind as a whole?

In other words, Covenant and Charter legitimized the presence of the macropolitical idea in the international system, a system in which micropolitics had so long and so decisively claimed a monopoly. The nineteenth-century Concert accepted and was designed to deal with the consequences of a system in which the parts counted far more than the whole. Its twentieth-century successor organizations were designed to alter the system so that the relationship between the parts and the whole would cease to be so one-sided and to assert the interest of the whole in issues that threaten violence.

The push in the macropolitical direction at once benefited and suffered from the fact that international organization was for the first time equipped with the makings of a constitutional legislature and an executive. It suffered because disillusion with political constructions that pretend more than they can deliver eroded the credibility of international organization. League credibility was bankrupt by the end of the Italo-Ethiopian war in 1936. In the case of the United Nations, credibility has risen and fallen with events. In dealing with the crises of Korea, Suez, and the Congo and with a number of lesser emergencies, the UN has demonstrated the capacity to use its legislative and executive competences with speed and with a creditable degree of effectiveness. Berlin, Hungary, Cuba, Czechoslovakia, and Vietnam, of course, are counterexamples. But the experience, even if intermittent, of making a decision and disposing of the power to implement it is the sine qua non of organizational survival. Without the admittedly ambiguous executive and legislative powers of the Charter—which nonetheless are far more tangible than were those of the Covenant—no such experience would have been possible.

MEMBERSHIP ISSUES

Twentieth-century international organization broke the precedent of previous centuries' practice in still another way: it moved toward universality of membership. From the age of discovery to World War I, the world offered no serious rival to European power. (If the Ottoman Empire is counted part of the European system, for nearly a millennium there were no great powers outside Europe.) Thus the only diplomacy that counted was European diplomacy, just as the only international law that counted was European-sired international law. The Concert of Europe was the world Concert; Europeans presumed to prescribe the conditions of life for Asia and Africa, and they had the power to back up their presumptions. Colonies had no sovereignty, and only sovereign voices could be legally (or psychologically) heard. Extra-European societies with sovereign status in the Western Hemisphere and the Far East—many in law but fewer in fact—were too weak either to desire or to be accorded entry into a Concert where power and Europeanness counted for everything.

Covenant and Charter, by contrast, were of non-European inspiration and used the language of universality. Any state in any part of the world was eligible for membership in the League if it offered "effective guarantees" of its will to abide by the purposes of the Covenant. "Fully self-governing" dominions and even colonies were also eligible under the same conditions. One must note, of course, that colonies and dominions, no matter how full the measure of self-government, invariably have a peculiar relationship which usually involves some degree of subordination to the metropolitan power. More important, very few colonies (India was one) were deemed ready for self-government, even in the rather modest degree symbolized by League eligibility. So long as the great European empires maintained themselves, the ideal of an authentic universality remained a matter for the future. In the meantime, the new applicant for League membership, whether self-governing colony or full-fledged state, had to gain the approval of two-thirds of the League Assembly.

The United Nations retained this numerical hurdle, so that the General Assembly also admits new applicants by a two-thirds majority. Indeed, in one significant respect, the UN is retrograde in comparison with the League: membership in the UN was made dependent on initial approval and recommendation by the Security Council. Thus each applicant has had to run the gauntlet of the great power veto, and more than twenty states had to wait up to ten years and more before they could get the nod from all the permanent members. Still, as of 1974 the United Nations counted 135 members, well over twice as many as the League at its zenith. Most of the gain comes from Asia and Africa, and the Europeans are dramatically outnumbered. After the admission of West and East Germany in September 1973, the only major membership issue remaining unresolved concerned the status of the two Vietnams and the two Koreas. A truly universal membership, then, is now almost within reach.

THE PROBLEM OF INTERNAL SOVEREIGNTY

Governments, of course, may or may not be representative of their peoples, so that even the presence of all the sovereign states on the rolls of the United Nations would not guarantee that all the peoples of the world would in fact have a voice in the world's governance. After all, as we have seen earlier, sovereignty can work not only to incorporate and protect a people's independence but also to seal off an oppressed population (or portion thereof) from any aid and comfort from beyond the sovereign borders.

European politics long reflected and contributed to the perennial debate concerning the expediency and morality of external interference in the internal affairs of states. Medieval institutions and the Holy Alliance are generally cited to uphold the affirmative, and the peace arrangements of Westphalia and the history of the Concert of Europe can be considered to support the negative to this question. Certainly sovereignty itself presupposes the inviolability of internal affairs, so that during its nineteenth-century apogee as a doctrine it is hardly surprising that the corollary of noninterference in internal affairs should have achieved ascendancy in European thinking about international politics.

There were, however, domestic events that threatened the rational calculations of international power politics. Among them were the massacres in the Ottoman Empire and the pogroms in Russia—as well as oppressive behavior by imperial powers within their various colonial domains. Such acts of cruelty by governments against their own populations sometimes provoked demands in other countries for international intervention and retribution. But the doctrine of noninterference generally prevailed, and states tended to follow the rule of thumb that what a government does on its own sovereign territory is its own business. Outrage over acts of terror might undermine a useful alliance or precipitate an unpromising war. Only if a given state were weak and without powerful friends was its internal behavior a safe target for foreign interference.

The principle of sovereign immunity in internal matters was carried

over into the Covenant of the League of Nations virtually without qualification. The single operative modification concerned the lost imperial
holdings of Germany and Turkey that were parceled out among the
several victor powers under a system of League Mandates (Article 22).[2]
The mandatory powers were required to administer these newly acquired
territories on the principle that "the well-being and development" of
the inhabitants should be the paramount consideration. More detailed
guidelines concerning the internal government of the mandates were also
stipulated, and the Mandatories were bound to submit annual reports,
designed to serve as an ongoing account of their stewardship, to the
Council of the League. The Mandatories (Britain, France, Japan, Belgium,
Australia, New Zealand, and South Africa) adhered to these legal commitments with varying degrees of scruple, but in all cases their behavior
in carrying out their responsibilities reflected their own colonial and
internal policies more than the standards set by the League. As we have
seen, the clash between national policy and international standard was
particularly blatant in the case of South Africa.

This first modest and ambiguous effort to establish international
norms for internal political administration was accompanied by a statement of intent on the part of the Covenant signatories to pursue a series
of social objectives both individually and jointly as circumstances might
require. These objectives were listed in Article 23 and included such
subjects as "fair and humane conditions of labor", "just treatment of
the native inhabitants of territories under their control," the banning of
traffic in women, children, drugs, and arms, freedom of communication
and transit, equitable commercial policies, and cooperation in the prevention and control of disease.

Some of these goals had more to do with international than domestic
behavior and are thus reminiscent of nineteenth-century international
efforts to abolish the slave trade rather than with new departures in
defining the role of internal sovereignty. The undertakings in the fields
of labor policy and treatment of colonial populations, however, were
squarely within those confines traditionally reserved to domestic jurisdiction. The commitment in regard to labor policy gave rise to the International Labor Organization (ILO), which functioned throughout the
life of the League and is now one of the specialized agencies of the
United Nations. But the members of the League (and later the UN) were
left free to accept or reject the conventions drafted by the ILO, and
there was no centralized enforcement machinery to ensure that signers
would honor the obligations they voluntarily assumed. Thus Article 23,

---

[2] The League Council also functioned as overseer of the rights of ethnic minorities
in a number of countries, primarily those created or enlarged by the peace settlements of 1919. This function of the Council, however, was authorized by the respective peace treaties and not by any specific provision of the Covenant.

as the more inclusive statement of international concern for domestic social, economic, and political behavior, was far more diluted than the mandate article (Article 22). The mandate article contained no policing provisions either, but at least there was an obligatory reporting requirement, and the Mandatories were made explicitly responsible to the League Council.

In sum, there was certainly no reversion anywhere in the language of the Covenant to the ideology of the Holy Alliance, which asserted on behalf of Christian Europe (that is, the conservative great powers) the right and duty to determine the legitimacy of the internal policies of the several European states. The interventionist policies of the Holy Alliance carried with them their own dangerous consequences for human freedom. But at least they operated on the principle that the internal practices of states have an inescapable effect on relations among states and that the domestic organization of societies cannot be ignored by those attempting to organize a viable international order. The rise of Hitler was the most dramatic restatement of this lesson during the life of the League. It was also the most toxic of the many causes that led to the League's death.

In contrast to the Covenant, the preamble to the United Nations Charter reads almost as much like the opening paragraphs of a civil constitution as it does like a document in international diplomacy. Three of the eight substantive statements of purpose concern themselves with such matters as the "dignity and worth of the human person," individual freedom and equality, and economic betterment. The Covenant preamble, on the other hand, adheres to language typical of the traditional international agenda: peace and war, the sanctity of international law, treaty obligations, and the like.

In regard to the issue of internal sovereignty, the most significant clause in the Charter preamble is the pledge "to employ international machinery for the promotion of the economic and social advancement of all peoples." The most significant part of the pledge is that it has been kept. It was fortified in the Charter itself chiefly by the detailed and remarkably comprehensive provisions establishing the Economic and Social Council or ECOSOC (Chapters IX and X), and, once again, by the standards set for the governing of "territories which may be detached from enemy states."[3] The implementation of the pledge has been primarily entrusted, on the one hand, to the growing number of specialized agencies linked to ECOSOC and, on the other, to the Trusteeship Council which inherited the mandate functions of the League.

---

[3] Article 77 was also designed to include "territories voluntarily placed under the [Trusteeship] system by states responsible for their administration." No such voluntary placement has ever occurred.

If the Charter's pledge to promote human liberty and welfare has been kept, however, the scope of implementation has been severely limited, and the achievements have been puny in comparison with the needs. What has so far been accomplished in the sphere of social and economic life by the United Nations as an international organization has been done on sufferance of the sovereign power retained by the individual members of the United Nations. The members have always been free to choose whether or not they would accept the standards and policies the UN or the specialized agencies might devise concerning social and economic matters. They have likewise been free to decide their share of the funding of UN programs in these fields. And they have guarded the right to carry out their own programs parallel to those of the United Nations, particularly in the key areas of foreign aid, technical assistance and training, and educational exchange. The result is that the bilateral programs under these headings invariably dwarf United Nations efforts. Here, as elsewhere, the power and prestige of the sovereigns continue to dominate the scene.

The language of the Charter, of course, does not fail to register, and indeed reinforce, this state of affairs. As if to balance the bold promises made in the preamble and echoed in Article 1, the first paragraph of Article 2 affirms the familiar doctrine of sovereignty: "The Organization is based on the principle of the sovereign equality of all its members." As we noted in the previous chapter, Paragraph 7 of the same article adds the redundant but obviously political guarantee of internal sovereignty: "Nothing contained in the present Charter shall authorize the United Nations to intervene in matters which are essentially within the domestic jurisdiction of any state or shall require the Members to submit such matters to settlement under the present Charter."

The League Covenant makes the same disclaimer of concern for domestic affairs (Article 15, Paragraph 8). The drafters were wholly consistent in this respect, for there was nothing anywhere in the constitutional arrangements of the League that could raise any real doubts about sovereign prerogatives. In the Charter, however, the preamble's expression of intent with regard to social and economic matters and human rights and the elaborate machinery foreseen to give effect to the intent did raise such doubts. Here was one reason, at any rate, for the reassuring if somewhat contradictory obeisance in Article 2, Paragraph 7.

COLLECTIVE SECURITY IN PRACTICE: THE LEAGUE

The most obvious threat to sovereignty, however, did not stem from United Nations enthusiasm for individual freedom and social welfare within the several states. Instead, it was external sovereignty—the state's freedom to make its own decisions in matters of peace and war, and foreign policy generally—that appeared to be most in jeopardy as a consequence of the Charter's language concerning collective security. The theory of collective security, as we have seen, does in fact conflict with the theory of sovereignty. It assumes that the war decision is no longer the exclusive prerogative of the individual state but is shared with, if not preempted by, the collectivity of states. It calls upon the state to entrust its ultimate security to the decisions of the international community rather than to its own sovereign judgment. It demands the renunciation of all the old techniques—alliances, balance of power, neutrality, the final reliance on the war-making capacity of the individual state—in favor of what Woodrow Wilson called a new "community of power." In return, the community would guarantee the security of each by the prohibition of aggression and a commitment to a community defense of the victim of aggression against the aggressor.

Articles 10 through 17 of the League Covenant, however, provided for a collective security process that amounted to only a blurred reproduction of the abstract doctrine. In essence, the League provisions did not require members to declare war on an aggressor (or violator of the Covenant) but only to refrain from going to war against the victim of aggression (Articles 13 and 15). It is true that the opening language of Article 16 takes a hard line: "Should any Member of the League resort to war in disregard of its covenants under Articles 12, 13 or 15, it shall *ipso facto* be deemed to have committed an act of war against all other Members of the League." But paragraph 2 of the same Article turns soft: "It shall be the duty of the Council . . . to *recommend* . . . what effective military, naval or air force the Members of the League shall severally contribute . . . to protect the covenants of the League. [Italics added.]" Members thus remained completely free to decide whether or not they would respond to the Council's recommendation to take military action against the transgressor state.

The gap between apparent promise and likely performance in matters of collective security became still wider as a result of a series of interpretive resolutions agreed to by the League Assembly in 1921. Resolution 3 came to the crux of the matter: "The unilateral action of the defaulting State cannot create a state of war; it merely *entitles* the other Members of the League to resort to acts of war or to declare themselves in a state of war with the covenant-breaking state. [Italics added.]"[4] If there was ever any concern that the language of the Covenant might

---

[4] The ambiguous sentiments in Resolution 4 added to the general confusion that effectively let everybody off the hook: "It is the duty of each Member of the League to decide for itself whether a breach of the Covenant has been committed. The fulfillment of their duties under Article 16 is required from Members of the League by the express terms of the Covenant, and they cannot neglect them without breach of their Treaty obligations."

imply a loss of sovereignty in matters of war and peace, the 1921 resolutions put all doubts to rest.

Article 16 also required members to sever diplomatic and economic relations with the covenant-breaking state and in general to force it into a kind of international quarantine. Woodrow Wilson used the terms "boycott" and "absolute isolation." Once again, however, the 1921 resolutions gutted the obligatory character even of these short-of-war sanctions. The resolutions legitimized variations in response to the League Council (or Assembly) should it call for a boycott against an offending state. "Certain States" might be free

> to postpone, wholly or partially, . . . the effective application of the economic sanctions laid down in Article 16 . . . insofar as it is desirable for the success of the common plan of action, or reduces to a minimum the losses and embarrassments which may be entailed in the case of certain Members . . . by the application of the sanctions. (Resolution 9)

> The interruption of diplomatic relations may, in the first place, be limited to the withdrawal of the heads of Missions. (Resolution 11)

> Consular relations may possibly be maintained. (Resolution 12)

> Correspondence and all other methods of communication shall be subjected to special regulations. (Resolution 15)

> Humanitarian relations shall be continued. (Resolution 16)[5]

Thus the boycott against a covenant-breaking state which Wilson envisaged as an isolation device became a sieve of fine-print evasions.[6] The qualifications attached to both military and nonmilitary sanctions prescribed (or, better, described) in Article 16 turned them into paper threats. So, in fact, they proved to be. They were not even invoked in the case of Japan's two major aggressions against China in 1931 and 1937. Nor were they applied against the Soviet Union in its war on Finland in 1939–1940, although the Soviets were rather superfluously expelled from the League. By then, of course, World War II had already broken out, and no significant action of any kind could be expected from an organization that had been advertising its own superfluousness for some years. In sum, during the entire life of the League there was not a single instance in which the Covenant provisions for military sanctions were activated.

---

[5] The full text of the Resolutions will be found in League of Nations, *Official Journal*, Special Supplement No. 6 (October 1921).

[6] See the close and penetrating analysis of League inadequacies in the realm of collective security in Hans J. Morgenthau, *Politics Among Nations* (New York: Knopf, 1973), pp. 293–299.

Economic sanctions were imposed on only one major occasion, when Italy set out to conquer Ethiopia in 1935. But Italy graphically demonstrated its ability to carry on a full-scale war effort despite the boycott measures. It was unqualifiedly dependent on only two items the outside world could withhold: oil, and unhindered passage for troops and supplies moving through the Suez Canal from Italy to the Ethiopian front. Mussolini threatened dire consequences for any state that sought to deny him the necessities of his war, and there was none bold enough to test his determination to carry out his threat. Oil continued to be shipped to Italian ports and the canal remained open, with the result that Ethiopia was subdued by force and annexed to the Italian empire in May 1936.

All the traditional considerations of diplomacy that collective security was designed to supplant asserted themselves in overwhelming combination to produce this most tragic of the League's failures. Balance of power was at stake. The ominous presence of both Germany and Russia in the European power equation helped to convince the British and French governments that they could not risk a war with Italy that might weaken them should they subsequently have to face still more powerful enemies. Alliance strategy was at stake. Britain and France had assiduously cultivated Mussolini's friendship; both were eager to retain Italy in the painfully constructed tripartite front against the rising power of Hitler. Enmity with Mussolini would break the front and, at worst, drive Italy and Germany into an alliance.

In order to avoid such an eventuality, Britain and France, while the outcome of the Ethiopian war was still in doubt and while officially leading the League's sanctions efforts against Italy, secretly offered Mussolini virtual control of approximately one-half of Ethiopia's territory if he would agree to end the war.[7] Here was collective security in reverse: the victim of aggression was to be sacrificed in order to appease the aggressor. There is perfect logic as well as tragedy in the fact that this classic maneuver of secret diplomacy marked the death of the League as an effective agency of collective action.

The Anglo-French intent to appease became public knowledge via a leak to the French press. The ensuing uproar, replete with withering commentaries on governmental hypocrisy and cynicism, forced an official disavowal by the British government and a less vocal retreat by the French. But repudiation of the offer after the fact could not restore the lost credibility of the sanctions procedure. Nor could it do much to repair the reputation of the League's two leading members. Both in name and in fact they were now irrevocably tied to the policies of appease-

---

[7] The offer was concocted by Sir Samuel Hoare, British Foreign Secretary, and Pierre Laval, Prime Minister of France, and was communicated to Mussolini in December 1935. It has gone down in history as the Hoare-Laval plan—or deal.

ment which yielded up a growing number of small nations to the growing appetite of aggressor states.

The immediate sequel was the total defeat of Ethiopia within months after the ill-fated appeasement enterprise. Britain and France had to accept Mussolini's defiance of the League and his triumph in Africa. They also had to stand by and watch the realization of their worst fear: spurred by anger and contempt for the Western powers and by larger imperial ambitions, Mussolini now made a decisive turn in policy and joined Hitler in the Rome-Berlin Axis. Attempting a selective application of the contradictory principles of collective security and traditional diplomacy, the French and British failed with both.

Other calculations of traditional diplomacy also played their role in the drama of the Italo-Ethiopian war. Assessments of the relative military strengths of the states concerned were more effective in governing policy than the paragraphs of the Covenant. Mussolini's boast that the Mediterranean had already become an Italian military lake—the Duce revived the ancient Roman claim to *mare nostrum*—had the desired effect in London. The top command of the British navy asserted that it could not defeat Italian air and sea power in the waters between Gibraltar and Suez. It was an assertion disproved in fact and retrospect after the Italian entry into World War II in 1940, but it was a crucial support for the arguments of the appeasers in 1935–1936. The sum of both real and spurious fears of military disaster, then, was a powerful factor in dissuading Britain, France, and some fifty other members of the League from effectively carrying out their pledges (if not obligations) to implement the principles of collective security.

A final major guideline and option of traditional diplomacy helped to frustrate the aspirations for a "community of power" protecting all members of the community from aggression. It was the classic option of neutrality. The strict theory of collective security rules out neutrality. Even though incomplete, the language of Article 16 reflects the theory with a fair degree of rigor: "Should any Member of the League resort to war in disregard of its covenants . . . it shall . . . be deemed to have committed an act of war against all other Members of the League." Thus the political-military configuration foreseen whenever a state initiated hostilities in violation of the Covenant would find the aggressor-violator on one side and the rest of the membership lined up in support of the victim on the other.

But the interests and plans of individual states, both powerful and weak, did not fit such a configuration. The Soviet Union was a new member of the League, having just emerged from the international ostracism to which it had been condemned since the Bolshevik Revolution in 1917. While it vigorously backed the League's economic sanctions, its own trade with Italy was minimal. Besides, the Soviets were much more concerned about Germany, and so they did not seriously try to influence the course of events in the Ethiopian crisis. For the Soviets, as for the British and French, Italian aggression in Africa was an unwelcome distraction from their preoccupation with the European power structure. In conformity with attitudes customarily evoked by distractions, the spirit (if not the letter) of neutrality dominated the calculations of all three.

The collective security front was still further weakened by the insistence of three smaller League members, Austria, Hungary, and Albania, that they could not undertake sanctions against Italy. All three had geographic, economic, and ideological ties to Italy and yielded rapidly and not unwillingly to Italian antisanctions pressure. Thus the paragraphs of the 1921 resolutions which had punched so many holes in the commitment to collective security now came to life in the form of the actual political behavior of League members. The result was evasion, dissembling, and ultimate betrayal of the principle of collective action.

There were three major "neutrals" who were not League members: Japan, Germany, and the United States. Japan had resigned from the League as a gesture of defiance in response to the League's condemnation of Japanese aggression in Manchuria. Having embarked on a policy in Asia that had nothing in common with the principles the Covenant was designed to uphold, the Japanese had no interest in cooperating with the League to apply these principles in the case of Ethiopia. Besides, it was already becoming evident that Japan's likeliest friends in Europe would turn out to be Germany and Italy, so that there was a double premium on noninvolvement. Finally, although there was some public sympathy in Japan for Ethiopia as a victim of white imperialism, the Japanese government acted on the correct assumption that Mussolini's humiliation of Britain and France as leaders of the League effort would weaken their power to interfere with Japanese plans in Asia.

Hitler, of course, was eager to gain Mussolini as an ally. And, like Japan, he wanted to encourage Britain and France to take further steps along the path of appeasement in regard to German expansionist ambitions. Hence he maneuvered in good neutralist (though hardly neutral) fashion to demonstrate to Mussolini that he would do nothing to hurt the Italian war effort. At the same time, Hitler was careful not to be ostentatious about his growing interest in a connection with Fascist Italy.

The official American response to the war was to embargo shipments of arms, munitions, and "implements of war" to both the aggressor and the victim. Since there was virtually no trade of any kind between Ethiopia and the United States, however, this act of American neutrality was tantamount to discrimination against Italy. On the other hand, American export trade to Italy in commodities other than armaments continued brisk in the face of the somewhat lax restraints placed upon it by a government-inspired but legally voluntary "moral embargo."

Above all, American oil flowed into Italy with little effective hindrance. Thus the United States and the League, each looking to see whether the other would take the first step in banning the shipment of oil, managed between them to postpone the whole issue until it became academic by virtue of Ethiopia's capitulation.

This tale of debacle and tragedy is a tale of constitutional permissiveness: almost nowhere in the Covenant did the language relevant to collective security go beyond recommendation into the realm of requirement. Where it did or seemed to do so, the 1921 resolutions effectively altered the intent or made it ambiguous. Hence every time the League faced the problem of activating its collective machinery it was evident that it had to depend on exhortation rather than legal obligation. This permissiveness, in turn, rested on the old penchant for anarchy in international politics. The connection is obvious in the unanimity provision in Article 5: "Except where otherwise expressly provided in this Covenant ... decisions at any meeting of the Assembly or of the Council shall require the agreement of all the Members of the League represented at the meeting." Thus with the exception of a joint session of Council and Assembly when a unanimous Council and a majority of the Assembly could decide League policy, one opposing vote by any member was sufficient to block League action on any matter on the agenda of Council or Assembly.

This extreme form of the veto system operating on the principle of almost undiluted anarchy necessarily reinforced permissive attitudes. After all, if every member could exercise a veto, only those measures could usefully be considered that were likely to earn 100 percent approval. Such measures, in turn, had to cater to or at least avoid offending the special interests of every member. Since no measure dealing with a highly political issue and involving most of the sovereign nations of the globe could possibly be drafted to these specifications, the obvious option was to let each member interpret the collective policy as it chose. There was no authentic alternative, anyway. Article 15, Paragraph 7, spelled out the consequences of failing to find policies pleasing to all:

> If the Council fails to reach a report [sic] which is unanimously agreed to by the members thereof, other than the Representatives of one or more of the parties to the dispute, the Members of the League reserve to themselves the right to take such action as they shall consider necessary for the maintenance of right and justice.[8]

The unanimity rule, in other words, was the ultimate assurance to members that action under the Covenant could not require of them

---

[8] Article 15, Paragraph 10, stipulates that the Assembly shall operate according to the same procedures except that, in cases referred from Council to Assembly, the Council-in-Assembly voting provisions shall apply.

anything they would not have wanted to do anyway in the exercise of their sovereign powers—just one dissenting vote and everyone could behave as he pleased.

COLLECTIVE SECURITY IN PRACTICE: THE UN

The framers of the United Nations Charter drastically curtailed the possibilities for constitutional resort to a veto, and for this reason the United Nations was initially considered a challenge to and a reduction of sovereignty to a degree never intended in the League. Article 25 was the Charter's key departure from League permissiveness: "The Members of the United Nations agree to accept and carry out the decisions of the Security Council in accordance with the present Charter." No longer was each member free to decide for itself whether the rules had been violated or not; it was bound by the decision of the Security Council. This farewell to individual discretion received added emphasis in Article 39 which stipulated that the Security Council "shall determine the existence of any threat to the peace, breach of the peace, or act of aggression."

The Security Council was given not only a virtual monopoly in terms of defining the problem but also in the delicate matter of what to do about it. It could decide to make a recommendation but, unlike the League Council when it came to matters involving the use of force, the Security Council was not limited to recommending. It could "decide" courses of action both military and nonmilitary and "call upon" members to aid in their implementation. Thus the circle that the League left open was theoretically closed: the Security Council had the power of command and the general membership took upon itself the obligation of obedience.

But the circle, as practice has demonstrated, sprang open again. While the general membership agreed to carry out Security Council decisions, the degree of vigor invested in implementing such decisions has largely been left for the individual member to determine. In the key area of military sanctions, Articles 43 and 45 provided for the signing of binding agreements between the Security Council and individual members (or groups of members) containing precise commitments of military resources members would make available on call. But in the more than quarter century that has passed since these articles were voted not a single member has entered into the projected agreements. Hence every member of the United Nations has retained its prerogatives in the crucial area of military sovereignty. This state of affairs was dramatically demonstrated in the one instance, Korea, when the United Nations responded to aggression with military force. Of the (then) sixty members of the organization, only sixteen contributed in one way or another to actual military operations; five other members supplied medical units. Thus under the banner of the United Nations, as well as of the League of Nations, collective security has remained a voluntary and not an obligatory enterprise.

What is at stake in all these considerations is the ability of an organization to make corporate decisions concerning those matters for which it has declared itself responsible. The League's declaration of responsibility rang hollow from the outset in light of the explicit requirement of a unanimous vote in Council or Assembly as a prerequisite for corporate action. The modified unanimity rule governing Council-in-Assembly sessions did not really alter very much. The United Nations, on the other hand, banished the unanimity rule from the General Assembly and, in the Security Council, restricted it to the permanent members. Article 27, Paragraph 3, sets out the celebrated veto clause in deceptively innocuous language: "Decisions of the Security Council on . . . [nonprocedural] matters shall be made by an affirmative vote of nine members including the concurring votes of the permanent members."[9]

Here is the crux of the matter. If the Charter did not follow the Covenant in equipping every member with a veto, it nevertheless placed the veto in the hands of those who could wield it most persuasively, the great powers. If any one of the permanent members refused to "concur" in any given substantive vote, the Security Council could not make a corporate decision. In turn, the command-obedience relationship between Security Council and General Assembly would be dissolved each time great power "concurrence" was unattainable. Unable, then, to require military contributions from the membership so long as Articles 43 and 45 remain dead letters, the Security Council cannot require the membership to do anything at all whenever it faces an issue upon which the permanent members are divided among themselves. In such circumstances the concept of corporate responsibility and the prospects for the effectiveness of corporate action must necessarily remain unpromising.

Each of the five permanent members, then, can individually block the United Nations from taking any binding action it deems inimical to its interests. The rest of the members cannot individually veto action, but they can in most situations withhold their cooperation from United Nations enterprises they may consider inopportune. The veto provision registers the great powers' constitutional right and opportunity to choose their own interests in preference to community interests—or to defend an interpretation of community interests different from that espoused by the other permanent members.

---

[9] In the original Charter, Security Council membership was set at eleven, and seven votes (including those of the permanent members) sufficed for binding decisions. A 1965 amendment raised the membership to fifteen and, correspondingly, the required majority to nine votes.

The failure to implement Articles 43 and 45 permits the rest of the membership to exercise the same preference in regard to the supreme issues of war and peace. Moreover, events since 1945 have confirmed what empirical observation has always been able to demonstrate: few major issues in international relations can arise in which all of the major powers will be found on the same side. Hence the frequency of unanimity among the permanent members must necessarily be minimal and the number of command decisions by the Security Council few. In consequence, the ordinary UN member had, and has, little to fear from constitutional compulsion under any provision of the Charter.

One can point to the divisive function of the veto without making it the villain of the piece. It is the direct heir of the generalized unanimity rule of the League which, in turn, was a slightly modified version of the standard unanimity procedures of traditional diplomacy. We have already noted the indissoluble tie between unanimity and anarchy and remarked its manifestations in both Concert and League. The common lesson the United Nations and its antecedent international organizations teach is that the unanimity procedure can be dispensed with only to the extent that common interests prevail in the international system.

The veto is the effect and not the cause of division; it is the necessary constitutional nucleus of an international organization built to function in a divided world. Without the veto there would have been no United Nations at all—neither the United States nor the Soviet Union, nor the other prospective members of the Security Council, would have signed the Charter without the unambiguous affirmation of their sovereign great power status firmly anchored in Article 27.

It follows that the recurrent agitation to abolish or sharply curtail the veto procedure is bound to be misleading and unproductive. A global organization in the contemporary world will either have some form of unanimity rule or it will cease to exist. It is not the veto that threatens the United Nations but the conflicts which persist among the membership. The real test of United Nations success will be what it always has been: the extent to which it can aid in ameliorating those conflicts. For this task, in the foreseeable future, it has no choice but to use methods that are basically voluntary in nature.

The Security Council may on occasion achieve the requisite unity to decree compulsory measures, as in the mandatory economic sanctions voted against Rhodesia in 1966. But even in this instance there was no inclination to proceed further along the path of compulsion by punishing South Africa and Portugal for their open defiance of the sanctions. The result was the same as in the Italo-Ethiopian war: the boycott became a sieve. The white-supremacy regime in Rhodesia demonstrated that it could effectively withstand economic pressures because it had like-minded friends beyond its borders. It also demonstrated, once again, that the will of an international organization with a highly diverse membership is seldom as vigorous as the will of one or more individual states when they believe their vital interests to be at stake.

Rhodesia only adds to the mass of evidence that compulsion cannot be the strong suit of international organization. The Soviet invasions of Hungary in 1956 and of Czechoslovakia in 1968, the American invasion of Santo Domingo in 1965, and the war in Vietnam all substantiate the constitutional infirmity of the UN and the sovereign strength of its members in matters of coercion. If the failure to implement Articles 43 and 45 has previously been analyzed as a back-door affirmation of sovereignty, particularly for the less powerful members of the UN, it is necessary at this point to stress the other side of the coin. Lacking the prescribed military agreements between the Security Council and the individual members, the United Nations is militarily helpless in that it can ask for, but cannot command, the use of force. In this area the members have retained their traditional monopoly and have ceded the organization nothing.[10] If, then, one is concerned with the role of compulsion in international relations, one must look beyond the United Nations to the members that retain the capacity to compel.

VOLUNTARISM AND THE GENERAL ASSEMBLY

These considerations suggest many of the reasons why there has been a long-term decline in the importance of the Security Council and a corresponding rise in the significance of the General Assembly in the political dynamics of the United Nations. The General Assembly epitomizes the spirit of voluntarism which in fact dominates the Charter. The General Assembly cannot decide substantive issues, it can only recommend. The members may accept or reject its recommendations at their discretion. Lacking the powers of compulsion, it did not need to be equipped with a veto procedure. A two-thirds majority on the principle of one state—one vote makes its recommendations official (but not mandatory) with no modifying provisions to give special privileges to great powers.[11]

There are many reasons why the small powers have been eager to

---

[10] A number of UN members, notably Canada, the Scandinavian countries, India, and Ireland, have earmarked small units of their armed forces for United Nations use. These arrangements are entirely voluntary, however, and they can be placed under United Nations command only at the discretion of the governments concerned. This arrangement is in part an outgrowth of the Uniting for Peace Resolution, to be discussed shortly.

[11] It should be noted, however, that in such matters as budget and membership, General Assembly votes do have binding force. Also, on issues not defined as "important questions" "decisions . . . shall be made by a majority of the members present and voting" (Article 18).

expand the prerogatives of the General Assembly. One, most obviously, is that less than 10 percent of the small power membership is represented on the Security Council at any one time. Thus the General Assembly is necessarily the forum in which the smaller powers can make their weight of numbers felt to best effect. Moreover, to function in the General Assembly, the great powers must leave behind their privileged citadel in the Security Council and play by the egalitarian rules of majority vote instead of the oligarchic rules of the veto. Egalitarianism in the General Assembly is, of course, a matter for qualification; knowledge of what a great power will or will not do affects the votes of lesser powers. But the reverse is also true: sentiment among the membership at large will have its impact on the debating and voting behavior of the great powers.

It is obvious that the great powers have a constitutional stake in shoring up the Security Council's position. What is more, there is a strong case to be made in support of a renewal of the Security Council's authority. If all the business of the United Nations were to be conducted on the floor of the General Assembly, decisions (to recommend) could be reached only by constant politicking to obtain, or to prevent, two-thirds majorities. The shifting composition of such majorities would necessitate the canvassing of every last ministate on every issue coming up for debate. Such a political procedure would be wholly out of balance in terms of the relation between franchise and executive responsibility.

At the same time, it is hardly possible for the great powers or anyone else to make too much of the evident weaknesses of the General Assembly or to idealize the Security Council as a stronghold of rational debate, realistic voting arrangements, and decisive action. As we have seen, the Security Council has been shackled by the antagonism between East and West, a political infirmity that the more than one hundred vetoes cast by the Soviet Union faithfully reflect. In their preferred forum the great power permanent members have usually exhibited not vigor but impotence in dealing with the world.

The nonbinding nature of General Assembly votes has been considered a hallmark of weakness. Yet the grant of mandatory powers to the Security Council has been no less debilitating to that body. Without the power to bind, the Security Council's permanent members might have been willing to place less reliance on the veto. The result would have been a Security Council more often capable of arriving at recommended positions, instead of a body striving to perform a largely illusory command function and constantly stymied by the great power unanimity rule.

In any case, a Security Council disencumbered of its constitutional power to decree would be closer not only to the spirit of the General Assembly but also to the micropolitical realities of the contemporary international system. The vision of a world jointly governed, at least in matters of peace and war, by the world's great powers must inevitably recede before the spirit of anarchy that infects, above all, the great powers themselves. The recommending powers of the General Assembly are far more attuned to the persisting condition of anarchy than are the pretentious and largely fictitious powers of compulsion conferred upon the Security Council.

If the League fell victim to its own permissiveness, the same disease is a constant threat to the existence of the United Nations. Yet the Charter laid sturdier foundations than the Covenant. It burdened the General Assembly neither with command responsibilities nor with the veto. A two-thirds majority could come up with resolutions that, while not binding, nonetheless had the merit of being official statements of United Nations policy. Here was room for the growth of authority on a voluntary basis: two-thirds plus of the membership could agree to collaborate and thus to assume the mantle of United Nations authority, and at the same time each remained free to specify the degree of its commitment.

This alternative structure for United Nations decision making was given concrete form in 1950 when the General Assembly endorsed the Uniting for Peace Resolution sponsored by the United States. The resolution was designed to permit the General Assembly to function as a substitute collective security mechanism, on a voluntary basis, whenever the Security Council might be incapable of action because of the veto. Uniting for Peace fulfilled the immediate need of enabling the General Assembly to continue to supervise the prosecution of the war against aggression in Korea.[12] But its long-range effect was to extend responsibility for dealing with any issue of aggression and at the same time to sidestep all the futile debates over the role of compulsion.

The resolution provided that the General Assembly can convene within twenty-four hours if, in the event of aggression or a breach of peace, Security Council action is blocked by veto. The key measure in the resolution authorized the assembly to vote recommendations for collective measures, including the use of armed force. It also converted the substance of Articles 43 and 45 into a voluntary arrangement whereby members could designate, if they so wished, military units to be made available to the UN on a standby basis. A Peace Observation Commission was established whose task was to investigate and report

---

[12] In response to the initial aggression of North Korea, the Security Council was able to order collective security measures only because the Soviet Union had withdrawn from Security Council meetings and was not present to cast a veto. The Soviet withdrawal was in protest against the failure of the United Nations to transfer UN membership from Nationalist China to Communist China. When the Soviets ended their boycott it was obvious that the veto would hamstring the Security Council once again and that it would no longer be capable of functioning as the political headquarters of the collective security operations resisting North Korean (and later Chinese) aggression. The Uniting for Peace Resolution in effect transferred that headquarters to the General Assembly.

threats to peace to the General Assembly. Finally, a Collective Measures Committee was charged with examining and recommending techniques that would contribute to more effective execution of collective security undertakings. The upshot was an international organization with two collective security systems: one with mandatory powers but crippled by the veto and one lacking mandatory powers but free of the veto.

Since the passage of the Uniting for Peace Resolution, the United Nations has resorted to both systems. In situations where the permanent members have been in agreement, the Security Council has functioned as the chief instrument to deal with threats to peace: in Cyprus in 1964, the Indo-Pakistani war of 1965, and Rhodesia in 1966. Where there has been permanent member disagreement, the Uniting for Peace option has been brought into play, most spectacularly in the Suez crisis of 1956. The Congo emergency of 1960 occasioned the use of both systems. At the outset, the Security Council was in charge; when the policies of the United States and the Soviet Union collided, the General Assembly assumed responsibility for the extensive military and civilian operations under the command of the UN Secretary-General.

This kind of flexibility, which permits a choice between Security Council and General Assembly as the collective security instrument, is clearly an asset. It increases the opportunities for resort to collective measures both by making possible an actual circumvention of the veto and by means of the pressure a prospective circumvention can exert on the permanent members of the Security Council.

COLLECTIVE SECURITY AND PEACEKEEPING

The existence of two procedural options, however, does nothing to enhance the substantive effectiveness of collective security measures. We have already noted the meager results of the sanctions voted by the Security Council against Rhodesia (as well as cases of flagrant aggression where no collective action was taken at all). The General Assembly, lacking mandatory powers, must necessarily follow the course of pragmatism and decide the collective-measures issue in accord with the concrete circumstances of each presumptive threat to peace. In the case of both the Security Council and the General Assembly, then, the cardinal question is: How far, in the specific instance, is the membership prepared to push the logic of collective security?

The double crisis of Suez and Hungary in the fall of 1956 brought this question to the fore with dramatic urgency. In regard to Hungary, the massiveness of Soviet power and the danger of nuclear warfare were sufficient to paralyze any impulse to advocate collective measures against the aggressor. In the Middle East, however, the power commitments of those involved were then more modest and the dangers of a major war correspondingly less. Or, more bluntly—and for Britain, France, and Israel, more bitterly—the Middle East aggressors were not so powerful and menacing as the Soviets. For this and other reasons there was a marked willingness to attempt a collective response to the aggression at Suez. After the Security Council had been immobilized in the Suez crisis by the double veto of Britain and France, the General Assembly convened in accordance with the provisions of the Uniting for Peace Resolution and voted to urge a cease-fire.

Since the belligerents soon complied with the General Assembly's recommendation, there was no need to press the collective security issue further. But the threat of activating collective security measures played its significant role in the aggressors' decision to draw back. And the negotiations for a cease-fire, by calling into being the United Nations Emergency Force (UNEF), opened up new possibilities for collective action in response to threats to peace. UNEF deployed a multinational cordon of uniformed men between the Egyptians, on the one hand, and the attackers on the other, thus easing immediate tensions and facilitating withdrawal operations. Eventually it took up positions on the Egyptian side of the border with Israel and for eleven years served as a buffer between the two hostile states. Even though, on Nasser's demand, Secretary-General U Thant withdrew the UN troops in 1967 on the eve of renewed war in the Middle East, UNEF earned its title as the most significant and successful experiment in what has come to be known as peacekeeping.

As a lightly armed military force, UNEF was obviously incapable of doing much in the way of coercion. Moreover, it was organized and deployed only after cease-fire agreements had been reached. Hence it was not a force designed to serve the classic purposes of collective security by repelling or punishing aggression. Most important, it was not cast in the role of partisan; for UNEF there was officially no aggressor and no victim of aggression but only a threat to peace. The corollary was that the viability of UNEF—and of the subsequent peacekeeping operations which drew inspiration from UNEF—depended on the readiness of all parties to a given conflict to welcome or at least tolerate the UN presence. Neutrality is therefore the normative essence of the peacekeeping approach. In this respect it is the categorical opposite of the partisan norm of collective security.

Finally, all peacekeeping operations have been designed to operate at the tactical and not at the strategic level. Where the power of the opposing forces is relatively modest (as in Cyprus or the Congo) or when the will to make war is quiescent (as it was during most of UNEF's existence), peacekeeping operations can perform valuable services in depressing the level and restricting the scope of conflict. But they are incapable of dealing with a determined and powerful aggressor or with two even moderately powerful states bent on settling their differences by force. In situations where violence has reached or threatens to reach the proportions, say, of the Korean War, there is no substitute available to international organization for the collective security procedures which have generally been assumed to be its most important set of functions.

Korea was, in fact, the first and last major test of the UN's collective security mechanisms, and they passed the test. If the United Nations did not then rise as a body united against aggression, neither was its corporate performance supine in the face of danger. Despite the disproportionate war burden carried by the South Koreans and the United States, and by fifteen other states that made much smaller military contributions, there was a roughly rational division of labor in terms of interests and capabilities among members who contributed troops, members who contributed in nonmilitary ways, and members whose main contribution was votes in the General Assembly. Members outside the Soviet bloc did what they thought they ought to do in terms of condemning aggression and what they thought they could afford to do in terms of actually combating it. At all events, in contrast to the outcome of the Italo-Ethiopian war, the effort made under the United Nations aegis in Korea sufficed to fulfill the collective security purpose of frustrating and punishing aggression.

Thus the outcome of the Korean War may have been an ambiguous triumph for the United Nations, but at least it was not a failure. Whereas the sanctions fiasco in the Italo-Ethiopian war signaled the death of the League, the successful defense of South Korea injected a crucial increment of confidence in the vitality and durability of the United Nations. The decisive factor at work in the two different outcomes was great power leadership. Both the sanctions procedures of the League and the military-economic-political effort of the UN rested ultimately on voluntary and not obligatory relationships among the members. But in the one case Britain and France believed their national interests to be at odds with collective security norms while in the other the United States believed that the two coincided. The differing perceptions sufficed to ensure debilitated leadership in response to Italian aggression and vigorous leadership fifteen years later in response to North Korean aggression.

It is likely that any future tests of the will to collective security will take place within the framework of these considerations. First, the Ethiopian and Korean cases both demonstrate that states will abide by collective security norms only to the extent that they do not conflict with their perceptions of their national interests; hence the prospect for the foreseeable future that collective security processes in the United Nations must rest on consent and not on obligation. Second, where one or more great powers in a given case equate their national interests with the collective security function, there will be sufficiently dynamic and persuasive leadership to make it likely that at least the bulk of the organization will perform more or less according to the spirit of the Charter. Great power leadership is capable of achieving these results to the extent that it is strong enough to offer members protection from the aggressor, to warn them of unpleasant consequences if they fail to support the joint enterprise, and to portray the collective security effort as generally advantageous and likely to succeed.

The point has just been made that states will not support collective security if it conflicts with their national interests. It should now be stressed that great power leadership is capable of *changing* national interest perceptions. National interest is not something immutable; changing environmental circumstances and changing evaluations of internal resources combine to produce constant reformulations of national interest. While there are durable elements in the national interest formulations of every state, there are inevitably transient factors as well. Moreover, even the most consequential and long-standing national interest doctrines can yield to change. The spectacular European abandonment of empire since 1945, America's definitive emergence since Pearl Harbor from more than a century of isolation, and Britain's decision to join Europe (bidding farewell to its four-hundred-year-old role of the aloof balancer) are cases in point.

The effectiveness of collective security is not dependent on such dramatic and massive shifts in national priorities. What is needed is great power leadership that by example, education, and pressure demonstrates that participation in the collective security enterprise is more in the national interests of UN members than nonparticipation. If no such leadership is available, the vast majority of the membership will almost invariably decide that collective security and national interest do not mix.

No international community can be built by exhorting states to sacrifice their individual interests in favor of the collective interest. Community purposes can be realistically pursued only if states can be convinced that their interests would be profited rather than subverted by loyal participation in community enterprise. Pressures and threats are useful up to a point in influencing a state's conduct, but nothing except conquest can force a state to yield up its sovereignty. Hence if collective security has a future, it must ultimately emerge from interaction between the free will response of the members and the leadership qualities exhibited by some or all of the great powers.

The imperative of great power leadership points to some other obvious lessons. Without initiative on the part of either or both the United States and the Soviet Union, there can be no leadership whatever. The United Nations has managed to take some major actions (Korea and the Congo) against the will of Moscow and some minor ones despite antagonism from Washington. But it cannot act in any significant way when both superpowers are united in opposition.

By the same token, the might of both superpowers places severe limits on the ability of one to press the United Nations into a course antagonistic to the other. In proxy wars or in other contexts in which Soviet and American interests confront each other only indirectly, there have been and will presumably continue to be opportunities for UN involvement. But any attempt by one superpower to lead the UN majority into a frontal engagement with the other in matters where both the stakes are high and the interests direct must necessarily fail. This is true because the enforcement effort would be the equivalent of global war in which not the United Nations but the nuclear arsenals of the superpowers would determine the outcome. Thus the superpower leadership is essentially immune to collective security processes. This is the basic explanation why Vietnam, during all the tragic years of war and agony, has never been entered on the UN agenda for formal consideration or action. A realistic assessment of leadership opportunities in the United Nations must take these unyielding facts into account.

The ability of great power leadership to elicit a creative and fundamentally unconstrained response from the members will decide the fate not only of collective security but of all the other functions of the United Nations as well. Any attempt to amplify the role of constraint in an organization whose membership remains so disparate in power and purpose cannot succeed. The great powers will not consent to grant the General Assembly the rights of enforcible decree in a situation where they are outnumbered roughly twenty to one and in which the vote of the Maldive Islands (population 97,743) weighs as much as that of the United States, the Soviet Union, Japan, or China. In the Security Council, the permanent members will certainly not abandon their powers of veto so long as their deep political and ideological divisions persist and so long as Security Council decisions in the crucial areas of war and peace are constitutionally binding. No permanent member has any more desire to be outvoted by a nine-man majority in the Security Council than by the membership at large in the General Assembly. On this issue, at least, the permanent members are united; they will therefore continue to see to it that no binding votes in either forum can be taken against their will.

Schemes for weighted voting as a device to overcome antipathy to extending the scope of mandatory powers miss the point. Criteria for assigning weights (population, gross national product, military power, contribution to the organizational budget) pose difficult but not impossible problems. The resort to weighting procedures in UN-affiliated bodies and the special voting privileges in the Security Council itself testify to this point. But the real issue at stake in those policy-making processes of the United Nations that touch on war, peace, and sovereignty is not whether there will be an accurate weighting of each nation's vote according to some generally accepted standard. Instead, it is the freedom of each nation, whatever its assigned weight, to decide for itself whether it will or will not abide by the outcome of any given vote. As we have seen, the smaller powers have guarded this freedom as resolutely, if not as ostentatiously, as the permanent members of the Security Council.

Despite the Charter's language in Article 25, then, the succession from the League of Nations to the United Nations has not witnessed a fundamental change in the readiness of nations to take on unambiguous obligations to international organization in matters of major political importance. But it is also true that the extent of national involvement in the fate and functions of the United Nations is qualitatively different from the relationship between the nation-state and the League. This difference must be credited primarily to the sharp contrast in the historical development of the two organizations. The history of the League is one of failure in every major test of its viability. The history of the UN has been marked by many failures and disappointments, but the larger record, including such critical confrontations as Korea, Suez, and the Congo, has been one of crisis surmounted. Though the credit and credibility of the United Nations sinks very low from time to time, its collective security and peacekeeping achievements and its demonstrated capacity for adaptation and innovation have made it a significant and indeed indispensable component of the contemporary international system.

ECONOMIC AND SOCIAL COMPONENTS

The political resilience and durability of the United Nations has been, in turn, the indispensable support for its efforts to infuse the concept of global community with social and economic content. As we noted earlier in the chapter, the Charter's terms of reference for the Economic and Social Council laid the foundations for international initiatives in nearly every area of human concern. Article 55 is the master formulation of this set of purposes:

> With a view to the creation of conditions of stability and well-being which are necessary for peaceful and friendly relations among nations based on respect for the principle of equal rights and self-determination of peoples, the United Nations shall promote:
>
> a. higher standards of living, full employment, and conditions of economic and social progress and development;
> b. solutions of international economic, social, health, and related problems; and international cultural and educational cooperation; and
> c. universal respect for, and observance of, human rights and fundamental freedoms for all without distinction as to race, sex, language, or religion.

The Article makes a number of points that deserve comment. First, it recognizes an indissoluble connection between the internal regimes of states and the probabilities of external peace and war. Second, it pledges UN action in all those phases of socioeconomic life which states have customarily reserved for themselves. Third, however, it repeats the genuflections in the direction of sovereignty and domestic jurisdiction contained in Article 2 with the ritual statement of deference to the values of "equal rights and self-determination of peoples."

Two conclusions emerge from these observations. One is that the prospects for peace will not be good unless some of the barriers are removed between domestic jurisdictions and the concerns of the international community. The other is that the change in jurisdictional relationships can occur only as a result of an essentially voluntary process. In turn, just as in the case of collective security, voluntary rearrangements of jurisdictional authority can come about only to the extent that the socioeconomic services and standards of the United Nations enhance the interests of the member states.

The specialized agencies associated with the United Nations by means of contractual agreements with the Economic and Social Council are among the most important sources of such standards and services. A complete list of these agencies offers a forceful illustration of the variety and scope of their activities:

> Food and Agriculture Organization (FAO)
> International Civil Aviation Organization (ICAO)
> International Labor Organization (ILO)
> Intergovernmental Maritime Consultative Organization
> International Monetary Fund (IMF)
> International Telecommunications Union
> Universal Postal Union
> United Nations Educational, Scientific, and Cultural Organization
>   (UNESCO)
> World Bank Group:
>   International Bank for Reconstruction and Development
>   International Development Association
>   International Finance Corporation
> World Health Organization (WHO)
> World Meteorological Organization

To these should be added a sampling of the more important autonomous agencies, commissions, and other functional organizations operating within, or having a specially defined relationship with, the United Nations structure:

> International Refugee Organization
> International Atomic Energy Agency
> Commissions for commodity trade, disarmament, human rights, narcotics, population, statistics, status of women

Regional economic commissions for Europe, Asia and the Far East,
    Latin America, and Africa
United Nations Conference on Trade and Development (UNCTAD)
United Nations Development Program[13]

The combined list suggests a resemblance to a somewhat incomplete
but nonetheless broad-based scheme of domestic governmental organization. This is hardly surprising since the organizations listed are for
the most part outgrowths of Charter pledges to involve the United
Nations in matters that have been traditionally assigned to domestic
jurisdiction. Indeed, agencies concerned with agriculture, health, education, labor, finance, commerce, transportation, and post office and tele-
communications conjure up a reflection of, say, the American cabinet
system operating at somewhat better than half strength.

To be sure, the reflection would be an illusion in most respects. Whatever command power is at the disposal of the international agencies has
an ultimately uncertain constitutional basis, and their work can more
often be classified as service-oriented, technical, advisory, and informa-
tional than as policy formation and execution. Moreover, their budget-
ary resources hover in the vicinity of .01 to .10 percent of their American
counterparts; hence their bureaucratic complexity and thrust—though
not necessarily their efficiency and imaginativeness—are incomparably
less. Yet the sense of similarity between national and international organization remains useful insofar as it underlines the far-reaching identity of
societal needs in international and domestic society. It also draws attention to the extent to which international organization is already engaged
in attempting to meet these needs at a global level.

In this sector of the United Nations, then, we observe an organization which has developed in embryonic form institutions and instruments more appropriately labeled transnational than international. That
is, most of the UN and UN-associated agencies are not so much concerned with the socioeconomic problems that arise *between* one sovereign and another as with those that exist *within* the sovereign boundaries of all or many members. We have already observed, in the case
of Namibia, among other examples, how difficult it is to penetrate the
province of sovereignty. It is easier to do so, of course, if one is bringing along a public health project or an economic development proposal
than if one is promoting a plan to implement the Declaration of Human
Rights. Yet the accumulation of UN experience with both failure and
success in transnational operations around the globe has strengthened

---

[13] For further information in succinct form concerning the organizations in both
parts of this list, see Inis L. Claude, Jr., *Swords Into Plowshares*, 3rd ed. (New
York: Random House, 1964), Chap. 17, and Appendix V in the fourth edition (1971).
Also see Ralph Townley, *The United Nations: A View from Within* (New York:
Scribners, 1968), Chaps. IX through XII.

the still tenuous hopes for a more rational and less national approach to the great social, economic, and political problems that oppress and endanger mankind.

It would be a mistake to assume that every breach of sovereign boundaries advances the cause of peace and every successful defense of sovereignty represents a setback. The prevailing distribution of power between nationalism, on the one hand, and internationalism and transnationalism, on the other, negates both the likelihood and the wisdom of precipitate efforts by the United Nations (that is, states within the United Nations) to diminish the ultimate authority of the members. After all, we have already observed that sovereignty embodies the principle of independence for the weak as well as the strong. As such, it is something not to be lightly put aside.[14]

Moreover, some of the issues involved in the sovereignty question are more likely to be resolved in the context of regional rather than global organization, as the experience of the European Community has already demonstrated. In any case, it should be evident that the values of internationalism and transnationalism, which the United Nations has been able to nurture, can be advanced only as they prove their compatibility with the national values they seek to supplement and their superiority to those they seek to replace.

THE MACROPOLITICAL CHALLENGE

Yet there is a pressing need for urgency in moving away from the parochialism of sovereignty. The global nature of the world's most critical problems is becoming more and more evident. Nuclear escalation, the population explosion, the pollution of the environment, the communications revolution, the world-wide concentration of wealth and the world-wide expansion of poverty are all essentially global and not local phenomena. They have given rise, in turn, to earth-spanning and revolutionary demands for mass education, mass health, mass welfare, and mass participation in the decisions affecting man's fate.

The ability of international organization at its present stage of development to respond to these kinds of challenges is obviously inadequate. At the same time, there is no reason to rule out the possibility of a rapid expansion of activities and a significant increase in the authority of the United Nations as the enormity of the problems confronting global society becomes more and more palpable.

---

[14] In this connection it is important to keep in mind that critics of the United Nations are to be found not only among Americans who charge the UN with subverting American sovereignty but also among nationals and even governments of weaker states who accuse the United States (or other large powers) of using the UN as an instrument to undermine the sovereignty of smaller powers.

After all, it has been often and truly said that the United Nations is what its members make it. If the international and transnational perspectives that have animated the United Nations have persisted, it is because these same perspectives have been present to a greater or lesser extent among the membership. Each member has had to ponder the antagonism between the essential isolation that characterizes the concept of sovereignty and the macropolitical idea of a community of man. And no state is comprised of a population unanimously agreed on sovereignty as a monolithic dogma that excludes all competing concepts from consideration. In these circumstances it is not unreasonable to anticipate that the member states will be moved to consider equipping the United Nations with more comprehensive powers as global pressures build.

The presence of cosmopolitan impulses among the members underscores the fact that cosmopolitan behavior in international politics can find expression outside the confines of the UN as well as within. The problem posed by the military might of the superpowers, as we have just noted in another context, is certain to remain beyond the competence of the United Nations for the foreseeable future. Yet the test-ban and the bilateral SALT agreements, for all their fragmentary character, reflect an authentic concern for the larger community of mankind as well as the parochial preoccupations of the nuclear powers. A similar judgment can be made about the postwar programs of bilateral foreign aid that have constituted a unique chapter in the history of international relations. The self-serving aspects of these programs do not negate the existence among donor states of a sense of transnational solidarity with human beings beyond their own borders.

International organization, then, is not the only instrument of macropolitics. The policies of the superpowers, the dialogue between the developed and underdeveloped worlds, the dynamics of regional organizations, and the ever more integrated structure of the international economy are among the key agencies for advancing or retarding the growth of a macropolitical consciousness. It follows that the world will continue to be one in which decisions of global consequence will be made by a multiplicity of centers of power and purpose.

A realistic projection of the kinds of decisions that need to be made and of how and where they are likely to be made requires a comprehensive understanding of the macrocosm of our contemporary world. It is a macrocosm in which the United Nations and other transnational structures play essential roles, but its dimensions are far larger and its dynamics far more complex. The second part of this book will seek to explore this global macrocosm. Without losing sight of the micropolitical realities it will undertake a macropolitical analysis of international society. It will also argue that in the absence of a macropolitical perspective our lonely planet can be neither understood nor rescued.

The boundary lines of the epoch are
not between nations,
                         but between
the Gullivers of all countries and
                    the Lilliputians
YEVGENY YEVTUSHENKO

PART TWO

The
Macropolitical
World

Expanding
Perspectives

Power, wealth, ideology, and nationalism (as the most pervasive and compelling manifestation of ideology in our time) are preeminent among the goals and values that shape foreign policy behavior in the contemporary international system. If we recognize that nationalism is only a modern counterpart of all the parochial ideologies of the past, then it is possible to say that these are the values that have chiefly set the course of international politics throughout history. One can say the same about the history of domestic politics. Power, wealth, and ideology are perennially at the center of political action both within the state and beyond it.

If domestic and international systems share common salient values, they also share common salient problems. One problem of the very first importance to both is that of cohesion and divisiveness. That is, every society, from the tribal system to the global system, faces the need to reconcile the often conflicting requirements of the parts and the whole. From the smallest to the largest, every society experiences more or less frequently the divisive struggle of part against part or of parts combining to challenge the authority of the overall system—or to withdraw from it. Conversely, there are more or less frequent occasions in each society when one or more parts seek or claim to articulate the needs of the total system and to subordinate other parts to them, by conciliation or force. In short, all societies have had to deal with internal challenges to their integrity, security, and survival. This is true because no society is indivisible, and there is always tension between the whole of the society and its parts as well as among the parts themselves.

In domestic politics, the parts have been castes, classes, priesthoods, parties, races, establishments, and revolutionary and counterrevolutionary movements. Again and again their members have looked upon power, wealth, and ideology in parochial, partisan terms. That is, they have regarded these values as theirs to possess, enjoy, inculcate, and monopolize to the exclusion of the larger society in which they exist. Whether conservative or revolutionary, whether in power or seeking to win it, those who exhibit such attitudes represent the historic incarnations of both parochialism and elitism. In terms of contemporary national societies, these parochial forces are commonly described as putting interests such as those of class, section, or race above the interests of the nation.

Arrayed against them have been groups and individuals who argue the necessities, advantages, and obligations of a social organization in which there is equitable access to the central political values for all its members. These are the historic exponents of cosmopolitanism and egalitarianism. They can be called cosmopolitan in the sense of valuing the larger unit over the smaller, of preferring the more spacious community to those more circumscribed and inward-looking. They are egalitarian to the extent that they resist parochialism and exclusivism and regard the purpose of society as an instrument for sharing rather than restricting access to power, wealth, and ideological values. They have been variously called centralizers, federalists, liberals—and sometimes empire builders.

Just like their antagonists, the cosmopolitan-egalitarians are also parts of the whole; hence they cannot themselves be entirely free of parochial interest. The unavoidable result is that the vision of the whole is repeatedly blurred in consequence of the divergence and contention of the parts. Marx was neither the first nor the last to observe the phenomenon of the politician or philosopher advocating the rights of all citizens or all men while in fact meaning only himself and his allies. Nor was Marx the first or last to fall prey to the same vice he condemned in others.

In international politics, elitism and parochialism have been still more entrenched. Here the contending factions have been states, and they have typically recognized no law beyond their boundaries other than their own will. Beginning with Bodin in the sixteenth century, the will of the state was termed sovereign. But the functions that sovereignty describes have set the fashion in international politics since the beginning of history. Factions within civil societies could at least invoke, more or less credibly, norms claiming legitimacy for the whole society. But states in international politics have operated in a world which has approximated a normative vacuum, a society essentially devoid of binding obligations. In such a context there is no reliable restraint on the arbitrary use of force except counterforce, and there is no way to modify the fundamentally arbitrary way in which the state conducts its diplomacy.

Imperialism, the rule of the strong over the weak for the benefit of the strong, is in all its many guises the inevitable product of a political system in which decisions are made almost exclusively by tests of strength. Since this condition is still the prevalent characteristic of international relations today, it is not surprising that charges of imperialism and neocolonialism fill the air even after most of the symbols of the old colonialism have vanished. A system that features an anarchic coexistence of the powerful and the weak must produce instances of tyranny and exploitation with almost rhythmic regularity. The structures of international law and international organization reflect far more than they restrain this systemic international anarchy and its compulsive bias toward tyrannical solutions.

Having reached that point in history where humanity has discovered the secret of its own annihilation, men now confront the necessity of building a different kind of international system from one which has locked them for so long into a single option between tyranny and anarchy. This is the option that perennially generates violence. And in the nuclear age it will condemn men to nuclear violence. Avoidance of nuclear destruction, then, requires that international society cease to be dominated by the overt clashes and covert collusion of tyranny and anarchy.

The vicious circle that produces both clash and collusion begins with anarchy's divisions. It develops with the fears that division generates. The junction is reached in the ensuing struggle when each part in the fragmented system seeks power as the only security against fear and reckons its gains in terms of the losses of others. These are the classic calculations of tyrants and the classic breeders of distrust. Distrust, in turn, as the enemy of unity, must also perpetuate anarchy—and the circle is complete.

These are the dynamics which in international politics express themselves in war, imperialism, and the rules of sovereign diplomacy. In every age they have been denounced as inhumane and dangerous. But they have more often been accepted, defended, and even idealized as the only effective techniques for attaining power, wealth, and ideological satisfactions in a world where these commodities are in short supply.

The scarcity of these commodities provokes competition and results in an unequal distribution of values among the competitors. Imbalance between demand and supply of power, wealth, and ideology has been at the heart of the perennial struggle between parochial-elitist and cosmopolitan-egalitarian forces in both domestic and international politics. In both contexts the parochial-elitist argument has prevailed more often than not because, more often than not, scarcity has been the prevailing human condition.

Scarcity, then, has provided the basic rationale for the parochial-elitist position that only some and not others could enjoy desirable values. With some reason, unequal distribution passed as the only feasible adjustment to the reality of limited supply. By the same token, competition was deemed the only conceivable method of distribution, and the only conceivable outcome was that the strong should have much and the weak little. The implication is clear: the rule of tyranny, anarchy, and violence will be curtailed only as scarcity and inequality yield to abundance.

The vision of abundance has always been linked with the cosmopolitan premise that values increase in worth to the extent that they are shared instead of hoarded. On the same premise, diffusion of power generates riches for society and all its members in far greater measure than the benefits minority rule can produce—even for the ruling minority. Abundance of human liberty and dignity, of material goods, of opportunities for autonomy in the development of individuals, groups, and societies, an abundant peace—these have been the professed objectives of the cosmopolitan-egalitarian argument. To the extent that these purposes have been approximated and abundance achieved within the state, the politics of force, oppression, and exclusivity have receded. The counterpart policies of force, imperialism, and sovereign autocracy in international politics will not yield unless the same cosmopolitan-egalitarian purposes are recognized to be as valid beyond the state as within it, and unless conscious efforts are directed toward their realization.

The fundamental lesson of our age is that there is no qualitative difference between international and domestic politics. Indeed, and despite numerous arguments to the contrary, no such difference has ever existed. The root problems of the state—civil peace or civil war, civil liberty or civil oppression, civil wealth or civil poverty—find and always have found their precise counterparts in relations among states. But the parallels have been obscured, often understandably, to the extent that geographic distance and cultural isolation produced a real contrast between the relative cohesion of at least some civil societies and the relative incoherence of the world beyond their borders.

Today that contrast is more shadow than substance. Every facet of contemporary technology relentlessly assaults the ancient barriers of distance and isolation. The assumption that every state has or must aspire to a destiny fundamentally detached from the others becomes untenable in a world in which the patterns of production and consumption, of transport and communications, and of the resultant political anticipations draw the global populations into an ever tighter network of interdependence. It is untenable, above all, in a world in which these same forces are making mankind into an increasingly compact target for nuclear bombardment.

Survival, liberty, justice, material wealth, and peace within the state have always been dependent to a greater or lesser degree on the state's international environment. Now the difference in degree is approaching the vanishing point. The fate of the civil society is becoming indistinguishable from the fate of the international society. It follows that the purposes and tasks of the civil society must become identical with the purposes and tasks of international society if either is to endure.

This kind of analysis and prescription necessarily leads to a demand for a radical departure from the traditional wisdom in international politics. It enjoins a break with the micropolitical assumptions that have dominated foreign policy discourse during most of history. That is, it requires what some have called a Copernican revolution in global politics, one in which men no longer attempt to define reality and purpose from the vantage point of the smaller part but to understand themselves and their environment from the perspective of the global whole.

To the extent that such a shift in the angle of vision takes place, the ancient distinctions of principle between foreign and domestic will fade and disappear, together with the rationale for the old tribal verities expressed in the terms "we" and "they." This shift away from the traditional sight lines of international relations is the indispensable condition for a transition from the paramountcy of micropolitics to the paramountcy of macropolitics, to an international politics which in theory and practice recognizes that the parts can function satisfactorily only within a satisfactorily functioning whole.

Macropolitics, then, necessarily treats international problems as the domestic problems of the global system. It discerns no essential differences between the problems of the whole and the problems of the parts, though it must recognize the continuing vitality and, within limits, the enduring legitimacy of micropolitical distinctions between foreign and domestic. Macropolitics and micropolitics are not mutually exclusive; they are complementary. But they are in unavoidable contest for ascendancy in human thought and behavior in the global system. The macropolitical purpose ought not to be the destruction of micropolitical behavior; such a goal is both illusory and undesirable. The objective should rather be a displacement of standards, in which macropolitical propositions replace micropolitical propositions as the governing considerations in international policy. Given the historic predominance of micropolitics, such a purpose assures contest enough. It is a contest that will decide the outcome of humanity's struggle to stay alive.

For the first time, the penetration of space has offered men a perspective from which to view the whole of the physical earth. Macropolitics attempts to achieve an analogous perspective from which to view the whole of the political world. A probe into political space will unavoidably produce distortions, but they can be progressively corrected if the contest between macropolitics and micropolitics engenders rational debate and adjustment. And error can be minimized to the extent that the debaters understand the true situation of the globe on which we live. It is a situation tellingly summed up by Adlai Stevenson in his last speech as ambassador to the United Nations: "We travel together, passengers on a little spaceship . . . preserved from annihilation only by the care, the work, and I will say the love we give to our fragile craft."

Chapter 12

Global Demand and Supply

Traditional thinking in international politics, insofar as it has employed the concept of demand and supply at all, has applied it almost exclusively to the nation-state. It has tried to ascertain the kinds of demands being placed on the state in terms of self-preservation, pressures for expansion, economic viability, and ideological toughness or creativity. In turn, it has sought to examine the supply of resources that the state possesses or could develop in order to deal with these demands. The best-known formulation of this kind of analysis has been the so-called elements of power—or foundations of national power—approach to international politics. The state's role in the world is appraised in terms of the ensemble of factors which strengthen or weaken it in the pursuit of its international goals.

The major categories of inquiry in the elements of power approach are geographic size and location, topography and climate, natural resources, population numbers and skills, economic productivity, military capability, effectiveness of social and political organization, and degree of diplomatic know-how. A balance sheet of the state's assets and shortcomings in each of these categories, and their ramifying subcategories, has been regarded as essential to an understanding of the state's behavior and experience in the world at large.

The ability of a state to exert or defend itself, in this view, depends on the nature of its physical base and the human superstructure that has developed from that base. An analytical examination of base and superstructure, then, could provide an empirical measurement of state power. Such an examination could also give rise to a prescriptive, or policy, science that could judge whether the state's foreign policy was overextended or undercommitted relative to the power resources available to it. Ideally, such a policy science could describe the optimum relationship between foreign policy goals and internal resources and prescribe the techniques best able to achieve such a relationship. Its fundamental theme is that the secret of solvency in foreign policy is to be discovered in the connection between the state's commitments and its resources.

The solvency prescription follows automatically: optimum power for the state depends on the maintenance of an equilibrium between commitments and resources, between demand and supply.

None of the elements of power, however, can be adequately analyzed simply by examining the state's own base and superstructure in isolation from the rest of the world. Power, after all, is a relational concept. It always assumes an object: Power in regard to what? And it can only be measured in comparative terms: Is the power of A more or less than—or approximately the same as—the power of X? It is obvious, then, that the external world must be included in the elements of power analysis. If elements of strength and weakness are present within the state, they are to be found in the state's environment as well. It is evident, for example, that a state will be able to exercise more external influence if its potential foreign enemies are at odds among themselves than if they form a united front. Or, to resort to a different illustration, a high degree of social and political vigor within a state in an international environment where these qualities are in short supply offers possibilities for the growth of influence that a less vulnerable environment would otherwise obstruct.

Hence the "foundations of national power" are found outside as well as within the state. The inherent relativity of power and the necessity for comparison force the analyst to consider the international context in order to assess the state's chances for survival or growth and to identify rational choices in foreign policy. The realization, in turn, that the nation's fate is to a significant degree dependent on the international system in which it operates transfers some of the analyst's, or politician's, concern for the state to a concern for the functioning of the larger system.

FROM MICROPOLITICS TO MACROPOLITICS

These kinds of considerations have at many different points in history provided the orthodox arguments on behalf of "internationalism" or, in more contemporary terms, of "globalism." They rebuke "isolationist" assumptions of state or national self-sufficiency by stressing the extent to which life in any given civil society is conditioned by the way the rest of the world is living. A case in point is the ultimate argument of many contemporary American internationalists. The contention is that the Soviet Union shares with the United States the capability of destroying civil society everywhere. If the balance of terror has so far inhibited the exercise of this fatal capability, its continuing effectiveness is in constant doubt and dependent on the prevailing level of rationality in both Moscow and Washington. The argument concludes that the manifest interdependence of the Soviet Union and the United States in the matter of safeguarding their very existence demands a measure of collaboration between them. In other words, the realities of the nuclear international system require the most powerful states of all to accept obligations and guidelines for behavior that derive not from their own internally generated aspirations but from the dynamics of their interaction.

For all the stress on the logic of interaction, however, orthodox internationalism still takes the state as its central point of reference. The state is the chief actor and reactor, and the welter of activity in the international system is scrutinized in order to gauge its impact on the concerns of the state. The state-centered vantage point of orthodox internationalism unquestionably offers insight into international reality. This is doubly true insofar as the analysts and politicians of all states take the same approach; then all can be said to be well attuned to the way the game is being played. In such circumstances each state is assumed to be pursuing its national interest, calculating its course of conduct according to its perception of both internal and external dangers and opportunities. This is the highest level of realism that the fundamentally micropolitical concepts of traditional internationalism can attain.

In the perspectives of micropolitics, the world is at best a vast extension of the state's internal resources. From the external resource system the state can extract elements of safety (an alliance), occasions for expansion (an empire), or opportunities for enrichment (international trade and investment). At worst, it is the chief source of threats to the state's survival, which must be countered with the methods appropriate to conflict. The practice of micropolitics is therefore characterized either by exploitation or defensiveness, or both. Since it assumes the good of the state to be its chief concern, micropolitics cannot easily conceptualize or generate policies that would subordinate extractive or defensive considerations to the greater good of the environment in which the state exists. The introduction of such policy considerations also introduces the idea of international interest alongside the national interest. The articulation of an international interest, in turn, marks the transition from micropolitics to macropolitics.

Macropolitics is concerned with the operation of the world political system as a whole. Its basic questions are: What is the nature of the system? What is the impact of parts on the system? How does the system affect the parts? How do the parts affect each other? These questions obviously require that macropolitical analysis understand the behavior of the parts as well as the whole. But the purpose of such an understanding differs from the purpose embedded in microanalysis. Micropolitics studies state behavior and the encompassing system in order to discover the conditions of the state's viability. Macropolitics studies the encompassing system and state behavior within it in order to discover the conditions of the system's viability.

If micropolitics accords priority to the fortunes of the state and macro-politics to the fortunes of the global system, it does not follow that the two approaches are in fundamental conflict. State and system each has a stake in how the other functions, and the rational goal of both is that their mutual relations should be harmonious and not antagonistic. It is the same stake and goal that characterize the assumptions of federalism or the relationship between the individual producer-consumer and the economy in which he subsists. In the economy, in the civil society—federal or not—and in the international society, the whole and the parts are mutually dependent. Mutuality of dependence, of course, supplies ample opportunity for hostility as well as harmony. But this basic truth does not negate the equally basic truth that in a state of interdependence it is rational to seek agreement in preference to disagreement.

Despite the potential compatibility of micropolitics and macropolitics, history has made them adversaries. The claims of the parts—the states—have consistently overridden the claims of the larger system. This is hardly surprising; only seldom in time or place has there been a realistic perception of the larger system in which the state must operate. To the extent that its very existence goes unrecognized, in turn, the survival requirements of the encompassing macrosystem will remain unremarked. The eventual outcome is the collapse of the system as a consequence of the myopia afflicting its component parts, the states. Even the European adepts in balance of power theory and practice could not recognize the true nature of the system on which each of the states of Europe depended. They failed because all were chiefly bent on exploiting the system rather than nurturing it. Two world wars and the end of Europe's historic ascendancy in international politics were the unavoid-able results.

Only in our own time has the international system begun to be intel-ligible in all its dimensions. It follows that previous ages cannot be faulted for failing to understand what they could not perceive, except in those cases—frequent enough—where failure of perception was more a matter of will than of ignorance. But in the late twentieth century evidence presses in from all sides that all states, great and small, are enmeshed in a global system that defines the ultimate conditions of their existence. The time has come to give the system its due.

It is at this juncture, however, that the dispute between micropolitics and macropolitics emerges. Micropolitics, with its stress on the claims of individual states, has dominated the entire course of international history. Macropolitics, concerned with the claims of the system as a whole, must necessarily contest the traditional micropolitical monopoly in defining the rules of the game. Its intellectual premises enjoin a still more radical objective: the displacement of micropolitics as the govern-ing approach in the theory and practice of international politics. The realization of such objectives would indeed constitute a Copernican revolution.

The causes for conflict between macropolitics and micropolitics are abundantly evident. The conflict is essentially the same as that engendered by the ecologist when he insists that a habitable environment will not survive the reckless behavior of its disparate populations and that the requirements of the balance of nature must have priority over the untutored predilections of individuals. Macropolitics confronts micropolitics with an analogous admonition: states must meet the needs of the political ecosystem in its global dimensions or court annihilation. Ecology holds out the promise of rescue from the dangers of resource pollution and depletion—if men will learn to nurture their natural environment. Macropolitics offers the same promise concerning the danger of physical annihilation—if men and states will learn to nurture their political environment.

Instead of beginning, then, with an inquiry into the elements of a nation's power and the demands made on that power, macropolitics examines the elements of global viability and the challenges to that viability. The central problem of our time is that men are burdening the global system with a whole battery of demands that threaten its capacity to survive. They run the gamut from basic food needs for multiplying billions to the insistence upon continuing the elite game of nuclear politics. Unless men reorder their demands and reorganize the arrangements for supply, the system in which they live will be destroyed.

A FIRST ASSESSMENT OF GLOBAL VIABILITY

An elements of power approach taking for its subject the entire globe rather than the individual state would have to consider the following data:

Geography: 196,950,284 square miles of surface area. This area, in turn, is divided into three basic components: land, 25 percent; sea and ocean, 70.8 percent; bodies of fresh water, 4.2 percent.

Topography: The earth's land surface can be subdivided into the following major categories: built-on land (human constructions), 14.6 percent; croplands, orchards, and gardens, 9.7 percent; pasture, 19.5 percent; forest, 29.6 percent; desert and wasteland, 23.3 percent. (Mountainous areas are located mainly in forest, desert, and wasteland categories.)[1]

Climate: Temperate climate prevails over 36.8 percent of the global land surface; tropical over 19.9 percent; arid and semiarid over 26.3 percent; arctic and subarctic over 17.0 percent.

---

[1] This does not include land under ice cap.

Population: Approximately 3.6 billion human beings in 1970. Very unevenly distributed both in terms of population density and in terms of the ability of societies physically to sustain present and projected population numbers. The current global rate of population increase is estimated at 70 million annually. Estimates of world population by the year 2000 vary between 6.5 and 7.5 billion, or roughly double the 1970 figure. At the current rate of increase, another doubling is projected by the decade 2020 to 2030 and further doublings thereafter at ever shorter intervals.

Population skills: Very unevenly distributed. High levels of education and skills for substantial majorities in most industrialized countries; average for nonindustrialized countries very low. Nearly 800 million people, almost all in the underdeveloped world, are totally illiterate. Almost half the world's children do not go to school.

Food supply: Growing but insufficient. Unequal productivity and distribution result in chronic malnutrition among large sectors of the global population. Approximately 3.7 million die annually from starvation and malnutrition-related disease. Rapidly expanding population is steadily escalating pressures on world food supplies.

Raw materials: Unevenly dispersed over the earth's surface. The capacity to extract and process raw materials into fabricated form is still more unequally distributed and is overwhelmingly in the hands of the technically skilled minority of the global population. The rate of raw materials exploitation threatens to exhaust or drastically restrict the availability of a whole series of major minerals within one generation.

Economy: The gross world product (GWP) in 1970 (the sum of the annual gross national products of the countries of the world) is estimated to have been—in 1970 dollars—approximately $3.22 trillion. An equal division of the GWP among the world's population would yield a per capita figure of $881. But the now familiar pattern of inequality finds its most pronounced expression in the realm of economics. The developed world (communist and noncommunist) alone accounts for approximately 83 percent of the GWP, or $2.664 trillion, leaving 17 percent, or $555 billion for the rest of the world. At the same time, the population ratio is almost the reverse: The developed world accounts for approximately 27 percent of the global population and the rest of the world accounts for the remaining 73 percent. Thus 73 percent of the world's population generates and consumes roughly 17 percent of the GWP and 27 percent generates and consumes approximately 83 percent. On the basis of this division, per capita GWP in North America and Europe averages $2701 and in the rest of the world $208.[2] Continuation of current trends will widen the gap

---

[2] Statistics in this section are taken from *World Military Expenditures 1971*, U.S. Arms Control and Disarmament Agency, Washington, D.C., July 1972.

between the rich minority and the poor majority to a point where the grotesque disparity of today will seem equitable in retrospect.

Political organization: Divided, as of 1973, into approximately 150 sovereign units, many of which are sovereign more in name than in fact. More than 60 colonial or otherwise dependent territories (mainly small in area and population) comprise the remainder of the globe's political subdivisions. In all of the subdivisions, sovereign or not, parochial concerns predominate to a greater or lesser degree over global or regional concerns. Political behavior in terms of global or regional values is thus persistently subordinated to values traditionally associated with sovereign advantage. With each of the parts in the international system deeming itself more important than the whole, the politics of divisiveness maintains a built-in ascendency over the politics of unity. Problems of a global or regional nature that rationally require action by governmental bodies of appropriate scale are in the main dealt with by or among the individual sovereign governments or left unresolved. The fragile sense of community beyond the sovereign boundaries results in a world political structure which is dangerously accident prone. and highly vulnerable to outbursts of violence of local, regional, or global dimensions.

The United Nations, as noted below, must presently be seen more as a forum for diplomacy than as an instrument of government.

Military capability: More than sufficient to bring an end to all life. The activation of the full capability, however, violates all military doctrine (to say nothing of other values) in that it would eliminate the traditionally inclusive military options of win, lose, or draw. Hence the chief military problem at the global level is to prevent all-out nuclear warfare in a situation in which none of the nuclear powers is willing to give up its capability to precipitate the holocaust. Techniques to deal with this problem include deterrence strategy, arms control devices, and hitherto successful efforts (after Hiroshima and Nagasaki) to prevent more limited forms of violence from crossing the nuclear threshold. The adequacy of all three techniques is in constant jeopardy due to the continuing arms race, both nuclear and conventional, to investments in new weapons of mass destruction, and to rising political, economic, and social tensions around the globe.

The spectacular inequalities in the distribution of political and economic power among the global populations are repeated in the realm of military power. The two superpowers all but monopolize the existing nuclear capability and command the lion's share of conventional military power as well. The three remaining nuclear powers are far down the scale in both categories, though Chinese conventional forces are formidable and Chinese nuclear capabilities are increasingly significant. Among the nonnuclear states, perhaps thirty maintain conventional military forces of major importance to their local or regional areas. Of the hundred and more remaining, it can be said that their military organizations are more relevant to internal than to international politics.

Diplomatic capability: Lacking an encompassing governmental structure, the globe depends for its survival on the diplomatic capabilities of its constituent states. It is dependent, above all—once again the pattern of inequality—on the diplomatic goals and capabilities of the two superpowers. All the rest can both create and resolve diplomatic problems, but it is the diplomacy of the superpowers which can either contain a local conflict or transform it into a major crisis. By the same token, only superpower diplomacy is capable of providing the leadership and a sufficient share of the resources necessary to reverse the accelerating trend toward ever greater inequality among the globe's inhabitants. Accentuation of the division between the rich minority and poor majority is the greatest single challenge to the survival of the global society. As long as there is no global government committed to relieving the inequities that burden most of its citizens, superpower diplomacy is the only available surrogate to perform such a function.

The United Nations is the sole quasi-governmental organization that spans the earth, and it faithfully reflects the fragmented structure of the international political system. Its activities are carried on at the pleasure of the parochial sovereignties; it follows that any gains by the UN in governmental effectiveness must stem from more cosmopolitan impulses from within the sovereignties. The UN as government has the potential to deal with the global problems of demand and supply, of imbalance between the rich and the poor, of security, and of disparities in political effectiveness—but only if the membership wills it.

This, in necessarily brief and sparse detail, constitutes a first sketch or abstract of an elements of power approach applied at a global rather than a national level. A signal characteristic of this description of global geographic base and human superstructure is the massive inequality in terms of power, wealth, education, and status that sets off the minority rich from the majority poor. The differential in the prevalence of education and technological and organizational skills is the fundamental dividing line between the minority and the majority. It follows that the rich sectors of the globe, possessing most of the wealth-building means of production, also possess most of the sophisticated means of destruction. The result is that the poor majority is dependent to an unprecedented degree on the behavior of the rich in matters of both life and death.

Were the foregoing the description of a single state instead of the globe as a whole, the observer would be forced to the conclusion that the unit analyzed is critically endangered. Although the earth faces no external enemy (the primary menace in the traditional elements of power approach), it is, in C. P. Snow's words, in a state of siege. First, total available resources are seriously insufficient to meet the needs of the total population. Moreover, accelerating population growth and rapid depletion of the present resource base threaten to produce an imbalance of catastrophic proportions within the span of one or two generations.

Second, gross inequality marks the distribution of presently available resources among the global population. A comparable division of wealth in a developed domestic society (27 percent of the populace commanding more than 80 percent of total property and income) would brand that society as monumentally unjust and in peril of revolution. The future frequency and intensity of violence (of "revolution" in the sense of destabilizing the global society) as a product of resource scarcity and extreme inequality of distribution defy precise calculation. But it is instructive to recall that the large majority of wars and other instances of political violence since 1945 have originated in the underdeveloped, resource-poor world. A prognosis for a rising curve of violence among the world's poor is in accord with all the indicators now available.

Third, the world's rich minority is profoundly divided within itself, most obviously between communist and noncommunist segments, but still more fundamentally in the fragmentation represented by the individual sovereignties. These essentially provincial divisions prevent the rich minority from jointly addressing itself to the global perils that menace both rich and poor. And, of course, the divisions specifically prevent a joint approach to, and defense against, the misery, hunger, disease, and violence that darken the existence of the poor three-quarters of mankind.

Fourth, the stocks of nuclear weapons already capable of destroying the earth continue to multiply, primarily in the arsenals of the super-powers. Except for China, the world's poor have access only to conventional arms, but the pressure for acquisition of nuclear capabilities will mount unless the imbalance between nuclear haves and have-nots is mitigated. At the same time, the fear of igniting the nuclear fires sharply reduces the otherwise overwhelming advantages of the rich in the use of threat and force in their dealings with the poor. Unwillingness to resort to the bomb functions as an equalizer between nuclear and non-nuclear societies and transmutes the anger and violence endemic in the world of the poor into a far greater menace to the rich than would otherwise be the case. It follows that the poor are not so weak as they seem, and the rich are more vulnerable than they may suppose.

Thus the global society bristles with monstrous weapons aimed at one another by antagonistic factions. A little more than one-quarter of the population controls so much of the wealth that the remaining three-quarters are left to hover at subsistence level. Meanwhile, the resource base for the whole of the global population and economy shrinks as demand swells. Finally, there are no adequate political processes or institutions which could enable earth's inhabitants to begin to emerge from chaos and to deal rationally and responsibly with the multiple hazards that beset the society of men.

This is what is meant by the earth's state of siege. It is an internal siege in which both inherited and newly created divisions immobilize the global society and so hinder it from dealing with the causes that threaten its extinction. Unlike the classic crisis situation in traditional—micropolitical—international relations, there is no enemy outside the walls. Modern means of production and destruction have extemporaneously created the macropolitical system that now encompasses the globe and have—necessarily—brought the enemy inside the gates.

An abstract of the global elements of power, the elements whose sum measures the ability of a society to influence events to its benefit, yields a result that signals weakness and danger rather than power and security. But the signal is not always easily detected and interpreted, and detection and interpretation are especially difficult for those who wield most of the available power. Just as the inhabitants of suburbia find it hard to see the ghetto, so the citizenry of the few affluent, militarily strong, and relatively well-ordered states find it hard to see what is happening to the rest of mankind. Failure to see and respond to the domestic ghetto and failure to see and respond to the global poor have the same results: the affluent become less able to understand themselves and the situation in which they exist.

POPULATION PRESSURES ON HUMAN SURVIVAL

The situation can be seen in more concrete terms than an elements-of-power abstract permits. It can be illustrated by the plight of India, burdened with a populace of more than half a billion. In 1970 21 million babies were born in India, and 8 million people of all ages died. The difference is the population growth rate that condemns an already poverty-stricken and hungry society to find food for an additional million-plus mouths every month. Each month's increase, in turn, expands the total population base and presages a still larger monthly production of consumers in each succeeding year. If the current population growth rate of 2.5 percent per year persists, India will have to provide sustenance for nearly a billion human beings before the century ends.

Despite the remarkable achievements of the green revolution in Indian agriculture, India cannot possibly meet the challenge of its own population explosion without massive changes internally and in its relations with the outside world. And meeting the challenge obviously cannot be defined simply in terms of food. Water supply, fertilizer, food distribution and storage facilities, clothing, housing, health services, education, employment, manufacture, capital, and governance are also crucial components in any formula to keep a society of a billion people alive and to prevent it from going out of control.[3]

By contrast, the United States, with less than 40 percent of India's population and almost 2,000 percent of India's wealth (in terms of GNP), adds only one-quarter as many people per year to its population base. It is estimated that the United States population in the year 2000 will reach approximately 300 million. Thus the projected ratio of the population of India to that of the United States rises from 2.7 to 1 in 1970 to approximately 3.33 to 1 in 2000, while the absolute GNP differential in favor of the United States grows from approximately $920 billion in 1970 to a fantastic $2.4 trillion in the year 2000.[4]

Yet responsible critics have contended that in terms of public health and resource consumption, even the United States had already exceeded its optimum population by the year 1969.[5] A calculation of the voracious consumption propensity of the average American helps to illustrate the case of the critics:

> Every 7½ seconds a new American is born. He is a disarming little thing, but he begins to scream loudly in a voice that can be heard for seventy years. He is screaming for 26,000,000 tons of water, 21,000 gallons of gasoline, 10,150 pounds of meat, 28,000 pounds of milk and cream, 9,000 pounds of wheat, and great storehouses of all other foods, drinks, and tobacco. These are his lifetime demands of his country and its economy. . . .
>
> He is requisitioning a private endowment of $5,000 to $8,000 for school building materials, $6,300 worth of clothing, $7,000 worth of furniture. . . . He is yelping for a Paul Bunyan chunk, in his own right, of the nation's pulpwood, paper, steel, zinc, magnesium, aluminum and tin.[6]

This gross portrayal—in more than one sense—of the average American consumer leaves out, of course, the creative capabilities of that same average American as producer. An equally vivid calculation of his productive capacities in the context of a rapidly changing technology is needed to draw an accurate balance between demand and supply for both the present and the future. Yet high levels of consumption are

---

[3] To this list must be added the pressures created by a still more populous China and a dozen other overpopulated countries in Asia, whose overall population in the year 2000 is projected to be 3.8 billion, or more than the entire world population in 1970.

[4] Projections are calculated in 1970 dollars and based on trends identified in the period from 1960 to 1970. They are, of course, subject to revision to the extent that trends are altered in future years. See population and GNP tables in Appendices B and C.

[5] See the assertion of Dr. John H. Knowles, Director of the Massachusetts General Hospital, that United States population has passed the optimum mark in respect to public health considerations. The article also records a variety of expert opinions concerning the extent of resource depletion. *New York Times*, December 30, 1969.

[6] Robert and Leona Rienow, *Moment in the Sun* (New York: Dial Press), 1967, p. 3.

obviously involved in the production process itself, before its fruits ever reach the consumer, so that there are limits, even for the richest nation in the world, to the formula of increasing productivity in order to meet rising consumer demand. Thus the population-resources imbalance, which constitutes the chief of many threats to the world's poor, also threatens the rich countries both in terms of the world-wide pressures it generates and in terms of their own prodigal patterns of production and consumption.

The pressure of population on resources can in some ways be more graphically portrayed in small-scale rather than large-scale terms. Mauritius, Indian Ocean island, sovereign state, and member of the United Nations, doubled its population in the fifteen years between 1955 and 1970.[7] Thirty-eight by twenty-nine miles in extent (roughly one-tenth the size of New Jersey), the island now carries a load of more than 850,000 people. If the present growth rate persists, there will be nearly 1.5 million by 1982 and nearly 3 million by 2000. The root cause for this human explosion is one common to most of the underdeveloped world since 1945: not a rise in the birth rate but a drastic decline in the death rate. In the case of Mauritius, as in India, Pakistan, Ceylon, and a number of other countries, the most dramatic drop in the annual death rate dates from the virtual eradication of malaria by DDT.

Mauritius is one of many stark examples of the revenge that technological progress and medical advances can take. The doubling of the available work force in fifteen years resulted in a 33 percent unemployment rate by 1970. The economy would founder without subsidy from Britain, the former colonial ruler, mainly in the form of purchasing more than half of the export sugar crop at 50 percent more than the prevailing world price. The governing apparatus is fragile and increasingly vulnerable to overthrow by sectors of the rebellious, multiracial, and ever growing populace. The population division of the World Bank describes Mauritius as "experiencing the first true Malthusian breakdown."[8]

---

[7] The material on Mauritius as well as the quotations are taken from Richard Critchfield's article, "Mauritius: A Sense of the Apocalypse" (New York: Alicia Patterson Fund, January 1970). By permission of the Fund and the *Washington Evening Star*. Population figures for Mauritius in Appendix B differ from those given here, particularly in the projections.

[8] Thomas Malthus, who developed the first systematic analysis of population problems, set forth in 1798 his fundamental theoretical proposition: "The Power of Population is indefinitely greater than the power in the earth to produce subsistence for man." Malthus concluded from this proposition that human demand always threatens to overwhelm available food supply and that temporary abundance merely serves to increase the number of human consumers and thus to reinforce pressures on the food base. When demand actually outruns supply, a Malthusian breakdown occurs, resulting in starvation and a struggle for survival in the most literal sense of the term. The quotation is from Malthus' *An Essay on the Principle of Population as it Affects the Future Improvement of Mankind* . . . , published anonymously in London in 1798.

What a Malthusian breakdown means can be illustrated on a still smaller scale. In Critchfield's report on Mauritius he records the experience of fishermen at Cap Malheureux on Mauritius' northern tip:

> With shouts, oaths, the rhythmic beating of sticks against hulls, hisses, splashed gaffs and the strain of shoulders and backs, the net is drawn in, dripping with sea grass. Until two years ago, it would have been heavy with parrot fish, spiny-backed Cordonier, the dazzling reds and yellows of reef fish or a big fifteen-pound carp. Then there were cries of "God is with us," "We can catch fish today."
>
> Nowadays there is usually only a bemused silence as the men see there are only a few small reef fish flopping in the bottom of the net. . . . The patron curses. . . .
>
> For two years now the lagoon around the island has been depleted of fish. With not enough work in the towns or sugarfields, the young men take to the sea. They hunt fish everywhere in the lagoon, with nets, lines, bamboo cages, or, risking sharks and barracuda, underwater with spears and harpoon guns or, risking imprisonment, at night with dynamite. Now if a patron is lucky, a crew of sixteen men must share earnings from a day's catch of twenty pounds. Three years ago it would have been a hundred pounds and the sea would have yielded a decent living.
>
> . . . the patron busies himself with the rigging as the small fleet of pirogues sets sail once more. But he watches, secretly, the hardening faces of his men and tells a visitor that the young ones are beginning to speak of revolution and the old of starvation and apocalypse.

Moving back again from the smallest scale to the larger dimensions of the population-resource imbalance, the bitter fact must be recorded that more than thirty countries are in the same category as Mauritius in terms of the rate of population increase (3 percent or more per year); among them are Brazil, Iran, Mexico, North Vietnam, Pakistan, Peru, the Philippines, South Africa, Turkey, and Venezuela. Of the remaining countries in the underdeveloped world, all but a few are growing at a rate of from 2.0 to 2.9 percent. For upward of 70 percent of mankind, then, a Malthusian breakdown is not an abstract concept but a concrete menace which may become a terrible reality during the remaining years of this century or early in the next.

With the single exception of Australia, the population growth rates of the developed countries are currently defined as "moderate" (1.0 to 1.9 percent) or "low" (0.1 to 0.9 percent). Yet even they are not immune to a Malthusian future of social breakdown resulting from a deterioration of the resource base to the point where it is no longer able to support the populations dependent upon it. The global population growth rate in 1970 approximated 2 percent (the beginning of the "high" growth rate category). The 2 percent figure functions as the true indicator that the population crisis of mankind is indivisible. After all, the industrial nations, with few exceptions, are dependent for important elements of their own nutrition on those countries where Malthusian forces may disrupt the supply.

But as always and in all places, food is a primary problem for the poor and a secondary one for the rich. The affluent societies are likely to go on eating when famine has already taken on massive proportions in the world of the poor. A more immediate material challenge to the affluent world is of a different order: it is a challenge to the whole technological infrastructure upon which the dynamic of life in the developed countries depends. It is a double-barreled threat: the global raw material base essential to industrial societies is rapidly contracting, and, at the same time, industrial societies are polluting additional resources crucial not only for production but for the very quality of life in the industrial societies themselves.

NATURAL RESOURCES AND HUMAN DEMANDS

Depletion of the resource base manifests itself most starkly in the depletion of the land—land as a producer of organic growths and land as a complex of inorganic constituents. Although the sea has been an important source of food (it is now also endangered as we have seen in the microcosm of Mauritius and in the macrocosm of competition among the major commercial fishing nations), land has been the prime source of man's food and fiber. Human dependence on the products of the land must necessarily increase as the number of human beings increases.

Yet the net amount of land available for agriculture has sharply decreased. Deforestation, erosion, and agricultural malpractice are responsible, along with other factors, for a seventy-year increase (from 1882 to 1952) in desert and wasteland area from 9.4 percent to an ominous 23.3 percent of the total land area of the globe. During the same period, acreage in crops, orchards, gardens (tilled land), and pasture also expanded, though more modestly, from 21.0 percent to 29.2 percent. Land devoted to urban and rural housing, industry, railroads, highways, military uses, and comparable purposes almost doubled, from 7.7 percent to 14.6 percent. The expansion of urban and agricultural land use, however, did not begin to match the destructive growth of the desert, and the percentage rise in all three categories of land took place in very large part at the ultimate expense of the world's forests. In 1882, 45.4 percent of the globe's land surface was forested; by 1952, this figure had dropped to 29.6 percent.[9]

---

[9] The material in this paragraph is taken from Robert R. Doane, *World Balance Sheet* (New York: Harper & Bros., 1957), p. 24. The percentages refer to total land area less land under ice cap.

The ecological implications of a contracting forest and an expanding desert are manifold and dangerous. But in terms of nutrition, the amount of food-producing land deserves special consideration. After all, the world is sustaining, if with difficulty, more than double the population of some ninety years ago. Intensive agriculture, and not the expansion of food-producing lands, has been the chief source of mounting food production. It is also the chief hope for sustaining a world population that will double again in only thirty years.

There is evidence, as we shall see, that it is not a vain hope. But it must be based on a realistic appraisal of all the factors involved, and one of the most basic factors is the quality of the soil itself. Robert R. Doane offers somber statistics (see Table 12.1) concerning the deterioration of the world's cropland during the period from 1882 to 1952.

Over a seventy-year period, Doane has calculated an appalling annual net loss of 5.179 billion tons of topsoil from the earth's land surface, including 110 million tons of nitrogen, 443 million tons of potassium, 672 million tons of calcium, 211 million tons of magnesium, and 3.6 billion tons of organic matter. If this rate of depletion cannot be reduced, the world's entire inventory of topsoil will have been exhausted somewhere around the year 2025.[10]

It is not necessarily beyond human capacity to remedy this situation. Yet Doane makes clear that as of the time he wrote, the human contribution to the annual replenishment of the soil by means of manufactured fertilizers and irrigation was a mere 27 and 60 million tons, respectively, of a total annual replacement figure of nearly 1 billion tons (90 percent of topsoil replacement takes place by natural processes). Human replenishment shrinks to minuscule proportions compared with the annual net depletion figure of more than 5 billion tons and with the gross annual loss of more than 6 billion. On the other hand, the manufacture and use of fertilizer has grown enormously since the early 1950s, when Doane completed his study. The 1968 Yearbook of the United Nations Food and Agriculture Organization (FAO) reports a world fertilizer production in the year 1967 to 1968 of more than 56

---

[10] Figures in this paragraph and the one following are drawn from tables in Doane, pp. 29–32.

Table 12.1
Deterioration of Cropland, 1882–1952

	1882	1952	NET CHANGE
Good land	85.0%	41.2%	−43.8%
50% topsoil lost	9.9	38.5	+28.6
Submarginal land	5.1	20.3	+15.2

million tons, more than double the 1952 figure. Moreover, in the four-year period from 1963 to 1967 production was registering a 12 percent annual increase.

Man's ability to replenish the soil is clearly increasing along with his ability to produce more food per acre. But many agronomists warn of the likelihood of an upper limit to the amount of fertilizer that can be productively applied to the land, after which diminishing returns will set in. Moreover, the runoff of manufactured fertilizers into streams and rivers stimulates the growth of algae which, in turn, consume oxygen in such amounts as to endanger the viability of fish and other animal life in the affected waters.[11] These negative life cycles join other evidence to demonstrate that there is a staggeringly long way to go before men can erase or compensate for the growing topsoil deficit.

The decline in the earth's fresh water resources is not yet as massive as the progressive loss of topsoil, but it is dramatic enough in its own terms. Doane calculates the 1882 global fresh water supply at approximately 292 quadrillion gallons (292 million billion) and that by 1952 it had diminished by 6.8 quadrillion gallons, or 2.33 percent.[12] Since both agriculture and industry are ravenous consumers of water, the burgeoning of industrialization and of intensive agriculture in the period from 1950 to 1970 has certainly accelerated the rate of water loss to the point where the world's water supply must be regarded as a critical issue.

The issue becomes still more serious when the geographic distribution of fresh water in relation to consumer populations comes into consideration. And, of course, the problem of water pollution is a further negative factor. Great hopes have been placed in the desalinization of sea water. But it is too early to judge whether these hopes will materialize on a scale adequate to meet the needs of some 7 billion human beings in the world of 2000 in which industry and agriculture must have enormously surpassed present levels in order to sustain the doubled population.

Only toward the end of the 1960s did men begin to perceive the air they breathe as a finite resource. The phenomenon of growing air pollution was the chief agent in bringing about the new awareness of the earth's atmosphere. Pollution rightly continues as the major concern,

---

[11] Insecticides, fungicides, and herbicides used in agriculture and chemical wastes from industry have added to the rising level of pollution. DDT has gained the greatest notoriety as a pollutant. But, in addition, such substances as cadmium, lead, and mercury salts have created serious water and fish contamination problems. By mid-July 1970, United States government investigators had found quantities of mercury approaching or exceeding the danger level in the lakes and streams of more than fourteen states. Mercury ingested in amounts above the human tolerance level (directly or by consuming contaminated fish) can cause kidney and nerve damage and, in larger doses, death (*New York Times*, July 9, 1970).

[12] Op. cit., p. 84.

but depletion is also a factor. Air can be and is used as a source of chemicals: the commercial extraction of nitrogen from the atmosphere is the most familiar process. More important is the intimate and dynamic interaction between the atmosphere, on the one hand, and sun, water, soil, and plant and animal life, on the other. The intricacies of this interaction and the scientific controversies concerning it are far too complex to attempt to describe and evaluate here. It must suffice to point out that air is no more an unlimited resource than land or water. All three are fundamental and irreplaceable elements in the global ecosystem, and their diminution or contamination must have profound effects on the earth's ability to sustain life.

The basic sustenance of the world's industry, as noted earlier, comes from the world's minerals. Of not quite 2,000 kinds of minerals (defined as inanimate chemical elements or compounds found in nature), about 100 are presently of economic importance. These valuable minerals are at the crux of the depletion problem. Charles Park, in his study of mineral extraction, concludes that there is already a world shortage of tin, silver, and mercury and that the shortage is likely to grow steadily more acute. On the other hand, iron and aluminum are among the few minerals whose reserves are sufficient to permit a steadily rising level of consumption in the foreseeable future. In between, Park observes,

> lie the great majority of mineral products. They are present in the earth's crust in amounts sufficient to satisfy current demands and to allow for moderate expansion. They cannot, however, over a long period of time keep abreast of the rapid increase in world population. . . . This is especially true of the fossil fuels that provide so much of the energy required by our civilization.[13]

Park drives home his point by noting the present huge differentials in mineral consumption between the developed and underdeveloped worlds. As the richest country in the developed world, the United States alone, on a per capita basis, annually consumes about five times the world per capita consumption of iron. The comparable ratio for copper consumption is nearly six to one; for lead, eight to one. If world population continues to grow at the present rate, and if development actually succeeds in transforming the countries of the presently underdeveloped

---

[13] Charles F. Park, *Affluence in Jeopardy: Minerals and the Political Economy* (San Francisco: Freeman, Cooper, 1968), p. 323. For data on 20 key minerals, including information on global reserves, rate of depletion, prime producers and consumers, and United States consumption as a percentage of the world total, see Donnella and Dennis Meadows *et al.*, *The Limits to Growth* (Washington, D.C.: Potomac Associates, 1972), pp. 56–60. Some of the statistics differ markedly from those of Park, but both studies affirm the preeminent position of the United States as the world's most ravenous consumer of minerals.

world into technologically advanced societies, the conclusion is obvious: the demand for minerals will skyrocket.

For purposes of illustration, Park makes the improbable assumption that the annual United States demand for minerals will not rise but remain constant during the balance of the century. If, then, the world per capita level of consumption in the year 2000 should rise to the level of United States consumption in 1968, the annual production of iron would have to increase by a factor of 12, of copper by a factor of 11, and of lead by a factor of 16.[14]

The assumption of world-wide affluence by 2000 implied in the projected level of mineral demands is, of course, as unrealistic as the assumption of constant demand in the United States. The two assumptions, in effect, cancel each other out; current trends point to a future characterized by an enormously increased minerals demand in the rich sectors of the world and a moderately increased demand in the poor sectors. In any case, total world demand at the end of the century is bound to strain the sources of supply for many key minerals and to threaten some with exhaustion.

ENERGY: CRISIS AND PROMISE

Finite limits to the quantity of mineral fuels, coal, oil, natural gas, and uranium, are as evident as with other minerals. The exceptional abundance in the earth's crust of the first three has made them by far the most important sources of fuel and energy for the industrial world. Experts are in disagreement concerning the size of both actual and potential reserves, but they do agree that coal, oil, and gas are being consumed at a prodigious rate.

It has been calculated, for example, that more coal has been mined in the twentieth century than in all previous history. As for petroleum, large-scale use developed only in the second half of the nineteenth century and is thus a wholly new demand on a previously untapped geological resource. In regard to natural gas, there is agreement that it is present in far smaller quantities than coal and oil and that its exhaustion early in the next century is in the realm of probability. In addition to the fossil fuels, hydroelectric power makes a significant but far more modest contribution to the world's energy needs. The development of water power resources can be considerably expanded—at considerable cost—but even the maximum utilization of hydroelectric resources would have only a minor impact on the world's energy economy.

Uranium is a fuel that represents a fundamental departure from recent as well as older energy technologies. Its first and most terrible use in

---

[14] Op. Cit., pp. 11–15.

the atom bomb demonstrated that men had discovered an energy resource several orders of magnitude greater than anything previously
known. Induced fission of the uranium atom was an historic achievement
not only in itself but also because it established the feasibility of a whole
new series of techniques to obtain massive releases of energy. The most
powerful and dangerous of these techniques is the fusion of hydrogen
atoms.

Growing numbers of nuclear reactors around the world are trans-
muting uranium into energy for peaceful purposes, and the relative
abundance of uranium ore ensures that it will be an increasingly important source of human energy needs. Yet the expense of processing
uranium ore into usable energy slows down the development of its full
potential. An additional inhibiting factor is the radioactive wastes generated by the refining process; the problem of permanent, safe disposal
of these wastes is still unresolved.[15]

Thermal pollution poses still another problem, since current reactor
technology requires huge amounts of water to be heated during use.
The ultimate environmental impact of emissions of hot water in such
massive volume is still uncertain, but it is the cause of considerable
concern. Still, as of 1973, there has been no definitive demonstration of
generic flaws in the operating reactor installations around the globe.
Hence the prospect is one of technological refinements and of accelerating expansion of reactor-produced energy (possibly using thorium and
other elements as well as uranium) to the point of cheapness and
abundance.

Just as nuclear fusion surpassed the capacity of nuclear fission to produce terrifying weapons—by a factor of 1000—so the taming of the
energy produced by fusion promises a plenitude of energy not readily
imaginable. While experiments with fusion processes have been carried on since the 1950s, the very high temperatures required in these
processes are not as yet controllable. Glenn Seaborg, former chairman
of the Atomic Energy Commission and one of the scientists most confident of ultimate success in controlling fusion, asserted that when such

---

[15] The world-wide danger from radioactivity and other by-products of nuclear testing for military purposes led to the nuclear Test Ban Treaty (except for underground
testing) in 1963. Since then, France and China, as nonsigners, have continued
atmospheric tests and so have added marginally to global levels of radioactivity.
But radioactive contamination from pre-1963 atmospheric and underwater nuclear
explosions by the United States, the Soviet Union, and Britain also persists. Rene
Dubos, professor of environmental medicine at Rockefeller University, provides an
example of the cumulative impact of radioactivity on the intricacies of the ecosystem: "Radioactive products from the fallout of nuclear explosions in the United
States were absorbed and concentrated by the lichens of the Arctic. From the
lichens, they reached reindeer which feed on these plants and eventually the Eskimos
who eat the reindeer" (New York Times, January 6, 1969).

a success is achieved "we shall have in the heavy hydrogen of the world's oceans a source of energy to sustain us for millions of years."[16]

Other dazzling prospects are held out by breeder-reactors which produce more fissionable materials than are consumed in the energy-creating process, thus adding to rather than subtracting from the raw materials of energy. The Soviet Union inaugurated the world's first commercial breeder-reactor on November 30, 1972. Similar installations were nearing completion in Britain and France, while American construction continued to be delayed by disagreements over a site.[17] It is in any case clear that in the 1970s the breeder-reactor's promise of an energy infinity will be subjected to the conclusive test of operating conditions.

Tapping the energy of the sun by means of solar energy devices has been providing men with power and heat for many years. But this rather simple technique of capturing and storing heat from the sun's rays has contributed very little to total energy supply. Costs of building and emplacing receptors and of energy storage have so far restricted its use to local and specialized purposes. The technical feasibility of widespread application, however, is not in doubt. Harnessing the energy of the tides at many locations around the world is also technically possible, but here, too, the cost factor has been a major stumbling block.

The fundamental importance of abundant and cheap energy is that it permits men to extract and process raw materials that would otherwise be out of reach because of high production costs. As Park points out,

> The greatest single factor in the price of any mineral product (or of almost any other commodity) is the cost of its energy requirement. Ore is of no real worth lying in the ground. The price of a copper bowl, a steel bar, or an asbestos siding is largely determined by the cost of the energy that was needed to mine, to fabricate, and to transport the mineral. Other factors, such as rarity, demand, and taxes play their part, but in general the monetary value and the energy cost of a mineral product are nearly the same.[18]

Hence the reduction of energy costs makes possible one or both of the following results: lower mineral costs or expansion of the mineral supply at constant or moderately varying prices by exploitation of lower grade or more inaccessible ores.

This has been the historic contribution of the fossil fuels to the burgeoning of the minerals industry since about 1750. Nuclear fuels promise results far more prodigal and open up the prospect for economic

---

[16] *New York Times*, January 6, 1969. By 1973, new techniques using laser beams and refinements in reactor processes had measurably increased the likelihood of success in controlling fusion.

[17] *New York Times*, December 5, 1972.

[18] Park, *Affluence in Jeopardy*, p. 170.

utilization of a whole new range of raw materials. Some see this new
bonanza as coextensive with the geological composition of the globe
itself, one in which men will be able both to fabricate and to extract
energy from ordinary varieties of rock. In the vernacular of nuclear
research this expectation is known as "rock burning."

Cheap energy is also the obvious key to the desalinization of sea
water on a mass basis and thus to converting the growing fresh water
deficit into a surplus. Cheap energy can make possible the expansion of
fertilizer production to the point where it could make a really significant
contribution to the replenishment of the soil. At the same time, its
capacity to convert volumes of sea water into fresh water could bring
new lands into agricultural production and halt and even reverse the
encroachment of the desert on the productive land surfaces of the
world.

In these terms, nuclear energy emerges as the salvation rather than
the doom of an overburdened world. This is clearly Seaborg's view:

> Perhaps few people realize how timely, in a historic framework, the dis-
> covery of nuclear fission was. Before the advent of nuclear power the days
> of our growing industrial civilization were numbered—in terms of the num-
> ber of years that the earth's supply of fossil fuels could last. At best this is
> estimated to be a few centuries.

Instead of a world decaying as a result of an irrational self-abuse, Seaborg's nuclear vision offers a world of abundance, sanity, and beauty:

> Abundant low-cost energy can radically affect our industrial production,
> the way we use our natural resources and control our waste, the way we use
> our water and produce our food. The extensive use of very large breeder
> reactors may make it possible for us to live one day in an essentially
> junkless and pollution-free environment, where much of our solid waste
> is recycled back into usable resources and air pollution is held to a minimum
> by a decreased dependence on combustion for power.[19]

But meanwhile the vast majority of mankind continues to be poor. As
we have noted earlier, hundreds of millions are malnourished and more
than 3 million of this number die annually from causes linked to nutrition deficiency and from outright starvation. Pending the fuller elaboration of a new technology, the resource base continues to contract. The
dominant technology, prodigal in its gifts and in its costs, pollutes the
air, the water, and the land at an accelerating rate. The extension of so
improvident a technology from the rich minority to all mankind, however desirable in the name of economic equality, must hasten the day

---

[19] Seaborg, *New York Times*, January 6, 1969.

when depletion and pollution will produce an unmanageable crisis. And each year that the world's population spirals upward lends increasing credibility to Malthus' dictum: the reproductive power of human beings is greater than their power to create sustenance for the numbers they produce.

These are some of the basic characteristics of the present-day world that lead many to discount the promise of a future technology. C. P. Snow conjures up a nightmare of famine for the world's poor in which we shall watch millions starving before our eyes—on our television sets. Others have developed a profound concern with the increasing carbon dioxide content of the earth's atmosphere. Due primarily to the combustion of fossil fuels, the amount of atmospheric carbon dioxide has risen by 10 percent since 1870; with combustion processes multiplying, the increase is likely to attain the 25 percent level by 2000. Since a growing volume of carbon dioxide reduces the volume of oxygen, some scientists have speculated that the apocalypse will come with the eventual disappearance of breathable air. Others, because carbon dioxide in the air warms the oceans, foresee the possibility of the polar ice caps melting to a degree where the coastal areas of the earth's continents would disappear beneath an irreversible flood. Still others see in contemporary statistics evidence that mankind will finally be smothered in its own junk:

> The increased use of modern technology has brought about major increases in the amount of waste products which serve as environmental pollutants. It has been stated that in the United States of America alone, this amounts each year to 142 million tons of smoke and noxious fumes, 7 million automobiles, 20 million tons of paper, 48,000 million cans, 26,000 million bottles and jars, 3000 million tons of waste rock and mill tailings, and 50 trillion gallons of hot water along with a variety of other waste products.[20]

RESOURCE ALLOCATION

Contemporary and projected statistics concerning massive production, massive consumption, and massive waste are relevant not only to the problems of resource depletion and pollution. They also document, if more documentation were needed, the radical inequities that characterize human life around the globe. An annual American per capita consumption of iron approximately five times the world average attests to a superabundance in the United States of the prime raw material for construction, vehicles, machines, and weaponry and a corresponding

[20] Report of the Secretary-General, "Problems of the Human Environment," United Nations Economic and Social Council, E/4667, May 26, 1969, p. 5.

dearth for the countries at or below the world average. As we have also seen, American consumption of copper and lead constitutes an even larger share of annual world production. Further, the United States accounts for approximately 50 percent of total world oil consumption and a still higher proportion of natural gas.

These specifics serve as graphic illustrations of the almost incredible consumption differential that divides the world's rich, with America as their archetype, from the world's poor. It is an across-the-board differential including food, water, fiber, fuel, and minerals. Production and consumption of these basic commodities, the volume of their import and export, and the superstructure of service industries they sustain, together comprise the bulk of that familiar entity, the gross national product. Hence the difference between a society with a per capita GNP of $4740 (the United States in 1972) and a per capita GNP of $100 is the difference between near-glut and virtual destitution, both in terms of the basics of food and housing and in terms of the commodities necessary to make the economy grow.

Gross national product, as its name implies, is fundamentally a measure of productivity. On a country basis, wealth and high productivity are synonymous. Hence the rich countries hardly need apologize for their productive capacity as such; after all, it has been the most palpable conqueror of their own former poverty. If apologies and amends are in order, they relate to the unheeded or insufficiently heeded misery of the rest of mankind to which the rich, with their imperialism, their science, and their racism, have made an indelible contribution.

More specifically in the context of the present chapter, the issue of apology and amends arises from the fact that the industrial base of the rich countries is the product of an eminently international process in which they have exploited not only the resources within their own borders but also in the lands of the poor. The nonindustrial world is a major and sometimes the chief supplier to the industrial world of a long list of crucial minerals including oil, copper, tin, chrome, cobalt, manganese, aluminum, and phosphorous. Without these minerals the technology of the developed countries could not have attained present levels of productivity. Should they become unavailable, present technology would falter—as tellingly evidenced in the energy crisis provoked (but not caused) by the Arab oil embargo in the wake of the Arab-Israeli war of 1973.

Of course, raw materials exported from underdeveloped countries command a price, and often, particularly in the case of oil, a fair and even handsome one. Generally, the raw material prices have risen steadily since the days of formal imperialism, but gains for the exporters are offset by the rising cost of imported manufactured goods in relation to raw materials. Thus the poverty of the raw material exporting countries is prolonged, and the ancient issue of the exploitation of the world's poor by the world's rich emerges in its most urgent contemporary form.

But the issue here is not primarily one of a differential in price levels between products in raw and finished form. It is instead the overall availability of raw materials in the foreseeable future. Just as the developed world struggled for access to raw materials in the building of its economy, so the goal of development for the rest of the world necessarily implies a comparable struggle. It will be a struggle for their reallocation, for a repossession of their ownership and management, for a rechanneling of their output into domestic industrial production, and for a repatterning of world trade away from raw material export by the poor and manufactures export by the rich. The objective of the poor countries is a world trade pattern in which they will produce, consume, and export their own manufactures, thus building their own internal wealth, raising the level of their internal consumption, and putting an end to the situation of chronic international price disadvantage that has characterized the economy of raw material export.

This set of objectives must conflict with both the present pattern of raw material consumption and the present dominant technology. The nature of the consumption conflict was pinpointed at the 1969 meeting of the American Association for the Advancement of Science. Harrison Brown asserted that the United States was "stripping the poorer countries of their resource heritage," leaving them "a dismal prospect for their future development." Preston Cloud then put the obvious question: "What kind of social and political turmoil will arise where aspiring nations discover, or think they have discovered, that exportation has handicapped their chances for development?"[21]

Whatever the degree of handicap, it is certain that underdeveloped countries will seek to reduce the industrialized world's share in the consumption of raw materials and increase their own, and this in a context of rising world demand and the threat of a declining world supply. Development *means* increasing resource consumption. Hence the allocation of raw materials is bound to be a crucial factor for global development and thus in the global relationships of rich and poor. On the basis of present reserves and supply arrangements and of future demand patterns, there simply may not be enough to go around of a whole series of key raw materials.

Thus the world faces an unprecedented challenge concerning the equitable and economic division of raw materials essential to industry and to industrialization. But it faces an additional and unprecedented challenge: how to cope not only with the allocation of the supply but also with the absolute limits of its availability. Many resource optimists and pessimists are in agreement that shortages will sooner or later develop among the raw materials on which industrial civilization has

---

[21] *New York Times*, December 30, 1969. Harrison Brown is a geochemist and professor of science and government at the California Institute of Technology. Preston Cloud is professor of biogeology at the University of California, Santa Barbara.

hitherto relied. They part company in their assessments of the promise of new technology: whether it can relieve the pressures on the existing inventory of marketable industrial raw materials by exploiting whole new grades and categories of natural resources. As noted earlier, Seaborg viewed the new technology as one which rescues, in the nick of time, an industrial world whose dominant technology is gobbling up at an ever faster rate the resources to which it is tied.

Thus there is little disagreement in the scientific community that the problem of resource depletion and exhaustion has become a potentially unmanageable one for contemporary technology. It follows that the elaboration of a new technology, with nuclear energy as its driving force, is essential to the future of both industrial and industrializing societies.[22] In its absence, absolute and differential shortages of the raw materials consumed by contemporary technology can only intensify conflict in a world already marked by extreme inequalities in access to and use of the earth's natural resources.

HUMAN NUMBERS ON A FINITE EARTH

Man is the most creative and the most destructive of earth's creatures. Both qualities combine to make him into the major consumer of the earth's resources. Thus the most obvious source of the human problem of demand and supply is the human population itself. The size of the population determines the problem's magnitude and also powerfully affects its qualitative characteristics. In 1970, 3.6 billion human beings put an enormous strain on the world's resources. But the extent of the strain can be measured accurately only if it is understood in the context of time. In the first seventy years of the twentieth century world population more than doubled. In the final thirty years, based on current trends, it will come close to doubling again.

The prehistory of this unprecedented century of population expansion is by now all too familiar to those who concern themselves with population matters. A time span from the beginning of human life until

---

[22] Geothermal energy may join nuclear fuels as a major new source of energy. As the name implies, its source is the interior heat of the earth itself. Several countries are already deriving electricity from wells up to 25,000 feet in depth which bring steam or boiling water to the surface to drive generators in power plants. New techniques are being tested that, by forcing cold surface water down to molten or dry hot rock, would produce steam and boiling water and thus vastly augment the existing natural reservoirs.

Proponents of geothermal energy stress that it can be tapped at lower cost than any other major energy source and that it is pollution free and virtually limitless in its abundance.

One major uncertainty is the effect of wholesale exploitation on the earth's crust and surface. If this issue and some attendant technical problems are resolved, however, it is likely that geothermal energy will be an important component in world energy supply by 1985 or 1990.

approximately 1650 A.D. was required before the global population reached a level of 500 million.[23] An additional two centuries sufficed to double human numbers to the billion mark. The fifty years from 1850 to 1900 added still another 500 million. Thus the twentieth century began with a global population approximating a record 1.5 billion, and it will end with somewhat more or less than 7 billion.

The population prospects beyond the twentieth century have also been analyzed, at least by calculation and projection. If current trends hold steady, larger populations will continue to produce larger populations. Thus when the year 2000 is reached it will require only an additional five years to produce a net increase of another billion—a feat that can be matched thereafter at ever shorter intervals. These calculations provide the basis for those monstrous predictions of 50 billion human beings in the late twenty-first or twenty-second century—at this remove one must take one's pick—or an eight-century projection of a land-man ratio of one square foot per person.

While these projections into a distant future have illustrative value, they do not help much in gaining a realistic understanding of the challenge posed here and now by a rapidly increasing population. On the way toward the global claustrophobia envisioned for the twenty-eighth century, men would find means, undoubtedly very unpleasant, to prevent themselves from arriving at the prescribed destination. The real challenge is to the present generations and their immediate successors. The task before them is to find ways to slow population growth over the remainder of this century and subsequently to stabilize human numbers by achieving a minimal or negative growth rate.

If this task is not accomplished, even a new technology cannot prevent increasingly bitter struggles in a situation of continuously and massively escalating demands on a resource inventory which may still be abundant for 7 billion consumers but eventually insufficient for 14, 28, or 56 billions. It seems apparent, then, either that men will resolve the problem of human numbers in the next thirty or fifty years or they will not have much of a future to look forward to beyond that time.

The developed world has generally reached a stage of very moderate population increase. Even the United States, whose birth rate was among the highest in the industrialized world in the postwar period, had dropped by 1972 to a .7 percent rate of increase. But this only illustrates one more gap between the world of the rich and the poor. The great and immediate tragedy of the population explosion is that it is generated mainly by the countries of Asia, Africa, and Latin America that can least afford to deal with it. They are the ones most rapidly adding to the human race. The more hopeful among population analysts stress the possibility that the growth rate of the underdeveloped world,

---

[23] This figure is identical with the ten year *increase* in world population from 1960 to 1970.

and hence of the world itself, may level off in two or three generations. They often cite the historical experience of industrializing Europe, in which sharply falling death rates and the resulting massive increases in population were eventually followed by sharp decreases in the birth rate. The result was that the growth in numbers leveled out to manageable proportions.

But the impact of the European population explosion from the eighteenth to the twentieth century was mitigated, at least for the Europeans, by large-scale emigration and large-scale imperialism as well as by the increased productivity brought about by the Industrial Revolution. Imperialism, however irrational, dangerous, and unjust, continues to be a live option today. But large-scale emigration, with or without an imperial connection, is far less feasible in the overcrowded world of the late twentieth century than it was in the preceding 300 years. Hence the countries of the underdeveloped world that are now experiencing the population explosion will have to find means of accommodating their growing numbers primarily within their own borders.

Moreover, the time frame for industrialization or modernization for presently underdeveloped countries is very much in doubt, particularly when burgeoning numbers are themselves one of the major hindrances to lifting these societies above subsistence level. Even if the phenomenon of rapidly falling birth rates in nineteenth-century Europe were likely to repeat itself as the countries of Asia, Africa, and Latin America move toward industrial economies, the build-up of misery and conflict in the intervening years may prove to be more than the world could bear. Finally, if the present annual global population growth rate of 2 percent were to be cut in half by the end of the century, or one or two decades thereafter, a 1 percent rate of growth for a 7 billion population base would still produce as great an absolute increase every year as the current 2 percent rate for a 3.6 billion base.

It follows that the fundamental terms for human survival prescribe enormously increased productivity and enormously decreased reproductivity. Only if these terms are met can supply meet the most basic global demands for food and water, housing and health services, education, and productive employment. As we shall see, the evidence suggests that the technological competence to convert scarcity into abundance is not lacking. The critical question, now as in the past, is addressed to human organizational capacity and political will. Are men, and most specifically men of the industrial world, capable of elaborating a less voracious technology within a political-organizational framework designed to share rather than hoard the fruits of productivity? The answer to this question will also decide the outcome of the issues raised by the concept of world demand and world supply: famine or plenitude, depletion or renewal, pollution or decontamination, equity or inequity of consumption patterns, conflict or cooperation—that is to say, war or peace.

Chapter 13

Rich and Poor in the Global Society

An examination of demand and supply at the global level necessarily stresses the status and prospects of the overall system. Insofar as it considers differentials in production and consumption among different sectors of the system it does so—in principle—in order to assess the viability of the system as a whole. While this kind of examination performs an indispensable function, it runs the risk of obscuring the concrete realities in the daily lives of individuals and societies whose existence is shaped by vast differences in what is demanded and what is supplied. These realities add up to a world-wide coexistence of surplus and want of appalling dimensions. An effort to grasp these dimensions is essential to an understanding of the intrinsic injustice in the way human values are now distributed around the world. It is also essential to realistic assessment of diverse and often competing proposals designed to bring about a more equitable distribution in the future.

Two initial observations are essential to any useful discussion of world wealth and world poverty. The first is that the global condition of a minority of rich societies and a majority of poor ones finds a parallel *within* each of the poor societies. That is, within the typical underdeveloped society a small segment of the populace controls most of the power and wealth that society is presently capable of generating while the vast majority lives in powerlessness and poverty. Thus a gulf separates rich minority and poor majority in the typical underdeveloped country as broad and deep as that which divides the few rich and the many poor societies at the global level. The second observation is that globally and, by some criteria, within the underdeveloped societies the numbers of the poor are growing relative to the numbers of the rich.

DISTRIBUTION OF WEALTH AND POVERTY

Calculations of gross national product and per capita GNP are only the first and second steps in assessing the wealth or poverty of a society.

Analyses of income distribution and property ownership are indispensable to a tolerably accurate portrayal of the way people actually live in
any given society. Unfortunately, the statistical data upon which to base
such analyses are almost universally lacking in the underdeveloped
countries. Even in the developed countries the data are often incomplete,
and the uses to which they are put frequently occasion sharp controversy. Despite such handicaps, however, it is possible to say that one of
the most significant differentials between developed and underdeveloped
countries is the degree of equity prevailing in the distribution of income
and owned wealth. The gross contrast between income and wealth distribution in the typical developed country (DC) and the typical underdeveloped country (UDC) are schematically portrayed in Figure 13.1.[1]

Figure 13.1
Proportions of Wealth and Poverty in
Developed and Underdeveloped Countries

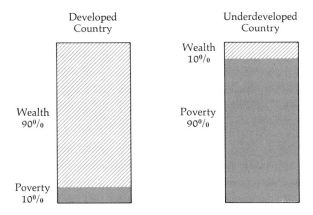

A calculation of the 1970 gross world product in the previous chapter
yielded a per capita GWP of $881. But it also showed that a simple
division of product by population produced an unreal "average" that
conveys little of the true conditions of the world economy. Only by sub-

---

[1] This figure is not based on calculations of the division of wealth actually prevailing in any given developed or underdeveloped country nor on any necessarily fic-
tional averages for the societies grouped under each of the two categories. It is a
schematic composite based on unavoidably incomplete data. As such, it can claim
only an approximate accuracy in portraying the incidence of wealth and poverty in
the two kinds of societies. Nor, of course, does it make distinctions of degree of
wealth and poverty within the two sectors.
  The "conditions of poverty" are those illustrated during the balance of this chapter. "Wealth" is the enjoyment, in moderate to superabundant degree, of all the
values lacking in the life of the poor, including education, status, and power.

dividing the world product into the component national products could one ascertain more pertinent averages: 27 percent of the world's population enjoyed a per capita product of $2,701 and 73 percent subsisted at a per capita level of $208. The calculations were then further refined by taking into account the mathematically obvious: the richest and the poorest of the countries of the world stood far above and far below the per capita figures representing the averages for the developed and the underdeveloped world.

These statistics and calculations can be represented schematically in yet another way (see Figure 13.2). Global wealth statistics are based on total products of national economies, and they do not take account of wealth distribution within these economies. Yet since more is known about GNPs than about their domestic distribution in most countries, it is ironically possible to achieve greater precision at the global level than in the internal analysis of most national economies. Thus a rough estimate is possible not only of the numbers of rich and poor in the world but also the amount of wealth the rich command and the extent of poverty the poor must suffer.

This grotesque imbalance in the production and distribution of wealth among the people of the world roughly reproduces the imbalance to be found within the typical underdeveloped country. But two significant variations are evident. Rich populations constitute a much larger percentage of the global society than the local rich in a given under-

Figure 13.2
Global Distribution of Wealth, 1970

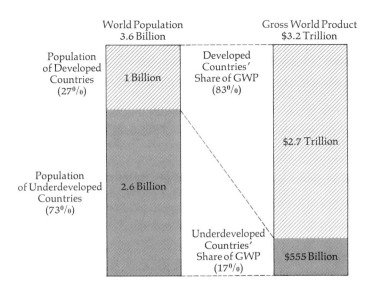

developed society. The global rich also command far greater resources absolutely and proportionally than the wealthy in each underdeveloped country, who typically comprise only a thin layer of affluence above the impoverished mass.

It follows that policies to achieve greater equality at both global and local levels will be fatally handicapped if they must be sustained only by the meager resources of local wealth in UDCs. In order to be successful, they must be able to draw on the vastly greater resources of the global rich. This prescription, of course, is derived from the domestic experience of already developed countries, where the resources of the richer regions have been tapped in order to develop the poorer for the benefit of the whole society. It is a prescription that will be discussed more fully in subsequent chapters.

At this point it is necessary to revert from macroanalysis to microanalysis. The dynamics of an economy, global or local, developed or underdeveloped, can be measured only if one goes beyond the size of the product and gains insight into how it is produced and distributed. As we observed earlier, knowledge of income and wealth distribution in underdeveloped societies is too meager to permit precise measurement of these dynamics. But evidence in particular cases can shed some light on the generality.

Venezuela is a case in point. As one of the world's leading producers of oil, it has registered for a number of years the highest per capita income in all of Latin America (with the special-status exception of Puerto Rico). Oil has brought riches to a few and considerable prosperity to some; oil workers command high wages and the services that go with them. Since oil has provided approximately three-quarters of the national income of Venezuela in recent years, owners, workers, middlemen, and the government sector of the petroleum industry have accounted for an enormous share of the total national product, which in the late 1960s averaged out to a per capita GNP of approximately $800.

But, as Josué DeCastro observes,

> . . . arithmetical averages are grossly misleading. Oil workers are in fact only a tiny fraction of the whole population, and the great mass of the people still live in the blackest misery. The $800-per-capita average actually comes from a purely imaginary distribution of multimillion-dollar incomes accruing to the very few.[2]

Thus despite a steady growth in GNP (plus serious efforts in education, health, and social services), oil-rich Venezuela has not yet significantly altered the ancient pattern in which a small elite virtually monopolizes wealth and power to the exclusion of the masses of poor.

Whether at the top or at the bottom of the GNP range that defines the underdeveloped world, the 120-plus countries that make up its num-

---

[2] Josué DeCastro, *Death in the Northeast* (New York: Random House, 1966), p. 146.

ber typically repeat this vast disparity in power, wealth, and life style of the few and the many. This is true in part because, as we have just observed, what power and wealth these societies have traditionally been able to generate has been severely limited. Hence the traditional argument that even an equitable distribution would only have succeeded in equalizing everyone at poverty's level. There followed the traditional conclusion: it is better that a few should enjoy wealth and exercise power than that all should be immersed in an anarchy of undifferentiated misery.

These doctrines, of course, are by no means unique to the political, economic, and social traditions of the underdeveloped world. They are instead the universal heritage of mankind. Those societies which are now termed developed began to find the means to break with the traditional way of life and its traditional rationale at various times only during the last 200 years. Prior to their breakaway they, too, exhibited the central characteristics of "underdevelopment": a tiny elite of wealth and power segregated from and governing a poverty-stricken and politically inert mass.

The continuing persistence among the now developed countries of minority poverty and of political, social, and racial discrimination in varying combinations and degrees of severity demonstrates that the breakaway is not yet complete and that for them, too, "development" is unfinished business. Yet it remains true that their achievement in converting poverty from a majority into a minority phenomenon represents a historical revolution without precedent. The same can be said for their sometimes ambiguous departures from elite rule. Even in the developed countries of the communist world the norm of popular rule is uncontested in theory; in the West the same norm has prevailed more often than some of its critics are willing to concede.

In sum, the developed societies have scored enormous successes in breaking with the universal heritage of elite wealth and rule and mass poverty and obedience. Success is something that is never complete or secure, and it always creates new problems of its own. But inability to recognize success is as unrealistic and self-destructive as an inability to recognize failure. With all their shortcomings, the societies that have been able to reverse the ratio between rich and poor have registered an achievement that merits closest attention at a time when the rest of mankind now also yearns for "development."

The very essence of economic development is a process in which the numbers of poor diminish as wealth spreads into ever larger sectors of the society. It was this process in the West that refuted Marx' apocalyptic prediction for the bourgeois society that the rich would become richer and fewer and the poor poorer and more numerous. In the Marxian prognosis the sheer weight of the growing masses of poor and the political organization born of their misery would precipitate a violent proletarian revolution in which the rich would be driven from power and the bourgeois state dismantled.

To the extent that Western societies "developed," they managed to avoid what Marx insisted was inevitable. A combination of motives among both elites and nonelites in these societies—profit, humanitarianism, the vision of a just society, the will to power of persons, parties, and nations, and fear of revolution in the absence of reform—combined to produce an expanding participation of the populace at large in the life of the economy and polity.

The indispensable fuel for the process of expansion, of course, was another unprecedented breakaway from the heritage of the past, the Industrial Revolution. In those societies where the Industrial Revolution took hold, it transformed, slowly at first and then at an accelerating rate, the static economy characteristic of all previous history into the dynamic economy of constantly rising levels of productivity. Because it produced a steady growth in the size of the economic cake, the Industrial Revolution made it progressively easier to share the cake more and more widely. Thus it altered the historic reality of scarcity economics, and it broke the historic rationale for a social structure typified by a thin layer of privileged persons on top of a mass of human beings whose lifetime experience was dominated by poverty, ignorance, and subordination.

There is sufficient evidence to assert that the same forces unleashed by the Industrial Revolution in the West are also at work in the Soviet Union and in the European communist countries where they emerged at a later date. The response of their elites to the growing economic cake and to the crumbling rationale for elite rule still awaits definitive forms. Whatever specifics these forms may develop, the world will be a much more hopeful place if the disciples of Marx can dismantle his elite-mass concepts of industrial society as effectively as his bourgeois targets have done.

GROWING NORTH-SOUTH INEQUALITIES

The overriding problems of wealth and poverty and elite and mass, however, are not to be found in the Cold War divisions of East and West but in the juxtaposition of developed North and underdeveloped South. The terms North and South are obviously as imprecise, geographically and otherwise, as the older East-West terminology. They do serve, however, to symbolize and dramatize the displacement of the world's chief danger zone from the confrontation of communist and noncommunist to the confrontation between the world's rich and the world's poor. The oversimplified juxtaposition of these terms also conveys the fundamental truth that the division between rich societies and poor societies is in fact a boundary line separating two different worlds. It follows that each world has its own priorities and preoccupations. Meaningful communication between them is therefore difficult—at least as difficult as communication between elite and mass in the traditional state.

One of the messages essential to North-South communication is that Marx's discredited prognosis for the bourgeois society can presently claim validity for the global economy. The rich societies are growing richer and the poor societies poorer. Concomitantly, the populations of the rich societies constitute an ever smaller fraction of mankind whose rapid growth in numbers is primarily the contribution of the poor. Contemporary global society is one in which poverty and misery are expanding, not contracting, and in which the concentration of wealth proceeds at an accelerated pace in the economies of the rich societies.

In the previous chapter it was noted that the GNP differential between the United States and India approximated $920 billion in 1970 and is projected to reach the level of $2.4 trillion in 2000. This growth in differential from the merely colossal into the realm of the macabre represents the rule and not the exception in comprehensive projections of the growth prospects of developed and underdeveloped economies. As noted in Figure 13.2, the combined 1970 GNPs of the developed countries amounted to about $2.7 trillion. They are projected to reach $9.2 trillion by the year 2000. During the same period the combined GNPs of the underdeveloped world are projected to rise from approximately $555 billion to approximately $1.65 trillion. Hence the differential between the GNPs of the presently developed and underdeveloped worlds rises from roughly $2 trillion in 1970 to more than $7.5 trillion in 2000. Converted into GNP per capita, the present and projected differential between the developed world (DW) and the underdeveloped world (UDW) appears in Table 13.1. It shows the difference in per capita GNP between the two worlds increasing from $2,493 in 1970 to $5,376 in 2000.[3]

It is evident that the rich are getting richer. To show that they are also

---

[3] The 1970 figures are again taken from *World Military Expenditures 1971*. Projections of GNP and GNP per capita are based on individual country and world aggregates to be found in Appendices A and C. See notes to Appendix A for an explanation of the discrepancies between figures used here and in the Appendix.

It should be stressed that it is impossible to assert the accuracy of any projections. In all cases they are based on the assumption that past and current growth rates provide a clue to the future and that the average growth rate registered over a given period in the past will tend to persist during the period for which projections are made. This is rather like assuming that the rate of compound interest offered by a bank will not deviate significantly from the level established during a base period from which projections into the future are calculated.

Such assumptions are highly vulnerable to unforeseen and unforeseeable events that can alter or reverse what are currently regarded as trends. Yet accurately identified trends are anchored in the realities of the present and the past and provide our only reasonably reliable signposts into the future. As such they can perform the signal service of indicating to men where they are currently headed and what is likely to happen if they keep going in the same direction. Thus projections function as heuristic devices and efforts at approximation and not as definitive predictions of things to come.

Table 13.1

Per Capita Product

	DW	UDW
1970	$2,701	$208
2000	$5,720	$344

becoming relatively fewer, one need only add projected percentages of world population for North and South (see Table 13.2). If the percentage changes fail to convey the full import of these projections, population projections in absolute figures can help to make the message clearer. The approximate 1970 population of the developed societies was 1 billion and of the underdeveloped societies 2.6 billion. In the most conservative projections for the year 2000 the two populations will rise to 1.6 billion and 4.8 billion, respectively.

The rich are becoming richer and fewer and the poor poorer and more numerous. A host of other indicators point in the same direction. Since 1964 the United Nations Conference on Trade and Development (UNCTAD) has become the major forum for what is often acrimonious and bitter debate concerning the economic status and relationships of the rich and poor countries. But in its first plenary conference with 121 nations attending (UNCTAD I, Geneva, 1964), no one debated the fact that between 1950 and 1960 the underdeveloped world's share in the money volume of world trade dropped from 30 percent to 20 percent. (In the same period the Western developed countries increased their share from 60 percent to 66 percent, and the share of the Soviet Union and the European communist countries rose from 8 percent to 12 percent.) During the same ten years, the value of exports from the poor countries dropped 26 percent. In a different time frame, the UDCs were able to attract 43 percent of all foreign investment in 1958; by 1963 the figure had fallen to 29 percent.[4]

---

[4] During this same period, UDCs were beginning to feel the pinch of servicing aid loans previously contracted. Concerning World Bank loans, for example, Escott Reid wrote that ". . . at the present time [1965] the low-income member countries of the Bank are paying out more in interest and repayments of principal on World Bank loans than the Bank is disbursing on those loans. In 1964 the cost to the very poor member countries of servicing Bank loans was $42 million more than the disbursement on those loans. . . . Bank loans therefore did not result in a flow of resources from the richer part of the world to the poorer part. Bank loans were responsible for a flow of resources from the poorer to the richer. The situation is likely to worsen." Escott Reid, *The Future of the World Bank* (Washington, D.C.: International Bank for Reconstruction and Development, 1965), pp. 36–37.

Reid argued that only a major expansion of the soft loan operations of the Bank's associate organization, the International Development Association, could rectify the worsening debt situation of the poor countries. Since he wrote, such an expansion has taken place, and the debt-service problem has been somewhat alleviated.

Table 13.2

Percentage of World Population

	DW	UDW
1970	27%	73%
2000	25%	75%

UNCTAD II, with 132 nations represented (New Delhi, 1968), offered the negative consolation that the UDW share of world trade value had dropped only a single percentage point during the six years from 1960 to 1966 in contrast to the average drop of 1 percent annually during the previous decade. But the delegates were also informed that the UDW economic growth rate had slowed to the point where the average increase in UDW per capita income stood at $2 per year as against an approximate average of $60 per year in the developed world. These are some of the considerations that prompted most of the poor countries to attend a pre-Delhi caucus in Algeria in the fall of 1967. There they adopted the Charter of Algiers whose text contained the now familiar description of the economic state of the globe: "the rate of growth of the developing world has slowed down, and the disparity between it and the affluent world is widening."

The charter asserted that the prospects for improvement held out at UNCTAD I remained unfulfilled and demanded drastic remedial action by UNCTAD II. Demands included far-reaching reforms in trade and aid policies, nonreciprocal tariff preferences in the developed world for manufactures from the UDCs,[5] and commodity stabilization agreements governing prices for a series of foodstuffs and raw material exports from the underdeveloped countries. None of these objectives was realized at New Delhi. All that emerged was a pledge by most of the developed countries to increase the level of aid to 1 percent of their respective GNPs by 1975. But this pledge did not arrest the downward trend in aid appropriations by many of the aid-giving countries—most conspicuously the United States. As of 1970 United States foreign aid had declined to .33 percent of GNP from a peak level during the Marshall Plan period of 3.0 percent. This percentage dropped still further in 1971 and 1972. In the fall of 1973 the House and Senate had passed separate bills authorizing foreign aid at the level of $1.2 billion—approximately .10 percent of GNP.

The delegates to UNCTAD II (including those from developed coun-

---

[5] The call for a manufactures tariff preference goes directly against the grain of the tariff structure typical of the industrialized state (raw materials: low tariffs or none at all; semimanufactures: moderate tariffs; manufactures: high to prohibitive tariffs). The tariff pattern is supplemented by nontariff restrictive techniques such as import quotas, licensing, and other devices.

tries) also called for an early general agreement to grant preferential tariff treatment to UDC manufactures and semimanufactures exported to developed countries. An agreement on this matter was in fact reached by UNCTAD's Special Committee on Preferences in the fall of 1970. But the developed countries could not agree to any uniform preferential treatment, with the result that each developed country remained free to establish its own preferential schedules and to be as restrictive or as open-handed in implementation as it saw fit.

A more serious deficiency of the preferential tariff arrangement is that only a few of the UDCs are industrially advanced enough to derive significant advantage from it. Most UDCs either do not produce sufficient industrial goods for export, or the goods are of inferior quality, or inefficiencies in production or marketing make them noncompetitive. As we shall see (Chapter 15), these are some of the reasons why increased trade, as desirable as it is, cannot in the foreseeable future replace aid as a stimulus to development.

The 1970 agreement was nonetheless a useful step, even a historic one in the sense that the developed countries agreed to depart from the most-favored-nation principle in order to benefit UDCs, and without demanding reciprocal concessions. Also, the preferential systems should be an inducement for the developed world to invest capital in new manufacturing facilities in UDCs capable of competing on the world market.

By the time UNCTAD III took place in Santiago, Chile, in the spring of 1972, both the developed and underdeveloped worlds were caught up in the ramifying effects of international monetary instability. The main effect was that developed countries, beset by their own economic problems, were even less disposed than before to make major concessions to the UDCs.

Still outstanding issues concerning preferential tariff treatment were deferred until the opening of the world trade conference scheduled to begin in 1974 and to continue into 1975. Action on losses in UDC foreign exchange reserves caused by devaluations and revaluations of developed world currencies was likewise postponed until the world monetary conference, also tentatively scheduled for 1974. With so little accomplished, the UDCs could only register once again their worsening plight in world trade: by 1970 their share had dropped to 17.6 percent.

THE FACE OF POVERTY

It is clear that Marx's prognosis of progressive impoverishment is manifest in a host of current trends in the global society (an application of his thesis that Marx himself did not make). As we shall see, there are also countertrends at work, but it is a moot question whether they will gather enough force to slow or reverse the present course of events. If they do not, the consequences for mankind are likely to be far more cruel than those Marx predicted for bourgeois society. But whether the present trends are long range or short, if the poor are getting poorer, it is important to know where they now are in order to comprehend better where they will be if present trends continue.

Poverty lies buried at the bottom of the affluent society, commanding attention only to the extent that those who live at the bottom become politically organized or violent, or both. The poor society, on the other hand, is one in which poverty is the way of life for the vast majority, existing apart from and beneath a thin layer of wealth and power. Hence the essential distinction between a developed and an underdeveloped country is not between wealth and the absence of wealth but between poverty as a minority and poverty as a majority phenomenon. In the North one finds enclaves of poverty embedded in a landscape of affluence. In the South one finds oases of wealth surrounded by a desert of misery and destitution.

The face of poverty in urban and rural slums has universal features, recognizable in Chicago and Appalachia, in the bidonville suburbs of French cities, and in the south of Italy and Spain as well as in the global South. But the massiveness of poverty in Latin America, Africa, and Asia is the overwhelming characteristic and dominant challenge to the viability of their societies. India is a country of a hundred Harlems; Latin America, Africa, and Asia harbor a thousand Appalachias. This difference in scale is the vital difference between the facts of life in rich lands and poor and between the roles North and South play in the global society.

One account portrayed the massive poverty and wretchedness in Latin America more dramatically than most; it was presented to the United States Senate in a four-hour speech by Robert F. Kennedy on May 9 and 10, 1968:

> The final legacy of this [traditional] pattern of development is poverty and degradation and want, the statistics of which have become almost a litany.
>
> Income per person is often less than $100 yearly; the average for all of Brazil is at most $300 and may well be less; 60 percent of the people of El Salvador have incomes of less than $55 a year.
>
> Ignorance is standard in nearly all the countries; in Colombia, for example, only 60 percent of all children enter the first grade—and 90 percent of these have dropped out by the fourth grade. Fifty percent of all Latin Americans are illiterate.
>
> Disease and malnutrition are almost everywhere; half of all people buried in Latin America never reached their fourth year.
>
> To travel in Latin America, to see the terrible reality of human misery, is to feel these statistics with stunning force.
>
> In Recife, there are people who live in shacks by the water in which

they dump their refuse and garbage; the crabs which feed on that garbage are the staple of their diet.

In fields nearby, men cut cane in the broiling sun from dawn to dusk, 6 days a week—and take home $1.50 for their week's labor; children under 16 make half as much; the minimum wage of 60 cents a day is not enforced. In some of their villages, and in others which we visited, 7 out of 10 children die before their first birthday—and there are primary schools for only one-quarter of those who do survive. In other villages nearby, a new factory has contaminated the water supply—and the mortality rate for children and adults is catastrophic.

In Peru, outside Cuzco, we met men working their landlord's fields for 45 cents a day, a good wage in an area where others must work 3 days with no pay beyond the right to cultivate a small mountainside plot for themselves. . . .

And everywhere, in and around every major city, were the slums—incredible masses of tin or tarpaper or mud huts, one room to each, with what seemed like dozens of children coming out of every doorway. Called barriadas in Lima, poblaciones callampas in Santiago, villas miserias in Buenos Aires, favelas in Rio de Janeiro, and ranchitos in Caracas, all are the same—vast numbers of peasants who have come to the cities in search of a better life, but find no work, no schools, no housing, no sanitary facilities, no doctors—and all too little hope. . . .

. . . there cannot be steady jobs and housing and economic security; there cannot be schools for all the children; and there can be no democracy or justice or individual dignity without revolutionary changes in the economic, social and political systems of every Latin American nation.

And these changes the people of Latin America are determined to have. The coal miners in Concepción, laboring 5 miles under the sea for $1.50 a day—the mothers in Andean villages where schoolteachers tell the children that their parents' tongue is the language of animals—the canecutters and laborers watching their children die—the priests who see the teachings of their church violated by the lords of the land—these people are the engines of change in Latin America.

These people will not accept this kind of existence for the next generation. We would not; they will not. There will be changes.

So a revolution is coming—a revolution which will be peaceful if we are wise enough; compassionate if we care enough; successful if we are fortunate enough—but a revolution which is coming whether we will it or not. We can affect its character; we cannot alter its inevitability.[6]

Two reports contemporary with Senator Kennedy's address supplement his Latin American compendium with the details of poverty in specific cities, Guayaquil, Ecuador, and Lima, Peru. Guayaquil:

[6] Robert F. Kennedy, "The Alliance for Progress: Symbol and Substance," *Congressional Record*, 89th Cong. (May 9 and 10, 1968).

There is no relief for the eye or mind. The dun-colored rows of mud and bamboo hovels stretch in four directions to the perspective's vanishing point. The summer dust seems to rise of itself from the baked earth to choke away the stench of sewage.

On the path next to the fetid drainage canal, a dog chews on a rat. A ragged child flogs a smaller one with a ruined fan belt; both are crying. An Indian woman as dusty as the road shambles along, clacking two sticks to advertise her jungle herbs. . . .

It is the "suburbio," 4000 blocks of human misery packed behind this sleepy Pacific port. Three hundred and fifty thousand people—about 60 per cent of the city's population—exist in the suburbio.

This morning Carlos Torroveles . . . was talking with a visitor. He was very tired. He had worked through the night at the market to earn $1.15 for his wife and five children. That is a lot of money in the suburbio, even for 10 hours work.

". . . the government doesn't do anything here. Every two weeks their water truck comes. But the thieves on it only give us half a barrel, and still charge us the full price."

An oil drum of water costs 12 cents in the suburbio. Few houses have running water.

. . . primary schools are fiercely overcrowded and turn away about half the applicants. The fee for a month is 8 cents. There are six hours of classes a day.

Olivia Tomala, the only teacher, said the school might have to close for lack of money. "There is nothing I can do," she added.

Behind a cardboard partition a little girl lay on a cot, moaning with stomach cramps from intestinal parasites. This is a frequent cause of death in the suburbio. Miss Tomala said she hoped a doctor might come before the day was out.

Probably the largest single "industry" is on 18th Street, the red light district. There, in a scene of unsurpassed wretchedness, perhaps 400 girls stand outside their stalls on an average night. Some are little more than frightened children. The standard fee is 35 cents.

On the western edge of the suburbio is a new cemetery. . . . For an adult, it costs $20 to be buried . . . payable over three years. There is a special rate for children—$10.80.

In the patch of ground for the dead of this month, there are 36 graves. Thirty-one are the graves of children.[7]

Lima:

Just outside the city limits of Lima, a narrow asphalt road runs north along the base of the Andean foothills. . . . On the dusty glacis and, behind,

---

[7] Paul L. Montgomery, *New York Times*, May 30, 1968.

up the stone-strewn ravines straggles the largest slum appended to Lima—
Pampa de Comas.

When I first came to this *barriada* in 1962, it was estimated to have
90,000 population after only five years of existence; revisiting it this year,
in February 1968, I was told it now had 340,000. . . .

The national government [in 1962] had set up a couple of schools on the
lower level [of the barriada], along the road, but there was always the problem of keeping teachers who had to commute from the city and instruct
under adverse conditions. Above this lower strip was sort of a no-man's land
for all services—no schools, no water supply, no sewerage system, no garbage
collection, no electricity.

Contributing to the marauding habits of the youth was the absence of
parental control. The priests estimated that about half of the homes were
headed by "abandoned mothers," their men unable or unwilling to bear the
responsibilities of the family. To make a living, many of them spent long
days in Lima, often as domestic servants; in season they also picked cotton
in the nearby hacienda, earning about 30 cents a day. There had been an
instance, only a week before our arrival, of a mother who had to work and
so locked her three small children in the *choza* [hut] during her ten hour
absence; but, one day, they found the matches and she returned to find the
children dead and home destroyed. . . .

Infant mortality in Pampa de Comas was very high. . . . there was little
doubt that about half of the babies up to the age of one were lost. The
major cause, in conjunction with intestinal parasites, was dehydration, either
because of the mother's ignorance or of a sheer lack of water. Since there
was no water system, it was brought from the city in tank trucks which
struggled up the rough terrain to fill the conglomerations of containers at
appointed supply points. The residents had to buy the water and guard it
in their own barrels and buckets. . . . The trucks serviced the higher reaches
but once every two weeks, and the last supply point was still far down from
the upper *chozas*.

And even above these houses there was one more institution. A well-
tred path led up through the barren height . . . and terminated in the wind-
swept cemetery. During our two weeks . . . in Pampa de Comas, no day
passed that we did not see cortéges winding upward, usually bearing small
caskets. . . .

. . . capacity for self-help and organization has brought Pampa de Comas
a long way since 1962. It is now incorporated and elects its own mayor
and council. . . . The municipal leaders are currently negotiating with those
of Lima to obtain electricity. There is already a water system, installed with
the help of the Alliance for Progress, and sewerage drains are available
to part of the area. . . .

A few asphalt streets start up the slope and, though they soon turn to
dirt, the bed is graded and runs purposefully in a straight line. Alongside, a
few *chozas* remain, houses of more solid construction dominating until the

uppermost ring where new *chozas* attest to the continuing growth of the city.

Pampa de Comas, 10 years old and with 340,000 population, is now an established urban center. Beyond, 13 miles from Lima's city limit, is the young upstart, Collique, two years old and building up rapidly from its current 50,000 inhabitants.[8]

None of the essentials and few of the details differ when one turns from the life of poverty in Latin America to its counterparts in Africa and Asia. Abidjan, Ivory Coast:

For tens of thousands of people, born in mud-walled huts, in villages where cowry shells have not yet been replaced by coins, where magic—"fetiche"— is commonplace, Abidjan is the irresistible magnet of modernity.

In Abidjan . . . there are buildings 20 and more stories high. They look like the illustrations from French and American magazines.

In Abidjan the streets are paved and lined with ornamental trees. Air conditioned stores display radios, and packaged food, and European clothes. The streets are crowded with the bustle of people and cars.

Not only are there street lights in Abidjan, they are left on all night, an intended ostentation. . . .

The architecture is showy, the restaurants deservedly famous. Night-spots even include a submarine with glass walls, where you can watch the fish for $4 a drink.

But for the other half or more of the city's residents, who do not see a wage from month to month, any restaurant, let alone a submarine in the lagoon, might as well be on the moon. . . .

These are the residents of Adjame and Treichville, the long-established "popular quarters," and of Port Bouet and Nouvelle Koumassi and the other newer shacktowns that dot out from Abidjan's center. The newest ones are not on the city's maps. Officially, they do not exist.

In actuality, it is the sewers that do not exist, and it can be a good long walk to the nearest water spigot. . . . .

The market is the hub of activities in a district like Treichville or Adjame. . . . These markets . . . were planned by the best architects in the country. Not so with the houses that stretch off all around. These are the places often described, as Barbara Ward did recently in the *Economist*, this way: "Looking down, the traveller catches a glimpse, under a pall of smoke from cooking pots in backyards, of mile on mile of little alleys snaking through densely packed huts of straw, crumbling brick or beaten tin cans." . . .

With 50,000 new residents a year, at least 10,000 new houses must be

---

[8] Frances M. Foland, "Pampa de Comas Revisited," Report for the Institute of Current World Affairs (New York, March 6, 1968). By permission.

built. This takes at least 500 acres of land. Since only housing for the rich is a good investment, only expensive housing is built, officially. All the rest just happens—"spontaneous housing" it is called here. There are a few public housing projects, but they don't begin to meet the need.

When a "spontaneous" neighborhood sprouts, there are no streets, no sewers, no schools, no markets and no plans for any. The city has lost control of itself. . . .

For example, the tidal flatlands next to the city's slaughterhouse, which has no walls, have been covered with houses. It would be a suitable place for the industry the planners wanted to put there. It is a horrible place for houses.[9]

Calcutta, India:

This is one of the world's largest cities, and it is in crisis—overwhelmed by runaway population, poverty, disease and illiteracy.

A third of its people live under conditions unfit for human habitation by Western standards. . . .

The city has a population of about seven million persons and gains 200,000 a year. The Hooghly river on one side and salt water swamps on the other keep Calcutta from spreading out; so the population density goes up and up.

Calcutta is estimated to have 102,000 persons a square mile, compared with 27,000 for New York. Thousands live on the sidewalks.

The lack of safe water supply, sewage facilities and proper housing has made Calcutta an endemic source of cholera and other diseases. The World Health Organization calls the city an international health hazard. . . .

No school is available for one-half million children. At the present rate of population growth, Calcutta would have to build 100 schools a year for 20 years and these would have to operate on double shifts. The city has not opened a single school in the past 10 years.

Hospitals are so overcrowded that patients pronounced incurably ill must leave. The city has 3.8 hospital beds for every thousand persons, a fairly good figure for India. But people come from all over eastern India for treatment. The city is building one hospital every 10 years.

---

[9] Andrew Barnes, "Abidjan—A Real New City," April 18, 1970. Mr. Barnes wrote this report for the Alicia Patterson Fund while he was on leave from the *Washington Post.* At the time of writing, the population of Abidjan was 500,000.

Another African city of 200,000 was described by the World Health Organization in these terms: "Seventy per cent of its homes are improvised, there is no public sewage system, and most homes have only open holes for latrines. Only 6 per cent of the houses have indoor piped running water. . . . There is no organized public waste collection service, and community clean-ups are not usually carried out until conditions have become unhealthy to a high degree" (*New York Times,* February 11, 1968).

It would take about 200,000 new houses to clear the present bustees or slums. At the present rate of building it would take 100 more years just to clear the present slums.[10]

Philip Appleman converts these statistics into a picture of the daily life of the poor in Calcutta:

> At Sealdah Station, Calcutta, misery radiates outward. In the station, displaced families from East Pakistan hover around little piles of possessions. Outside, dusty streets straggle away in every direction, lined with tiny shacks built of metal scraps, pieces of old baskets, strips of wood, and gunny sacks. In the dark interiors of the shacks, small fires glow through the smoke, and dark faces gaze out at children playing in the urinous-smelling, fly-infested streets. In a few years the children who survive these conditions will stop playing and become adults; that is, they will grow taller and thinner and stand in the streets like ragged skeletons, barefoot, hollow-eyed, blinking their apathetic stares out of gray, dusty faces.[11]

One hundred million Latin Americans live in the urban and rural slums that together constitute the economic cellar of society. Most of the remaining 150 million live only a few levels above the pit. These are the realities of a 1970 per capita GNP of $514. The corresponding figure for Asia (excluding Japan, Israel, and Kuwait) is $160; for Africa it is $155.[12] These figures too often lose their power to convey the reality of North and South in the global system: North coexists with South as an island of wealth surrounded by an ocean of poverty. And if the per capita GNP in the South rises from year to year, and characteristically it does by very small increments, it often obscures additional realities. That is, the painfully slow economic growth rate of the underdeveloped countries is not sufficient to deal with the massive new problems that emerge out of the very process of development itself.

The rapid expansion of populations due to medical advances is, as we have seen, the most obvious novelty envenoming all the other problems of "development." It is the great multiplier of demand for food (and for more productive agriculture), for water, land, housing, health care, education, and employment. Overpopulation in the countryside and the often illusory hope of a better life drives masses of human beings into

---

[10] *New York Times*, May 5, 1966. Two years later the World Health Organization reported that "In Calcutta about 70 per cent of families live in single rooms 'or less,' and in some districts of the city 30 to 50 persons share a single latrine. . . . The population of the city is growing at such a rate that by the year 2000 it may well be over 30 million" (*New York Times*, February 11, 1968).

[11] Philip Appleman, *The Silent Explosion* (Boston: Beacon Press, 1965), p. 3.

[12] Agency for International Development, *Selected Economic Data for the Less Developed Countries* (Washington, D.C.: AID, June 1972).

the cities—more accurately, into the urban slums, whose connection with the city's services and the city's culture is fundamentally one of malignance. Indeed, the *barriadas*, *favelas*, and *bustees* can only be termed anticities in the sense that they are nightmare caricatures of urban living. They are anticities in the political sense as well: they constitute the main reservoir of revolutionary anger directed against the traditional rulers of society. The analogy with slums in developed societies is obvious.

This is the social and political malignancy that moved U Thant to assert in a September 1969 report to the United Nations Economic and Social Council that "throughout the developing world the city is failing badly." The report describes the spectacle of "exploding cities in unexploding economies," many of which "are racing toward a population of a million . . . before even 5 percent of their residents are absorbed into industry."

Urban experts who helped to prepare the report predicted that by 1980 Latin America, Asia, and Africa will have 360 cities of at least one-half million.[13] (In 1920 there were only thirteen cities of this size in all three continents.) These nightmare cities are the chief pressure points of a population explosion that in a fifteen-year period is adding 177,000,000 human beings to the population of India (a 41.8 percent increase), 50,243,000 in Pakistan (52.7 percent, including Bangla Desh), 44,032,000 in Indonesia (47.2 percent) and 379,800,000 in mainland China (51.8 percent).[14] They are the most hideous and dangerous products of a process that threatens Mexico with a population in 2000 eight times as large as it was in 1900 and Brazil with a thirteenfold increase during the same period.

POVERTY'S DIET

Urban or rural, the most basic human need is food. Poor families in the underdeveloped world spend by far the largest part of their income on

---

[13] *New York Times*, September 3, 1969. See also United Nations Economic and Social Council Document E/C.6/90, 24 July, 1969. Still another slum city adds credibility to these forecasts. Metzahuacoyotl, fifteen miles outside Mexico City, counted 540,000 residents in April 1969. Its population had increased sixfold since 1960. Its growth rate points to a population of well over 1 million in the early 1970s. Living conditions are virtually identical to those in Guayaquil's suburbio or in Pampa de Comas in Lima. "There is one policeman to ten thousand people, and the crime rate is skyrocketing" (*New York Times*, April 20, 1969).

[14] Irene B. Taeuber, "Asian Populations: The Critical Decades," in Larry K. Y. Ng and Stuart Mudd (eds.), *The Population Crisis* (Bloomington: Indiana University Press, 1965), p. 80. The projection period for India and Pakistan is 1961–1976; for Indonesia, 1960–1975; and for China, 1963–1978.

food, sometimes in excess of 90 percent. Food is the first priority of the hungry. By contrast, the food expenditure of the average family in the United States amounts to about 16 percent of disposable income. These figures do much to explain why the economies of the underdeveloped world are typically agricultural and the economies of the developed world typically industrial. In most of Asia, Africa, and Latin America the bulk of economic effort is devoted to the production and procurement of food.

In the developed world, industrial production of machines and fertilizers and the growth of a scientifically based agricultural technology have increased food yields to a point where only a small part of total economic activity is required to satisfy the needs of human nutrition, and satisfy them abundantly. Thus the average family budget in a developed country is devoted overwhelmingly to commodities other than food.[15] This pattern of expenditures in developed countries, in turn, explains the enormous demand for industrial goods and for services, a demand which in the underdeveloped countries is infinitesimal by comparison.

The priority task of a poor country, almost by definition, is the attempt to feed its people. It is a task of formidable proportions. Hunger and malnutrition are massive and endemic phenomena in the contemporary world, overwhelmingly concentrated in the three "agricultural" continents. In the late 1960s the average number of calories per person consumed daily ranged from 3,290 in New Zealand and 3,240 in the United States to 1,900 in India and 1,770 in Somalia. On the basis of earlier data, averages for China and communist Asia would rank somewhere between the two lowest figures. Thus there is a differential of 1,500 calories between the averages of the best and the most poorly fed nations. It is the difference between a daily superabundance of food and daily hunger.

On a world basis in 1970, the average calorie consumption per person was 2,409. The position of the average is much closer to the bottom of the calorie intake than to the top. The Food and Agricultural Organization of the United Nations has set 2,385 calories (with some variations according to region) as the average daily minimum for normal activity and health. This figure, along with the average caloric intake, testifies to the fact that the majority of the world's people have been (and still are) unable to obtain a quantitatively adequate diet.

The FAO summed up the world nutrition problem in the period from 1960 to 1970 with the observation that there had been a slight improvement in per capita consumption in underdeveloped countries and further

---

[15] It should cause no surprise, however, that among the minority poor of the developed world the allocations of family expenditure resemble the typical patterns found in the underdeveloped world.

major increases in high quality diet in the developed countries. The percentage estimate of actual undernourishment in the South declined, but because of population increase the estimate in absolute numbers of undernourished people remained the same in 1970 as in 1960: 300 to 500 million.

Malnutrition (qualitatively inadequate diet) is harder to measure than undernutrition (quantitative deficiencies in foodstuffs). The FAO's third *World Food Survey* in 1963 estimated that 60 percent of the population in the underdeveloped world lived on diets deficient in nutritional quality. By 1972 the FAO conceded that the earlier estimate had probably been too high. But its current estimate was somber enough: "Protein/calorie malnutrition . . . affects one-quarter to one-third of the population in many of the developing countries for which data are available." It added the pathetic statistic that clinical studies between 1952 and 1966 in twenty-six countries established that the "prevalence of moderate protein/calorie malnutrition (PCM) varied between 4.4 and 57 percent in children up to five years of age."[16]

The nutrition data for the late 1950s and 1960s were gathered at the start of a decade when awareness of massive population growth in the underdeveloped world was just beginning to be acute. At the same time, the production inadequacies of agriculture in most of Asia, Africa, and Latin America were not yet fully apparent. By 1960, grain production, the basic food supply indicator, had recovered from a postwar decline on the three continents and was 42 percent higher than the average for the period from 1934 to 1938. This would have been an impressive performance (the comparable increase for North America, Europe, and Oceania was 51 percent) had population grown at the same rate in North and South. But the respective increases were 20 percent and 46 percent, with the result that the per capita output of grain rose by 26 percent in the developed world and fell by 3 percent in the underdeveloped world.[17]

The ratio of population to grain production is, of course, only part of the larger ratio of population to total food supply. The two ratios, however (in partially overlapping time periods), are markedly similar. World production of all foods in 1969 was 50 percent higher than the average for 1952 to 1956. But again this unprecedented increase averaging 3 percent annually was almost cancelled out by the unprecedented world

[16] The nutrition data in this and preceding paragraphs are derived from *The State of Food and Agriculture* (Rome: FAO, 1970 and 1972). This publication is the most comprehensive of the annual surveys of the world's agriculture, forestry, and fisheries issued by the Food and Agricultural Organization of the United Nations.

[17] Lester R. Brown, "Population Growth, Food Needs and Production Problems," in L. A. Richards *et al.*, *World Population and Food Supplies, 1980* (Madison, Wis.: American Society of Agronomy, 1964), p. 5.

population growth. The result was a seventeen-year per capita food gain of only 11 percent.

A breakdown of these totals yields still more discouraging findings. Once again the growing gap between developed and underdeveloped is in evidence. Food production increased equally rapidly in North and South during the period from 1952 to 1969. But the differential in population growth resulted in a per capita gain of 25 percent for the developed nations and only a 4 percent gain for the underdeveloped countries. All these ratios remained ominously constant in the production figures for 1970 and 1971.[18]

In sum, since World War II, the underdeveloped South as a whole has been barely able to sustain itself at a tragically inadequate level of nutrition. Throughout most of the period food reserves in most countries have been slim or nonexistent, so that crop failures, drought, floods, or other natural or manmade catastrophes have necessitated vast transfers of food from the industrial to the agricultural continents.

Again, grain serves as a basic indicator. Before World War II, the underdeveloped world had been a net exporter of grain, exports averaging 11 million tons annually from 1934 to 1938. After the war it became a net importer, averaging 4 million tons a year in the period from 1948 to 1952 and 13 million tons in the period from 1957 to 1959. By 1961 the figure was 20 million tons, and by 1966, 31 million.[19] In 1966 India alone received about 8.5 million tons of grain from the United States and some 5 million tons from other governments. The years from 1965 to 1967 were the famine years in north India, when rainfall failure caused a disastrous drop in domestic grain production from 89 million tons in 1964–1965 to 72 million tons in 1965–1966 and 76 million tons in 1966–1967. Without the tremendously increased importation of grain from the developed world, hundreds of thousands would have died of starvation. As Carroll Streeter, former editor of the *Farm Journal*, observed, India's people were living from ship to mouth.

These desperate middle years of the 1960s need to be understood not only because of the misery they inflicted at the time. They are also important because they set off a panic reaction among a considerable number of both seasoned and novice observers of the underdeveloped world. There resulted a spate of articles and books that continue to influence the thinking of those concerned with the relationship between population and food. Some flatly asserted that the long-range battle to feed the growing populations of the underdeveloped world had been irretrievably lost and that death by starvation was to be the inevitable lot of countless millions by 1975, 1980, or some later date.

---

[18] *The State of Food and Agriculture*, 1970 and 1972.

[19] Brown, in Richards, *World Population and Food Supplies*, p. 7. The final figure is from Orville L. Freeman, *World Without Hunger* (New York: Praeger, 1968), p. 8.

In many cases, however, the data used to support these prophecies was neither complete nor convincing. Some of the proposals for saving what could be saved from the anticipated wreckage displayed a glaring lack of political and economic understanding. Still more deplorable, they were sometimes short on human compassion. Their most valuable contribution was to dramatize the need for world-wide action to reduce the rates of population growth and to stress the urgency of increasing agricultural and general economic productivity in the South.

The late 1960s offered at least a temporary rebuke to the prophets of inevitable disaster. After the drought years India resumed its long-run increase in grain production, which had peaked at 89 million tons in 1964–1965. Production for the period from 1967 to 1968 yielded 95.6 million tons, an increase of nearly 20 million tons over the second drought year production of 76 million. Crop levels rose steadily; in 1970–1971 India produced 108 million tons of food grains. On the strength of this performance the Indian government announced that the goal of self-sufficiency in food grains had been reached.

The chief heroes in this dramatic comeback were the high-yield cereals whose seeds first became available in quantity during 1967. These are the seeds that produce "miracle" wheat, rice, and corn, miraculous because they increase per acre yield by such enormous percentages that they have given rise to the term "green revolution." By the early 1960s, the top wheat yield in India had risen to eleven or twelve bushels an acre. The change by 1969 is best described by a special report of the Rockefeller Foundation whose sponsorship of twenty-five years of research and experiment in improved varieties of grain resulted in a spectacular payoff:

Today, just two years . . . [after the drought years], the Gangetic and Indus plains of northern India (and of neighboring West Pakistan) are one vast carpet of beautiful wheat—short, stiff strawed, thick in stand, as level as though just mowed, heavy with big heads loaded with plump kernels. The better farmers in this region are regularly achieving yields of 60 to 70 bushels an acre, and some have passed the hundred bushel mark. One Punjabi farmer was recently awarded a medal for top yield of 150 bushels an acre. The transformation has been nothing less than miraculous.[20]

India was not alone. In the same year, Pakistan nearly doubled its wheat yield in comparison with the predrought 1964–1965 season. In both countries rice yields increased impressively, if not nearly so dramatically as wheat. Where "miracle" rice demonstrated its growing power most spectacularly was in East Asia and Southeast Asia. The Philippines, where the rice phase of the green revolution began in 1965, had con-

---

[20] Carroll P. Streeter, *A Partnership to Improve Food Production in India*, a Rockefeller Foundation special report (New York, December, 1969), p. 10.

verted from a net importer to a net exporter of rice by the late 1960s. The same phenomenon occurred in Japan in roughly the same time span. Indonesian rice production rose by approximately 160 percent in the period from 1963 to 1971.

But these remarkable achievements must be seen in perspective; East Asia and Southeast Asia's gains during this period were not duplicated in other areas of the global South. Dependence of high-yield seed varieties so far developed on irrigation and intensive fertilization, together with problems of disease resistance and grain quality, place limits on their use. However, experiments both with new high-yield strains and with growing techniques should push back these limits significantly.

Indeed, by 1972 the increase in acreage planted in high-yield varieties in Asia threatened to produce glut conditions in both rice and wheat. Less than a year later, however, severe drought in some areas, floods in others, and generally poor growing conditions resulted in a return to grain shortages of major proportions. India, which had declared itself self-sufficient in grain production in 1971 and expected to become a major exporter beginning in 1972, instead had to spend precious foreign exchange on grain imports in 1973. The years of drought and famine in six sub-Saharan African countries which reached a devastating climax in human and animal suffering in 1973 illustrate the fragile base of food production in all parts of the underdeveloped world.

These fluctuations between hope and disillusionment have characterized a green revolution which, by 1973, was not much more than a half-dozen years old. While the miracle seeds have not yet demonstrated that they are the answer to the world's hunger, their performance during a short initial period provides the single greatest hope that it is not beyond earth's capacity to feed its inhabitants.

Once again, however, a qualification must be entered. The green revolution will not solve the problem of human hunger unless it achieves a double objective. First, it must increase food production by enough to feed a world population that by the year 2000 will be approximately double the population of 1970. Second, it must eliminate the current world food deficit that condemns half of present humanity to life-long hunger. Miracle seeds may—at some point—permit India to dispense with food imports permanently, but even so remarkable an achievement cannot be termed self-sufficiency unless domestic production can feed all Indians adequately. The lot of the hungry poor in Calcutta was changed very little by the first exhilarating successes of miracle wheat in the Indian countryside.

Around the world each year 3 million die from outright starvation or from disease and infirmity related to nutritional deficiencies; hundreds of millions suffer physical and mental ill health as a result of insufficiencies of diet; a hundred societies are hampered in their efforts to attain higher levels of productivity by the limited energies of undernourished populations. The half-diet of half of mankind needs to be made whole. Unless it is able to bring an adequate diet to all human beings in this century as well as the next, the green revolution will have failed.

Water is as essential as food to men and animals and to the plants that provide their nutritional base. Oceans and fresh water are also direct sources of food, primarily in the form of fish. There is promising potential for greatly increasing the yield of food from water by such techniques as aquaculture, or farming the sea and fresh water bodies for both fish and vegetable matter. But the immediate problem is a shortage of water for conventional uses. The truck dispensing water to the slum dwellers in drums and cans testifies that, as with all other human needs, the shortage of water is most acute among the world's poor.

At the same time, water usage patterns in the industrial countries identify water as another in the long list of indicators registering a fantastic imbalance in the way supply operates for the poor and the rich. The industrial countries use water at a prodigious rate: 45,000 gallons of water are needed to make an automobile; 120,000 gallons to make one ton of aluminum; 240,000 gallons to make a ton of newsprint. In 1965 the United States alone was using about 270 billion gallons a day from a daily water yield of approximately 1.45 trillion gallons. The differential between yield and usage is currently more than adequate. But it is bound to become less so in view of the fact that United States water consumption doubled between 1945 and 1965 and is likely to double again by 1985. Industrial water usage in the United States, which accounted for more than 130 billion gallons of the total in 1965, is expected to quadruple by the year 2000.[21]

Thus, as with other natural resources, high consumption of water in rich countries threatens to strain their supplies, while low-consumption poor countries already experience shortages. Like the problem of food, then, the global water problem is a double one: to meet the needs of future populations and to supply water to the hundreds of millions to whom it is presently a luxury commodity. It is also evident that the water-poor societies must enormously increase the availability of water not only for human consumption but also for agricultural and industrial use if they are to become developed. These needs clearly cannot be met without a global effort in water conservation, water storage, and expansion of existing supplies through exploration of underground water sources and refining desalinization technology to the point of general applicability at low cost.

The poor countries variously lack the technology, the capital for research and construction, the internal market, and sometimes the phys-

---

[21] John Laffin, *The Hunger to Come* (London: Abelard-Schuman, 1966), pp. 150, 152. The statistics specific to the United States are taken from T. E. A. van Hylckam, "Water Resources," in William W. Murdoch, *Environment* (Stamford, Conn.: Sinauer Associates, 1971).

ical access to water sources. With such handicaps they cannot cease being poor unless there is a joint effort of poor and rich to make water available in sufficient quantity to meet the human needs of the individual consumer and to provide an adequate hydrological base for rising productivity in presently underdeveloped economies.

THE DEFICIT IN HEALTH AND HOUSING

The basic indicator of health in a society is the life expectancy of its population—how long the average person can expect to live. In the early 1960s, the average life span for the globe as a whole was moving upward in the range between 40 and 50 years. The developed countries, in this as in all other material matters, ranged high above the world average. The average person in Sweden and the Netherlands lived 73 years; in the United States and Australia, 70 years; in the Soviet Union and Japan, 68 years. India and Pakistan were close to the global average with life expectancy ranging between 40 and 45 years. Life was most fragile in some parts of Latin America and in Black Africa: Guatemala's average life expectancy was 40 years, Senegal's between 35 and 40, and that of Guinea and Ivory Coast between 30 and 35.

This contrast between life expectations in North and South, however, represents an extraordinary change for the poor countries from the conditions that prevailed only twenty years earlier. In India, for example, the Government of India census in 1951 set average life expectancy at 32 years; in the 1961 census life expectancy was found to be 42 years. In December 1968 President Husain of India, in an address on population problems, reported that average life expectancy had passed the 50-year level, as against a 27-year average in 1947. He also noted the consequence: during the same period India's population had climbed from 344 million to 528 million. Underdeveloped countries, as noted in the previous chapter's discussion of Mauritius and other cases, have generally experienced sharp drops in the death rate. The result is longer lived populations and, consequently, more people at any given time dependent on the resources of these countries. Between 1940 and 1950 the death rate dropped 46 percent in Puerto Rico, 43 percent in Taiwan, and 23 percent in Jamaica. The average decline in death rate for a sample of eighteen underdeveloped areas between the years 1945 and 1950 was 24 percent.[22] In the all-encompassing gap between North and

---

[22] All but one of the sets of life expectancy figures in this paragraph and the one previous are taken from the *Population Bulletin* 19, 6 (October 1963), 146–147. The percentages of decline in death rates are taken from Paul Ehrlich, *The Population Bomb* (New York: Ballantine Books, 1968), pp. 33–34. President Husain's address was reported in *India News* 40 (December 20, 1968). *India News* is published by the Indian Embassy in Washington.

South, the disparity in life expectancy is the only gap that has been perceptibly reduced—and the tragic result is the population explosion.

The result has been tragic in the classic sense of the word. Hundreds of millions of people have a firmer grip on life, with vastly improved chances of emerging from infancy into childhood, maturity, and old age. This achievement of science can only be seen as a good in itself. But this good is the direct cause of the Malthusian evils that arise when there are too many people and too few resources to sustain them. The population explosion is the most massive and dramatic episode in history to illustrate the Greek lament that tragic man, seeking good, unleashes evil instead. The narrowing of the gap in life chances between North and South has widened the gap in life conditions. There are now more people living longer lives than ever before; in the starkest terms, this means that the number of people whose lot in life is poverty, hunger, and ill health is greater by far than at any time in all previous history.

Adequate medical care for their citizens is quite beyond the capacities of the governments of underdeveloped countries. This is evident not merely in the data concerning the health problems of the poor but in the inadequacy of the objectives set forth to alleviate their situation. When, for example, the United Nations designated the 1960s as a "Development Decade," the World Health Organization (WHO) prescribed as a goal for 1970 a ratio of one doctor to every 10,000 inhabitants in the developing countries. The significance of this ratio is best understood when compared with the doctor-population ratio in the developed countries which ranges between 1:500 and 1:1,000.

As of 1970, however, even so inadequate a goal was far from being met in many countries in the underdeveloped world, and particularly in Africa. In the whole of Africa, by 1967, the doctor-population ratio ranged between 1:25,000 and 1:50,000. In twenty-six African countries it was established that the situation had deteriorated rather than "developed"; the number of doctors dropped from 4,700 in 1962 to 4,400 in 1965. Part of the explanation for the decrease lies in a still more discouraging circumstance of African medicine. Of the 4,400 doctors remaining in the countries surveyed in 1965, only 1,700 were Africans; the rest were foreign doctors and missionaries. One country had no African doctor, and in another the ratio was one African doctor to each million of population. The deterioration was evident as well in regard to other health personnel: in the same twenty-six countries the number of registered nurses and midwives fell from 1:5,800 persons in 1962 to 1:7,500 in 1965.[23]

India, on the other hand, has made extraordinary progress. In 1946 there were just fifteen medical colleges admitting approximately 1,000

[23] Report of Dr. Alfred Quenum, Regional Director for Africa of the World Health Organization, *New York Times*, April 4, 1967.

students a year; in 1970 there were ninety-four medical colleges admitting about 12,000 students annually. By 1960 India was already well above the minimum doctor-population ratio set by WHO as a 1970 target; by 1968 India's ratio was 1:5,112. Yet this remarkable accomplishment still left India with a doctor-population ratio less than one-tenth that in the Soviet Union and one-eighth that in the United States.

Thus despite a tremendous expenditure of effort, India continues to be burdened with massive health problems. They are exacerbated by a persistent shortage of medical teaching personnel, by a high dropout rate among medical students, and by a preference on the part of new doctors to practice in urban areas instead of in the countryside where more than 80 percent of the Indian population lives.[24] In addition, India has lost the services of many thousands of doctors who emigrated abroad in search of better pay and better facilities for practice. India's difficulties in these areas of medical training and practice are variations on a theme typical of the experience of the underdeveloped world as a whole.

Although there has been a recrudescence in the late 1960s of some of the major communicable diseases, the spectacular gains made since World War II against such mass killers as malaria and smallpox are generally being held and extended. The urgent health problems of the world's poor now derive from malnutrition, inadequate water supply, overcrowding, and generally unsanitary living conditions. Malnutrition, by definition, makes its victims prone to diet-deficiency diseases. But the resulting body weakness increases vulnerability to all other forms of illness, a situation (it bears repeating) in which more than half of mankind finds itself. This is the half chiefly referred to in a study on water-borne disease cited in the *1967 Report on the World Social Situation* by the United Nations Economic and Social Council (ECOSOC):

> Every year an estimated 500 million people suffer from disabling diseases related to the lack of clean water. Contaminated supplies are associated with widespread epidemics or with endemic patterns of disease. The loss of man-hours arising from this is stupendous. Water-borne diseases are also the leading cause of illness and deaths among infants and children.

The report also cited WHO surveys of 75 countries in Asia, Africa, and Latin America which ascertained that in 1963 only 33 percent of the urban population had piped water in their homes; another 26 percent had access to public outlets within a reasonable distance.

> This means that nearly 130 million of the total urban population depend for their water on wells, rivers and other sources generally open to contamination or of doubtful quality.

---

[24] *India News*, January 6, 1967, and February 27, 1970.

By 1977, as many as 337 million persons will be in the same situation if existing services are not increased. . . .

The results of a qualitative assessment by the WHO regional offices present an even more disturbing picture. Only 11 per cent of the population surveyed were described as having good or fair water supplies, leaving 89 per cent whose supplies were unsatisfactory or grossly unsatisfactory.[25]

Wretched housing and surroundings in the urban and rural slums are an integral part of the massive problems of poverty and disease. A 1965 ECOSOC report estimated that 900 million people in the third world of Asia, Africa, and Latin America lacked proper housing. The victims of this gigantic deficiency run the gamut from the pavement dwellers of Calcutta, the shacktown millions surrounding all the third world's cities —to the inhabitants of the slum tenements in the central cities of the richest nation in the world. It is evident that the deficiency has become still more grotesque since the 1965 survey. At the outset of the UN's first Development Decade, ECOSOC had specified a construction goal of 10 dwelling units per 1,000 population in the underdeveloped world as a minimum requirement to replace buildings deteriorating in the normal course of events and to achieve a significant reduction in the number of people living in substandard housing or having no shelter at all. By 1969 ECOSOC's Committee on Housing, Building and Planning reported that:

> progress toward this goal has been disappointing. Only two new dwellings per thousand inhabitants are being produced per year in many developing countries. Without doubt the projected goals have been overwhelmed by high and increasing rates of population growth, heavy migration from rural to urban areas, and the rising costs of land, labor, and materials. In many countries, the housing situation has deteriorated, and in some it verges on disaster.[26]

India, as usual, provides the bleakest example of the housing crisis. After constructing 400,000 low cost housing units in fifteen years during three consecutive five-year plans, the Indian government in the mid-

---

[25] *1967 Report on the World Social Situation* (New York: United Nations, Department of Economic and Social Affairs, 1969), pp. 29–30. These are the conditions that have given rise to a resurgence of cholera in the particularly virulent form known as El Tor. Spreading out from Southeast Asia during the 1960s, El Tor had, by 1973, penetrated into the Middle East, the southern Soviet Union, and East, West and Southern Africa. After a period of quiescence in 1971–1972, cholera (El Tor and other strains) became epidemic once again in 1973, most notably in Southern Italy, where the last such epidemic had occurred in 1911.

[26] United Nations Economic and Social Council, Committee on Housing, Building and Planning, Sixth Session, 2–12 September 1969, Document E/C.6/90, 24 July 1969, p. 4.

1960s planned to step up its efforts by projecting 600,000 units for a single five-year span under its fourth plan. At the same time, it estimated the overall "deficit ... at the beginning of the Fourth Five Year Plan is 74.1 million houses—11.4 million in the urban areas and 62.7 million in the rural areas."[27] At the increased rate of construction set for the Fourth Five Year Plan it would require more than 120 years just to erase the current deficit.

A realistic projection of India's housing needs, of course, would have to take into account the housing demand of a doubled and perhaps redoubled population in the period under consideration, as well as replacement of existing units as they become obsolete. To return from a forbidding future to an equally forbidding present, a conservative calculation of 4 persons per dwelling yields a total requirement of approximately 135 million houses for India's 550 million citizens as of 1970. A deficit of 74.1 million houses means that well over half of India's total population lives in conditions for which the term substandard housing provides a wholly inadequate description.

Chile provides a less awesome but more revolutionary example of the housing emergency in the underdeveloped world. With a population of approximately 9 million, the Chilean government built 180,000 homes between 1958 and 1964, and the private and public sectors together built another 126,000 from 1965 to 1967. Since 1959 Chile has actually reduced the number of people living in squatter settlements, and in the late 1960s it was the only country in Latin America where the rate of housing construction kept ahead of the rate of population increase. Yet by the end of the decade only a moderate dent had been made in a deficit estimated in 1964 at 420,000 houses—in a population of 9 million. Among other things, Chile has to contend with earthquakes that destroyed 58,000 homes in 1960 and another 23,000 in 1965.[28]

Thus by the turn of the decade, nature and the insufficiencies of human effort in Chile had conspired to produce attempts to satisfy the hunger for housing and land by force:

A sea of Chilean flags fluttered over tattered tents and cardboard shelters as some 1,200 indigent families founded a new Marxist community in a field here this week.

Residents struggled with their mattresses and pots, arranged their belongings, and somewhat self-consciously addressed each other as "comrade." Militiamen wearing red armbands quickly fortified the site against Government policemen and all comers.

---

[27] *India News* (October 27, 1967). The Fourth Five Year Plan spans the period from 1968–1969 to 1973–1974.

[28] Thomas G. Sanders, "Juan Pérez Buys a House," Report of the American Universities Field Staff (Hanover, N.H., April 1969).

The new squatter camp, dubbed Che Guevara Encampment, was the latest in a series of a dozen or so similar camps organized in various parts of Chile this year by the Revolutionary Junta of Homeless Ones.

The Sin Casa, or the Homeless, as the organization is familiarly known, is an appendage of the Chilean Socialist Party, a Marxist party with close ties to Cuba.

In the latest land seizure, families organized by Sin Casa in a suburban Santiago slum called Las Barrancas moved quickly in the night to occupy a field owned by the Government. The field had been allocated for public housing, but spokesmen of Sin Casa insisted that the Government was moving too slowly and in a discriminatory way.

Their backs loaded with kitchen utensils, clothing and odds and ends of material for making tents and shanties, the families completed their land grab in a few hours. Socialist party cadres established rigid discipline within the camp, giving immediate attention to sanitary projects and the posting of guards.

Young men and women with clubs along the fence surrounding the field barred not only would-be visitors and policemen, but hundreds of indigent families not belonging to the group. A certain amount of political orientation appeared to have been a prerequisite for participation in the land seizure.

The land grab was illegal, and the police could easily have overpowered the militia guarding the camp, but the political cost to the Government would have been high. . . .

Last year, the police tried to evict Socialist-led squatters from a camp near Puerto Montt in Southern Chile. The squatters resisted, and policemen opened fire, killing nine of them. About 30 persons were wounded, including some policemen.

The incident rocked the Government of President Eduardo Frei Montalva, which was accused by leftist parties of maintaining a police force of "butchers." . . .

Sin Casa camps have not progressed beyond tent communities. A few have electricity, and most are supplied with water.

Money to buy food and emergency supplies apparently comes mostly from the Leftist Revolutionary Movement, known as the M.I.R., which carries out several bank robberies each week. Few of the camp dwellers have jobs. The unemployment rate in Santiago is at present more than 20 per cent, and beggars congest downtown streets.

Rules are about the same in all of the camps, and they are strict. Alcohol, wife-beating and gambling are prohibited. Each tent is inspected by militiamen twice weekly for cleanliness and at unannounced times for alcohol raids.

Members of encampments must attend meetings of a highly political character every few days. Failure to attend three meetings in succession without authorization by the camp central committee results in expulsion from the camp. . . .

The Sin Casa leaders say that their popular militias, whose weapons are believed to include submachine guns, will one day govern the nation. This they say, will represent the final triumph of Chilean socialism.[29]

The homeless ones and their leaders made their full contribution to the social ferment and to the electoral victory that, a few weeks after the founding of the Che Guevara encampment, made Salvador Allende the first Marxist president of Chile.

POVERTY, EDUCATION, AND CHANGE

Food, health, and housing are at once basic human demands and indispensable indices in the measurement of poverty and wealth. But if one moves on from the initial task of recording the data of poverty to the question of how the conditions of poverty might be altered, the overriding need becomes one of education. Enhancing the individual's productivity in agriculture, industry, and services is the only remedy for his poverty and for that of his family and his society. The only method by which individual productivity can be enhanced, in turn, is education—sometimes outside but mostly within a system of formal schooling. It follows that if poverty is to be transformed into abundance in any society, education must be recognized as the single most important agent of change.

The first and indispensable educational achievement in a world governed by the written symbol (Marshall McLuhan notwithstanding) is literacy. In 1970, 34.2 percent of the world's population over the age of fifteen lacked that fundamental requirement for entry into modern society.[30] This is a vast improvement over the situation twenty years earlier, when it was estimated that the world's adult illiteracy was more than 45 percent. The overwhelming majority of illiterates are found in the underdeveloped world. In 1968, 82 percent of the population above 15 years of age in Africa was illiterate, 54 percent in Asia, and 34 percent in Latin America. Percentages for some individual countries in the same year are shown in Table 13.3. These figures provide a stark contrast to the 1 to 3 percent illiteracy average in Western and Northern Europe, the Soviet Union, and Japan, and the 2 percent for the United States and Canada.

Expansion of education and adult literacy campaigns in the underdeveloped world began to effect massive changes in the 1950s and 1960s. Between 1950 and 1960 the world-wide illiteracy rate estimate dropped from 44.3 percent to 39.3 percent, and the estimated number of literate persons (over 15) rose from 878.9 million to 1,141.3 million. But during the

---

[29] Malcolm W. Browne, *New York Times*, August 31, 1970.

[30] See Appendix F for literacy rates by continent and country.

Table 13.3

Percentage of Illiteracy, 1968

COUNTRY	PERCENT ILLITERATE (ESTIMATE)	COUNTRY	PERCENT ILLITERATE (ESTIMATE)
Algeria	75-85	India	70-75
Nigeria	80-88	Pakistan	75-85
Senegal	90-95	Indonesia	55-60
Zaïre (formerly		Guatemala	60-70
Congo, Kinshasa)	80-85	Mexico	30-35
South Africa	65-70	Brazil	30-35
Turkey	60-65	Peru	35-40
Saudi Arabia	85-95	Bolivia	55-65

same period the population explosion took its toll here as elsewhere: the total number of estimated illiterates also rose from 700 to 740 million. Thus the extraordinary educational achievements in all parts of the underdeveloped world could only slow down the rate of increase in the numbers of human beings entering the adult world without the ability to read and write.

A special international commission on education reported to UNESCO in 1972 that the world total of illiterates had increased during the sixties to 783 million. The commission estimated that by 1980 there would be 820 million illiterates. The 1950–1960 pattern repeats itself: the percentage of illiteracy falls while the absolute number of illiterates rises in a rapidly expanding population. To these somber figures must be added more hundreds of millions who might qualify as literate by a multiplicity of widely varying standards but whose facility with language in its written form does not enable them to use it as an effective working instrument. These uncounted numbers of disadvantaged people are variously labeled semiliterates or functional illiterates.[31]

The category of functional illiterate lends emphasis to the fact that literacy is only the bare beginning of education. The magnitude of the demand for basic education is most succinctly stated in terms of the

---

[31] Data in this and the two previous paragraphs are taken from Sir Charles Jeffries, *Illiteracy: A World Problem* (New York: Praeger, 1967), p. 26; *1967 Report on the World Social Situation*, p. 62; *New York Times*, October 19, 1969; and *Literacy 1967–1969* (Paris: UNESCO, 1970). The illiteracy percentages by continent and for individual countries are taken from the *World Population Data Sheet—1968* (Washington, D.C.: Population Reference Bureau, March, 1968). (The percentage for Latin America in this source is much lower than the 50 percent figure cited by Senator Kennedy and is probably closer to the real figure.) For the 1972 report of the international education commission to UNESCO, see *The New York Times*, October 2, 1972.

numbers of school-age children living at any given time. To take some major countries of Asia as an example, there were approximately 325 million children between the ages of 5 and 14 living in India, Pakistan, Indonesia, and mainland China in 1960. Taking into account population growth rates then prevailing, the governments of these four countries had to anticipate that the number of children in that age category would have increased by nearly 200,000,000 by 1975. The figures for the individual countries are shown in Table 13.4. The political, economic, intellectual, and psychological strains in societies involved in attempting to provide education for this mass of young people, massively expanding, defy description. It is certain that the closing down of the Communist Chinese school system from the elementary level through university for varying periods during the "Great Cultural Revolution" of 1966–1968 was in part a reflection of these strains.

At least for the next two decades, most Asian governments will not be in a position to meet the needs of their citizens for education. In connection with a 1965 blueprint for education in Asia drawn up under the auspices of UNESCO (the Karachi Plan), Asian governments, not including Communist China, North Korea, or North Vietnam, "hoped that, between 1965 and 1970, 38.3 million students can be added to the primary school enrollment, 11.6 million to the secondary school enrollment, which will require an additional 245,000 teachers, and 1.1 million to the enrollment at higher educational establishments." But even assuming success, this outsized educational effort necessarily failed to reach millions of Asian school-age children, for in this same five-year period their numbers increased by more than 60 million. By 1967 only eight of thirty-five Asian countries had 90 percent or more of their primary school-age groups actually enrolled (an increase, at any rate, from 1955 when there were just two: Japan and Thailand). The majority of Asian countries were nowhere near this level of enrollment.

Table 13.4
Numbers of children aged 5 to 14 (in millions)

	1960	1975
India	100	150
Pakistan		
(including Bangla Desh)	24	40
Indonesia	21	35
China	180	300
Total	325	525

Source: Irene B. Taeuber, "Asian Populations: The Critical Decades," in Ng and Mudd, *The Population Crisis*, pp. 83–84.

Similar situations prevail in Latin America and Africa. Increases in the number of children attending school are far from making up the combined deficit produced by an inherited insufficiency of schools and teachers and a burgeoning school-age population. Between 1956 and 1965 the percentage of the population of Latin America enrolled in some kind of school rose from 13.3 to 17.1. (Of the latter figure, primary school enrollment accounted for 82.2 percent.) But entered against this significant gain is a statistic that records a still more significant—and tragic—loss: in 1968 approximately 28 percent of the total population of Latin America was of school age (5 to 15 years), but only 17.1 percent of the total population (including secondary and university students) was in school.

In Africa there were 25 million school-age children at the beginning of the 1960s. A generous estimate was then made that 50 percent would complete primary school. A less generous estimate at the same time foresaw only three of every 1,000 having a chance for higher education. By 1966, 6 percent were entering secondary schools. This modest result at least began to alter the prevailing situation south of the Sahara (excluding South Africa) in which no more than 2 percent of any age group had any form of secondary education. The growing numbers of universities and university enrollments in Africa thus rest on a very narrow preuniversity base. This structure of the educational pyramid in Africa is repeated, with only slight modifications, in most of Asia and Latin America.

The global result that emerges from these figures is an educational gap between developed North and underdeveloped South even more ominous than the gap in economic productivity. The gap is perhaps most in evidence at the top of the educational pyramid. In 1968 there were nearly two and a half times as many college students in North America as in all the rest of the world. In North America, 1 in 8 students attended an institution of higher learning; in Europe 1 in 20. The corresponding figures in Asia were 1 in 38; in the Arab states 1 in 45; in Latin America 1 in 49; and in Africa 1 in 90.

These disparities in access to higher education are the end product of radically unequal opportunities for education in North and South at every level. The percentages of school enrollments in Table 13.5 offer a dramatic demonstration of this situation. The enrollment figures reflect and are reflected by the huge difference in educational expenditures of North and South. In 1968 the South spent $11.35 billion on education; the North spent $120.29 billion.[32]

---

[32] Data and table are taken from the *New York Times* report on a special international commission on education study for UNESCO, October 2, 1972. Budget expenditures in the commission's study are totals for "industrial" and "developing" countries with China, North Korea, and North Vietnam omitted.

Table 13.5

World School Enrollment Rates, 1967–1968

REGION	CHILDREN OF PRIMARY SCHOOL AGE (%)	YOUTHS OF SECONDARY SCHOOL AGE (%)	20–24 YEAR OLDS IN HIGHER EDUCATION (%)
North America	98	92	44.5
Europe and USSR	97	65	16.7
Oceania	95	60	15
Latin America	75	35	5
Asia	55	30	4.7
Africa	40	15	1.3

School enrollment figures, of course, constitute only a crude index of the extent of educational opportunity. Schooling is a long-term process; one who participates in the process but fails to complete it may serve as a school enrollment statistic, but he will not gain a useful education. Thus the dropout rate is a crucial additional measurement if one is to judge degrees of success and failure in any educational enterprise. In Latin America the statistics reveal at least some progress from worse to bad. In 1957, 41 percent of the primary enrollment in all of Latin America was concentrated in the first grade and only 7 percent in the highest primary grade. By 1965 the figures had changed to 38 percent and 8 percent respectively. In rural areas the situation was typically much more severe. In eleven Latin American countries the percentage reaching the final primary grade in rural schools was less than half the corresponding percentage for urban schools. In Asia, "drop-out rates in the first four years of primary school range up to 80 percent or more of original enrollment in some . . . countries, and rates of more than 50 percent are common." Only in Japan, Taiwan, Malaysia, and the Republic of Korea are the dropout rates lower than 15 percent.

The underlying cause that produces all these discouraging statistics is poverty. The poverty of governments and societies is reflected in the shortage of schools, books, and the still more severe shortage of properly trained and adequately paid teachers. The poverty of individuals and families is evident enough in their meager resources. But it is also reflected in the fact that education is an alien and often threatening phenomenon for most of the older generation. Thus wherever there is a history of poverty and cultural deprivation, whether in an underdeveloped country or in an American ghetto, psychological impediments join the ensemble of factors obstructing the purposes and hopes of the educational enterprise. Friction between the student and his unlettered family in home conditions wholly unsuited to study is a universal drama in the contemporary world of the poor. The United Nations *1967 Report on the World Social Situation* identifies as most important among the operative causes for the school dropout rate "the lack of sufficient employment opportunity to justify the family sacrifices entailed in keeping a child in school." Thus the vicious circle is at full turn: a poverty-stricken society is able to offer its poverty-stricken citizens only limited employment opportunities, whatever the level of their educational achievements, with the result that education appears to many to be just another blind alley instead of a pathway to significant change.[33]

India again provides a sobering example. In 1970 there were approximately 50,000 engineers unable to find employment in their profession and a still higher number of degree holders at the bachelor of arts level who could not find positions for which they were qualified. Moreover, the relevance of the education offered at all levels of the Indian system to contemporary social and economic needs is in serious question. Education is often seen as a passport from the countryside to the urban sector, but the overcrowded cities are already filled with unemployed. Hence the need, only beginning to be recognized, to gear more of primary education to prepare students for a rural life. At the university level, among India's eighty institutions of higher learning, the centers of real excellence are far outnumbered by those which range from mediocrity downward.

This unhappy situation is an almost unavoidable result of the otherwise admirable investment of energy that has brought education to scores of millions since Indian independence in 1947. A crash program has transformed India from a society where education was restricted to a tiny minority into one in which there are more students in school and college than in the United States (in absolute numbers). But the problems compounded of massive population growth and a forced-pace attempt to liquidate the huge educational deficit of India's colonial past are evident to a disheartening degree: depressed educational standards, inadequacy of curricula, overcrowding of school facilities, and a society hard pressed to find employment for the products of its educational system.[34]

---

[33] Data in this and the preceding four paragraphs are drawn from the *1967 Report on the World Social Situation*, pp. 63, 118, 143–144, 159–160, 161. The percentage figure for persons in Latin America under 15 years of age is from *World Population Data Sheet—1968*.

[34] Harold Howe, "What Kind of Education in Poor Lands?," *New York Times*, January 12, 1970. As a commentary on failures to relate the classroom to reality, Howe points to the lack of understanding of India's most desperate problem, runaway population growth: "A high school graduate in India is not likely to have learned that his country has such a problem. If he had, he would be unlikely to learn how serious it is or what might be done about it. A few efforts are being made to fill this vacuum."

Since this report, efforts by the Indian government have made population control a much more widely understood issue.

With all the dilemmas and insufficiencies that afflict the Indian effort in education, the achievements have also been enormous. Most important, there can be no doubt concerning the sincerity of India's commitment to education for all its citizens. This commitment, it must be stressed, is far from being universal in the underdeveloped world. If education is the chief agent of change, developing countries have an enormous objective stake in the school house. But not everyone in these countries is committed to development; there are those who are unenthusiastic about social change because it will alter their favored position in society. Precisely because a functioning program of mass education will produce major changes in any society, those who are opponents of social change are also unenthusiastic about the spread of education. A mass citizenry that is educated—or even partly educated—will espouse different values and demands than one whose great majority is wholly or functionally illiterate. These new values and demands—or rising expectations—on the part of the mass convert a somnolent society and a stagnant economy into a political and social battleground, and the old verities of government by and for the elite are called into question.

The struggle between the traditional elite state and the nascent mass state is exacerbated by the harsh and stubborn fact that underdeveloped societies, by definition, have yet to generate a level of productivity capable of sustaining realistic policies directed toward growing economic and political equality. In such a context, policies in education as in other fields are doubly vulnerable to subversion and abuse. It is often difficult to judge where intellectual or financial shortcomings in these policies leave off and where deliberate starving of the educational effort begins as a method of perpetuating elite privilege. Without attempting to pass such a judgment in this specific instance, the following appraisal of the educational situation in Brazil describes facts and effects that speak for themselves:

Every commission that has studied education in this country of 88 million people has pronounced it a national scandal. Although Brazil has a burgeoning industrial complex and leads Latin America in the production of everything from automobiles to television tubes, she has only 175,000 students in universities.

Most education in Brazil is financed by the government, and most critics say its inadequate performance is due primarily to inadequate funds. Since the military coup, education's share has grown progressively less, from 11 percent of total government expenditures in 1965 to 7.7 percent this year.

Comparing budgets for 1967 and 1968, the army got 45 percent more money this year, the navy got 42 percent more and the air force got 46 percent more. Education's increase was 26 percent, or slightly less than the rate of inflation in Brazil in the same period.[35]

Concerning student protests against government educational policies, the same report went on to note that "the Government has repeatedly stated that the student movement ... [in Rio de Janeiro] and in other major cities is under the control of 'international agitators.'" This kind of reaction, of course, is hardly unique to Brazil or to the underdeveloped world. But wherever it appears, and whatever the degree of truth or falsehood in the associated allegations, it never suggests a readiness to come to grips with real grievances and fundamental causes underlying the problems at issue. Remedies for most of the real problems can in any case be found only gradually, but remedies are not likely to be found at all where those with power regard the remedy as more dangerous than the complaint. This is notably the situation in Rhodesia, South Africa, and Portuguese Africa, where access to secondary and higher education is reserved for the white elites and a minute fraction of the black masses.

But southern Africa is not the only place where elites are determined to defend their inherited privileges, nor is skin color the only basis for discriminatory practices. Wherever the fear of equality is present in the contemporary world, it is always accompanied by the fear of universal education. If explanations are sought for failures and successes in the educational efforts of both the underdeveloped and developed worlds, population pressures, economic capacities, training facilities for teachers and students, and, in the South, the newness of the concept of mass education must all be subjects of inquiry. But no explanation will be complete without an examination of the way in which ideas of equality and inequality are manifested in the society under consideration.

These observations point back to the issues raised at the outset of the chapter. First is the fantastic disparity between the developed North and the underdeveloped South: in gross national product, in GNP per capita, in levels of nutrition, in population growths, in life expectancy,

---

[35] Paul Montgomery, *New York Times*, June 27, 1968. Montgomery's university enrollment figure is more than 100,000 less than the Brazilian government's official 1968 figure of 278,295 undergraduate and 4,358 graduate students. See Riordan Roett (ed.), *Brazil in the Sixties* (Nashville, Tenn.: Vanderbilt University Press, 1972, p. 281.)

Given the generally low quality of university education in Brazil, it is doubtful if the larger enrollment figure is an unambiguous plus. Even the larger figure is quantitatively disheartening: it is equivalent to 0.3 percent of the total Brazilian population. The comparable percentage for 1967–1968 in France is approximately 1.2; in the United States it is 3.5. Thus, in proportional terms, the 1967–1968 university student population was thirteen times greater in the United States than in Brazil.

in health and housing, in education, and therefore in power. Second, there is a disparity just as fantastic within each underdeveloped society between the lives of the few and the many. It is essentially the same disparity: a radically unequal distribution of basic human needs and values. In each underdeveloped country there is a small percentage of the total population that lives above the internal world of want and whose life style is as alien to the poverty surrounding it as the life of the global North is from that of the global South.

The presence of a small minority who are rich and a vast majority who are poor defines the underdeveloped society. This is the dominant presence in some 120 underdeveloped countries. It is also the dominant presence in the global society—which must, then, itself be characterized as underdeveloped.

Development, by definition, is a process in which the disparity between rich and poor is progressively alleviated. The developing society is one that moves away from the traditional antithesis of elite and mass and toward a community in which all the population has an authentic opportunity to share in the production and uses of power and wealth. There is no other way for poor countries to join the ranks of developed societies. There is no other way for the world as a whole to "develop."

The gap of wealth and power between North and South cannot diminish until the same gap that divides underdeveloped societies within themselves—into the privileged few and the miserable many—begins to close. It follows that the heart of the development problem is to set in motion a continuous process of internal reform designed to achieve ever greater degrees of political, economic, and social equality in the underdeveloped countries. Those who oppose this process can be fairly identified as the enemies of development. It is their opposition that must be overcome if, now at the global level, Marx's prediction of an expansion of poverty among the growing many and a steady concentration of wealth among the diminishing few is to be confounded.

Chapter 14

Development: Politics and Economics

"Development is the new name for peace." These words provide the intellectual and moral climax to the papal encyclical of March 1967, which Paul VI entitled "Populorum Progressio," or "On the Development of Peoples." They proceed from the proposition that only political, economic, and social development that enables men to move away from poverty and coercion and toward abundance and freedom can realize justice, and that only justice can bring peace.

The equation of development to peace and of peace to justice necessarily points to a judgment that development is something more than a drive toward higher levels of production and consumption. It is instead a process whose purpose is to create economic, social, and political conditions conducive to the pursuit of justice, to a world in which men and cultures are treated as ends in themselves and not as instruments to serve the ends of others. Only such a concept of development, applied both within and among nations, can warrant the multidimensional assertion that development equals peace.

In this formulation the heavily economic overtones of the conventional concept of development are subordinated to considerations of morality and the issue of human security and survival. Increase in living standards is seen as a necessary (but not sufficient) condition of peace and justice. After all, rich societies have been both unjust and warlike. Hence the papal dictum is perhaps better understood in its negative form: without development there can be no peace or justice. Development will not guarantee them. But development is their precondition.

The pope linked the new alliance of development and peace to the historic encyclicals of his predecessors that addressed themselves—in the classic phrase—to the "social question." These papal documents of the nineteenth and twentieth centuries were landmarks in the continuing critique, both Catholic and non-Catholic, of the evils of economic and social inequality within societies. In "Populorum Progressio" Pope

398

Paul broadened the tradition of Catholic social criticism when he observed that "the social question has become world-wide."

The inference is clear: social evils and society's obligation to eliminate them can no longer be understood and acted upon only within the confines of the sovereign state. Instead, both the evils and the obligations are transnational in nature and will yield only to transnational solutions. It will be noticed that these propositions are hardly original: they are found in Marxism, the UN Charter, in much of Western development theory, and, after all, in the founding tenets of Christianity. But their similarity to other doctrines only enhances their importance by underscoring the agreement among some of the world's major ideologies concerning the transnational character of the major issues of our time.

If the "social question" is worldwide and a proper matter for world concern, it follows that this concern cannot be confined to issues among states or between developed and underdeveloped countries. It must instead be directed primarily to the issues generated by the internal structures of societies. Social change within these structures is the only presently available path for greater justice for all men. For the developed countries, democratic and communist, social change is imperative if they are not to be immobilized or torn apart by their still imperfect understandings of liberty and justice and by the persisting inequities of their economic systems. For the underdeveloped countries, vast changes in their domestic social orders are indispensable if they are to "develop."

It is true that international peace and justice and internal peace and justice are mutually dependent. But the safety of the world today depends less on the foreign relations of states than on their internal dynamics. China, Vietnam, Cuba, Zaïre, Nigeria, Cambodia, Laos, Jordan, and Pakistan have offered bloody confirmation for this proposition—and they stand as tragic symbols of the interior anguish that convulses all societies in the underdeveloped world.

Development is the prime requirement for peace. Social change is the prime requirement for development. If these two propositions are valid, it follows that the seeker of peace must examine and then attempt to influence the social forces at work within a vast array of diverse societies around the world. Otherwise, his efforts to comprehend, adjust to, and influence the external behavior of these societies will fail to achieve his goal. The same may be said, incidentally, for the seeker of war, although a laissez faire policy in the contemporary world is about as likely a method of producing war as deliberate manipulation.

The implications of these observations are far-reaching. They are indeed revolutionary in relation to orthodox prescriptions for international behavior, which assert that states must not concern themselves with the internal affairs of other states. Practice, of course, has repeatedly subverted doctrine, and nowhere more systematically than in colonial empires and "spheres of influence." But as a norm, the doctrine of noninterference in the domestic affairs of sovereign states has long stood uncontested as a rule of the international system (which even the communist states have generally found it opportune to affirm).

The coupling of social change with development and development with peace, however, necessarily leads to a counternorm. It can be expressed by the proposition that every state has a stake in the domestic structures of all other states from which it derives both legitimate interests and legitimate obligations. It can also be stated less austerely: every man is involved in the life of all men. Departing from austerity altogether, it can find expression in the best of all the revolutionary ideas: all men are brothers.

But just as practice undermined the old norm of noninterference to the point of bankruptcy, so practice will determine the fate of any counternorm. One can offer benign interpretations of a norm that asserts the interdependence of all the world's societies in both their internal and external behavior. But they will persuade no one if the idea of interdependence only functions as one more imposture camouflaging the ancient game in which the rich and powerful oppress the poor and the weak.

After all, the ideas of sovereign inviolability and noninterference in domestic affairs were designed to erect barriers around states that other states, even if richer and stronger, had no legal right to violate except in case of outright war. Moreover, the concept of sovereignty generated a whole series of restrictions on state behavior so that even in war there were generally recognized limits to what states might legitimately do to each other and to what the victor might do with the vanquished. Even if the concept of sovereignty has been mocked again and again and is now in conflict with the imperatives of development, its protective function still commands high esteem. This is particularly the case among the poor societies, which are generally so little able to protect themselves against the political, economic, and military giants of the world. For them, any doctrine of sovereign rights is bound to be profoundly congenial.

The antagonism between the concept of sovereignty and the concept of development may often be concealed, but it is at the very center of relations between North and South. The conflict can never be fully resolved, but any successful development policy must find ways of reducing it to manageable proportions. This means that development policy must strive to bring about the domestic social change requisite to economic and political movement in the direction of equality; at the same time it must value sovereignty insofar as it functions to protect and promote the cultural and political individuality of underdeveloped societies. In sum, a commitment to development requires a new conceptualization of sovereignty. It must stress that many of the inherited attitudes toward sovereignty will have to yield before the new imperatives of development. But it must also protect the central idea of sovereignty, the yearning of individuals as well as societies to govern themselves in accordance with both inherited and emerging values unique to their own cultural experience.

DEVELOPMENT ISSUES: THE ALLIANCE FOR PROGRESS

The difficulty of achieving such a balance in policies for development is everywhere evident. Perhaps the greatest single source of such evidence is to be found in the history of the Alliance for Progress. The launching of the Alliance in 1961 marked the most comprehensive American commitment to development yet undertaken. It was hardly surprising that the commitment should be made in that area of the underdeveloped world to which the United States has had its closest historical ties. In the view of most articulate Latin Americans, however, the chief significance of these long-standing ties had been to bolster the hegemony of the United States in the hemisphere and to perpetuate Latin American subordination.

The reasonableness or unreasonableness of these views is the subject of a long-standing debate which has no foreseeable end. (In this sense, at least, these views bear comparison with attitudes toward Yankees that have found expression south of the Mason-Dixon line from colonial times to the present.) Whatever their validity, the ancient and widespread conviction below the Rio Grande that the United States would exploit Latin American weakness and intervene in the external or internal policies of Latin American states whenever it suited Washington's purpose heavily mortgaged the prospects for achieving the development goals of the Alliance.

The goals were themselves provocative—as any meaningful articulation of the objectives of the development process must be. But given the historic suspicions of the Latin South concerning the motives of the Yankee North, the official rhetoric of the Alliance was bound to heighten both misgivings and skepticism. We have already seen Robert Kennedy predict for Latin America the coming of revolution in his Senate speech of May 1968. Both Presidents Kennedy and Johnson also resorted to revolutionary phraseology and defined the purpose of the Alliance as the launching of a political, economic, and social revolution on a continental or hemispheric scale. Given the premises of the Alliance and the objective requirements of the development process, these were fair statements of intent. Further, they were accompanied by assurances that the revolution could and would be peaceful and that United States policy would be designed to promote changes advantageous to Latin American societies as a whole and not work to the detriment of some groups while benefiting others.

As might have been anticipated, however, the Alliance suffered a credibility gap from the outset. The goal of revolution was suspect among the Latin American left because of the long record of United States support for the oligarchical status quo. The right, for its part, could hardly be expected to relish the prospect of revolution. Both factions, in turn, exhibited well-founded skepticism concerning the proposition that "revolution" could take place without damaging the interests of some groups while promoting those of others.

In his Alliance speech in the Senate, Robert Kennedy discussed fundamental issues of development in Latin America with a candor that fully justified this skepticism. After pointing to the necessity of progressively expanding internal markets in Latin American countries, Kennedy went to the heart of the matter:

> But the greatest part of the expansion of internal markets is not a matter of trade barriers between countries; it is a matter of class barriers within countries. Small internal markets are the inevitable result of social and economic systems in which wealth is concentrated in the hands of the few—in which investment is made only in the cities, and not in the countryside—and where the great majority live at a level of bare subsistence. Widening internal markets—like land reform or education, or indeed any major progress in Latin America—will require a conscious effort at lessening social and economic inequalities, ending the isolation and poverty of the masses of the people. Without that change—without that social revolution for which President Johnson called—no economic assistance or devices will be successful.[1]

The diagnosis is accurate, but the resulting prognosis and prescription are aimed directly against the privileges and power of the oligarchical systems that dominate most of Latin America. One can argue, as Mirabeau did in the French Revolution, that the long-term interests of the ruling groups require that they renounce some of their prerogatives before all of them are taken away by force. But elites accustomed to a monopoly of power for centuries find it difficult to conceive of their interests in any other terms than the perpetuation of their minority rule. Hence the insistence on class barriers as the paramount obstacle to development is necessarily (and correctly) perceived as an attack on all those interests dependent upon the immutability of the oligarchic state.

Kennedy's speech probed still deeper into the internal structures of

---

[1] This and the two subsequent quotations are taken from "Alliance for Progress: Symbol and Substance," *Congressional Record*, 89th Cong. (May 9 and 10, 1968).

Latin America. He identified education and land reform as the two great problems "at the heart of the revolution," noting the impact that mass education must inevitably have on the internal political balance of any state where education has been traditionally restricted to the few. As for land reform, Kennedy cited familiar figures:

> Throughout Latin America it is estimated that more than 70 percent of the landowners control less than 4 percent of the land. Ninety percent of all land is controlled by less than 10 percent of the landholders; and there are nations in which less than 1 percent of all landholders control nearly 70 percent of the land.

In such circumstances, those paragraphs in the Charter of Punta del Este[2] which called for a redistribution of land on the basis of equitable tenure (and which Kennedy repeated) must have seemed like a declaration of war on those who benefit from the fantastic inequities characterizing the existing distribution.

But most of the governments that signed the Alliance in 1961, including the United States, subsequently demonstrated their reluctance to translate paper statements of purpose into operative policies, so that the statistics of land distribution that Senator Kennedy cited in 1968 were not significantly different from what they had been seven years earlier.[3] He had a remedy for that, too:

> . . . we can help Latin Americans meet the political challenges of land reform—above all, by clearly identifying and associating ourselves with the forces of reform and social justice. . . . Strong association of the United States with land reform will everywhere help its supporters, and make others more reluctant to oppose it.
>
> The basic work of reform, of course, is and must be for the people and governments of each Latin American nation. . . . But we can help; and we certainly can help by not extending our material and moral support to those who actively oppose necessary political, economic, and social change, including the comprehensive land reform which is at the heart of development efforts.

---

[2] The initial multilateral document that set forth the aims of the Alliance for Progress. The Charter was signed by all Latin American states (except Cuba) and the United States at Punta del Este, Uruguay, on August 17, 1961.

The text of the Charter is available in numerous publications, including *American Foreign Policy: Current Documents, 1961*, Department of State Publication 7808, 1965, pp. 393–409.

[3] By 1973 land redistribution programs had altered these statistics noticeably but not to the point of effecting a drastic change in the overall pattern of land ownership in Latin America.

The significance of the remedy is manifest: the active engagement of United States influence in the internal politics of Latin American countries on behalf of those groups committed to social change and against those that oppose it.

American intervention in the domestic politics of Latin American states was, of course, not a new idea. But in both the nineteenth and twentieth centuries virtually every American decision to intervene was made in order to prevent any rocking of the boat of American governmental or business interests in Latin America. The composition of internal social structures in Latin American countries was a matter of indifference except insofar as it affected these extrinsic interests, frequent declarations from Washington about the principled importance of democracy and constitutionality in the hemisphere notwithstanding. Against this background, the Alliance for Progress promised three major departures from the historic record of the United States in hemisphere relations.

First, America committed itself as a matter of policy to support the forces of change in Latin America and explicitly judged the status quo to be unviable. This position coincides with the general theory of development, which prescribes that societies must initiate a transforming process leading from the status of "underdeveloped" to "developed," during which they will necessarily undergo a whole series of profound internal changes.

Second, the United States asserted its concern for internal Latin American affairs not because of their effect on any specific American governmental or business interests but because of a general commitment to the growth of social justice and material prosperity for all people living in the hemisphere. It is hardly surprising that this statement of intent invited the attention of skeptics. American businesses and the oligarchical states of Latin America had understood and accommodated each other for a long time; both occupied positions of elite privilege in Latin American societies. Since development presumes a movement away from elitism and toward egalitarian principles of government, both were bound—in terms of the stated objectives of the Alliance—to lose an indeterminate share of their disproportionate political-economic power. Critics on the left insisted that American policy would not sacrifice existing American business interests to hemispheric social reform; critics on the right insisted it should not. The role of American corporations in Latin America thus became a key issue in the ensuing history of the Alliance.

The actual record in this prickly aspect of Alliance relationships has been a mixed one. The United States has often reverted to its old preference for the politics of the status quo, sometimes in specific defense of American business interests. But its efforts on behalf of social change have also had their effect in altering the conditions under which American firms operate in Latin America. The policies and operational programs of the Alliance have contributed to a situation, for example, in which stricter controls by Latin American governments over American corporate activities became more lively policy options. At the same time, the Alliance commitment reduced Latin fears that the institution of such controls (or even the extreme alternative of expropriation) would provoke Washington into severely punitive retaliations—at least until the Chilean copper expropriations discussed below. This atmosphere, in turn, has stimulated self-reform efforts by American businesses and an increased sense of responsibility to the societies in which they carry on their activities.

Fair judgment must find that United States policy has alternately cooperated with and yielded to pressures generated on both sides of this crucial issue of inter-American relations. The reactions from Washington to expropriations in Brazil (1962) and Bolivia (1970) were relatively mild. In Chile, both the United States government and the Anaconda and Kennecott corporations cooperated in the "Chilenization" of the copper industry during the Frei administration (1964–1970). In this process, Chile became majority stockholder in the several mines the corporations had owned for more than forty years. Similar cooperation has marked the "Mexicanization" of various sectors of the Mexican economy, including auto parts, tobacco, sulphur, and the national telephone company, all of which were owned or in effect controlled by American or other foreign interests.[4]

These examples contradict the standard left-wing accusation that the Alliance was just another smokescreen to conceal collusion between American government and business in the game of exploiting Latin America. On the other hand, the Peruvian expropriations of American-owned oil and sugar properties in 1968 and 1970 provoked sharper controversy and some largely ineffectual acts of retaliation by the United States.

The most severe conflicts arose in Chile after the advent of the Allende regime in 1970. The new Chilean government (with unanimous support in the Chilean parliament) repudiated the Chilenization solution and decreed the outright expropriation and nationalization of the copper industry. Moreover, the Chilean government refused to indemnify the corporations on the ground that they had for years piled up superprofits, most of which should rightfully have gone to Chile.[5] Balancing the cur-

---

[4] *New York Times*, November 24, 1972.

[5] In a speech before the United Nations General Assembly on December 4, 1972, President Allende asserted that in forty years of operations in Chile, with an initial investment of $30 million, the copper companies had extracted more than $4 billion in profits. He also stated that Kennecott Corporation had averaged 52.8 percent profit annually during the period from 1955 to 1970 and had realized 205 percent profit in the single year of 1969. Needless to say, these figures, like all other aspects of the expropriations, are the subject of bitter controversies among the contending parties.

rent value of the corporation properties against what were considered the unjust profits of the past, the Allende government declared that the copper corporation had no just or legal claim to compensation.

The Nixon administration responded by acting to dry up Chile's sources of external credit. For their part, the copper companies have attempted to lay legal claim to Chile's copper exports to other countries. Litigations arising from these claims are likely to bedevil American-Chilean relations for years to come. But the most damaging blow to the now tired spirit of the Alliance for Progress came when documents were made public implicating the International Telephone and Telegraph Corporation (ITT) in covert efforts to overthrow the Allende regime. Against this background, the successful military coup and Allende's death in September 1973 inevitably provoked charges, notably by Fidel Castro, that the United States government and American corporations were prime movers in the military takeover.

Historians will have much to sort out in weighing relations between the United States and Allende's Chile. But the hostilities between them have resurrected the image of the imperial Yankee in Latin America and have at least temporarily soured the hopes attending the birth and early years of the Alliance for Progress.

Yet the larger and more generous purposes of the Alliance have registered achievements as well as failures since the signing of the Charter of Punta del Este. In any reckoning the achievements need to be weighed along with all instances of backsliding by the United States into the old policy habits defending the status quo. And both the implementations of new policy positions and the backsliding need to be assessed in light of the fact that—contrary to some leftist mythology—the most ardent and effective defenders of the status quo in Latin America are not the United States government or American corporations but the oligarchies indigenous to the Latin American societies themselves.

This fundamental fact in the life of oligarchies (in the rest of the underdeveloped world as well as in Latin America) is directly related to the third major departure from previous practice signaled by the signing of the Alliance Charter. Its text abounds with tacit and sometimes explicit propositions that the signatories have a legitimate concern with one another's internal political, economic, and social structures. The Alliance certainly did not imply a renunciation of sovereignty on the part of its members. But it did establish a set of transnational norms for internal development and a set of transnational institutions designed to make possible their realization. It asserted that the underdeveloped countries had to move toward the goal of development in concert and identified mutual assistance as an essential partner of self-help. Its explicit exhortations concerning the need for land reform, mass education, expansion of social services, and other portentous changes had the interesting effect of placing on record the signatories' opposition to the perpetuation of one another's oligarchical systems.

If any part of the Alliance was handled with caution, it was this. Whatever their own representatives had agreed to in order to get the Alliance under way (and to start the flow of development dollars from the North), the oligarchies were clearly unenthusiastic about the prospect of their own disappearance. Already coping with various forms of domestic opposition, the oligarchs were still less cheered by any implications that their local opponents might attract outside assistance inspired by the antielitist and transnational ideology of the Alliance.

So far their fears have proved to be groundless. The Latin neighbors have generally left each other alone. As for the United States, its opposition to Castro's style of transnationalism and to his abortive efforts at revolutionary intervention in other Latin states has blocked the effective consideration of any Washington-sponsored policies in direct support of antioligarchical forces. In other words, Robert Kennedy's plea for active assistance to those committed to social reform and active opposition to those who resist it within the domestic political framework of Latin American states has been officially turned aside.

The first decade in the history of the Alliance for Progress thus confirms the proposition that there is a profound antagonism between the concept of development and the concept of sovereignty. Outside intervention in the domestic affairs of states is an intricate and risky enterprise in all circumstances. It has a bad name, and deservedly so in light of the record of great power interventions, whose purpose has usually been to stifle social change rather than encourage it. In the Western Hemisphere, the United States is particularly vulnerable in this respect. Hence the political premium on avoiding policies liable to accusations of interventionist intentions.

Yet the language of the Alliance stands, and it has not proved wholly rhetorical: the internal structure of each signatory is a proper concern of the others. If the United States has not often openly supported the political efforts of the antioligarchs, it has done things that have added significantly to the ferment of internal change in Latin American societies. However insufficient, American funds and training programs in support of expanding educational opportunities, modernization of agriculture, and improved public health have not bolstered the defense of the status quo. Nor has the annual injection of Peace Corps volunteers, many of whom have criticized the failings of both their host societies and the United States with impartial abandon. Further, American prodding of Latin American governments in the sensitive areas of inflation control, tax reform, and regional economic integration has fostered the spirit of innovation, even though ineptitude or indigenous oligarchical reaction has often resulted in backfire effects.

On the other hand, American-financed training programs for Latin American military and police forces, particularly in the area of antiguerilla operations, have bolstered the status quo. Some exceptions to this generalization might be found in countries where those who com-

mand armed power are sympathetic, or at least neutral, toward advocates of social change.

In sum, under the auspices of the Alliance there has been a tangible
if equivocal United States presence in the internal structures of most
Latin American countries. Prior to the Alliance, an American presence
in the domestic politics of Latin America was common enough. But
experience since 1961 documents at least a partial change in its purposes
in accord with the American commitment to development and the social
changes which development postulates. The directions taken by this
presence in the future will depend to a very great extent on the degree
of vigor animating the development commitment.

Unfortunately, by 1970 this kind of vigor and support had become a
scarce commodity in Washington, and in many Latin American countries as well. The experience of the early 1970s moved many among
both friends and enemies of the Alliance to pronounce it dead. Certainly
in terms of leadership, vision, commitment, and the level of United
States appropriations the most optimistic diagnosis would be one of
stagnation. Yet the goals of the Alliance should not on that account be
condemned as unrealistic or hypocritical. The task to which the Alliance
addressed itself was far larger and more complex than its founders and
sponsors were prepared to recognize. The task grows, and solutions are
more urgent than ever. There is no reason to assume that this urgency
will not once again become manifest in the consciousness and conscience
of the hemisphere. On the other hand, in the absence of a new rationale
for development policies in the world at large as well as in Latin America,
there is no reason to assume that it will.

THE ECONOMICS OF DEVELOPMENT

Even a brief and incomplete probe into the workings of the Alliance for
Progress reveals the intricate interconnections between economics and
politics in the development process. Any analysis that fails to stress
these interconnections fails to deal with the central problems of development. As part of a more comprehensive inquiry, however, it will be useful at this point to set out at least the major economic considerations
relevant to development policy before placing them once again in the
larger context of which they are part.

In economic terms, productivity (of material goods and the services
related to them) is the master standard that measures the level of development of any given society. The developed countries are high production societies; underdeveloped countries are low production societies.
No country can be said to be developing unless it is increasing its
productivity. But the increase, in this context, must be calculated in
terms of the per capita production of any given country and not in

terms of a rise in the country's total product. If the gross national product is rising at an annual rate of 2 percent and the annual population increase is 3 percent, the productivity of the society is not increasing but decreasing in relation to the demands being placed upon it.

In such a situation the society is not only straining its existing productive capacities but is also producing more and more individuals whom it cannot afford to feed and educate and who are therefore fated to swell the ranks of the underproductive. This is the situation, in fact, of most underdeveloped countries today. In only a minority of these countries has the rate of growth of production significantly exceeded the rate of population growth; the majority barely manage to keep the growth in productivity ahead of the expansion of population. In some countries, human numbers have outdistanced productive capacities. All three categories illustrate the necessity of dividing the national product by the number of those consuming it in order to approach an accurate measure of national productivity.

If per capita productivity is the standard yardstick for measuring the stages of development, it is not equivalent to development. Increase in per capita productivity may be so fractional as to be indistinguishable from stagnation. At the beginning of the 1970s many countries had per capita incomes slightly above or below $100. An annual per capita productivity increase of 1 percent would condemn them to wait the better part of a century for productivity to reach the $200 level.[6] In other words, the underdeveloped, after three generations, would remain underdeveloped. In reality, such a course of events would represent not simply stagnation but retrogression, since the demands and expectations of a more populous, urbanized and complex society would inevitably rise at a faster rate than the snail's pace of productivity increase.

Development, then, requires a *rapid* increase in productivity, one that is capable, at an accelerating rate, of supplying rising levels of consumption and of generating the investment capital necessary for furthering economic expansion. This requirement is reflected in the target set for the growth of developing countries in the 1970s by the United Nations Committee on the Second Development Decade and by the World Bank's Commission on International Development: a minimum per capita annual growth rate of 2.5 to 4 percent.[7]

---

[6] While the actual growth performance of most underdeveloped countries has bettered this example, it is not an unrealistic illustration. In the previous chapter we noted that the average per capita growth rate in the underdeveloped world from 1960 to 1966 was $2 per year.

[7] Cited by Robert S. McNamara in his address to the Board of Governors of the World Bank Group in Copenhagen, September 21, 1970, published by the International Bank for Reconstruction and Development, Washington, D.C., p. 21. The report of the Commission on International Development, chaired by the late Lester

Even rapid growth in per capita productivity, however, is not identical with development. The previous chapter pointed to the deceptiveness of per capita GNP figures as indicators of the real social and economic conditions prevailing in any society because of the often drastic unevenness in the distribution and consumption of the national product. The pattern of distribution plays an equally important role in assessing the impact of productivity increases on development. If sustained development is to take place, productivity increases must be linked to and reflected in an expanding internal market. That is, a larger and larger segment of the domestic population must be able to purchase a growing supply of goods.

In the absence of such internal economic expansion there are immutable limits to long-term economic growth even though marked increases in productivity are registered on a short-term basis. So long as increased productivity (along with consumption) is concentrated in a minority sector of the society, it is impossible to generate that volume of national product which is the hallmark of the developed country. A developed economy is by definition a mass participation economy, one in which all or the overwhelming majority of the members of the society live well above the poverty level and are thus part of the economic mainstream as producers and consumers.

Those countries where productivity increases have historically been confined to relatively narrow sectors of the society can be defined as cases of arrested development. A number of Latin American countries fall into this category, notably Argentina, Brazil, Chile, Mexico, and Venezuela. A have-not nation can never become a have nation in terms of either wealth or power so long as the bulk of its population lives in poverty and therefore does not significantly contribute to or benefit from the total economic effort.

THE EXPORT ECONOMY

One of the most important factors inhibiting broad-based economic growth is a complex of legacies from the colonial or quasi-colonial past. The past expansion of economic activity in almost all underdeveloped countries was geared to the needs of the industrial world and not to those of the indigenous populations. Responsibility for this situation of economic imbalance, which helped to perpetuate and in some cases

B. Pearson, was published under the title *Partners in Development* (New York: Praeger, 1969). It will be referred to hereafter by its published title.

The two groups actually set a 6 percent GNP growth rate as the annual target. Currently obtaining population growth rates between 2 percent and 3.5 percent would therefore result in a per capita productivity increase of 2.5 to 4 percent. Since the 6 percent GNP growth goal is defined as an average for all UDCs, those with exceptionally high population growth would have to better the average figure in order to meet the growth norm stipulated by the commission.

intensify the miseries of mass poverty, lies heavily on the industrial and imperial world. Responsibility must be shared, however, by the local oligarchies in the countries now termed underdeveloped, and most particularly in Latin America.

Whatever the burden of responsibility, the economic pattern which obtained between the industrial North and the colonial South was one in which the North invested in the development of agricultural and mineral resources in the colonial areas in order to maintain the rapid expansion of its metropolitan manufacturing enterprises. The typical result was that economic growth in the South was concentrated in the production of one or a few raw materials on a massive scale to feed the populations or the factories in the North. This pattern of production and distribution came to be known as the export economy.

In an export economy such as that of Venezuela, a small percentage of the total population can achieve considerable, and in some cases formidable, economic gains. But the price of these gains is an almost total dependence upon and orientation toward the external markets provided by the industrial countries. In a society where the vast majority is poor and uneducated, the internal market is necessarily minuscule, so that what local capital and entrepreneurial skills exist must inevitably be attracted to the profits found in export. The tangibility of export opportunities and the single-minded interest of Northern capital in their exploitation powerfully inhibited the channeling of energies into the development of internal markets.

This inhibition was and is decisively reinforced by traditional class attitudes which regard a social system characterized by a few rich and many poor as inevitable, normal, or desirable—or a combination of all three. Thus the oligarchies of the South typically wedded themselves to their export partners from the North. They profited from the export of cotton, coffee, wheat, bananas, rubber, beef, copper, tin, and later oil, but they also became dependent on the sometimes sharply fluctuating prices these commodities commanded in the Northern market.[8]

Hence even those societies in the South not formally incorporated into imperial or colonial systems were not masters of their own fate once they became dependent on Northern markets and Northern capital. In this they developed a strong resemblance to the economically less advanced regions within the Northern countries themselves. The bitter complaints, persisting well into the twentieth century, of American farmers in the Midwest and South, and of miners and loggers in the

---

[8] "Almost 90 percent of the export earnings of the developing countries derive from primary products. Moreover, nearly half of these countries earn more than 50 percent of their export receipts from a single primary commodity. As many as three-quarters of them earn more than 60 percent from three primary products. Many of these products have been subject to a high degree of price instability, and a few have suffered continuing adverse price trends in the last decade and a half." Pearson, *Partners in Development*, p. 81.

West, against the power of Eastern banks and railroads and the vagaries of the populous Eastern markets were functionally similar to those heard throughout the colonial and quasi-colonial world as the global North-South relationship developed. Agrarian and mining areas located within the imperial North and the colonial economies of the South alike were "export economies."

A combination of political reforms and rapidly increasing wealth within the industrial countries during the middle third of the twentieth century brought relief to their domestic agricultural and mining sectors, as well as a considerable measure of equalization in standards of living and economic power on a nationwide basis. No such process of equalization is yet under way, however, on a global basis. On the contrary, we have seen that the inequalities of wealth and power that divide the industrial North from the agricultural and mineral-producing South are becoming steadily more pronounced—and at an accelerating rate.

The rational goal of development policy can only be to slow down and then reverse this retrograde trend. To achieve this goal, in turn, internal markets in the underdeveloped countries must be expanded to the point where the volume of domestic economic activity overshadows foreign economic relations (as it does in every developed country).[9] In short, the process that transforms the economically underdeveloped into the economically developed necessarily destroys the export economy and replaces it with an economy in which all sectors of the society participate. Rising productivity of a steadily growing portion of the population, a sustained upward curve in internal investment, a decrease in the proportion of export in the total volume of production and sales, and continually higher levels of consumption in all sectors of society—these are the indicators and prerequisites of a developing economy.

The fundamental obstacle to economic development is that all these factors are interdependent. That is, increased internal investment is needed to initiate the process of rising productivity, but capital tends to be attracted to enterprises that have already demonstrated rising productivity or that are directed to the supply of an already affluent market. It follows that commercial or private capital (i.e., profit-seeking investment) will generally avoid undertakings in areas where productivity and consumption have been chronically low.[10]

---

[9] In the United States, for example, foreign trade in the twentieth century has averaged less than 5 percent of GNP. Japan's foreign trade amounts to approximately 10 percent of GNP.

[10] These are the facts of (unregulated) investment behavior that explain the traditional and contemporary pattern of private capital transactions in the global context. The overwhelming percentage of international investment by the capital-rich industrial countries is to be found in other industrial countries and not in the capital-poor underdeveloped regions. Private investment by the North in the South, in turn, is overwhelmingly concentrated in export economies.

The typical result in the underdeveloped world has been that the internal economy, and with it the life situation of the great bulk of the indigenous populace, has stagnated. The export economy, on the other hand, involving only a small percentage of the population, has had easy access to capital precisely because it has already demonstrated its productivity growth and because of the active international demand for the things it produces. Under these conditions, the export economy will continue to grow, the internal market will continue to languish, and the economy as a whole will remain "underdeveloped." A rapidly growing population, in turn, will ensure that the underdeveloped country's plight will not be one simply of standing still; instead, it will deteriorate.

The most basic elements in the vicious circle are the interrelated ones of inadequate productivity and capital. High productivity generates capital, and capital generates high productivity; low productivity cannot generate capital and cannot attract external sources of profit-motivated investment to raise its own level of performance. In order to break this vicious circle, nonprofit-seeking capital must be introduced into areas of low productivity. This kind of capital may be defined as capital grants or as loans at a very much lower rate of return or with a very much more extended repayment period than is typical of standard commercial capital transactions. Nonprofit-seeking capital, of course, is available primarily from government-sponsored bilateral or multilateral development assistance programs, including operations of the International Development Agency of the World Bank Group, and also from private foundations with large overseas commitments, such as Ford and Rockefeller.

Capital expenditure of this nature is invested, ideally at least, in such undertakings as the development of agricultural productivity, transportation and communications infrastructure, education, housing, and surveys of resources. Investment objectives in these areas include an adequate level of food production, growing numbers of better educated and healthier people, a progressive linking together of hitherto isolated markets for produce and labor, increasing employment opportunities, housing that nurtures family life instead of destroying it, and a context of life conducive to innovation and enterprise instead of stagnation.

Such a set of objectives is a formidable investment challenge. It comprehends by far the largest sector in the economic life of the typical underdeveloped country in terms of population and employment—though not, unfortunately, in terms of profitability. Yet only this kind of investment can provide the catalytic agents to transform a low-level equilibrium into an economy capable of self-sustaining growth. Significant expansion of the internal market within, say, the span of a generation can take place in no other way. This, then, is the condition for any meaningful success in the process of development.

THE TVA MODEL

Apart from the factor of scale and the special role of hydroelectric development, this pattern of investment and investment objectives finds many parallels in the policies that initiated and expanded the Tennessee Valley Authority (TVA), beginning in the 1930s. The first priority then was not the development of new sources of water power. Instead, the intention was to convert a vast internal watershed of the United States from a situation of chronic depression in terms of every criterion from agriculture to transport into a region capable of participating productively in the mainstream of American economic life and society in general. TVA's massive undertakings in hydraulics, navigation, land conservation, and power and fertilizer production were of enormous value in themselves. But their chief purpose was to facilitate the realization of such essentially social objectives as lifting the standard of living and stimulating the social energies of the entire population of the region.

In short, TVA sought to equalize the life situation of people living in the Tennessee Valley relative to the rest of American society. For that purpose it invested nonprofit-seeking capital (federal government funds) in a specific geographical region in an effort to stimulate across-the-board internal economic growth to the point where it became self-sustaining. The results achieved have made TVA one of the most successful development enterprises ever attempted.[11]

The developmental model provided by TVA, then, has involved these major components:

---

[11] Per capita income in the TVA area, for example, increased by 73 percent between 1933 and 1940 as against an increase of 56 percent for the nation as a whole. While this differential must be attributed in part to the fact that the regional economic base was at a very much lower level than the national average, its significance is not thereby seriously diminished. On the contrary, in some ways it is enhanced. TVA expenditures reversed a growing disparity of wealth between a depressed area and other regions of the United States and thus realized one of the prime purposes of contemporary development theory: halting the growth of the gap separating rich and poor and beginning the work of narrowing it. See David E. Lilienthal (then Chairman of the TVA), *TVA: Democracy on the March* (New York: Harper and Bros., 1944), p. 34 and *passim*.

Other indicators of the narrowing gap cited by Lilienthal include a 76 percent increase in regional bank deposits for the years 1933 to 1939, while the national average rose only 49 percent. During the same period, regional retail sales increased 81 percent compared with a 71 percent increase on a nationwide basis. In 1933, per capita electricity production in the TVA area was 60 percent below the national average. In 1943, it was 150 percent above the average. In terms of actual customer usage of electricity, the twelve agencies originally selling TVA power to private homes recorded a 196 percent increase in sales between 1934 and 1942, as against a nationwide average increase of 63 percent (see pp. 17, 21, 34).

Throughout his appraisal, Lilienthal stresses that the most important contribution of TVA was the stimuli it generated to effect changes in people's attitudes toward the possibilities of new technology, new enterprise, and new social techniques and purposes.

Transfers of capital, most of which was nonprofit-seeking, from a richer to a poorer sector of the economy. (Investment in hydroelectric installations began to produce power at a profit beginning in 1938, and part of these investment funds derived from the flotation of bonds.)

Transfers of technology and technological skills

Educational undertakings running the gamut from modern farming methods through home economics to real estate appraisal

Administrative structure and authority, in part imported from outside the region and in part developed out of the interaction of federal and regional institutions, both governmental and nongovernmental

A commitment to social and economic change

A doctrine based on the premise that improvement in the economic conditions and the general living conditions of a depressed area is a value in itself and that it will also benefit the larger politico-economic unit of which it is part

These same components, or their analogues, are essential to successful development programs at the international level. They have obvious social and political implications as well as implications for the economics of development.

In assessing the international relevance of the TVA model, the most evident problem is the problem of scale. The challenge of international development concerns more than 2 billion people around the globe, rather than the 4 to 5 million residents of the Tennessee Valley. On the other hand, as far as individual underdeveloped countries are concerned, the majority have populations smaller than that of the TVA area, and many do not exceed it in geographical extent. Still, it is the aggregate of the underdeveloped countries rather than individual cases that sets the true dimensions of the development problem. It is one thing for an American population of 135 million (in the 1930s) to effect a major transfer of resources to 5 million of its own number. It is another for a developed world population of approximately 1 billion to transfer resources to an external population roughly two and one-half times its size. The TVA operation in the 1930s foreshadowed the sometimes less effective efforts of affluent societies of the postwar period to deal with domestic "pockets" of poverty. For international development, however, poverty is not a pocket but an ocean.

Yet the contrast is not so great if we turn from the ratios of population to the ratios of wealth. In 1970, United States GNP was just under $1 trillion, while the gross product of the entire developed world approximated $2.7 trillion. This is a total more than five times as great as the combined product of the underdeveloped world. In terms of population, then, international development involves transfers of resources from

27 percent of the global population to the remaining 73 percent. But in terms of economics, the transfers occur between that sector of the global economy which generates 83 percent of the world product and the sector generating only 17 percent. Hence, if one applies the key criterion of economic productivity, the developed North is clearly capable of making significant contributions to the growth and development of the depressed economies of the South. The dimensions of the problem are formidable but not so enormous that they must confound rational policies of development assistance.

DEVELOPMENT ASSISTANCE AND RESOURCE TRANSFERS

In 1960 the United Nations General Assembly passed a resolution calling upon all developed countries to effect an annual transfer of resources, equal to 1 percent of their national incomes, to the less developed countries. In 1968, as we have seen in the previous chapter, UNCTAD II called for such a transfer at the level of 1 percent of GNP (GNP represents an economic aggregate approximately 25 percent larger than national income; hence the UNCTAD resolution upped the aid target by a corresponding percentage). The new target was subsequently adopted by the United Nations as indispensable to the "Second Development Decade" (1970–1980), specifying that the 1 percent goal should be met not later than 1975 and then should be sustained through the rest of the decade. This target could hardly be regarded as placing excessive demands on the economies of the developed countries.

At the turn of the decade, however, the actual volume of resource transfers from developed to underdeveloped was so much less than the target figure that skepticism was widespread concerning the likelihood of its being met by the mid-1970s. In 1968, the peak year of resource transfers, the fifteen richest noncommunist countries in the developed world effected transfers totaling $12.8 billion. By estimate of the Pearson Commission, communist countries (including mainland China) added a meager $350 million. Together, these flows added up to less than 70 percent of the objective. Subsequently, there has been a further downward trend. While some developed countries, notably Germany and Japan, have increased their volume of aid and private investment in the underdeveloped South, the United States, as chief source of both public and private capital, continued on a course of retrenchment already in evidence by the mid-1960s. Unless the United States reverses the direction of its aid policy, there is no possibility of achieving the 1 percent goal to which it and the other members of the United Nations pledged themselves.

In sum, the first Development Decade of the 1960s witnessed an enormous increase in the wealth of the developed countries and a disappointing decline in the percentage of resource transfers from North to

South. In 1960 this percentage—in terms of the combined GNPs of the fifteen most affluent Western countries (including Japan)—was 0.89. By 1968 it had fallen to 0.77.[12] The percentages gain in significance when placed in the context of the increase in productivity achieved by these same fifteen countries during the same period. In 1960 their combined GNPs totaled nearly $1 trillion; in 1968 the figure was approximately $1.6 trillion. Even discounting price rises, this vast enrichment of the developed West in nine years presents a painful and dangerous contrast to the simultaneous spread of poverty in the underdeveloped world and the slackening effort on the part of the rich to arrest and reverse the process of global impoverishment.

The contrast becomes still more extreme when one analyzes the components of "resource transfers." All resource transfers can perform a useful function in stimulating development, though those which serve only to enlarge the export economy are often, as we have seen, counterproductive. The most urgent needs of development, as we have also noted, require that nonprofit-seeking capital spur the growth of the internal markets in the countries of the South. Only this kind of capital, provided for the most part by donor governments under bilateral or multilateral arrangements, is properly called development aid. The other components in the flow of resource transfers, private capital investment or credits extended by one government to another for commercial reasons, do not constitute "aid."

This clarification of terminology identifies profit-serving investment and nonprofit aid as two distinct subcategories of the resource transfer process. The Pearson Report deemed such a clarification essential in order to dispel misapprehensions and resentments concerning North-South economic relations in general and aid flows in particular. It certainly did not imply a disparagement of non-aid capital flows. On the contrary, the report recognized that they will continue to be indispensable instrumentalities of economic growth. The point is simply that profit-seeking investments are by definition intended primarily to benefit the investor. They may and often do generate benefits for the recipient countries. But they cannot for that reason be credited to the aid efforts of developed countries.

The real target of the Pearson Report in this matter, then, was not private investment but the governments of the developed countries. By separating private investment from government aid in the resource transfer aggregates, the report was able to specify the true volume of development aid flowing from North to South.

---

[12] Pearson, *Partners in Development*, pp. 137, 145. The fifteen countries comprise the membership of the Development Assistance Committee (DAC) of the Organization for Economic Cooperation and Development. They include most of the original Western European recipients of Marshall Plan assistance plus Sweden, Switzerland, Canada, Australia, the United States, and Japan.

In 1961 the volume of authentic aid (for the fifteen Western countries, including Japan) was $5.2 billion; in 1968 it was $6.4 billion. Thus the combined GNPs of the donors rose during this period more than 60 percent, but their donations to the underdeveloped world rose only about 20 percent.

In response to these disheartening statistics, the Pearson Commission went beyond the 1 percent of GNP figure applied to resource transfers (which, it stressed, constitutes a minimum standard). It built into this figure a target of 0.70 percent of GNP constituting bona fide aid "deliberately conceived as development assistance and not incidental to normal commerce and finance." The Commission thus established a more meaningful criterion by which to judge the aid performance of developed countries in North-South relationships: annual resource transfers at a minimum of 1 percent of GNP including a .70 component comprised of government grants or noncommercial loans. Since the official development aid flow from the DAC countries had declined to 0.36 percent of their combined GNPs in 1969, the Pearson Commission in effect challenged them to double their aid giving during the 1970s.

Many of the DAC countries have since significantly increased their aid programs and have explicitly accepted the Pearson Commission targets. By 1971 resource transfers from the DAC countries had risen to approximately $18.1 billion, of which about $7.7 billion constituted development aid in terms of the standards set by the Pearson Commission.[13] But despite the encouraging increase in absolute terms, the aid figure still amounted to less than 0.4 percent of their combined GNPs. Here the downgrading of foreign aid in the United States has played a decisive role. By 1970 American aid programs had shrunk to approximately 0.3 percent of GNP, and they declined to somewhat lower levels in the period from 1971 to 1973. During this period the United States has ranked eleventh or twelfth among the fifteen DAC countries in percentage of GNP devoted to aid.[14] Thus the recent record of the world's richest country puts the fate of the "Second Development Decade" very much in doubt.

---

[13] *The German Tribune Supplement*, No. 3, Hamburg, January 18, 1973, p. 16.

[14] McNamara, *loc. cit.*, p. 9. There is perhaps an unfair stress here on the shortcomings of the DAC countries. They obviously do not include all the developed countries that could be termed underachievers. The developed countries of the communist world (plus mainland China), for example, accounted for an average of only "about 3 percent of the total resource flow to developing countries in 1965-67" (*Partners in Development*, p. 139). The gap between aid capability and aid performance is vastly wider in the communist world than in the Western world. One can only hope that this gap, too, will begin to narrow as the needs of the underdeveloped world become more urgently manifest.

DEBT, TRADE PATTERNS, AND SUBSIDIES

The Pearson Commission targets for resource transfers and development assistance were formulated not only as a response to a perceived need for an increase in the gross volume of flow from North to South. They were also designed to reverse the trend of mounting indebtedness that has burdened many of the underdeveloped countries. In 1968 the external public debt of the developing countries approximated $50 billion, a five-fold increase since the mid-1950s. Debt service in the form of interest payments and amortization has thus come to siphon off a significant portion of the foreign exchange earnings of the underdeveloped countries back to the creditor countries in the developed world. The result is a severe strain on the balance of payments positions of the countries of the South and a corresponding weakening of their capacities to stimulate internal economic expansion.

In absolute figures, underdeveloped countries returned $4.7 billion in debt service payments to developed countries in 1967, thus reducing the total transfer of resources from North to South (both official grants and loans and private loans and investments from DAC countries) from a gross of $11.2 billion to a net of $6.5 billion. Hence the actual transfer of resources from North to South was nearly 43 percent less than the gross figures for 1967 indicate. The gap between gross and net was still wider in 1968: the gross flow from North to South was $12.8 billion, but the net was only about $6.3 billion. That is, nearly 51 percent of the gross flow was in effect a bookkeeping operation; only 49 percent was actually available to the underdeveloped countries for development and investment purposes. By 1970 the net figure had dropped to 48 percent. The growth of interest payments to service mounting debts reflects both the rising level of private investment and lending in the total volume of resource transfers from North to South during the 1960s and the increasing proportion of loans to grants within official development assistance programs.[15]

In order to prevent debt service payments from canceling out ever larger percentages of annual development assistance and private investment, the World Bank Group and the Pearson Commission recommended two essential steps. One is to refinance the existing debt structures of the underdeveloped countries presently overburdened with interest payments. The second, far more important, is a major increase in the official development assistance component in the total volume of resource transfers (to the minimum level of 0.70 percent of the developed countries' GNPs). Within this component, moreover, the recommendations call for a reduction in the amount of lending at quasi-commercial rates and an increase in the amount of grants and of loans whose terms are soft enough (long-

---

[15] Pearson, *Partners in Development*, pp. 72–74, 137–140, 153–167.

term repayment provisions—25 to 40 years—and very low—2 percent—interest rates) to make them almost the equivalent of grants.

A growing share in the volume of international trade is an essential element in the development of the South. As the previous chapter pointed out, that share has been decreasing instead of increasing since the 1950s, not because the overall foreign trade activity of the underdeveloped countries has not been expanding but because its rate of expansion has been far less vigorous than that of the developed countries. The chief difficulty, however, is that, both relatively and absolutely, the South's foreign trade is not producing enough export earnings to finance the volume and range of imports required for sustained internal development. Given this situation, the importance of governmentally sponsored grants and grant-like loans as one means of financing adequate import programs should once again be evident.

For the long run, of course, policy in the North should be geared to a timetable in which, after currently necessary increases, development assistance should gradually diminish and finally be phased out as countries in the South demonstrate a capacity for self-sustaining growth. Such a capacity, in turn, can only be a joint product of accelerating internal economic expansion and growing vigor in the export market.

Within the familiar triad of primary products, semimanufactures, and manufactures, the South is overwhelmingly dependent on the export of primary commodities. In the early 1970s, they comprised about 80 percent of the value of all exports from the underdeveloped world. In the international economy as in the domestic economy, these primary products produced by farms and mines are notoriously subject to sharp and sometimes disastrous fluctuations in price. Within the domestic economies of the developed countries, the analogous problems of price instability have typically been met by governmentally administered price stabilization techniques, so that producers of agricultural and mineral products are financially buffered against the vagaries of the market.

These same kinds of techniques are reflected at the global level in international agreements that have brought some stability into prices for such commodities as coffee, sugar, wheat, and tin. Informal arrangements and consultations concerning other primary products have also brought additional elements of stability to international marketing. But neither formal nor informal measures in the international economy approach the scope or effectiveness of the stabilization programs that have brought relief to the domestic agrarian and mining sectors of developed economies. An expanded complex of financial and administrative undertakings to provide the primary producers of the South with more stable prices for their products is therefore an obvious item on the agenda of world economic development.

The developed countries, of course, have gone much further than price stabilization programs in their efforts to deal with the problems of their own agrarian and mineral producers. In those areas where productive capacity consistently threatens to outrun effective demand, they have resorted to government subsidy to producers, enabling them to restrict production without economic loss. Alternatively, governments have used subsidies as a means of expanding consumption by maintaining market prices below production costs and remitting the difference (plus a profit margin) to the producers. The problems attending subsidy programs are formidable, as the internal economic histories of most developed countries will attest. Nonetheless, they have largely succeeded in their primary purpose of achieving a more equitable distribution of income between the industrial and the agrarian-mining sectors of their economies.

If, on a global scale, the underdeveloped countries constitute the main agrarian-mining sector of the international economy, it is not unreasonable that the global industrial sector should take the subsidy route as one means of forwarding the development process. The economic aim of development, after all, is to lift the income of the underdeveloped world to the point where a growing global income is more evenly distributed between North and South. This double goal of economic growth and economic equalization is precisely the objective long pursued with impressive success within the domestic economies of the industrial North. The success was not merely one of lifting their agrarian and mining sectors out of recurrent or chronic depression but of achieving a situation of steadily rising demand in the economy as a whole. The second achievement, of course, resulted in large part from the fact that subsidization and other techniques converted the agrarian and mining sectors from negative into positive factors in the overall domestic demand structure.

The presence or absence of similar results at some point in time will measure the success of global development. The growth and equalization of income in the world economy depends on many things, but a more comprehensive resort to subsidization is indispensably one of them. Development assistance programs on a nonprofit basis are, of course, in themselves subsidy operations. Any capital gifts or any transfer of capital without requiring the full returns that a market transaction would bring is subsidy, whether the recipient is a depressed Tennessee Valley or a depressed global South. But present subsidization policies need to be extended to the point where they are specifically addressed to the global problems of agricultural and mineral production.

This does not mean that the industrial countries should grant bounties to the producers of primary commodities in the South indiscriminately and for an indefinite period of time. It does mean that a series of long-term production and price agreements need to be worked out that will ensure a primary commodity price level sufficient to enhance the purchasing power of primary producers and thus to stimulate the internal economic expansion of the countries in the agrarian-mineral producing South.

Price stabilization alone is not enough; after all, prices can be stabilized at a level that yields only a subsistence return to a majority of producers. The purpose of subsidy, insofar as it is designed to further the goals of development, is not to stabilize income but to increase it—to the point where those subsidized make a significant contribution to the growth of demand for commodities of all kinds both within their domestic economies and in the international market.

Production limitation agreements are essential counterparts of price support agreements. Otherwise the rush to convert to the production of commodities commanding a bounty would raise the costs of subsidization to unacceptable levels and create conditions of glut or aggravate such conditions where they already exist. Production agreements are also essential to the general development process which requires increasing diversification of production in the underdeveloped countries. Societies whose economic life is dominated by the production of one or a few commodities for export (for which, in most cases, the demand is relatively inelastic) cannot significantly increase opportunities for productive employment for their total populations. Nor can these societies be very effective in augmenting mutually profitable international trade among themselves as long as so much of their economic effort is geared to supplying the industrial North with primary products for which there is little or no demand in the underdeveloped and undiversified economies of the South.

Economic diversification is the standard—and appropriate—prescription for remedying the poverty of the underdeveloped society. Ideally, the agricultural sector should produce a diversity of crops. Minerals extraction should be only the first stage in a series of pyramiding domestic enterprises: refining, processing, and manufacture of semifinished and finished goods. In addition, manufactured and semimanufactured commodities that do not require domestic mineral resources should become an ever larger component in the developing economy.

In general, then, the countries of the underdeveloped South should repeat the essentials of the economic development experience of the North to the point where they, too, become predominantly high technology producers in both industry and agriculture. Outside the realm of economics, recipes calling for imitation of the North are bound to fail. But for any society today whose aim is to move from poverty toward wealth, the economic history of the North provides a model for which, in its main characteristics, there is no rational alternative.

Economic diversification in the South would clearly be stimulated if its manufactures and finished goods of all kinds could gain easy entry into the markets of the industrial North. Hence the drive by the underdeveloped countries in 1968 at UNCTAD II in Delhi to obtain nonreciprocal preferential tariff treatment for their manufactures from the industrial nations. Although no concrete concessions were granted then, by 1970 some of the developed countries, including the United States, were beginning to adopt concessionary policies in this area. But we have also seen that the issue remained mostly unresolved and the subject of bitter dispute both before and after UNCTAD III at Santiago in 1972.

Concessionary tariff policies can make a valuable contribution to development. But they can address themselves to only a small part of a large problem. The greater part of the problem is the prevailing scarcity of capital and skills with which to finance and manage a variety of more sophisticated enterprises which will supply the local market economically and will be competitive in the export trade. Both these desiderata will be difficult to achieve. Quality products in large quantity at low prices are broadly characteristic of advanced economies and not of underdeveloped or even transitional economies. It follows that manufactures from the South, even with a favorable tariff position, will face formidable challenges from competing manufactures fabricated in the industrial North. The underdeveloped countries' insistence on nonreciprocal tariff preferences, by the same token, is the clearest possible indication that protectionist policies in the countries of the South are essential if their own manufactures are to withstand competition from foreign products in their own domestic markets.

THE CRUCIAL ROLE OF CAPITAL

The growing indebtedness of the underdeveloped countries, the characteristics of their role in international trade, the need for price supports and production controls as well as price stabilization in order to remedy the vulnerability of their primary producers, and the prime requirement for the expansion of their internal markets—all these problems point back to the crucial role of capital transfer from North to South. Capital is the fuel without which the development process must come to a halt.

It should be added that technical assistance and the transfer of technology and skills ought to be seen as an integral part of capital flow. Knowledge is as vital as money in any enterprise, private or public. Indeed, in the most fundamental sense, knowledge is the source of money and not the other way around. It is the ultimate foundation of all the wealth of the developed North. Hence the transfer of knowledge is the most precious of capital gifts. Without it, the mere transfer of funds is a flow without direction.

Capital transfer on terms that will enable the recipient to generate new and independent wealth is in effect a redistribution of wealth. When new wealth emerges where none was before, the *share* of total wealth held by the previously affluent necessarily diminishes. But the classic compensation to the suppliers of capital in this process is an *absolute* and double gain in wealth for the investors: return on investments and the emergence of new customers as the developing economy generates increasing numbers of people with buying power. Thus a rational policy of wealth redistribution can result in gains for both North and South. But such a policy presupposes an understanding on the part of the rich that it is more profitable—and safer—to trade some of their comparative and overwhelming advantages against absolute gains more equitably distributed.

The investment yield of these kinds of capital transfers can be calculated only partly in commercial terms. All of it is long range, many of its risks are indeterminate, and some of it is indefinable. But if development assistance is well managed and adequate in volume, the yield prospects are there. Economically, they are connected with the generation of new wealth that stimulates the internal growth of the underdeveloped country and thus increases its capacity to engage in profitable transactions with the developed world. Politically, they are linked to success in significantly diminishing the prevailing disparities in wealth and power between North and South so that peaceful change toward the goal of a global social justice becomes possible.

Both public and private capital can contribute to this effect. Because government grants and grant-like loans in a development assistance program constitute nonprofit-seeking capital they are uniquely suited to assist in the building of the infrastructure necessary to a modernizing economy: mass education, productive agriculture, adequate housing and health services, an expanded transport and communications network, and rational exploration of economic potentials.

Private capital can play a vital supplementary role in development, and one that increases as the process gains momentum. Since private investment requires that the flow of profits commence relatively soon after the initial outlay, it is uniquely suited to making more immediate contributions to economic growth. These contributions can include payrolls, taxes to the host country, local purchase of equipment and services, and importation of advanced technology and skills. They can also include stimuli to and frequently direct participation in the building of new infrastructure, demonstration effects, new demand configurations, export promotion, and import-saving. Such contributions can be significantly amplified by policies on the part of the private investors, their home governments, and the host country that promote the local reinvestment of profits, local sharing of ownership, and a purposeful coordination of the enterprise with the overall needs of the developing society.[16]

---

[16] See Pearson, *Partners in Development*, pp. 100–102. One of the most spectacular successes achieved as a result of these kinds of impacts of private investment, in tandem with subsidy capital, is the development of Puerto Rico. If Puerto Rico is

As more of a modern infrastructure comes into being with the aid of governmental capital transfers on a subsidy basis, the need for subsidy will decline while the attractiveness of the society for private investors will increase. This set of consequences, in turn, should hasten the day when subsidy financing can cease altogether, at which point the developing society has become economically self-sustaining for the balance of its journey from underdeveloped to developed.[17]

If there is no substitute for international capital transfer in the development process, it follows that the frequently repeated arguments for trade instead of aid as the better answer to the South's predicament cannot be persuasive. We have already seen that a greater share in international trade for the underdeveloped countries is an important component in any program for a more equitable sharing of global wealth. But we have also seen that the countries of the South are overwhelmingly dependent on the export of primary commodities, with all the attendant disadvantages in terms of foreign exchange earnings and internal economic effects. The main problem is that, with the exception of a few major oil-producing countries, the present structure of their exporting capacity is simply insufficient to finance the imports necessary to an adequate developmental effort.

Capital transfers are therefore essential to improving the trading potential of the underdeveloped world. Once the export-import potential is more fully realized by means of product diversification and increased productivity, the need for capital transfers on a subsidy basis will decline, along with a parallel decline in consequence of the expansion of internal markets. Until that point is reached, however, the development formula must be one of trade plus aid, with aid ranking first in the order of priorities.

The central place given to capital transfer in the development process finds its most comprehensive rationale once economic analysis is rejoined to political analysis. If the North-South flow of capital dwindles, or merely stagnates, one underdeveloped country after another will reach a point where it must make a desperate choice. One option is to permit development efforts to founder and to slide into the economic chaos and political violence that a rapidly increasing population with rapidly rising

---

admittedly a special case politically, the history of its economic development nonetheless deserves close attention. In twenty years it has more than quadrupled GNP and also enjoys a more equitable income distribution than any other Latin American society, or any other society in the underdeveloped world, for that matter. It is noteworthy and indicative that Puerto Rico's university student population doubled in the decade from 1959 to 1968. Per capita GNP in 1968 was $1129 (*New York Times*, January 6, 1969).

[17] The Pearson Commission asserts that "In most instances, . . . we believe that developing countries can achieve self-sustaining growth at reasonable levels by the end of the century." Ibid., pp. 125–126.

demands must necessarily produce. The other is to embark on a program of internal capital formation on the Stalinist model of forced saving imposed by governmental repression. This option, of course, would have to be implemented in the context of economic and social conditions far bleaker than those which attended the internal development of Soviet Russia. Hence there must be an extra premium on harshness of method while, at the same time, the prospects for actually achieving developmental objectives must be heavily discounted.

It is likely that many underdeveloped countries would oscillate between these two options and so suffer the unhappy consequences of both. Indeed, this kind of oscillation between chaos and tyranny can already be observed in a number of countries in the South. A variation is the regime of force without any authentic program for capital acquisition and development, employing pragmatic and sometimes ruthless methods to keep the lid on while drawing most of its support from those who benefit from the status quo. All these kinds of "government" must obviously take a terrible toll in human lives and human values in the global South. Their impact on the global system as a whole, as we shall see, will express itself in more indirect and complex ways. But the portents are ominous: if development is the path to a peaceful world, then the failure of development is the road to a world at war.

Chapter 15

Development as a
Global Political Process

At every point in the development process there is interaction between politics and economics. The previous chapter sought to separate out some of the major economic considerations in development as a means of highlighting their role in the process as a whole. Here the focus will be on development as a political process.

Economics analyzes that aspect of human behavior concerned with material wealth (or its scarcity). Politics refers to the part of human behavior concerned with influencing or governing forces and events that affect the destinies of the society as a whole. Individual or group political behavior, of course, may concern itself exclusively or selectively with any of a variety of social wholes—from the local precinct to the nation-state to the global system. At each level, however, political activity attempts to deal with the composite functioning of the social whole, or system. In so doing, it must address itself to the two-way relationship between the political system and its internal components, on the one hand, and between the system and its external environment, on the other.

Both economics and politics are complex matters, but the greater complexity of politics is evident in the sheer variety of phenomena that enter into the destinies of social wholes. In the previous chapter's brief analysis of the Alliance for Progress, historical experience, demography, class structure, ideology, education, and culture were shown as inextricably intertwined with considerations of wealth and power. These interconnections emerge wherever politics is involved. Thus an inquiry into development as a political process requires, in addition to the joining of political and economic considerations, consideration of all aspects of man's life in society.

In order to deal with development as a political process, then, it must be understood as a phenomenon that affects and is affected by the entire range of social and individual values. Hence the central thesis of this book set out at the close of the introductory chapter finds a corollary in the imperatives of development: *development requires an expanding economy and a broadening sense of political responsibility that will gen-*

erate local and global redistributions of power, wealth, education, and status on the principle of equal access.

Only one of these terms needs elaboration here: status refers to the sense of dignity and freedom residing in—and accorded to—individuals and groups. A redistribution of status values as part of the developmental process requires the dismantling of superior-inferior relationships and the building of a global society, and local societies, with equal dignity for all men and cultures. Kenneth Kaunda, the President of Zambia, gave expression to the true meaning of the concept of status and status change:

> The challenge is not just simply the elimination of poverty, ignorance, and disease. It is first and foremost a question of building a world in which every man, woman, and child, without distinction, will have and exercise the right to live a full human life . . . free from servitude, oppression, and exploitation imposed . . . by other fellow human beings; a world in which freedom, peace, and security will have practical meaning to each and every member of the human race.[1]

With these words status becomes the ultimate value of the development process and status redistribution the essential change that transforms oppression into freedom.

POWER CONFRONTS WEAKNESS

Subsequent analysis will explore linkages among the several values of the development formula just offered. But power comes first in the sequence of analysis because, as we have seen, it is the indispensable coin of politics. The relationship of power to weakness is at the center of the development process; it is also the key element in the coexistence of developed North and underdeveloped South. Preponderant United States power is the most conspicuous fact in the inter-American experience. At the global level, disparity in power between the developed and underdeveloped worlds is again the dominant factor affecting their mutual transactions. The existence of this disparity in power gives rise, unavoidably and continuously, to two basic phenomena of the development process: first, temptation of the strong to dominate the weak, and second, the fear and resentment aroused in the weak by the threat or reality of domination by the strong.

The confrontation of power and weakness is the perennial source from which such contemporary concepts as neoimperialism and neocolonialism

---

[1] Speech at the Fourth Assembly of the World Council of Churches, Uppsala, Sweden, July 1968.

gain vitality and conviction. However justly or unjustly they are used in specific situations, these concepts are profoundly germane to the dynamics of contemporary international politics. Imperialism is a doctrine that prescribes rule by one group over another for the benefit of the ruling group. Neoimperialism, or neocolonialism, follows the same prescription but denies it. It therefore disavows the explicit doctrine of imperialism, abandons obvious techniques of imperial rule in favor of more subtle ones, and declares itself anti-imperialist. Hence neoimperialism compounds the tyranny and injustice of imperialism with subterfuge, deceit, and hypocrisy. This is a bitter ideological brew, and it is distilled from an aggregate of bitter experiences inherent in the coexistence of great power and great weakness.

Taken at face value, then, the accusation that a country (or an ideology, a racial or ethnic group, a party, a corporation) pursues a policy of neoimperialism is one of the most serious and inflammatory charges that can be made in contemporary world politics. Although the concept has been diluted and debased by excessive and indiscriminate use, international events continually revive its power to explain and convince.

The concept of neoimperialism lives in part because classic world-wide imperialism is still a recent memory and because local remnants of formal empire, most notoriously in southern Africa, still persist. It lives, too, because communist and noncommunist countries in the developed world frequently find it useful to pin the label of neoimperialism (sometimes justifiably) on each other's policies. Governments in underdeveloped countries also find the accusation useful when they desire to distract attention from their own shortcomings. But the explanatory and propagandistic effectiveness of the neoimperialism concept is most forcefully renewed whenever a developed country pursues its own purposes at the expense of an underdeveloped country. Since this practice will continue to occur with considerable frequency, the issue of neoimperialism will be a fixture in international politics for a long time to come— as long as power and weakness coexist.

In this situation the goal of development cannot avoid becoming entangled with the problem of neoimperialism. This is, of course, a corollary of the proposition that there is an unavoidable antagonism between development and sovereignty. But the linkages between the process of development and the problem of neoimperialism are visible without reference to deductive reasoning. They are in evidence wherever contact is made between developed and underdeveloped.

Every underdeveloped country has officially expressed its desire to develop. All have called upon the industrialized countries for aid in getting the process underway. And all have received some measure, however adequate or inadequate, of assistance. But the appeal to the industrialized societies reestablishes (or continues) a dependency relationship in varying degree with the very world of empires and hegemonies from which colonial liberation movements in Asia, Africa, and Latin America sought to free themselves.

In the context of a continuing dependency on the industrial world, then, assistance programs in the form of grants, loans, technical training and advice, military training and funding, educational planning, and the physical presence of varying numbers of personnel from the assisting country bear more than a passing resemblance to life under the former colonial or quasi-colonial regime. The resemblance is more marked to the extent that personnel from the assisting country occupy positions of power. There may, in fact, be less dependency than in the old colonial relationship. But a measure of dependency remains, and, more important, the long familiar juxtaposition of foreign power and domestic weakness continues visible within the internal structure of the under-developed society receiving assistance.

The development relationship thus becomes the most fertile source for charges that the old imperial game of domination and subordination continues essentially unchanged and that only a set of different and sometimes only supplementary techniques justify the prefix "neo." Reality, subjectivity, and distortion all contribute to these charges in a context where the temptation to dominate and the fear of domination are inherent and constant factors. The issues of development and development assistance thus become inextricably intertwined with the issue of neoimperialism.

After all, the bulk of the governmental relationships between the industrial powers of the North and the basically agricultural countries of the South are carried on in the name of development. This is as true of Soviet-Chinese relations before the split between Moscow and Peking as it is of the United States in Latin America or France in West and North Africa. Development and development assistance are at the center of the political interaction between the powerful North and the fragile and fearful governments of the South. It follows that the fundamental long-term questions for the South must be: Will development efforts achieve the goals set forth in development rhetoric and result in economic growth and political freedom? Or will development be transformed into a new set of mechanisms which perpetuate poverty and impose new forms of subordination?

DEVELOPMENT: THE DISTRIBUTION OF BENEFITS

The answers to these questions are not yet available. But both the past and the future course of development can be better assessed if a simpler and more abstract question is asked first: Who is likely to benefit from development?

There are, initially, four basic categories of beneficiary:

Underdeveloped countries (UDCs)
Certain groups and individuals in underdeveloped countries
Developed countries (DCs)
Certain groups and individuals in developed countries

As soon as a plurality of beneficiaries is indicated, still another question suggests itself: Who is likely to benefit more and who less? While equal distribution among the beneficiaries is a conceivable outcome of the development process, development theory itself, as we shall see, prescribes unequal benefits. Moreover, experience has shown that development practice has consistently resulted in unequal distribution of benefits, in configurations which are often enough at variance with those development theory prescribes. Thus inequality of benefits is built into both development theory and practice.

The issue of inequality is directly posed by two additional possible outcomes of the development process:

Some underdeveloped countries may benefit more than others.
Some developed countries may benefit more than others.

These additional outcome possibilities testify to the fact that the variable effects of development are not limited to relationships within or between rich countries and poor countries. They also influence the status of poor countries among poor countries and rich among rich.

Taken together, these six possible outcomes in the distribution of development benefits and their mutual relationships provide a set of indicators for understanding development as a political process. The remaining indicator, of course, is the relative magnitude and quality of the development effort by both the developed and the underdeveloped countries.

As we have already seen, development presupposes change. In political terms, this means that developmental change will result in a different distribution of benefits and values from that which previously obtained. The norms of development theory rule out any assumption that development is merely a matter of producing a greater abundance of benefits for all parties while leaving the ratios of distribution unaltered. The initial inequities in distribution are too great. Consequently, development is properly seen not simply as a scheme to increase benefits but also to effect a progressive reduction of inequalities in their allocation. *Equitable* distribution of benefits by definition requires *unequal* distribution—in favor of those previously disadvantaged. This is the meaning of the frequent pronouncements that development must close the gap between rich and poor and that this gap is the central fact of political life both within underdeveloped societies and in the confrontation of the developed and underdeveloped worlds. Development requires a steadily increasing production of benefits and a progressive equalization of consumption patterns.

In these terms, development must lead to outcomes in which some benefit more than others, even though, as we shall see, all may make some gains. This statement can serve as a brief definition of the central political problem of development. Its implications may become clearer if we now incorporate the six possible outcomes just listed into a schematic projection of functional and dysfunctional results of the development process (see Table 15.1).

The table lists "best possible" and "worst possible" outcomes in terms of the development formula offered at the beginning of the chapter. Many variations between the two extremes of functional and dysfunctional are obviously possible. Should the time ever come when a definitive assessment of the development process might be feasible in the sense that it was possible to survey the results of the Marshall Plan, it is certain that reality will be different from either extreme. But the "functional" outcome realistically states the norm for development policy, and the "dysfunctional" outcome just as realistically states its perversion.

The juxtaposition of the two outcomes illustrates the kinds of hopes and fears that attend the development process. The functional outcome provides more benefits to those who now have less and therefore harmonizes with the principle of equalization. The dysfunctional outcome provides more benefits to those already advantaged and thus accentuates

Table 15.1
Projected Distribution of Development Benefits

	Functional	
MORE BENEFITS	FEWER BENEFITS	EQUAL BENEFITS
UDCs	DCs	UDCs as a group
Less advantaged	Advantaged groups	DCs as a group
groups in UDCs	in UDCs	All groups within DCs

	Dysfunctional
MORE BENEFITS	FEWER BENEFITS
DCs	UDCs
Some DCs	Other DCs
Some UDCs	Other UDCs
Advantaged groups	Less advantaged groups
in UDCs	in UDCs
Advantaged groups	Less advantaged groups
in DCs	in DCs

prevailing inequalities. The difference between the two outcomes defines the difference between policies aimed at creating a greater equality and community among men and policies which merit the neoimperialist accusation. The norm of development leads to a diffusion of power, wealth, knowledge, and status. Its perversion leads to a further concentration of these values in the hands of minorities.

The norm provides, in addition, for an equal division of benefits for three other sets of claimants: among the developed countries as a group, among the underdeveloped countries as a group, and among the internal populations of developed countries. If one or more developed countries accumulate the benefits of development to an extent that puts other developed countries at a disadvantage, the process will be in danger of breaking down under the pressures of great power rivalry. Development is by definition a cooperative effort; while it can tolerate a degree of rivalry and conflict, it cannot endure long if it comes to be dominated by power struggles. Military and other kinds of combat considerations will then play an overweening role in the allocation of development resources to the point where development goals become unattainable.

The experience of the United States in South Vietnam has been a bitter lesson in this regard, both locally and in its impact on American development policy throughout the world. A similar lesson can be found in the policies of both the United States and the Soviet Union in the Middle East. Soviet ambitions in Southeast Asia provided still another example when Moscow pandered to Sukarno's mania for armaments and thus contributed to the ruin of the Indonesian economy and Sukarno's own ultimate downfall.

If great power rivalry can distort the purposes of development, so can conflicts among the developing countries. Disproportionate advantages accruing to one or several underdeveloped countries are bound to provoke contentious reactions on the part of others. The quarrel between India and Pakistan and the strife among Arab states as well as between Arabs and Israelis are classic examples. The task of effecting a rough equality in the apportionment of benefits among underdeveloped countries is still more difficult than among developed countries; in the short run it is impossible. But unless the norm of equality shapes long-run policy with reasonable effectiveness, development goals will be aborted by the appearance of whole new sets of enmities in the underdeveloped world—with corresponding effects on the international relations of the developed world. If development is the new word for peace, it will have meaning only to the extent that it provides the most gains to the presently disadvantaged within an overall concept of equality of benefits.

As for the internal populations of developed countries, it is obviously desirable to remedy the situation of any seriously deprived groups. But equalization efforts at this level do not depend on global development, though they will clearly be affected by it; the developed countries possess sufficient internal resources and sophistication to evolve the necessary remedies without reference to external concerns. The equality principle in this context properly functions as a restraint where there is a danger that certain groups profit inordinately from development operations while others experience severe losses. Development presupposes accelerating changes in the world economy as well as in the world power structure. In these changing circumstances, developed countries must be able to meet the needs of all sectors of their populations in an even-handed way. Otherwise the forward thrust of the development effort threatens to be stopped in its tracks by the pressures arising from their own domestic dissensions.

FOES OF DEVELOPMENT

Development as a formula for equalization is bound to provoke opposition. Those who enjoy the most advantages under a given system of distribution are prone to resist any changes which might erode their position. Those who already possess power and wealth generally desire to remain powerful and wealthy. Moreover, the evident differential in power and wealth that almost always prevails between the educated and the uneducated has prompted privileged elites throughout most of history to prefer the restriction of education to its universalization. The preference of these elites for a hierarchy of status follows logically. Hierarchy maintains social distance and prevents those whom the system disadvantages from gaining access to any of the values that could aid them in redressing their situation of inequality.

Philosophically, hierarchy and equality are conflicting though not irreconcilable concepts. But when hierarchy reflects and perpetuates radical inequalities in the distribution of human values, the antagonism between the two concepts must be correspondingly radical. Antagonisms at this level of intensity now characterize the relationships of elites and masses within underdeveloped countries and, on the global scale, between underdeveloped South and developed North. Hence development policies designed to diminish these antagonisms run the constant risk of being undone by them.

This double set of antagonisms subjects development efforts to a double set of hazards and criticisms. We have already seen the neoimperialist label affixed, almost inevitably, to the development policies of the North. This labeling refers not simply to a presumed relationship between dominant North and subordinate South. It also embodies the charge that development aid has only served to shore up the very elites in the countries of the South who, because they are determined to perpetuate their local monopolies of power, wealth, education, and status, are the necessary enemies of development. The conclusion can then be drawn that there is a coincidence of interest between global and local elites in defending the present distribution of benefits in the world at large and in the underdeveloped countries in particular.

In this interpretation the North gains in two ways. First, it can exploit the economies of the South with the connivance of the local elites. Second, since economic exploitation prevents authentic development, the North secures a guarantee that its world preeminence will not be challenged by new centers of modernity and power which, in the absence of exploitation by the North, would emerge in the South. The local elites, in turn, obtain political and economic support from the North and so strengthen their ability to maintain control of the internal political and socioeconomic structure.

This critique of North-South relations, disseminated generally by the political Left and widely accepted in all parts of the underdeveloped world, dispenses with nice distinctions between imperialism and neo-imperialism altogether. The relationship as described is identical with one of the favorite methods of classic imperialism: the deal with the tribal chief which rendered him subservient to the imperial power in exchange for imperial support within his own political bailiwick.

The double-barreled attack from the Left finds its counterpart among hostile attitudes of the political Right. If development is an equalization process, then it must necessarily erode the internal power of traditional elites. For those among the elites who do not choose to see their power diminished, the developed countries of the North are not allies (contrary to the assertions of the Left) but are antagonists. Pressures from the North to universalize education, modernize agriculture and land-tenure systems, upgrade the economic and social status of labor, and expand the internal market are wholly inimical to the traditional power structure of the underdeveloped country. Of course, countries in the North with development assistance programs can choose to exert these kinds of pressures vigorously, half-heartedly, or not at all, and the amount of resistance among local elites is inevitably a major factor in the choice made. Whatever degree of vigor countries of the North may exhibit in these matters, the obvious diplomacy of the local oligarchs resisting change is to give lip service to development goals in order to obtain intrinsically desirable grants and loans and then to subvert the purposes they were designed to serve.

To the extent that developed countries willingly or unwillingly lend themselves to this diplomacy, they give substance to the charges of imperialism-neoimperialism emanating from the Left. On the other hand, in cases where donor countries of the North have acted vigorously to implement the publicly professed goals of development and "modern-

ization," those among the privileged classes of the underdeveloped countries who do not wish to modernize have often matched their counterparts on the Left in vitriolic and imaginative denunciations of neoimperialism. The most obvious and persistent theme in these political
exercises is the charge that the economic changes or social reforms projected in development assistance programs traduce the underdeveloped
country's sovereignty.

It must be added that defense of traditional power structures is by no
means a monopoly of the political Right. On the Left, too, the preference for status quo unrelieved by reform is often enough in evidence.
The ideological rationale is that the prevailing arrangements governing
society must be prolonged until social conditions have deteriorated to
the point where popular wrath brings down the ruling oligarchy—and
entrusts power to the revolutionary counteroligarchy.

But there is a more expediential, and reactionary, rationale which
finds adherents among the Left opposition as well—notably among many
in the communist parties of Latin America. They have opposed the development process in the fear that it will generate new social forces unre-
sponsive to orthodox communist leadership and that the role the party in
opposition politics will in consequence be diminished. This penchant for
monopoly has been one of the major bones of contention between
Moscow-oriented Latin communists and the more eclectic new-style
communism of Castro.

Thus the preference for perpetuating a ruling elite is duplicated in
the preference for perpetuating a ruling counterelite. The symmetry is
complete when elite and counterelite are discovered to share the same
motivation: a predilection for a politically passive society minimizing
the risks of competition for leadership which a politically dynamic
society invariably brings with it. On both Right and Left, then, there are
forces committed to maintaining the status quo. Since these forces make
up very large segments of the power structures of a very great number
of underdeveloped societies, efforts in both North and South to forward
the development process necessarily encounter determined resistance.

It follows that a rational development policy must anticipate purposeful opposition by contriving antidotes to immobilize or circumvent
obstructionist tactics. In turn, a rational assessment of the achievements
and failings of development efforts must be sophisticated enough to
understand that disappointments and criticism are among the unavoidable consequences of the commitment to change. It must also learn the
political lesson that setbacks and hostile invective are produced not
simply by incompetence, lethargy, or random ill will but also by deliberate efforts at sabotage by those who fear the changes that development brings. The path to development, in short, is studded with political
as well as economic, demographic, and cultural roadblocks. One can test

the validity of this proposition not only in underdeveloped countries but also in any American ghetto.

STATIC AND DYNAMIC UNIVERSES

In a static universe, one in which one party's gain in benefits must necessarily result in another's loss, the antagonisms created between the forces of change and those who resist change are virtually insoluble. Such a universe has, in fact, been the condition of life for most societies for most of history. In consequence, an oligarchical hierarchy marked by extreme disparities in power, wealth, education, and status has been the dominant social form to date. The first sustained breakaway from this vicious circle, as we have seen, came when the Industrial Revolution began to create the conditions for a dynamic universe, one in which a growing volume of benefits permitted more and more people to share in them without necessarily causing losses to others.

As imperfect as that process has been in what have become the developed societies, it has now brought men to the point where it is possible to expand the dimensions of the dynamic universe to coincide with the globe itself. Now, on a world scale, one society's gain need not be another society's loss. On the contrary, the gains of one can enhance the gains of all. Keynes argued this in economic terms: gains in wealth by one country can make it a more efficient supplier and a better customer for others. It can also be argued in political terms: the satisfaction of one society can augment the security of all. By the same logic, whatever holds true in the arguments at the global level also holds true for the internal social orders of individual states.

All such benign effects, of course, are matters of possibility or probability and not of certainty. Wider distribution of benefits in greater volume involves unavoidable risks. Even a major increase of supply may not satisfy the pent-up demand of those who have long been deprived of most of the benefits of life. Unless new demand-supply relationships can be generated, the society will arrive at an impasse typical of pre-revolutionary situations, in which "concessions" come too late to convert antagonists from political violence to political reform. In these circumstances, moreover, concessions are at the same time likely to polarize the society still further and to place more power in the hands of those who prefer violence to argument. Fragments of this explosive pattern have been clearly visible in the United States since the beginning of the 1960s, when the struggle over civil rights moved to the center of American political life. The emergence of this pattern is an ominous indication that it is very late in the day to redeem the original American promise of equality.

Timing, then, affects the prospects for success or failure in any scheme to redistribute social values. In the case of global development, it is also very late in the day. Poverty, humiliation, and all the other stigmata of human misery have existed in so much of the world for so long and now exist on so massive a scale that there is abundant evidence from which to argue that the situation is beyond repair. But there is persuasive counterevidence as well in the efforts being made by many countries of the South. The programs of assistance from the North, though still inadequate, provide further counterevidence. On balance, the sum of evidence suggests that world society has not yet arrived at the impasse of prerevolution. It also suggests, however, that unless present trends in demography, economics, and political radicalization are reversed during the remaining years of the century, the world will be inexorably driven to the point of no return.

Time's formidable pressures on policies for development are less intense, however, than the pressures created by the central concept of redistribution itself. It is true that the transition from a static to a dynamic universe eases the pressure: no longer must one's advance be another's retreat. A dynamic universe makes possible gains in material productivity and in the rationality and equalization of political and social arrangements that will increase benefits to all human beings. It does require, of course, adjustments to change—new methods in the exercise of power and new ways of making profit—and such adjustments are bound to be less attractive for some parties than for others. Cutting far deeper than adjustment, however, is the basic developmental requirement of a reapportionment of benefits. It is a requirement with a double imperative: a relative decline in the power, wealth, and status of those already powerful and wealthy and a relative increase in the power, wealth, and status of those now weak and poor.

Here is where the opposition of oligarchies will be most easily aroused. It can be softened by demonstrating the difference between relative and absolute changes in the distribution of benefits. Even should, for example, the share of benefits enjoyed by the presently advantaged be reduced over time by 50 percent, if the total volume of benefits available to all parties increases during the same period by 300 percent, all parties can register absolute gains. This is precisely the kind of arithmetic which powered the dynamic growth-redistribution relationship of those societies that industrialized during the century preceding World War I. This was the dynamism that lifted the once static and therefore underdeveloped economies and polities of the North into their present "developed" condition of abundance and power. The inequities in the distribution of benefits were progressively, if unevenly, reduced in a context where the growing quantity of benefits made redistribution economically and politically less painful.

As more and more people shared in the increasing volume of benefits, these beneficiaries in turn became new sources of power and wealth for the society as a whole, so that the process of growth began to profit all sectors of the population. The burgeoning of production, consumption, savings, capital investment, and tax revenues and the equalizing functions of government (education, social services, progressive taxation, compensatory economic and fiscal policies) contributed to a process in which all parts of the society—even established as well as aspirant elites—recognized a growing stake.

THE INTERDEPENDENCE OF DEVELOPMENT AND COMMUNITY

The very success of equalization in the North makes the continuing exclusion of racial or cultural underclasses indefensible on yet another count. The practical and moral anomaly of underclass exclusion, however, provides an explanation for the limits that presently prevent the equalization process from expanding further. In the developed countries, these limits are essentially national. That is, a wide distribution of benefits among all who are members of the national community is politically, economically, and socially acceptable to all or most of those concerned. Acceptability, in turn, is principally a product of the mutually profitable social and economic results of the equalization process.

Beyond the national community, however, ventures in equalization are still novel. Internally, countries like the United States, with large racial and cultural minorities, have not yet been able to define their nationhood in a way that encompasses these minorities on the basis of voluntary choice and equality. Hence they remain essentially alien to the nation and outside the implicit social contract that sanctions the equalization principle. Externally, with the partial exception of the Common Market, the policies of the developed countries are at best only pale and ambiguous reflections of their commitments to internal equalization. At worst, which is most of the time, their external and internal policies are in flat contradiction. That is, except for the underclass phenomenon, their domestic policies are based on the principle of inclusiveness while the fundamental principle of their foreign policies remains one of exclusivity.

In the underdeveloped South, almost the reverse is true, at least wherever the local oligarchies can be defined as colonized elites. Here the exclusivity principle embodied in the idea of external sovereignty is breached to the extent that these elites are dependent on their relations with the industrial North for the continuance of their privileged status. Internally, as we have seen, the exclusive principle of class, rather than the inclusive principle of nation, defines the outer limits within which the distribution of values for mutual benefit takes place.

In both North and South, and for both international and internal development, the problem is identical, obvious, and difficult: how to develop more spacious concepts of community than those which have been built on class, ethnic group, race, or nation. The chief obstacle impeding solution is the fear of equality. It is a fear that persists despite the power, the riches, and the knowledge generated by those societies now termed developed and which have themselves produced irrefutable evidence that the equalization principle is an indispensable guideline in men's search for the good society. If equalization in practice has raised new problems of mass conformity, organizational unwieldiness, bureaucratic rigidity, and degradation of the environment, it is nonetheless true that their solutions cannot be found without new applications of the very same principle: the equal right of all men to live freely in societies which nurture rather than subvert their material welfare and their intellectual and moral potentials. Indeed, only the further extension of the equality principle can create new communities capable of replacing the present global coexistence of privilege and deprivation with a cooperative effort to share benefits and thus to increase their quantity.

But the implementation of egalitarian doctrines comes hard to those who consider one another alien. Equality of status and power among those who have no bonds of mutual or common loyalties invites anarchy, and anarchy raises the specter of force. As in the anarchy characteristic of traditional international politics—or of a domestic political system when it is moving toward civil war—the idea of equality is sure to be trampled in the rush to build up superior power of all kinds in order to prevail against all comers. Thus the great impediment to expanding the equalization process is the fear that it will only serve to multiply and strengthen those who are, at best, regarded as aliens and, at worst, as enemies. Machiavelli gave classic expression to this fear and offered a classic remedy when he advised the ruler never to enhance the power of another prince.

THE PROBLEM OF SAFETY

Machiavelli's recipe was only a restatement of a political doctrine of much more ancient heritage. Among those who have, there is a propensity to maintain intact their advantages over those who have not. This phenomenon cannot be explained by assuming that privileged minorities begrudge in principle the good things of life to underprivileged majorities. It must rather be traced to the tendency among the rich and powerful to see the totality of their interests linked to existing structures of inequality. That is, they are prone to believe that the preservation of these structures is essential to their own continuing enjoyment not only of wealth and perquisites but of physical safety itself.

Wealth, rank, and knowledge, after all, are convertible into coercive power. Desirable in themselves, they are also coveted for their utility in conflict. Oligarchies have often enough used wealth, rank, and knowledge as weapons. They have just as often been fearful that a wider diffusion of these commodities could be turned into weapons against themselves. Hence the proclivity among oligarchs to look upon the idea of equalization as an invitation to place themselves up against the revolutionary wall.

This built-in—and not wholly irrational—bias among oligarchs will harden to the degree that equalization proposals are designed to include aliens: individuals, classes, or societies who would presumably feel least inhibited about transforming their gains into weapons against the hitherto privileged minorities. In the West, nationalism provided tolerably effective constraints on these kinds of dangers by evoking a sense of community within which gradual transfers of power and gradual reductions in the disparity between wealth and poverty could take place. Common loyalties to the nation as well as a growing volume of benefits in most instances helped to protect both the retreating oligarchs and the advancing mass from full-scale revolution and its bloody consequences. But within the typical underdeveloped society, the internal class barriers—like the sovereign barriers that divide international society —now constitute formidable obstacles to further exercises in community building. To overcome these obstacles, it is necessary to demonstrate that a growing volume of benefits can in fact be generated and that the equalization process of growth redistribution will benefit the oligarchs more than any available realistic alternative.

But, once again, it is difficult to reconcile people to the loss of advantages they have traditionally enjoyed. This is true even if there is a plausible prospect of compensation in the form of different kinds of gains. Whatever the compensation, the idea of development poses a central political question bound to cause uneasiness among all oligarchs: Will the global establishment and the establishments within the underdeveloped countries be willing to accept an outcome of the development process that lessens their comparative advantages in wealth and power and in other values that contribute to wealth and power?

As we have seen, even the arithmetic of a dynamic universe promising greater gains for all cannot alter the blunt terms of this question. Even if development adds to the riches of the presently wealthy, their *share* of the total production and consumption of wealth will be less. Even if a more equitable sharing of power would pacify societies in the underdeveloped South, and in the international society as a whole, those who now control most of the power at both levels would have to give up the deceptive but flattering assumption that their security depends exclusively on their own wills. Instead, their security would become the joint product of their own more modest resources and the growing resources of the newcomers to power.

In a word, a successful process of development entails the dismantling of the superior-subordinate relationship characteristic of oligarchy and, therefore, the dismantling of oligarchy itself. The presently poor and powerless would move away from a position of dependency, while the rich and powerful would gradually forfeit their present position of sovereign license. In turn, both haves and have-nots would begin to move slowly and unevenly toward the only situation offering a long-run prospect for peace: interdependence.

If oligarchs at the global level and in the underdeveloped societies were to ponder a diminution of their own power as a policy option, at least four major issues would come under scrutiny: justice, profitability, feasibility, and safety. All these issues will be subjects for investigation in the ensuing chapters. At this point, the issue of safety demands particular attention. Assuming that the oligarchs could be persuaded on other counts that extreme inequalities in the distribution of benefits are undesirable, one is still faced with the question, How can the possessors of inordinate power and wealth *safely* renounce their quasi-monopolies?

It would be idle to argue that a dilution of oligarchy would not involve risks to the oligarchs because the argument would be neither true nor persuasive. A demonstration that the risks could be made manageable and losses limited rather than total would have greater credibility. But the decisive argument could only be one that made it manifest that there will be fewer risks and losses attending a policy of redistributing power, wealth, and their associated values than in policies designed to perpetuate the status quo. In other words, those commanding power and wealth —the developed countries of the world and the oligarchies in the countries of the South—will have to be convinced that a continuation of present configurations in the distribution of values and benefits will lead them to a general catastrophe. They might then be persuaded that their best chance for safety lies in a policy whose purpose is a progressive dismantling of oligarchy by means of a more equitable distribution of benefits.

THE VULNERABILITY OF THE STATUS QUO

The most extreme form of catastrophe, of course, is the nuclear Armageddon that obliterates mankind and all its works. In this particular denouement the oligarchs and the powerless, the rich and the poor, would finally be united in the equality of oblivion. But while all men fear the ultimate cataclysm, for most human beings, for most of the time, the threat is remote and little related to their daily behavior. Problems of perception therefore compound the intrinsic difficulties in demonstrating an unambiguous cause-effect relationship between any particular policies and nuclear incineration. Nevertheless, the nuclear danger cannot be conjured away, and policies must be tested for their potential to increase or diminish the danger.

Superficially, policies involving conflicts and arms races between the superpowers—that is, between the leaders of the global oligarchy—generate the most plausible contexts in which the nuclear furies might be unleashed. Yet those who make policy for the superpowers are more aware than most of the suicidal nature of nuclear war. Hence they assign first priority to holding their conflicts to levels below the nuclear threshold. In so doing, they are constantly enticed by the idea that enduring safety would result from a reciprocal legitimation of one another's oligarchical positions. Such a "peace" formula obviously implies the perpetuation of oligarchy rather than its disappearance.

The concept of a Soviet-American duopoly whose governing purpose is to maintain the global supremacy of the two superpowers has made notable gains in credibility since the Cuban missile crisis of 1962 and the Soviet invasion of Czechoslovakia in 1968. The suspicion of oligarchical collusion has grown with the rapid pace of Soviet-American detente policies in the early 1970s; the simultaneous American wooing of Communist China has done little to allay it. Both in the countries of the South and in the smaller powers of the North, many have come to employ this concept as the master formula for explaining contemporary world politics. Their bitter complaint is that the two superpowers have become the guardians of the status quo.

Both the United States and the Soviet Union are accused of being essentially indifferent to the misery and injustice that crush the majority of mankind. The necessary conclusion is that they will involve themselves in the problems of the weak only if involvement serves their own particular interests and only to the extent that it does not endanger the stability of their duopoly. These are some of the assumptions that in the 1960s split apart almost every communist party in the underdeveloped South and many in the developed North. It is hardly surprising that many of those who adopted such assumptions should turn for inspiration to new champions of revolution: Communist China, Castro's Cuba, Nasser's Egypt, and later, the Palestinian guerrilla organizations, or Hanoi. Many also turned to ideologically more circumscribed nationalist-military regimes as models for radical change.

It could be argued, of course, that the fragmenting of revolutionary forces in the underdeveloped world testifies to the success of the alleged duopoly, at least from the point of view of the United States. Historically, oligarchs have been able to bolster their positions when revolutionaries begin to fight among themselves more fiercely than they fight against the oligarchy. But it is difficult to judge when revolutionaries will once again coalesce. In China, the divisions that were both cause and effect of the almost psychotic excesses of the Cultural Revolution of 1966 to 1968 appeared at least outwardly healed two years later. At the beginning of the 1970s, particularly in Latin America, some of the estranged communist and radicalized socialist factions began to initiate attempts to collaborate with one another again. One result was the election in 1970 of Salvador Allende as president of Chile; upon his inauguration the first freely elected Marxist government in the Western Hemisphere took office.

In assessing the viability of a politics of duopoly and status quo, however, there is a consideration far more important than the ebb and flow of tactical alignments. It is the growing misery of the vast majority of mankind that lives in the underdeveloped societies of the South. The conditions that make for radicalization are built into the present structure of world politics and will not be easily altered. These conditions arise not only from the fact that the world is now populated by the largest mass of poverty-stricken human beings in history but also from their coexistence with the largest mass of affluent people in history. Mass majority and mass minority, in turn, are bound together in an ever more intricate network of global communications.

As is always the case with outsiders looking in, the poor majority is more sensitive to the messages coming over the network than the rich minority: the dissatisfaction and the envy of the poor make them more attentive. The very massiveness of the affluent minority and the multiplicity of its enterprises around the globe are a constant stimulus to envy. Because affluence has become a mass phenomenon relatively recently, it is also a stimulus to the conviction among the global majority that the prevailing radical inequalities in the world society are not matters of unalterable fate but human arrangements crying out for radical change.

Those who subscribe to the theory of duopoly and decry its impact on the countries of the South must logically develop policies to undermine the duopoly's power. In addition to the third force options represented by China, Castro, and others, such policies can seek to enlist the industrialized powers of Western Europe and Japan as partners in efforts to reduce and counter American and Soviet influence in the underdeveloped world. Indeed, France under De Gaulle nurtured a special sense of mission with regard to such possibilities and options. But the most direct and generally the most effective method is one that creates or increases friction between the duopolists themselves. Observers in the South have not failed to note that the economic aid programs of both superpowers in the underdeveloped countries diminished after the 1962 Cuban crisis and the subsequent Soviet-American detente. It was hardly illogical to conclude that the interests of governments, factions, or peoples in the South might be better served by intensified conflict rather than by increasing cooperation between Washington and Moscow.

Governments and other political forces in the underdeveloped countries, then, have a variety of options to choose from in shaping their relations with the superpowers. Because of their own weakness, however, no one of the options promises to yield more than limited successes. Hence they will be prone to try combinations and to oscillate between one and another option. In such a context the only element of consistency will be the fundamental one of a persistent search for ways to obtain the leverage to pressure the powerful into political and economic investments in the underdeveloped world beyond what a status quo–oriented policy of duopoly would deem prudent.

The now hoary gambit of extorting money, arms, or both from Washington, presumably to prevent the petitioner's country from going communist (or from Moscow to frustrate factions that allegedly want to sign up with American imperialism), is still a favored technique. It has, of course, been tried many times in situations where the payoffs to the donor have been disappointing. The Vietnam war is a frightening commentary on the excesses that can be justified in the name of this particular political exercise. Yet as the ongoing international traffic in armaments testifies, political and military extortion continues to be a fixture in North-South relations.[2] And as worsening social conditions produce a rising tide of violence in the underdeveloped South, resort to policies of extortion is likely to increase. Whatever the degree of disillusion created by the experience in Vietnam, acts of wholesale repression, overthrow of governing elites, and civil wars cannot fail to involve the interests of the superpowers (and other militarily strong states) in the affairs of the South.

As their doubling populations place ever greater strains on their resources, the countries of the South will be propelled more and more into the center of global politics. In these conditions the pressures on Moscow and Washington to intervene on behalf of opposing sides must increase. A Brazil, for example, with a projected population of more than 200 million in the year 2000 is bound to have still more difficult political problems and to command more political attention in the world

---

[2] This traffic accounts for an indeterminate share of the approximately $5 billion dispensed by the United States in foreign military assistance in 1970. A Defense Department breakdown of this figure included $2.4 billion in grants, primarily to Southeast Asian countries, $1.4 billion in military sales, $518 million in military support assistance, and $224 million in transfers of surplus military equipment. Not included in the total was the value of installations turned over to South Vietnam and Thailand (*New York Times*, January 7, 1971).

Western European, Soviet, Czech, and Chinese arms also continue to flow to the underdeveloped world in significant quantities, sometimes on commercial terms but often on a give-away basis with all the obvious political implications. Soviet military aid to Egypt had reached a total of about $5 billion by March 1972, and was at that time flowing in at the rate of $5 million a day (*New York Times*, March 31, 1972). The Egyptian decision to eject thousands of Soviet military technicians occurred later in the Spring of 1972.

at large than the Brazil of 1970 with roughly 90 million inhabitants. The same is obviously true for the other countries of the South caught in the flood tide of population growth, but the largest among them make the point most spectacularly (see Table 15.2).

If it is true that politics is people, then it is evident that the dimensions of global politics are in process of drastic alteration. By the conservative estimate of Chapter 13, the total population of the developed world will rise from 1 billion in 1970 to 1.6 billion in 2000; during the same period the population of the underdeveloped world will rise from 2.5 to 4.8 billion. These massive growths and growth differentials are inexorably altering the terms of the world power equation. Their proximate effect will be to increase the likelihood of social chaos and of repressive attempts to bring it under control. In such a context neither the superpowers nor other states of the developed world with global commercial and industrial interests can be consistently indifferent to upheavals in the South, no matter how much they might prefer to maintain low profiles.

If advocates of the low profile can argue persuasively that in the 1960s interventionist policies by the superpowers and others in Southeast Asia, the Middle East, Africa, and the Caribbean frequently lacked a viable rationale, it is a still more powerful argument that the interventions occurred nonetheless. If it is asserted that they were often compounded with large elements of confusion and aggravated by irrational fears and pride, the rebuttal can only be that these states of mind will continue to

Table 15.2

Estimated Population Increases 1970–2000 (approximate) in Selected Major Countries of the Underdeveloped World (in millions)

	1970	2000
Mexico	51	135
Nigeria	55	131
Morocco	16	41
Burma	28	53
China	760	1165
India	550	1084
Indonesia	121	255
Iran	29	66
Pakistan	134	334
Philippines	38	98
Thailand	36	83
Turkey	35	73

NOTE: See Appendix B for population projections on a continent by continent and country by country basis. The figures for Pakistan include Bangla Desh (seceded in 1971).

bedevil high profile as well as low profile policy making. The lesson to be drawn from the mistakes of the past is not that the powerful should disengage themselves from the affairs of the weak. It is rather that the powerful must rethink their unavoidable involvement with the weak so that their global presence will be more creative and less destructive, more benign and less oppressive.

Since social chaos invites oppression (a variation on the ancient theme of orthodox international doctrine that political systems abhor power vacuums and that those with power will strive to fill them), the impact of North on South must inevitably be repressive to the extent that the South is characterized by social disorganization. Since the threat of social breakdown is endemic to the South, it follows that there is a premium on authoritarian politics and foreign support for authoritarian regimes.

Only if the South succeeds in mastering the problems of social disorganization that increasingly threaten to tear it to pieces can it hope to avoid repressive interventions by the North—and repressive indigenous governments tolerated or encouraged by the North. Only the North, in turn, can supply the South with that margin of capital and technology transfer that might be able to make the difference between social breakdown and political tyranny, on the one hand, and evolving social order and justice, on the other. In sum, there is no way to escape the Northern presence in the South; only the quality of that presence is at issue.

It is evident that there is a congenial relationship between the low profile preference and the arguments of neoisolationism. The relationship is particularly apparent whenever advocates of reduced foreign aid spending join hands with those who favor increased military appropriations. Often, of course, the two kinds of advocacy are put forward by the same persons and groups. Whatever its source, this is advocacy of the impossible. There can be no peace in the South if the North does not help build conditions for peace. And the more often peace breaks down in the South, the more pressures there will be on the states of the North to exercise police functions. This is an inescapable lesson taught by the history of international and domestic politics alike.

The lack of realism of the low profile persuasion is evidenced in still another way. The trillion dollar economy of the United States cannot, by definition, manage to project a low profile. If one then places the American economy in the global context—it accounts for approximately a third of the world's total economic product—the low profile concept becomes ludicrous.

If the advocates of low profile policies merely sought to renounce self-serving interventionist policies in the South, one could laud their purpose. But when they also call for cutbacks in development assistance, they multiply rather than diminish the probabilities of interventionary activity, and the sincerity of their purpose is placed in doubt. Moreover, deception and self-deception insinuate themselves into the argument to the extent that the low profile image can be nothing more than camouflage for the continuous and unavoidable presence of the United States and other major countries of the North in affairs of the South.

The short-range prospect, then, is that the superpowers and other powers of the North cannot escape being caught up in the turbulence of the South. A corollary is that the more frequent, widespread, and violent the turmoil, the more likely it is that the states of the North, and particularly the superpowers, will intervene on behalf of opposing sides. Hence if the states of the North are concerned for peace among themselves, they have a vital stake in preventing the spread of violence in the South. It follows that they have a vital stake in providing effective development assistance as the only alternative to a situation where the politics of desperation reaches epidemic proportions. Aerial hijackings, guerrilla warfare in cities and countryside, hit-and-run massacres at airports and other public places, diplomatic kidnappings, and assassinations are the kinds of actions that desperate people will turn to in deteriorating situations. Already international in scope, these techniques can be refined and extended until no part of the globe is safe from their explosive effects.

But it is in the longer range prognosis that the ultimate danger looms largest. Herman Kahn is not alone in foreseeing the day of "cheap" nuclear warheads and missiles that relatively poor countries could afford to produce or purchase and a traffic in nuclear arms that would render them accessible to guerrilla organizations or even ordinary criminal gangs.[3] No nuclear nonproliferation treaty will prevent such a disastrous multiplication of the sources of destruction if the political and economic demands now accumulating in the underdeveloped world remain unsatisfied.

Before such conditions came to pass, already industrialized but non-nuclear states would have anticipated them by abandoning the nonproliferation treaty in the name of their own safety in an intolerably dangerous world. One underdeveloped country is already a nuclear power; by the year 2000 China's own nuclear arsenal and its capacity to supply weapons from it to those it chooses to support outside its borders offers a prospect of terrifying proportions. It is not an unalterable prospect, but it cannot be altered if three-quarters of mankind has not by then become less resentful and violent, and therefore more hopeful, than in the 1970s.

---

[3] Herman Kahn, *On Thermonuclear War* (Princeton, N.J.: Princeton University Press, 1960), pp. 489 ff.

THE FUSION OF NORTH AND SOUTH

It is an illusion to suppose that no one will ever pull the nuclear trigger in a world in which political attitudes are dominated by hatred and fear. Such a world is as dangerous for the oligarchs—despite their power and wealth—as it is for the rest of humanity. The situation lends itself to analogy with the plight of urban America: the streets of even the most opulent sections of New York, Washington, and Chicago are no longer safe, and for comparable reasons. One cannot live on the edge of a slum, whether urban or global, and escape violence. At the global level, the slum dwellers are not a small minority but the vast majority; in consequence, their capacities for violence are enormously magnified. At the same time, the physical and psychological distance between the affluent North and the blighted South steadily diminishes.

In his celebrated speech on wars of national liberation in September 1965, Lin Piao made an analogy between the city and the world that has become the centerpiece of Chinese communist revolutionary strategy: "Taking the entire globe, if North America and Western Europe can be called the cities of the world, then Asia, Africa and Latin America constitute the rural areas of the world."[4] Having drawn the analogy, Lin concluded that the most significant confrontation in our time is between the three "rural" continents, on the one hand, and the urbanized industrial societies headed by the United States on the other. (It was not lost on the Soviet Union that its position in the confrontation was passed over in silence.) Lin's purpose followed from his conclusion: global revolutionary strategy must unite the world countryside against the world city.[5] It must unify all the antioligarchical forces in the underdeveloped world and within the countries of the developed world, and by infiltration, sabotage, and terror it must prepare the way for the climactic assault on the oligarchical world "city."

Lin indicts the world city as the enemy of the world countryside on the grounds that it uses its superior power to conquer and oppress the rural continents and that it seeks to perpetuate the conqueror-conquered relationship. There follows the familiar assertion that the phasing out of formal imperialism merely made way for the advent of neoimperialism and did nothing to alter the essential terms of the struggle between oppressor and oppressed. Necessarily imperialist because it is capitalist, the West, with the United States as the leader, is arraigned as the prime cause for the poverty and humiliation of the masses in the underdevel-

---

[4] Lin Piao, "Long Live the Victory of People's War," New York Times, September 4, 1965.

[5] In terms more specific to contemporary America, one might alter Lin's prescription to read: unification of the world ghetto, and its rural wellsprings, against the world suburb.

oped world. To the extent that they have yielded to the blandishments of capitalism internally and externally, the Soviet Union and its allies have joined the ranks of imperialist exploiters. Hence, Lin concludes, the power of the urban, industrialized, and white North must be destroyed if the rural, agricultural, and nonwhite South is to be freed from bondage.

One need not play with Lin the ancient game of blaming others for all one's own troubles in order to recognize the power of his indictment. Whatever weight one assigns to imperial injustice in accounting for the wretchedness of the rural continents, the global coexistence of massive affluence and productivity alongside still more massive poverty and misery is itself the most radical affront to any concept of justice that embraces the principle of human equality. Those who suffer because of inequalities, whatever their cause, will always brand as unjust those who tolerate or benefit from them.

The disappearance of all the varieties of polycentric communism would not alter this basic fact of life. Envy, hatred, and desperation would find new means of ideological expression and new methods of political organization to challenge the oligarchical structure of world society. Particular political movements, under any banner, are only surface manifestations of threats to peace in the South or in the world. The fundamental threat to peace derives from the general global conditions of radical inequality and hence of radical injustice.

The quest for peace, then, is inseparable from the quest for equality, and thus for justice in the form of a more equitable distribution of human values and benefits. The classic alternative strategy, of course, seeks to secure advantages for one party from an unequal distribution of values and then to overawe or outfight others from a position of superiority. Here safety rather than peace is the primary policy goal, though the two concepts are often used interchangeably. The result of this practice is that the multilateral connotations of the latter (peace for all) are obscured by the unilateral assumptions of the former (safety for some).

The chief instrument of such a strategy is necessarily, in Machiavelli's words, fear rather than love.[6] Those in the inferior position will not voluntarily support policies designed for the unilateral benefit of the superior. Hence the superior must rely on fear and on the threat or use of force as the mainstays of policy. A policy of unilateral superiority must pursue "law and order" rather than justice. It must assume that repression rather than satisfaction is the more rational way to deal with grievance—because satisfaction points toward a dissolution of the superior position. In a word, it must subordinate all other considerations to

---

[6] Niccolò Machiavelli, *The Prince*, XVII.

preserving the situation of inequality from which the superior benefits. To revert to Machiavelli's terminology once again, such a policy can have nothing to do with love.

From an historical perspective, it is something of a misnomer to label a policy of superiority as an alternative to the quest for peace. More often than not, it is the reverse: the quest for peace is relegated to the alternative position, and the search for safety in superiority is the norm of policy. This is the unavoidable outcome in every situation where those who interact politically are not bound together by a sense of community. As we have seen, this is the classic situation which has characterized the international political system. More fundamentally, it is the standard context for all forms of oligarchical politics, domestic or international.

In the absence of equality, community cannot develop. In the absence of community, peace cannot endure. And wherever these conditions are absent it is hardly surprising that safety via inequality should be the preferred expedient, particularly when those who adopt it fail to consider what they might contribute to fill the voids. The will to community and equality is the first condition for the realization of community and equality; their mere absence in no way precludes the effort to bring them into being. But the difficulties of such an undertaking—and its attendant dangers, real and imagined, for those who benefit at any given time from the politics of inequality—inhibit the act of will that alone makes possible the first steps toward equality, community, and peace.

Policies of safety through superiority have often achieved successes in the past in the sense that those groups that were powerful and rich successfully used fear or force, and sometimes favors, to keep their domestic or international enemies at bay. Their reward was a more or less enduring preservation of their own privileges. In the long run (sometimes a very long run), however, every one of these groups has succumbed to internal disintegration, to a new center of superior external force, or to both. By definition, these exercises in the politics of conflict could produce only armistices and not peace. Still, they did provide a suspenseful safety for those who were strongest.

But the outcomes of these struggles and the weapons with which they were fought were roughly proportional to the stakes. Victory assured survival and often enough an increase in power and wealth, while defeat almost never excluded recovery. With a few exceptions, annihilation remained a specter in the background; even in those instances where annihilation was the policy of the victor, this ultimate cruelty was visited only on the vanquished. The majority, comprised of the victors and those who were uninvolved, survived. Now, however, men have conjured away the limits to their powers of destruction. The specter of annihilation has emerged from the background into the foreground of global politics. It no longer threatens only a particular population occupying a limited area of the earth's surface but all men in every part of the globe. The danger of annihilation as a consequence of political behavior has ceased to be infrequent, local, and abnormal and has become constant, universal, and normal.

The observation that the arrival of the nuclear age is a revolutionary event in the history of mankind has long been a commonplace. The deepest significance of the new age, however, has been obscured by the failure to draw the appropriate conclusions in the realm of politics—that realm where men decide how they will live with one another in society. In an age of unlimited perils, political behavior continues to be guided by the suppositions and standards developed during an age of limited perils. Since old habits always die hard, the lag in effective response to a fundamentally changed situation is hardly surprising. But understanding why the political answer has not yet caught up with the nuclear question does nothing to diminish the dangers that burden all men as long as the international system is run according to prenuclear formulas.

The basic formula of the oligarchic tradition is that inequality and the violence it generates is normal, that violence is the ultimate court of appeal—the *ultima ratio*—and that no level of violence is essentially unmanageable. The advent of the nuclear age most obviously nullifies the final part of the formula, but it also negates the first two parts as well. If some levels of violence are recognized as unmanageable, then it becomes imperative to find methods of settling conflict that place restraints on all levels of violence. If some forms of violence must be banished in the name of safety, then all forms of violence must be placed under restraint lest the pressures generated by the limited use of force crumple agreements not to resort to unlimited force.

In turn, if inequality generates violence, it cannot be accepted as normal. As the prime cause of potentially unmanageable violence, the phenomenon of inequality requires still more urgent attention than the methods of conflict settlement which, after all, can only deal with symptoms. If the present dimensions of inequality persist, the victims will risk all forms of violence, manageable or not. Those presently advantaged will inexorably be driven to respond in kind. In such a context there can be no hope for the growth of processes of accommodation capable of preventing conflict from becoming unmanageable. Only a joint effort to dismantle the structures of inequality can begin to reduce the historic premiums on violence and to protect men from the unmanageable—and unimaginable—punishments at the disposal of a nuclear court of appeal.

What is suggested here, then, is that history has provided a new rationale for human equality. Before 1945 the proposition that all men are created equal could be debated in terms of empirical observations, economic and social utilities, and moral imperatives. With the arrival of the nuclear age a new dimension has been added to the debate: a linkage between the problem of equality and the capacity of humanity to survive. If the argument is accepted that inequality is the great breeder of violence, it follows that political behavior can no longer afford to resist or evade the egalitarian case long since made in the name of empiricism, social utility, and moral norms. Survival itself dictates the rejection of all forms of the doctrine of human inequality as false, and now intolerably dangerous.

Nothing is inevitable. Thus it cannot be proved that the persistence of oligarchical forms in world politics is bound to produce general nuclear war. It can only be demonstrated that the policy which perpetuates prevailing inequalities must necessarily accentuate them and runs greater risks of catastrophe than any alternative policy. In a world convulsed by the processes of change, this holds as true for the oligarchies that govern in the countries of the South as for those at the summit of the global power structure. At this point one can only say that the deeper one gets into the politics of inequality, the more the danger signals multiply. It is therefore appropriate to examine more intensively whether the politics of equality involve fewer risks and offer better prospects for peace and safety. Since, as we have seen, development is a fundamentally egalitarian concept, an assessment of the politics of equality should also advance our understanding of the problem of development.

Chapter 16

Sovereignty and the Global Society

Underdeveloped countries in the twentieth century bear a strong resemblance to the presently developed countries as they were two centuries ago. The resemblance becomes virtual identity in the matter of the distribution of social values or benefits. That is, in underdeveloped societies of today such values as power, wealth, education, and status are typically the monopoly of a small percentage of the total population. The same pattern of value distribution characterized the presently developed societies before they became involved in the development venture, anywhere from 100 to 200 years ago. Depending upon the particular society, the monopolizing elite constitutes 1, 3, 5, or possibly 10 percent of the total number of human beings in the society. The remaining 90-plus percent is powerless, poor, uneducated, and disregarded.

The similarity between today's societies in the global South and the societies of the North in the eighteenth and nineteenth centuries is easily understood. The politics and economics of the traditional North and of the contemporary South share the age-old characteristic of all societies prior to the Industrial Revolution: they are predominantly static. In such societies only elite minorities engage in socially significant political, economic, or intellectual activities. Since in any state there are always elites and counterelites, persons, families, and groups within these minorities may change over time. What does not change in the static society is the phenomenon of elite rule itself. Only the minority possesses the franchise in every major aspect of social life; the vast majority is, in effect, disfranchised.

The basic significance of development is that it is a process which, unless arrested, progressively extends the franchise to larger and larger sectors of the population. Extension of the franchise, in these terms, is not simply a matter of the vote. It is political in many other ways, and it is economic, educational, and psychological as well. It narrows the gap between the powerful and the weak and between the rich and the poor. Education becomes widely accessible instead of tightly restricted, and the status of citizen-participant, and hence of full membership in the community, is at least formally accorded to all and not just to a small in-group at the top of the social pyramid.

Development is therefore intrinsically a process of equalization—or democratization. But for the society as a whole it is also a process of power agglomeration, of the multiplication of wealth and intellectual resources, and of the strengthening of social allegiances. As the dynamic of equalization in a given society produces more and more people who are politically active and economically and intellectually productive— and who value the society because they feel valued by it—the cumulative power and wealth of the society itself grows at a pace undreamed of before the age of development made its first appearance in the eighteenth century. At least, this has been the history, with communist, fascist, or racist modifications, of those countries now termed developed. All developed countries have gone through some variant of the equalization process; as a consequence they have arrived at a state of power and affluence that towers above the weakness and poverty of the majority of mankind, whose societies have yet to begin, or have barely begun, the process.

The late twentieth century has thus brought about a confrontation between haves and have-nots on a global scale comparable to conditions prevailing within national or other kinds of geographically delimited societies prior to the onset of development. The developed North now plays the role of elite to the South's mass. It commands the lion's share of the world's power, wealth, and educational resources; it constitutes the global establishment, and its perquisites are comparable to those of the elites that once governed or still govern in the static and traditional territorial societies. The parallels can be graphically illustrated by reverting to the columnar models introduced in Chapter 13 and adding a time dimension (see Figure 16.1).

The magnitudes in the model can obviously be only approximate, but they do not thereby lose their power to convey reality. The estimate that 10 percent of the population constitutes the elite sector in the typical undeveloped society of the eighteenth century and in the typical underdeveloped society of the twentieth is nearer the maximum than the average. The 27 percent figure depicting the portion of the world's population (including elites in underdeveloped countries and excluding deprived groups in developed countries) having adequate or extravagant access to the values represented in the model may be slightly low. Whatever modifications a fully empirical investigation might yield, however, the model faithfully represents the radical inequality characterizing minority-majority relations in all societies before the Industrial Revolution, in all presently underdeveloped societies, and in the collectivity of human beings inhabiting the globe today.

Inequality has been a fundamental phenomenon of human history,

Figure 16.1

Distribution of Power, Wealth, Education, and Status (Crosshatched Areas)

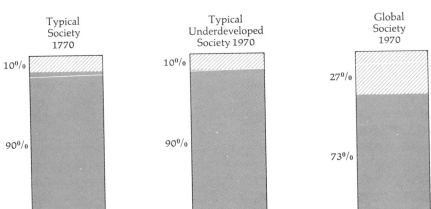

and it is common to both domestic and international society. It follows that any adequate discussion of development must consider both domestic and international distributions, or maldistributions, of human values. Most attention has so far been given to domestic inequalities, that is, to the first two columns in the model: the history of equalization in the now developed countries and the requirements for equalization in the still underdeveloped countries. Now it is time to expand on the global themes introduced in the previous chapter and symbolized by the third column: the problem of equalization in international society. We have noted resistance to development within individual societies in significant part because of its equalizing tendencies. The obstacles to equalization in the global context are far more formidable, qualitatively as well as in terms of scale. What is at stake here is nothing less than the revamping of the global power structure.

After all, every country completing the passage from underdeveloped to developed will have generated a level of power, wealth, and other resources that must necessarily augment its weight and role in the international system. When a score of countries in the South reach the point where they can be regarded as developed, a whole new set of international relationships will have emerged. On the unforeseeable day when all nations have left behind the miseries of underdevelopment, the international system will have changed beyond recognition. All will have—by the very definition of development—populations enjoying high standards of living generated by high levels of education, skills, and productivity.

Those with the largest populations and territories, in turn, would have the capacity to become superpowers. A fully developed China or India, to take the most obvious examples, would possess a capacity for civilian and military production that must necessarily outclass the productivity of the smaller populations of the United States and the

Soviet Union. Thus the outcome of development might trade old inequalities for new. At the very least, a fully developed world will radically alter present structures of international inequality.

The foregoing can hardly qualify in any exact sense as handwriting on the wall. The difficulties that beset the many paths to development make time projections, persistence of purpose, and success itself uncertain. At a minimum, however, at least a modest number of societies in the South are likely to realize enough of their development goals before the end of the century so that they can begin to play the kinds of roles in the international system that until now have largely been reserved to the countries of the North. To this extent there will have occurred something of an equalization in the global system, representing a minimum realization of global development goals.

But this minimal attainment of development goals by a few societies must necessarily take place in a world context that increasingly threatens not only the modest gains in the South but also the security and prosperity of the North. If, by the year 2000, most peoples and most societies on earth still remain far down on the development scale, it will mean that the global ratio between the poor and the rich and the weak and the strong will have reached grotesque proportions.[1] In most areas of the South multiplying populations will have strained available resources to the point of social breakdown and mass starvation.

But within this vast area of poverty and exhaustion there will be a number of societies, thousands of groups, and millions of individuals with sufficient resources to mobilize mass misery and hatred against the most obvious target: the richest and most powerful. They will be joined by allies in the North motivated by conscience or opportunism. Thus the minimally developed world of 2000 will not only be chaotic, engulfed in misery, and riven by conflict; the South will also have the means to divide the rich and powerful North and to inflict upon it grievous and perhaps irreparable injury.

A fully developed world within a generation is an impossibility. A minimally developed world is a far more realistic projection in light of present trends. But minimal development is also an intolerable outcome for both North and South. Rational policy must therefore speed up the development process, multiply the kinds of investments necessary to an accelerated effort, and aim at as high a level of development as policy and technology can achieve. If the effort must necessarily fall far short of full development, it must also far surpass the minimum if major disasters are to be avoided.

This means that rationality impels men in the direction of global equalization. By the same token, it is irrationality which deludes them

---

[1] See Chapter 13 and Appendix A.

into supposing that the status quo can be indefinitely perpetuated. If one links reason to morality, it is also evident that the perpetuation of the present distribution of values around the globe is both irrational and unjust. It follows that both reason and justice prescribe as the prime international task a massively enhanced development program that will progressively dismantle global inequalities.

SOVEREIGNTY AND INEQUALITY

But both reason and justice always need to be tested against the facts of the case. If the equalization process has met with opposition in domestic societies, it also meets with obstacles in the global context, and the nature of those obstacles must be identified and analyzed. The list is long: sovereignty, ethnocentrism (disregard for the out-group and loyalties limited to the in-group), mistrust, fear, and truculence in the face of challenge. To these must be added the general human vices of greed, shortsightedness and narrow-mindedness, preoccupation with one's own power and security, and readiness to resort to coercion rather than take the risk that one's own interests might be diminished.

Undergirding most of these resistances is the concept of the contemporary state as a limited liability enterprise, that is, a society responsible only to itself and for itself. That, as we have seen, is the meaning of sovereignty, which recognizes no will or obligation beyond what it wills itself. It may take on international obligations so long as they are judged to be consonant with its own interests, but the concept of binding obligations is inherently repugnant to the sovereign will, whose policy is to make and break obligations at its own pleasure.

Sovereignty, as the embodiment of self-sufficient and arbitrary power, excludes the concept of a more encompassing community built on foundations of mutual allegiance and obligation. Thus the sovereign state bears resemblance to the sovereign ruler within the state in the age of divine right. The absolute monarch refused to share his power with nobility, parliament, or people. Government was a matter of royal prerogative, and the political and economic destinies of the society, in theory, at least, depended not on many wills but on one. Throughout the long decline and final fall of the absolute monarchy—in England, France, Austria, and the states of Germany, in other European countries, and in the American colonies—the monarch resisted infringement of his monopoly of authoritative power. His antagonists were individuals and groups representing new political, economic, and social interests and power; they sought first a share of the monarch's authority and finally all of it.

At all stages in the process the new forces insisted that the political and economic systems of which they were part could not be governed rationally or justly—nor, most importantly, could their own interests be adequately served—by an absolutist regime based on the narrow foundations of monarchical will. They rebelled against the concept of the state as the king's realm and demanded that all articulate interests have a voice in the governing of the realm. In what was in most cases an excess of rhetoric, many asserted at various times that the sovereignty of the monarch must be transferred to the people.

The rhetoric was excessive because the prime antagonists of absolute monarchy were the new monied and educated classes whose use of the term "people" generally referred to themselves and not to the sum of all those who inhabited the realm. The predominant assumption among the bourgeoisie was that only those with property and education could be safely and fairly admitted to the governing process. Once admitted, the bulk of the propertied middle class looked upon itself as the only legitimate bearer of sovereignty. Thus a fresh struggle ensued. On one side the new parochialism of the triumphant bourgeois minority claimed for itself a monopoly of power, wealth, education, and status, thus replacing monarchical sovereignty with class sovereignty. On the other side a more spacious concept of sovereignty was embedded in the ideology of nationalism that accorded all citizens the right to participate in the political, economic, and intellectual life of the nation, a right stemming simply and solely from their status as nationals.

The ideology of nationalism, in varying forms, triumphed in all the countries now termed developed.[2] None have realized all the democratic norms implied by the national concept of an inclusive political community; some have realized very few. But in all of them the development process under the aegis of nationalism and industrialization converted elite monopolies of power, wealth, and education into mass phenomena and so gave substance to earlier doctrines of popular sovereignty. Even where governing power continues to be restricted to elites, the exercise of power nonetheless occurs within the context of a mass society whose wishes cannot be ignored with impunity as they were in the days when the mass was politically inert and simply did not count in the calculations of the governors. Mass education, mass wealth, and mass political participation—in stark contrast with the underdeveloped South—are the prime characteristics distinguishing developed from underdeveloped. They are also the characteristics that differentiate the concept of national sovereignty from the sovereignty of monarch or class.

Whether sovereignty is located in an absolute monarch, in a class oligarchy, or in the mass of the citizenry, its internal function is to secure and maintain a monopoly of power for its possessors. This monopolistic stance also characterizes the external functions of sover-

---

[2] See Chapter 7.

eignty. First, the sovereign state resists any intrusions from outside its boundaries into its domestic political, social, and economic structure. Second, as previously noted, it rejects any notion of obligation or accountability to the international system with which it coexists; international commitments are made and broken at its convenience. The essential characteristic of arbitrary will in the concept of sovereignty is thus evidenced both within and beyond the state—wherever one group claims to incorporate a sovereign will from which all others are excluded. This is the politics of disjunction, apparent alike in the gulf that isolates the absolute monarch from the people he rules and in the barriers that separate the sovereign state from other states and from the international system as a whole.

INTERNAL AND EXTERNAL SOVEREIGNTY

In the international system, of course, there is a multiplicity of sovereignties. The aspiration of one group to achieve exclusive and formal sovereignty at the global level has emerged only infrequently in history and never to the point of actually realizing an effective monopoly of global power. The imperial will, in other words, has always encountered limits beyond which it has been unable to expand either because of internal fatigue or external counterpower. While monopolistic ambitions for global power are persisting issues in both the reality and propaganda of the contemporary world, the dominant characteristic of the present international system continues to reside in a plurality of local territorial sovereignties. Each of the territorial sovereignties relies on power to defend its internal monopoly, to pursue its external interests, and, not infrequently, to contest the power and internal monopolies of other sovereignties. But historically the outcomes of these contests have never changed the fundamentally pluralistic character of the international system, and even the strongest sovereignties have not been able to establish the kind of paramountcy externally that monarch, class, or nation have been able to achieve within the state.

But too rigid a differentiation between a pluralism of sovereignties in the international system and a sovereign monopoly in domestic systems is deceptive. After all, if absolute monarchy, class rule, and the national state are characteristic of the historical development of the modern West, they are not typical of most of history nor, indeed, of most societies in the contemporary world. If all of history is taken into account, the territorial state displaying a high degree of internal cohesion and thus of uncontested sovereignty within its borders is a minority phenomenon. The majority of human societies over time have been fragmented by the internal presence of multiple power centers and of a plurality of institutions claiming allegiance from the members.

In the thousand-year history of the medieval West this phenomenon found its most dramatic expression in the struggle for supremacy between church and state and, of course, pervaded the entire structure of feudalism. Medieval societies thus bear more resemblance to the persistent pluralism of the international system than to the modern integrated Western state. This proposition is the more poignantly true for the corruption of feudalism called warlordism. And it also holds true for dozens of contemporary states where tribal, ethnic, or religious identifications contest the state's claim to supreme loyalty from its citizens.

Indeed, in more muted form the international pattern of multiple sovereignties is evident in even the most integrated and centralized societies. Domestic pressure groups, voting blocs, and power structures in the government and in the economy also play the game of internal monopolies and external exertions of power in order to pursue the goals they define. These generally competitive activities are typically carried on with a show of deference for the more encompassing goals of the domestic society as a whole. But whatever the degree of sincerity in the manifestations of deference, there are always internal pressures to make the larger society accommodate to the desires of the parochial interest group rather than the other way round.

Where such pressures are strong enough, they produce the familiar phenomenon of the state within a state: armies, parties, police organizations, trade unions, business and financial associations, and criminal groups have all exemplified this phenomenon in various contexts. This usurpation of public interest by private interest, if carried to extremes, can result in the disintegration of society to the point of civil war.

The lesson is that *all* societies operate along a continuum stretching from unity to disunity. International society can also be located along this continuum, whether one considers the global system itself or the subsystems that link states by means of alliances, blocs, regional organizations, or economic unions. The pluralism of sovereignties in the international system differs in degree, not in kind, from even the highly integrated state. In the case of loosely integrated states, the degree of variance from some international systems is frequently negative. The measure of unity achieved among the countries of the European Community, to take the most obvious example, is greater than that attained within the domestic political systems of most of the underdeveloped countries today. The NATO alliance has demonstrated a greater degree of political solidarity than has the state of Pakistan, and the governments of the Warsaw Pact powers have often been closer to one another than some of these same governments have been to their own peoples.

At the global level, nuclear weaponry, the revolution in economics and communications, the population explosion, and the growing ecological crisis are only some of the major contemporary challenges to the proposition that a plurality of sovereignties is the "natural" and immutable state of the international system. These global challenges have placed human survival in unprecedented jeopardy, and a successful response can emerge only from greater unity and less disunity in international behavior. It is therefore a matter of necessity to reject the traditional compartmentalization that divides international and domestic systems as if they constituted two essentially different kinds of politics. And in this case there is a coincidence of the necessary and the possible. The politics of both unity and disunity are products of the ever new possibilities generated by changing historical circumstances. Their dynamics cannot be confined to arbitrary categorizations eternally separating domestic from international. The history of Rome, the global expansion of the world religions, the medieval system of Europe and its destruction by the wars of religion, the French Revolution, and Marxist communism all offer irrefutable testimony to this point.

It would be neither realistic nor desirable to seek an end to the multiplicity of power centers in the global system. The prescription of both necessity and realism is a different one: to create conditions in which these many power centers are able to realize a greater sense of concert in their interactions with one another. It is a prescription, in other words, for policies that will move the global system further along the continuum, away from the politics of disunity and closer to the politics of unity. Such a movement does not require the disappearance of centers of independent decision. What it does require is the recognition of interdependence and an understanding that independence and interdependence are not mutually repugnant.

It is at this point, however, that the idea of sovereignty reenters the argument. The prescription for a politics of interdependence is unquestionably irreconcilable with the principle of sovereignty. The arbitrary will of sovereign monarch, class, or state is, by definition, unable to build larger political structures in which it becomes one of the interdependent parts in a system designed for mutual benefit. It must necessarily repel potential partners in such an enterprise because it cannot accept the common obligations that flow from interdependence. It follows that an international politics of interdependence requires a dilution of state sovereignty in the same way that monarchical sovereignty and class sovereignty yielded up their monopolies of governing power in the process of building the nation-state.

Lest the prescription for a politics of interdependence at the international level appear too formidable in its requirements, it should be stressed that what the sovereign monarch and the sovereign class yielded up was a *monopoly* of power. Their characteristic fate was not one of instant powerlessness; they simply had to reconcile themselves to a new situation in which their share of the available power was no longer close to 100 percent. This relative decline in power, at the same time, meant that they had to accept restraints on the considerable power remaining to them, because the amount of power in the hands of the newcomers made it prudent to do so. The new power relationships, in turn, joined the new economic and social enterprises characterizing a developing society to form the foundations for a set of mutual obligations. These obligations were honored to the extent that the new partnership proved mutually beneficial.

So far the argument has sought to dismantle the conceptual barriers between international and domestic politics. The international system is characterized by a multiplicity of sovereignties, but the sovereign stance is sometimes significantly modified by cooperative undertakings, such as the Common Market. Far more often, of course, it is undermined or negated by stronger sovereigns converting weaker sovereigns into vassals or parts of imperial systems. These kinds of operations are also observable in domestic political systems. Cooperative undertakings among economic groupings or political blocs[3] are pursued alongside efforts to control, annex, or suppress weaker companies, unions, or political factions.

In highly integrated nation-states common laws, common government, and common or overlapping interests tend to mute the conflict relationships and enhance opportunities for cooperative solution—but this has by no means been a uniform tendency. As we have seen, the highly integrated society is a historical rarity; in most societies the internal plurality of power centers has usually blocked the creation of bonds that could unite all or almost all people living on a given territory in a common allegiance. These kinds of domestic political patterns approximate far more closely the divisions of international politics; where they disintegrate into civil war, the struggle often exceeds in ferocity any but the most major international conflicts of history.

There is, then, an interchangeability of parts and behavior between international and domestic politics which demonstrates that their essential dynamics are identical. The identity becomes still more striking in the concept of sovereignty itself which, in both its internal and external manifestations, claims a monopoly in the exercise of power. Sovereign monarch or sovereign class excludes the rest of the population from sharing in the governance of the realm and defends its internal monopoly against all comers from abroad. Theoretically, the sovereign nation dissolves internal governing monopolies but asserts its own territorial omnipotence against the rest of the world. In all these instances of the exercise of sovereign power the common theme is political exclusivity: the contention that no other parties in society, whether domestic or international, have a right to trespass on the province that the governors have reserved for themselves. In the profoundest sense of the word, sovereign government is provincial government.

---

[3] Often called coalition politics, thus lending stress to the parallel with alliance, or coalition, politics in the international arena.

Sovereignty is not necessarily an evil. On the contrary, it has provided indispensable political services by giving form to content in the building of viable societies. But it must necessarily be obstructive when social forces emerge that make viability dependent on building more spacious and more cosmopolitan political communities. Whether the new forces are internal or external to the society, they press for a departure from the old patterns of exercising power. In each case the established sovereign will resist, and conflicts of varying intensity must ensue. For the first time in history, these kinds of conflicts have taken on global dimensions. In the ancient struggle between narrower and wider concepts of political community, the modern state has now become the province—and the cosmopolis is the earth itself.

At the outset of this chapter, comparisons were drawn between the typical eighteenth-century society, the typical underdeveloped society of the twentieth century, and then the contemporary global society. The similarity of their political, economic, and social structures provides insight into the nature of the current struggle between province and cosmopolis. It is once again the struggle for a redistribution of power, wealth, education, and status. Redistribution can be sought by the now intolerably dangerous methods of violence in which one's gain is another's loss—or the loss of all. Or it can be sought by attempting to build a community, transcending but not necessarily obliterating the state, in which there would be joint gains for all parties. As we have seen in previous chapters, the model for this latter course of action is the process that has produced the modern developed state. And central to this model was the presence of forces whose interests lay in transforming the old and narrower political and economic structure into a new and broader one.

In order to assess the possible outcome of the current international struggle for redistribution, one must seek answers to questions analogous to those raised by the historian of domestic development. What social forces feel cramped in the existing system of territorial societies? Which have already expanded beyond the confines of the sovereign state? What are the potentials for further expansion? What are the resistances to this expansion? In short, what are the strengths of the forces of provincialism and the forces of cosmopolitanism? The short answer is that both are very strong but that the sovereign province remains clearly dominant. Still, the evidence reveals a multiplicity of forces at work in the world today that have already brought about a whole series of mergers joining the life of international and domestic societies. Their cumulative effect, as we shall see, can only be termed momentous.

Chapter 17

The Transnational
Economy

Of all the tangible forces joining human beings together in a global network of interdependence, the strongest by far is the quest for wealth. A lowering nuclear presence threatens mankind with a common and ultimate fate; but in the immediate world it is the unprecedented surge of human economic activity since World War II which is the chief architect of transnational unities. This is the dynamic that daily elaborates an increasingly complex and world-spanning maze of wealth relationships from which no country or individual can exit.

From the beginning of history the urge for riches has been a crucial factor in the building, and destroying, of territorial societies. At the same time, it has constantly driven men beyond the confines of these societies so that the annals of economics typically reveal the double entry of local enterprise and distant transactions. Until recently, the volume of business registered under these two entries (measured in terms of total world economic activity) was overwhelmingly greater in the local sector. But the Industrial Revolution inaugurated a qualitative change in the relationships between domestic and foreign economics. Not only did foreign enterprise increase as a percentage of domestic economic activity, but the growth in its absolute volume introduced a new phenomenon in international life. As industrialization-development began to create mass economies in the societies of the West, their economic relations with the rest of the world also began to be massive.

If the money value of imports and exports typically continued to be far less than that of domestic production, a steadily growing portion of production and consumption in the mass economies became directly or indirectly dependent on foreign supply and demand. In the rest of the world still untouched by development, the needs of the mass societies of the West (or North) stimulated the growth of narrowly based export economies. Colonies or not, the countries of the South provided agricultural and industrial raw materials for processing and consumption in the burgeoning North on terms that proved disastrous for their own prospects for growth.

What economic dynamism the South developed was attracted or coerced into the export sector. The result was that industrial and commercial growth remained confined to enclaves, usually port and capital cities, while the mass of population continued to live in the traditional world of the static, subsistence economy. Both North and South, then, became more and more involved with each other in international economic relationships. Here, as in the political, military, and technological contexts, it was once again an involvement of strength with weakness—with most of the benefits going to the strong.

THE INTERNATIONAL MOVEMENT OF GOODS

Whatever the distribution of benefits, the unprecedented expansion of international economic activity in the last two centuries has connected the countries of the world into a global economic system. Moreover, the pace of expansion in the earlier stages has been overshadowed by the spectacular acceleration marking the later stages. Marx's dramatic evocation in the Communist Manifesto of bourgeois enterprise penetrating every corner of the earth is only a tale of pygmies compared with the explosive growth of the international economy in succeeding generations. In the seventy-year period from 1880 to 1950, for example, there was approximately an 800 percent increase in the money volume of world exports. In just twenty additional years (from 1950 to 1970) volume soared to 600 percent of the 1950 level. Thus the increase in world export money volume over the entire period from 1880 to 1970 approximated 4400 percent.[1] Even when these figures are discounted by rising prices, it is evident that a growth of extraordinary proportions has occurred. It is still more evident that in the period since World War II international trade has accelerated its growth to the proportions of a full-fledged economic giant.

[1] Monetary values of world trade in the years selected for comparison are as follows:

	1880	1950	1970
Exports	$7,042,000,000	$55,400,000,000	$309,400,000,000
Imports	$8,162,000,000	$58,200,000,000	$324,800,000,000

(The 1950 figures do not include communist countries. The 1970 figures do not include Mainland China, North Korea, North Vietnam, Mongolia or Albania.) See Appendix G for sources of data and for a more comprehensive record of the growth of world trade from 1867 through 1971.

The International Monetary Fund reported that world trade volume in the first quarter of 1973 had risen to the equivalent of an annual rate of trade of $429.2 billion. This boom figure represents a 24 percent increase over 1972, well above any depreciating allowances that must be made for inflation factors. (*New York Times*, September 4, 1973.)

In absolute figures, the world's total exports in 1970 were valued at nearly $310 billion and imports at nearly $325 billion. The export figures alone are equivalent to nearly 10 percent of the total goods and services produced around the globe in the same year. When they are measured against comparable figures of an earlier period, the growing importance of the world's trade to the world's economy is manifest. In 1938 world exports were valued at $13.4 billion and world imports at $14.3 billion; exports alone then comprised barely 4.6 percent of the world's production of goods and services.[2]

The far lower ratio of exports to world income reflects the economic nationalism that marked the policies of the industrialized countries after World War I—and particularly after 1929, when each sought refuge from world-wide depression behind protectionist barriers with the consequence that the volume of world trade plummeted. But it also reflects only a dip in the 200-year growth curve of international trade and only a low plateau before the steep rise of the postwar years, in which the actual volume of commodities traded internationally as well as their monetary value has been doubling roughly every decade.

The message of these statistics is that the countries of the world are dealing today with an international economic entity of unprecedented magnitude. They are profiting by it as never before; by the same token, they have become dependent upon it as never before. The only rational conclusion must be that they have a major stake in its continued expansion and that any repetition of the restrictive economic nationalism of the interwar period must have far more disastrous effects today. Rationality in the quest for wealth therefore requires a commitment to an increasing global economic interdependence, which, in turn, must put increasing pressure on the concept of national economic sovereignty. As we shall see, however, the rapid growth of the international economy has generated mounting counterpressures that may make it difficult for rationality to prevail.

In a process where nations are annually doing hundreds of billions of dollars worth of business with one another, cooperative decisions are essential. The postwar emergence of such institutions as the International Monetary Fund (IMF), the General Agreement on Tariffs and Trade (GATT), and the International Bank for Reconstruction and

---

[2] League of Nations, *Review of World Trade 1938* (Geneva, 1939), p. 8. The export percentage of gross world product is based on a 1938 world income estimate of $260 billion. See W. S. and E. S. Woytinsky, *World Population and Production: Trends and Outlook* (New York: Twentieth Century Fund, 1953), p. 393. A 10 percent increase has been added to the estimated world income figure. This a standard differential between national income and GNP—in this case world income and GWP—magnitudes. (Export-import figures and the world income estimate are expressed in terms of gold dollars.)

Development (IBRD, also known as the World Bank) testifies to growing recognition of the need for international economic cooperation. Considered individually and together, these and other international institutions have registered many significant accomplishments. But their functions and authority constitute only a beginning phase in the building of a fully collaborative decision-making structure that could nurture, regulate, and expand international economic exchange.

Meanwhile, the existing institutions themselves have exhibited serious shortcomings in their efforts to cope with rapid change. Most of these shortcomings can be traced to the fact that there is far more chaos than order in the world's burgeoning economic life. It is a situation which derives in turn from a still more fundamental reality: in international economics, as in international politics, decisions continue to be made primarily from the perspective of the national parts rather than from the perspective of the global whole.

GATT is the best-known contemporary example of an institution designed to further international economic cooperation. Founded in 1947 by agreement of twenty-three countries, its membership had grown to seventy-seven countries by 1970.[3] Yet this means that more than sixty countries remained nonsignatories, including the Soviet bloc and many from the underdeveloped world. GATT's major purpose is to reduce trade barriers among member countries and in the world at large, and it has had some impressive successes. Undoubtedly the most impressive was the Kennedy Round, the sixth in a series of general tariff negotiations since GATT's founding. In response to a previous initiative of President Kennedy, more than fifty countries began negotiations in 1964 which lasted into 1967. When the agreements were signed, the negotiators had committed themselves to tariff reductions approximating 35 percent on more than 6,000 products, mainly manufactured goods. The reductions took effect during the period from 1968 to 1972.

The Kennedy Round was thus a major step forward in international cooperation to achieve freer trade and therefore a greater volume of trade at lower prices. Nevertheless, the result fell short of the original goal of a 50 percent across-the-board cut, and tariffs on such key commodities as steel, textiles, and foodstuffs were left virtually untouched. Also, since the Kennedy Round reductions applied mainly to the more sophisticated manufactured products, the underdeveloped countries derived few benefits from the agreements. Indeed, by facilitating trade among the industrial countries the Kennedy Round has accelerated the long-term decline in the underdeveloped countries' share of total world trade.

---

[3] At that time fourteen additional countries were operating according to GATT's rules on a de facto basis.

Moreover, although GATT has competence to deal with nontariff restrictions on trade, negotiations under its auspices have largely been confined to tariff issues. Nontariff restraints on trade constitute a formidable list: import quotas, unilateral export controls, bilateral agreements to limit exports, restrictive import licenses, currency exchange controls, credit restrictions on traders, and customs legislation that values specified imports above the exporter's price and thus subjects them to correspondingly higher duties. To these must be added governmental purchasing policies that discriminate against foreign goods and services in favor of domestic suppliers and government subsidies of domestic producers, exporters, and shippers. Antidumping legislation can serve as another restraint on trade. Overtly directed against the unfair trade practice of deliberately flooding the importing country with commodities at below-cost prices, antidumping restrictions often function covertly as techniques for stifling foreign competition.

Nor is this the end of the list; it also includes domestic price controls depressing the price of imported commodities below the level of international market prices, domestic excise taxes imposed on specified imported items after they have already passed customs, and various kinds of regulations involving public health, packaging, or weight and measurement standards that often interfere unjustifiably with trading activity.[4]

There are other and still more intricate techniques in use that can be as effective as tariffs in restraining world trade. Thus there remains a tangled accumulation of both tariff and nontariff hindrances to freer international economic exchange. They owe their origin and persistence, for the most part, to the fact that important segments of business, labor, and agriculture in the several nations have perceived and often realized economic gains from protectionist policies.

Without probing the past and present arguments of those who have benefited from restaints on international trade, it must suffice to say that tariffs and other protectionist devices have, in fact, often served larger economic and social purposes than simply private profit. But it must also be said that the only legitimate rationale for governmental interference with the flow of commerce is public and not private interest and that departures from this rationale have been frequent and frequently harmful to the economic life of both individual societies and international society as a whole.

---

[4] The material in this paragraph and in the two preceding it is drawn from Karen Bivens, "After the Kennedy Round: Outlook for World-wide Trade Liberalization," National Industrial Conference Board Research Report (New York, 1968), and Committee for Economic Development, "Nontariff Distortions of Trade" (New York: CED, September 1969).

Reference to the concept of public interest in economic matters reintroduces the issue of which public shall be served. Prior to World War II the answer was virtually unambiguous: the public interest was assumed to be the national interest. John Maynard Keynes was one of a very few to point in the direction of a larger public interest arising from the fact that nations, and major trading nations in particular, share a mutual interest in one another's prosperity. Keynes said, in effect, that national economies which are efficient and prosperous internally are the best of partners in international trade. This is because they will be exporters of desirable goods at desirable prices and, at the same time, the most affluent customers for imports.

The validity of this commonsense insight was documented in the actual patterns of world trading long before Keynes articulated it. But those in the mercantilist tradition of economic nationalism clung to the illusion that internal prosperity and a favorable balance of external trade for one's own state are the only really meaningful guides to policy making. The parallels with equally provincial approaches to military security and to the political and social viability of the state are obvious.

In the interwar years all the major trading nations attempted to insulate themselves from the world market and the world economy, with the result that their domestic economic positions only became more critical. This was the experience that moved them to incorporate Keynes' insight into their postwar policies. The stake of each in the prosperity of all has as its corollary the venerable free trade doctrine of comparative advantage: that maximum benefits for all members of the system flow from a division of labor in which each concentrates production in those areas where it can produce more efficiently and cheaply than any other member of the system. The necessary companion proposition, of course, is that each must have unhindered access to the markets and the produce of all the others. Taken together, the Keynesian and free trade doctrines add up to a momentous thesis and prescription: there are no theoretical differences between rationality in domestic economics and rationality in international economies, and the political barricades separating the two should therefore be pulled down.

International free trade has been a subject for hot debate ever since Adam Smith. The most durable and telling point for the negative position is that it favors the stronger and disadvantages the weaker members of the system. Should a government or an entrepreneur want to establish a new industry that might eventually perform in accord with the principle of comparative advantage, for a given time its products are not likely to be able to compete—at home or abroad—in price or quality with comparable products of a long-established industry in another country. In this situation a government is under enormous pressure to build a tariff wall to protect the fledgling enterprise.

Infant industry is the classic name for such an enterprise. Linked historically to the names of Alexander Hamilton and Friedrich List, the term has figured prominently in the policies of almost all the great trading nations of the West. The United States, France, and Germany, for example, each resorted to the tariff to protect the growth of its own industrial and trading base. The defense of the industrial infants was directed primarily against the superior competitive position of Britain which, as the first to industrialize, was also—not surprisingly—the foremost advocate of free trade. Today the infant industry argument is heard most persistently in the underdeveloped countries as they, too, seek to develop industries that cannot now, but may eventually, be competitive.

The problem of competitive weakness reappears at the other end of the development process in what could be called industrial geriatrics. Coal, steel, ship building, and textiles in one or more developed countries have been in this state of superannuation for some time. Suffering from varying combinations of obsolescent plant and equipment, high-priced labor, unenterprising management and merchandising, inadequate financing, and deterioration in raw material supply, they are no more equipped to meet the challenge of efficient foreign competitors than is the infant industry.

Once again government is under pressure to raise tariffs, or to employ other protectionist techniques, in order to save a long-established industry whose production in the past may have contributed significantly to the growth of the national economy and that may still be providing tens of thousands of jobs for unionized workers. The protectionist arguments of such an industry are reinforced to the extent that it can claim a relationship to the needs of national defense—and there are few branches of industry, or agriculture, that have not made, or could not make, that claim plausible.

The problems of infant and superannuated industries provide only an indication of the range of issues that beset the doctrine of international free trade. Enough has been said, however, so that it should be evident that they reflect on the world scale the same kinds of problems that plague the internal economic life of industrial nations. Free trade versus protectionism confront one another both within and among nations.

This is particularly true in the case of the United States, which for more than a century has been the most dynamic and fast-changing of all industrial economies. The American South, of course, long remained a static economic appendage of the dynamic North. As it began to recover from the Civil War, however, it launched its own infant industries, attracting Northern capital with its major asset: cheap labor. Since the Constitution forbids internal tariffs (as do all modern industrial states), Southern entrepreneurs turned to nontariff devices in the form of subsidies from local and state governments and finally from Washington to protect themselves from Northern competition. Once Southern industrial viability was established, however, the problem of protection began to shift to the counterpart industries of the North. The textile and shoe industries of New England provide classic examples: old mills and factories with old equipment, an aging and relatively expensive unionized work force, and old ways of doing things were the tell-tale signs of senescence.

Firms left New England for the South, shut down or curbed production, or went bankrupt. In the struggle for survival they, too, went the subsidy route in the form of tax easements from local and state governments. The federal government contributed its share with defense contracts and capital funding to permit diversification of production and, later, the retraining of labor. These and other measures have registered both successes and failures, but the long-range effect of all these developments is that textiles and shoes in the one-time center of American production of these commodities have become residual industries.

The next chapter in the story of comparative advantage in fabrics and footwear returns us to the international economy. New areas of industrialization with new sources of cheap labor have emerged around the world: notably, Japan,[5] Korea, Taiwan, Hong Kong, Singapore, Mexico, and some of the Mediterranean countries of Europe. National tariffs and other protectionist devices have displaced sectional subsidies as the chief bone of contention in the conflict between free enterprise and protection which has for so long characterized the American shoe and textile industries. Early in the 1970s, pressure for higher tariffs from American producers of these particular commodities became the first major internal challenge to the postwar American commitment to freer international trade.

At the same time, production itself was once again migrating—this time not to the American South but to the new cheap labor areas abroad. The proliferation in these areas of shoe and textile factories, wholly or partially American-owned, or licensed to use American-developed technology at amply profitable royalty fees, repeats and magnifies the earlier lesson of New England and the South: the superior mobility of capital as compared with labor. The result is to stimulate high-tariff sentiment among American unions in these industries and in others similarly affected. On the other hand, American capital, to the extent that it is involved in production abroad, tends to take a low-tariff position—with the proviso that imports do not significantly depress the internal American price structure.

---

[5] Japan's status as a low wage economy has been changing rapidly since the mid-1960s.

THE INTERNATIONALIZATION OF ENTERPRISE

It is evident that the issues surrounding the production of shoes and textiles extend far beyond the realm of trade and protectionist techniques, whether internal or international. The same is true of virtually every other branch of modern industry. Mobility of capital, the capacity to build new or relocate established industries, and the migration of technology and management skills play an ever greater role as the industrial economies grow steadily more complex.

Observable in the early stages of industrialization largely within the confines of the domestic society, expanding or migrating industries nevertheless spilled across the boundaries of the home state and into foreign areas from the beginning of the industrial era. These international businesses were, in part, continuations of the earlier investments and colonial enterprises of the mercantile age. By the beginning of the twentieth century they had become very visible on the international scene. But only since World War II have they assumed a role of major proportions in the world's production and trade. Only since then did the internationalization of enterprise reach the takeoff stage, a stage symbolized by, but not confined to, the rise of the multinational corporation.

It should be stressed from the outset that the migration of enterprise is the product of a multiplicity of causes. If cheap labor has been a major lure in the ongoing relocation of the American shoe and textile industries, it is only one component in the more basic calculation of the profit margin, existing somewhere between the costs of production and the return on sales. Multinational corporations seek out both low-cost labor areas and expanding markets, but most of their energy is now spent in pursuing the latter objective. The large majority of wholly or partially owned subsidiaries are established abroad in order to produce goods for the market of the host country unhindered by tariffs and other impediments to competitive pricing that these same goods would face if they were export items in international trade.

Getting inside the tariff wall has been a particularly strong motivation in the expansion of American industries into Canada and Western Europe.[6] These two areas constitute the world's most affluent consumer market outside the United States itself. It is no coincidence that approximately two-thirds of total American investment abroad is located in this market. In the late 1960s, Japan, responding to both external and internal pressures, began a staged relaxation of its previously strict limitations on the importation of capital. The result was that American and

---

[6] A far higher percentage of American investment has gone into production for markets in Europe than for markets in Canada since a significant portion of American capital in Canada is invested in the production of raw materials for export. And Canada, of course, constitutes a much smaller aggregate of consumers.

other foreign enterprises promptly stepped up their investments as a means of getting a larger share of the booming Japanese internal market. The move was once again predicated on the assumption that goods will be more profitably produced and marketed in Japan than produced abroad and exported to Japan.

Establishing subsidiaries or buying into the management of ongoing enterprises abroad has another signal advantage for the multinational corporation or the multinational investor. Decisions concerning product design, manufacturing schedules, merchandising, and other key operations can be made within the country or region to be supplied. They can therefore be responsive to the demands of the specific market to a degree unattainable where some or all of these activities are carried on at a distance within the borders of an exporting country. In addition, when the multinational company disposes of advanced technology or managerial skills developed in the home country, its subsidiaries abroad can import them to the benefit of their competitive position. These assets, along with unrivaled financial strength and expertise in large-scale organization, have been the particular strengths of American corporations operating abroad. The American advantages are often resented; on the other hand, they are also often emulated and welcomed as stimulants to greater prosperity, dynamism, and efficiency in the host economy.

The attractions of multinational business operations are clearly reflected in the spectacular increase in the volume of private international capital flow since World War II. With approximately 500 major companies engaged in overseas operations, the United States alone accounts for well over half the volume. In the twenty-year period from 1950 to 1970 the book value of all American private investment abroad increased by 600 percent: from $19.9 billion in 1950 to $119.4 billion in 1970. During the same period the book value of direct foreign investment by United States companies increased almost 700 percent, from $11.8 billion to $77.2 billion.[7]

These figures reveal a colossal expansion of American corporate and

---

[7] *Federal Reserve Bulletin* (April 1971), p. 280. *Market* value is the presumed worth of assets held were they to be sold at the time the value is estimated. *Book* value is the original purchase price of the assets less depreciation. In a rising market, therefore, book value is almost always considerably lower than market value. In a declining market the reverse relationship often asserts itself. *Direct* investment could be likened to active investment. That is, the investor allocates capital in order to build plant and equipment and to hire personnel and build an organization to produce goods and services for the market. *Indirect* investment is more passive; it is the purchase of stocks or bonds in enterprises managed and controlled by others. The two together constitute the sum of investment assets in any given context.

financial activity abroad, but it is important to add that the other non-communist developed countries have also played a significant role in the burgeoning growth of foreign investment. In 1966 the book value of direct foreign investment around the world had reached approximately $90 billion, of which the United States accounted for about $55 billion; the remaining $35 billion had its origin primarily in Western Europe, but Canada, Japan, Australia, and New Zealand also contributed to the total.[8]

The full significance of the growth in international investment becomes apparent only when it is recalled that investment generates productivity. By a standard calculation, a direct investment will annually produce goods or services worth twice its book value.[9] Hence if, over the years, the accumulated book value of American direct investments abroad reached $77 billion by 1970, those same investments would be producing in that single year some $154 billion worth of goods and services. As for indirect investment ($42.2 billion in 1970), Polk estimated the ratio between the book value of indirect investment and annual production value at 1:1. Applying Polk's estimates to both direct and indirect investment, one arrives at a figure of nearly $200 billion worth of goods and services being produced in 1970 by American investment abroad.

Polk also calculated (for the previous year) that production around the world attributable to direct and indirect international investment from all investing countries was about $400 billion.[10] This was twice the size of the 1969 GNP of any single country on earth except for the supereconomies of the Soviet Union and the United States. The nearly $200 billion worth of goods and services generated just by American investments abroad in 1970 is itself equal to 20 percent of the 1970 United States GNP. It is evident that the international economy has provided the supports for a massive extension of the American economy; the same is true, on a smaller scale, for the other investing countries.

It is also now evident that the spectacular growth of international trade which we observed earlier is overshadowed by the still more spectacular growth of international investment. This is particularly true for the United States. One need only compare the $200 billion product of American foreign investment with the 1970 value of American exports:

---

[8] Sidney E. Rolfe, *The Multinational Corporation* (New York: Foreign Policy Association, 1970), pp. 27–32.

[9] See Judd Polk, "The Rise of World Corporations," *Saturday Review* (November 22, 1969).

[10] Polk's figures and estimates may be found in ibid, and in his article "The New World Economy," *Columbia Journal of World Business* 3, 1 (January–February 1968).

$42 billion. The comparison demonstrates that American enterprise abroad is producing and marketing five times the value of the goods and services it is producing at home and exporting abroad. This ratio is sharply reduced if the focus is shifted to total international investment and total world exports: approximately $400 billion worth of output from all international investments in 1969 as against the world export total of $311 billion in 1970. But whether the reference point is the United States, the industrial nations of the West as a group, or the world economy as a whole, it is apparent that for the first time in history trade has taken second place to investment in the dynamics of these economies. As Polk puts it: "In place of the old order of national producers and international traders we now have international producing facilities as the most important link between national economies."[11]

By one standard, there were in 1970 some 150 major "international producing facilities" operating around the world.[12] The European companies account for roughly half this number and include such immense complexes as Imperial Chemical and Leyland Motors in England, Volkswagen and Bayer in Germany, Michelin and Renault in France, Montecatini-Edison and Olivetti in Italy, and Shell Unilever in the Netherlands. As for the United States, the list reads like a Wall Street register of blue chip securities. It is manifest that the larger the corporation, the more likely it is to have become an "international producing facility"—though the total investment by smaller companies in international operations is also very large.

The proliferation of international production facilities, paced by those

---

[11] "The Rise of the World Corporation," p. 34.

[12] Rolfe, *The Multinational Corporation*, p. 34: "If we accept an arbitrary definition that a multinational company is one with six or more producing plants in other countries, then some 62 American companies and 49 non-American companies fall into this category. If by multinational we mean a company in which 25 percent or more of its earnings, assets, employment or sales (excluding exports) is in countries other than its origin, then . . . the United States has about 75 to 80 companies in this category . . . [and] Europe appears to have about 75."

For a listing of individual multinational companies and more specific data concerning their activities, see Professor Rolfe's article "The International Corporation in Perspective," in Sidney E. Rolfe and Walter Damm (eds.), *The Multinational Corporation in the World Economy* (New York: Praeger, 1970).

Using different criteria, Raymond Vernon identifies 187 American companies as multinational corporations. He documents their spectacular growth by enumerating the foreign manufacturing subsidiaries of these companies over time:

1901:	47	1939:	715
1913:	116	1950:	988
1919:	180	1959:	1891
1929:	467	1967:	3646

See Raymond Vernon, *Sovereignty at Bay: The Multinational Spread of U.S. Enterprises* (New York: Basic Books, 1971), p. 62.

based in the United States, explains why, by 1968, the big three of the American automobile industry accounted for 15 percent of all auto production in France, 30 percent in Germany, and nearly 50 percent in Britain. In 1971, after the lowering of Japanese investment barriers, Chrysler, General Motors, and Ford in sequence bought into the Japanese automobile industry as well.[13] An incomplete 1965 statistical listing shows seven American corporations registering more than 50 percent of their sales abroad and forty-five between 25 percent and 50 percent. Among companies from this same list, the percentage of corporate assets of fifty-eight companies held abroad ranged from 20 percent to 64 percent. Eight employed more personnel abroad than at home; for an additional fifteen, foreign operations accounted for from 20 percent to 50 percent of the total payroll.[14]

As the head of one multinational corporation observed:

> In these circumstances, the company finds it has not just grown—it has been transformed. In making direct investments abroad, it has become multinational. In such a situation, though the headquarters of the company is in the United States and though it has the large U.S. market at hand, it must now be organized as a world enterprise. The company's assets and efforts must now be managed multinationally, in accordance with market opportunities wherever they may be.[15]

These sentiments were strongly seconded in 1972 by William Spencer, president of the First National City Corporation with banking operations in ninety countries and stockholders in sixty-three: "The political boundaries of nation states are too narrow and constricted to define the scope and sweep of modern business." Mr. Spencer called businessmen "the new globalists" who "see the entire world as a market and as a site for the production of goods and services."[16]

The chairman of the board of Dow Chemical Company pushed the logic of multinational enterprise a few steps further at a White House Conference in 1972:

> We appear to be moving strongly in the direction of what will not be really multinational or international companies as we know them today, but what

---

[13] *New York Times*, October 1, 1968, and June 12 and July 17, 1971. In 1973, Chrysler Corporation introduced to the American market its Japanese-made Dodge Colt.

[14] Rolfe and Damm, *The Multinational Corporation in the World Economy*, pp. 18–19.

[15] John J. Powers, Jr. (President of Charles Pfizer & Co.), "The Multinational Company," address to the Manufacturing Chemists' Association (New York, November 2, 1967).

[16] *New York Times*, October 25, 1972.

we might call "anational" companies—companies without any nationality, belonging to all nationalities.

. . . I have long dreamed of buying an island owned by no nation, and of establishing the World Headquarters of the Dow company on the truly neutral ground of such an island, beholden to no nation or society . . .[17]

One inevitable result of this trend toward internationalization is that larger and larger percentages of profits are earned outside the corporation's home country. In 1970, for the first time, IBM's international profits exceeded its domestic profits. The foreign earnings of Standard Oil of New Jersey (now Exxon) have exceeded domestic earnings for some time. During the decade from 1961 to 1970 only once, in 1969, was the earnings distribution reversed. Total earnings in 1970 were $1.310 billion, foreign and domestic operations accounting for 52 percent and 48 percent, respectively.[18] The 1965 list in Rolfe and Damm identifies thirteen major American corporations deriving more than half their earnings from abroad. No less than another thirty-two realized between 25 percent and 50 percent of their total profits from their international operations.[19]

The increasing internationalization of corporate investment, employment, production, sales, and profits has made a major contribution to the world's productivity. If the calculation is correct that production generated by total international investment in 1970 approximated $400 billion, then it also accounted for about 12.5 percent of the gross world product. If one adds the 1970 total of world exports (less 20 percent to allow for duplications), the sum of international production and international trade constitutes approximately one-fifth of all goods and services produced annually around the world.

Thus the long static ratio between local and global enterprise has been drastically altered. If current trade and investment trends persist, by the year 2000 the ratio will have been reversed and the world's economy will have become more than half internationalized.[20] Should this degree of fusion in local and global economic life actually be reached, the functions of nation-states and the lives of their citizens are bound to be profoundly altered. The historic dominance of the territorial society in defining the terms of livelihood for its members will be at an end. In its place will be a global network of investment, production, and

---

[17] Charles A. Gerstacker at the White House Conference on the Industrial World Ahead (Washington, D.C., February 7–9, 1972).

[18] For details on IBM's status, see *New York Times*, January 16, 1971. Figures for Standard Oil are taken from Standard Oil Company (New Jersey) Annual Reports for 1961–1970, New York.

[19] Rolfe and Damm, *The Multinational Corporation in the World Economy*.

[20] Polk, "The Rise of World Corporations."

marketing in which territorial societies can maintain prosperity and autonomy only if they are able to respond creatively to a wholly new economic environment. Such an outcome would duplicate, on a global scale, the experience in national development since the eighteenth century that linked rural areas, cities, agriculture, and industry into an integrated national economy.

But where there are trends there are also countertrends. A globally integrated economy is only in its beginning stages, and there are formidable barriers in the way of its further progress. The multinational corporation, in particular the American corporation, has functioned as the leading edge in this progress. It is also in particular the experience of American multinationals which has revealed the difficulties of economic internationalization in a world which continues to be organized politically in accordance with the premises of national sovereignty.

Specifically, as Chapter 19 will demonstrate, American foreign investment has contributed powerfully to the growing instability of the world monetary system. The outflow of American investment dollars has joined American governmental expenditures abroad and domestic inflation to produce a glut of American currency on international money markets. The result has been the crisis devaluations of the dollar in 1971 and 1973 that brought to a climax the rising balance of payments difficulties the United States began to experience in the mid-1960s.

Reserving discussion of more technical considerations until Chapter 19, it can be said at this point that the very massiveness of American corporate enterprise abroad has helped to create a situation in which it must cope with a shrinkage of its liquid dollar assets through inflation and devaluation. As long as the value of the dollar and other currencies remains uncertain and subject to major fluctuations, the multinationals must also cope with international monetary speculation, in part by themselves engaging in speculation and thus creating further instability. What the multinationals do with their huge pools of dollars has a powerful effect on the financial positions of both their host countries and the United States. Pressures to restrict the multinationals' freedom of action are the unavoidable consequence.

Similar pressures are in evidence within the United States itself. The Johnson administration imposed moderate limits on foreign investment activities which, in diluted form, were still operative in 1973. But much more intense pressures have been generated by American labor as the issue of "exporting jobs" has spread from textiles and shoes to other industries. In 1972 the AFL-CIO Council endorsed the Hartke-Burke bill,[21] which seeks to protect American industry and jobs from foreign

---

[21] The bill was introduced in Congress as The Foreign Trade and Investment Act of 1972 by Senator Vance Hartke of Indiana and Representative William Burke of Massachusetts.

competition by restricting both imports and American corporate activity abroad. Whether or not the legislation is passed in original or modified form, it is symptomatic of the hostility that the new transnational economy has provoked among those who are tied to the inherited national economic systems.

The Nixon administration's decision in 1973 to propose comprehensive trade legislation permitting the President to "raise as well as lower tariffs" was a still more telling symptom. By 1973 it was clear that international trade, investment, and monetary institutions were in the process of major change. The spectacular growth of the international economy may be due for at least a short-term setback. Even should there be a leveling off in the rate of economic internationalization, however, it is already true that hundreds of millions of people, hundreds of corporations, and scores of governments are profoundly dependent on the efficient functioning of the transnational sector of the world's economy. Among them are to be found some of the major forces at work loosening the constraints of the nation-state system—as their entrepreneurial and governmental predecessors once loosened the internal rigidities of feudal, monarchical, and class structures.

THE INTERNATIONAL MOVEMENT OF PEOPLE

The unprecedented acceleration in the flow of capital and goods in the contemporary world has also stimulated the movement of labor. We have already noted the superior mobility of capital and the constraints that will always set limits on labor mobility. Yet economic pressures and opportunities, rapid communications and transport, and human venturesomeness and need have combined to produce a more mobile labor force than any in previous history. This mobility is most evident, of course, within the confines of the domestic society. The United States leads the world in people ready and able to move to new places of work, a leadership that is the product of the general rule that the higher the level of industrialization and technology, the greater the mobility of the internal work force.

But the work force crossing international borders has also become massive.[22] Here the European Economic Community holds the lead, both in numbers of foreign workers and in the historic decision to dis-

---

[22] The millions of political refugees since World War II are not included in this account. In their great majority, they have been forced to change their residence from one country to another, often with agonizing delays; once settled in the new country, they are no longer mobile in an international sense.

mantle national barriers to the flow of labor. In accordance with the sequential commitments undertaken in the Treaty of Rome, citizens of the member nations may now seek employment in any part of the Common Market on the same terms and with the same rights as nationals of the member country where employment is offered. This has contributed importantly to a Europeanization of the labor market for relatively small but still significant numbers of highly skilled and middle-level personnel and for masses of semiskilled and unskilled labor.

In the Common Market, Italy has been the chief source of mobile labor and the German Federal Republic and France the chief employers. During the five-year period from 1964 to 1968 more than 340,000 Italians entered West Germany to take up employment while nearly 307,000 were leaving the German labor force and returning to Italy. During the same period, 82,000 Italians entered the French work force and 73,000 left it. This cyclical flow of labor, of course, is not confined to the Common Market. Italians have found their greatest opportunity for foreign employment in Switzerland, where Italian inmigration and outmigration for the same five-year period approximated 490,000 and 433,000, respectively. For Europe as a whole during the period from 1964 to 1968, the flow of Italian labor totaled nearly a million each way.[23]

The Italian statistics are obviously only a part of a far larger process of international labor mobility. The whole of the Common Market, for example, granted about 890,000 work permits to foreign workers from both member and nonmember nations in the single year 1965. West Germany alone accounted for 525,000.[24] By 1970 there were 1,575,000 temporary to quasi-permanent foreign nationals in the West German work force, including hundreds of thousands of Italians, Spaniards, Greeks, Yugoslavs, and Turks and considerable numbers from such countries as Iran and Pakistan.

By 1968 more than 500,000 Algerians were resident in France, the bulk of whom were in the work force or seeking work. During that single year Algerian inmigration totaled 230,000 and outmigration 198,000. Britain has become a center for both temporary and permanent immigration from the Commonwealth countries, with West Indians, Indians, and Pakistanis constituting by far the largest percentages. In 1969 the combined inmigration-outmigration figures for these three groups alone were 127,000 and 104,000. By way of comparison, in 1970 the United States admitted a total of 86,000 "temporary workers and industrial

---

[23] The statistics in this paragraph are taken from *International Migration*, 8, 1–2 (1970), 88, statistical appendices.

[24] Jacques R. Houssiaux, "The European Common Market," in Walter Adams (ed.), *The Brain Drain* (New York: Macmillan, 1968), p. 192.

trainees" (nonimmigrants). But the United States also admitted some 373,000 immigrants for permanent residence.[25]

This massive and largely circulatory flow of labor across national boundaries bears witness to the powerful attraction exercised by highly industrialized and urbanized societies for unemployed or underemployed people whose home country economies are primarily agricultural and operating at lower technological levels. There is a clear though not complete parallel with the familiar pull that cities exert on countryside within the confines of a single state. The defect in the parallel, of course, is that in the domestic growth of the modern industrial state there has been, so far, at least, no significant reverse flow accompanying the trek to the cities. Migrants have been permanently absorbed into the industrial and urban economy and way of life, and the rural population has steadily declined in numbers.

Cultural and political barriers at the international level prevent duplication of the historic one-way flow in the domestic society. This is not necessarily to be deplored; both the host country and the foreign sojourner have legitimate attachments to the uniqueness of their cultures. Moreover, the permanent concentration of populations in urban areas with the resulting depletion of the countryside is no longer looked upon as an unambiguous good in any context. Nor could the less developed countries afford the permanent loss to the more developed economies of what must be among the most venturesome and adaptable members of their work force. At the same time, the postwar experiences of massive numbers of sojourning labor—experiences of the workers themselves and of the country in which they are resident—may con-

---

[25] German statistics: *Statistisches Jahrbuch 1970*, p. 127. French statistics: *Annuaire Statistique 1970*, p. 62 and *New York Times*, July 8, 1968. British statistics: *Whitaker's Almanac*, 1971, p. 593. United States immigration statistics: Department of Justice, Immigration and Naturalization Service, *1970 Annual Report* (Washington, D.C.: Government Printing Office), p. 32. (The figures in the *Annual Report* refer to fiscal and not calendar years.)

Note that East Germany, the most highly industrialized country in the Soviet bloc, is also the first communist country to import large numbers of skilled and unskilled workers from abroad. This particular international labor flow has been restricted to Soviet-oriented Eastern Europe; Hungary has been a prime source of labor export. See *New York Times*, November 18, 1967.

Mid-1973 unofficial statistics on migrant labor in Europe dwarf the numbers of foreign workers cited in official sources only two or three years earlier. The London *Economist* of August 15, 1973, estimated the size of the 1973 foreign labor force in Western Europe at more than 8 million, plus 4 million dependents. The *Economist's* estimates, for 1972, of the number of foreign workers in individual Western European countries are (in millions): Germany, 2.4; France, 2.0; Switzerland, .6; Benelux, .35. These figures translate into percentages of the total labor force of the host countries as follows: Germany, 10 percent; France, 10 percent; Switzerland, 25 percent; Belgium, 7 percent; Holland, 3.5 percent.

tribute to the growth of a stronger conviction that the individual ought to enjoy greater freedom to choose his place of residence and work internationally as well as in his own country.

If most foreign workers seek or are able to hold employment abroad only temporarily, the foreign work force to which they constantly add or from which they detach themselves is a continuing presence. It is because of this enduring presence, which as yet gives no sign of diminishing, that one can speak of an internationalized labor market. The market has become vital to both labor-importing and labor-exporting countries—in relation to the production processes and labor shortages of the former and to the labor surplus and foreign exchange earnings[26] of the latter. And it has become vital to the individuals concerned in terms of better opportunities for employment and better pay for the migrating workers and in terms of more abundant production of goods and services for individuals as employers or consumers in the host country.

The more somber aspects of these arrangements—frequent instances of economic, legal, and cultural discrimination, inadequate housing (usually wretched in the case of Algerians in France), and of human estrangement and alienation—do not negate the intrinsic value of the international labor market. The problems and abuses are not too dissimilar from those that have accompanied domestic rural-urban migration. As in the domestic analogue, the remedy must be directed to the problems and abuses themselves. The shutting down of the international labor market and the freedom of human movement that it has encouraged would be an irrational and counterproductive response.

THE BRAIN DRAIN

A specialized and highly visible sector of the international labor market is comprised of people with professional or technical skills. Since the early 1950s, doctors, lawyers, scientists, engineers, teachers, nurses, and technicians have left their countries of origin in extraordinary numbers in order to take up employment abroad. In contrast to less skilled migrant labor, the intention of most of the professionals has been a long-term or permanent change of residence. Yet it is also true that many would return to their native country, and many would never leave it, if the combination of economic, professional, and social opportunities

---

[26] Derived from income in foreign currency, a portion of which most workers abroad remit to their families at home. With approximately 400,000 workers abroad in 1969, the Turkish government realized $140 million in foreign exchange earnings from remittances. This sum was by far the largest item in Turkey's "export" account. Cotton was second at $113 million. Remittances were expected to exceed $200 million in 1970 and the total numbers of Turkish workers abroad to rise above 600,000 in 1971. *New York Times,* December 12, 1970.

at least began to approach the attractiveness of these same opportunities which they anticipate and often find in the country of immigration. In this sense, then, they must be counted as part of the mobile international labor force.

The direction of this specialized labor flow is the same as that for the masses of less skilled laborers: from the less-developed regions to the more developed. Hence the epithet brain drain, coined in the 1960s to underline the damage to any society that must result if a significant percentage of its most highly skilled people is constantly being drained off via emigration. Excepting the communist countries, the brain drain is a world-wide, though unevenly distributed, phenomenon. The main flows are from East and Southeast Asia, Latin America, and Canada primarily to the United States; from South and West Asia and Africa primarily to Western Europe; and from Western Europe primarily to the United States and Canada. This pattern, one which has provoked controversy around the globe, repeats the experience of domestic urbanization still more exactly. The largest and wealthiest cities in the country attracted the largest numbers of immigrants from the countryside. At the same time, the larger the city, the more likely it was to attract a disproportionate number of people with special talent or skills not only from rural areas but from lesser cities as well.

The United States, as the largest and wealthiest urban complex in the world—the biggest "city" of all—has become the immediate or ultimate goal of by far the largest number of skilled emigrants. During the period from 1952 to 1970 a total of some 5,650,000 immigrants were admitted to the United States for permanent residence. Of these, approximately 500,000 were classified by immigration authorities as "professional, technical and kindred workers."[27] This is a massive international transfer of talent, and it is also growing in size. For the entire period in question, persons in this category of the highly skilled comprised about 9 percent of total immigration. But in more recent years the percentage has steadily risen. In 1970, 12.4 percent of all immigrants to the United States were in the high-skills category (46,151 of 373,326).

In 1968, the peak year in post–World War II immigration to the

---

[27] Statistics for total immigration during the period are taken from Immigration and Naturalization Service, *1970 Annual Report*, p. 35. Figures for "professional, technical and kindred workers" are compiled from the same source and from a graph covering the years from 1952 to 1969 in Gregory Henderson, *Emigration of Highly Skilled Manpower from the Developing Countries* (New York: United Nations Institute for Training and Research [UNITAR], 1970), p. 196. "Professional, technical and kindred workers" is a classification established by the International Labor Organization and widely used among governments. It includes doctors, lawyers, academicians, engineers, clerics, artists, nurses, and technicians with a wide variety of skills.

United States (454,448), the following professionals were among the immigrants:[28]

2,461 natural scientists
498 social scientists
3,514 physicians, surgeons, and dentists
6,942 nurses (including student nurses)
2,692 persons in other medical and related fields
9,310 engineers
8,238 persons in other technology and related fields
331 editors and reporters
315 lawyers and judges
1,653 professors and instructors
1,764 religious workers
6,049 elementary and secondary teachers
3,107 other professional, technical, and kindred workers

Including other categories not listed here, the total number of professional, technical, and kindred workers who immigrated to the United States in the fiscal year 1968 was 48,753. Of these immigrants 34 percent came from North America, 30 percent from Europe, and 27 percent from Asia.[29] The steady increase in immigrant professionals from Asia during the 1960s became spectacular in the following year: in fiscal 1969 Asians accounted for 41 percent of the total, while the proportion of immigrant professionals from Europe and North America had declined to 24 percent and 23 percent, respectively.

The significance of these figures is twofold: their sheer size and their documentation of the growing proportion of immigrant professionals from areas of the underdeveloped world. The significance of size is revealed by comparison. During the nine-year period from 1962 to 1970 the United States gained nearly 54,000 engineers via immigration. This is roughly half again the increase in the number of new engineers produced by American educational institutions during the same period.

In 1967 it was estimated that every sixth doctor in the United States was foreign born and the holder of a foreign medical degree (approximately 50,000 of 309,483). The major role of immigrant doctors from underdeveloped areas is evident in the 1967 estimate that they

---

[28] Data of immigration to the United States of aliens in professional and related occupations, fiscal year 1968, are from Department of Justice, Immigration and Naturalization Service, *Annual Indicator* (Washington, D.C.: Government Printing Office, June 1970), pp. 2–3.

[29] Ibid., p. 29. Data for 1969 in the sentence immediately following are from the fiscal year 1969 volume, p. 29.

accounted for more than 60 percent of the foreign born and educated
doctors resident in the United States. As for engineers from underdeveloped countries, in the single year 1967 they accounted for about 50
percent of all immigrant engineers (4229 of 8682); their numbers alone
were greater than the increase in the number of new engineers produced
that year within the United States.[30]

These statistics are typical for the entire spectrum of immigrant professionals, and they have far-reaching implications. First, the United
States, and to a lesser extent other developed countries, is a magnet for
talented people from all over the world. In this sense it continues to play
its legendary role as a land of opportunity and joins the other developed
societies in reproducing, now on a global scale, the historic magnetism
of city for countryside. The result, on first calculation, is mutually beneficial. The immigrant professional generally realizes his hopes for better
opportunities in the metropolis, and the metropolis is enriched by the
increased numbers of highly skilled people.

But this set of mutual interests, of course, created the dynamo that
sparked, intensified, and now prolongs the brain drain. The mutual
gains of immigrant and country of immigration must be weighed against
the losses to the countries of emigration. In terms of educational investment alone, it has been estimated that in the period from 1953 to 1969
the underdeveloped countries lost close to $1.5 billion with the presum-
ably permanent departure of some 150,000 scientists, engineers, and
medical personnel to the developed countries. When the projected career
earnings of the emigrant professionals are added to the calculation, the
presumptive loss soars to tens of billions.[31]

Of course, these sums must be discounted because they represent
anticipated earning power of the emigrants in the developed world; had
they not emigrated their income would have been far lower. Even so,
the magnitude of the loss is a staggering one—to the point where many
have called the brain drain foreign aid in reverse, a process in which the
aid donors receive more than they give and the recipients of aid give
more than they receive. A frequent and equally bitter observation is that
the rich countries are recruiting professionals on the cheap: limiting
their domestic educational investments to the point of insufficient supply, they make up the difference with already educated professionals
imported from abroad.[32]

---

[30] The information in this paragraph is drawn primarily from Henderson, *Emigration
of Highly Skilled Manpower*, pp. 29–32, and is supplemented by data from the
Annual Indicator and *Annual Report* prepared by the Immigration and Naturalization Service for the relevant years.

[31] Henderson, *Emigration of Highly Skilled Manpower*, pp. 131–133.

[32] This calculation, too, requires some discounting because a large number of immigrant professionals receive some or all of their professional education in the country
of immigration (or another developed country) before assuming immigrant status.

The underdeveloped world desperately needs professional skills, and its losses via the brain drain have been grievous. Yet, in a very crucial sense, they can also be viewed as paper losses. That is, the capacity, and sometimes the will, of underdeveloped societies to offer their native professionals productive and remunerative employment is severely limited. An economy in which the per capita annual income is $100 or even $500 has room for only a minimal number of professionals. Only a small percentage of the total population can afford the services of professionals, and governmental revenues are too meager to provide these services at public expense in any comprehensive way to the masses who need them.

All this points to a fundamental reality—and tragedy—of the brain drain: a high percentage of those who emigrate are surplus commodities in the countries of their origin. Nor is economics the only element in the tragedy. Traditional elites in the underdeveloped society typically resist the emergence of new claimants to positions of power and wealth, and precisely the professionally skilled comprise the bulk of such claimants. To oligarchs suspicious of social change, therefore, the brain drain appears less like a loss and more like the exporting of trouble. Even where ruling groups are less resistant to change, the physical and organizational infrastructure necessary to support significant numbers of professionals is typically minimal. The combined result is that the professional, to a greater or lesser degree, feels alienated from his tradition-bound and poverty-stricken homeland.[33]

For the professionals, then, the brain drain represents a passage from unemployment to employment, from ill-paying to well-paying positions, from restricted to abundant professional opportunities, from social rigidity to social mobility, from a provincial to a more cosmopolitan style of life. This complex of motivations draws still closer the parallels between international and intranational rural-urban migration—and most particularly of the above average in talent. It is the same configuration of motives that has produced the unceasing internal movement from coun-

---

[33] Henderson (ibid., pp. 146–147) and others have noted that many underdeveloped countries suffering from the brain drain at the same time employ considerable numbers of foreign experts. Among several explanations for this phenomenon is the frequent assertion that ruling groups regard noncitizen professionals as politically more antiseptic—that is, they will do their jobs as technicians and not demand changes in the social order.

The Brazilian scholar Helio Jaguaribe lends forceful support to this assertion. Underdeveloped countries of Western or Westernized tradition "are not underdeveloped because they cannot master the appropriate skills. They are underdeveloped because their own elites want it that way. In order to maintain their privileges they are dependent on the perpetuation of the status quo. . . . What is important is to force social change by giving new qualifications to the new generation . . . to create a new functional elite whose interests are compatible with and dependent on an increase in the general welfare" (quoted in Walter Adams, "How to Stop the Brain Drain," NATO Letter [May 1968], p. 5).

tryside to city characteristic of Western societies since they began to industrialize. On a smaller scale, of course, this movement has been in evidence in all parts of the world since the beginning of urban history. Similar motives and opportunities usually produced similar results: the cities abounded in talent, and the rural areas suffered chronic scarcity.

If it is evident that there is desperate need for the professionals in the world countryside—to revert to Lin Piao's phrase for Africa, Asia, and Latin America—it is also evident that there is little effective demand. That is, however great the human needs for professional skills, most societies in the underdeveloped world do not offer the kinds of economic, psychological, social, and political incentives that transform authentic needs into authentic demand.

The diagnosis points directly to the remedy: raise the level of demand. But as we have already seen in the earlier chapters on development, the remedy is expensive and difficult. It requires a massive increase in external aid and an effective commitment both internally and externally to the social change that alone can move the societies of the world countryside from the category of "underdeveloped" into the category of "developing" countries. Once such a movement is underway, the pressures and lures that have swelled the brain drain from a trickle to a flood will begin to recede.

Meanwhile, it cannot be doubted that the hundreds of thousands of professionals together with the millions of less skilled immigrants act as a cosmopolitanizing force throughout the developed world. Nor can it be doubted that if their homelands quicken the pace of socioeconomic change many will be induced to return. Whether the returnees will continue to stimulate the growth of cosmopolitan values in the new-old surroundings will depend very much on local conditions. But it will also depend on the quality of professional and life experiences they will have accumulated during their sojourn in the urban North.

POLITICAL COROLLARIES

Consideration of the international movement of goods, capital, and people returns the argument to the issues of development raised in the beginning of the preceding chapter. These issues revealed similarities between the problems of development within the domestic society and at the level of the world society. In essence, they demonstrated that the world itself must be looked upon as an underdeveloped society since it is characterized by the condition typical of all underdeveloped societies: the juxtaposition of a minority rich in the whole ensemble of material values of life and a majority desperately deficient in all of them. The enormously expanded international flow of goods, money, management, and technology has so far functioned to enrich still further the already rich minority of the global population. The flow of professional people from the underdeveloped South to the developed North contributes to the same effect. These conclusions are in accord with the evidence provided by every available indicator for measuring the state of global society: the gap between minority rich and majority poor is not narrowing but widening.

This widening gap is the overriding threat imperiling the survival of world society. It is the same gap, now grown to macropolitical dimensions, that once threatened to tear apart the domestic societies of the industrializing North. We have already seen how the industrial societies reversed course, enabling them at once to prevent civil disaster and to disprove the scientific pretensions of Marxist determinism. The turnaround was effected by the progressive, if not everywhere complete, dismantling of domestic monopolies in politics, economics, and education. The consequence was participation in the state and society on steadily improving terms by a steadily growing proportion of the total population.

If the threat to the last century's industrializing societies and to this century's industrializing globe is the same, so is the remedy. It requires the progressive dismantling of the international monopolies of class, nation, and race so that the hitherto excluded global majority can begin to gain access to power, wealth, and knowledge on steadily improving terms. If, in turn, prime threat and rational response have become the same in both international and domestic society, the assertion that the two forms of society have begun to merge achieves its most important meaning. Underlying all the similarities, and differences, between domestic and international life is the fundamental fact that the main conditions governing their continuing existence have become identical.

The analogy goes further. The redistribution of values that took place in the domestic societies of the industrializing North could not have occurred without the emergence, in Helio Jaguaribe's words, of "a new functional elite whose interests are compatible with and dependent on an increase in the general welfare [see Note 33]." New science, new education, new technology, new entrepreneurial skills, and new concentrations of urban labor were the most tangible forces enlarging and transforming the social structure of the industrializing societies in the North. They both stimulated and reflected the appearance of new social philosophies and new concepts of the scope and meaning of the economy and the state. The representatives of these new forces exercised the pressures indispensable to successful change, resorting to negotiation, compromise, and sometimes coercion in the process of divesting the traditional elites of their traditional monopolies.

We have now seen that similar forces have made their appearance in international society. The massive movements of men, ideas, commodities, technology, capital, and enterprise across national boundaries have not yet begun to halt the widening of the gap between North and South. That is, they have not yet duplicated the strategic turnaround that ultimately saved the Northern industrial societies from disaster. But they are nonetheless the main forces now at work eroding the parochial assumptions and monopolies of the traditional nation-state system.

These economic, social, political, technological, and cultural forces have created a world economy that is already 20 percent internationalized in terms of production and trade; they have built up an investment in its profitable functioning that no national government can afford to undo. They are the generators and carriers of rapid global transport and instantaneous communication. They contribute powerfully to the fact that the impact of cosmopolitan on national values is qualitatively and quantitatively greater than ever before in history. They have reinforced the lesson of global interdependence for which nuclear weapons offered the first irrefutable demonstration.

This is the combination of forces and events that has begun to lay the foundations for a world society as well as a world economy. It has created new problems, as we have seen. But it is here, if anywhere, that realistic hopes for global development are in order. Development is far more than economics, but it is crucially important that the economic rationale for development has already been demonstrated by the now massively accumulated experience of transnational economic enterprise. The rationale is that profitability requires innovation and growth and that both demand the creation of new markets.

The world economy repeats the lesson of the domestic economy: people with many needs but no purchasing power do not constitute a market. It is the rise in purchasing power that brings a market into existence where none existed before. But as the domestic history of the industrialized countries demonstrated, any sustained rise in purchasing power requires investment in education, agricultural modernization, public health, housing, transportation, and working conditions. These are the indispensable stimulants to raising the productivity of the work force, and only a productive work force develops the purchasing power, or effective demand, that forms a viable market. These same kinds of investments are now required on a global scale—far larger and more purposeful than those the developed countries have undertaken hitherto—if the world majority is to emerge from the wasteland of poverty.

Such a prospect—such a global turnaround—is ardently to be desired on many counts, some of which are still to be considered. But the economic implications are already clear enough. The wasteland would be turned into a market. Development, to put it baldly, is good for business. Those already involved in the transnational economy and society are the most likely to recognize these implications. They are also in the best position to know that the global minority has now become so rich that it can *afford* to finance the development of the majority poor.

This investment capability of the industrial North endows the prospects for global development with an advantage lacking in the domestic underdeveloped societies of both the eighteenth and twentieth centuries. On a global basis, the number of people already having at least adequate access to power, wealth, and education (populations of the developed countries) approximates 27 percent of the total world population. These numbers represent an accumulation and diffusion of affluence never before achieved in history. It follows, as the model at the beginning of Chapter 16 illustrates, that they constitute an international base from which to effect change proportionally and absolutely far broader than the thin layer of affluent and educated people typical of the domestic underdeveloped society.

If, then, sober appraisal must recognize the formidable impediments to world development, it must also recognize the formidable resources available to overcome those impediments.

Chapter 18

Transnational Society: Region and Globe

Success in building new communities cannot be achieved by the sacrifice of established interests. Instead, new communities emerge because established interests perceive them as contexts in which to pursue their aims on more favorable terms than in the old communities to which they had previously confined their activities.

New communities are no different from old ones. Both emerge, persist, or dissolve according to their abilities to attract a set of supporting interests. Even tyranny—the antithesis of community—cannot govern by force and fear alone. Its viability as a political form is also dependent upon the presence of supporting interests. This is all the more true for the authentic community: one whose boundaries are determined by the numbers of persons who voluntarily identify with it. Its roots are to be found in the propensities of its members and not in the commands of its governors. It follows that community exists, or comes into being, according to the principle of attraction.

This is the principle that attended the birth and has fostered the spectacular growth of the Common Market. The magnetism of the European Economic Community has proved so great that neither the nationalism of De Gaulle nor the historic aloofness of Great Britain has been able to withstand its powers of attraction. An analogous magnetism has been at work wherever successful federations have been created: in the eighteenth century among the newly free American states, in Switzerland, and, subject to more complex qualifications, in Canada, India, South Africa, and the Soviet Union. It was also everywhere in evidence in the national unification process that gradually destroyed the political forms inherited from medieval Europe.

If new communities cannot be built without satisfying established interests, it does not follow that no sacrifice of interest will take place in the process. The proper inference is simply that the extent of anticipated sacrifice indicates the intensity of probable resistance to the community-building enterprise. The extent of prospective satisfaction, on the other hand, measures the probable strength of those in favor of the enterprise. The relative power of those who fear losses and of those who seek gains in the new community will therefore be crucial in deciding whether the new community will or will not come into being. In other words, proposals for new communities always originate with those who foresee greater satisfactions from them than from existing communities. Their prospects for realization rise and fall with the political strength their advocates are able to muster. Satisfaction of interests, then, and not their surrender, creates and sustains communities.

TRANSNATIONALISM: TERMS OF DEBATE

These rather simplistic truths require extra emphasis in a world in which parochial values still dominate political thought. The European-sired nation-state system inherited by the contemporary world created a set of domestic and international norms among which the indivisible sovereignty of a politically and, where possible, culturally homogeneous people has traditionally occupied first place. As we have noted earlier, the creative and interest-satisfying results of this system have contributed powerfully to its longevity and to the nationalist fervor of its partisans. They also do much to explain the system's latter-day extension to the entire globe when those in the former European imperial territories decided they could achieve similar results via the territorial nation-state.[1] Until the twentieth century, the destructive costs of a system in which political loyalties are organized around parochial and territorial values were generally regarded as acceptable.

This is the historic context which accounts for the emptiness of much of the debate concerning the future of the nation-state system. The differences among those who dominate the debate are overshadowed by an inherited agreement to treat the nation as if it were a secular deity. In consequence, the argument becomes one between the orthodox and the heretical. One side is ready to offer up the nation as the supreme sacrifice to the still greater deity of world peace. The other side, resisting the heresy, insists that such an act of sacrifice must be illusory and ruinous in a world where only national egos count. For both sides, the nation is either adjacent to or at the summit of the value hierarchy. If the transnationalists assign a still higher value to peace than to the nation, the nationalists couple their dissent with the contention that the pursuit of peace is quite compatible with, and indeed dependent upon, the continued supremacy of national sovereignty.

In both camps, therefore, commitment to a transnational community is portrayed as a wrenching farewell to the supreme political values men

---

[1] See Chapter 7.

have hitherto cherished.[2] The difference between them is that the transnationalists portray the sacrifice as painful but necessary, while the
nationalists denounce it as a folly whose only outcome must be disaster.
Formulated in these terms, the debate is bound to result in victory for the
nationalists. Proponents of transnational structures are cast in the role
of other-worldly advocates of radical self-denial, while nationalists play
the part of hard-boiled connoisseurs of the primacy of self-interest in
realistic politics. The nationalists' advantage is thus reinforced: they
defend a status quo that is treated with reverence even by its opponents.

The sterile quality of the debate, however, is a sure indicator that
objective conditions for constructing a given transnational community
are lacking. Wherever these negative circumstances obtain, the transnationalists are in the notoriously impossible position of trying to beat
somebody with nobody. This is the situation in which they found themselves whenever they offered the flawed and failing League of Nations
or the still weak United Nations as universal replacements for the territorial nation-state. Proposals for world government were and are pale
attractions in comparison with the robust and idiosyncratic realities of
national or regional interests.

Life and meaningful choice come into the debate only when new
robust and idiosyncratic realities emerge which begin to erode the territorial structures: as when the nation ceases to be an adequate market
for business or is unable to offer sufficient employment for labor, or
when it is no longer able to provide effectively for its own defenses.
In these cases the national government must either seek cooperative
international or transnational solutions or continue the attempt to rule
a society whose economic and security interests are increasingly at odds
with the political structure constraining it. If a government vulnerable
in these ways holds aloof from the transnational associations of other
nations that bring them palpable economic and security gains, it will
come under additional pressure to put an end to isolation. These have
been some of the factors at work in Britain's long and ambivalent debate
with postwar Europe. They can also be observed much further back in
history: during the rise of the national monarchy as it demonstrated its
increasing capacity to provide security and economic opportunity more
successfully than the provincial feudal barons.

Whatever the historical period, major political transformations come
about as a result of the push and pull of powerful interests in which one
set of interests may first be weaker, then equal to, and finally stronger
than the opposing set. Once this process is under way, the nation (or

---

[2] The argument is further skewed by the tendency to forget that "men" really means
only "men of the West since the eighteenth century." Chapter 7 documents the
newcomer, minority status of the nation-state as a framework for political organization.

whatever political unit incorporates the status quo) begins to lose the aura of sanctity. The debate begins to be carried on more frequently in terms of comparative advantage rather than of self-denying sacrifice. Instead of being frozen into a state of immobility by opposing sides that demand all or yield nothing, the issue is broken down into its component parts. The opportunity for change comes when the debaters become negotiators and begin to discover which parts of the old structure and which of the new aspirations are compatible, expendable, or nonnegotiable.

The opportunity for negotiated major change is not always realized, in which case the alternatives are either maintenance of the status quo, limited rearrangements within existing structures, or violence. But if a cooperative redesign of crucial relationships among nations is, in fact, consummated, it will have gone through the pragmatic bargaining among interests just described. This was preeminently the case in building the European Coal and Steel Community (ECSC), the European Economic Community (EEC),[3] and the counterpart of the EEC, the European Free Trade Association (EFTA).

All these enterprises involved assessments of the status quo and proposals for new departures. Their outcomes demonstrated that in most cases the pragmatic European eclipsed the ideological nationalist. Since it is precisely the nature of pragmatism to pursue the attainable and to eschew unattainable goals, the makers of the European Community (EC) did not seek to abolish treasured national identities. Instead they yoked them to a supranational entity whose authority was spacious but still limited and many of whose jurisdictions had to await the passage of time before becoming binding. National independence was not eliminated but only curbed, precisely because traditional nationalism retained sufficient vigor to resist any more drastic measures.

The old and the new were fitted together in relationships that were sometimes contradictory or ambiguous. But the result was the emergence of a new supranational political-economic structure to which the old nations made an initial grant of power and pledged themselves to cede additional powers as the new organization demonstrated its capacity to benefit the members. EEC has dramatically manifested such a capacity, and so far its members have honored their pledges, sometimes well ahead of the dates on which they fell due. As a result, the power of the Community has grown and, along with it, the power of its members. What has diminished is the members' ability and will to use their power independently of or against one another. Multiplying benefits through

---

[3] ECSC and EEC, together with the European Atomic Energy Commission, are now jointly known as the European Community (EC). The founding members ("the Six") are the German Federal Republic, France, Italy, the Netherlands, Belgium, and Luxembourg. Britain, Denmark, and Ireland joined the Community January 1, 1973.

cooperation have thus made a return to isolation and rivalry increasingly unattractive and structurally difficult.

REGIONAL COMMUNITIES

ECSC and EEC resulted from the first serious efforts to break with the fundamentally parochial assumptions of the nation-state system. The League of Nations and the United Nations, despite (and in part because of) their outsized mandate to foster global cooperation, left the essentials of national sovereignty intact. Some of their constitutional language notwithstanding, neither Covenant nor Charter challenged in any fundamental way the parochial egotism which is the paramount characteristic of the inherited international system.

The emergence of the European communities was marked by a different spirit. Their founders made the first decisions by major members of the nation-state system that the costs and destructiveness of that system had become too great for them to bear. Their remedy was to create a larger political-economic entity which would presumably be better equipped than the individual members to fashion a viable future for their populations. And they accepted the proposition that this joint effort could not succeed without significant limitations upon each member's freedom of action.

The negotiators of the Coal and Steel Community and of the EEC (or Common Market) were careful to enumerate and specify the sacrifices entailed in the new arrangements. But they then built into the treaties both unilateral and community measures designed to cushion their impact and create offsetting advantages. They did this for a combination of normative and instrumental reasons. Their prime responsibilities were still to their national constituents, and their mandate in transnational negotiations was to maximize the gains and minimize the losses of these constituents. The negotiators' self-awareness as delegates of nations was reinforced by the knowledge that their mandate could be revoked by these same national constituents if, in their judgment, the results did not register a surplus of gains over losses.

In seeking to limit sacrifices, however, the negotiators were also guided by the axiom that combinations of interests are always temporary and their components changeable. A supporting interest, under changing conditions, might become an opposing interest. While cultivating the support of the currently well-disposed, therefore, the governments concerned were prudent enough to remove as much of the sting as possible for the presently disadvantaged in order that their future willing partnership in the new community might not be precluded. These are some of the essential but not always sufficient means of stimulating the organic growth of a new community as a set of expanding and mutually supporting interests. Mediating between the old national needs and the new transnational needs, the negotiators proceeded to create arrangements that held out the prospect of immediate or potential advantage to as broad an array of interests within each nation as possible. Thus opportunity—and not sacrifice—was the *leitmotif* in the negotiations that gave birth to the European communities.

The subsequent realization of opportunities foreseen in 1957 when the six signatories of the Treaty of Rome created the European Economic Community has been the prime cause for both the stability and the growth of the Common Market. Diminishing trade barriers within the Community contributed significantly to rapidly rising levels of production in all the member states.[4] Intra-Community and extra-Community foreign trade moved up with and sometimes paced the members' domestic productivity. The spectacular improvement in the economic situations of all the members led them to speed up some of the timetables agreed to in the Treaty of Rome. As a result, all customs duties and quantitative restrictions on intra-Community trade in industrial goods were abolished by mid-1968, eighteen months ahead of schedule. At the same time, the remaining tariffs and other restrictions on agricultural trade among the six members were removed, the objective of full mobility of labor within the Community was achieved, and a common Community tariff on goods imported from nonmembers was established.

By the early 1970s the remaining nontariff barriers to intra-Community trade in industrial goods were being phased out. Major elements of common policies were already operative in the areas of foreign trade, transport, Community agricultural production and pricing, regulation of business practices, and quality controls for industrial and agricultural products. Still more significant were the agreements that for the first time gave the Community its own financial resources of more than $4 billion a year deriving from tariff, tax, and agricultural equalization monies collected by the national governments. A corollary agreement for the first time gave the European Parliament more than consultative status: a (limited) supranational supervisory function over the European Commission, the bureaucracy of the Community.[5] The commission is the central agency implementing Community policies, and it spends the bulk of the yearly appropriations.

---

[4] Intra-Community trade (among the six original members) increased sixfold during the years from 1958 to 1970: from $6.8 billion to $42.8 billion. In the period from 1958 to 1969 the per capita gross national product of the Six increased from $965 to $2271 (135 percent). European Communities Press and Information, *The Common Market and the Common Man*, 3rd ed. (Brussels: May 1971), pp. 5, 13.

[5] In 1972, before the six members grew to nine, the commission was headed by nine commissioners directing the work of about 6,000 civil servants drawn from the member countries.

If the record of achievement is impressive, it is nonetheless far from complete. The components crucial to full economic integration are still missing: a common currency and Community authority to make common policy for all aspects of economic life. That is to say, effective control over internal economic and fiscal policies remains in the hands of the member governments. At the December 1969 summit conference at The Hague, the Community foreign ministers officially stated their intentions to move toward a full economic and monetary union. But the projected dates for implementation (1980 and beyond) are indicators of the difficulties that retard and could even prevent these ultimate steps in the process of economic integration.

The difficulties, of course, stem from the continuing reluctance of the members to relinquish to the Community what they still control: the essentials of national economic sovereignty. The transfer of political power is a still more difficult problem than the transfer of economic power. Hence the statements at The Hague conference concerning the objective of political unification promised nothing more than the initiation of a process of continuing consultations and avoided any kind of timetable at all.

The period of international monetary crisis beginning in 1971 strained intra-Community relations, particularly between Germany and France. But it also spurred the Six, and then the Nine, to make the Community as a whole better able to weather financial storms created by the falling value of the dollar and by devaluations and revaluations of most of the world's currencies. The Nine took a small but significant step in October 1972, establishing a European cooperative monetary fund which was activated in April 1973. The fund establishes lines of credit totaling $1.4 billion (with a proviso for possible subsequent expansion to $4 billion). These credits would be available to assist a Community member with balance of payments difficulties. Most significantly, the agreement also authorized a study of the feasibility of reconstituting the fund so that it will cease to be simply an instrument of credit availability and will instead be a source of currency—in effect, the first authentic European currency.

At the same time, the Nine agreed on a Community effort to finance development programs for economically depressed areas in the Community, such as parts of Scotland and Southern Italy. Finally, and in what is at least for the short run the most difficult matter, the Community members pledged themselves to speak with a unified voice in international monetary negotiations. Despite the pledge, however, continuing political and economic differences among members were very much in evidence by early 1973 when the international monetary system was once again in crisis.

Even if it is still uncertain whether all the goals of the Treaty of Rome will be achieved, the Community's sturdiness and capacity for growth are not in doubt. These characteristics have been exhibited not only in its successful integration of some of the major aspects of its members' economic life, but also in its demonstrated ability to withstand distintegrative forces. The Common Market surmounted the crisis over agricultural policy in 1965 as well as the 1968–1969 crisis precipitated by unilateral reversions to a variety of protectionist practices which altered the members' competitive positions in both intra-Community and extra-Community trade. The Community has weathered the series of international financial crises since 1971 with considerable success. It also survived the unrelenting skepticism of General de Gaulle throughout his long term of office (1958–1969).

The most notable and prolonged crisis in the Community's external relations, of course, was the issue of Britain's connection to the Common Market. After ten years of intermittent negotiations and two French vetoes, the Community and Britain finally signed the long elusive agreement in June 1971[6] providing for the membership of Britain, which took effect January 1, 1973. (Simultaneous membership agreements were also signed with Denmark, Norway, and Ireland. Norway, however, failed to ratify.)

Both the triumphs and the unresolved issues in the historic efforts to build a European community demonstrate that any transition from narrower to wider allegiances is likely to be difficult, protracted, and uncertain as to outcome. The absence elsewhere in the world of any transnational communities of a comparable degree of integration reinforces the lesson. Competing and often half-hearted efforts at Arab or African unity and Nehru's vain hopes for Third World solidarity illustrate the difficulties, as do the several agreements to promote economic integration in Latin America. Since its inception in 1960, the Latin American Free Trade Association (LAFTA) has failed to generate significant economic gains or cooperation among its members. The commitment to develop a Latin American common market during the period 1970–1985, signed by the hemisphere presidents in Punta del Este, Uruguay, in 1967, still awaits serious efforts at implementation.

The Andean Common Market agreement signed in Bogota in 1969 (Bolivia, Chile, Colombia, Ecuador, and Peru) was in some respects a breakaway from the hemispheric commitment. The five signatories, all small countries and most of them among the economically weakest in South America, resented the footdragging and the predominance of Brazil, Mexico, and Argentina in LAFTA. The tendency to fragmentation was further evidenced when Venezuela, the richest of the Andean group and a participant in the nearly three years of negotiations, at the last minute refused to sign the Bogota agreement.

After a difficult beginning, however, the Andean group in less than

---

[6] The House of Commons approved British membership in the EEC October 28, 1971, by a vote of 356 to 244.

three years managed a near-doubling of the volume of trade among its members. More important, in August 1972, the five members reached a decision without precedent in international economic cooperation. They agreed to a regional allocation of seventy-three basic industries, so that most industrial production of the members would be complementary instead of competitive. If successfully implemented, the agreement would in effect give rise to a joint industrial development program.[7] But the effectiveness of implementation has still to be tested. Because the existing industrial base and the financial resources of the membership are very limited, the tests are likely to be severe.

In its early years, the Central American Common Market (CACOM) compiled an impressive record. It had apparently survived the 1969 war between two of its five members (Honduras and El Salvador) and had gone furthest in the direction of economic integration of any grouping of nations in the underdeveloped world. Trade among the members increased nearly sevenfold in the first seven years of CACOM's existence (1961–1968), an increase the more notable when compared with the twofold increase in intraregional trade among LAFTA members during the same period.[8]

Because of persistent political and economic disagreements among the CACOM countries, however, the community began to deteriorate in the early 1970s. Honduras suspended its participation in early 1971, with the result that Costa Rica was flooded with imports from other CACOM members that otherwise would have been destined for Honduras. Costa Rica responded by reimposing duties on imports from Guatemala and El Salvador. The disintegration of free trade among the members was then temporarily halted, only to resume its course in 1972 when Costa Rica again attempted to restrict imports. The outcome was a stoppage of all trade with Costa Rica by the three remaining active members of CACOM.[9]

The precarious economic balance and the political rivalries rending CACOM may or may not come to endanger the Andean group. But there is a structural defect underlying both groups that is likely to impose stringent limits to the extent of integration attainable and to the economic benefits integration can provide.

As we noted earlier, the identifying economic characteristic of underdeveloped countries is that only a small percentage of their populations is involved in the modern sector of the economy and society. In turn, it

---

[7] New York Times, August 26, 1972. Venezuela finally joined the Andean group in 1973.

[8] Galo Plaza, "A Common Market: Neighbors Advance on a Difficult Road," New York Times, January 20, 1969. CACOM was established in 1960 by the Treaty of Managua.

[9] New York Times, November 8, 1971 and September 11, 1972.

is mainly the goods and services generated or managed by this small percentage that enter international or intraregional trade. Thus regional integration policies tend to be concerned primarily with what might be called these pockets of modernity. The mass of society, still bound to the traditional economy, gains only marginally from integration or regional free trade policies. This contrasts sharply with the achievements of EEC or EFTA, in which all sectors of the populace have benefited from the dismantling of trade barriers and other economic barriers among the members.

We have also seen in the underdeveloped country the virtual equivalency of the modern sector with an export economy geared to the markets of the developed North. The typical pattern of international economic activity in the countries of the South, in consequence, has been one in which their most significant trade and other economic relations (investments and loans, for example) have bound them to the North, and not to one another. Trade among the underdeveloped countries currently accounts for only 20 percent of their total international trade. The result is another striking contrast between the industrial North and the underdeveloped South: the industrial countries are characteristically one another's best customers and suppliers, while the economic ties among underdeveloped countries have been minimal and tenuous.

The North-oriented export economy, however, only aggravates but does not explain the contrast. The economic intimacy of the industrial countries is a product of their high levels of productivity, which are reflected, in turn, in rich domestic markets. The incentive to buy and sell within the industrial sector of the world economy is therefore very great—that is where the customers and the money are. On the other hand, a society at a low level of productivity necessarily generates only a very limited purchasing power. By definition, it cannot be an attractive economic partner, and this is the basic problem which dogs economic integration schemes among the countries of the South.

Regional economic collaboration or integration of poor countries, then, cannot do much to alleviate their poverty. Certainly it cannot begin to enrich them to the extent that EEC and EFTA have enriched Western Europe, nor could it begin to match the more modest collaborative achievements of the Soviet Union and its Eastern European political and economic allies. If the basic problem is that the typical underdeveloped country is not an economically attractive partner, the basic question must ask how it can become more attractive. As we have observed in earlier chapters, the answer is easily given and difficult to act upon. The underdeveloped society must expand its internal market. It can do this only by raising the level of productivity which, in turn, requires a rising volume of investment. In short, it must develop, and development depends first of all on internal effort and only marginally upon closer economic relations with other still underdeveloped countries.

All this is not to say that economic collaboration among countries of the South cannot produce useful results. But these results must necessarily be meager so long as the main political, economic, and social task of internal development languishes. It is therefore far more important that the underdeveloped country seek to create an internal community of rising productivity and political solidarity than to go in search of communities beyond its borders with counterparts whose plight also dictates the priority of internal concerns.

GLOBAL COMMUNITIES: NORTH AND SOUTH

Like transnational community, domestic community also rests on the principle of attraction: on reciprocal gains by the parties concerned. But within the typical underdeveloped country, the principle lies buried in the chasm separating the privileged few and the aggrieved many. And the typical policy of the privileged few has been to perpetuate the chasm, just as the traditional nationalist has insisted upon perpetuating the gulf between sovereign state and sovereign state. Even in those underdeveloped societies where some of the privileged have the will to build an authentic internal community, however, the poverty of the internal resource base condemns the community-building effort to constant setbacks.

As we have seen, the chief problem of underdeveloped societies is the scarcity of capital and of skilled people at all levels of society able to invest their assets rationally—that is, to extract increased productivity from investments made. As long as this condition obtains, hopes for a wider distribution of benefits among the population as a whole must founder on the insufficiency of the sum total of benefits available for distribution. It follows that the will to transform a divided and elitist society into a united and democratic community must also founder. Those who exhibit such a will will either succumb to illusions or be forced back to the ancient choice between dogged and violent defense of the status quo or unrelenting and violent revolution.

This kind of internal impasse can be avoided or overcome throughout the underdeveloped world only by significantly and continuously increasing the total benefits available for internal distribution. Such an increase cannot be generated by the limited resources indigenous to the typical underdeveloped society. The productivity of the modern sector in the average country of the South, which accounts for a high percentage of GNP but involves only a fraction of the total population, is inadequate for the task. Societies in which only 1 or 2 or 8 or 10 percent of the population is "modern" (that is, possessing power, wealth, and education) face almost insuperable obstacles in launching programs of sustained development designed to galvanize the other 90-plus percent, even if they desire to do so. Prospects for such programs cannot improve unless a much larger resource base can be tapped than any indigenous to the underdeveloped countries. This larger base is to be found only in the modern sector of the globe itself, the quarter of the earth's population living in the developed North.

Underdeveloped countries can realize aspirations for development only in an evolving community relationship with the developed world. The importance of that relationship is underlined by the network of economic agreements of long standing between the Common Market and former colonies of Common Market members. The network was significantly enlarged in 1973 upon Britain's formal accession to the EEC, since Britain added to the outreach of the Common Market structure a new series of economic agreements negotiated with her ex-colonies, now members of the Commonwealth.

Like the North-South pattern of Latin American trade and economic ties, the array of contractual interconnections between the Common Market and a large number of Asian and African states further documents the paramount importance of the developed world in the economic life of the underdeveloped countries. Even without drawing up a balance sheet of the equities and inequities involved in these interconnections, it can nonetheless be asserted that they are products of mutual interest, that indispensable, though not sufficient, prerequisite for community.

The developed North can supply—and has been supplying, though very inadequately—what the South needs most: capital, technology, skills, and markets. The underdeveloped countries cannot obtain them from one another above the level of token exchanges precisely because the scarcity of these necessities is a prime characteristic of all underdeveloped countries. For the South, then, the obvious partner in a community relationship is the North—or parts of the North—because the North is the only external source of the essentials for development and for survival itself.

But in this context, as in any other, successful construction of community relationships depends on the presence of expectations of benefits accruing to all the prospective members. Development and trade as an exercise in transnational community must promise gains to both North and South. The obvious corollary follows: the anticipated gains must outweigh the risks and sacrifices unavoidably linked with major changes in North-South relations.

For the countries of the South the risks are formidable. Closer ties to the North bringing with them more adequate imports of capital, technology, and skills render the countries of the South more and not less vulnerable to the policies and the economic power of the developed countries. Factories and farm equipment imported from the North or built to specifications developed in the North require a flow of parts and replacements also built or designed in the North. Financing new facilities is not a one-shot affair but requires assurance of capital availability over time. It follows that the countries of the South, to the extent that they accept development aid, must also accept long-term dependence on the North as a supplier of capital.

Increases in production generated by investment must be matched by increases in sales; insofar as the internal market of a developing country cannot immediately absorb the increases in productivity, access to the markets of the North becomes more important than in the earlier stages of development. Hence the preoccupation of UNCTAD, since its founding in the 1960s, with obtaining from the industrial North tariff concessions for the manufactures of the South. Thus the dependence on the North for capital, technology, and markets must grow during an indeterminate period of transition—until the development process is so far advanced that capital, technology, and purchasing power can be generated domestically in adequate volume and quality. Only then can the developing country move away from dependency to at least a qualified independence. By the same token, only then can emerge a community between North and South in the full sense of the concept: an interdependence among equals engaged in joint enterprises.

COMMUNIST AND WESTERN DEVELOPMENT MODELS

An obvious question in any appraisal of North-South relations is: Which North? The South is in most respects far more diverse than the North, but its universal weakness and poverty and its common need for development assistance constitute elements of homogeneity which are manifestly missing in the developed world. The North, by contrast, has been divided both by the rivalry of communism and democracy and by divergent approaches to the problem of development—to which substantive ideological differences and the phenomenon of rivalry itself have contributed.

Thus it is that ever since development became a major issue in the international system, the North has confronted the South with two conflicting models of the developmental process. With due regard for variations within every developed country, these models can be broadly labeled capitalist democracy and socialist dictatorship. As the (imperfect) incarnations of these models, the United States and the Soviet Union have been their most active sales representatives throughout the underdeveloped South.

Partisans of the Soviet model began with some formidable advantages. First, the colonial empires had been built largely under the aegis of capitalism; hence Lenin's argument that capitalism and imperialism are synonymous was eminently plausible to imperialism's victims. Lenin's further assertion that socialism and imperialism are inherently antipathetic was contradicted primarily by Soviet policies in Eastern Europe and within the Soviet Union itself—far away from Africa, Latin America, and most of Asia. In the experience of the colonized people of the global South, the imperial masters had always been Western capitalists and never Eastern socialists.

Quite apart, then, from the substantive merits of the various forms of socialism as ways of organizing societies, ideological commitment to socialism as an alternative and rebuke to capitalism and its imperialist history had and continues to have enormous appeal. This is an important reason why the governments of most of the major countries in Africa and Asia profess socialist goals. In Latin America, where in most countries traditional elites remain in power, socialism is the battle cry of the opposition.

Second, the communist concept of dictatorship, or oligarchic rule, corresponds closely with the political realities of the underdeveloped world. The nearly universal absence of a vigorous entrepreneurial middle class means that there are no real alternatives to the domination of society by government. The government, not the private sector, is typically the major producer of goods and services, the prime generator of jobs, the chief investor, and the leading borrower at home and abroad. It is all these things because only very few private individuals dispose of capital and only a very small percentage of the total population has the power or the knowledge to participate meaningfully in the modern sector of society. The small minority of moderns tends to be concentrated in the civilian and military bureaucracies.

The characteristic social structure of the underdeveloped country is therefore fundamentally at variance with democratic premises and aspirations. By the same token, it is fundamentally akin to the hierarchical rigidity characteristic of the various forms of contemporary communism. Power, wealth, and education are not diffused but compacted, so that the Leninist prescription for dictatorship by the governing minority harmonizes neatly with the prevailing patterns of political, economic, and social inequality. Whatever the political coloration of the governing minority—from Rightist-traditional to Leftist-revolutionary—the most familiar path to follow is one that presupposes continuance of elite rule.

Third, dictatorship commends itself not only as being consonant with the social structure of the typical underdeveloped country. A powerful case can be made that it is also the only form of government that can successfully take on the task of development. By definition, development calls for more or less rapid, but cumulatively drastic, breaks with the patterns of life characterizing the traditional society. There is ample evidence in every society that significant percentages of both elites and masses will resist departures from established institutions and patterns of behavior. As a result, many analysts as well as practitioners of development have drawn the conclusion, or accepted the Marxian premise, that coercion is the only way to effect genuine social change.

Robert Heilbroner offers a telling illustration of the relevance of coercion to social change by drawing an analogy between land reform in an underdeveloped society and a reform in the distribution of corporate holdings in a developed society. Noting that land holdings and corporate holdings are the chief forms of wealth in the respective kinds of societies, Heilbroner invites his American readers to make the following experiment in self-examination:

> . . . supposing that *we* were an underdeveloped country and that some superior power offered us aid on the condition that we would undertake "share reform"—that is, the redistribution (or even the abolition) of our present concentrated ownership of corporate securities. How rapidly would our own powers-that-be acquiesce in such a proposal?[10]

The experiment inevitably concludes with a corollary question: "How rapidly will Latin America, where 10 percent of the people own 90 percent of the land, acquiesce in land reform?" The implication is obvious: in the typical underdeveloped country a thoroughgoing program for transferring acreage from the landed to the landless strikes at the heart of the inherited socioeconomic and political structures. It will meet with such strong opposition that coercion and countercoercion in varying degrees of intensity must unavoidably come into play.

Whatever the attitudes toward the desirability of change in the underdeveloped South, change itself—massive and rapid to a degree unprecedented in history—cannot be halted. Nor can it be significantly slowed down; successful prevention of change in one area is likely to speed up changes in others. The dragging pace of land reform, to use the example just cited, has multiplied the miseries and intensified the militancy of the landless. Moreover, it has driven tens of millions of them to the cities to augment the revolutionary potentials in the massive urban slums. The raw population problem itself provides still another illustration of unstoppable change. Wherever the population of a country doubles in a generation's time—and this is the fate of most societies in the global South—the dislocations in the life of the country are fundamental and universal, no matter what institutions appear to survive unscathed by the process.

The population explosion joins other intrinsically unpolitical phenomena in forcing political, social, and economic change. Accelerated discovery, exploitation, and exhaustion of the earth's resources, a technology that emerges from the laboratories to speed up both productivity and obsolescence, and ever more pervasive and intricate communications systems—these are only some of the other major nonpolitical forces in

---

[10] Robert Heilbroner, *The Great Ascent* (New York: Harper Torchbooks, 1963), p. 129.

the world today that are fast altering contexts in which political decisions must be made.

In utilitarian terms, then, all developmental models—capitalist, communist, and their variants or alternatives—will be tested chiefly in terms of their capacity to adapt to, initiate, and manage immense processes of change. So far, both models from the North have generally failed this test. In part, of course, the failure is economic. Neither the communist nor the Western world has mounted the kind of rational and adequately financed aid program sufficient to try the strength of—let alone prove out—the development models they espouse.

Too many of the aid billions from the West have been dissipated through irrational allocation, deliberate decisions to sacrifice development objectives to political sensibilities within the recipient country, or to Cold War considerations, or all three. The inordinate amount of money that has gone into military or "defense support" aid is a notorious case in point. The Soviet aid program can be faulted for precisely the same reasons, as well as for an overall level of aid expenditure that can only be described as niggardly.

But more than parsimony inhibits the effective working of the imported developmental models. The basic difficulty is that they do not really address themselves—rhetoric to the contrary—to the problem of change. This is a common accusation, of course, against the West in general and the United States in particular. It is charged (supported by formidable documentation and refuted by some counterevidence) that the West prefers to cooperate with existing elites in the name of business efficiency, profits, and anticommunism and thus consciously and unconsciously hobbles and resists the forces making for large-scale change. Soviet and other varieties of communism, on the other hand, derive ideological profit from the Marxist promise of total and even apocalyptic change. Thus they continue to command a degree of credibility in the underdeveloped world as the prime challengers to the status quo and champions of societies made wholly new.

Yet the communist claim is spurious so long as the Leninist component remains central to its sociopolitical model—that is, the insistence upon the primacy of a conspiratorial and highly disciplined party dictatorship both before and after the seizure of power. In practice, the dictatorship's tenure has proved to be indefinite; nowhere since 1917 has communism been able to make the transition from government by an elite to government by the mass. It is hardly surprising, therefore, that the developmental model it proffers to the underdeveloped world is not a very promising instrument to bring about the change the underdeveloped country needs most: a steadily expanding proportion of its population endowed with wealth, knowledge, and political power. No less than the traditional elites, the Leninist party aspires to control and not to liberate the masses. It follows that both elites aim to monopolize power—and the wealth and knowledge that contribute to power—and not to share it. Yet without a diffusion of power, wealth, and education a society cannot, by definition, develop.

The gap between communist ideological claim and practical performance is duplicated in the West. The ideas of liberty and equality are exported perhaps as vigorously as communism broadcasts its commitment to fundamental social change. But, as in the classic age of Western imperialism, the political and social applications of these ideas are characteristically obstructed, both by intrinsic difficulties of implementation and by the arrangements considered necessary by the West to do business in, or to dominate, the South. These arrangements are typically designed to reach an understanding with the representatives of an anti-democratic status quo.

The result is a radical distortion of the Western developmental model. This result produces a further contradiction in Western behavior in the underdeveloped world. A reasonable correspondence obtains between the communist model for development and the dictatorial regimes that continue to characterize the more developed countries in the communist world. But the West's affinity for the status quo in the South stands in glaring, though not total, contrast to the currently operating models of Western democracy.

The basic component of these models has been a commitment to rapid and massive social change in the direction of equality. Since World War II, the measures taken to implement this commitment, whatever their shortcomings, have succeeded in bringing an ever larger percentage of the populations of the Western countries into the mainstream of the national (or in some respects transnational) political and economic life. All Western democracies have arrived at the state of mass affluence. In some—West Germany, Sweden, Denmark, and the Netherlands, for example—it is possible to apply the term "affluent society" to nearly 100 percent of the population.

Economic gains for both individual and society have been organically linked to expanding access to education and information and to increasing social mobility and political participation. During this period change itself has been the chief agent of what political unrest there has been in the affluent societies. And except in the United States, whose rending racial and cultural predicaments are unique among the democratic developed countries, only small and transient minorities have advocated rejection of the basic political forms of the West. Hence the overall record of the Western democracies in the postwar period is one of rapid and massive social change joined with an exceptional degree of political stability, both domestically and in their mutual international relationships.

Thus the two major developmental models proffered by the North confront the South and one another in puzzling juxtapositions. The communist model, promising to change everything, prescribes the time-worn recipe of oligarchy as the way to construct a new life. The Western model, more selective but still wide-ranging in its advocacy of change, is theoretically hostile to oligarchy. But the scruples of theory are challenged by the fact that oligarchy is the dominant way of life in the underdeveloped world. Given the existing distribution of power and wealth, it could not be otherwise. Some degree of accommodation to oligarchy is therefore unavoidable.

But the West, moved by its anticommunist preferences and adjusting to the prevailing distributions of power in the South, characteristically (but not always) all too readily aligns itself with the status quo. Communism, for its part, typically (but not always) attacks the status quo—only to prescribe a successor status quo with a different elite and a different combination of dominant interests. By so doing, both betray their ideological promises to liberate men from the tyrannies of minority rule.

If expediency and current necessities can make a case for adapting to the rules of oligarchy, it is nonetheless true that both individual freedom and societal development require a fundamental break with the oligarchic principle. The authenticity of any developmental model, therefore, must be judged by the way it proposes to effect that break. And the difficulty with such proposals, of course, is that they necessarily call for the eventual dissolution and reformation of the total social structures of the underdeveloped countries.

The result is a formidable dilemma for any imported, and intellectually defensible, model for development. The requirement that it be anti-oligarchic in concept also forces it into a veiled or open declaration of war against the oligarchic status quo. The next inevitable step is that the proponents of the imported model are engaged on the main domestic political battlefields of the underdeveloped South. The ancient and bitterest issue is thereby reopened: interference by the North in the internal affairs of the South.

Such considerations make it imperative that the underdeveloped countries evolve their own development models. They join other and still more weighty considerations pointing to the same imperative: the requirement that development models sensitively reflect the particular capacities and needs of each underdeveloped country and region and that each culture experience its development effort as an essentially autonomous, rather than as an imitative, process.

A developmental model from the North must therefore be supplementary rather than comprehensive in application. Those who implement it should seek to reconcile the assumptions and goals of the model with the assumptions and goals of the underdeveloped country's own model. They should be eclectic, which means abandoning dogmatic attitudes about capitalism and socialism in the development process and welcoming experiment. Eclecticism also means willingness to collaborate with opposing models imported from the North—developmental projects jointly undertaken by the United States and the Soviet Union, for example—where political and technical considerations permit. In the midst of all this flexibility there is only one unyielding requirement: that the application of the development model, however supplementary in scope and open to modification, resists the perpetuation of oligarchy and helps to move the society toward greater equality.

NORTH AND SOUTH: CHANGING COURSE

It has been a fundamental argument of this book that optimum conditions for the global South's transition from underdeveloped to developed require a major and sustained input of development aid from the North. It follows that development assistance—designed to benefit the recipients rather than the donors—is the precondition for building transnational communities between rich and poor societies. If the North cannot meet the needs of the South for capital, technology, and markets, the two worlds will be driven still further apart. Present alienation will become implacable enmity, for the same reasons that long-oppressed majorities within states have finally confronted their internal ruling elites in revolutionary hatred. The result must be that the already limited opportunities for building transnational communities by fostering mutual interests, mutual obligations, and joint enterprises will vanish.

Yet it is evident how difficult it is to bring the two worlds closer together when the divisions are already so deep. The nations of Western Europe formed a regional community of approximate equals—if not in national size, power, and wealth, then in the living standards of their citizens and confidence among the members in the vigor of their cultural identities. Most important of all was their conviction that they could fashion from their mutual interests a community structure which would prevent discrimination and promote equal advantages for all the members.

In the North-South relationship none of these conditions are met. Its fundamental characteristic is inequality in every political and economic category. In the countries of the South, cultural self-confidence is precarious in the face of Northern power and opulence—and hence all the more fiercely asserted and defended against contamination. The historic experiences of imperialism join the South's perceptions of the present global system to undermine credibility in any association with the North that purports to offer mutuality and equality, let alone preferential advantages for the Southern partners.

Distrust will diminish only as results of Northern policies provide concrete demonstrations that inequalities have grown less rather than more. But these first beginnings in global equalization will, in most cases, be separated by decades from the actual achievement of equality in the sense that the nations forming the European Common Market were equal. The distance in time between reality and expectation is alone enough to jeopardize all joint enterprises between North and South. Disappointment and recrimination are inevitable on the long journey toward change. But the heart of the difficulties besetting any scheme for global equalization lies not in the time factor nor in the specifics of North-South interaction. It is found instead in the necessity that the countries of the South must themselves be the chief architects of their equality in the international system, a function they can perform only by carrying out drastic changes in their internal social systems.

The parallel gap between rich and poor at the global level and between elite and mass within the underdeveloped societies has been stressed often enough. It follows that those seeking to close the gap in either of the two contexts will experience comparable difficulties, because the dynamics produced by the radical inequalities characteristic of both are functionally identical. To the extent that the countries of the South must draw on the Northern resource base in order to bring about fundamental changes in their present status, they invite the Northern presence into their internal affairs. For if Northern aid does not assist in stimulating internal change it will have failed the only purpose that could unite North and South in the building of community: working toward the goal of equality.

In these circumstances the specter of Northern intervention will haunt the development enterprise as long as it lasts. Even the internationalization of development assistance, desirable as it is, cannot banish it. It can, however, be offset in the degree to which the North understands that it is rational as well as just, in the development relationship, to prefer the South's advantage to its own.

If that seems like a great deal to ask in the way of political understanding, it is much less if considered from the perspective of a global system in which the prevailing distribution of advantages is grotesquely lopsided. From such a perspective it is clear that the presently advantaged would have to give more than they receive, on a massive scale and for a very long time, before they would have reasonable cause to regret their magnanimity. But a realistic program of development does not in any case ask the rich countries for such massive sacrifices. It only asks for an annual 1 percent of their GNPs, allocated in the interests of the recipients instead of the donors.

The aid relationship between North and South points once again to the central problem of inequality in that relationship—and to the difficulties which must beset any attempt to create a sense of community among unequals. In these circumstances, community structures must be far less elaborate and binding than those to which the European equals agreed in their joint search for solutions to common problems. The dominant purpose of the Europeans has been to tie themselves into an ever more intricate network of integration in order to free themselves from the many curses of nationalism. The dominant purpose among the countries of the South has been to assert their nationalisms and to free themselves from the bonds of Northern domination. Hence they will willingly accept only those relationships with the North which will increase their capacity to break away, if they so choose, from the Northern connection.

The South will resist the ties that bind. The Western Europeans reached the conclusion that their national destinies, at least as untrammeled independent sovereignties, had played themselves out. The countries of the South see their national or cultural destinies just emerging from the colonial straitjacket, and they demand independent expression without restraints of any kind, particularly those of Northern origin.

Northern power and Southern weakness, Northern oppression and Southern anger—these are not promising circumstances in which to build community relationships.[11] Yet even in these circumstances the one essential for any community enterprise remains clear: mutual attraction based on anticipation of mutual advantage. For the South, as noted earlier, the advantage is evident and immediate: a more extensive access to Northern capital, technology, and markets. And the attractiveness of the advantage will grow if the qualitative terms of access improve. An increase in the volume of outright grants, a decrease in interest rates on loans, private investment that expands internal markets, preferential tariff concessions by the North to stimulate the export of the South's manufactures, and the assignment of a growing role to international agencies in the funding and administration of development assistance— these are some of the measures that could strengthen the sense of trust that has all but vanished in the South.

For the North the economic advantages are more remote, but remote in the same sense in which the capital yield on investments is also ordinarily remote. The basic economic rationale for the North's role in the development partnership is the same as that for the investor in classic capitalist doctrine. The investor foregoes a portion of current consumption (in this case a very small portion) and decides to make an outlay of capital in the expectation that subsequent returns will be greater than current sacrifices. The returns from investment in development, however, are not in the form of interim dividends or capital appreciation benefiting specific individuals. Instead, they result from the formation in the South of new centers of production where none existed before and, consequently, new markets and sources of supply.

Development assistance, then, is an investment in the maturation of the global economy. It is an investment whose purpose is to transform a

---

[11] Just as white power and black weakness, white oppression and black anger repeatedly confound efforts to build a community among races in the United States.

world of paupers into a world of producers and customers. Such a world (assuming rationality in ecology as well as in economics) would contribute immeasurably more to the wealth of an already affluent North than all the riches extracted from the imperial economies of exploitation. From the perspective of the global economy, moreover, colonialism and neocolonialism have not increased the sum total of human wealth but diminished it, for the South's losses have been greater than the North's gains.

As Hobson already demonstrated at the turn of the century, there was no exception to this rule within the imperial metropoles themselves.[12] A small group of Northern investors profited handsomely from buying into specific economic enterprises in colonial territories, but these profits yielded no measurable benefits for their countries' economies. Indeed, so long as majorities in the societies of the North were themselves poor, most imperial investments were demonstrably counterproductive. That is, they drained off capital which, if invested in the expansion of the North's internal markets, would have averaged far larger and more lasting returns than imperial stocks and bonds, both to the individual investor and to society.

It should be evident, then, that the maturation of the global economy is equivalent to a vast expansion of economic activity on a world-wide scale. At some point along the way it would take on the characteristics of a global economic boom. A number of impediments to the achievement of such an objective have already been discussed, and more remain to be considered. But if it is assumed for purposes of immediate argument that they can be overcome, there might be wide agreement that a uniformly productive and prosperous globe is an economically rational goal and certainly preferable to a world that is one-quarter rich and three-quarters desperately poor. After all, it has been the ever more conscious preference for an economy of the mass instead of the minority that has brought the national economies of the developed countries to their present state of affluence. As the interconnections among national economies steadily multiply, the analogy between national and global economic rationality and preference acquires growing force.

However strong the analogy, a host of unresolved questions remains. Is the preference for a fully developed global economy also a necessity? That is, will the failure to realize such a preference bring with it unacceptable penalties? Or is it only one preference among several, each of which can claim equal, nearly equal, or even superior rationality? Are there risks as well as gains connected with this preference?

Evidence still to be considered—both economic and noneconomic in nature—should provide firmer grounds for judgment. But at this point one basic reality should be quite clear. A commitment by the countries

---

[12] See Chapter 8.

of the North to global development, together with a rational implementation of that commitment, is the indispensable condition for the growth of a community relationship between North and South.

Development and independence (complementary but also often contradictory, as we have seen) are the governing aspirations in the countries of the South. Even the elites who fear development as a danger to their power must now use the rhetoric of development and conceal their anxieties and their opposition. In this, they resemble the elites of Europe in their struggle with the nationalism of the French Revolution: in the end the European aristocracies had to adopt the language and much of the substance of nationalism in order to save what they could of their own positions in their societies. If the will to develop cannot be termed universal, it is enough to say that it is the strongest social force now at work in the global South. Political reason, therefore, joins economic considerations in recommending a partnership with this force. And, since the developed world is divisible, those parts of the North that hold back from such a partnership can expect to incur the enduring hostility of the majority of mankind.

Chapter 19

Transnational Society:
The West

The growth and expansion of the European Community has taken place within the framework of a still larger community, composed primarily of the democratic states of the developed West and led by the United States.[1] The communal bonds were forged, and American leadership established, during World War II and in the early postwar years. Exhibiting far greater variety and looser and more diverse organizational ties than the Common Market countries, the community of the West owes its identity and cohesion to the same principle of attraction on which the Common Market was founded. The similarity, of course, is not incidental but organic—because no community of any kind can emerge or endure if it does not incorporate the principle of attraction. In the case of the West, the principle of attraction has drawn its vitality from common security interests, mutual economic advantage, and generally similar ideological values.

Concerns over common security resulted in a global network of multilateral and bilateral military treaties directed against the communist East. But some of these agreements also regulated military relationships internal to the West, including the integration of Germany and Japan into the Western community, the balance between Greece and Turkey, and the relations between the American superpower and the other community partners.

Economic cooperation, and economic competition governed by cooperatively formulated rules, has showered wealth upon the countries of the West beyond the most utopian expectations of those who in 1945 hoped for a better postwar world. Moreover, the economic activity of the West has not been simply a matter of mutual enrichment. It has also been the indispensable agent in the massive internationalization of the world economy examined in previous chapters. Further, the West has

---

[1] The "West" is here taken to include northern and western Europe and Italy, the United States and Canada, Japan, Australia, and New Zealand.

been chief aid donor to the global South, accounting for more than 90 percent of the total world flow of development assistance since the late 1940s. It has played a comparably dominant role in the world trade of the South and in the volume of foreign investment in Southern economies.

During this long period of Western military, economic, and political collaboration—and of prodigious changes accompanying and flowing from it—the basic commitments to common ideological values have held steady. The shortcomings and perversions of these values have been on view often enough, but none of the societies of the West has renounced the norm of individual freedom nor the institutions of government by democratic choice.

This series of achievements offers sufficient testimony to the presence of a dynamic and intricately linked community of states. If any further evidence is needed, it can be found in an irrefutable summation of internal Western experience since 1945: cooperation has been the major theme and conflict the minor. The summation, of course, leaves ample room for the fact that at no time has conflict been absent. But it also stresses the far more important fact that at no time has conflict nullified the principle of attraction which holds the community together.

Community strength has been tested at various times since its inception: by the issue of German rearmament during the period from 1949 to 1955, by the Suez crisis of 1956, and frequently during the long presidency of General de Gaulle and the long agony of Vietnam. But the most formidable challenge to Western unity began to build up in the 1960s and became fully manifest in 1971 in the form of an accelerating deterioration in economic relations among the community members. In a fundamental sense, the deterioration was a product of the very success of the Western community in helping to generate an unparalleled enrichment of its members.

Rapid economic growth has been the common denominator in the community experience. But rates of growth have varied over time, as have the economic magnitudes of the growth units. Outside the Common Market, the nations of the Western community were essentially free to set their economic policies without regard, if they chose to withhold it, to the needs of the community as a whole. (As an entity dealing with the outside world, the Common Market enjoyed and exercised the same sovereign prerogatives.) The result was an inadequate set of regulations governing their mutual economic and financial relations and a correspondingly inadequate set of facilities through which new policies could be cooperatively devised to meet new situations. Thus the international economic crisis of the early 1970s reveals much more than just the specific conditions upon which continued Western unity depends. It also reflects the classic problem of all communities: the never-resolved tension between the needs and wills of the whole and of the parts. As such, the crisis merits more detailed attention.

THE NEW INTERNATIONAL ECONOMY
IN THE POSTWAR WEST

Since 1945 the United States has been the kingpin of the Western international system, most visibly in matters of military security and economics. Toward the close of World War II the primacy of American
economic power was symbolically and practically confirmed by the end
of the long reign of the British pound as the prime currency of international transactions. In its stead, the dollar became the universally
accepted instrument of trade and exchange. The transition was made
official at the international economic and monetary conference of 1944
in Bretton Woods, New Hampshire.

The Bretton Woods agreements, among other things, created a new
monetary base for international trade and finance. All the world's currencies were valued against what some economists dubbed the gold-dollar
standard. That is, the worth of each currency was calculated in terms of
the dollar which, in turn, was valued against gold at the fixed rate of
$35 an ounce. The system provided not only a standard unit for mone-
tary measurement; it also provided a stable standard, so long as the
dollar itself remained stable. Still another provision buttressed the stability of the system: the Bretton Woods signatories pegged their currencies
to the dollar and agreed not to permit them to fluctuate more than a percentage point above or below their pegged value without consultation
with the other signatories.

There was a growth as well as a stability factor in the Bretton Woods
agreements. It is a standard rule of economics that an expanding volume
of economic activity requires an expanding volume of currency; an
inadequate monetary base must slow, halt, or even reverse economic
expansion. Thus within domestic economies, the policies of government
and of central banks attempt to foster a regulated growth in the volume
of money in circulation; the growth should be rapid enough to stimulate
steady economic expansion, but not so rapid as to cause inflation. But in
the international system there is no central government or central bank.
Hence there has been no centralized making of international policy to
establish a rational relationship between the amount of economic activity desired and the amount of money in circulation.

The traditional reliance on gold as the only universally accepted standard of value meant that the international economy was tied to a money
supply that could increase, theoretically, only as rapidly as it was mined
from the ground. What happened in practice was that the national currency of the strongest economy (the largest international trader, investor,
and banker) came to supplement gold as a universally acceptable medium
of exchange. This was the function performed by the British pound
through the nineteenth century and until World War II, then to be succeeded by the American dollar.

The availability of a universally acceptable, or key, currency alongside gold meant that international business activity could rely on two sources of monetary supply. Because the key currency, especially after the ascendancy of the dollar, has been much more abundant than gold (and since it does not need to be mined but only printed) the continuing growth of the international economy is far more dependent on the key currency than on gold. Consequently, the more vigorous the internal and external economic performance of the country whose currency is also the key currency, the broader the base for expansion of international economic activity. The Bretton Woods consecration of the dollar as the new key currency to spark international economic growth paid off spectacularly as the postwar levels of trade and investment reached the historic heights described in Chapter 17.

It should be evident, then, that the key currency performs a crucial service for the international economy. But it also brings some disadvantages with it, disadvantages that made themselves increasingly evident and played a major role in the severe international monetary crises of the late 1960s and early 1970s. A key currency is obviously only a make-shift surrogate for the lack of a rationally governed international monetary supply. Moreover, it is supplied by only one member of the international economic society and is thus influenced primarily by the circumstances, needs, and wishes of that member. Thus United States policies with economic impact at home and abroad—and the activities of American corporations and individuals—have had an inordinate influence on the key currency, far greater than even the size and power of the American economy as such would warrant. This has led other nations, particularly the major industrial countries of the West, to resent what they argue has been their undue dependence in economic transactions on the vagaries of American economic behavior.

Economic dependence of whatever degree always raises issues of political prestige, and it was France, in particular, that vented its resentment against an international monetary system so heavily dominated by one country. But the economic issues per se have been the most important. As key currency, the dollar has been a privileged international monetary unit. It gave to American investors abroad an additional advantage on top of their already strong economic position: they were paying in coin of the realm, so to speak, and not, like other foreign investors, in unmistakably foreign exchange.

It was theoretically possible for the American government to pay off its debts abroad simply by printing sufficient dollars to do so. Most important, under the rules of the International Monetary Fund, established at Bretton Woods, the dollar was exempt from the ordinary laws of supply and demand applicable to the rest of the world's currencies. That is, if the supply of dollars abroad exceeded the demand, it was difficult for foreign governments and private dollar holders to unload on the open market. For both, the dollar was the prime reserve currency.

Large-scale selling would cause the dollar to decline in value with a consequent shrinkage of their own reserves. Moreover, the governments, as members of the International Monetary Fund, had pegged their currencies to the dollar. Thus they felt obliged to buy dollars and accumulate surpluses in order to keep the international value of the dollar steady. To do otherwise, to free their currencies from a fixed dollar rate, would be tantamount to abandoning the international monetary stability that had energized the whole era of postwar economic boom.

INFIRMITIES IN THE NEW SYSTEM

These and other ills of the system remained latent or bearable so long as the dollar's real value continued steady. They were activated or aggravated the moment the purchasing power of the dollar declined in relation to the purchasing power of other currencies. Such a decline began to manifest itself in the late 1950s, but it did not take on serious proportions until the mid-1960s, when rising American expenditures for the Vietnam war produced an increasingly severe internal inflation.

The result was that while the dollar could buy fewer goods and services at home, the fixed relationship between the dollar and other currencies permitted dollar holders to continue to buy goods and services abroad at a constant dollar price. Thus purchases made abroad by American importers and investors—and by the American government—were paid for in a currency whose value to foreign holders steadily shrank in terms of its ability to purchase goods and services produced by the American economy. In sum, American private and public purchases abroad were being acquired with fewer dollars than the real value of the dollar warranted. Hence the growing conviction by critics of American economic policy, at home as well as abroad, that the dollar was overvalued.

The bargain acquisitions by dollar holders of foreign goods, services, and capital assets were in themselves enough to cause rising resentment. With respect to capital assets, the resentment was compounded by an already lively concern over the expanding role of American investments and enterprise in foreign economies. The magnitude of this investment activity, described in Chapter 17, has been such as to arouse fears that American-based multinational corporations might come to dominate the economic life of the host countries and thus to compromise their economic independence.[2] The unduly low prices at which foreign assets were

---

[2] The most widely known treatise on this subject is Jean Jacques Servan-Schreiber's *The American Challenge* (New York: Atheneum Press, 1968). First published in France in 1967. It immediately became a best seller; the number of sales was without precedent in the history of economic literature.

available to dollar holders obviously accelerated American capital acquisitions abroad, so that foreign economies were in effect subsidizing their own Americanization.[3]

The American urge to buy and invest abroad was further reinforced by high prices at home; rising domestic costs were counterpart to the foreign bargains. One result was a rapid increase in American imports until, in 1971—and for the first time in the twentieth century—the value of imports exceeded the value of exports.[4] Another result was that American corporations and stockholders found investments in foreign operations and the establishment of foreign affiliates more and more attractive as a way to escape high production costs at home. The domestic cost-price push was in large part the result of the Vietnam war. But it was stimulated by a number of other factors as well, including large federal deficits to which tax reductions and increased expenditures on social programs contributed. One of the most significant factors has been the rising cost of labor.

The relevance of the American wage structure to the economics of the Western community is evident in a comparison of wage levels in the United States and other developed countries (see Table 19.1). These comparisons of wages actually earned in the industrial sector reveal drastic differences in labor compensation in the countries listed. American factory workers in 1970 were earning considerably better than 3 times as much as their counterparts in Italy, Japan, and France and more than 2.7 as much as those in Britain, the Netherlands, and Belgium. With respect to West Germany and Sweden, the ratio drops to approximately 2:1 and 1.5:1, respectively. Only in Canada did industrial earnings come close to the American level.

The disparity between industrial wages in the United States and in other Western countries has been a major factor in the outflow of American industrial capital in search of lower production costs. (The process bears comparison to the exodus of the service sectors of corporations from New York City to urban and suburban areas across the United States in quest of reduced operating costs.) The impact on American labor has been discussed in Chapter 17: feeling threatened in its prosperity it moves toward protectionism to stem the flow of imports. At the same time, it seeks restrictions on American investment abroad, contending that the export of capital, and technology, also exports jobs. That is, foreign investment is seen as opening up new employment

---

[3] The political aspects of the Americanization phenomenon should be obvious. One specific political issue bears mention. Foreign critics of American policies in Vietnam made a telling point that their own countries, by selling supplies for overvalued dollars, were in fact subsidizing the American war effort in Indochina.

[4] In 1971 the import excess was $2.7 billion; in 1972 it more than doubled to $6.9 billion.

Table 19.1

Average Hourly Earnings of Wage Workers in Manufacturing, 1970

Italy	$0.96	Belgium	$1.32
Japan	0.96	West Germany	1.62
France	1.01	Sweden	2.33
United Kingdom	1.25	Canada	2.98
Netherlands	1.27	United States	3.36

SOURCE: Peter G. Peterson (Assistant to the President for International Economic Affairs), "Report on the International Economic Situation of the United States," *New York Times*, December 30, 1971.

opportunities for workers outside the United States at the expense of employment opportunities for Americans at home.

This is the two-edged rationale of the Hartke-Burke bill: curbing imports of goods and exports of capital will increase domestic production and domestic employment. Without going further into the arguments of its partisans and opponents, it is evident that the bill intends a double effect: to reduce the role of the international economy in American society and to diminish the impact of the American economy on international society. No fair-minded observer could deny that certain sectors of American labor have cause for complaint. Nor can it be maintained that the internationalization of large segments of American business has occurred without damage as well as benefit to the American economy. But the proposed remedies of the Hartke-Burke bill are not really addressed to the dynamics of the new transnational economy; instead they purport to offer safety by backing away from it.

Like the protectionist Smoot-Hawley tariff legislation forty years earlier, the Hartke-Burke curbs on imports would provoke retaliatory curbs abroad on American exports. Restrictions on American foreign investment would make American international business less competitive. From a macropolitical perspective, the result would be a reversal of momentum in which the transnational economy has functioned as the drivewheel generating a complex and increasingly tangible global interdependence. In short, the Hartke-Burke bill proposes an isolationist answer to problems created by the dynamics of a world economy already well along in the process of internationalization. Should its objectives be attained, the disruptions of both international and national economies would produce external and internal conflicts far more massive than those which ravaged the more self-contained national economies during the period of economic isolationism and nationalism in the 1930s.

It is evident, then, that protectionist policies constitute the most serious challenges to the viability of a community of Western industrial states. Moreover, they can find advocates in any country where relatively high wage scales prevail, so long as there are foreign areas where mark-

edly lower levels of compensation attract large inflows of capital. It is
no accident that American enterprise, with the most internationalized
system of production, should also be most subject to domestic pressures
to renationalize. Other industrial countries will feel similar pressures as
they proceed further along the path of internationalization. The resulting conflicts can be lessened only as the geographic differentials in wages
are reduced. Their lasting resolution enjoins the transformation of the
lower wage areas into high wage areas—pointing once again to the indispensable requirement of a global redistribution of wealth and other
values on a more equitable basis.

THE WESTERN ECONOMIC CRISIS

The issues discussed above are clearly related to the observation in
Chapter 17 that the superior mobility of capital and the relative immobility of labor combine to produce recurrent tensions in economic and
political life. These tensions were much in evidence when the international economic life of the West reached the crisis stage in 1971. But
they were only part of an ensemble of factors affecting the American
international economic position. All these factors combined to make the
crisis extraordinarily complex and protracted:

> High costs of production relative to other countries in the Western
> community
>
> Rapid expansion of capital investment abroad
>
> Balance of payments deficits
>
> Rapid rise in the level of imports to the point of import surplus
>
> Inflation attributable primarily to expenditures for the war in Vietnam
> but also to other public outlays making for federal deficits and to
> forces in the private sector prodding the wage-price structure upward
>
> Large scale government expenditures abroad including military ex-
> penditures in Vietnam and in other parts of the world as well as non-
> military outlays
>
> The gold-dollar standard which offered dollar holders added induce-
> ment to import and to invest abroad
>
> A huge pool of dollars held abroad and growing to the point where
> supply far exceeded demand
>
> A consequent overvaluation of the dollar

These factors, in turn, activated the deep-seated defects in an international monetary system dependent on the national currency of a single
state. But it was not just a matter of the weakening of that currency
because of internal inflationary pressures in the United States. As the
de facto international currency, the dollar was required to serve as the

financial basis of the world economy. With the expansion of world economic activity the problematics of this role became increasingly evident. The United States experienced more and more difficulty in financing with its own currency the accelerating demands for economic growth. Moreover, its own relative position in the world economy declined as the economies of other countries recovered from the war and then began to register spectacular gains. The American economy was no longer a giant among midgets but a giant among young and rapidly growing giants, notably the Common Market and Japan.

With the new situation, the potentiality inherent in the key currency system of Bretton Woods became manifest: the pace of long-term world economic expansion could be maintained only if chronic United States dollar deficits were acceptable to all parties concerned. That is, world economic expansion *required* American balance of payments deficits if there was to be a sufficient volume of money to finance further expansion. Continuing expansion was dependent on more and more dollars in circulation outside the United States. The United States and its foreign creditors finally found the system intolerable and, in 1971, began to chart a new course. The major lesson of the crisis was that no longer has one country the economic strength to offer or impose its national currency as the world's money.

All these phenomena contributed to a vast and continuing outflow of dollars far in excess of the inflow of foreign exchange or returning dollars derived from American exports, dividends on foreign investments, investments made in the United States by foreigners, and other sources. This situation has been reflected in the long-term decline in United States gold reserves as foreigners exercised their right, until 1971, to trade excess dollars for gold from the United States Treasury at the fixed convertibility rate of $35 per ounce of gold. More importantly, the glut of dollars abroad was registered in deficits in the American balance of payments.[5] From 1960 to 1964 these deficits averaged $.7 billion; in the 1965 to 1969 period the average deficit was $2.2 billion. The year 1970 closed with a negative figure of $3.1 billion; in 1971 and again in 1972 the deficit soared to an unprecedented $9 billion plus.[6]

The effect of these mounting deficits was a crisis of confidence in the

---

[5] Essentially, the balance of payments measures a country's total annual flow of expenditure and income arising from transactions abroad. In addition to foreign trade, the balance of payments includes payments to and receipts from foreigners for services (travel, of which tourism is a major component in the West, transport, interest and dividends, banking and insurance, and government expenditures). It also includes short- and long-term flows of capital investment, the flow of gold, and unilateral transfers (such as government grants for economic or military aid and nongovernmental gifts or grants). The sum of these items yields the balance of credits and debits in a country's international account.

[6] "U.S. Balance of Payments and Investment Position," *Federal Reserve Bulletin* (April 1973), p. 246. The figures pertain to the so-called basic balance (the balance on current accounts and long-term capital).

dollar. The course of crisis accelerated with the growing conviction in international money markets that the American government would have to resort to devaluation of the dollar in order to eliminate or reduce balance of payments deficits and to bring down the high costs of American exports. The conviction grew so strong that in the single week before August 15, 1971, approximately $4 billion flowed out of the United States to purchase foreign currencies whose values were expected to, and did, increase once the anticipated dollar devaluation took place.[7] These were the international circumstances surrounding the Nixon administration's August 15 declaration of a "new economic policy" aimed at rescuing the American economy from its domestic as well as international inflationary predicament.

With respect to the international economy, the new policy signaled two momentous departures from previous American behavior: convertibility of dollars into gold was suspended and a 10 percent temporary import surcharge imposed. Both measures were designed to stem the dollar outflow. The purpose of the surcharge on tariffs was to reverse the balance of imports over exports. It also served to pressure the other industrial countries of the West to revise those aspects of their trade policies which the United States claimed were discriminatory or otherwise disadvantageous to the American economy. The suspension of convertibility was a very much more far-reaching step. It was tantamount to a unilateral declaration that the Bretton Woods gold-dollar system was at an end. The language of the "new economic policy" asserted that the convertibility suspension was temporary. But the American guarantee to convert dollars into gold, once revoked, could not easily be resurrected, if only because confidence in the longevity of any new guarantee would be lacking.

The most immediate impediment to restoring convertibility, however, was the enormous sum of dollars held abroad. Until convertibility suspension they represented claims against American gold. In 1971, there were upwards of 50 billion of these expatriated dollars, a sum nearly five times the value of the remaining gold reserves of the United States. Renewed convertibility in these circumstances would expose the United States to the constant danger of a run on its gold supply, with the consequent necessity, should the threat materialize, of retreating to inconvertibility once again. Only a long-term effort to restore a balance between American economic productivity and the volume of dollars in international circulation can resolve the convertibility problem. In other words, the United States must combat inflation abroad as well as at home until the supply of goods and services produced by the American economy is in equilibrium with the demand that the volume of currency represents.

---

[7] Edwin L. Dale, Jr., *New York Times*, January 9, 1972.

The immediate impact of the convertibility suspension was to loosen the ties of the international monetary system to gold, thus introducing a new element of flexibility into currency valuation. The United States then sought to turn the new flexibility to its advantage by persuading its major trading partners to upvalue their currencies while leaving the value of the dollar formally unchanged. The American government anticipated a number of benefits from this course of action. Chief among them was the expectation of a rise in American exports, because foreign buyers could purchase them more cheaply, and of a decline in imports, because American buyers would have to pay out more dollars for foreign goods. By the same token, foreign capital assets would rise in value and thus be less attractive to American investors, with a consequent decline in the emigration of investment dollars.[8] Finally, avoidance of a formal devaluation of the dollar would also avoid offending congressional and other political sensibilities which entertained a simplistic but still tenacious belief that devaluation must necessarily result in loss of prestige for the dollar as the symbol of American wealth and power.

The 1971 crisis was chiefly the product of the economic difficulties of the United States as a nation and as the kingpin of the world economy, particularly of its crucial Western component. But the United States was not the sole contributor to the deteriorating Western economic partnership. Western Europe and Japan, far more dependent on foreign trade than the United States, have also been more protectionist in many areas. Agricultural protectionism in the Common Market is a particularly noteworthy example. The Common Market's preferential trading arrangements with a large number of Mediterranean and African countries also favor narrower regional interests at some expense to the larger trading community.

The disproportionate role of the United States in Western security has also meant a disproportionate American share of defense costs. Thus the other Western partners have been able to forward economic expansion while carrying a comparatively lighter burden of defense expenditure to support what all partners have agreed is a common task and obligation. Also, as we have seen, the international economic position of the other partners has been advantaged by their lower wage structures. Hence their living standards are lower than in the United States and, in gross terms, their products go for lower prices on the international market.

All these issues, as well as those generated primarily by the United

---

[8] Most of these expectations failed to materialize. As noted earlier, the trade deficit more than doubled in the period 1971–1972. Exports did indeed spurt as anticipated, from $42.8 billion in 1971 to $48.8 billion in 1972. But import volume in the same period grew still more rapidly: from $45.5 billion in 1971 to $55.7 billion in 1972. At the same time, the rate of private American investment abroad held steady over the two year span. See *Federal Reserve Bulletin* (April 1973), p. 246.

States, require fair resolution if the Western economic partnership is to endure. Together, they pose a fundamental challenge to the whole post-war economic structure built on freer international trade and investment and on monetary partnership. The basic issue in the 1970s is whether the members of the Western community can find a way to continue their economic collaboration under new conditions and with new means, or whether they will revert to traditional behavior in which each state sees the others mostly as rivals and seldom as partners.

The crisis of 1971, in short, raised the threat of a wholesale reversion to economic nationalism. As the prime example, the American surcharge on imports was a clear violation of multilateral treaty obligations under the General Agreement on Tariffs and Trade. Its practical effect for the five-month period of its duration was unilaterally to abrogate all of the American tariff reductions reciprocally negotiated since 1945. Moreover, although the surcharge was advertised as temporary, the conditions under which it would be rescinded were unclear enough to excite speculation that it might be indefinitely prolonged.

In such a contingency other industrial countries would be bound to retaliate by raising their tariffs against American goods. In this event, a new era of trade protectionism would emerge whose impact would be compounded by restrictions on international investment and by competitive monetary policies. The result could only be a halt to the spectacular twenty-five-year boom in the international economy and to the benefits it conferred on the participating national and regional economies. And to the extent that the new era of protectionism turned economic partners into economic rivals, it would enfeeble the attraction holding the Western community together.

THE SMITHSONIAN ADJUSTMENT

The magnitude of the danger produced a series of negotiations among the countries of the West culminating in the Smithsonian Agreement[9] of December 18, 1971. The United States agreed to end the import surcharge without demanding prior concessions from other trading nations. The unconditional annulment of the surcharge removed the threat of retaliatory actions. It also dismantled at least one major obstacle to subsequent trade negotiations: the growing conviction that America's trading partners were being pressed to make concessions in order to appease

---

[9] So named because the negotiations took place in the Smithsonian Institution in Washington. The negotiators represented the so-called Group of Ten, the ten most important economic and financial powers in the world economy. They are: the United States, Britain, France, West Germany, Japan, Italy, Netherlands, Canada, Belgium, and Sweden. Switzerland attends meetings of the Group of Ten as an observer.

the United States into revoking what was a unilateral and massive act of protectionism.

The most significant part of the Smithsonian Agreement, however, was monetary. For the first time in history, the major trading nations abandoned the sovereign prerogative of unilateral monetary valuation and engaged in a multinational negotiation of currency exchange rates. The United States ended its resistance to dollar devaluation while several of the other negotiating nations, most notably Japan, agreed to upvalue their currencies to levels they had previously been unwilling to consider. The combined effect of these devaluation and revaluation negotiations was a dollar worth approximately 12 percent less in the international market.

Buoyed by the resolution of these immediate issues, the Smithsonian negotiators encouraged the view that their collaboration represented the beginning of a long-range effort to reform the international monetary system. First, they anticipated that a more realistic dollar valuation would gradually reduce the deficits in the American balance of payments. The result would be a reduction in dollar surpluses abroad and hence a mitigation of pressures for further devaluation. These effects, in turn, would restore confidence in the dollar as the key currency in the international economy, at least for a transitional period. It would benefit the trading partners of the United States by enabling them gradually to divest themselves of excess dollar holdings and to use dollars as international currency again with less reason to fear a repetition of unwanted inundations. (These expectations, as we shall see, were not to be realized.) In addition, the parties to the agreement gave evidence of a will to go beyond the restoration of the dollar and to move, cautiously, toward a truly international currency as the prime medium of exchange in international transactions and as the monetary base to finance world economic expansion.

Those who hoped to move in this direction had a means of implementation already at hand. In 1970 the International Monetary Fund had begun issuing an embryonic international currency after its 111 member nations voted in October 1969 to establish Special Drawing Rights (SDRs), to be administered by the Fund.[10] SDRs—or paper gold, in the metaphor of international finance—are the creatures of prescribed quotas of financial-contributions that members make to the International Monetary Fund. In the past, these quotas had provided the capital base for the general lending activities of the Fund. Beginning in 1970, they were increased so that some of the Fund's assets could serve as the financial base for debit and credit transactions in settling current international accounts. SDRs are the instruments of these transactions. Prior to the new system, a state was effectively obliged to settle most of its inter-

---

[10] No negative votes were cast; South Africa abstained. By 1973, IMF membership had reached 126.

national transactions in gold or dollars. Henceforth it could also use SDRs; that is, it could draw on its line of credit at the International Monetary Fund to settle deficits in its balance of payments. Thus a new internationally issued money, or credit instrument, took its place alongside gold and dollars as a universally accepted medium of exchange.

The prime significance of the SDR agreement was that it incorporated the principle of cooperative international regulation of the world's monetary transactions. The world economy was no longer dependent solely on the vagaries of gold supply or on the performance and availability of a single national currency. The prime weakness was that the regulation exercised was limited to SDR transactions and thus to only a fraction of the total international monetary flows, which continued to be made up overwhelmingly of dollars and gold.[11] Accordingly, it was the dynamics of supply and demand in gold and dollars that led to the crisis of 1971, a crisis in which the still marginal volume of SDRs could have no effect.

But the emergence of the SDR held out a promise for the future. Excess holdings of dollars abroad, reflected in the mounting deficits in the American balance of payments, led to the 1971 declaration ending dollar convertibility. No longer convertible into gold, the overabundant dollar was also no longer so attractive as an international reserve currency. Its allure was further diminished by subsequent devaluation. In consequence, the major trading nations, including the United States, evidenced readiness to explore possibilities for a more far-reaching reform of the international monetary system, whereby a modified form of SDR would play a leading role instead of a secondary one. This would, in effect, extend international control into the mainstream of the world's international financial transactions. It would also make an internationally issued and regulated currency a major agent in the expansion of world trade and, more indirectly, of world economic development.

Readiness to move in new directions was subsequently given its most concrete and authoritative expression by George Shultz, United States Secretary of the Treasury, at the 1972 annual meeting of the International Monetary Fund and the World Bank. Shultz called for the gradual curtailment of the role of gold, dollars, and national currencies generally in international monetary affairs. As these traditional instruments of exchange declined in importance, SDRs would become the chief vehicle of international monetary transactions and "the formal numeraire of the system."[12]

---

[11] As of 1972, $9.5 billion in SDRs had been added to the reserves of International Monetary Fund members. This amounts to about one-quarter of the approximately $40 billion in gold held by individual countries and is dwarfed by the massive role of the dollar in international accounting.

Each member of the International Monetary Fund was credited with SDRs in an amount proportionate to its quota contributions. Hence the richest countries, contributing the largest quotas, also disposed of the largest quantities of SDRs.

The secretary's use of this technical term had a far-reaching significance: it was a proposal that the nations of the world should work toward a system in which they would cease to define the exchange rate values of their currencies in terms of gold, dollars, or any other national currency and, instead, adopt SDRs as the international and universal standard of currency valuation. If this proposal is a logical companion to expectations that the SDR would become the chief currency and credit instrument in the international economy, it was also something more. If adopted, it would signal a formal farewell to an international monetary system dominated for nearly two centuries by a single national currency (the pound and then the dollar). Simultaneously, it would represent the legitimation of a new order regulated by an internationally managed monetary instrument. As subsequent events were to dramatize, however, Secretary Shultz's macropolitical prescription for the global macroeconomy will not be adopted easily.

At the same meeting the IMF membership voted to transform the Group of Ten into the Committee of Twenty, with nine seats going to underdeveloped countries. With this action major decisions in international monetary matters ceased to be the exclusive and uncontested province of the rich countries. The Committee of Twenty was charged with responsibility to formulate proposals for international monetary reform. Representatives of the underdeveloped countries immediately made their voices heard by proposing an increase and reallocation of SDRs to serve as a resource for development loans and as credits to pay for current imports and interest obligations on previously contracted foreign loans.

At this point the problem of excess dollars emerged once more. A superabundance of dollars means a superabundance of available international credit: the classic inflationary situation of too much money chasing too few goods. Some developed countries, in particular West Germany, argued that an expansion of SDR credits must aggravate international inflationary pressures. As these and other pressures brought on renewed monetary crises in 1973, the hopes of the underdeveloped countries for new and easier sources of credit once again had to be deferred until the rich countries could restore some order to the chaos of their own monetary affairs.

---

[12] Secretary Shultz's speech of September 26 was reprinted in the *New York Times*, September 27, 1972. Mr. Shultz did not let subsequent adversity deflect him from promoting the SDR as "numeraire." On the occasion of the second devaluation of the dollar on February 12, 1973, his official description of the decision was "a formal 10 percent reduction in the par value of the dollar from 0.92106 SDR to the dollar to 0.82895 SDR to the dollar " (Washington, D.C.: Bureau of Public Affairs, Department of State, News Release, February 12, 1973).

The West German government followed suit and announced in conjunction with its 3 percent revaluation of the mark on March 17, 1973, that it would henceforth express the parity value of the mark in SDRs instead of dollars (*The German Tribune*, No. 573, Hamburg, April 5, 1973).

RENEWED CRISIS

The course of events in 1972 made it clear that the Smithsonian agreements and subsequent efforts at regulation had failed to provide that order. American deficits in both trade and balance of payments persisted and grew, with the inevitable result that the volume of excess dollars abroad continued to increase. By 1973 estimates of dollar amounts in the international money market went over the 100 billion mark with billions more unaccounted for.

These colossal sums pointed up still another major issue of international finance, and not only for the dollar. A United States Tariff Commission study concluded that at the turn of the year 1971–1972 the sum of all national currencies in the international money market had reached $268 billion.[13] Of this huge total, United States privately owned banks and corporations controlled some $190 billion. The full significance of these figures is revealed when they are compared with the total official currency reserves of the governments of all the industrial countries: $88.5 billion. Thus, the liquid assets controlled by private enterprises operating in the international economy had grown to more than three times those commanded by their governmental counterparts.

In consequence, private financial resources decisively outclassed governmental resources in the international money market. Official reserves are the chief instruments at the disposal of governments to defend the stability of the international exchange rates of their currencies. They are obviously at a great and growing disadvantage in pursuing stability when their reserve instruments are dwarfed individually and jointly by private and essentially uncontrolled international monetary forces.

These private international assets were the catalysts of monetary crisis on no less than six separate occasions during the years from 1968 to 1973. The catalytic mechanism has worked roughly as follows. A given nation's economy exhibits weakness: among the familiar symptoms, usually interrelated, are inflation, declining productivity, poor export performance, and balance of payments deficits. These indicators give rise to anticipations that the government of that nation will consider devaluing its currency as a means of restoring at least its international economic position. The intended result of devaluation, as we have seen, is to make its exports cheaper and therefore more attractive to the foreign buyer. In turn, increased exports would presumably reduce or even eliminate balance of payments deficits. The remedy does not, however, alleviate the problems of domestic inflation or productivity, and it can indeed aggravate them.

---

[13] United States Tariff Commission, *Implications of Multinational Firms and World Trade and Investment for U.S. Trade and Labor* (Washington, D.C.: Government Printing Office, 1973).

What is certain is that a decision to devalue must injure those engaged in the international economy with assets in the currency in question. Thus if devaluation is anticipated, there is a powerful incentive to sell off these assets and to buy up the national currencies of stronger economies, the so-called hard currencies. The value of the latter necessarily increases once the devaluation of the "soft" currency actually occurs. Hence those who have correctly anticipated the course of events in their selling and buying of currencies will have minimized their losses and maximized their profits.

This mechanism is an international version of the familiar dynamics operating in any stock market and goes by the name of speculation. Those involved are also familiar: banks, corporations, and individuals and organizations mainly or exclusively preoccupied with playing the market. This speculation is inseparable from the economic system in which it occurs. As long as that system is in reasonable economic health and financial equilibrium, speculative activities are usually contained within tolerable limits and often perform a useful function as extremely sensitive indicators of economic performance. When economies fall into disequilibrium, however, private speculation aggravates and exaggerates the difficulties of the system, sometimes to the point of panic.

In the international as in the domestic economic system, then, it should be evident that massive and frequently reckless speculative behavior is far more symptom than cause of the system's difficulties. Once the frequency and severity of these difficulties begin to increase, however, speculation starts to make its own contribution to further deterioration. Thus speculative flows from one currency into another have precipitated situations in which governments have been forced to devalue or revalue against their original intention and will—and sometimes in the absence of any objective economic rationale. The greater the sums involved in these speculative flows, the more of this kind of leverage they are capable of exercising, and we have seen that these sums have now become enormous.[14]

Speculative flows reached massive proportions three times in the fif-

---

[14] The pool of international private assets (and of governmental assets not performing a reserve function) is now being rapidly augmented by funds from oil-producing Arab countries. It is estimated that almost $1.5 billion of Arab oil money was converted from dollars to marks in a single day (March 1) in the renewed speculative crisis following the February 1973 dollar devaluation. The rate at which the developed countries are purchasing Arab oil indicates that within a few years assets controlled by Arab governments or corporations will be among the largest in the international money market.

Horace Bailey, president of the Chemical Bank of New York, estimated that oil revenues accruing to countries in the Middle East would soon reach a level of $30 to $40 billion a year and that by 1980 Middle Eastern governments may command liquid assets in the vicinity of $175 billion (New York Times, March 16, 1973).

teen months following the Smithsonian agreements. All three times they took the form of flights from the dollar and multibillion dollar purchases of harder currencies, chiefly German marks and Japanese yen. In each case, they were triggered by the expectation either that the American government would further devalue the dollar or that the prevailing exchange rate between the dollar and other currencies would be altered in some other way. Each time the speculative movements were stimulated by persisting and observable weaknesses in the American economy.

The first speculative surge occurred in July 1972, less than seven months after the Smithsonian agreements. Speculators unloaded hundreds of millions of dollars and bought up (mainly) marks. The German Central Bank responded by issuing sufficient paper marks to buy the proffered dollars at the Smithsonian rate—to the point where the volume of dollar selling and mark buying subsided, and the crisis was resolved. Thus the West German action made a major contribution both to the newly established valuation of the dollar and to the hopes for international monetary stability in general. But it did so at the cost of expanding the total volume of marks in circulation and at the consequent risk of triggering inflationary pressures in the German domestic economy. It was therefore obvious that there were limits to the extent and frequency that West Germany, or any country faced with a massive speculative demand for its currency, could resort to this expedient.

The second speculative wave began to build up in late January and early February of 1973. Once again the mark was the chief target of buyers seeking to sell dollars, with the yen as a second preference. This time the greater volume of speculative activity and the doubtful ability and willingness of the Germans to repeat their bailing-out performance of the previous July contributed to a different result. But the most important factor in the outcome of the February crisis was the fundamental one of American economic performance. It was this factor that forced the American government to take direct action to end the monetary crisis. On February 12 it abandoned the Smithsonian solutions and devalued the dollar for a second time in fourteen months, in this instance by 10 percent.

The decision was reached by intense negotiations between the United States and other leading nations in trade and finance. Since dollar devaluation would make their exports relatively more costly and American exports relatively cheaper, their assent and cooperation were essential. The assent was given and cooperation to maintain the new value of the dollar promised on condition that American policy would avoid future actions that might further disadvantage other nations in international trade.

There was irony in the new manifestation of the dollar's weakness since it came at a time when both the American domestic economy and its export volume were visibly gathering strength. But the import surplus and balance of payments deficits persisted, with the consequence that the sum of excess dollars abroad continued to mount. Above all, rising prices and the Nixon administration's decision to shelve most of the governmental controls on the domestic price structure stimulated international fears that the United States might be headed for a major bout with inflation. The necessary consequence would be a further decline in the purchasing power of the dollar to the obvious disadvantage of those who hold dollars.

Faced with these prospects, the only recourse for dollar holders in the American domestic economy would be internal political and economic action to increase productivity and thus decrease prices—necessarily a long-term undertaking. But international dollar holders (including American banks, corporations, and speculators) had at hand the immediate remedy of selling their dollars for other currencies likely to maintain or increase their purchasing power. They availed themselves of this remedy in February 1973 as they had done the previous July and prior to the crisis of August 1971. When the United States yielded to these pressures by resorting to a further devaluation, those who had sold their dollars had escaped a significant loss and realized a handsome profit.

NEW EXPEDIENTS: THE FLOAT

Once dollar devaluation had taken place, other currencies became more expensive to buy. Hence the incentive to purchase them by selling more dollars was sharply reduced. But confidence in the American economy and in the stability of the dollar's new international value was still not repaired. Two weeks after the February 12 devaluation a new wave of dollar selling for higher priced currencies began to build. Once again the German mark was the buyers' target. On March 1 the German Central Bank, in accordance with the February agreement to uphold the new dollar exchange rate, was forced to sell more than 7.5 billion marks in exchange for $2.7 billion—an all-time record volume for a single day. The result was that on March 2 official exchange markets around the world shut their doors for a period of a little more than two weeks.[15] By this action the governments hoped to cool the speculative fever and buy time in which to find new solutions.

---

[15] The French government at first attempted to keep its exchange market open only to close later in the morning of March 2 after it had been obliged to purchase $500 million of American currency in a single hour.

Over the six-week period spanning the two crises that climaxed in February and March, the German government paid out some 23 billion marks for more than $8 billion.

The resolution of the March crisis was achieved not by dollar devaluation but by a wholesale departure from the fixed exchange rate which was a central principle of both the Bretton Woods and the short-lived Smithsonian systems. That is, the major industrial countries decided to permit the values of their currencies to float upward or downward against the dollar in response to forces in the monetary market.[16] The float offered the advantage of releasing governments from the obligation of intervening in the money market to maintain a fixed value relationship between their own currencies and the dollar. The United States benefited from the float because it resulted in a slight additional increase in the value of foreign currencies and so further stimulated American exports.

It was anticipated that the floating system would serve the general advantage by discouraging further repetitions of wholesale speculative activity. By permitting the value of their currencies to fluctuate in response to market activity on a day-to-day basis, governments could hope to avoid repeating the unhappy experiences of the fixed-rate system. Since 1968 their attempts to defend established currency values against large scale speculative flows had invariably resulted in crisis. By resorting to the float, governments anticipated an end to the sudden devaluations and revaluations that had come to be the standard outcomes of crisis. Consequently, they anticipated an end to rewarding speculators with huge profits that could only whet the speculative appetite for further gambles with international monetary instabilities. In short, it was hoped that the floating system with its flexible exchange rates would be an effective step to restore confidence in the world's currencies as instruments of world trade, banking, and investment.[17]

Yet the new system left the basic problems of the world economy unresolved. If in theory there should be much less incentive to speculators, there is no guarantee that they would cease to seek opportunities to profit by driving the value of a particular currency up or down beyond limits tolerable to the government concerned. Given the enormous resources of private currency holders in the international money market, the wherewithal to engage in such speculative raids will be a continuing and growing presence.

---

[16] A number of currencies, including the British pound, the Swiss franc, the Italian lira, and the Japanese yen had already been floating for varying lengths of time. The Canadian dollar had been floating for some years.

[17] In a rather remarkable feat of diplomacy and finance, six of the nine Common Market countries agreed on March 11 to a common float in which their currencies would float against the dollar but would be held to a fixed relationship (with some flexibility) to one another. The move was made in order to preserve and even enhance the economic cohesion of the European Community.

Because of their special economic circumstances, the remaining European Community members did not join the common float but expressed their official intention to do so as soon as their individual monetary situations would permit.

The float is, therefore, only an uncertain defense against speculation, if only for the reason that no government can permit the value of its currency to depend solely on forces beyond its control. As we have seen, international monetary values have a powerful effect on the volume of imports and exports, on international investment and banking activities, and thus on the vigor of each country's domestic economy. If the value of a given country's currency is bid up as a result of buying pressures, the resulting increase in its export prices may cause domestic unemployment and internal economic dislocation. This is the point at which the government concerned will modify or abandon the floating system and reimpose exchange controls to defend the value of its currency. This kind of government intervention is known in the jargon of the trade as "dirty floating."

Neither will a government permit its currency to be driven down to a level where the stability and productivity of its economy is placed in doubt—or to the point where it is forced to pay ruinous prices for essential imports because its money has lost value on the international market. Devaluation, whether as a result of forces in the international money market or of a formal government decision, is hardly a painless remedy. After all, when devaluation cheapened American exports, increased foreign demand for American agricultural products contributed powerfully to soaring domestic food prices. Conversely, a dollar worth less on the international market bought a smaller quantity of foreign oil, resulting in domestic price increases for gasoline and other oil products and still another stimulus to inflationary pressures.

The Bretton Woods system was designed to end the anarchy that had traditionally characterized international economic exchange and which led in the 1930s to chaos, international and domestic economic collapse, economic nationalism, and war. Bretton Woods established a set of controls and standards designed to ensure orderly financial and economic relations at the international level and to provide the basis for orderly economic growth. The controls and standards gained their force from stable relationships among the world's currencies and from an internationally recognized medium of exchange (the dollar) in whose value all participants had confidence. The mainspring and chief guarantor of the system was the world's most powerful national economy, the United States. As we have seen, the system performed its intended function with remarkable success until major shifts in the structure and dynamics of the world economy—and, above all, its colossal growth—produced stresses that once again plunged international economic life into chaos. At that point the Bretton Woods system was abandoned.

The crucial question is: What will take its place? If, for convenience' sake, floating can be called a system, it is not a system in the sense of providing for long-term orderly relationships in the international economy. It has served as a helpful device in freeing governments from having to uphold unrealistic fixed exchange rates, and it may be useful in the short term by permitting market forces to establish new and more realistic valuations of the world's currencies. But floating is intrinsically a retreat from the concept of cooperative controls over the international economy. As such it expresses the principle of anarchy and not of order. It cannot be expected to be very effective as a constraint when new economic dislocations again undermine confidence in stability—or when individual nations are tempted to resolve their difficulties with the old methods of economic nationalism.

A floating world is one in which the ties binding national economies together have been loosened. That is why the European Community members decided to float against the dollar but not against one another's currencies. If each of the Community's members had permitted its national currency to find its own level in the world market, the long-sustained momentum toward greater economic unity would have been arrested and possibly reversed. Certainly the projected European currency union would have suffered a major setback. The world is not as closely knit as the Common Market, but the analogy holds: a system in which each currency floats independently is an agent of disunity and not of unity.

The Bretton Woods international monetary system and its Smithsonian extension collapsed because they were unable to cope effectively with the pressures of market forces. Floating, in effect, is a bandwagon reaction: if these forces cannot be adequately regulated by governments, then governments should cease attempting to regulate and permit market forces themselves to function as the international regulating mechanism. But we have already seen that governments have too much at stake to concede to market forces unlimited power to define national status in the international economy. If nationalism is no longer unchallenged as the ideal way to organize political and economic life of the world's peoples, it still remains the reigning orthodoxy. So long as the nationalist orthodoxy prevails, governments will prefer the welfare of the domestic economy to the welfare of the international economy. This means that governments will interfere with market forces in the international economy in order to prevent unacceptable domestic consequences—or to capitalize on the difficulties of other governments.

MICROPOLITICAL AND MACROPOLITICAL PERSPECTIVES IN THE WORLD ECONOMY

The real issue, then, is not one of free market versus controls. It is instead one which poses two basic questions: What kind of balance will be struck between the free play of market forces and devices of control or regulation? Will the controls adopted be national or international? The first question assumes the unavoidable presence of some kinds of governmental control mechanisms. The second highlights once again the familiar confrontation between micro and macro considerations in both politics and economics. Economics necessarily conforms to the same rules governing all other aspects of international life. National solutions to international problems tend to be micropolitical in substance and effect. International solutions to international problems tend to be macropolitical in substance and effect. That is, micropolitical nationalism puts the interest of the sovereign nation ahead of all other considerations. Macropolitical internationalism advances the claims and concerns of the global society of which each nation is an increasingly integral and dependent part.

Micropolitical behavior in the international economy does not exclude cooperative behavior on a transnational basis. But it is at best fair weather cooperation. When serious dislocations arise, micropolitical assumptions dictate competitive rather than cooperative solutions. Secretary Shultz stated the problem very effectively when he observed that if international economic cooperation falters, "the pressures to retreat inward will be intense." He added: "We must avoid that risk, for it is the road to international recrimination, isolation and autarky."[18]

Unregulated market forces in both domestic and international economies have consistently demonstrated their long-term tendencies to favor the stronger at the expense of the weaker. To counteract these tendencies, and to obtain more equitable economic outcomes, political and governmental forces have intervened in the domestic market place. Such intervention came to be justified as a means of avoiding civil divisiveness and strife and to promote economic justice. The economic rationale for such intervention drew on the powerful argument that producers ultimately depend on consumers: the greater the number of disadvantaged and impoverished consumers, the fewer the producers' customers; conversely, the greater the number of affluent consumers, the greater the number of customers.

Until Bretton Woods, political and governmental intervention in the international market place had been largely of the self-help variety. That is, governments attempted to regulate international economic forces to their own advantage and independently of other governments. The system worked tolerably—for its stronger members at least—in times of market expansion. But whether strong or weak, a government's only defense against market contraction or other kinds of dislocations was to impose unilateral restrictions on the free flow of trade and investment. Other governments would follow suit, either in response to the same general market forces or in retaliation against specific restrictive prac-

---

[18] Statement by Secretary of the Treasury George Shultz at a press conference called to discuss the new devaluation of the dollar (Washington, D.C.: Bureau of Public Affairs, U.S. Department of State, February 12, 1973).

tices. The result was inevitably a shrinkage of trade and a general contraction and depression of the world economy. In these circumstances nations were transformed from trading and financial partners into trading and financial rivals—and, often enough, enemies.

The chief economic need of the West today is to prevent a repetition of these adversary dynamics. It is a need of governments because each is responsible for the economic welfare and peace of its people. It is also a need of private industry and finance, which has a profound stake in the annual flow of exports and imports, now nearing the $400 billion level, and the more than $400 billion worth of goods and services produced every year by multinational corporations.

Government and business now face together at the international level the same basic problems they faced earlier within the national economy. From the domestic economic experience they learned that neither can afford to permit uncontrolled market forces to propel them into cycles of boom and bust. Corporations, with their huge investments in money, men, and technology, require a secure, and preferably expanding, market for optimum returns. In order to obtain these ends, they have accepted government intervention in the domestic economy to regulate levels of consumer demand, and of their own profits as well. By the same token, the stability of governments in the industrial world depends on a high level of employment and a satisfactory relationship between wages and prices for the mass of their citizens. And governments have repeatedly intervened in the domestic economy to secure these ends.

The attainment of such domestic objectives is now increasingly dependent on the forces generated by a new factor: a giant and growing international economy. As Chapter 17 pointed out, business investment, sales, and profits in the transnational economy have been enormous. This is true because business has enjoyed relative freedom of movement in a relatively liberal international system of trade and finance. This is also true because business has had the benefit (until the early seventies) of being able to rely on relatively stable international currency relationships. All industrial governments, with their obligatory commitment to domestic prosperity, have benefited correspondingly. It follows that both government and business—as well as labor, agriculture, and the populace at large—have a profound stake in protecting and nurturing international economic life.

But the international economy can be protected and nurtured only if those who participate in it collaborate more than they compete. Without a mutually agreed on set of regulations and controls, analogous though not identical to the array of domestic regulators, competition will take the upper hand and fresh crises will produce varying intensities of economic warfare. The accumulation of crises since the late 1960s has already produced instances of such warfare. Indeed, crises have never been really absent at any period of international economic life. But for more than twenty years the Bretton Woods system demonstrated its capacity for constraining rivalries and adjusting clashing interests in a manner tolerable to those concerned.

The particularities of Bretton Woods have outlived their usefulness. But the general principles cannot be abandoned without grave political as well as economic dangers. Collaborative efforts by governments to facilitate the free flow of currency, investments, and goods, cooperative regulation and expansion of the international monetary base essential to the growth of the international economy, and a joint guarantee of a stable and therefore universally acceptable international reserve currency—these are the principles whose sacrifice would convert the new and incredibly rich transnational economy into a wealth-destroying battleground. They require a new articulation and a new embodiment in international economic organization. Otherwise, the growing wealth and spaciousness of the world economy will shrink, and with it the wealth and spaciousness of every domestic economy.

By the spring and summer of 1973 the danger signals were very much in evidence. The value of the dollar was again declining, not because of formal devaluation but because of renewed doubts among buyers and sellers of foreign currency concerning the dollar's stability. Their skepticism was aggravated by events within the United States. Sharp increases in domestic price levels and the Watergate scandals generated insecurities regarding the future course of both American politics and economics. As a result, other currencies were preferred to dollars in international money markets and therefore sold at higher prices.

Gold commanded the highest prices of all. Soaring to $127 an ounce in June 1973, gold was bought and sold at nearly quadruple the fixed value of $35 an ounce which had prevailed from the mid-1930s until the demise of Bretton Woods in 1971. A rush to gold is the classic symptom of failing confidence in monetary systems. Together with the further decline of the dollar, it provided new evidence that the resort to a floating system could serve only as a prelude to more basic remedies capable of dealing with the severe imbalances that have developed in the international economy. Among these are the continuing world-wide oversupply of dollars and the inflationary pressures which, by 1973, had spread to every economy in the West.

Yet the cumulative record of Western economic behavior, including most aspects of the 1973 Nixon trade bill,[19] demonstrates an awareness of many of these dangers and a readiness to combat them. So far, at least, one can conclude that the principle of attraction in the Western community has remained operative in conditions of major change and severe crisis: cooperation has continued to outweigh conflict in the

---

[19] Transmitted by President Nixon to Congress, April 10, 1973.

behavior of the members. So far, they have showed themselves unwilling to permit even major economic differences to endanger the alliances which bind them to one another militarily. Nearly a quarter-century of political and ideological solidarity has played at least as important a role in holding the community together through a time of stress. Above all, cooperation among Western nations has built so massive a structure of international trade and transnational investment that they could not allow conflict to place it in jeopardy without each one inviting upon itself the direst internal economic consequences.

Thus the community of the West has repeatedly exhibited a compelling will of its own greater than the wills of the members; the concern for the whole has significantly modified the behavior of the parts. Whether the community will prevails in future tests is a moot question. But the stake of the West in international economic, and therefore political, collaboration grows with the continuing growth of an already enormous transnational economy. It is this shared transnational interest that has become the prime warranty for the future vigor of the community will.

The world at large, in turn, has its own high stake in the continuance of Western community. A West riven by conflict will be crippled in its ability to generate the capital, technology, markets, and financial instruments essential to world development. The hopes of the poor societies for adequate levels of development assistance and internationalization of aid funding and management must founder if economic nationalism regains its old ascendancy among the rich. Justified criticism of the past behavior of the industrial West ought not to obscure the calamitous consequences for the underdeveloped South if the richest nations in the world forsake international collaboration for an uninhibited pursuit of their self-formulated national interests. Pending the emergence of a still larger community, the erosion of Western solidarity would run wholly counter to the objective survival requirements of the world economy and the world society.

Chapter 20

Transnational Society: West and East

Enmity has been the central characteristic of the relationships between the West and the communist East. Since the close of World War II—but with roots going back a century earlier—conflict has been the dominant theme, and cooperation has been sporadic and minimal. West and East have been ideological, political, and military enemies, and all attempts over the years to reach mutual accommodations on specific issues have not altered these enmities. These observations hold true even amidst the spectacular efforts at détente in the early 1970s. At no time in the history of negotiations between the antagonists has there been any intention by either side to bring an end to hostility, or even to moderate it in any significant way. The periodic agreements that have been reached have simply registered the outcomes of threat and counterthreat. Or they have been mutually agreeable tactical arrangements enabling the contestants to carry on hostilities on somewhat more convenient and less expensive terms without, presumably, impairing their combat capacities.

Since the leading powers in East and West both dispose of sufficient nuclear force literally to stop the world, their struggle places all mankind in mortal peril. As long as the struggle continues the peril must persist, its consummation postponed only so long as the mutual fear of the antagonists also persists. These are the circumstances, unique in human history, that have created the central mechanism of the contemporary international system: the bipolar balance of terror. It is a mechanism that cannot soon or easily be replaced; it follows that the threat of annihilation will be a condition of man's existence into the foreseeable future.

Even the blurring of lines between East and West cannot alter this prospect. American initiatives toward China in the early 1970s and Soviet countermoves in seeking agreements with India and Japan—like the sporadic efforts of France to insulate some of its policies from East-West antagonisms—merely represent tactical regroupings in the continuing struggle. The same is true for the spectacular break between Russia and China that occurred more than a decade earlier.

Chinese defection diminished and weakened the Soviet bloc, but it has not revised the basic conditions governing the international system. It could not do so because China did not, and does not, have the power to challenge the supremacy of the American and Russian superpowers. Chinese policy both before and since the warming of American-Chinese relations leaves no doubt that it ultimately intends such a challenge. But its timing will depend on the growth of Chinese power far beyond current levels. In the meantime, China, like all other states, can only make tactical adjustments to gain a more advantageous position within the balance of terror system.

The beginning of American and Chinese efforts at détente in 1971 coincided with the deterioration and crisis of American relations with Europe and Japan. At the same time, the Soviets were showing themselves more forthcoming toward old antagonists in Europe as well as in Asia. It was also the period in which Common Market negotiations with Britain finally achieved success, with the result that an enlarged European Community would soon be able, at least in economic terms, to claim superpower status. All these events were both cause and effect of an increase and acceleration of diplomatic activity without precedent in postwar history.

The result was a new international climate; the old criteria used to distinguish friend from foe no longer seemed so clear. Both fears and hopes centered on portents of new combinations and alignments. Important changes were indeed under way, greater than any since the onset of the Cold War. But systemic change—the replacement of the balance of terror system by another kind of system governed by fundamentally different rules—remains confined to the realm of long-range possibilities. In terms of probabilities, the preeminence of the United States and the Soviet Union is likely to persist beyond the turn of the century. This means that America and Russia will continue to be the foremost powers in West and East, however fluid or rigid the dividing line between them. It also means that in the coming decades they will continue to bear the heaviest burdens of responsibility for world peace or world war.

AMERICA AND RUSSIA: CONFLICT AND PARTNERSHIP

At center stage in the confrontation of East and West, then, is the Soviet-American duel. Communist China, on the occasion of its entry into the United Nations in 1971, made a barbed acknowledgment of Soviet-American preeminence when it accused the two superpowers of monopolizing UN decision-making processes. The new Chinese chief delegate reinforced the acknowledgment by stressing that "China is still an economically backward country as well as a developing country" and therefore "belongs to the Third World." He promised that China would never imitate superpower behavior: "The superpowers want to be superior to others and lord it over others. At no time, neither today nor ever in the future, will China be a superpower subjecting others to its aggression, subversion, control, interference or bullying."[1] The self-serving character of these sentiments is obvious: they were another manifestation of China's long-standing ambition to gain acceptance as the selfless leader of the underdeveloped world. They also gave expression to China's still deeper purpose to dismantle the American and Soviet preeminence it presently acknowledges.

However artful the Chinese formulations, they are in tune with the resentments and fears that the strong have always inspired in the weak, and since the world's weak are in the vast majority, they appeal to majority sentiment. Moreover, the relative decline of American and Russian power is already under way, and every indicator in the international system testifies to the irreversibility of this trend. The crucial qualifier, of course, is that the same indicators point to a very gradual decline. Thus by the end of the century, the United States and the Soviet Union, even with relatively less power at their disposal in dealing with the rest of the world, are still likely to represent the two largest concentrations of power in the international system. This projection does not, however, alter the fact that the Chinese aspiration to reduce the world roles of America and Russia is in accord, and not in conflict, with historical trends. It hardly needs saying that China is interested in accelerating these trends.

There are, therefore, certain elements of similarity in American and Soviet relations with the rest of the world, the most basic being that they alone rank as superpowers. Both look out upon the rest of mankind as giants, and each provokes emotions ranging from acquiescence through unease and discomfort to fear and hatred. Each sees these emotions as the unavoidable but acceptable costs incurred in maintaining its leadership position. Each assumes that its relations with the other will have the decisive influence in determining the course of world events. And both have difficulty in imagining an international system that could function in any other way. In short, both in their own view and in that of outside observers there is a Soviet-American resemblance that persists despite the profound differences in their social systems and despite their long-standing enmity. And as the Chinese have long in-

---

[1] Chiao Kuan-Hua, *New York Times*, November 16, 1971. Chou En-Lai made the same point a few weeks earlier in an interview with a Japanese newspaper editor: "Our principles are clearcut ones. We are opposed to the 'major powers,' to power politics and to domination. We will not become a major power under any circumstances" (*New York Times*, November 9, 1971).

sisted, this resemblance indicates a certain coincidence of Soviet and American interests.

The supreme interest for both the United States and the Soviet Union is survival. In this they are not different from other states; what does differentiate them, however, is that their survival is a function of their mutual dependence. In the abstract, at least, all other states are free of this kind of dependence. While their continued existence may depend on the will of one or both of the superpowers, it does not depend on one another. That is, outside the circle of the superpowers, state A may threaten the survival of state B without *necessarily* jeopardizing its own survival. This generalization has held good since the beginning of history: victories, defeats, truces, and renewed hostilities or peaceful settlements were phenomena that have only rarely involved the actual annihilation of one of the contending parties.

The generalization continues to hold for most of the world today. Evidence to support the generalization is provided by the outcomes, since the dawn of the nuclear age, of the wars accompanying decolonization and of the civil and international wars that have lacerated every part of the underdeveloped world. Victory for one side has not meant annihilation for the other. Nor—and this is the crux of the matter—has military conflict meant annihilation for both. The United States and the Soviet Union are unique because military conflict between them does indeed pose the gravest risk of mutual annihilation. Measured against this risk, victory and defeat are drained of meaning.

The result is that America and Russia have been forced into a measure of joint management of their conflict so that it will not become unmanageable. Hence the reluctant but persistent efforts at reciprocal arms control described in Chapter 5. But the range of common interest extends beyond limitations on weapons. Stable or even reduced levels of armament cannot conjure away the threat of reciprocal extinction—unless, indeed, nuclear weapons were to disappear altogether and with them all knowledge of nuclear and missile technology. Barring this improbable contingency, there is a joint Soviet-American interest in preventing situations that could provoke resort to even the diminished arsenals which arms agreements might permit. The fear of destroying one another therefore generates a parallelism of interest not only in the realm of weapons capabilities but also in the world political and economic pressures that could activate their use.

The burdens of maintaining superpower status must be reckoned in terms of costs as well as risks. Both compel the superpowers to search for ways to cooperate despite their enmity. These are the common considerations that have unfailingly pushed them to the bargaining table in preference to the battlefield. Concerning costs, each knows that significant relief from the monstrous overloads of military expenditure can come only from mutual agreement. The steadily rising pressure for more consumer goods in the Soviet Union and the explosive problems of poverty, race, and environmental degradation in the United States have made such relief into domestic issues of first importance. The demands of the military are increasing internal economic and political tensions in both systems. The inevitable result is the strengthening of opposing demands, most overtly in the United States, for a different allocation of national resources in which the military would play a more modest role.

The pace of the superpower arms race also generates external costs and tensions. It reduces the capabilities of America and Russia to play an effective role in responding to the development needs of the global South, not to mention the more self-serving aspirations of various Third World governments. In the early 1970s, the ratio between expenditures on defense and foreign aid in the United States was approximately 31:1, and the Soviet ratio was still more extreme. This pattern of resource allocation by the superpowers cannot fail to increase the number of their enemies in the underdeveloped countries.

In all states in both the developed and underdeveloped world, the unrelenting growth of Soviet and American arsenals reinforces the already well-established argument that the unwillingness or inability of the superpowers to scale down their military might requires others to increase theirs. This has been the unyielding position adopted by China and France, dramatized by their refusal to sign the nuclear nonproliferation treaty. The longer the United States and the Soviet Union pursue the arms race, the more likely and numerous the converts to that position—and consequent denunciations of the treaty by those who signed it.

These considerations lead from present costs into future risks. It is futile to dwell on the risks to which the superpowers and all mankind would be exposed should a nuclear war actually break out. This is the ultimate catastrophe that all rational policy making must seek to avoid. A calculation of risks is meaningful only as it is addressed to policies that lead men closer to or further from the final risk.

The enlargement and proliferation of nuclear arsenals can only move the world nearer the brink. If unchecked, such a development would undoubtedly restore a degree of multipolarity to the world balance of power and reduce the American-Russian preponderance that has characterized the bipolar system. Greater equality in the distribution of power is indeed intrinsically desirable in the world society, but nuclear proliferation as a means to achieve it effectively negates its value. Greater equality would be purchased at the risk of greater fear, greater uncertainty, and greater probabilities of miscalculation and accident as the number of players in the nuclear game multiplies. Under these conditions, the road to equality and to the nuclear brink are the same—and at the cost of a still more immense and reckless diversion of resources from needs that, if unmet, menace human existence in a number of ways other than nuclear destruction.

It is evident, then, that all mankind has an objective interest in preventing the spread of nuclear weapons. Within this circle of universal interest, it is equally evident that the United States and the Soviet Union have a particular and joint interest, whose most emphatic manifestation was their common sponsorship of the nonproliferation treaty. But this near-consensus of interest cannot stand by itself. France and China, as the major treaty holdouts, demonstrate that nuclear safety has no automatic priority over other considerations. If America and Russia remain chained to the status quo of their own preponderance, the near-consensus against nuclear proliferation will crumble before rising demands for greater equality in the world power structure.

Insofar as these demands include nuclear armament, the joint American-Soviet interest in blocking proliferation can be defended by only two courses of action: One would require threats or force as a means to convince the other states concerned to shelve their nuclear intentions. The other would require a tandem decision by Russia and America voluntarily to reduce their own preponderance. The reduction would have to diminish nuclear inequality to a level acceptable to the non-nuclear states. And it would have to be accompanied by measures to give nonnuclear states a more equal international voice in all nonnuclear matters.

In short, the United States and the Soviet Union confront a world in which demands for greater equality are at the center of every major issue in international life. Nuclear armaments, political independence, economic opportunity, levels of development, access to the daily essentials for maintaining human life itself—inequality is the common mark of all these phenomena and a basic explanation for the venom they inject into the international system. America and Russia are the obvious and chief targets for the anger of those with inferior resources; if they are not the cause of all earthly inequities, their position at the summit is the most massive reminder of the gulf separating the powerful from the weak and the rich from the poor. It is also a reminder of the various levels of political subordination that bar most of mankind from any meaningful participation in decisions affecting the life and death chances of all of mankind.

CHOICES FOR THE SUPERPOWERS

The demands for greater equality once again re-create, now on a global scale, the classic confrontation between democracy and oligarchy. The superpowers, as the chief oligarchs, or dyarchs, also once again confront the classic choice: to defend their privileged position or to dismantle it to the point where the inequities inevitably remaining will be tolerable to the rest of the world. If status quo is the choice, their joint interests would become stronger. Mutual fear would be joined by a more resolute common interest in preventing third parties from sharing and thus diluting their power. As we have already noted, the superpowers would have a mutual interest in a stable world system and in preventing disturbances that might threaten the established order of power and privilege.

Such a policy would in fact be in keeping with the definition of community as a manifestation of the principle of attraction. The superpowers would be attracted to one another because each would be indispensable to the other, both for its immediate safety and in executing the status quo policies jointly agreed upon. But reciprocal attraction and the sense of community generated by fear of one another and by a coincident fear of the rest of the world are necessarily fragile. So long as the superpowers' marriage of convenience is marked by hostility, each must anticipate treachery from the other. This antagonism among the governors introduces another classic predicament of oligarchic rule. The solidarity imperative is constantly at odds with the counterimperative admonishing each oligarch to put his own interest ahead of the collective interest.

A Soviet-American duopoly is unavoidably subject to the rule that no oligarchy is ever monolithic; it is always composed of contending factions. Each faction, fearing treachery from the other, is driven to seek unilateral advantages in order to bolster its power against the other. At some stage in this jockeying for position, one faction may find itself decisively outmaneuvered and no longer able, with its own resources, to contest the ascendancy of the other. This is the moment when the weaker side abandons the solidarity ground rules of oligarchy and solicits allies outside the charmed circle of the oligarchic elite. But this is only one scenario; the fact is that these ground rules are vulnerable to constant violation. Given the uncertainty of information and the suspicions generated by hostility, each faction, no matter what its power position within the oligarchy, must constantly reckon the risks and gains of extraoligarchical alliances.

Oligarchy, then, is an inherently unstable form of government. The principle of the oligarchic community is to reserve to its members a monopoly of the crucial decision-making powers affecting itself and the larger society subject to its rule. But the oligarchs themselves are necessarily ambivalent toward their own monopoly and must constantly calculate whether their interests are better served by defending the oligarchy or betraying it. The more hostility prevailing among the oligarchs, the less scruple will restrain their calculations.

As long as there is a rough equilibrium among the oligarchs and a vast inferiority of forces outside the oligarchic circle, these maneuverings for position cannot fundamentally alter the total power structure. This has been the characteristic pattern of postwar international relations that produced the novel configurations of the Cold War and the bipolar system. No quantity of extraoligarchic alliances on either side could decisively change the terms of the contest between the superpowers themselves. Yet by the early 1970s, the rising power of Europe, Japan, and China had put the longevity of the bipolar system in question. In 1950 the superpowers were the *only* powers; by 1970, however great their continuing superiority, they were no longer alone in the world power structure. And, as noted earlier, they are due to find themselves ever more crowded. Hence the probes on both sides in the direction of new extraoligarchical alignments that sooner or later may indeed have major consequences for their bilateral relationships.

In these circumstances, both the United States and the Soviet Union must inevitably ask whether they can afford to continue the level of mutual hostility that prevailed during the period of their monopoly, or duopoly, of the world's power. We have already noted their collaboration to hinder the further spread of nuclear weapons and their efforts to reduce mutual fear of each other's weapons. In the evolution of deterrence strategy, the basic search for safety in a system of nuclear threat and counterthreat has come to include the doctrine that neither side must look *too* threatening lest miscalculation or panic touch off the very holocaust deterrence is designed to ward off. The series of arms control agreements from the test ban treaty of 1963 through the first official accord reached in 1972 by the SALT[2] negotiations constitute, among other things, mutual reassurances that neither side wishes to put the other in an intolerably dangerous position. Insofar as both America and Russia have evidenced the will to coexist on these terms, their enmity toward one another is now manifestly further from the ultimate degree of hostility than it was during the height of the Cold War.

In a world of increasingly volatile power distributions, of ever more sophisticated weapons, and of steadily tightening constraints on the relationships between man and his environment, rational policy making requires that the superpowers continue their efforts at rapprochement. Of course, rationality may not prevail. But the prospects for rational policy can never be ascertained by posing the either-or question which asks whether men will behave rationally or irrationally. This is because there is only one possible answer: men will always behave both rationally and irrationally, and the behavior of the superpowers has not been and will not be an exception to this rule. The more apposite question, then, concerns the premises of their efforts at collaboration: What kinds of shared goals—and policies designed to attain them—will increase the

---

[2] Strategic Arms Limitations Talks; see Chapter 5.

probabilities of future rational behavior and diminish the number of irrational choices?

THE CONSTRAINTS OF OLIGARCHY

Collaboration for the purpose of freezing the bipolar status quo has already been considered. It implies perpetuating the extremes of inequality toward which the international system has been moving for two centuries and which are epitomized in the postwar oligarchy, or dyarchy, of the superpowers. But the thrust of new forces and the Soviet and American responses to them are signals that the preeminence of the superpower dyarchy has already peaked. The odds are now against rather than for protracting the life of an international system dominated by a club of two.

An attempt by the superpowers to prolong the dyarchy cannot help but make their policies progressively more desperate and less rational. As they become less able to play the game of world supremacy and their own game of mutual enmity wholly by themselves, they must permit others to come closer to the center of power. But the purpose of preserving the dyarchy dictates that the intrusion of other powers must be temporary. When lesser states have served their purpose of restoring the bilateral balance between the superpowers, they must be removed once again to the sidelines—and with as few lasting gains as possible. In this situation each superpower must prefer unstable to stable combinations in its policies toward the rest of the world, a preference that may become manifest in the evolution of Chinese-American and Soviet-Japanese relations.

A political structure marked by gross inequalities in which the most powerful are sworn to defend the status quo against those with lesser power is nothing new. It can be observed again and again in the history of international and domestic politics. In the presently underdeveloped countries it typifies the domestic system—as it did in the traditional societies of the West before the Industrial Revolution. In international politics, almost without exception, oligarchy has been the name of the game, as the persistence of the ancient hierarchical concept of "great and small powers" attests. In both domestic and international politics, recurring pressures from the less powerful have intruded into the oligarchs' mutual rivalries and suspicions to plunge the system into periodic crisis. In the resulting breakdown of oligarchic solidarity, the oligarchs war on one another until one side gains ascendancy over the other.

The consequence in international politics has invariably been a reconstitution of the oligarchy, either by a calculated rehabilitation of the beaten oligarch (France after the Napoleonic wars) or the introduction of new oligarchs in place of old (the rise of the United States and Japan and the fall of Germany and Russia in World War I). This recurrent pattern is a faithful reflection of the anarchic context characteristic of international politics. Where there are no bonds of community and obligation among the oligarchs, and still less between the oligarchs and the rest of the world, the strong will seize and secure what they can and the weak will suffer what they must. For the oligarch, the will to superior power is tempered only by the fear of losing it; hence there is "respect" for the power of the other oligarchs, some of whom may be useful allies and others too dangerous to challenge.

As for the world outside the oligarchy, the same ambivalence prevails: the oligarch desires to maintain the oligarchy but "respects" new forces hostile to the status quo that generate enough strength to be useful as allies or to be dangerous if courted by rival oligarchs. These were some of the facilitating considerations at work when both Germany and Russia climbed back into the arena of oligarchs after World War I. They were as much in evidence in the West's rapid rehabilitation of Germany, Japan, and Italy after World War II. And they are manifestly present in the 1970s as China and India demonstrate power as well as weakness, and as it becomes evident that Japan's capability to become a nuclear power is also the capability to demand entry into the oligarchy.

Gaining or retaining membership in the oligarchy is thus a function of power. Since the decisions of the international oligarchies through most of history have been decisive for the fate of men subject to their dominance, membership in the oligarchy has consistently been an alluring prize. It has meant the difference between being the hammer of international politics and being the anvil. In such a context the zeal to gain power and the jealousy with which it is guarded should hardly occasion surprise; it is inherent in the system.

By the same token, the essential helplessness of the vast majority beneath the oligarchy in the face of war, oppression, or poverty is also an inherent part of the system. In the absence of shared values modifying and countervailing the role of power among the participants in any human society, considerations of strength and weakness must crowd out all other criteria in the making of decisions, and what is weak will not count. As long as these conditions prevail, new forces will make the journey from weakness to strength only to join the oligarchy. They may pull down established members or merely augment the population at the summit. But the result will be no more than a changing of the oligarchical guard—no matter how often China vows not to behave like a superpower.

The rule of oligarchy can be broken only by the disappearance of the anarchic context that gave it birth and whose persistence guarantees its continuance. For in anarchy there is no sanction other than that which strength can impose; it follows that the strong will call the tune, and it is precisely this which constitutes the formula for oligarchic rule.

It must be evident, then, that the reinforcing interaction between oligarchy and anarchy will weaken only to the extent that an increasing number of participants in all parts of the system perceive that it is generating intolerable dangers to their interests and aspirations. But the threat of bankruptcy is not enough to persuade the participants to abandon the system. They must also perceive the possibility of viable alternatives to the existing system which promise fewer dangers and greater benefits. Otherwise, there is no apparent option but to play according to the rules of the prevailing system and hope, or pretend, that its future is less sinister than the available evidence indicates.

The juncture at which signs of the impending bankruptcy of a society confront articulated alternative proposals for its reorganization has been throughout history the classic occasion for fundamental change. In domestic politics, the most momentous of all previous such junctures was reached in the eighteenth century when the rapid development of Enlightenment thought, of nationalism, and of the Industrial Revolution began to challenge the idea of the class state with the idea of the mass state. The main theme, no matter how often it was compromised or muffled, asserted itself as revolutionary and egalitarian, as democracy versus oligarchy. But democracy was not championed as an alternative in the abstract. The Industrial Revolution offered a concrete complement to the developing formula for universal political franchise: the growing prospect of a material abundance sufficient to meet the economic demands of newly awakened mass populations. And nationalism offered a new and magnetic set of loyalties to replace the old hierarchical principle of social cohesion.

Most important, the rising forces of democracy, nationalism, and industrialization created a situation in which the old and new did not necessarily have to face off in a zero sum game. Events proved—not always, but often enough—that gains for the new order did not automatically occasion equivalent losses for the old. As it evolved toward national democracy, the new and more spacious society demonstrated its capacity to attract erstwhile antagonists from the old order as well as the new mass constituencies.

In international politics, so portentous a juncture has yet to be reached. The menace of bankruptcy is evident enough. But the magnitude of the threat—the bankruptcy of human civilization itself—alternately staggers and freezes the imagination. At the same time, there is no obvious and immediate alternative to the system of international oligarchy. The option of transnational community based on egalitarian principles has already taken form in the West and is at least a relevant goal in the developing relationships between North and South. But in the East-West confrontation of the superpowers such an option has not yet emerged as a plausible objective. The global system remains in thrall to the interactions of anarchy and oligarchy, and the political, ideological, and military tensions between the chief oligarchs are not as amenable to resolution as are the economic issues in the West or even the massive issues of development between North and South.

Yet if there is now no probable replacement for the present structure of East-West relationships, and therefore no replacement of the global system dominated by them, pressures for and possibilities of fundamental change are nonetheless evident. Even if the intolerable dangers of nuclear war are partially offset by the balance of terror, its precariousness prods the superpowers to search for alternatives to an open-ended race in competitive armaments. As we have seen, the economic burdens of the nuclear contest and opposition to the entry of new members into the nuclear club add their own urgencies to the search.

Moreover, at the very largest order of magnitude, the global system itself threatens to become unmanageable. The exponential growth of world population is generating a larger and larger majority of the angry, the sullen, and the apathetic. Whatever the ratio in this mounting majority between those robust enough to be revolutionary and those too hungry and diseased to care much, none can be counted as supporters of the global status quo—and all must be reckoned among its liabilities. In radical effect, the population explosion is matched and magnified by the growing crisis of the biosphere. Resource exhaustion and resource pollution on a global scale put in question the survival prospects of mankind on any societal and technological terms heretofore devised.

The widening gap between global demand and global supply poses an unambiguous challenge to the prevailing international system. Any effort to reverse trends—to close the gap or even to narrow it—will require a reallocation of resources and a reordering of priorities clearly incompatible with current patterns of consumption and with the inherited patterns of international political behavior. The growing visibility of the threat and of the directions that must be taken to combat it offer the best hope for rational responses by those in the present international system whose response counts most. As the chief oligarchs and rivals in the global hierarchy, the superpowers can hardly be expected to join forces in a movement to revolutionize the existing system. But it is not unrealistic to anticipate that they could reach incremental agreements to reform the system in order to cope more effectively with the dangers that threaten its collapse.

A POLICY OF DEVOLUTION

The key requirement for effective reform is the reallocation of resources away from armaments budgets and into undertakings that will offer all human beings a better life and a better chance to live it. This means a renewed and far more massive—and culturally sensitive—commitment to the development of the South. It also means a simultaneous commitment to the conservation of the biosphere and to the development of the technology necessary to its preservation. A political corollary is attached to these reallocations of military, economic, and technological investment: a commitment to accommodate and accord legitimacy to new forms of political pressure that must necessarily emerge in a world less cowed by nuclear fears and less constrained by the scarcity of resources to sustain everyday life.

The political corollary, better than anything else, suggests the price tag for meaningful reform of the international system. In a world moving away from the point of desperation, political pressures must become more and not less numerous, and the violence potential of these pressures must increase. In a system that perpetuates inequality, the weak see violence as the sole alternative to acquiescence, but their very weakness severely inhibits recourse to it. But in a system moving at least some distance toward greater equality, the resources of the weak must, by definition, increase.

In such a context, violence may no longer be the only plausible way to effect further change. But the weaker side will have a greater will to violence and a greater capacity to use it if other methods fail to achieve its purposes. For the strong, of course, resort to counterviolence and suppression does not become impossible. But it does become more difficult and costly, and mastery of the system is no longer indisputably in their hands.

Whether they will it or not, events are pressing in on the superpowers to make a momentous choice between two courses of action. One is undoubtedly attractive as the line of least resistance: continuing to put their own preeminence above all other considerations. But the inexorable price is to be fettered to a system that grows less and less viable. Even if the superpowers can fortify their competitive advantages as against the rest of the world, they cannot eliminate competition from others—and certainly not between themselves. The terms of competition, in turn, would necessarily become fiercer and the risks more deadly. A world whose resources go unconserved is one that must sooner or later move from anarchy toward chaos. In such a context the ability of even the strongest to exercise control must diminish, and the probabilities of catastrophe, nuclear or otherwise, must increase.

The other course of action is also filled with peril, belying the innocuous label of reform. Choosing this course, the superpowers would by mutual agreement reduce their military superiority over the rest of the world and therewith their ability to coerce it. By shifting freed resources to human development and global conservation they would narrow still further the distance that separates them from the weaker and weakest members of the international system. In short, some of their power would devolve upon others. The dangers are obvious. The superpowers are not the only ones inclined to oligarchy, and the ruling ambitions of rival powers may expand as the old inequalities grow less.

The choice for reform may also come too late—or the measures for its implementation may consume too much time—to repair the social and physical damage already sustained by the world at large. In this case, a choice for reform would degenerate into a futile attempt to parcel out insufficient resources among unappeasable appetites, not only for food and health but also for revenge. Faced with this predicament, the superpowers' most likely reaction would be to try to reverse course and restore the dyarchy. But the perils entailed in a subsequent policy of restoration would be still greater than those attending a policy of devolution.

Yet the risks inherent in a dying system cannot be rationally preferable to the risks accompanying an attempt to renew the chances for life. Besides, in the latter course there are compensating elements of safety. The margin of military superiority of the superpowers is so great that much of it could be ceded without irreparable damage to their defensive capacities. Their economic, technological, and population advantages would remain largely intact, while their political advantages might even increase.

Despite the turmoil that any policy of devolution—of equalization—must bring with it, some of the forces set free by the new dispensation will begin to regard the superpowers with hope instead of despair, as political leaders instead of immovable and self-obsessed tyrants. In sum, the presently favored position of the superpowers is so formidable that they could divest themselves of some of their advantages over a long period of time before having to fear that they might be squandering them. And the losses in coercive power could be compensated by gains in the numbers of those they could attract on the basis of consent.

It is obvious, however, that a calculus of gains and losses for a policy of devolution must remain in the realm of contingency as long as a prior condition is unmet: the readiness of the superpowers jointly to pursue such a policy. Their mutual enmity is the most evident obstacle hindering the superpowers from satisfying that condition. But the novelty of the devolution concept (in international politics but not in domestic politics, as we have seen) is itself a formidable deterrent. Moreover, political internationalism at the global level has not yet developed a degree of force and tangibility comparable to the rising nationalist movements, which offered alternative and attractive ways of organizing domestic societies when domestic oligarchies faced the choice between status quo and reform. An international policy of devolution, then, would commit the oligarchs to move away from the old order without the materialized presence of a new order rising to replace it.

Finally, a joint policy of devolution assumes the ability and willingness of the superpowers to effect a retrenchment of power in tandem. Both must be able to feel confident that the relative equality of their power will be maintained during the process of retrenchment. The history of Soviet-American arms negotiations amply illustrates the difficulties surrounding the tandem concept. Of the handful of arms control agreements that have been reached, all have been designed to inhibit the acceleration of the arms race; only the treaty on biological weapons (see Chapter 5) ranks as a bona fide disarmament agreement. In particular, all proposals for mutually verified destruction of currently stocked nuclear weapons in matching quantities and qualities have died at the bargaining table.

The refusal to date by the superpowers to engage in any joint ventures in genuine arms curtailment only underlines the problematics of a joint policy of devolution. Moreover, to bring about a more peaceful world, such a policy on the part of the superpowers would have to go beyond a mere scaling down of their armaments in tandem. It would also require of them a measure of cooperation in the alternative allocations of resources made available as a result of their diminished military expenditures. Indeed, it has been the argument throughout this book that armaments constitute only one element among the factors of power. It follows that altering the world military structure also implies a reallocation of the entire inventory of world resources.

The connection between armaments and other elements of the international complex was amply documented during the Washington meetings between President Nixon and General Secretary Brezhnev in June 1973. Among a whole series of agreements, conventions, and protocols signed on that occasion by the two heads of state, one concerned itself directly with armaments: a commitment to speed up SALT II negotiations by bringing forward from 1977 to 1974 the deadline for new agreements to limit strategic weapons. Another agreement pledged the superpowers to avoid policies that could provoke nuclear confrontations and to mutual consultations should the risk of such a confrontation appear imminent. All the remaining agreements concerned themselves with such diverse matters as bilateral trade expansion, agricultural, environmental, and space cooperation, joint oceanographic projects and exploration of new energy sources (including nuclear energy), and collaborative research in specialized aspects of biological and physical sciences and in transportation engineering.

Soviet-American détente, then, manifestly requires much more than agreements to curb the arms race. So does a global détente. Suspicion and antagonism between North and South cannot be dissipated simply by a superpower pact to freeze the armaments status quo. Only if SALT II achieves an actual reduction in the overwhelming superiority of American and Soviet arms will confidence have a chance to grow—in the rest of the world as well as between the superpowers themselves. Above all, arms reduction must be accompanied by superpower initiatives to reduce their lopsided preponderance over the rest of the world in wealth, technology, and educational opportunity. In other words, relationships of peace between East and West and between North and South share an identical requirement: not just better techniques for conflict settlement but concrete and comprehensive changes in the prevailing power relationships that produce conflict.

It should be clear, therefore, that the implications of a devolution policy add up to a radical departure from the present international system. But it is not so radical as to be beyond reach and practicality. The United States and the Soviet Union, and other countries in the developed world as well, have power and wealth enough to venture the sharing of them in comparative safety. Moreover, experience gained by the superpowers in pursuing a common and cooperative path of sharing can achieve additional safety, because it is this kind of experience which creates the basis for a growing sense of community between them.

The obvious sources and strengths of resistance to such a policy do not detract from the fact that devolution is the only rational option open to the superpowers in a world whose prevailing trends of demand and supply are on a collision course. The collision quite simply cannot be prevented unless the two greatest consumers and producers in the system join hands to prevent it. Otherwise, the world's poor majority will double itself by the year 2000 and double again less than twenty years after that. Depletion and pollution of the earth's resources would inexorably accelerate, first, as a result of the population explosion itself and, second, because of the reckless allocation of resources that sacrifices conservation and replenishment to the priorities of competitive consumption and the arms race. The resulting constriction of global society must produce rising levels of fear and violence to a point where the cumulative probabilities of a resort to nuclear arms will become a certainty.

The superpowers have already demonstrated that they do not desire to precipitate their joint suicide in a nuclear war. It is therefore not unrealistic to expect that they will consider measures which will increase their chances of avoiding such an outcome in the future. The imperative of survival is often—though not always—a compelling force in the formulation of policy. That imperative requires the superpowers to move the world away from the brink to which it has been driven by the ancient game of oligarchy and to begin to build those conditions of equality indispensable to safety and peace. Whether and when the superpowers will recognize the interdependence of survival, equality, and peace is uncertain, but events are bound to make the point with increasing frequency and emphasis.

Chapter 21

Justice in the Global Society

Justice is the end of government. It is the end of civil society. It has ever been and ever will be pursued until it be obtained, or until liberty be lost in the pursuit. In a society under the forms of which the stronger faction can readily unite and oppress the weaker, anarchy may as truly be said to reign as in a state of nature, where the weaker individual is not secured against the violence of the stronger.[1]

These sentiments of the *Federalist* authors faithfully reflected the revolutionary spirit of their times. Their more conservative persuasions notwithstanding, they were here at one with the central concerns of the Declaration of Independence for life, liberty, and equality. And they foreshadowed the triad of liberty, equality, and fraternity that became the domestic and international battle cry of the French Revolution. Like the revolutionary theses of 1776 and 1789, these makers and advocates of the American Constitution declared justice and oppression to be the great antagonists in the drama of politics.

If the proper end of government is justice, then oppression must be repugnant to any government properly constituted. The antipathy of justice and oppression necessarily follows from the characteristics attributed to each. Concerning oppression, Federalist 51 is explicit: it is any situation in which the weak are defenseless against the will of the strong. Lacking defenses, the weak must be constantly vulnerable to subjugation, violence, and all manner of constraints. The authors persuasively used history to reinforce logic in demonstrating the truth of these arguments (a reinforcement that subsequent events have in turn reinforced). The function of justice, then, is clear: to rescue men from the anarchy whose general property is conflict and whose particular characteristic is the victimization of the weak. Justice replaces constraints

---

[1] *The Federalist*, Number 51. It has never been established whether Hamilton or Madison was the author of this key essay in the classic series that they jointly produced and to which John Jay also made significant contributions.

with liberty and subjugation with equality. Its instrument is a civil society united by the proposition that equality and freedom are the inalienable rights of all its members. Completing the circle of reasoning, the right use of political liberty is defined as service to the cause of justice. The premise that justice is the proper object of government—and therefore of political activity—permits no other conclusion.

These propositions about political norms, in their interaction and in their sum, correspond faithfully to the categorical ethic of Kant for the whole of human behavior: men should be treated as ends in themselves and not as means to the ends of others. But norms, whatever their validity, are by definition prescriptions for man's conduct and not descriptions of it. The distance between norm and reality may vary, but it never reduces to zero; a degree of divergence and conflict is consequently inevitable. A chain of events may promote the realization of norms, but the realization is always a transient one, or at best recurrent, because events are by nature time-bound. Yet if events collaborate in realizing norms, it follows that there must be an interdependence between norms and events, between norm and reality, that makes for mutual ambivalence rather than for a necessary hostility.

Hostility, however, is usually more visible than ambivalence—to the point where norms and events typically appear to be at war with one another. This was dramatically true concerning the norms of the Constitution-makers. Their propositions concerning justice and oppression were stated in the same universal language which marked the Declaration of Independence when it asserted that equality is the birthright of all men. The words of 1787 as well as of 1776 were a plain declaration of war on slavery, racism, and oligarchy. But slavery, racism, and oligarchy persisted; further, they received sanction from the very men who used the language of equality. Under the American Constitution justice, in fact, rescued only some men from subjugation, violence, and all manner of constraints. And of those who were rescued, some were endowed with legal rights themselves to play the oppressor. If events surrounding the birth of the United States collaborated to bring norm and reality close, they subsequently demonstrated the imperfections and transience of their coming together.

MICROPOLITICS: THE VULNERABILITIES OF JUSTICE

The fundamental difficulty with the norm of justice is that it both attracts and repels. Men generally desire not to be victims of oppression, but the admonition against oppressing others has less appeal. Hence that repetitive set of events in which men attempt to seize the good of justice for themselves without accepting the obligation it lays upon their behavior toward others. Hypocrisy and cynicism are not the only motivations for or consequences of this option. The more extensive and diverse the social circumstances to be subjected to the government of justice, the more complex the relationship between norm and reality must be. Since the establishment and defense of justice in any set of circumstances is a task that is never easy and never finished, there are always formidable pressures to set limits to its jurisdiction. The most formidable of these pressures derives from the voluntaristic nature of justice itself. That is, justice cannot be imposed; it can only be defended. Successful defense, in turn, depends on the availability of a sufficient number of people who will freely obey the rule of justice and freely unite to defend it.

The unavoidable dependence of justice on consent is the fundamental, though not inclusive, explanation why justice has always achieved only incomplete, parochial, and transient victories in human societies, why justice characteristically finds expression in micropolitical rather than macropolitical forms. The ambivalent attitudes toward suffering and inflicting oppression furnish the largest part of the reason why consent to justice is so often withheld and why, once given, it is often so tenuous. In these circumstances, fear that others will not honor their obligations to the just society is rooted in the recognition of the self's own ambivalence. It is this fear, then, that operates as a permanent threat to the coherence of the just society, a fear all the more formidable because it is realistic and not illusory. The reality of the threat, however, does not mean it cannot be dealt with realistically. Fear of the destruction of social obligations and of oppression can be successfully countered as long as the society is able to demonstrate the vigor of its commitment to justice and its continuing ability to create conditions of consent.

The fear of being dominated—and the hankering to dominate—are the principal subverters of justice in established societies. Still more are they the chief adversaries to the extension of justice, whether within a society or between societies. The greater the psychological, social, and cultural distances among members of a society, the more prevalent the fear of oppression and the stronger the inducements to oppress. Shrinking these distances is an obvious and proved remedy, but the indestructable fact—and value—of diversity always sets limits to its application. Physical distance also makes its variable contribution to social remoteness within a society. Between societies it has characteristically been the chief impediment to just relationships because the sense of physical separation has usually negated the sense of interdependence.

The most generous and complete concept of justice wills it for all, but throughout history every social expression of this will has always restricted it to some. The specific causes are varied and related: insufficient power to extend the rule of justice beyond given physical or cultural limits; cultural disagreements concerning the meaning of justice and, even where there is agreed meaning, disputes over the terms of its implementation; the illusion that the form a particular society gives to the rule of justice is as universal as the principle it (imperfectly) reflects; the consequent penchant to assume that a more extended rule of justice can only come about when outsiders conform to the local articulations of justice as well as to its general principles. Social and physical distances interact with and reinforce all of these constraining forces. But they derive the largest part of their energy from the corrupting ambivalence of human attitudes toward oppression and, therefore, toward justice itself.

In the face of all these impediments even dedicated seekers of justice must be tempted to settle for half a loaf. If the external world proves intractable, the sole choice is to abandon the search or to delimit the enterprise and stake out defensible boundaries within which to undertake the nurture of justice. What durable social expressions of justice there have been are in fact products of the option for boundaries. The result is a world marked by the coexistence of injustice and justice with the latter characteristically manifesting itself in enclaves.

THE COMMUNITY AS ENCLAVE

The earliest and most enduring of these enclaves is the family. From the beginning of history the family, both nuclear and extended, has functioned as a refuge from the anarchy of the larger society. Within its confines the family has characteristically valued collective loyalty, mutual support, individual rights and obligations, protection of the weak, and restraints on the strong. Even when these norms have been honored more in the breach than in the observance, the cumulative record of the family as a social organization for the promotion of justice surpasses that of any rival. For much of history there was no rival; beyond the family there were only tyrants and oligarchs battling for preeminence in an anarchic void. In much of the underdeveloped world today, the family continues to outperform the rival organizations of state, nation, party, and class as a bulwark against the ravages of anarchy and tyranny. Even in the West, the family remains a sometime refuge from the harshness that often enough marks the terms of existence in larger collectivities.

In its ideal form and in much of its historical record the family displays the familiar characteristics of community. That is, the family whole is greater than the sum of its individual parts, if only because the unity of the collectivity is the indispensable condition for effectively protecting the individual members from the storms beyond its confines. There are the obvious needs for protection against other families, against other kinds of social organizations, against tyrants and oligarchs. In meeting these needs the family functions as an instrument of power.

But the anarchy of battle in the outside world is not the only threat.

Family solidarity, with its corresponding rights and duties, represents one of the historic choices between order and anarchy as a way of life. If the individual members fail to honor family solidarity and fail to abide by its rules, the community becomes prey to anarchy not by the acts of external foes but by internal subversion. Community is the existential antithesis of anarchy; without it there is no refuge from the chaos where none have rights or duties. Community therefore has an intrinsic value independent of the presence or absence of external threats. It is the only context within which men can combat oppression by nurturing a community-based concept of justice.

With suitable modifications to allow for time and circumstance, the analysis of family as community can be applied to all social organizations. This is so because the functioning of all organizations necessarily depends on a measure of solidarity among their members. The general norms and dynamics of social cohesion in the family are therefore no different for tribe, nation, state, class, party, ideology, religion, or race. Whether the community is great or small, all share the characteristics of the enclave. At various points in history each of these enclaves has offered a set of ordered relationships constructed from the proposition of solidarity which the members were invited to contrast with the relatively unstructured and anarchic outside world.

Moreover, though their practice has often been otherwise, all these enclaves have represented themselves ideally as voluntary organizations designed to benefit the members. Since oppression must conflict with the promise of benefits, the enclave, again ideally, must function as a context in which the members are able to pursue their aspirations for justice. To the extent that they are satisfied in this respect, their loyalties to the enclave-community are reinforced.

Because of the ambivalence of human attitudes toward justice and the resulting difficulties in its nurture, the satisfactions of the enclave dwellers may often be spurious. But as long as satisfactions are perceived, whether authentic or bogus, the conviction that the enclave-community is dispensing justice will persist. So will a morale whose most common expression assumes the superiority of the particular community to any alternative—not only to anarchy but also to other communities or other forms of community.

In short, the enclave-community is typically vulnerable to the familiar dynamics of in-group psychology. Their consequences for relations with out-groups are also familiar, running the gamut of hard-heartedness from alliances of convenience to conflict, hatred, and war—and oppression. It follows that in-group psychology necessarily subverts the idea of a universal justice. The contradiction between the proclamation of human equality in the Declaration of Independence and the American reality is only one of many such conflicts rooted in the in-group mentality of the enclave.

Yet the vices of the in-group mentality ought not to obscure the real services of the enclave-communities to human justice. They have often been, in fact, a refuge from and a grateful contrast to the harshness of the world outside their gates. Even a deficient observance of the rules specifying reciprocal rights and duties generates conditions of life preferable to those where the only rule is coercion. These enclaves of imperfect justice have provided the indispensable contexts for the growth of trust, for the sense of familiarity that makes living less risky, or at least more congenial, than in an alien world of strangers. All these are qualities for which the civil society is typically celebrated and preferred over the state of nature.

The preference for civil society—for civil behavior—is no abstract option offering protection against the perils of some mythical primeval chaos. Insofar as the state of nature depicts a realm devoid of social loyalties and rules of social conduct, it has been a continuously evident and concrete presence in human history.[2] It exists in the indifference and corruption of many of the societies within which the extended family system still prevails as a sanctuary in the social wilderness. It is to be found in the cash nexus which Marx excoriated, that market place where human values are reduced to economic utility and where the economically stronger exploits the weaker as a matter of course.

It is inherent in the propositions of racism that deny the humanity of those not belonging to the chosen race and so give over relations among races to anarchy and coercion. The state of nature has been most characteristically evoked to describe the relations among states for which the law of the jungle has been the favorite metaphor. In fact, however, the state of nature concept and the jungle metaphor pertain to every condition where human beings interact in the absence of felt mutual obligations.

Man is properly labeled a social animal because he has consistently and universally preferred some historically concrete form of civil society to some historically concrete form of the state of nature. It follows that the civil society, whatever its shortcomings, is a powerful magnet for human loyalties. Moreover, since civil society is typically parochial— that is, it is built on the principles of the enclave-community—human loyalties are typically concentrated in particular civil societies and not in the idea of social civility as such.

This pattern of investing social loyalties does much to explain the persistence of particular civil societies over time. It also helps to account for the coexistence of a multiplicity of civil societies at any given time. Finally, it contributes significantly to the explanation for the recurrent fierceness with which a particular civil society is defended or aggran-

---

[2] The state of nature concepts of Locke and Rousseau were less anarchic than those of Hobbes, but all three were agreed on the imperative of social contract if men were to be spared the evils of life without community.

dized. Members are often persuaded that only their own enclave-community can offer them the reality or the prospect of justice and that its erosion or destruction must deliver them up to conquest. Since conquest means being helpless before the will of the stronger, to be conquered is functionally identical with anarchy—the state of nature against which all civil societies attempt to insulate themselves.

The fears of the enclave dwellers are real; the bitter experiences of minority groups within states, the consequences to societies vanquished in war, and the fate of victims of imperial expansion provide sufficient and terrible testimony to that point. The link between the fall of the community and the triumph of injustice has shown itself to be one of the great and tragic regularities of history. Hence it is an understandable and sometimes heroic choice to put the preservation and the power of a particular civil society above all else. The attraction of the enclave-community must therefore not be underestimated in any realistic assessment of its present role and future prospects. Nor should it be undervalued. The material satisfactions and moral opportunities with which it has enriched men's lives are beyond reckoning. In consequence, any proposal for alternative strategies for social organization cannot be persuasive unless it is sensitive to the values of the enclave.

ENCLAVE AND SOCIAL CHANGE

Yet if man's attachment to the enclave has been a mighty and constant force in the shaping of history, it has also yielded periodically to a still mightier counterforce: the will to social change. The struggle between status quo and innovation is the very stuff of history, but the still accumulating sum of outcomes on this perennial battleground always records the eventual surrender of the old to the new. The whole record of human events, then, shows that the tenacity with which men cling to inherited social arrangements finally yields to the desire for or acceptance of new social forms.

Often enough coercion is the cutting edge of change, and even voluntary change never occurs without conflict. But whether change is willed or imposed, the new order cannot maintain itself unless it can eventually attract the same kinds of loyalties and attachments that defined the old order's capacity to endure. It follows that any proposals for new social arrangements must be tested in terms of their probable capacities to attract loyalties sufficient in strength and scope to warrant confidence in both their consummation and their durability. Failing this test, proposals for social change—for abandoning any given enclave—must be visionary, violent, or both.

The evident theme of the argument (which appears in one form or another throughout this book) is that men will give their loyalties to social arrangements they deem just and will resist those arrangements they hold to be unjust. This hardly results in straightforward choices, however. The fundamental ambivalence toward the reciprocity requirements of justice repeatedly distorts the perception of its nature, and the enclave mentality functions as a persistent pressure to restrict its jurisdiction.

But ambivalence, distortion, and parochialism are only recurrent and not incessant phenomena. Otherwise, it would be impossible to explain the revolutionary social impact of those religious as well as secular movements that have rebuked human ambivalence toward justice and have asserted its universal authority over the particular jurisdictions and practices of the enclaves. All these movements, of course, have exhibited their own particularities, but their historical longevity has been and is a product of that part of their doctrines which transcends time and place. They have lived because human ambivalence toward justice has never irrevocably accepted the unambiguous proposition that justice is something to be coveted only for the self and never for others.

The quality of justice which both repels and attracts defines its weaknesses in competition with other values in political life. But there are also compensating strengths: the organic connection between justice and survival and the link between justice and the good life. Injustice threatens the survival of the individual to the degree that he is left defenseless against coercion and oppression. Injustice also threatens social survival to the extent that a society's members, perceiving themselves oppressed, withdraw their allegiance from it. Only the presence of justice can make individuals feel secure in their social existence. Individual security, in turn, translates into community allegiance and thus becomes the strongest of all the forces sustaining the life of a society.

Security, so construed, is the good life. It is not the same as survival on any terms or at any price, and it is therefore not the same as survival in misery and fear. The purpose of justice is to secure the safety and rights of all within its jurisdiction and thus to replace the constant menace of arbitrary coercion with the constant expectation of free choice— within a framework of social obligations based upon consent. How to create, maintain, and expand these conditions of social life is the key question in all of politics, from the level of the family unit to the global macrocosm. Justice is the evident answer, and therein resides its claim to be first among political values and the proper object of government. But because it requires great exertions in order to obtain the benefits it promises, justice often enough loses out in the competition with lesser political values.

Dependent on a sense of community and trust, justice is at a particular disadvantage where there is no perceived need for community. This lack —or failure—of perception is the chief reason that justice has typically found social expression in enclaves rather than among men at large.

Wherever the jurisdiction of justice has expanded, it is because the enclave mentality has given way to a larger sense of community. That is, there has been a recognition among men of different enclaves (families, tribes, classes, nations) that they could not defend their survival and their security independently of one another. Without the perception of interdependence, there can be no extension of community. Without the extension of community, there is no way for justice to expand its jurisdiction.

MACROPOLITICS AND JUSTICE

Of the possible jurisdictions in which to extend the rule of justice, the international system is the largest of all. It is the macrocosm of all human societies; as such, its vastness and diversity have so far fated justice to be a consistent loser in the international competition with such other political values as power, wealth, and parochial interest. The idea that there could be a community of interests at the global level—and hence a context conducive to the pursuit of justice in global relationships —could attract very little practical attention in a world where physical and social remoteness defined political assessments and decisions. For at least two thousand years, religious leaders, philosophers, international lawyers, and both conservative and revolutionary politicians have occasionally come forward to assert the unity and interdependence of all human beings. But the historic case for the community of man has clashed with powerful realities as well as powerful illusions; it has been perennially confounded by this combined opposition.

Any present assessment of the prospects for international justice must give the somber record of repeated experience full weight; otherwise it would forfeit its claim to realism. But this is only the first step in realistic analysis. The next is the recognition that the problem of justice for all men is posed today in a context fundamentally, though by no means completely, different from any in which human beings have ever lived before. It is a world in which human capacities for productivity have expanded beyond all verifiable finite limits—to a point where the material conditions and potentials of man's life are qualitatively different from previous history. It is also a world in which, for the first time, human capacities for destruction have literally become infinite. This fantastic amplification of the powers of production and of destruction has wrenched these powers loose from their familiar geographic and cultural confinements, and they have become world-wide in scope and impact. Because of them the globe has lost its immemorial vastness; science, wealth, and weapons have compressed it into a local habitation in which men everywhere are linked together by common bonds of life and death.

In short, the world of the late twentieth century is a transformed world, a world which must deal with phenomena of giant magnitude and import never before encountered. Unprecedented acceleration in the growth of human numbers, of wealth and poverty, of technological innovation, of the production and consumption of energy, and in the exploitation and abuse of the environment has populated the world with sudden and huge mutations. The historic patterns of long and slow evolution in both nature and society have been ruptured by the emergence of these mutant prodigies.

Thus the world is transformed, in effect, in time as well as space. Both of these basic dimensions of life have been radically compressed; so altered, they are the most momentous of the new realities with which man's political and social practices must reckon. In their old and extended forms space and time favored the politics and society of the enclave; at the global level this meant the enclave of the (sometimes) sovereign state. In their new compressed forms they have made the state-enclave, as traditionally constituted, into a deathtrap. In other words, powerful realities that formerly stood against and blocked the realization of a community of man have switched sides.

The moral case for the global community is now buttressed by practical imperatives. In consequence, the traditional case for the state-enclave as the only practical response to man's needs for political, economic, and social organization and to his yearnings for justice is correspondingly weakened. This change in the terms of debate, of course, does not mean that the enclave called the state is suddenly bereft of all the objective supports that contributed to its persistence throughout history. Nor does it mean that it necessarily faces imminent demise because it is no longer a realistic way to structure man's political life. What it does mean, however, is that the historically invincible coalition of objective forces on which it based its claims to sovereign self-sufficiency has been broken.

The problem for the state, then, is not automatic doom, but a problem which is far more difficult (since nothing can be done about automaticity). It is to assess the present and future impact of the massive shift in the configuration of natural and historical forces and to draw the consequences for its own behavior. The most difficult moment of this exercise will come when there is recognition of the basic political change produced by the transformed world: the state can no longer be both sovereign and secure. That is, human security and human survival can be rationally sought only through cooperative efforts at the global level and not behind the ramparts of the inherited enclaves.

As a result, the sovereign state as an effective and comprehensive solution to the problem of security has reached the terminal point of its development. It follows that it must begin to divest itself of the ancient sovereign claim to the exclusive loyalties of its inhabitants. It must be willing instead to foster a sharing of loyalties between the states and transnational institutions that will assume or share functions previously reserved to the state alone. The sharing of loyalties is crucial because no new institution can survive if it cannot make its own compelling claims to allegiance.

This is the indelible lesson of all transfers of function from smaller to larger and more comprehensive units of organization: the operation of the federal principle in the European community and in the United States itself provides obvious examples. It is also the lesson of federative enterprises that the transfer of functions can be gradual and selective. There is no need, for example, to assume that only an international body with total control of the means of coercion could save mankind from itself. Indeed, such a solution is neither possible nor desirable in the foreseeable future. What is possible and desirable is an end to the arms race and a radical reduction in existing armaments—within a negotiated framework of mutual verification that permits the state-enclaves to come to terms with other aspects of their new environment without being harassed by the constant dread of their own extinction.

What is required of the state-enclaves is not that they should disappear but that they should change. Neither is there required for the community of man some impossible feat that suddenly engineers a full-blown superstate. The requirement set by the new realities of the international system is at once simpler and, again, more difficult (for one can do no more about impossibility than about automaticity). It is to recognize that the idea of the human community has moved from the realm of illusion into the practical realm of the attainable—and that human survival and security depend on human behavior directed toward reaching that attainable end. It is to recognize that a new imperative has been injected into human history and that men must govern themselves accordingly or perish.

The new imperative is manifest in the massive forms with which we are already familiar. All men are now caught between the upward curve of population growth and the downward curve of resource availability. There is passionate argument whether it is possible to escape the final trap these curves project. But there can be no argument that rescue is more likely in a world that invests in cooperative solutions than in a world ridden by divisiveness and conflict.

All men are now caught in the global economic net in which social and individual wealth and poverty in one society are inextricably bound up in the social and individual wealth and poverty of all other societies. All men now experience the global impact of a constantly changing technology. As a result, they have at last achieved equality as candidates for extinction—but much less than equality in their opportunities for creative and life-enhancing use of technology.

THE NEW TERMS FOR SURVIVAL

These giant new forces of the political cosmos at once beckon and admonish men to emerge from their deteriorating enclaves so that they can examine realistically the new terms that have been set for survival and security. The new terms are recognition of global interdependence, cooperative efforts to protect and enhance the vitality of the interdependent parts, and a will to defend the integrity of the global whole as the necessary condition for the continuing life of the parts. Of course, the terms are new only in the magnitude of their dimensions. Substantively, they merely restate the ancient requirements that all communities of whatever scope, each in its specific way, must meet.

The community norm requires that all members share a common concern for the rights and welfare of each member and that the nurture and defense of this common concern be recognized as the condition for the survival and security of both the community as a whole and the individual members. Of course, the reality of any given community—family, tribe, religion, nation—is never identical with the norm, and communities have survived even spectacular deviations from it. But tolerance for deviations has its limits; if they are exceeded, the norm loses its vitality and the community disintegrates. This follows because the more numerous and extreme the deviations, the closer will be that anarchy in which rights and welfare are safeguarded not by mutual obligations but only by superior strength. Then the weak, unprotected by community, will deny it their allegiance, while the strong, unrestrained by community, will destroy it.

Like justice, then, community involves obligations and restraints as well as the promise of survival, security, and peace. Like justice, community both attracts and repels because it couples its offer of safety and freedom from fear of oppression with the commandment not to oppress. The result is that men are as ambivalent toward the requirements of community as they are toward the requirements of justice. More than any other factor, it is this fundamental ambivalence that causes the death of existing communities and impedes the birth of new ones. When a global community is posited as an objective, distances, diversities, inequalities, and inherited traditions all present formidable obstacles. But none is so formidable as the ambivalence that values the benefits community offers but hankers for a shortcut which will yield the benefits without requiring the constraints.

Success in the building of community, then, depends on the satisfaction of a set of increasingly difficult conditions. First, there must be a genuine and comprehensive interdependence among those to be embraced by the community. For a global community this condition could not be met until the science and technology of our own time suddenly created it.

Second, the interdependence must be perceived. Here the perennial struggle between old perceptions and new realities continues unabated and unresolved. If men around the globe recognize that they are dependent on one another for survival in the nuclear age, other interdependencies are less easily apprehended. The great juxtapositions of industrial North and agrarian South, of a capitalist West and a communist East, are evident to many. But their interactions are so complex and so punctuated by hostilities that the global interplay of economics, technology, population growth, and ecology in which they are enmeshed is more often obscured than obvious.

Parochial perceptions—the psychologies of the enclave—are still in the ascendancy. Yet the growth rate of comopolitan perspectives since mid-century has been spectacular; the result is that the distance between the new global realities and the perceptions of them has sharply diminished. It is fair to assume that the social, economic, and technological forces which have stimulated a growing cosmopolitanism will continue to provide further stimuli.

But the assumption will mislead unless the resistances to these stimuli are given full weight in calculating the future. And it will be doubly misleading if one forgets that the multiplying cosmopolitan perspectives have yet to attain the forms of persuasiveness that might begin to move mass nationalism in the direction of mass internationalism. The only inference the assumption permits—and that is already a great deal—is that the problem of perception of those issues requiring global solutions is not insoluble.

Neither does the third condition present insoluble problems—only ones of maximum difficulty. If interdependence exists, it means that those who are interdependent profoundly affect one another's existence. If interdependence is perceived, then men become capable of responding to it. But there is more than one possible response to the perception. It is the choice of what to do about interdependence that creates the most difficulties. The strong are tempted to respond by exploiting the interdependence for their own benefit and the weak to insulate themselves as best they can from the incursions of the strong. In international politics this response takes the form of conquest, empire, and colonialism. In domestic politics it finds expression in class or ethnic domination.

The concept of community as a response to interdependence, therefore, is not one abstract option alongside others for the organization of perceived interdependencies. It is, instead, an idea which has been engaged throughout history in a two-front war against the temptations of the powerful and the fears of the weak. The war is all the more bitter precisely because the fears of the weak are often justified, and such fears are as inimical to the prospects for community as the depredations of the strong. This war, moreover, has no likely end; hence the concept of community is always embattled. To achieve and sustain community at the global level, as at any other level, must always be the supremely difficult political feat.

BUILDING GLOBAL COMMUNITY

The global community can be attained only to the degree that macropolitics gains ascendancy over micropolitics, to the degree that the interests of the whole gain precedence over the interests of the parts. The postponement effect of this proviso should be evident: if there is to be a community of man, it will come at a point in time beyond present calculation, and its realization depends upon a series of momentous and difficult choices whose outcomes are now unknown. But that does not mean that the community enterprise must therefore live only on hopes and speculations about an uncertain future. It has other, immediate sources that can supply the necessary energy for momentum and growth. These are the same globe-spanning forces which, now eroding the functional effectiveness of the national enclaves, simultaneously generate stimuli and opportunities to build transnational structures and to reallocate or redefine functions the enclaves are performing with diminishing returns.

The immediate community-building task, then, is to alter existing political arrangements and policies so that they will cope more realistically with the transformed world in which they must function. Such a task requires realistic community builders. They must anticipate resistance to change and be willing to lose arguments where the resistance is strong. Change can come only piecemeal and only where it promises more gains than sacrifices to the parties concerned. (Even violent change cannot wholly disregard these rules, and violence is, in any case, at odds with the purposes of community.)

Pressures for change must be applied where the advantages of change are most evident: in economic and development policy, in the conservation and replenishment of the environment, in the sharing of science and technology, and in arms control, including arms reduction. Pressures must also be applied in the knowledge that in resisting or accepting change, members of the international society will vary with each substantive issue. Growth of a global community must, therefore, be the product of transnational arrangements of varied purpose, scope, and membership. The number and authority of truly universal global organizations can increase only as they command universal assent.

The pertinence of these prescriptions is confirmed, at least in part, by the fact that they are also descriptions of international processes already in motion. Today's global system is already an agglomeration of transnational institutions with universal, regional, ideological, or functional memberships coexisting harmoniously or otherwise with the still sovereign states. The approaches to world community must necessarily be many in order to accommodate the diverse needs and urgencies of the individual states whose commitment to membership must sooner or later be obtained. Thus the United Nations, though it is history's first institution designed to serve all mankind, ought not to be regarded as the only foundation on which to build the community of mankind. The flaws in its charter as the world's peacekeeper and the tragic inadequacy of its financial resources warn against pushing the logic of its purposes too far or too soon.

The United Nations needs the company and support of transnational enterprises of lesser scope, including regional political and economic associations as well as bilateral and multilateral undertakings to advance specific functional purposes. It needs to encourage private as well as governmental behavior that breaks out of the national enclaves and seeks transnational answers to the new problems and opportunities created by a new environment. Above all, the United Nations needs the support and company of the still sovereign governments, and not only because its own effectiveness as an organization continues to depend on their will. The impact of converging global forces on the *internal* interactions of peoples and their governments is crucial to the community-building process. It cannot be otherwise as long as the state-enclaves remain the most effective instruments for both precipitating change and adjusting to it—or for defending the status quo.

Hence the pressures for new transnational policies to accord with the needs of a new world must first be felt within the confines of the sovereign states and then be articulated by them. The resulting policies may or may not be incorporated in the formal structure of the United Nations. But any transnational enterprise designed to further the growth of the human community will also further the growth and purposes of the United Nations.

If the maturation of the human community must depend on a variety of methods and institutions, it also depends on a unity of substantive purpose. Injustice is the great ailment and oppressor of mankind. Since justice is the only evident remedy, it is also the only purpose that can advance mankind toward the goal of community. The underdeveloped world of the South chiefly suffers, and inflicts, the injustices of poverty. There the oppressors are hunger, ill health, political elitism, and the tragic vulnerability to exploitation that has always been the lot of the poor and uneducated. The developed North chiefly suffers and inflicts the injustices spawned by fear. Having amassed wealth and power, it is oppressed by the fear of their loss.

Destruction by holocaust or by Third World revolution is not an everyday anxiety in the industrial societies. Yet the North cannot liberate itself from the nemesis of the arms race nor from the specter of an ever more populous and turbulent South by ignoring their presence and potential. Reliance on competitive armaments and defense of the status quo can fortify only the illusion of safety because it is an expedient that can only produce more menacing realities. Thus the countries of the North continue to threaten and fear the cruelest injustice of annihilation. At the same time, their great and small competitions cripple their capacities to act with reason and compassion in response to the growing desperation of the poverty-stricken South.

Injustice is oppression, and oppression exists wherever men are ruled by fear. Fear, in turn, is the enemy of human freedom and equality, if only because the power of those who govern by fear must chiefly depend on the constraints that weakness and subservience impose on the governed. Where fear governs, justice must languish; where men are afraid of one another they will not easily heed the proposition that all men should be treated as ends in themselves. It follows that oppression will yield to justice only where mutual confidence has replaced fear as the dominant relationship among individuals, groups, or societies.

The rule of fear in society is historically the product of poverty. That is, fear is a typical response to a perceived scarcity of those things humans need and desire. Since there is not enough for all, the distribution must be unequal, and the characteristic division is one in which the strong obtain more and the weak less. The beneficiaries of this mode of distribution are also those who are most likely to desire its perpetuation. Thus the strong are moved to fortify their advantage by husbanding and increasing their power and by keeping the weak in their place.

Marxist analysis generally attributes this outcome to the perception of a scarcity of material wealth, but the perceived scarcity of other values can produce similar outcomes. Wherever values like safety, status, or even knowledge itself are judged to be in short supply, there will be an impulse to hoard them for oneself and deny them to others—an impulse as familiar to individual psychology as it is to social behavior. When different orders of scarcities produce similar responses, it must be evident that material poverty is not the only source of injustice. But another conclusion is also unavoidable. Poverty in any dimension of human life is conducive to fear and oppression; the replacement of injustice by justice is therefore dependent upon creating situations of abundance.

It follows that the conversion of scarcity into abundance must be the chief aim of policy in a world where fear and oppression have now come to threaten the continued existence of all its inhabitants. The countries of the North, at least in material terms, have now very largely succeeded in effecting this transformation within their own societies. In so doing they have developed powers of productivity whose magnitude is great enough not only to supply their own prosperity but also to stimulate and accelerate the same transformation in the countries of the South. Both the flows of development aid and of private investment attest to the prodigious capacities of the industrial North. But as the need has grown their volume has declined—a bitter witness to the inconstancy of will and reason among the countries of the South as well as of the North.

At the root of this inconstancy is the impulse to hoard. Fearful that safety is a scarce commodity, the countries of the North lavish their resources on their own defenses in the quest for an illusory impregnability. Discounting their own productive vitality, they are reluctant to allocate enough of it to alleviate the remaining poverty in their midst, let alone the poverty of the encircling South. And they are moved, too, by that primitive urge which counsels the strong to look first to their own strength and let the weak remain weak.

The South, for its part, typically reproduces all these syndromes in microcosm. Governing elites, fearing domestic factions more than external enemies, squander resources on armies and police forces by whom they are more often than not undone. Discounting or fearing the potential returns of economic growth, they are moved to invest for their own enrichment rather than for the enrichment of society. Such choices, in turn, only reinforce the conventional wisdom in poverty-stricken societies: the governors will care most for their own strength and will understand that strength chiefly to be a function of weakness among the governed.

The transformation of scarcity into abundance on a global scale, then, confronts obstacles at all points of the compass. They are not confined to one part of the world or another nor to any particular social system. They are created not simply or even mainly by the shortage of physical resources or by insufficient productivity or productive potential. The chief impediment is rooted in the human will, of those who prefer not to recognize that their survival depends upon that transformation and of those who fear that their privileges will not survive it. In order to conquer poverty, then, the promise of abundance must overcome not only the scarcity of physical resources but the inertia and active opposition of those whom poverty has benefited.

It follows that the task can be made easier if the opposition can be persuaded that abundance can yield richer and more durable benefits than all the contrivances spawned by the politics of poverty. The most persuasive demonstration is the power and affluence of the mass societies in the developed countries themselves. To the extent that poverty, inequality, and oppression persist in the developed societies the case is only strengthened, for wherever they continue to prevail the society is by so much impoverished and debilitated. The developed countries, having created abundance, provide the most tangible evidence that justice and equality impart strength to individual and society alike, and that oppression and discrimination can only weaken the social fabric and degrade the quality of individual lives.

The experience of history confirms that the distribution of values always defines the chief political issues for all societies. That a distribution takes place at all is evidence enough that the members of societies are interdependent. In the politics of poverty the perquisites of the powerful are ultimately linked to the deprivations of the weak; in the politics of abundance the wealth and freedom of the whole society is ultimately linked to the wealth and freedom of all its members. Given the interdependence that society connotes, the option for equality or inequality in the distribution of values, and consequently for justice or injustice as the instrument of government, is the fundamental political choice open to those who have the power to choose. In the newly manifested interdependence of the world society this same choice now confronts those with the power to choose on a global scale.

THE PREMISES OF MACROPOLITICS

To elect equality is to prefer macropolitics to micropolitics as the policy model. Unlike micropolitics, macropolitics gives precedence to the interests of the entire society rather than to its individual parts. Skepticism can summon up forceful arguments against the possibility of such a displacement of interests. Yet the requirements of the macropolitical model are here not so very different from those of the traditional balance of power model. The theory and practice of balance of power also declare the parts dependent on the whole and that the state's power is ultimately a function of the power configurations of the environment in which it exists. On this premise the state must be as concerned for the dynamics of its political cosmos as for its own narrower interests.

The practitioners of the balance of power have conclusively demonstrated the possibilities and advantages of cosmopolitanism in politics, and the most skillful have shaped policy to accord with their understanding that the interests of other states set limits on the assertion of their own. Where balance of power and macropolitics differ is in purpose. In the balance of power system both self-assertion and self-restraint are practiced in order to enhance the state's capacities for conflict. In the macropolitical system both are designed to enhance the state's capacities for cooperation.

The presumption of conflict must conclude that superiority is the key to political rewards. The presumption of cooperation must conclude that political rewards are generated by equality—because neither men nor states will willingly cooperate to accomplish or perpetuate their own inferiority. The politics of cooperation therefore depends on an equitable distribution of values, and where values are already unevenly divided it must foster their redistribution. The extremes of inequality in the world society warn that policies of cooperation confront enormous difficulties and that their objectives can be attained only as the result of long and arduous effort. Yet the resources for cooperation are also enormous. For the first time in history the capacity for producing wealth is equal to any reasonable demands that can be placed upon it. At the same time, the world system has attained a political and military equilibrium that allows the strong to meet the demands for equality at minimal risk.

For the North, and particularly for America and Russia, this juncture of events has deprived the old micropolitical superiority doctrines of their meaning. The nuclear balance has created an equality of both vulnerability and invulnerability which it is in the profoundest interest of all parties to maintain. Finding safety in equality, the countries of the North are free to reallocate resources away from futile and dangerous exercises in conflict that disturb the equilibrium. If they can find ways to act jointly so that the equilibrium is safeguarded, they can invest these resources on a scale sufficient to give hope that the demands in the South for equality and abundance can eventually be met.

The present superiority of the North in wealth and power is so great that there are no rational grounds for fearing the day when the South might draw even. For on that day abundance will have become global, and the conditions for policies of cooperation and equality will have been enhanced and fortified. As for the elites in the South, if they can conquer their fear of equality, growing abundance in their societies could make the internal processes of social change more benign than they now imagine.

The application of the macropolitical model must obviously revolutionize the prevailing world system. The norms of macropolitics are cooperation instead of conflict, equality instead of inequality, and trust instead of fear. The practical realization of these norms, in turn, depends on the human capacity to produce abundance, because to the extent that scarcity persists the old micropolitical model will appear to be more realistic and compelling to those who have the power to choose.

The transformation from micropolitics to macropolitics cannot be accomplished by violence. Though resorts to violence will unavoidably mark such a change, they must be counted as tragic costs that serve to obstruct the process rather than to quicken it. This follows because the purpose of macropolitics is to draw man into community, and a community cannot be the product of force. It also follows because the quest for a global community must perish along with the existence of all lesser communities the moment the fires of global violence are ignited. Finally, violence as a method for social change has historically succeeded only in replacing one micropolitical system with another and has only given new forms to old inequalities, old fears, and old injustices. Insofar as a society sheds its micropolitical characteristics after undergoing violent revolution, it does so primarily as a result of the processes of reconciliation that take place once violence is spent.

An interdependent and imperiled world can no longer ignore the ancient lesson of domestic politics that peace is a function of justice and not of arms and conquest. Peace cannot be built on injustice for the simple reason, as John Locke observed, that injustice and war are one and the same. Who wills peace must will justice and the conditions that make justice possible. Just as a domestic society cannot become an authentic community until the needs of all its members receive equal consideration, so the global community cannot be consummated until all men and all societies are valued as ends in themselves and therefore as equals.

If there is no certainty that such an objective can ever be reached, there are at least probabilities that favor its approximation. To the extent that the requirements of the macropolitical model are met the probabilities will be enhanced, for even its initial effects on policy will demonstrate the value of its norms. Holding out the promise of abundance and justice, they are norms that correspond to the real interests of all men. It is true that men are often blind to their real interests—or, more accurately, they often doubt whether their real interests can ever be gratified. But wherever policy is able to demonstrate with deeds the coincidence of norm and interest, skepticism recedes and the norm attracts growing assent.

Appendices: Introduction

The data contained in the following appendices vary considerably in degree of reliability. This is necessarily true in any compilation of wide ranges of information derived from a large number of diverse sources.

A cautionary statement is particularly in order concerning projections into the future. The only available technique for projecting is one that extrapolates from past and current trends. Hence any "statistics" purporting to represent future circumstances are nothing more than inferences drawn from past and present experience.

Projections are not predictions; they can only indicate what the future might look like if one assumes that the future will be congruent with current trends. Such an assumption is open to many obvious objections. Yet it provides the only empirical reference point from which to calculate future developments in terms of rationally defined probabilities instead of mere possibilities.

Given these limitations, then, much of the data and all projections in the following tables can at best offer only approximations of reality, present and future, and not reality itself.

Appendix A

Model of World Population, Gross World Product (GWP), and Per Capita GWP, 1970 and 2000 (Totals and Distribution Between Developed and Underdeveloped Worlds)

Population, GWP, and Per Capita GWP, 1970 and 2000

	1970	2000
WORLD		
Population (in thousands)	3,422,566	6,239,542
Gross World Product (in millions of 1970 dollars)	2,985,144	11,217,124
Per Capita GWP (in 1970 dollars)	872	1,798
DEVELOPED COUNTRIES (DCS)		
Population	834,270	1,153,779
Gross Product	2,421,670	8,296,094
Per Capita GP	2,903	7,190
UNDERDEVELOPED COUNTRIES (UDCS)		
Population	2,588,296	5,085,763
Gross Product	563,474	2,921,030
Per Capita GP	218	574

Per Capita GP: Absolute Differential Between DCs and UDCs

1970:	2,685	2000:	6,616

Ratios Between Developed and Underdeveloped Countries

	1970		2000	
	DCS	UDCS	DCS	UDCS
Population	0.32	1	0.23	1
Gross Product	4.30	1	2.80	1
Per Capita GP	13.30	1	12.50	1

NOTES REGARDING APPENDIX A

All figures in Appendix A derive from a basic model that reflects but is not identical with the actual world. The model is composed of 116 countries listed in Appendices B and C for which current population, GNP, and growth data are all available and thus permit projection to the year 2000. Consequently, of the country listings in Appendices B and C, the eleven countries for which there is incomplete data are not included in the totals of Appendix A.

Two further countries listed in Appendices B and C are omitted from the model despite the availability of sufficient current data to permit projections. They are Japan and Libya. References to their individual listings in Appendices B and C and at the end of the statement on notes and sources in Appendix C will explain their omission. In brief, the current growth rates of these two countries deviate so sharply from probable long-term growth that projections based on current performance produce highly inflated distortions instead of realistic expectations about future performance. These distortions have been allowed to stand on an individual country basis in Appendix C. Here, however, they have been omitted so as not to introduce them into a world summation of productivity and its distribution.

In addition, nineteen very small countries have been omitted from all three appendices. Finally, with the exception of Angola and Mozambique, all remaining colonial or otherwise dependent territories have been omitted from Appendices A, B, and C.

The 116 countries included in the world model account for approximately 95 percent of 1970 world population.

Countries with $1,200 per capita GNP or above in 1970 have been designated as developed, and countries below that level as underdeveloped. Like any classification, this one is arbitrary in some obvious respects. Yet it corresponds fairly closely to development-underdevelopment indices other than the single yardstick of per capita GNP. Thus the classification used here defines as underdeveloped all countries of Africa, all countries of the Western Hemisphere except the United States and Canada, and all countries of Asia except Israel and Kuwait. (Libya and Japan, if included in the model, would be classified as developed.) In the remainder of the world, Australia and New Zealand are defined as developed, as is Europe except for Bulgaria, Greece, Portugal, Romania, Spain, and Yugoslavia. (Albania, if included in the model, would also have been classified as underdeveloped.)

Appendix B

Population by Continent and Country for 129 Countries, 1940–2000 (All Figures in Thousands of People)

Population–Africa

COUNTRY	1940	1950	1960	1970	1980	1990	2000
Algeria	7,717	8,753	10,800	14,100	19,869	28,481	39,177
Angola	3,553	4,093	4,841	5,600	7,138	9,227	12,095
Botswana	—	308	483	650	792	1,031	1,317
Burundi	—	—	2,908	3,600	4,634	6,147	8,225
Cameroon	3,769[b]	4,124	4,700	5,840	7,343	9,691	12,857
Central African Rep.	—	1,072	1,227	1,520	1,948	2,581	3,442
Chad	—	2,241	3,070	3,710	4,785	6,349	8,415
Congo (Brazzaville)	—	684	773	940	1,202	1,595	2,128
Zaire (former Congo–Kinshasa)	10,399	11,313	14,139	17,420	22,439	29,920	39,994
Dahomey	—	1,570	2,050	2,690	3,550	4,833	6,631
Ethiopia	—	15,000[b]	20,700	25,050	31,516	40,831	53,344
Gabon	—	409	446	500	536	615	712
Gambia	193	296	299	360	454	586	763
Ghana	3,659	4,275	6,777	9,030	12,577	17,336	22,746
Guinea	—	2,250	3,072	3,920	5,016	6,613	8,787
Ivory Coast	—	2,170	3,230	4,310	5,578	7,437	9,991
Kenya	—	5,579	8,115	10,900	15,109	20,943	27,898
Lesotho	—	596	724	1,040	1,283	1,620	2,054
Liberia	—	—	988	1,170	1,446	1,851	2,395
Libya	900[a]	1,195[a]	1,349	1,900	2,602	3,646	4,925
Malagasy Rep. (Madagascar)	4,087	4,305	5,393	6,750	9,276	12,763	17,652

NOTE: All references follow the table.

580

Population–Africa (*continued*)

COUNTRY	1940	1950	1960	1970	1980	1990	2000
Malawi	1,686	2,290	3,500	4,530	5,834	7,894	10,717
Mali	—	3,445	4,062	5,020	6,580	8,784	11,848
Mauritania	—	546	970	1,170	1,506	2,012	2,700
Mauritius	417	465	645	810	1,107	1,399	1,696
Morocco	7,642	8,953	11,640	15,530	22,203	30,679	40,523
Mozambique	5,086	5,739	6,579	7,575	9,722	12,707	16,737
Niger	—	2,165	2,850	4,020	5,265	7,414	10,485
Nigeria	—	24,300	52,000	55,070	72,784	98,659	131,374
Portuguese Guinea	—	—	—	—	—	—	—
Rhodesia (Southern Rhodesia)	1,461	2,170	3,840	5,270	7,184	10,420	14,783
Rwanda	—	—	2,665	3,590	4,869	6,804	9,567
Senegal	—	2,093[b]	3,110	3,930	5,084	6,770	9,072
Sierra Leone	—	1,880	2,228	2,790	3,388	4,437	5,721
Somalia	—	1,886	2,010	2,790	3,654	4,924	6,572
South Africa	10,353	12,447	15,925	20,110	25,952	33,988	43,927
Sudan	8,500[a]	9,750[a]	11,770	15,700	21,946	30,637	41,289
Swaziland	—	—	316	410	575	807	1,133
Tanzania	—	7,732	10,328	13,270	17,475	23,688	32,158
Togo	834	990	1,444	1,860	2,457	3,338	4,561
Tunisia	2,877	3,470	3,896	5,140	7,041	9,637	12,601
Uganda	—	5,199	6,677	9,760	11,336	15,263	20,123
United Arab Republic	19,484	23,608	25,922	33,330	45,432	59,824	75,536
Upper Volta	—	3,126	4,406	5,380	6,770	8,825	11,651
Zambia	1,500	1,860	3,210	4,300	5,911	8,349	11,792

Population—The Americas

COUNTRY	1940	1950	1960	1970	1980	1990	2000
Argentina	14,169	17,189	20,850	24,350	27,830	31,376[c]	35,351[c]
Bolivia	2,690	3,019	3,825	4,930	6,006	7,782	10,081
Brazil	41,114	51,976	69,730	95,310	123,717	163,994	215,012
Canada	11,682	13,712	17,909	21,410	25,299	29,607[c]	34,700[c]
Chile	5,063	6,073	7,683	9,780	12,214	15,173[c]	18,862[c]
Colombia	9,094	11,334	15,397	21,120	30,238	41,579	54,691
Costa Rica	619	801	1,254	1,718	2,650	3,822	5,337
Cuba	4,566	5,508	6,826	8,390	10,068	11,927	14,018
Dominican Republic	1,674	2,131	3,036	4,320	6,118	8,752	12,378
Ecuador	2,466	3,197	4,358	6,090	8,526	11,894	16,314
El Salvador	1,633	1,868	2,454	3,530	4,922	7,149	10,411
Guatemala	2,201	2,805	3,810	5,110	6,822	9,174	12,168
Guyana	360	423	565	760	993	1,309	1,649
Haiti	2,751	3,112	3,991	4,870	6,836	9,144	12,347
Honduras	1,146	1,428	1,849	2,580	3,832	5,424	7,542
Jamaica	1,212	1,403	1,629	2,000	2,382	2,751	3,102
Mexico	19,815	25,826	36,046	50,670	71,375	99,653	135,067
Nicaragua	825	1,060	1,411	1,980	2,818	3,951	5,460
Panama	620	797	1,062	1,460	2,068	2,938	4,159
Paraguay	1,111	1,397	1,751	2,390	3,437	4,868[c]	6,867[c]
Peru	7,033	8,521	10,025	13,590	18,529	25,145	33,494
Trinidad and Tobago	476	632	831	1,070	1,253	1,410	1,556
United States	132,594	152,264	180,684	205,400	235,212	271,075[c]	311,507[c]
Uruguay	2,155	2,407	2,540	2,890	3,247	3,655[c]	4,118[c]
Venezuela	3,710	4,974	7,349	10,400	14,979	19,952	26,100

Population–Asia

COUNTRY	1940	1950	1960	1970	1980	1990	2000
Aden (Southern Yemen)	—	—	1,000	1,280	1,731	2,358	3,120
Afghanistan	10,000[a]	12,000	13,800	17,120	22,006	28,173	35,131
Burma	16,119	18,489	22,355	27,580	35,063	43,665	52,533
Cambodia	3,400[a]	4,074	5,440	7,330	9,724	13,086	16,777
Sri Lanka (Ceylon)	5,972	7,678	9,890	12,510	15,931	19,482	22,776
China (Mainland)	452,326	546,815	650,000	759,620	893,900	1,003,499	1,165,138
China (Taiwan)	5,987	7,619	10,612	14,040	17,423	21,301	24,665
Cyprus	401	485	573	630	674	710	755
India	316,004	358,293	429,016	550,380	717,380	901,375	1,084,291
Indonesia	70,476	76,000	93,506	121,200	161,362	207,437	255,253
Iran	14,000	16,276	21,520	28,660	38,769	51,757	65,574
Iraq	—	5,278	6,870	9,440	13,910	19,964	27,484
Israel	461	1,094	2,114	2,940	3,613	4,257	4,710
Japan	71,400	82,900	93,216	103,540	116,347	126,278[c]	136,752[c]
Jordan	—	1,296	1,695	2,320	3,255	4,599	6,320
Korea, North	—	9,740	10,600	13,890	18,207	23,325	28,194
Korea, South	—	20,513	24,695	31,790	40,831	51,159	61,091
Kuwait	—	—	278	710	1,638	3,346	4,951
Laos	1,075[a]	1,360[b]	2,337	2,960	3,901	5,035	6,241
Lebanon	—	1,257	2,110	2,790	3,771	4,981[c]	6,566[c]
Malaysia	—	—	8,113	10,080	14,342	18,567	22,602
Mongolia	750[a]	732[b]	953	1,290	1,739	2,273	2,821
Nepal	7,000[a]	8,000[a]	9,245	11,200	14,136	17,504	20,819
Pakistan	70,000	75,040	92,696	134,000	191,407	259,718	334,271
Philippines	16,459	19,910	27,410	38,490	54,095	74,895	98,088
Saudi Arabia	—	—	—	7,350	10,460	14,247	18,853
Singapore	751	1,022	1,634	2,050	2,645	3,258	3,757

Population–Asia *(continued)*

COUNTRY	1940	1950	1960	1970	1980	1990	2000
Syria	—	—	4,561	6,100	8,778	12,586	17,320
Thailand	15,296	18,488	26,392	35,810	49,775	66,198	83,193
Trucial Oman	—	—	—	—	—	—	—
Turkey	17,821	20,947	27,509	35,230	46,527	59,603	72,926
Vietnam, North	—	—	16,100	21,150	25,645	30,854	35,718
Vietnam, South	—	—	14,100	18,330	21,763	26,184	30,311
Yemen	—	—	5,000	5,730	7,748	10,553	13,965

Population–Europe

COUNTRY	1940	1950	1960	1970	1980	1990	2000
Albania	1,088	1,219	1,607	2,170	2,837	3,750	4,942
Austria	6,705	6,935	7,048	7,420	7,778	8,261	8,771
Belgium	8,301	8,639	9,153	9,680	10,150	10,695	11,242
Bulgaria	6,344	7,251	7,867	8,490	9,173	9,665	10,159
Czechoslovakia	14,713	12,389	13,654	14,470	15,772	16,581	17,429
Denmark	3,832	4,271	4,581	4,920	5,325	5,660	6,010
Finland	3,698	4,009	4,430	4,700	4,925	5,125	5,334
France	39,800	41,736	45,684	50,780	55,320	59,918	64,888
Germany, East		18,588[b]	17,241	17,250	17,680	18,342	19,089
Germany, West	69,838	47,847	53,224	59,550	61,054	65,290	67,950
Greece	7,319	7,566	8,327	8,890	9,479	9,986	10,497
Hungary	9,287	9,341	9,984	10,310	10,793	11,232	11,689
Iceland	121	143	176	210	252	302	361
Ireland	2,958	2,969	2,834	2,940	3,273	3,728	4,242

Population—Europe (*continued*)

COUNTRY	1940	1950	1960	1970	1980	1990	2000
Italy	43,840	46,603	49,642	53,670	57,855	62,102	66,588
Luxembourg	296	297	314	340	391	432	477
Netherlands	8,879	10,114	11,480	13,020	14,468	16,153	18,020
Norway	2,973	3,265	3,581	3,880	4,288	4,697	5,137
Poland	—	24,824	29,561	32,810	36,557	40,000	43,750
Portugal	7,696	8,405	8,826	9,630	10,283	11,141	12,065
Romania	15,907	16,311	18,403	20,250	22,417	24,257	26,269
Spain	25,757	27,868	30,303	33,290	36,413	39,805	43,536
Sweden	6,356	7,014	7,480	8,040	8,553	8,971	9,430
Switzerland	4,234	4,694	5,362	6,280	7,040	7,767	8,580
United Kingdom	48,226	50,616	52,352	55,710	59,548	64,338	69,674
USSR	191,700	181,000[b]	214,238	242,770	270,634	304,513	343,092
Yugoslavia	15,811	16,346	18,402	20,530	22,834	24,941	27,278

Population—Oceania

COUNTRY	1940	1950	1960	1970	1980	1990	2000
Australia	[a] 7,039	8,179	10,275	12,550	15,365	18,753	22,860
New Zealand	1,636	1,908	2,372	2,820	3,420	4,131	4,987

SOURCES FOR APPENDIX B

1940, 1950:   United Nations, *Demographic Yearbook* (New York: UN, 1960).
United Nations, *World Population Prospects,* Population Studies No. 41
(New York: UN, 1966) (*notation a*).
United Nations, *Statistical Yearbook* (New York: UN, 1967), pp. 15ff.
(*notation b*).

1960:   United Nations, *Monthly Bulletin of Statistics* (October 1970).

1970:   United Nations, *Monthly Bulletin of Statistics* (November 1971). Ex-
ception: the 1970 figure for Saudi Arabia is from an estimate in Richard
Stebbins and Alba Amoia (eds.), *The World This Year* (New York: Simon &
Schuster, 1971).

1980, 1990, 2000 Projections: United Nations, *Monthly Bulletin of Statistics*
(April 1971). Exceptions: figures for Europe and Oceania (1990, 2000) and
figures with *notation c* are computer projections based on 1985 population
estimates and 1980–1985 average growth rate estimates in United Nations,
Monthly Bulletin of Statistics (April 1971).

The projections for Pakistan were calculated before the secession of Bangla
Desh.

Appendix C

Gross National Product (GNP) and Per Capita GNP by Continent and Country for 129 Countries, 1940–2000

Gross National Product (GNP) and Per Capita GNP, 1940–2000

CONTINENT AND COUNTRY	BASE PERIOD GROWTH RATE OF GNP	GNP in Millions of Constant 1970 Dollars (Upper Figure) and Per Capita GNP in Constant 1970 Dollars (Lower Figure)						
		1940	1950	1960	1970	1980	1990	2000
AFRICA								
Algeria[2]*	6.9	—	—	2,776[e]	4,180[d]	8,146	15,875	30,938
				257	296	410	557	790
Angola[3]	3.1	—	—	422[e]	573[e]	778	1,056	1,433
				87	102	109	114	118
Botswana	—	—	—	—	66[g]	—	—	—
					102			
Burundi[2]	5.3	—	—	—	230[g]	385	645	1,081
					64	83	105	131
Cameroon[2]	3.9	—	—	398[a]	990[d]	1,451	2,127	3,118
				85	170	198	219	243

NOTE: All references follow the table.

Gross National Product (GNP) and Per Capita GNP, 1940–2000 *(continued)*

CONTINENT AND COUNTRY	BASE PERIOD GROWTH RATE OF GNP	GNP in Millions of Constant 1970 Dollars (Upper Figure) and Per Capita GNP in Constant 1970 Dollars (Lower Figure)						
		1940	1950	1960	1970	1980	1990	2000
Central African Rep.	—	—	—		200[d] / 132	—	—	—
Chad[3]	7.3	—	—	128[a] / 42	259[d] / 70	524 / 110	1,060 / 167	2,144 / 255
Congo (Brazzaville)[2]*	11.1	—	—	38[a] / 49	233[d] / 248	668 / 556	1,914 / 1,200	5,484 / 2,577
Zäire (Dem. Rep. of Congo)[1]	5.2	—	—	1,545[a] / 109	1,947[d] / 112	3,232 / 144	5,366 / 179	8,909 / 223
Dahomey[2]	5.7	—	—	93[a] / 45	235[d] / 87	409 / 115	712 / 147	1,239 / 187
Ethiopia[1]	4.7	—	—	1,158[b] / 56	1,738[d] / 69	2,751 / 87	4,355 / 107	6,894 / 129
Gabon[2]	—	—	—	82[a] / 184	309[d] / 618	—	—	—
Gambia[2]	7.4	—	—	24[e] / 34	46[g] / 238	94 / 318	192 / 642	392 / 1,089
Ghana[1]*	1.9	—	—	1,920[b] / 283	2,239[d] / 248	2,703 / 215	3,263 / 188	3,939 / 173
Guinea[3]	3.0	—	—	235[f] / 76	315[d] / 80	423 / 84	568 / 86	763 / 87

GNP in Millions of Constant 1970 Dollars (Upper Figure) and
Per Capita GNP in Constant 1970 Dollars (Lower Figure)

CONTINENT AND COUNTRY	BASE PERIOD GROWTH RATE OF GNP	1940	1950	1960	1970	1980	1990	2000
Ivory Coast[2]	5.4	—	—	618[a] / 191	1,424[d] / 330	2,409 / 432	4,076 / 548	6,897 / 690
Kenya[1]*	8.0	—	—	—	1,582[d] / 145	3,415 / 226	7,373 / 352	15,918 / 571
Lesotho[2]	1.1	—	—	—	94[g] / 90	105 / 82	117 / 72	131 / 64
Liberia[2]*	8.9	—	—	—	352[d] / 301	826 / 571	1,938 / 1,047	4,546 / 1,898
Libya[1]*	16.3	—	—	—	3,140[d] / 1,653	14,214 / 5,463	64,345 / 17,648	291,281 / 59,143
Malagasy Rep. (Madagascar)[2]	2.1	—	—	784[e] / 145	878[d] / 130	1,081 / 117	1,331 / 104	1,638 / 93
Malawi[1]	4.7	—	—	163[f] / 47	319[d] / 70	505 / 87	799 / 101	1,265 / 118
Mali[3]	6.9	—	—	261[a] / 64	510[d] / 102	994 / 151	1,937 / 221	3,775 / 319
Mauritania	—	—	—	—	180[d] / 154	—	—	—
Mauritius	—	—	—	193[e] / 299	189[g] / 233	—	—	—

589

Gross National Product (GNP) and Per Capita GNP, 1940–2000 (*continued*)

CONTINENT AND COUNTRY	BASE PERIOD GROWTH RATE OF GNP	GNP in Millions of Constant 1970 Dollars (Upper Figure) and Per Capita GNP in Constant 1970 Dollars (Lower Figure)						
		1940	1950	1960	1970	1980	1990	2000
Morocco[1]	4.6	—	—	2,280[b]	3,341[d]	5,238	8,213	12,877
				196	215	236	268	318
Mozambique[3]	2.8	—	—	664[e]	875[e]	1,153	1,520	2,003
				101	116	119	120	120
Niger[3]*	8.6	—	—	138[a]	315[d]	719	1,641	3,745
				48	78	137	221	357
Nigeria[3]	3.8	—	—	3,983[e]	5,800[d]	8,422	12,229	17,757
				77	105	116	124	135
Rhodesia (Southern Rhodesia)[1]	3.4	—	—	984[b]	1,427[d]	1,994	2,786	3,892
				256	271	278	267	263
Rwanda	—	—	—	—	195[g]	—	—	—
					54			
Senegal[3]*	0.5	—	—	664[a]	700[d]	736	774	814
				214	178	145	114	90
Sierra Leone[2]*	0.2	—	—	—	425[d]	434	443	452
					152	128	100	79
Somalia[2]	7.0	—	—	102[a]	181[d]	356	700	1,377
				51	65	97	142	210

GNP in Millions of Constant 1970 Dollars (Upper Figure) and Per Capita GNP in Constant 1970 Dollars (Lower Figure)

CONTINENT AND COUNTRY	BASE PERIOD GROWTH RATE OF GNP	1940	1950	1960	1970	1980	1990	2000
South Africa[1]	6.8	4,936e	—	9,691b	16,690d	32,223	62,213	120,114
		477	—	609	830	1,242	1,830	2,734
South-West Africa[3]	2.1	—	—	84e	103e	127	156	192
Sudan[2]*	2.2	—	—	1,419b	1,890d	2,349	2,920	3,630
				121	120	107	95	88
Swaziland[2]*	7.5	—	—	—	90g	185	381	785
					220	322	472	693
Tanzania[1]	5.7	—	—	966e	1,332d	2,319	4,037	7,028
				94	100	133	170	219
Togo[2]	4.7	—	—	84e	267d	423	670	1,061
				58	144	172	201	233
Tunisia[1]	2.8	—	—	871b	1,225d	1,615	2,129	2,806
				224	238	229	221	223
Uganda[1]	5.4	—	—	604e	1,297d	2,195	3,714	6,284
				90	133	193	243	312
United Arab Republic[2]*	0.4	—	—	—	6,580d	6,848	7,127	7,417
					197	151	119	98
Upper Volta[2]	2.3	—	—	175a	305d	383	481	604
				40	57	57	55	52
Zambia[1]*	8.4	—	—	883b	1,682d	3,768	8,441	18,910
				275	391	637	1,011	1,604

Gross National Product (GNP) and Per Capita GNP, 1940–2000 (continued)

CONTINENT AND COUNTRY	BASE PERIOD GROWTH RATE OF GNP	GNP in Millions of Constant 1970 Dollars (Upper Figure) and Per Capita GNP in Constant 1970 Dollars (Lower Figure)						
		1940	1950	1960	1970	1980	1990	2000
THE AMERICAS								
Argentina[1]	3.8	6,438[e] 454	11,329[b] 659	15,256[b] 732	23,830[d] 979	34,602 1,243	50,243 1,601	72,954 2,064
Bolivia[1]	5.2	—	—	598[b] 156	976[d] 198	1,620 270	2,690 346	4,466 443
Brazil[1]	6.6	4,520[e] 110	10,678[b] 205	20,622[b] 296	35,440[d] 372	67,153 543	127,244 776	241,107 1,121
Canada[1]	4.7	12,876[e] 1,102	29,715[b] 2,167	47,355[b] 2,644	84,700[d] 3,956	134,076 5,300	212,235 7,168	335,957 9,682
Chile[1]	3.4	1,864[e] 368	3,122[b] 514	4,447[b] 579	6,670[d] 682	9,318 763	13,018 858	18,187 964
Colombia[1]	5.7	—	2,445[b] 216	4,209[b] 273	7,070[d] 335	12,307 407	21,424 515	37,295 682
Costa Rica[1]	7.8	—	316[c] 395	506[e] 404	904[d] 526	1,916 723	4,061 1,063	8,606 1,613
Cuba	—	—	2,511[c] 456	3,538[e] 518	5,200[d] 620	—	—	—
Dominican Republic[1]	6.6	—	544[b] 255	982[b] 323	1,500[d] 347	2,842 465	5,385 615	10,204 824

GNP in Millions of Constant 1970 Dollars (Upper Figure) and
Per Capita GNP in Constant 1970 Dollars (Lower Figure)

CONTINENT AND COUNTRY	BASE PERIOD GROWTH RATE OF GNP	1940	1950	1960	1970	1980	1990	2000
Ecuador[1]	6.1	—	705[b] / 221	1,141[b] / 262	1,800[d] / 296	3,254 / 382	5,883 / 495	10,635 / 652
El Salvador[1]	4.9	—	461[c] / 247	590[b] / 240	977[d] / 282	1,609 / 327	2,596 / 363	4,189 / 402
Guatemala[1]	4.9	—	764[b] / 272	1,106[b] / 290	1,786[d] / 350	2,882 / 422	4,650 / 507	7,503 / 617
Guyana[2]*	0.6	—	—	—	250[d] / 329	265 / 267	281 / 215	298 / 181
Haiti[2]*	8.9	—	—	—	360[d] / 74	844 / 123	1,980 / 217	4,645 / 376
Honduras[1]	5.7	—	278[b] / 195	454[b] / 246	685[d] / 266	1,192 / 311	2,075 / 383	3,612 / 479
Jamaica[1]	4.3	—	—	742[b] / 455	1,156[d] / 578	1,761 / 739	2,683 / 975	4,088 / 1,318
Mexico[1]	7.2	—	9,471[b] / 367	16,684[b] / 463	33,060[d] / 652	66,260 / 928	132,800 / 1,333	266,162 / 1,971
Nicaragua[1]	3.7	—	259[b] / 244	430[b] / 305	772[d] / 390	1,110 / 394	1,596 / 404	2,295 / 420
Panama[1]	7.8	—	292[b] / 366	481[b] / 453	1,016[d] / 696	2,153 / 1,041	4,563 / 1,553	9,670 / 2,325

Gross National Product (GNP) and Per Capita GNP, 1940–2000 (*continued*)

CONTINENT AND COUNTRY	BASE PERIOD GROWTH RATE OF GNP	GNP in Millions of Constant 1970 Dollars (Upper Figure) and Per Capita GNP in Constant 1970 Dollars (Lower Figure)						
		1940	1950	1960	1970	1980	1990	2000
Paraguay[1]	4.6	—	296[b] / 212	386[b] / 220	600[d] / 251	941 / 274	1,475 / 303	2,313 / 337
Peru[1]	2.9	—	2,167[b] / 254	3,571[b] / 356	4,800[d] / 353	6,388 / 345	8,502 / 338	11,316 / 338
Trinidad and Tobago[3]	4.0	—	—	565[c] / 680	850[d] / 794	1,258 / 1,004	1,862 / 1,321	2,756 / 1,771
United States[1]	3.9	—	477,855[b] / 3,138	656,145[b] / 3,631	974,100[d] / 4,742	1,428,101 / 6,072	2,093,700 / 7,724	3,069,516 / 9,854
Uruguay[1]*	1.5	—	—	1,915[b] / 754	2,145[d] / 742	2,489 / 767	2,889 / 790	3,353 / 814
Venezuela[1]	4.2	—	2,702[b] / 543	5,967[b] / 812	10,300[d] / 990	15,542 / 1,038	23,452 / 1,175	35,388 / 1,356
ASIA								
Aden (Southern Yemen)	—	—	—	145[b] / 145	140[g] / 109	—	—	—
Afghanistan[3]	3.9	—	—	1,026[b] / 74	1,500[d] / 88	2,199 / 100	3,224 / 114	4,727 / 135

GNP in Millions of Constant 1970 Dollars (Upper Figure) and
Per Capita GNP in Constant 1970 Dollars (Lower Figure)

CONTINENT AND COUNTRY	BASE PERIOD GROWTH RATE OF GNP	1940	1950	1960	1970	1980	1990	2000
Burma[3]	1.2	—	1,002[c] 54	1,848[c] 83	2,080[d] 75	2,344 67	2,641 60	2,976 57
Cambodia[3]	1.8	—	—	633[b] 116	706[d] 104	908 93	1,085 83	1,297 77
Sri Lanka (Ceylon)[1]	5.6	—	—	1,364[b] 138	2,117[d] 169	3,651 229	6,296 323	10,857 477
China (Mainland)[3]*	0.5	—	—	108,620[f] 167	120,000[d] 158	126,137 141	132,588 132	139,369 120
China (Taiwan)[1]*	9.7	—	—	2,154[b] 203	5,460[d] 389	13,780 791	34,779 1,633	87,778 3,559
Cyprus[1]	7.2	—	—	298[b] 520	540[d] 857	1,082 1,605	2,169 3,055	4,347 5,758
India[1]	4.4	—	23,950[b] 67	36,078[b] 84	52,920[d] 96	81,400 113	125,207 139	192,590 178
Indonesia[1]	4.7	—	—	—	7,600[d] 63	12,030 75	19,043 92	30,144 118
Iran[1]*	9.2	—	—	4,851[b] 225	10,180[d] 355	24,546 633	59,184 1,143	142,702 2,176
Iraq[2]	3.5	—	—	1,680[c] 245	2,693[d] 285	3,799 273	5,359 268	7,559 275

Gross National Product (GNP) and Per Capita GNP, 1940–2000 (continued)

CONTINENT AND COUNTRY	BASE PERIOD GROWTH RATE OF GNP	GNP in Millions of Constant 1970 Dollars (Upper Figure) and Per Capita GNP in Constant 1970 Dollars (Lower Figure)						
		1940	1950	1960	1970	1980	1990	2000
Israel[1]*	7.6	—	1,071[b] / 979	2,327[b] / 1,101	5,500[d] / 1,871	11,442 / 3,167	23,803 / 5,591	49,517 / 10,513
Japan[1]*	12.3	—	—	67,851[b] / 728	197,400[d] / 1,907	629,716 / 5,412	2,008,826 / 15,908	6,408,256 / 46,860
Jordan[1]*	8.3	—	—	350[c] / 206	575[d] / 248	1,276 / 392	2,832 / 616	6,286 / 995
Korea, North[1]	—	—	—	2,172[f] / 205	4,500[d] / 324	—	—	—
Korea, South[1]*	12.1	—	—	3,366[b] / 136	8,213[d] / 258	25,737 / 630	80,652 / 1,576	252,738 / 4,137
Kuwait[2]*	9.2	—	—	905[e] / 3,255	2,750[d] / 3,873	6,631 / 4,048	15,988 / 4,778	38,550 / 7,786
Laos[3]	6.0	—	—	121[e] / 52	216[d] / 73	387 / 99	693 / 138	1,241 / 199
Lebanon[3]	7.7	—	—	724[e] / 343	1,525[d] / 547	3,202 / 849	6,723 / 1,350	14,116 / 2,150
Malaysia[1]	6.9	—	—	2,226[b] / 274	3,837[d] / 381	7,478 / 521	14,573 / 785	28,401 / 1,257

GNP in Millions of Constant 1970 Dollars (Upper Figure) and
Per Capita GNP in Constant 1970 Dollars (Lower Figure)

CONTINENT AND COUNTRY	BASE PERIOD GROWTH RATE OF GNP	1940	1950	1960	1970	1980	1990	2000
Nepal[3]	3.9	—	—	604ᵉ	685ᵈ	1,004	1,472	2,158
				65	61	71	84	104
Pakistan[1]	5.2	—	8,064ᵇ	10,500ᵇ	17,500ᵈ	29,053	48,233	80,076
			107	113	131	152	186	240
Philippines[1]	5.9	—	2,727ᵇ	5,132ᵇ	10,230ᵈ	18,148	32,195	57,115
			137	137	266	335	430	582
Saudi Arabia[2]*	11.4	—	—	1,569ᵉ	3,140ᵈ	9,242	27,203	80,070
					427	884	1,909	4,247
Singapore[2]*	10.7	—	—	—	1,970ᵍ	5,444	15,045	41,578
					961	2,058	4,618	11,067
Syria[2]	7.8	—	—	870ᵃ	1,590ᵈ	3,370	7,142	15,136
				191	261	384	567	874
Thailand[1]*	8.8	—	—	3,289ᵇ	6,510ᵈ	15,131	35,169	81,743
				125	182	304	531	983
Turkey[1]	6.8	—	2,866ᵇ	5,019ᵇ	9,000ᵈ	17,376	33,548	64,771
			137	182	255	373	563	888
Vietnam, South[3]	4.9	—	—	1,992ᵉ	3,200ᵈ	5,163	8,330	13,440
				141	175	237	318	443
Yemen[3]	3.5	—	—	325ᵉ	600ᵈ	846	1,193	1,683
				65	105	109	113	121

Gross National Product (GNP) and Per Capita GNP, 1940–2000 (continued)

CONTINENT AND COUNTRY	BASE PERIOD GROWTH RATE OF GNP	GNP in Millions of Constant 1970 Dollars (Upper Figure) and Per Capita GNP in Constant 1970 Dollars (Lower Figure)						
		1940	1950	1960	1970	1980	1990	2000
EUROPE								
Austria[1]	4.9	—	4,935[b] / 712	8,925[b] / 1,266	14,300[d] / 1,927	23,072 / 2,966	37,225 / 4,506	60,061 / 6,848
Belgium[1]	4.4	—	11,970[b] / 1,386	15,855[b] / 1,732	25,700[d] / 2,655	39,531 / 3,895	60,805 / 5,685	93,529 / 8,320
Bulgaria	—	—	—	4,345[f] / 552	9,800[d] / 1,154	—	—	—
Czechoslovakia[3]	6.1	—	—	18,103[f] / 1,326	30,500[d] / 2,108	55,138 / 3,496	99,679 / 6,012	180,201 / 10,339
Denmark[1]	4.3	—	7,035[b] / 1,647	9,660[b] / 2,109	15,600[d] / 3,171	23,767 / 4,463	36,209 / 6,397	55,164 / 9,179
Finland[1]	4.5	—	3,885[b] / 969	6,405[b] / 1,446	10,200[d] / 2,170	15,840 / 3,216	24,599 / 4,800	38,201 / 7,162
France[1]	5.7	—	53,130[b] / 1,273	82,530[b] / 1,807	147,500[d] / 2,905	256,769 / 4,942	446,984 / 7,460	778,112 / 11,992
Germany, East[3]	5.7	—	—	22,931[f] / 1,330	32,300[d] / 1,872	56,228 / 3,180	97,882 / 5,336	170,393 / 8,926
Germany, West[1]	4.5	—	49,770[b] / 1,040	114,030[b] / 2,142	186,300[d] / 3,128	289,318 / 4,739	449,302 / 6,882	697,752 / 10,269

GNP in Millions of Constant 1970 Dollars (Upper Figure) and
Per Capita GNP in Constant 1970 Dollars (Lower Figure)

CONTINENT AND COUNTRY	BASE PERIOD GROWTH RATE OF GNP	1940	1950	1960	1970	1980	1990	2000
Greece[1]	6.9	—	2,603[b] 344	4,617[b] 554	9,500[d] 1,069	18,514 1,953	36,081 3,613	70,316 6,699
Hungary	—	—	—	8,448[f] 846	14,300[d] 1,387	—	—	—
Iceland[1]*	1.7	—	210[b] 1,469	315[b] 1,790	500[d] 2,381	592 2,349	701 2,321	830 2,299
Ireland[1]	3.5	—	2,205[b] 743	2,625[b] 926	4,100[d] 1,395	5,783 1,767	8,157 2,188	11,506 2,712
Italy[1]	5.9	—	30,345[b] 651	53,130[b] 1,070	93,200[d] 1,737	165,339 2,858	293,315 4,723	520,348 7,814
Luxembourg[1]	3.5	—	525[b] 1,768	735[b] 2,341	1,000[d] 2,941	1,411 3,609	1,990 4,606	2,807 5,885
Netherlands[1]	5.1	—	12,075[b] 1,194	19,110[b] 1,665	31,200[d] 2,396	51,308 3,546	84,375 5,223	138,753 7,700
Norway[1]	4.4	—	4,620[b] 1,415	6,615[b] 1,847	13,400[d] 3,454	20,612 4,807	31,705 6,750	48,768 9,493
Poland[3]	3.5	—	—	32,586[f] 1,102	39,400[d] 1,201	55,578 1,520	78,398 1,960	110,588 2,528
Portugal[1]	6.2	—	2,310[b] 275	3,465[b] 393	6,200[d] 644	11,315 1,100	20,649 1,853	37,683 3,123
Romania[3]	4.1	—	—	14,483[f] 787	22,300[d] 1,101	33,328 1,487	49,810 2,053	74,443 2,834

Gross National Product (GNP) and Per Capita GNP, 1940–2000 (*continued*)

CONTINENT AND COUNTRY	BASE PERIOD GROWTH RATE OF GNP	GNP in Millions of Constant 1970 Dollars (Upper Figure) and Per Capita GNP in Constant 1970 Dollars (Lower Figure)						
		1940	1950	1960	1970	1980	1990	2000
Spain[1]	6.5	—	10,741[c] / 385	15,540[b] / 513	32,300[d] / 970	60,632 / 1,665	113,815 / 2,859	213,646 / 4,907
Sweden[1]	3.9	—	14,070[b] / 2,006	19,635[b] / 2,625	32,600[d] / 4,055	47,794 / 5,588	70,069 / 7,811	102,726 / 10,894
Switzerland[1]	3.7	—	8,610[b] / 1,834	13,230[b] / 2,467	20,500[d] / 3,264	29,481 / 4,188	42,396 / 5,458	60,969 / 7,106
United Kingdom[1]*	2.0	—	69,090[b] / 1,365	90,090[b] / 1,721	121,000[d] / 2,172	147,498 / 2,477	179,799 / 2,795	219,174 / 3,146
USSR[3]	3.4	—	—	319,828[f] / 1,493	497,000[d] / 2,047	694,323 / 2,566	969,989 / 3,185	1,355,103 / 3,950
Yugoslavia[3]	5.2	—	—	7,845[e] / 426	19,000[d] / 925	31,544 / 1,381	52,369 / 2,100	86,942 / 3,187
OCEANIA								
Australia[1]	5.1	—	13,755[b] / 1,682	20,370[b] / 1,982	32,990[d] / 2,629	54,251 / 3,531	89,214 / 4,757	146,710 / 6,418
New Zealand[1]	2.4	—	—	3,990[b] / 1,682	5,330[d] / 1,890	6,757 / 1,976	8,566 / 2,074	10,859 / 2,177

NOTES ON APPENDIX C: SOURCES AND METHODS

Per capita Gross National Product (GNP) figures result from a division of GNP (or GNP projections) by the population totals (or projections) of the corresponding country for the corresponding year (see Appendix B). The numbers in the column immediately following the country name denote in percentages the annual rate of growth of GNP. The reference number with a country name identifies the source from which the growth rate figure was obtained.

Projections to the year 2000 are products of assumptions that GNP will, on average, increase each year from 1970 to 2000 by the growth rate percentage specified. Per capita GNP figures are also governed by the assumption of a constant growth rate and, in addition, by assumptions about anticipated population growth as set out in Appendix B.

All growth rates are calculated in terms of constant 1970 dollars. Thus the data for 1940, 1950, 1960, and 1970 as well as the projections reflect 1970 dollar prices. It follows that all growth rates are "real" growth rates and exclude inflationary, or deflationary, inputs. (For a cautionary statement concerning the interpretation of projections see the Introduction to the Appendices.)

Growth rate figures are derived either from public sources or from computations based on publicly available estimates of national economic performance during a specified period of years. Sources follow in order of numerical notation:

1. Agency for International Development (AID), *Gross National Product* (Washington, D.C., May 15, 1971). The base period used in this publication to calculate growth rate is 1965–1970.
Exceptions are Jordan, the United States, and certain other countries.

The most recent estimate of Jordan's growth rate appears in *Gross National Product* (March 31, 1967). The base period is 1960–1966.

The growth rate of the United States during the 1965–1970 period was abnormally low (3.0). Consequently, it provides an unreliable base from which to project growth estimates. A different and longer base period was therefore substituted (1960–1971) during which the annual average growth rate was 3.9. This figure yields projections that are likely to be more accurate, but it is probably still too low.

Growth rates for some countries are calculated from base periods varying slightly from the standard 1965–1970 base. Consult *Gross National Product* (March 15, 1971), for variant cases.

2. Computations are based on GNP performances for 1967–1970 as recorded in AID, *Selected Economic Data* (Washington, D.C.: AID, 1969, 1970, 1971, 1972).

3. Computations are based on GNP performances in the two years 1960 and 1970. Sources for 1960 and 1970 GNP data are identified by lettered notations explained in the list that follows. (No projections have been made for countries where growth rate data were unavailable.)

The lettered notations in the columns for 1940, 1950, 1960, and 1970 refer to the following sources:

a. Population Reference Bureau, *Population Bulletin* (Washington, D.C., October 1963), pp. 161–167.
b. AID, *Gross National Product* (May 15, 1971).
c. AID, *Gross National Product* (March 31, 1967).
d. United States Arms Control and Disarmament Agency, *World Military Expenditures, 1971* (Washington, D.C., July 1972).
e. P.N. Rodenstein-Rodan, "International Aid for Underdeveloped Countries," *Review of Economics and Statistics*, 43, 2 (1961), 119–121, 126–127.
f. Escott Reid, *The Future of the World Bank* (Washington, D.C.: International Bank for Reconstruction and Development, 1965).
g. AID, *Selected Economic Data for the Less Developed Countries* (Washington, D.C.: AID, June 1972).

The GNP performances of all countries were projected in accordance with a standard procedure, with the exceptions indicated above. Standardization required that the constant growth rate calculated from performance during the specified base period be adhered to even though the growth rate during that period was, on the basis of other data and considerations, manifestly high or low. Very high or very low growth rates computed from a specific base period are far less likely to hold constant over two or three decades than are more moderate rates. In these cases, the assumption of constancy of growth is particularly likely to produce distorted—and sometimes spectacularly distorted—projections. The countries where distortion of this kind is evident are asterisked.

Appendix D

Ethnic Composition by Continent: Number of Countries in Each of Five Ethnic Categories (Total Number of Countries is 134)*

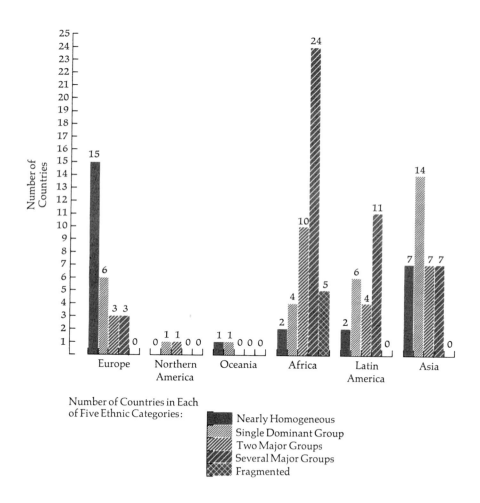

Number of Countries in Each
of Five Ethnic Categories:

Nearly Homogeneous
Single Dominant Group
Two Major Groups
Several Major Groups
Fragmented

*In some cases linguistic or religious groupings provide the basis for classification.

Appendix E

Ethnic Divisions by Continent and Country for 134 Countries

Africa

LESOTHO	SWAZILAND
Total: 1,040,000	*Total:* 410,000

MAURITANIA
Total: 1,170,000

Moors	72.0%
Fulani	4.6
Non-Africans	11.0

UNITED ARAB REPUBLIC
Total: 33,330,000

Arab Muslims	92.0%
Coptic Christians	7.7

TUNISIA
Total: 5,140,000

Tunisians	94.5%
Muslim Foreigners	2.6
Other Foreigners	3.3

UPPER VOLTA
Total: 5,380,000

Mossi	48.0%
Bobo	8.5
Mande	6.5
Gurunshi	5.7
Fulani	5.7

ALGERIA
Total: 14,100,000

Arabs	81.5%
Berbers	17.9

CHAD[1]
Total: 3,710,000

BURUNDI
Total: 3,600,000

Hutu	84.0%
Tutsi	14.0

LIBYA[2]
Total: 1,900,000

[1]No exact data available, but major division exists between black Africans and Arabs, with blacks slightly outnumbering Arabs.

[2]No exact data available. Arabs are in great majority, but there are large groups of Berbers as well.

Note: Country population totals are 1970 figures (see Appendix B). Subgroup percentages in most cases reflect data recorded in the 1960s. A few of the percentages refer to ethnic composition in the mid-1950s.

Where ethnic subgroups are listed for a given country, the percentages of the entire population represented by the subgroups often do not add up to 100 percent of the total. In such cases varying numbers of smaller subgroups have not been included in the enumeration.

In some cases religious or linguistic rather than ethnic subgroups are listed.

Africa (continued)

MAURITIUS
Total: 810,000

Indians	67.0%
Creole (Afro-Indian and	
Afro-European)	25.0
Chinese and Europeans	5.0

MOROCCO
Total: 15,530,000

Arabs	64.3%
Berbers	33.4
Non-Moroccans and	
Others	2.3

RWANDA
Total: 3,590,000

Hutu	81.4%
Tutsi	17.5

SIERRA LEONE
Total: 2,790,000

Temne	33.0%
Mende	30.0
Eleven Other Small	
Groups	37.0

SOMALIA
Total: 2,790,000

Somale	84.5%
Sab	15.5

SUDAN
Total: 15,700,000

Blacks	43.2%
Arabs	38.9
Mixed (Beja and Nubian)	9.5

ANGOLA
Total: 5,600,000

Ovimbundu	34.0%
Kimbundu	24.0
Bakongo	10.0
Nganguela	7.0
Lunda-Quioco	5.8
Europeans	3.6
Nyaneka-Humbe	4.2
Mestiços	1.1

BOTSWANA
Total: 650,000

Bamongwato	34.2%
Bakwena	13.6
Bangwaketse	13.2
Batawana	13.2
Bakgatla	6.8

CAMEROON
Total: 5,840,000

Kirdi	33.0%
Beti-Pahouin	19.8
Bamileke	14.7
Fulani	15.2
Tikar	9.1
Bussa-Bakoko	5.9

CENTRAL AFRICAN REPUBLIC
Total: 1,520,000

Banda	21.8%
Baya	20.9
Mandia	18.1
Ubangi	10.4

CONGO (BRAZZAVILLE)
Total: 940,000

Kongo	45.0%
Bateke	20.0
Boubangui	16.0
Gabonais	15.0

ZAIRE (FORMERLY CONGO-KINSHASA)
Total: 17,420,000

Ba-Kongo	21.4%
Ba-Mongo	14.3
Ba-Luba	10.7
Ba-Lunda	No Data
Several Smaller Groups	

Africa (*continued*)

DAHOMEY
Total: 2,690,000

Fon	40.7%
Adja	12.8
Bariba	10.0
Yoruba	9.3
Aizo	5.4
Somba	5.2

ETHIOPIA
Total: 25,050,000

Abyssinians	31.6%
Galla	31.0
Somalis	18.4
Blacks	13.2
Others	5.9

GABON
Total: 500,000

Fang	30.0%
Eshira	20.0
Mbede	15.0
Bakota	13.0
Omyene	5.0

GAMBIA
Total: 360,000

Mandingo	41.0%
Fula	13.6
Wolof	13.0
Jola	7.0
Serahuli	7.0

GHANA
Total: 9,030,000

Akan	44.1%
Mole Dagbani	18.4
Ewe	13.0
Ga-Adangbe	8.3

GUINEA
Total: 3,920,000

Mande Groups	47.0%
Peul Groups	28.6
Forest Groups	18.1

IVORY COAST
Total: 4,310,000

Immigrated Peoples (Mossi, Bobo, and Other Voltaic Groups)	31.4%
Western Forest Groups	28.0
Akan-Lagunaires	26.8
Senoufo	14.9
Malinke and Dioula	10.6

KENYA
Total: 10,900,000

Bantu	62.7%
Hamitic and Nilo-Hamitic	20.2
Nilotic	13.3

MALAGASAY REPUBLIC
Total: 6,750,000

Merina	25.3%
Betsimisaraka	15.5
Betsileo	12.4
Tsimihety	6.8
Sakalava	5.7
Antaisaka	5.5
Antandroy	5.0
Nine Other Tribal Groups	21.0

MALAWI
Total: 4,530,000

Chewa	28.0%
Nguru	19.0
Nyanja	15.0
Yao	14.0
Ngoni	9.0

Africa (*continued*)

COUNTRIES WITH SEVERAL MAJOR ETHNIC GROUPS (*continued*)

MOZAMBIQUE		SENEGAL	
Total: 7,575,000		Total: 3,930,000	
Makua	19.4%	Wolof	36.0%
Tribes of the		Peul	17.5
Lower Zambesi	19.4	Serer	16.5
Thonga	19.4	Tukolor	6.5
Lomwe	10.2	Diola	9.0
Nguni	9.8	Mandingo	9.0
Maravi	7.9		
Whites	1.0		
Asians and Mestiços	0.7		
NIGER		REPUBLIC OF SOUTH AFRICA	
Total: 4,020,000		Total: 20,110,000	
Hausa	46.7%	Blacks	68.1%
Djerma-Songhai	22.5	Whites	19.0
Fulani	17.3	Colored	9.9
Tuareg	10.4	Asians	3.0
NIGERIA		SOUTH-WEST AFRICA	
Total: 55,070,000		Total: 620,000	
Hausa-Fulani	40.0%	Ovambo	44.4%
Ibo	24.0	Whites	15.7
Yoruba	20.0	Dama	8.2
		Herero	6.6
		Hottentots	6.5
		Okavango	5.2
RHODESIA		TOGO	
Total: 5,270,000		Total: 1,860,000	
Shona	72.0%	Cabrai	18.2%
Ndebele	19.2	Ewe	17.8
Whites	7.2	Watchi	14.6
		Moba	6.4
		Cotocoli	5.5
		Other Small Groups	36.1

COUNTRIES WITH MANY SMALL ETHNIC GROUPS (FRAGMENTED)

LIBERIA		MALI	
Total: 1,170,000		Total: 5,020,000	
Kpelle	8.6%	Bambara	22.1%
Gola	7.5	Fulani	12.3
Bassa	5.0	Marka	5.7
Kru	5.0	Songai	5.3
Mandigo	5.0	Malinke	5.1
Loma	5.0	Tuareg	5.0
Americo-Liberians	2.0	Seventeen Other Small	
Nineteen Other Small		Groups	44.5
Groups	62.9		

Africa (*continued*)

COUNTRIES WITH MANY SMALL ETHNIC GROUPS (FRAGMENTED) (*continued*)

TANZANIA
  Total: 13,270,000

Sukama	12.4%
Nyamwezi	4.1
Makonde	3.8
Haya	3.7
Chagga	3.6
Five Other Tribes Over 200,000 Each	15.4
Thirteen Other Tribes Over 100,000 Each	23.0
Ninety-seven Other Tribes Under 100,000 Each	34.0

ZAMBIA
  Total: 4,300,000

Tonga	11.0%
Bemba	8.0
Chewa	5.7
Nsenga	4.4
Sixty-nine Other Small Groups	70.9

UGANDA
  Total: 9,760,000

Baganda	16.2%
Banyankole	8.1
Iteso	8.1
Basoga	7.8
Bakiga	7.1
Banyaruanda	5.9
Lango	5.6
Acholi	4.4
Bagisu	5.1
Eleven Other Small Groups	31.7

North, Central, and South America[3]

COUNTRIES WITH NEARLY HOMOGENEOUS ETHNIC COMPOSITION

ARGENTINA
  Total: 24,350,000

PARAGUAY
  Total: 2,390,000

COUNTRIES WITH A SINGLE DOMINANT ETHNIC GROUP

COSTA RICA
  Total: 1,718,000

Whites	90.0%
Blacks and Mulattoes	10.0

EL SALVADOR
  Total: 3,530,000

Mestizos	80.0%
Amerindians	10.0
Whites	10.0

[3]Considerable discrepancy exists among the countries of the Americas in the definitions of the ethnic categories white, black, mestizo and mulatto. This must be kept in mind when interpreting the percentage size of any of these groups, especially when making comparisons between countries.

North, Central, and South America *(continued)*

HAITI
  Total: 4,870,000

Blacks	90.0%
Mulattoes and Others	10.0

UNITED STATES OF AMERICA
  Total: 205,400,000

Whites	87.8%
Blacks	11.1
Indians, Mexicans, Puerto Ricans, and Others	1.1

HONDURAS
  Total: 2,580,000

Mestizos	90.0%
Others (Blacks, Whites, Mulattoes, and Amerindians)	10.0

URUGUAY
  Total: 2,890,000

Whites	90.0%
Mestizos	10.0

NICARAGUA
  Total: 1,980,000

Mestizos	77.0%
Blacks	9.0
Black and Indian Mixed	9.0
Amerindians	4.0
Whites	1.0

BOLIVIA
  Total: 4,930,000

Amerindians	70.0%
Mestizos	25.0
Whites	5.0

GUATEMALA
  Total: 5,110,000

Amerindians	55.0%
Mestizos	45.0
Whites	1.0

CANADA
  Total: 21,410,000

English-speaking Whites	67.1%
French-speaking Whites	30.4
Indians, Eskimos, Blacks, and Others	2.5

JAMAICA
  Total: 2,000,000

Blacks	78.0%
Mulattoes	14.0
Afro-Orientals	2.3
Others	6.0

CHILE
  Total: 9,780,000

Mestizos	68.0%
Whites	30.0
Amerindians	2.0

North, Central, and South America (continued)

BRAZIL
Total: 95,310,000

Whites	60.0%
Mixed (Mulattoes, Mestizos, and Combination)	25.0
Blacks	15.0

COLOMBIA
Total: 21,120,000

Mestizos	40.0%
Whites	30.0
Mulattoes	18.0
Indians	7.0
Blacks	5.0

CUBA
Total: 8,390,000

Whites	73.0%
Mulattoes	14.5
Blacks	12.5
Chinese	1.0

DOMINICAN REPUBLIC
Total: 4,320,000

Mixed (Indian, Black, and White)	60.0%
Whites	28.0
Blacks	11.0

ECUADOR
Total: 6,090,000

Mestizos	41.0%
Amerindians	39.0
Whites	10.0
Blacks	10.0

GUYANA
Total: 760,000

East Indians	51.0%
Blacks	31.0
Mixed	12.0
Amerindians	5.0

MEXICO
Total: 50,670,000

Mestizos	60.0%
Amerindians	30.0
Whites	10.0

PANAMA
Total: 1,460,000

Mixed (Mestizos and Mulattoes)	65.0%
Blacks	13.0
Whites	11.0
Amerindians	10.0

PERU
Total: 13,590,000

Mestizos	46.0%
Amerindians	42.0
Whites	12.0

TRINIDAD AND TOBAGO
Total: 1,070,000

Blacks	43.5%
East Indians	36.5
Mixed	16.3
Whites	2.0

VENEZUELA
Total: 10,400,000

Mestizos and Mulattoes	65.0%
Whites	21.0
Blacks	7.0
Amerindians	7.0

Asia

JAPAN
Total: 103,540,000

JORDAN
Total: 2,320,000

NORTH KOREA
Total: 13,890,000

SOUTH KOREA
Total: 31,790,000

Asia (*continued*)

MALDIVE ISLANDS
Total: 93,000

YEMEN
Total: 5,730,000

SOUTH YEMEN
Total: 1,280,000

COUNTRIES WITH A SINGLE DOMINANT ETHNIC GROUP

BURMA
Total: 27,580,000

Burmese	75.0%
Karens and Kayahs	12.0
Shan	6.0
Indians and Pakistani	3.0
Chinese and Others	4.0

MONGOLIA
Total: 1,290,000

Khalkha Mongols	70.0%
Western Mongols	6.0
Buryat and Bargut Mongols	3.0
Other Mongols	11.0
Turks	10.0

CAMBODIA
Total: 7,330,000

Cambodians	85.0%
Vietnamese	5.0
Chinese	6.0
Others	4.0

SAUDI ARABIA
Total: 7,350,000

Arabs	93.0%
Blacks	7.0

PEOPLE'S REPUBLIC OF CHINA
Total: 759,620,000

Chinese	93.0%
Zhuang	1.8
Hui, Uighur, and Yi	2.5
Tibetan, Miao, Manchu, and Mongol	2.2
Forty-six Other Small Groups	.5

SYRIA
Total: 6,100,000

Arabs	90.0%
Kurds	4.8
Armenians	3.2
Turkomans, Circassians, Assyrians	2.8

CHINA (TAIWAN)
Total: 14,040,000

Taiwanese	86.4%
Mainlanders	11.6
Aborigines	2.0

THAILAND
Total: 35,810,000

Thai	85.0%
Chinese	11.0
Malays and Others	4.0

ISRAEL
Total: 2,940,000

Jews	89.0%
Arab Muslims	8.0
Arab Christians	2.0

TRUCIAL OMAN[4]
Total: 120,000

---

[4]No precise data are available, but population is predominantly Arab with several small minorities, especially in Muscat.

Asia (*continued*)

TURKEY
  Total: 35,230,000

Turks	91.1%
Kurds	6.6
Arabs	1.3
Others	1.0

SOUTH VIETNAM
  Total: 18,330,000

Vietnamese	85.0%
Chinese	6.3
Montagnards	4.7
Cambodians	3.8

NORTH VIETNAM
  Total: 21,150,000

Vietnamese	85.1%
Upland Tribes:	
Tay	2.7
Muong	2.2
Thai	2.0
Nong	2.0
Chinese and Others	6.0

AFGHANISTAN
  Total: 17,120,000

Pushtun	60.0%
Tajiks	30.0
Uzbeks	5.2
Turkomans, Kirghiz, and Others	4.8

IRAQ
  Total: 9,440,000

Arabs	79.0%
Kurds	16.0
Persians	3.0
Turks	2.0

CEYLON (SRI LANKA)
  Total: 12,510,000

Sinhalese	70.0%
Tamil (Ceylonese, Indians, and Pakistani)	21.0
Ceylon Moors	5.0
Veddas and Others	4.0

LAOS
  Total: 2,790,000

Lowland Lao	67.0%
Lao-Theung (Upland Tribes)	29.7
Vietnamese, Chinese, and Others	3.3

CYPRUS
  Total: 630,000

Greeks	78.8%
Turks	17.5
Others	3.7

NEPAL
  Total: 11,200,000

Pahari	49.0%
Indians of the Tarai	24.0
Tamang	6.0
Newar	4.7
Tharu	4.4
Several Other Small Groups	12.0

IRAN
  Total: 28,960,000

Persians	55.0%
Turks	18.5
Gilac	5.5
Lur	5.2
Kurds	5.2
Mazandarani	4.4
Others	7.0

Asia (*continued*)

COUNTRIES WITH SEVERAL MAJOR ETHNIC GROUPS

INDIA

Total: 550,380,000

Linguistic Groups:

Hindi	30.0%
Telugu	8.6
Bengali	7.7
Marathi	7.6
Tamil	7.0
Urdu	5.3
Gujarati	4.6
Kannada	4.0
Malayalam	3.9
Bihari	3.8
Oriya	3.6
Rajasthani	3.4
Punjabi	2.5
Ten Other Groups with Over 1,000,000 Each	3.7
Twenty-five Other Groups with over 100,000 Each	2.0

INDONESIA

Total: 121,200,000

Javanese	45.0%
Sundanese	14.0
Madurese	8.0
Coastal Malays	8.0
Makassarese-Buginese	4.0
Menangkabau	3.0
Balinese	2.0
Batak	2.0
Atjehnese	1.0
Others	13.0

KUWAIT

Total: 710,000

Kuwaitis	51.0%
Jordanians	9.4
Iraqis	8.5
Iranians	5.5

KUWAIT *(con't)*

Syrians and Egyptians	5.1
Lebanese	5.0
Omanis	4.2
Indians and Pakistani	4.5

LEBANON

Total: 2,790,000

Ethnoreligious Groups:

Maronites	30.0%
Sunnis	22.0
Sh'is	18.0
Greek Orthodox	10.0
Greek Catholic	6.0
Druzes	6.0
Other Christians	8.0

MALAYSIA

Total: 10,080,000

Malays	42.0%
Chinese	35.0
Indigenous Tribes	7.5
Tamils	9.5

PAKISTAN[5]

Total: 134,000,000

Bengali	55.48%
Punjabi	29.02
Sindhi	5.51
Pushtu	3.70
Urdu	3.65
Baluchi	1.09
Brahui	0.41
Others	1.14

[5]The following 1961 tabulation of ethnic groupings in West and East Pakistan helps to explain the pressures that led to the secession of East Pakistan in 1971 and its emergence as the independent state of Bangla Desh.

	(West) Pakistan	Bangla Desh (former East Pakistan)
Bengali	0.12%	98.42%
Punjabi	66.39	0.02
Sindhi	12.59	0.01
Pushtu	8.47	0.01
Urdu	7.57	0.61
Baluchi	2.49	—
Brahui	0.93	—
Others	1.44	0.93

Asia (*continued*)

COUNTRIES WITH SEVERAL MAJOR ETHNIC GROUPS (*continued*)

PHILIPPINES
Total: 38,490,000

Linguistic Groups:	
Cebuano	24.10%
Tagalog	21.00
Iloko	11.70
Panay-Hiligaynon	10.40
Bikol	7.80
Four Other Large Groups	12.20
Thirty-eight Other Small Groups with 1 Percent or Less	12.80

SINGAPORE
Total: 2,050,000

Chinese	75.00%
Malays	14.00
Indians and Pakistani	8.20
Others	2.80

Europe

COUNTRIES WITH NEARLY HOMOGENEOUS ETHNIC COMPOSITION

ALBANIA
Total: 2,170,000

AUSTRIA
Total: 7,420,000

DENMARK
Total: 4,920,000

FRANCE
Total: 50,780,000

EAST GERMANY
Total: 17,250,000

WEST GERMANY
Total: 59,550,000

ICELAND
Total: 210,000

IRELAND
Total: 2,940,000

ITALY
Total: 53,670,000

LUXEMBOURG
Total: 340,000

NETHERLANDS
Total: 13,020,000

NORWAY
Total: 3,880,000

POLAND
Total: 32,810,000

PORTUGAL
Total: 9,630,000

SWEDEN
Total: 8,040,000

COUNTRIES WITH ONE DOMINANT ETHNIC GROUP

BULGARIA
Total: 8,490,000

Bulgarians	84.8%
Turks	9.1
Others	6.1

FINLAND
Total: 4,700,000

Finnish Speaking	92.4%
Swedish Speaking	7.4

GREECE
Total: 8,890,000

Greeks	92.8%
Turks	3.8
Slavs and Others	3.4

HUNGARY
Total: 10,310,000

Hungarians	95.7%
Germans and Others	4.3

Europe (*continued*)

ROMANIA
Total: 20,250,000

Romanians	88.5%
Hungarians	8.4
Germans	2.0

UNITED KINGDOM
Total: 55,710,000

Regional Divisions:	
England	83.0%
Scotland	9.8
Wales	5.0
Northern Ireland	2.0

COUNTRIES WITH TWO MAJOR ETHNIC GROUPS

BELGIUM
Total: 9,680,000

Flemings	62.5%
Walloons	37.5

CZECHOSLOVAKIA
Total: 14,470,000

Czechs	65.0%
Slovaks	29.3
Magyars, Germans, and Others	5.7

SPAIN
Total: 33,290,000

Spanish Speaking	77.5%
Catalan Speaking	20.0
Basques	2.5

COUNTRIES WITH SEVERAL MAJOR ETHNIC GROUPS

SWITZERLAND
Total: 6,280,000

Germans	74.4%
French	20.2
Italians	4.1
Others	1.3

UNION OF SOVIET
SOCIALIST REPUBLICS
Total: 242,770,000

Russians	54.7%
Ukrainians	17.7
Byelorussians	3.8
Uzbeks	2.9
Tatars	2.4
Kazakhs	1.7
Six Other Groups with Over 2,000,000 Each	7.3
Seven Other Groups with Over 1,000,000 Each	4.6
Others	3.2

Europe *(continued)*

COUNTRIES WITH SEVERAL MAJOR ETHNIC GROUPS *(continued)*

YUGOSLAVIA
  Total: 20,530,000

Serbs	42.0%
Croats	20.5
Slovenes	8.6
Macedonians	5.6
Montenegrans	2.8
Others	11.0

Oceania

COUNTRIES WITH NEARLY HOMOGENEOUS ETHNIC COMPOSITION

AUSTRALIA
  Total: 12,300,000

COUNTRIES WITH A SINGLE DOMINANT ETHNIC GROUP

NEW ZEALAND
  Total: 2,944,000

Whites	92.7%
Maoris	7.5

SOURCES FOR APPENDIX E

Africa

Algeria: *Annuaire de L'Afrique du Nord* (Paris, 1968), p. 275.

Angola: *U.S. Army Area Handbook, Angola* (Washington, D.C.: American University, 1967), pp. 82–98; and D. L. Wheeler and R. Pellissier, *Angola* (New York: Praeger, 1971).

Burundi: *Statesman's Yearbook,* 1970, p. 790; and *Encyclopedia Britannica,* 4 (1969), 463.

Cameroon: Victor T. LeVine, *The Cameroons* (Berkeley: University of California Press, 1964).

Central African Republic: *Encyclopedia Britannica,* 5 (1969), 173.

Ethiopia: G. A. Lipsky, *Ethiopia* (New Haven, Conn.: HRAF Press, 1962), pp. 34–36; and E. Ullendorf, *The Ethiopians* (London: Oxford University Press, 1965).

Gabon: Brian Weinstein, *Gabon* (Cambridge, Mass.: MIT Press, 1966), p. 31.

Gambia: *The Gambia,* Reference Pamphlet #70 (Bathurst: Central Office of Information, 1965).

Ivory Coast: Samir Amin, *Le Développement du Capitalisme en Côte d'Ivoire* (Paris: Les Editions de Minuit, 1967), pp. 29–42.

Lesotho: *Lesotho* (London: British Information Service, 1966), p. 3.

Liberia: *U.S. Army Area Handbook, Liberia* (1968), pp. 39–54.

Libya: *Statesman's Yearbook*, 1970, p. 1133; and *Encyclopedia Britannica*, 13 (1969), 1064.

Malagasy Republic: Richard Adloff and Virginia Thompson, *The Malagasy Republic* (Stanford, Calif.: Stanford University Press, 1965).

Mauritius: *Statesman's Yearbook*, 1970, p. 504; and *Encyclopedia Britannica*, 14 (1969), 1129.

Morocco: *U.S. Army Area Handbook, Morocco* (1965), pp. 69–75.

Mozambique: *U.S. Army Area Handbook, Mozambique* (1969), pp. 49–67; and A. Ehnmark and P. Waesberg, *Angola and Mozambique* (New York: Roy Publishers, 1963).

Nigeria: W. Schwartz, *Nigeria* (New York: Praeger, 1968), p. 14.

Republic of South Africa: *Fifth Special Report to the Director General on Apartheid in South Africa* (Geneva: ILO, 1969), p. 33.

Rwanda: P. B. Gravel, *Remera* (The Hague: Mouton, 1968), p. 21.

Sierra Leone: *West African Directory* (London: T. Skinner, 1967–1968), p. 416.

Sierra Leone, Congo (Brazzaville), Dahomey, Mali, Senegal, Zambia: *Africa* (Paris: Special publication of *Jeune Afrique*, 1969–1970).

Somalia: I. M. Lewis, *Modern History of Somaliland* (New York: Praeger, 1965), pp. 1–7.

South-West Africa: *South West Africa Survey* (Pretoria: Government of South Africa, 1967), pp. 16–23.

Sudan, Ghana, Guinea, Kenya: *United Nations Demographic Yearbook*, 1963 and 1964 (New York: UN, 1963 and 1964).

Swaziland, Mauritania, Tunisia, UAR, Upper Volta, Chad, Botswana, Congo (Brazzaville), Dahomey, Gambia, Malagasy Republic, Malawi, Niger, Rhodesia, Senegal, Togo, Mali, Tanzania, Uganda, Zambia: Violane Junod and Idrian Resnick, *Handbook of Africa* (New York: New York University Press, 1963).

Tanzania: Hugh W. Stephens, *The Political Transformation of Tanganyika* (New York: Praeger, 1968).

Zaïre (former Congo-Kinshasa):   *U.S. Army Area Handbook, Congo (Kinshasa)*, 1968.

North, Central, and South America

Argentina, Chile, Panama: *Worldmark Encyclopaedia of the Nations*, Vol. 3 (New York: Moshe Sachs, 1967).

Canada: *Canada Yearbook, 1969,* Ottawa: Dominion Bureau of Statistics, 1969.

Cuba: Boris Goldenberg, *The Cuban Revolution and Latin America* (New York: Praeger, 1965).

Guyana: *West Indies and Caribbean Yearbook, 1969.*

Jamaica, Trinidad, and Tobago: *United Nations Demographic Yearbook,* 1963.

Paraguay, Costa Rica, El Salvador, Haiti, Honduras, Nicaragua, Uruguay, Bolivia, Guatemala, Brazil, Colombia, Dominican Republic, Ecuador, Mexico, Peru, Venezuela: A. Marshall, *South American Handbook* (London: Trade and Travel Publications, 1970).

United States of America: U.S. Bureau of the Census: *Statistical Abstract of the United States, 1969* (Washington, D.C.: Government Printing Office, 1970).

Asia

China, People's Republic of: *China* (Geneva: Nagel Publishers, 1968).

China (Taiwan):   Chiao-min Hsieh, *Taiwan—ilha Formosa* (1964).

India: *India, 1968* (Delhi: Ministry of Information and Broadcasting, 1968).

Indonesia: Leslie Palmier, *Indonesia* (London: Thames and Hudson, 1965).

Iran: S. M. Aliyev, "The Problems of Nationalities in Contemporary Persia," *Central Asian Review,* 14, 1 (1966).

Iraq: *The Middle East and North Africa, 1968–1969* (London: Europa Publications, 1969).

Japan, Jordan, North Korea, South Korea, Maldive Islands, Burma, Cambodia, Israel, Saudi Arabia, Syria, Trucial Oman, Turkey, North Vietnam, Afghanistan, Ceylon, Cyprus, Laos, Kuwait, Malaysia, Singapore: *Worldmark Encyclopaedia of the Nations,* Vol. 4 (New York, 1967).

Lebanon: L. Z. Yamak, "Party Politics in the Lebanese Political System," in L. Binder (ed.), *Politics in Lebanon* (New York: Wiley, 1966).

Mongolia: *Encyclopedia Britannica,* 15 (1969), 728.

Nepal: *U.S. Army Area Handbook, Nepal,* 1964.

Pakistan: American University, *Pakistan Area Handbook* (Washington, D.C.: American University, 1971).

Philippines: Jean Grossholtz, *Politics in the Philippines* (Boston: Little, Brown, 1964).

Southern Yemen: A. Cohen, "The People's Republic of South Yemen," *New Outlook* (Tel Aviv, March–April, 1968), pp. 13–19.

South Vietnam: *Encyclopedia Britannica,* 23 (1969), 7.

Thailand: *Encyclopedia Britannica,* 21 (1969).

Yemen: M. W. Wenner, *Modern Yemen* (Baltimore: Johns Hopkins Press, 1967).

Europe

Albania, East Germany, Poland, Portugal, Bulgaria, Finland, Romania, United
  Kingdom, Switzerland: *Statesman's Yearbook,* 1970.

Austria, Denmark, France, West Germany, Greece, Hungary, Iceland, Ireland,
  Italy, Luxembourg, Netherlands, Norway, Sweden, Belgium, Czechoslovakia,
  Yugoslavia: *Worldmark Encyclopaedia of the Nations,* Vol. 5 (New York,
  1967).

Spain: *Encyclopedia Britannica,* 3 (1969), 254 and 5, 60.

USSR: Vernon Aspaturian, "The Non-Russian Nationalities," in A. Kassof
  (ed.), *Prospects for Soviet Society* (New York: Praeger, 1968).

Oceania

Australia: *Official Yearbook of the Commonwealth of Australia* (1969).

New Zealand: *Statesman's Yearbook,* 1970.

Literacy Rate by Continent and Country for 134 Countries

Africa

Algeria	15	Mauritania	3
Angola	3	Mauritius	62
Botswana	20	Morocco	15.5
Burundi	12	Mozambique	2
Cameroon	10	Niger	3
Central African Republic	15	Nigeria	32.5
Chad	5	Republic of South Africa	35
Congo(Brazzaville)	22.5	Rhodesia	20
Zaïre (former Congo-Kinshasa)	58	Rwanda	7.5
Dahomey	5	Senegal	6
Ethiopia	5	Sierra Leone	7
Gabon	12	Somalia	5
Gambia	10	South-West Africa	27
Ghana	22.5	Sudan	16
Guinea	10	Swaziland	36
Ivory Coast	20	Tanzania	17.5
Kenya	22.5	Togo	7.5
Lesotho	40	Tunisia	30
Liberia	10	Uganda	20
Libya	22	United Arab Republic	19.5
Malagasay Republic	35	Upper Volta	7.5
Malawi	7.5	Zambia	20
Mali	2		

America

Argentina	91	El Salvador	48
Bolivia	32	Guatemala	38
Brazil	61	Guyana	80
Canada	98.5	Haiti	10
Chile	84	Honduras	45
Colombia	62	Jamaica	85
Costa Rica	84	Mexico	71
Cuba	80	Nicaragua	50
Dominican Republic	64	Panama	78
Ecuador	68		

Note: All figures in Appendix F represent the percentage of total population, age 15 and above, having the ability to read and write. Data are taken from surveys conducted during the 1960s.

America (*continued*)

Paraguay	68	United States	98.5
Peru	61	Uruguay	91
Trinidad and Tobago	80	Venezuela	80

Asia

Afghanistan	8	Lebanon	86
Burma	60	Malaysia, Federation of	n.a.
Cambodia	31	Maldive Islands	n.a.
Ceylon (Sri Lanka)	75	Mongolia	95
China (Mainland)	55	Nepal	10
China (Taiwan)	78	Pakistan	20
Cyprus	76	Philippines	72
India	28	Saudi Arabia	10
Indonesia	43	Singapore	75
Iran	20	Syria	35
Iraq	20	Thailand	68
Israel	90	Trucial Oman	n.a.
Japan	98	Turkey	38.6
Jordan	37.5	North Vietnam	n.a.
North Korea	n.a.	South Vietnam	45
South Korea	71	Yemen	10
Kuwait	47	Southern Yemen	n.a.
Laos	15		

Europe

Albania	75	Italy	90
Austria	99	Luxembourg	98
Belgium	98	Netherlands	99
Bulgaria	90	Norway	99
Czechoslovakia	98	Poland	97
Denmark	99	Portugal	65
Finland	99	Romania	90
France	98	Spain	90
East Germany	99	Sweden	99
West Germany	99	Switzerland	99
Greece	85	United Kingdom	99
Hungary	98	USSR	98
Iceland	99	Yugoslavia	80
Ireland	99		

Oceania

Australia	99	New Zealand	99

SOURCES FOR APPENDIX F

With the exceptions noted below, all data are from the Agency for International Development's Regional Pamphlet Series entitled "Economic Growth Trends" (Washington, D.C.: AID, 1967–1968).

Data for the countries that follow are from *World Population Data Sheet* (Washington, D.C.: Population Reference Bureau, 1968): Burundi, Sudan, Canada, Cuba, Guyana, China (Mainland), Mongolia, Nepal, Albania, Austria, Belgium, Bulgaria, Czechoslovakia, Denmark, Finland, France, East and West Germany, Greece, Hungary, Iceland, Ireland, Luxembourg, Netherlands, Norway, Poland, Portugal, Romania, Spain, Sweden, Switzerland, United Kingdom, USSR, Yugoslavia, United States.

The data for Ecuador and Turkey are from the United Nations *Statistical Yearbook, 1967* (New York: United Nations, 1967).

Appendix G

International Trade

World Export and Import Totals for Selected Years, 1867 to 1971*
(In Millions of U.S. Dollars)

YEAR	EXPORTS	IMPORTS	YEAR	EXPORTS	IMPORTS
1867–1868[a]	4,979	5,554	1888	7,053	8,056
1872–1873	6,355	7,405	1889	7,542	8,750
1877	6,457	5,826	1890	7,771	9,052
1880	7,042	8,162	1891	7,853	9,178
1881	7,197	8,142	1892	7,730	9,047
1882	7,430	8,560	1893	7,763	8,941
1883	7,513	8,653	1894	7,564	8,815
1884	7,248	8,256	1895	7,949	9,005
1885	6,864	7,832	1896	8,171	9,524
1886	6,540	7,525	1897	8,480	9,799
1887	6,777	7,760			

YEAR	SUM OF EXPORTS AND IMPORTS	YEAR	SUM OF EXPORTS AND IMPORTS
1901[b]	22,291	1907	31,752
1902	23,055	1908	29,620
1903	24,392	1909	31,561
1904	24,999	1910	34,980
1905	26,940	1911	36,761
1906	29,704	1912	40,287

Note: The Export Quantum Index is included for the years 1913–1971. Quantum figures measure the physical volume of exports as percentages of the base year (1963) volume: (1963 = 100).

[a]1867–1938: Amounts are in gold dollars.
1938–1971: Amounts are in current U.S. dollars (current for each of the years indicated).
1938 figures are calculated twice to demonstrate the difference between gold dollars and the value of 1938 U.S. currency. Note that the Export Quantum Index remains the same for both sets of figures.

[b]For the years 1901–1912 only the combined export-import totals are available.

World Export and Import Totals for Selected Years, 1867 to 1971 *(continued)*

YEAR	EXPORTS	IMPORTS	EXPORT QUANTUM INDEX	YEAR	EXPORTS	IMPORTS	EXPORT QUANTUM INDEX
				1948	52,800	58,400	39
1913	19,800	20,800	31	1949	53,700	58,500	43
				1950	55,400	58,200	48
1920	31,600	34,200	19	1951	82,400	87,200	53
1921	19,700	22,100	23	1952	80,000	86,400	52
1922	21,700	23,600	25	1953	82,000	83,700	55
1923	23,800	25,900	28	1954	85,500	87,900	58
1924	27,850	28,980	32	1955	93,100	97,800	63
1925	31,550	33,150	35	1956	103,100	107,900	69
1926	29,920	32,120	36	1957	111,100	118,700	72
1927	31,520	33,760	39	1958	107,300	112,600	71
1928	32,730	34,650	41	1959	115,100	120,300	76
1929	33,024	35,595	43	1960	127,500	134,300	84
1930	26,480	29,080	35	1961	134,000	141,000	88
1931	18,910	20,800	36	1962	141,400	149,800	93
1932	12,885	13,970	32	1963	154,100	162,300	100
1933	11,710	12,460	32	1964	172,400	181,900	110
1934	11,300	12,000	33	1965	186,400	197,400	118
1935	11,600	12,200	35	1966	203,600	215,600	127
1936	12,600	13,100	36	1967	214,600	227,000	134
1937	15,000	16,100	41	1968	239,200	251,900	151
1938	13,400	14,300	38	1969	272,700	285,100	167
				1970	309,400	324,800	182
1938[ac]	20,700	23,200	38	1971	343,000	360,400	192
1947	48,300	50,100	38				

[a]1867–1938: Amounts are in gold dollars.
1938–1971: Amounts are in current U.S. dollars (current for each of the years indicated).
1938 figures are calculated twice to demonstrate the difference between gold dollars and the value of 1938 U.S. currency. Note that the Export Quantum Index remains the same for both sets of figures.

[c]Figures for 1938–1950 do not include China, USSR and nonreporting countries of Eastern Europe. Figures for 1951–1971 do not include Mainland China, North Korea, North Vietnam, and Mongolia.

SOURCES FOR APPENDIX G

1867–1868 to 1951: Wladimir S. and Emma S. Woytinsky, *World Commerce and Governments* (New York: Twentieth Century Fund, 1955), pp. 38–39.

1951–1969: United Nations, *Yearbook of International Trade Statistics, 1960, 1967,* and *1969.*

1970 and 1971: United Nations, *Monthly Bulletin of Statistics* (May 1972), pp. viii, 110, 116. The 1970 totals are the sum of the "world" totals and the Soviet and Eastern European totals that the *Bulletin* records separately. The 1971 totals are the sum of the "world" totals, recorded in the *Bulletin* and an estimate of the Soviet and Eastern European totals based on the growth of their foreign trade during the period 1967–1970.

Bibliography

The primary purpose of this bibliography is to draw attention to books of enduring importance to the study of international politics. Sources providing specialized or technical information may be found in footnotes to the text and in notes following the Appendix tables. Except for the first group of titles, books are listed according to chapter sequence. However, many have a relevance going far beyond the subject matter of a single chapter.

GENERAL REFERENCES

Aron, Rymond. *Peace and War.* Garden City, New York: Doubleday, 1966.

Carr, E. H. *The Twenty Years' Crisis, 1919–1939.* London: Macmillan, 1946.

Deutsch, Karl W., *The Nerves of Government.* New York: Free Press, 1966.

Hoffman, Stanley (ed.). *Contemporary Theory in International Relations.* Englewood Cliffs, New Jersey: Prentice-Hall, 1960.

Morgenthau, Hans J. *Politics Among Nations.* New York: Knopf, five editions, 1948 through 1972.

Wolfers, Arnold. *Discord and Collaboration.* Baltimore: Johns Hopkins Press, 1962.

INTRODUCTION: MACROANALYSIS

Barraclough, Geoffrey. *An Introduction to Contemporary History.* Baltimore: Penguin, 1967.

Fanon, Frantz. *The Wretched of the Earth.* New York: Grove Press, 1968.

Heilbroner, Robert. *Understanding Macroeconomics.* Englewood Cliffs, N.J.: Prentice-Hall, 1965 and 1970.

Herz, John. *International Politics in the Atomic Age.* New York: Columbia University Press, 1959.

Keynes, John Maynard. *The Economic Consequences of the Peace.* New York: Harcourt, Brace, 1920.

Marx, Karl, and Friedrich Engels. *The Communist Manifesto* (1848). Many editions.

Morgenthau, Hans J. *Scientific Man vs. Power Politics.* New York: Knopf, 1951.

PART ONE. THE MICROPOLITICAL WORLD

1. Power

Butterfield, Herbert. *Christianity, Diplomacy and War.* London: Epworth Press, 1953.

Dahl, Robert A. *Modern Political Analysis.* Englewood Cliffs, N.J.: Prentice-Hall, 1963.

Lasswell, Harold, and Abraham Kaplan. *Power and Society.* New Haven: Yale University Press, 1950.

Machiavelli, Niccolò. *The Prince and The Discourses.* Many editions.

Meinecke, Friedrich. *Machiavellism,* translated by Douglass Scott. New Haven: Yale University Press, 1957.

Niebuhr, Reinhold. *Christianity and Power Politics.* New York: Scribner, 1940.

Sterling, Richard W. *Ethics in a World of Power.* Princeton: Princeton University Press, 1958.

Thompson, Kenneth W. *Political Realism and the Crisis of World Politics.* Princeton: Princeton University Press, 1960.

2. Power and Purpose

Dehio, Ludwig. *The Precarious Four Centuries of the European Power Struggle.* New York: Knopf, 1962.

Hume, David. "Of the Balance of Power." In *Essays, Moral, Political and Literary.* London: Henry Frowde, 1904.

Kautilya. *Arthasastra.* Mysore, India: Wesleyan Mission Press, 1929.

Langer, William L. *European Alliances and Alignments 1871–1890.* New York: Knopf, 1950.

Schwartzenberger, Georg. *Power Politics.* New York: Praeger, 1951.

Spykman, Nicholas. *America's Strategy in World Politics.* New York: Harcourt, Brace, 1942.

Thucydides. *The Peloponnesian Wars.* Many editions.

Wight, Martin. *Power Politics.* London: Royal Institute of International Affairs, 1946.

Wolfers, Arnold. *Britain and France Between Two Wars.* New York: Harcourt, Brace, 1940.

3. Force

Aron, Raymond. *A Century of Total War.* Garden City, New York: Doubleday, 1954.

Clausewitz, Karl von. *On War.* Many editions.

Kahn, Herman. *On Thermonuclear War*. Princeton: Princeton University Press, 1960.

McNamara, Robert S. *The Essence of Security*. New York, Harper & Row, 1968.

Waltz, Kenneth N. *Man, the State, and War*. New York: Columbia University Press, 1959.

4. Force and War: Stimuli and Restraints

Kahn, Herman. *On Escalation*. New York: Praeger, 1965.

Kissinger, Henry. *Nuclear Weapons and Foreign Policy*. New York: Harper & Brothers, 1957.

Rosenau, James N. (ed.). *International Aspects of Civil Strife*. Princeton: Princeton University Press, 1964.

Schelling, Thomas. *Arms and Influence*. New Haven: Yale University Press, 1966.

————. *The Strategy of Conflict*. Cambridge: Harvard University Press, 1960.

Wright, Quincy. *A Study of War*. 2 vols. Chicago: University of Chicago Press, 1942.

5. Force and War: The Weapons Dynamic

Barnet, Richard. *Who Wants Disarmament?* Boston: Beacon Press, 1960.

Bull, Hedley. *The Control of the Arms Race*. New York: Praeger, 1961.

International Peace Research Institute (SIPRI). *World Armaments and Disarmament*, Stockholm. (Annual publication.)

Spanier, John W., and Joseph L. Nogee. *The Politics of Disarmament*. New York: Praeger, 1962.

Tate, Merze. *The Disarmament Illusion*. New York: Macmillan, 1942.

United States Arms Control and Disarmament Agency. *World Military Expenditures*. Washington, D.C.: G. P. O. (Annual publication.)

————. *Arms Control Achievements 1959–1972*. Washington, D.C.: G. P. O., 1972.

Wheeler-Bennett, John W. *The Pipe-Dream of Peace*. New York: William Morrow, 1935.

6. Ideology

Mannheim, Karl. *Ideology and Utopia*. New York: Harcourt, Brace, 1936.

Marx, Karl, and Friedrich Engels. *The German Ideology* (1846). Many editions.

Ward, Barbara. *Nationalism and Ideology*. New York: Norton, 1966.

7. Nationalism

Carr, E. H. *Nationalism and After.* New York: Macmillan, 1945.

Emerson, Rupert. *From Empire to Nation.* Cambridge: Harvard University Press, 1960.

Hayes, Carleton J. H. *The Historical Evolution of Modern Nationalism.* New York: R. R. Smitz, 1931.

Kohn, Hans. *The Idea of Nationalism.* New York: Macmillan, 1961.

Meinecke, Friedrich. *Weltbuergertum und Nationalstaat.* Munich: R. Oldenbourg, 1908.

Nehru, Jawaharlal. *Toward Freedom.* New York: John Day, 1941.

8. Imperialism

Gandhi, Mohandas K. *Non-Violent Resistance.* New York: Schocken, 1961.

Hobson, John A. *Imperialism.* London: Allen and Unwin, 1938.

Koebner, Richard, and Helmut Schmidt. *Imperialism: The Story and Significance of a Political Word, 1840–1960.* Cambridge: Cambridge University Press, 1961.

Langer, William L. *The Diplomacy of Imperialism.* New York: Knopf, 1935.

Lenin, V. I. *Imperialism: The Highest Stage of Capitalism.* Moscow: Foreign Languages Publishing House, 1950.

Moon, Parker T. *Imperialism and World Politics.* New York: Macmillan, 1926.

Schumpeter, Joseph. *Imperialism and Social Classes.* New York: Augustus M. Kelley, 1951.

Thornton, A. P. *Doctrines of Imperialism.* New York: Wiley, 1965.

Weinberg, Albert K. *Manifest Destiny.* Chicago: Quadrangle, 1963.

9. Diplomacy

Callières, François de. *On the Manner of Negotiating with Princes.* Boston: Houghton Mifflin, 1919.

Craig, Gordon, and Felix Gilbert (eds.). *The Diplomats, 1919–1939.* Princeton: Princeton University Press, 1953.

Ellsberg, Daniel. *Papers on the War.* New York: Simon and Schuster, 1972.

Iklé, Fred C. *How Nations Negotiate.* New York: Harper & Row, 1964.

Jones, Joseph M. *The Fifteen Weeks: An Inside Account of the Genesis of the Marshall Plan.* New York: Viking, 1955.

Kennan, George F. *American Diplomacy 1900–1950.* Chicago: University of Chicago Press, 1951.

Mattingly, Garrett. *Renaissance Diplomacy*. Boston: Houghton Mifflin, 1955.

Nicolson, Harold. *Diplomacy*. London: Butterworth, 1939.

————. *The Evolution of Diplomatic Method*. London: Constable, 1954.

Pannikar, K. M. *The Principles and Practice of Diplomacy*. Bombay: Asia Publishing House, 1956.

Sheehan, Neil, *et al. The Pentagon Papers*. New York: Bantam, 1971.

10. International Law

Black, Cyril, and Richard Falk. *The Future of the International Legal Order*. Princeton: Princeton University Press, 1969.

Brierly, J. L. *The Law of Nations*. 6th ed. New York: Oxford University Press, 1963.

Deutsch, Karl W., and Stanley Hoffman (eds.). *The Relevance of International Law*. Garden City, New York: Doubleday, 1971.

Grotius, Hugo. *De Jure Belli ac Pacis Libri Tres*. Oxford: Clarendon Press, 1925.

Kaplan, Morton A., and Nicholas deB. Katzenbach. *The Political Foundations of International Law*. New York: Wiley, 1961.

Kelsen, Hans. *Principles of International Law*. New York: Rinehart, 1952.

Lauterpacht, Hersch. *The Function of Law in the International Community*. New York: Oxford University Press, 1933.

Nussbaum, Arthur. *A Concise History of International Law*. New York: Macmillan, 1962.

Visscher, Charles de. *Theory and Reality in Public International Law*. Princeton: Princeton University Press, 1957.

11. International Organization

Bloomfield, Lincoln. *The United Nations and U.S. Foreign Policy*. Boston: Little, Brown, 1960.

Claude, Inis. *Swords into Plowshares*. New York: Random House, 1971.

Kelsen, Hans. *The Law of the United Nations*. New York: Praeger, 1950.

Kissinger, Henry. *A World Restored: Metternich, Castlereagh, and the Problem of Peace, 1812–1822*. Boston: Houghton Mifflin, 1957.

Nicholas, Herbert. *The United Nations as a Political Institution*. New York: Oxford University Press, 1959.

Nicolson, Harold. *The Congress of Vienna*. New York: Harcourt, Brace, 1946.

Zimmern, Alfred. *The League of Nations and the Rule of Law*. New York: Macmillan, 1939.

PART TWO. THE MACROPOLITICAL WORLD

12. Global Demand and Supply

Brown, Lester R. *World Without Borders*. New York: Random House, 1972.

Doane, Robert R. *World Balance Sheet*. New York: Harper & Brothers, 1957.

Ehrlich, Paul R. *The Population Bomb*. New York: Ballantine, 1968.

Falk, Richard A. *This Endangered Planet*. New York: Random House, 1971.

Laffin, John. *The Hunger to Come*. London: Abelard-Schuman, 1966.

Meadows, Donella, *et al. The Limits to Growth*. New York: Universe, 1972.

Ng, Larry, and Stuart Mudd (eds.). *The Population Crisis*. Bloomington: Indiana University Press, 1965.

Park, Charles F. *Affluence in Jeopardy: Minerals and the Political Economy*. San Francisco: Freeman, 1968.

Richards, L.A., *et al. World Population and Food Supplies 1980*. Madison: American Society of Agronomy, 1964.

Russett, Bruce M., *et al. World Handbook of Political and Social Indicators*. New Haven: Yale University Press, 1964.

Sprout, Harold, and Margaret Sprout. *Toward a Politics of the Planet Earth*. New York: Van Nostrand, 1971.

Ward, Barbara, and René Dubos. *Only One Earth*. New York: Norton, 1972.

13. Rich and Poor in the Global Society

Beckerman, Wilfred. *International Comparisons of Real Incomes*. London: Organization for Economic Cooperation and Development, 1966.

Brown, Lester R. *Seeds of Change: The Green Revolution and Development in the 1970s*. New York: Praeger, 1970.

Cochrane, Willard W. *The World Food Problem*. New York: Crowell, 1969.

DeCastro, Josué. *Death in the Northeast*. New York: Random House, 1966.

Jeffries, Sir Charles. *Illiteracy: A World Problem*. New York: Praeger, 1967.

Myrdal, Gunnar. *Asian Drama: An Inquiry into the Poverty of Nations*. 3 vols. New York: Pantheon, 1968.

Reid, Escott. *The Future of the World Bank*. Washington, D.C.: International Bank for Reconstruction and Development, 1965.

Ward, Barbara. *The Rich Nations and the Poor Nations*. New York: Norton, 1962.

14. Development: Politics and Economics

Birmingham, W., and A. G. Ford (eds.). *Planning and Growth in Rich Countries and Poor Countries*. New York: Praeger, 1966.

Heilbroner, Robert. *The Great Ascent.* New York: Harper & Row, 1963.

Hirschman, Albert O. *The Strategy of Economic Development.* New Haven: Yale University Press, 1958.

Horowitz, David. *Hemispheres North and South.* Baltimore: Johns Hopkins Press, 1966.

Myrdal, Gunnar. *The Challenge of World Poverty.* New York: Pantheon, 1970.

Pearson, Lester B. *Partners in Development.* New York: Praeger, 1969.

Raffaele, Joseph A. *The Economic Development of Nations.* New York: Random House, 1971.

15. Development as a Global Political Process

Almond, Gabriel, and James S. Coleman. *The Politics of Developing Areas.* Princeton: Princeton University Press, 1960.

Casanova, Pablo Gonzales. *Democracy in Mexico.* New York: Oxford University Press, 1970.

Jaguaribe, Helio. *Political Development: A General Theory and a Latin American Case Study.* New York: Harper & Row, 1973.

Kautsky, John H. *The Political Consequences of Modernization.* New York: Wiley, 1972.

Lewis, Oscar. *A Study of Slum Culture: Backgrounds for La Vida.* New York: Random House, 1968.

Montgomery, John D. *The Politics of Foreign Aid: American Experience in Southeast Asia.* New York: Praeger, 1962.

Pye, Lucien. *Aspects of Political Development.* Princeton: Princeton University Press, 1960.

16. Sovereignty and the Global Society

Beard, Charles A. *The Idea of National Interest.* New York: Macmillan, 1934.

de Jouvenel, Bertrand. *Sovereignty: An Inquiry into the Public Good.* Chicago: University of Chicago Press, 1957.

Laski, Harold. *Studies in the Problem of Sovereignty.* New Haven: Yale University Press, 1917.

Mark, Max. *Beyond Sovereignty.* Washington, D.C.: Public Affairs Press, 1965.

Morgenthau, Hans J. *In Defense of the National Interest.* New York: Knopf, 1951.

17. The Transnational Economy

Adams, Walter (ed.). *The Brain Drain.* New York: Macmillan, 1968.

Galbraith, John Kenneth. *The New Industrial State.* Boston: Houghton Mifflin, 1967.

Heilbroner, Robert. *The Making of Economic Society.* Englewood Cliffs, New Jersey: Prentice-Hall, 1962.

Rolfe, Sidney, and Walter Damm (eds.). *The Multinational Corporation in the World Economy.* New York: Praeger, 1970.

Servan-Schreiber, Jean-Jacques. *The American Challenge.* New York: Atheneum, 1968.

Vernon, Raymond. *Sovereignty at Bay: The Multinational Spread of U.S. Enterprises.* New York: Basic Books, 1971.

18. Transnational Society: Region and Globe

Deutsch, Karl W. *Political Community at the International Level.* Garden City, New York: Doubleday, 1954.

————. *Political Community and the North Atlantic Area.* Princeton: Princeton University Press, 1957.

Haas, Ernest. *Beyond the Nation State: Functionalism and International Organization.* Stanford: Stanford University Press, 1958.

————. *The Uniting of Europe: Political, Social and Economic Forces, 1950–1955.* Stanford: Stanford University Press, 1958.

Hallstein, Walter. *United Europe: Challenge and Opportunity.* Cambridge: Harvard University Press, 1962.

19. Transnational Society: The West

Brezezinski, Zbigniew. *Between Two Ages: America's Role in the Technotronic Era.* New York: Viking, 1970.

Diebold, William. *The United States and the Industrial World: American Foreign Economic Policy in the 1970s.* New York: Praeger, 1972.

Kindleberger, Charles P. *Power and Money: The Economics of International Politics and the Politics of International Economics.* New York: Basic Books, 1970.

20. Transnational Society: West and East

Fox, William T. R. *The Super-Powers: The United States, Britain, and the Soviet Union—Their Responsibility for Peace.* New York: Harcourt, Brace, 1944.

Khrushchev, Nikita. *For Victory in the Peaceful Competition with Capitalism.* Moscow: Foreign Languages Publishing House, 1959.

Le Feber, Walter. *America, Russia and the Cold War, 1945–1971.* New York: Wiley, 1972.

Pisar, Samuel. *Coexistence and Commerce.* New York: McGraw-Hill, 1970.

Roberts, Henry L. *Russia and America.* New York: Harper & Brothers, 1956.

Sakharov, Andrei. *Progress, Coexistence and Intellectual Freedom.* New York: Norton, 1968.

Ulam, Adam. *The Rivals: America and Russia Since World War II.* New York: Viking, 1971.

21. *Justice in the Global Society*

Hamilton, Alexander, John Jay, and James Madison. *The Federalist.* New York: Modern Library, n.d.

Kant, Immanuel. "To Eternal Peace." In Carl J. Friedrich (ed)., *The Philosophy of Kant.* New York: Modern Library, 1949.

Niebuhr, Reinhold. *Moral Man and Immoral Society.* New York: Scribner, 1932.

Toynbee, Arnold. *America and the World Revolution.* New York: Oxford University Press, 1962.

Ward, Barbara. *The Lopsided World.* New York: Norton, 1968.

Index

About the Author

Richard W. Sterling is Professor of Government at Dartmouth College, where he teaches international and comparative politics and political theory. He received his B.A., M.A., and Ph.D. degrees in international relations, all from Yale University. After army service in World War II he did research for the prosecution's case against the S.S. at the Nuremberg Trials. He returned to Germany in 1948 as a Foreign Service Officer, serving in Berlin for three years and in Frankfurt and Bonn for shorter periods.

In the course of Professor Sterling's teaching career, travel and research in Canada, the Middle East, and Puerto Rico extended his interests beyond an initial European specialization and have led to an overriding concern with relations between the developed and underdeveloped worlds. This concern is central to *Macropolitics*.

Professor Sterling's first book was a study of a German intellectual historian, *Ethics in a World of Power: The Political Ideas of Friedrich Meinecke*. He is currently engaged in an examination of international labor mobility in Europe, the United States, and Mexico.

A NOTE ON THE TYPE

The text of this book was set in Palatino, a type face designed by the noted German typographer Hermann Zapf. Named after Giovanbattista Palatino, a writing master of Renaissance Italy, Palatino was the first of Zapf's type faces to be introduced to America. The first designs for the face were made in 1948, and the fonts for the complete face were issued between 1950 and 1952. Like all Zapf-designed type faces, Palatino is beautifully balanced and exceedingly readable.

Composed by Cherry Hill Composition, Pennsauken, New Jersey
Printed and bound by Halliday Lithograph Corp., West Hanover, Mass.